U0577985

越 南 义 立

——冯原文化遗存发掘报告

四川省文物考古研究院

陕西省考古研究院　编　著

越南国家历史博物馆

文物出版社

北京·2016

图书在版编目（CIP）数据

越南义立：冯原文化遗存发掘报告：中文、英文／
四川省文物考古研究院，陕西省考古研究院，越南国家
历史博物馆编著. —北京：文物出版社，2016.7
　ISBN 978 - 7 - 5010 - 4646 - 1

　Ⅰ.①越…　Ⅱ.①四…②陕…③越…　Ⅲ.①文化遗存
（考古学）- 发掘报告 - 越南 - 汉、英　Ⅳ.①K883.338.05

中国版本图书馆 CIP 数据核字（2016）第 150412 号

越南义立——冯原文化遗存发掘报告

编　　著：四川省文物考古研究院　陕西省考古研究院　越南国家历史博物馆

责任编辑：杨冠华
封面设计：程星涛
责任印制：梁秋卉

出版发行：文物出版社
社　　址：北京市东直门内北小街 2 号楼
邮　　编：100007
网　　址：http：//www.wenwu.com
邮　　箱：web@ wenwu.com
经　　销：新华书店
印　　刷：北京京都六环印刷厂
开　　本：889×1194　1/16
印　　张：30.75　插页 2
版　　次：2016 年 7 月第 1 版
印　　次：2016 年 7 月第 1 次印刷
书　　号：ISBN 978 - 7 - 5010 - 4646 - 1
定　　价：280.00 元

本书版权独家所有，非经授权，不得复制翻印

序　言

　　您看到的这本书，记录的是四川省文物考古研究院和陕西省考古研究院联合在越南所做的 2006 年田野考古发掘报告。2006 年的这次看似普通的考古发掘，是我国内陆省级考古研究机构在国外的第一次田野考古工作。也有人说这是国内考古机构第一次在国外独立完成田野发掘所形成的考古报告。多年来，每谈及此，总不断有朋友同行问起我们早在 2006 年就去国外发掘的原因。借报告出版机会，同时也受陕西省考古研究院前任院长焦南峰、现任院长王炜林的委托，我把发掘的缘起、过程以及发掘的收获体会做一介绍。

　　1992 年夏天，在邓小平同志南行讲话精神的鼓舞下，全国各行业思想大解放。在此背景下，又逢香港中文大学召开郑德坤教授八十寿辰的纪念大会。鉴于郑德坤教授在四川工作时收集研究过广汉三星堆出土的玉器，所以这次大会是一个以古玉为主题的国际学术研讨会，内地参会学者空前踊跃。因为四川刚发现了举世闻名的三星堆遗址，尤其是遗址中出土了大量的玉器，又加上四川是郑德坤教授工作过的地方，四川省文物考古研究所和四川大学多位专家受邀参加大会。当时的我，尚在四川大学历史系考古教研室工作，个人的兴趣也有一部分在考古出土古玉器方面，而且，正在参加由李学勤先生主编、漓江出版社计划出版的《文物鉴赏丛书》中《玉器鉴赏》一书的撰写，因此之故，本人对玉器研究的学术动态尤为关注。当听到参加香港会议的专家介绍大会情况时，也格外留心。也就是在会上第一次听说越南学者带去了在越南冯原文化遗址中出土的玉牙璋照片，这位越南学者认为这与三星堆是有联系的。听此消息，当时感到吃惊，也留下了深刻的印象，但在当时也就是听听而已，绝没想到我们会在十多年后到越南考古发掘以探究竟。1998 年，香港中文大学邓聪教授发起召开了比 1992 年规模更大的东亚古玉研讨会，内地参会的学者有数十人之多，本人很荣幸也在受邀之列，得以在香港中文大学和越南参会学者面对面交流并看到了越南出玉牙璋的照片。在会上，越南学者还表示可以和中国学者共同研究而且欢迎中国考古机构去越南考古调查发掘，当时在场的中国学者并没回应。本人以为是说给在场的考古同行听的，虽然听到越南学者发出的英雄帖后，心中曾怦然一动。但彼时我供职的四川省博物馆，没有田野考古职能，所以几乎没考虑过去越南考古发掘这事。光阴荏苒，到了 2004 年夏，我调到四川省文物考古研究所工作已有两年，承蒙广西壮族自治区博物馆黄启善馆长的邀请，去参加他们 70 年馆庆大会。会后，我报名参加了中越边境学术考察，考察团里来自国内各博物馆的专家馆长不少，考察的重点是越南国家历史博物馆。广西壮族自治区博物馆组织得很好，越方非常重视，馆长出面接待，参观完陈列后，还举行了座谈。自从踏上越南国土我就一直惦记着 1998 年越南专家曾提及的欢迎中国考古机构到越南发掘一事，在越南国家历史博物馆展厅里第一次见到玉牙璋实物；现在有机会和越南国家历史博物馆馆长座谈，机会难得。在自由发言环节，我向馆长提出我们单位希望到越南考古发掘，有无可能性？馆长立即向我介绍了越南的考古管理机制和考古工作情况，说非常欢迎中国的考古同行到越南考古，并十分肯定地说就可以和他们合作。得到这样的回答我自然喜出望外，我也当着大家回答说，我回去后立即研究并向上级汇报，争取能够成行。当时，参与座谈的中国同行，一部分人认为这事不可能，一部分人私下还不以为意，以为我逢场作戏。

其实我是非常认真的。回到四川后，我立即向院里通报了有关情况，出乎意料的是马上得到了大家的赞成和支持。大家认为，中国考古是该走出国门了，而去越南发掘一处与三星堆遗址同时代且出过与三星堆相近文物的遗址，对我院的考古事业发展是个机遇，对推动三星堆文化的学术研究意义深远，我们应该抓住这个机会。于是我们做了初步论证后，向四川省文物局做了报告，省文物局也认为我院若能去国外考古发掘，特别是发掘点可能与三星堆有一定的关系，是件大好事，能有力扩大四川考古的影响力，省文物考古研究院的闯劲和主动作为的精神可嘉，很快同意了我们的报告并转呈国家有关部门。但是，这个报告近一年没有得到批复。经了解，该部门对此事高度重视并认真研究，他们认为虽然是件好事，但这事从没遇到过，上级部门也没有赋予他们审批到国外考古发掘的职能，所以没法批复。等不到批复，怎么办，放弃还是继续？我们觉得机会难得，不能轻易放弃。于是我们决定作为院里自拟项目来实施。我们认为，我们的想法虽是地方考古所所为，但若成行，在国外一定程度上也代表中国考古的形象，为了把工作做到尽善尽美，我们应找田野考古力量更强、经验更丰富的考古所合作。我向时任陕西考古研究院院长的焦南峰先生通报了情况并征求合作意向，焦院长听完后当即表示，这是件大好事，感谢我们对他们的信任，他们愿和我们一起去越南考古发掘。我同时也谈到我们遇到的困境，焦院长爽快地答应和我们工作共进退、风险共担当，很是令人感动。这也更增强了我们去做这件事的决心和信心。2006 年秋，我院和陕西考古研究院自立项目、自筹经费、各出两人组成的赴越南考古队终于成行了。

考古队到越南后，受到越南国家历史博物馆的热烈欢迎，他们派出了专人配合我们考古队的业务和后勤工作。我方考古队详细调查了越方提供的几处遗址，最后选定永福省义立遗址作为发掘点，发掘前进行了考古调查、钻探，最后才选定发掘地点，每次布 5 米×5 米探方四个，共布方两轮。在越南工作近三个月，发掘取得了丰硕成果，尤其是我们亲手发掘出了与三星堆同时期的、与三星堆文化有一定联系的一批遗物遗迹，收获远超预期。

发掘期间，考古队开放工地让当地民众参观。结束后，还在永福省组织了新闻发布会，向媒体和社会展示出土文物。这支来自中国的考古队的工作得到了越南国家历史博物馆的首肯和当地社会的好评，考古队员的敬业精神、认真态度都给越方留下深刻印象。在国内名声大噪的洛阳铲在越南考古工地的使用效果极佳，令越南同行大感兴趣。中国考古从调查、发掘、到修复、整理自成体系的理论方法也在越南的考古工地中得到了较好的应用展示。

2007 年春，四川省文物考古研究院和陕西省考古研究院在中国文物报社的帮助下，在北京举行了越南义立遗址发掘汇报会，邀请老一辈考古学家徐苹芳、张忠培、严文明、李学勤等先生二十多人和各大媒体到会听取汇报。汇报会由我主持，发掘领队之一的雷雨做了汇报。专家们对这项工作给与了高度评价，认为川陕两家考古研究院在越南的考古发掘在中国考古发展史上有极其正面的示范效应，给中国考古走出国门开了个好头，中国考古发掘应该走出去，也到了能走出去的时候。专家们对出国考古发掘应该着手的语言、专业、文化、外交上的准备也提出了很多好的指导意见，令我们多受益良多。汇报会上专家们的发言在《中国文物报》上整版刊出。会上，焦南峰院长代表川陕两家单位做的总结中有一段话令大家印象深刻。他说，高深道理大家都知道，文化交流的需要，学术研究的需要，我们也不用多讲。我们自己国内发掘都忙不过来，可为什么还要去国外考古呢？我们从进大学起，受到的考古史教育都在讲外国人在中国考古，改革开放以来，我们和国外考古合作发掘不少，可都是在中国境内进行的。现在中国开放了，我们也想去国外考古发掘，于是就有了这次越南考古。他这番朴实无华的话语，把大家都逗乐了。

随后，我们还邀请越南国家历史博物馆的同行到陕西、四川两地访问交流。2010 年后，陕西考古研究院王炜林院长也一如既往地支持越南的考古工作。2011 年底，应越南国家历史博物馆的邀请，我、焦南峰和当年参加发掘的队员们组团专程前往越南访问，主要商讨考古资料的整理和出版事宜。此后，报告编写驶入快车道，今年春节后，报告正式交付文物出版社，今年 7 月，报告即将出版。我们的第一次国外考古——越南考古，算是画上了圆满的句号。

如果一定要对这次行动做个总结的话，我以为，我们的第一次国外考古有如下几个鲜明的特点。

第一点是我们自发、自觉去做的。它既不是上级下达的任务，也不是去争取来的科研项目。

第二点是遗址和发掘点都是我们自选的。如前所述，我们向越方提出要求后，他们给了我们一片区域任我们挑选。

第三点是我们在越南的调查、发掘、整理都是独立、自主进行的，越方做了积极的配合。

第四点是我们的调查、发掘、整理、出版经费全是我们两院自筹的。

回顾中国一百多年的考古历程，若按从事考古工作的机构和参加者的国籍来划分，20 世纪 20 年代中期以前，主要是外国人在我国境内的河南、新疆、甘肃、四川、陕西、山西做探险和考古调查。20 世纪 20 年代后期，才有中国机构和学者独立开展的考古发掘。20 世纪 30年代，除中国考古机构自主的发掘外，也有中外合作的考古调查项目开展。20 世纪 50 年代后，中国在大学设立了考古专业，从中央到各省市纷纷成立考古研究机构，考古事业蓬勃发展并取得了辉煌成绩。这期间，几乎没有外国机构和学者在中国考古发掘。改革开放后，中国考古的大门也慢慢向国外打开，西方发达国家的考古学者接连来中国访问讲学，有的直接和中国考古机构进行了联合发掘，中外考古学术交流一派繁荣。但是，冷静思考中国的考古发展史就很容易发现一个现象，从初期的外国人来、到中外合作、到拒绝外国人来、再到中外合作，都是在中国土地上考古，还没有中国考古机构有组织有目的地到外国考古的，从学术和文化交流来说不应该也不正常。我们认为，中国考古界上必须尽快补上这一课。这是我们恢复高考后的第一代考古人的共同心愿。后来，当我们具备一定的专业能力，走上考古院所领导岗位。虽地处内陆，又还是两个省级考古所，但位卑未敢忘忧国，时逢国家经济腾飞，我们更有把愿望变成行动的冲动，才有了2006年的越南考古行动。

我们非常高兴地看到，在我们越南考古之后不久，国内就陆续有考古机构去俄罗斯、肯尼亚、越南、老挝、孟加拉……等地开展考古工作。特别是在今年初的全国两会期间，全国人大代表、中国社会科学院考古研究所所长王巍先生和全国政协委员、中国社会科学院考古研究所研究员袁靖先生同时呼吁国家应高度重视中国考古走向世界，提请国家把考古走出国门作为国家间文化交流项目，上升到大国的文化发展的战略高度来对待。而一周前在郑州召开的首届中国考古学大会，主题就是走向未来、走向世界，大会特别安排了国内四家考古机构近年在柬埔寨、洪都拉斯、蒙古、乌兹别克斯坦的考古报告，国际味很浓。

最近，有朋友对我们说，从十年前你们出国考古的一小步，到今天中国考古界出国考古迈大步；从十年前你们出国考古的一个蝴蝶翅膀振动，到今天中国考古即将刮起的走向世界的大风，很佩服你们两院当年的勇气和担当。我回答他们说，别把我们当年的决定和行动拔得那么高，我们只不过是把考古当事业在做；是职业使命感的驱使、时代和机遇、同事们的努力和担当、领导们的支持、老专家和同行们的鼓励成就了我们这次国外考古数据。仅此而已。

感谢参加越南义立考古发掘的川陕两省考古研究院的考古队员的辛勤劳动。感谢对本次考古行动给予过支持的国内外领导专家和本单位的同事们。感谢越南国家历史博物馆和馆长对我们的充分信任和在越期间给予我们的各种帮助。

四川省文物考古研究院　高大伦

2016 年 5 月 30 日于成都

总　目　录

目　录

插图目录

彩版目录

第一章　地理环境与历史沿革

第一节　自然环境、地理和气候

越南社会主义共和国位于亚洲的东南部，其北部与中国的云南、广西接壤，西部和老挝、柬埔寨毗邻，东南濒临南海，西南靠近暹罗湾，南扼太平洋和印度洋海上交通要道，自古以来，战略地位极其重要。面积约 33 万平方公里，人口 7300 万（1996 年）。境内共有京、岱依、傣、芒、苗、高棉、汉等 54 个民族，其中 89% 是京族（即越族），通用越南语。主要宗教有佛教、天主教、和好教、高台教。全国共划分为 57 个省和 4 个直辖市（河内市、胡志明市、海防市、岘港市），首都为河内。

越南处于印度支那半岛东侧，地形由西北向东南倾斜，南北狭长，弯曲呈 S 形，北部和南部突出，中部狭窄，南北全长 1650 公里，东西最宽处 650 公里，最窄处近 50 公里（图一）。山脉和高原约占全国面积的四分之一，集中在北部和中部，大致可分为三个区域——红河以北山区，红河、兰江之间的山区和长山山脉，西原区。长山山脉位于西侧，蜿蜒在越南中部，斜贯南北，是越南与老挝的天然国界。最大的平原是北部的红河三角洲和南部的湄公河三角洲。平原面积约占越南总面积的四分之一，大部分由河流泥沙冲积而成，北部平原是北方最富饶的地区，南部平原是南方最富庶的地区。这两个平原是世界上著名的产米区，更是越南的天然粮食仓库，亦是越南古代文化的酝酿和发展的主要区域。

越南山多水也多，全国共有大小河流 1000 余条，纵长约 41000 多公里，河水大部分是自西北向东南而入海。红河（珥河）和湄公河（九龙河）是越南境内两条主要的河流，发源于中国的云南和西藏高原。越南海岸线纵长约 3000 公里，水利资源较为丰富。

越南属于热带季风气候。各地气候因与赤道的距离和地形不同而有差异。南部靠近赤道，全年温差较小，最热是 4 月，月平均气温 29℃。北方气候差别较大，最热为 7 月，月平均气温 23℃；最冷在 1 月，月平均气温 15℃；西北部的山区冬季夜间温度可到 0℃ 以下。越南的雨量丰富，年均降水量 1800～2000 毫升。越南全年有雨季和旱季之分，雨季降雨量占全年降雨量的 80%，5 月至 10 月北部处于雨季，8 月至次年 1 月中部处于雨季，5 月至 11 月南部处于雨季；11 月至次年 4 月北部处于旱季，11 月至次年 5 月南部处于旱季，2 月至 7 月中部处于旱季。全年日照时间不低于 1500 小时，年均湿度约为 82%[1]。

---

〔1〕　郭振铎、张笑梅主编：《越南通史》，中国人民大学出版社，2002 年。

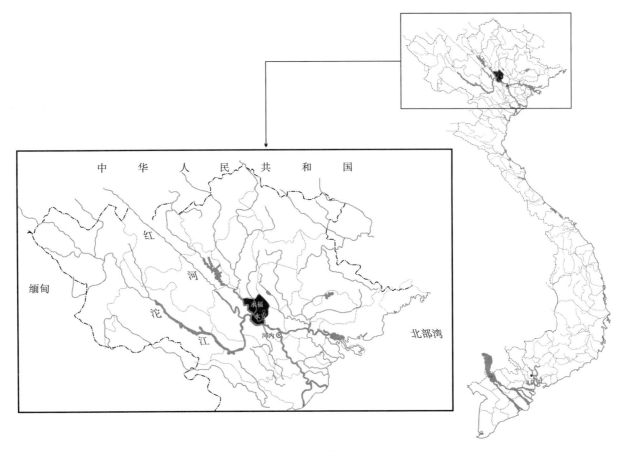

图一　永福省在越南的位置

第二节　历史沿革

山韦（Son Vi）文化和和平（Hoa Binh）文化的发现，说明在旧石器时代，越南北部的红河流域就有人类生存。

新石器时代的越南北部先后经历了北山（Bac Son）文化—查阜（Cai Beo）文化、多笔（Da But）文化、琼文（Quynh Van）文化—冯原（Phung Nguyen）文化、下龙（Ha Long）文化和保卓（Bau Tro）文化等阶段，这一时期遗址众多，分布范围较大，说明新石器时代越南北部聚落大量出现，人类活动频繁。这一时期也是中国和越南史书上所称的"文郎国"时期。

约在公元前250年，越南东北部的蜀部落打败了居住在红河流域的文郎部落，蜀部落首领蜀泮建都于螺城，取国号为瓯雒国，建立了越南历史上的第一个国家。

秦统一中国后，开始向南扩张领土。公元前214年，秦置桂林、南海、象郡，其中象郡就包括今越南的北部。公元前207年，南海都尉赵佗乘秦末战争之际，吞并桂林和象郡，自立为南越王，建立南越割据政权，控制了越南的北部和中部。

公元前111年，汉武帝派遣大将路博德平定南越，并在当地设立南海、苍梧、郁林、合浦、交趾、九真、日南、珠崖、儋耳九郡，其中交趾、九真、日南位于今越南北部和中部。

203 年，汉合并交趾三郡和南海、桂林三郡，称为交州。

三国时期，交州属吴国管辖，并重新交割成广州（范围包括广东、广西）和交州（原交趾三郡）两个行政区域。280 年，晋灭吴，交州牧陶璜投晋。

544 年，交趾李贲、并韶起义，建立万春国。建都龙编，李贲为南越帝，并韶为相。586 年，隋灭陈统一中国。602 年，隋大将刘与灭万春国。交州重新又分为交趾、九真、日南三郡。618 年，唐灭隋，设交州总管府。679 年，由于军管不力，起义频发，所以将交州总管府改为安南都护府。

938 年，吴权建立了越南封建社会的第一个朝代——吴朝。968 年，越南朝代更迭为丁朝。980 年，中国宋朝以丁朝不稳为由，出兵越南。越南黎恒继位，建立黎朝。1010 年，越南李公蕴建立李朝。1225 年，越南陈守度建立陈朝。

1400 年，越南胡季犛建立胡朝。1406 年，明朝以讨胡复陈的名义进攻越南并占领全境，取消越南国号，直接委派官吏统治越南。1418 年，越南黎利起义。1427 年，起义军与明朝和谈，明军撤出越南，黎利于 1428 年称帝，定都东都（现河内），国号大越，史称黎朝。

1527 年，莫登庸废黜黎帝，建立莫朝。1530 年，黎大将阮淦立黎氏后人为帝，恢复黎朝，双方形成黎朝在南，莫朝在北的对峙状态，越南史称南北朝。中国明朝出兵干涉，莫登庸割现高平一带予明朝，后莫朝被黎朝所灭，在明朝的保护下，偏安于高平。此后，越南各派势力重新洗牌，形成郑氏（北方）与阮氏（南方）继续割据的局面。1697 年，南明杨彦迪残部退入越南南部，被驱逐至现越南最南部地区。1733 年，阮氏攻占该地区，越南现代的疆土范围基本形成。1771 年，阮岳、阮惠、阮吕兄弟发动西山起义，先后击败南阮北郑，立黎氏后人昭统为帝。其后郑氏后人作乱，黎昭统逃亡至中国清朝；清朝派两广总督孙士毅以两广、云贵之兵入越。1789 年，阮惠击溃清兵，立西山朝，同时向清朝称臣。1802 年，原南阮贵族在法国人的支持下，灭西山朝，成立阮朝。1862 年，法国进入越南；1844 年，越南完全沦为法国殖民地[1]。

---

〔1〕　金旭东：《越南古代史概述》，《东南亚》1986 年第 2 期；［越］陶维英著，刘统文著、子钺译：《越南古代史》，商务印书馆，1976 年；郭振铎、张笑梅主编：《越南通史》，中国人民大学出版社，2002 年。

第二章　考古发掘及研究概况

第一节　发掘背景

东南亚地区一直是国际考古学界关注的焦点之一，特别是东南亚史前文化的研究上，多年来一直是国际学术界的热点之一，亦是我国考古人类学界的重要研究领域。近二十年来，东南亚地区一系列新的重要考古发现，为研究东南亚地区文化的统一性和特殊性、稻作农业的起源与传播、南岛语族的迁徙、金属冶炼等问题，提供了新的线索。东南亚地区成为考古学界万众瞩目的地区，中外学者对这一地区给予了很多关注，并进行了大量的研究。

本项目将研究的目光聚焦在越南北部这一区域进行重点研究。纵观整个东南亚地区，越南与我国的联系最为紧密。越南有两千多年可考的信史，其中约一千余年曾是中国封建王朝直接治下的郡县，约一千余年是作为中国的"藩属"而存在的独立国家。1884 年，越南政府被迫与法国签订了第二次《顺化条约》；1885 年，法国强迫清政府在天津签订了《中法会订越南条约》，清政府正式承认越南是法国的保护国，结束了中国与越南之间的"藩属"关系。越南与中国山水相连，相互之间有着悠久而密切的历史联系。但是这种联系最早开始于什么时候，并以什么样的方式和哪种文化为主？史料并未给出我们完整的答案。

20 世纪 80 年代以来，越南北部的永福省和富寿省陆续出土了几件形制与三星堆文化同类器极其相似的玉器（牙璋），经报道后，引起了中国学术界的关注。而更早以前，一批关注东南亚考古的中国学者就已经注意到——越南北部青铜至铁器时代的考古学文化与四川地区同时期或稍早时期的考古学文化面貌存在着某些相似性或一致性[1]。另外，有关古蜀国与位于现越南北部的古文朗国的交流和来往，在中越两国的史籍中均有或多或少的记载和暗喻[2]。

---

[1] 这种相似性或一致性主要表现在两地的遗存上，如船棺葬、青铜器、玉器等。参阅童恩正：《试谈古代四川与东南亚文明的关系》，《文物》1983 年第 9 期。

[2] 中越两国的文献中均记载。越南早期的历史，是由雄（或雒）王建立的文郎国开始的，文郎国传到十八世王时，被蜀王子泮攻占，并建立瓯貉国，自称安阳王。越南文献中关于蜀安阳王与文郎国的关系，最早见于《岭南摭怪·金龟传》中，其载："瓯貉国安阳王，巴蜀人也，姓蜀名泮，因先祖求雄王之女媚娘为婚，不许，怨之，泮欲成前志，兴兵攻雄王，灭文郎国，改曰瓯貉国；筑城于越裳之地"。随后的《史记全书》、《安南志略》、《越史考》等文献均记载该事件。中国文献中关于这一段历史的记载最早见于《水经注·叶榆河注》，其载："交趾昔未有郡县之时，土地有雒田，其田从潮水上下，民垦其田，因名为雒田。设雒王、雒侯主郡县。县多为雒将，雒将铜印青绶。后蜀王子将兵三万来讨雒王、雒侯、雒诸将。蜀王子因称安阳王。后南越王尉佗举众攻安阳王"。随后的历代文献记载或索隐中均援引该条记载。参见［越］陶维英著，刘统文、子钺译：《越南古代史》，商务印书馆，1976 年；蒙文通：《越史丛考》，人民出版社，1983 年。

因此，了解四川盆地与越南北部青铜时期考古学文化的关系，特别是三星堆文化对东南亚文化的影响，就显得十分必要，这也是本次考古发掘的初衷。

第二节 考古发掘及研究概况

（一） 考古发现概况

在越南北部的红河流域，现已发现并确定了冯原文化、铜荳文化、扪丘文化和东山文化等几种考古学文化，但关于以上各考古学文化的具体年代范围，包括越南学者在内的各国学者还持有不同观点，分歧较大。不过，各考古学文化的前后发展序列以及总的年代范围已基本确定，它们是冯原文化→铜荳文化→扪丘文化→东山文化，总的年代范围大致为铜石并用时代至铁器时代早期。其中材料较多，我们较为熟知的两个重要的考古学文化当属冯原文化（Phung Nguyen Culture）和东山文化（Dong Son Culture）[1]。

迄今已调查发现和发掘冯原文化时期的遗址 100 多处，经正式发掘的遗址 70 余处，主要分布于红河流域的富寿（Phu Tho）、永福（Vinh Phuc）、河内市（Ha Noi）、河西（Ha Tay）、北宁（Bac Ninh）等省市，遗址一般以山麓高原、河川两岸阶地分布较多，沿海则发现较少[2]。其分布区域恰好是越南历史记载和传说中的文朗国（Van – Lang kingdom）的区域。其早期连接铜石并用时代，历史上称为前文朗时期，中晚期为文朗国时期，下接青铜器时代晚期的东山文化。冯原（Phung Nguyen）遗址于 1959 年被发现，并于 1961 年进行了大规模的考古发掘，因其发现最早且文化内涵丰富，因而被命名为"冯原文化"。

（二） 越南学者研究概况

对冯原文化遗存的发掘始于 1959 年的冯原遗址的考古发掘。随后的 20 世纪 60～70 年代，一批重要的冯原文化时期的遗存陆续被发现（朋丘、峦河、姜堆等遗址），这促使越南学者开始重新思考越南古代史问题；这一时期也是越南考古学大发展的时期，许多新的观点在此形成[3]。20 世纪 90 年代至今，随着一些新的重要的遗存被发现，如"仁村"遗址的发掘（2002 年、2003 年、2004 年），丰富了冯原文化的内涵。基于新的考古学材料，越来越多的越南学者开始关注本土的冯原文化，其研究主要集中在冯原文化的年代、源流、文化内涵、族属、文明程度等问题上。这一时期最有代表性的著作为何文瑨的《越南考古文化》[4]和韩文

〔1〕 郭振铎、张笑梅主编：《越南通史》，中国人民大学出版社，2002 年。

〔2〕 邓聪：《越南冯原遗址与香港大湾遗址玉石器对比试释》，《南中国及邻近地区古文化研究》，香港中文大学出版社，1994 年。

〔3〕 [越] 陶维英著，刘统文、子钺译：《越南古代史》，商务印书馆，1976 年；[越] 黎文兰、范文耿、阮灵编著，梁志明译：《越南青铜时代的第一批遗迹》，河内科学出版社，1963 年。

〔4〕 [越] 何文晋著，[日] 菊池诚一译：《ベトナムの考古文化》，（日）六兴出版社，1991 年。

恳的《冯原文化》[1]。何文瑨对越南古代史进行了全面梳理,并重新构建了旧石器时代至铁器时代的年代框架,同时对冯原文化进行了较为深入的研究;而韩文恳的《冯原文化》一书则对冯原文化的发现、调查、发掘史进行了全面的回顾,并就冯原文化的年代、源流和文化内涵进行了全面概括。但因区域局限性和民族心理等因素,使得越南学者很难在更广泛的范围内探讨其与周边文化的关系,这也就制约了越南本地学者对冯原文化更为深入的研究。

(三) 国外研究概况

越南近代以来的考古学起源于西方,特别是法属时期,一批收藏越南青铜器、石器的学者,着眼于整个东南亚地区,以期全面地理解东南亚地区的古代文化。西方学者和日本的研究视觉主要着眼于整个东南亚地区,如澳大利亚的彼得·贝尔伍德(Peter Bell wood)教授从农业和南岛语族的迁徙角度探讨越南在亚洲及太平洋地区所发挥的作用[2];新西兰学者查尔斯·海厄姆(Charles Higham)则侧重于研究整个大陆东南亚的史前文化,从宏观角度解读大陆东南亚地区的史前文化[3];法国学者索兰[4]和英国伦敦大学的戴维森(Jeremy H. C. S. Davidson)[5]深入分析了越南地区从新石器时代到金石并用时代的文化,构建出该地区的文化发展序列。日本学者西村昌也[6]是国外学者中研究越南古代文化最有代表性的人物,其对越南古代文化遗存进行了全面的梳理,并构建出越南早期文化的序列。而日本学者吉开将人以中国与东南亚出土的"T"形陶环为线索[7],从更广泛的范围论述中国与东南亚特别是与越南的关系。

总体来看,国外学者的研究视角较广,不局限于某一个国家或地区的单一文化,而是从整个东南亚地区出发,进行更广泛的研究,涉及的课题亦较多,如文化的统一性与特殊性、稻作农业的起源与扩散、金属器的起源与扩散、南岛语族的迁徙等问题。但其局限性在于其很难利用中国东南沿海和西南、华南的考古材料,影响了其从更广阔的范围探讨东南亚地区的考古学文化。

(四) 中国国内研究概况

中国学者对越南地区的研究开始得较晚,其研究主要集中在中国西南与越南的关系、云南与越南的关系、两广地区(广东、广西)与越南的关系、四川与越南的关系以及稻作农业的起源、南岛语族的起源等问题上。

---

〔1〕 Han Van Khan, *Van Hoa Phung Nguyen*, Nha Xuat Ban Dai Hoc Quoc Gia Ha Noi, 2005。
〔2〕 [美]彼得·贝尔伍德、洪晓纯采访:《彼得·贝尔伍德教授访谈录》,《南方文物》2001年第3期。
〔3〕 Charles Higham. *Early Culture of Mainlant southeast Asia*. Bangkok: River Book Ltd 2002.
〔4〕 [法]埃德蒙·索兰等:《印度支那半岛的史前文化》,《考古学参考资料》2,文物出版社,1979年。
〔5〕 [英]杰里米·戴维森:《越南近年来的考古活动》,《考古学参考资料》2,文物出版社,1979年。
〔6〕 [日]西村昌也:《红河平原とメコン·ドンナイ川平原の考古学の研究》,东京大学大学院人文社会研究科,2006年博士学位论文。
〔7〕 [日]吉开将人著、陈德安译:《中国与东南亚的"T"字形环》,《四川文物》1999年第2期。

20 世纪 80 年代，童恩正开始关注中国西南地区与东南亚地区的考古文化交流与互动，于 1983 年发表《近二十年来东南亚地区的考古新发现及国外学者对我国南方古文明起源的研究》[1]一文，探讨了东南亚地区和中国南方农业的起源问题。吴春明致力于研究东南亚地区史前文化与华南的关系和南岛语族的起源问题，并且在整个大陆东南亚的大背景下研究越南北部的史前文化。他在《红河下游新石器时代文化与华南的关系》[2]一文中总结了前人对越南北部新石器文化谱系的研究，并深入分析了红河下游新石器时代文化内涵的发展，最后将越南北部的新石器文化与华南地区进行对比研究。20 世纪 80 年代以来，香港、台湾地区的学者也将目光投向了这一地区，研究的角度较广，且不仅仅局限于将越南北部与华南地区的对比上。台湾地区学者臧振华将台湾纳入到华南与东南亚史前文化的对比当中，发表《华南、台湾与东南亚的史前文化关系》[3]一文，从南岛语族的起源和迁徙这一角度来进行研究。香港中文大学教授邓聪则将研究的目光放到香港以及整个东亚、东南亚地区，并与越南学者合作研究越南北部地区的文化遗址，于 2003 年共同发表《越南海防长晴遗址的考古发现》[4]一文。

20 世纪 80 年代末，云南学者王大道开始关注云南青铜文化与越南、泰国等东南亚地区青铜文化的关系，相继发表了《云南青铜文化及其与越南东山文化、泰国班清文化的关系》[5]和《云南青铜文化的陶器及其越南东山、泰国班清文化陶器的关系》[6]，详细解读了云南青铜文化因素与越南东山文化之间的关系。近年来，李昆声和陈果所著《中国云南与越南的青铜文明》[7]则全面梳理了两地新石器时代至青铜时代的遗存，并对文化因素、农业、青铜器进行了比较研究。

两广地区特别是广西地区与越南山水相连，地理环境、气候条件和生态系统等基本相似，广西南部与越南的红河流域都位于北部湾沿海区域，水路和陆路都较为方便，相应的在史前文化上就有相同或相近的文化特征。广西感驮岩遗址的发现就是两地早期文化互动的最好证明[8]。目前关于两地的早期文化的研究还较少，相关的跨国研究尚未形成，制约了两地早期文化的研究。

最早关注四川与越南关系的是童恩正，在《试谈古代四川与东南亚文明的关系》一文中，他详细探讨了四川古代的文化因素与越南的关系[9]。随后更多的学者开始关注四川与越南的

〔1〕 童恩正：《近二十年来东南亚地区的考古新发现及国外学者对我国南方古文明起源的研究》，《西南民族大学学报》（人文社科版）1983 第 3 期。
〔2〕 陆勤毅、吴春明：《红河下游新石器时代文化与华南的关系》，《百越研究》第 2 辑，安徽大学出版社，2011 年。
〔3〕 臧振华：《华南、台湾与东南亚的史前文化关系：生态区位、文化互动与历史过程》，《新世纪的考古学一文化、区位、生态的多元互动学术研讨会》，2003 年。
〔4〕 邓聪、阮金容：《越南海防长晴遗址的考古发现》，《东南考古研究》2003 年第 3 期。
〔5〕 王大道：《云南青铜文化及其与越南东山文化、泰国班清文化的关系》，《考古》1990 年第 6 期。
〔6〕 王大道：《云南青铜文化的陶器及其越南东山、泰国班清文化陶器的关系》，《南方民族考古》第 3 辑，四川大学出版社，1991 年。
〔7〕 李昆声、陈果：《中国云南与越南的青铜文化》，社会科学文献出版社，2013 年。
〔8〕 广西壮族自治区文物工作队：《广西那坡感驮岩遗址发掘简报》，《考古》2003 年第 10 期。
〔9〕 童恩正：《试谈古代四川与东南亚文明的关系》，《文物》1983 年第 9 期。

关系，但这些研究主要集中在蜀人南迁的路线及其对越南的影响上[1]。近年来，四川的考古学者开始关注越南与四川古代文化的交流，雷雨的《从考古发现看四川与越南的关系》[2]揭示了从冯原文化至秦汉时期四川与越南文化的交流情况。而彭长林将越南出土的 8 件牙璋与四川三星堆遗址出土的牙璋进行了比较研究，探讨了四川盆地与越南红河平原早期文化的互动[3]。

总体来看，中国国内的研究主要集中在中国华南地区与东南亚特别是越南北部文化交流互动上，同时亦涉及南岛语族的起源与扩散、金属器的扩散、高等级玉器（如玉璋、玉戈）的起源与扩散等问题。但研究视角较窄，很多新的材料未能及时应用，已落后于西方和台湾、香港学者的研究。

〔1〕 王有鹏：《犍为巴蜀墓葬的发掘与蜀王的南迁》，《考古》1984 年第 12 期；孙华：《蜀人南迁考》，《四川盆地青铜时代》，科学出版社，2000 年。

〔2〕 雷雨：《从考古发现看四川与越南的关系》，《四川文物》2006 年第 6 期。

〔3〕 彭长林：《越南北部牙璋研究》，《华夏考古》2015 年第 1 期。

第三章　工作经过

第一节　考古发掘经过

2004 年 7 月，四川省文物考古研究院院长高大伦在南宁参加会议后前往越南访问，在参观越南国家历史博物馆时向对方表达了双方开展合作的意愿，越南国家历史博物馆对此予以了积极响应。2005 年 2 月，四川省文物考古研究院首次派出李昭和、陈德安、张肖马、胡昌钰、雷雨、孙智彬等人组成的考察组对越南国家历史博物馆进行了访问，双方初步达成合作意向。鉴于到陕西汉中盆地与成都平原青铜时期的考古学文化存在较为密切的联系，四川省文物考古研究院邀请陕西省考古研究院一道派出由陈德安、雷雨、王占奎和王炜林组成的联合考察组，于 2005 年 12 月对越南河内市、富寿省、永福省、头顿省、胡志明市等地的博物馆以及相关遗址进行了学术考察，并选定了发掘地点。2006 年 7 月，越南国家历史博物馆、四川省文物考古研究院和陕西省考古研究院在成都签订了长期合作的框架性协议，并将第一年度（2006 年度）发掘地点选择在越南永福省永祥县的义立遗址。

义立（Nghia Lap）遗址位于越南永福省（Vinh Phuc）永祥县（Vinh Tuong）义兴社义立村，处于红河（Song Hong）和泸江（Song Lo）的交汇地域，西距泸江 1.2 公里，南距河内至安沛省的铁路约 1.5 公里，东面与义立村相连（图二；彩版一）。遗址中部坐落一座寺庙。遗址中心点的地理坐标为北纬 21°18′，东经 105°30′，海拔 11 米，遗址面积约 10 万平方米，该遗址在 1963 年和 1967 年先后经过两次调查。1967 年 12 月至 1968 年 2 月，越南社会科学委员会考古学院对其进行过正式发掘[1]。2006 年 12 月，应越南国家博物馆邀请，四川省考古研究院、陕西省考古研究院和越南国家历史博物馆组成联合考古队，对义立遗址进行第二次考古发掘。

在考古发掘前，联合考古队对遗址进行分区，以义立寺为中心点，将遗址分为 A 区和 B 区，其中 A 区位于义立寺的南部，B 区处于义立寺的北部。越南国家历史博物馆原将本年度的考古发掘地点选择在遗址 B 区，随后联合考古队对遗址进行了广泛的调查和勘探（彩版二），这也是首次在越南使用探铲进行的考古勘探工作。通过调查和勘探，发现遗址的 A 区文化层堆积较厚，保存较好，故将发掘地点最终选择在 A 区。选定发掘地点后，按照当地的传统做法，

---

[1]　Nyuyen Van Hao（1968）：*Bao cao khai quat di chi Nghia Lap—Vinh Phu*，Tu lieu Vien Khao co hoc，Ha Noi。

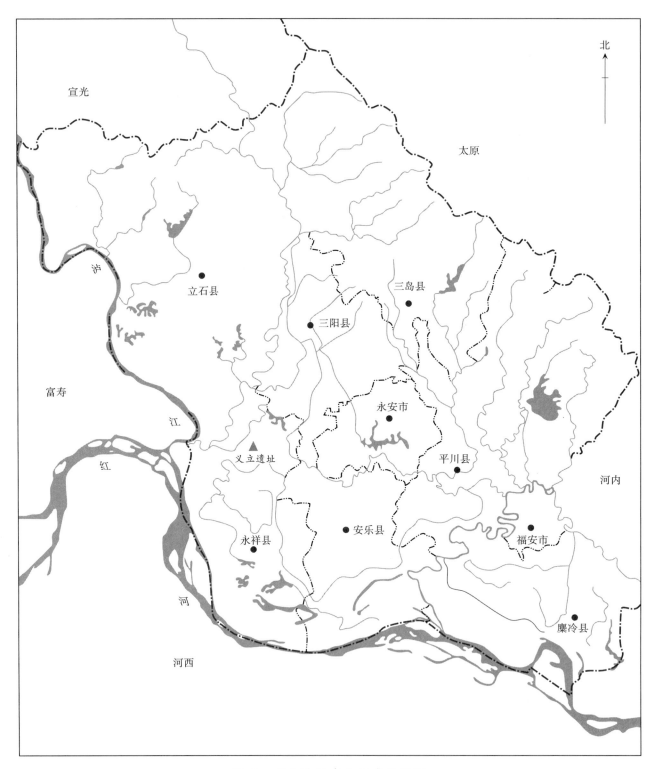

图二　义立遗址在永福省的位置

越南国家历史博物馆的工作人员前往义立寺进行祭拜（彩版三：1），并请义立寺的法师在即将发掘的工地上进行祭祀（彩版三：2）。

　　本次发掘在 A 区共布 5 米 × 5 米探方 8 个（图三；彩版四~七），中越两国联合考古队负

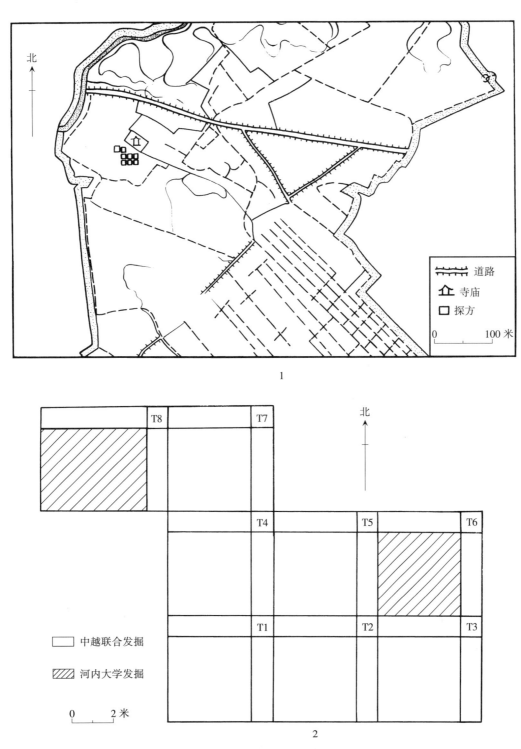

图三　遗址地形图及布方图

1. 地形图　2. 布方图

责发掘 T1 ~ T5 和 T7，越南河内国立大学负责发掘 T6 和 T8（同时，河内国立大学在 A 区发掘 1 个探方，编号为 T9），发掘面积 200 平方米（本报告不包含越南河内国立大学发掘的 T6、T8 和 T9 的材料）。发掘共清理遗迹 303 个，包括灰坑 34 个、墓葬 1 座以及与房屋建筑有关的柱洞或小坑 268 个（彩版八 ~ 一〇）。出土了大量的陶片和少量的玉器、石器，共挑选标本 834 件（图四；彩版一一 ~ 一四）。

本次考古发掘领队为四川省文物考古研究院的雷雨和陕西省考古研究院的岳连建，参加发掘的中方人员有四川省文物考古研究院的陈卫东、陕西省考古研究院的孙伟刚；越方人员有越南国家历史博物馆的 Vu Quoc Hien（武国贤）、Vu Quoc Hien（吴世丰）、Nguyen Van Doan（阮文团）、Truong Dac Chien（张德战）、Le Hoai Anh（黎怀英）、Chu Van Ve（周文卫）、Le Ngoc Hung（黎玉雄）、Nguyen Quoc Binh（阮国平）和越南国家社会科学与人文中心考古学研究院的阮文好（Nyuyen Van Hao），发掘中的翻译由阮文好（Nyuyen Van Hao）和武氏娟承担（彩版一五: 1）。

第二节　整理经过

发掘甫一结束，发掘人员即对发掘材料进行了初步整理，随后便在永福省博物馆召开了新闻发布会。中越联合考古队、越南国家历史博物馆、河内国立大学、胡志明纪念馆等相关人员就本次考古发掘的成果、意义及人骨的处理等方面进行全面的说明（彩版一五: 2），越南主要的媒体亦先后报道了本次考古发掘的成果。

2007 年 1 月中下旬，雷雨、岳连建、陈卫东分别对发掘的 T1、T2、T3、T5 及这 4 个探方内所有遗迹出土的陶片进行了统计工作，并挑选出标本[1]。随后，越南国家历史博物馆的相关人员对挑选出的标本进行了绘图、修复和拍照工作。2011 年，四川省文物考古研究院和陕西省考古研究院相关人员再赴越南，对出土的标本进行核对工作，同时亦考察了冯原文化的相关遗迹和遗物。另外，还请越南国家历史博物馆的相关人员对 T4 和 T7 内出土的陶器进行统计，并挑选标本。因四川和陕西参与本次考古发掘的人员国内发掘任务较重，致使考古发掘报告迟迟未能完成。2015 年，四川省文物考古研究院重新启动该项目的资料整理工作，由陈卫东负责对其进行全面的整理，因原始资料缺失严重和中越两国对器物存在一些分歧，致使编者在 2015 年 5 ~ 9 月，又对所有原始材料进行补充和完善。随后于 2015 年 10 月开始撰写本报告，并于 2016 年 3 月完成初稿。

本报告分 6 章，第一章介绍越南的地理环境及历史沿革，第二章介绍发掘背景与缘起，第三章介绍工作经过，第四章介绍各探方的发掘材料，第五章介绍初步研究。其中各探方材料将主要按照探方的地层堆积、遗迹和地层出土器物分别予以介绍。遗迹中主要介绍冯原文

---

[1] T4 和 T7 由孙伟刚负责发掘和整理，但因其国内有事先行离开越南，故这两个探方的统计材料和挑选标本的工作由越南国家历史博物馆派人进行。

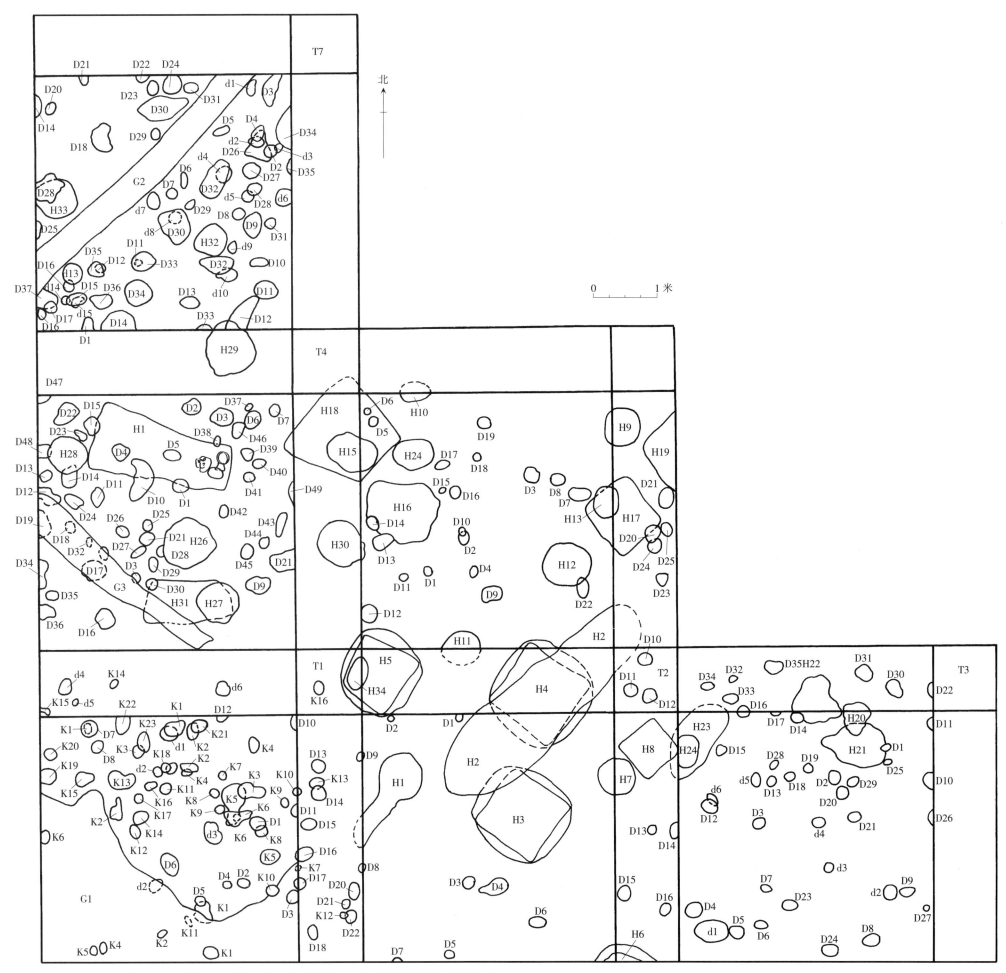

注：坑（K）和灰坑（H）均按照探方进行编号，大写均为⑤a层下，小写为⑤b层下或⑥层下。

图四 遗迹分布图

化时期的遗迹，对于近现代遗存不予以介绍。

　　为使学术界能够全面了解本次考古发掘的情况，避免著者对材料的取舍，我们对每一个探方进行全面介绍，著者的论断将放在材料的后面一并介绍。

　　义立遗址 2006 年度的考古发掘，出土了大量的遗迹和遗物，已有机构和学者曾发表了多篇相关的简报或研究性文章，凡已发表的原始材料与本报告有不符之处，均以本报告为准。

第四章　探方材料

第一节　T1

T1 位于整个发掘区的西南角，2006 年 12 月 3 日开始布方发掘，于 2007 年 1 月 8 日清理完毕，岳连建负责进行发掘、记录并绘图。

一　地层堆积

依据土质土色和包含物的不同，本探方的地层经统一后可分为 6 层（图五；彩版一六），但除第①层、②层、⑤a 层、⑥层为连续分布地层外，其余地层单位在探方内的分布并不是连续的，反映在探方四壁上就是有些地层单位的缺失。如 T1 东壁缺第③层、④b 层、⑤b 层；西壁缺第④层、⑤b 层；南壁缺第③层、④层；北壁缺第③层、④b 层、⑤b 层。现将 T1 的地层堆积情况分述如下。

第①层：厚 8 ~ 10 厘米。黄灰色耕土层，土质疏松，包含有少量的瓷片、塑料、植物根茎等。本层下叠压 G1。

第②层：厚 0 ~ 30、深 10 厘米。黄红色土，土质较硬，包含有大量的红色砖块、少量的青花瓷片、白瓷片和极少量的石器。为近现代堆积。

第③层：厚 0 ~ 16、深 20 厘米。浅灰色土，土质细密。包含有少量的砖块、瓷片等物。为近现代堆积。

第④层：分布在探方东隔梁的东北部，仅有第④a 层，厚 0 ~ 12 厘米，深褐色颗粒状土层，含有大量的铁、锰成分。包含有极少量的瓷片、陶片等。为丁朝至前黎朝时期堆积。

第⑤层：依据土质土色的不同，本层可分为两个亚层。为冯原文化时期堆积。

第⑤a 层：厚 20 ~ 52、深 34 厘米。黑灰色土，土质疏松，含有较多的红烧土颗粒。包含有大量的陶器和少量的石器。本层之下叠压有 23 个坑或柱洞。

第⑤b 层：厚 12 ~ 20、深 60 ~ 90 厘米。灰黄色土，土质较硬。包含物较少，主要是陶器和石器。本层下叠压有 16 个坑或柱洞。

第⑥层：厚 12 ~ 24、深 56 ~ 90 厘米。黄褐色土，夹杂有少量的灰土斑点，土质较硬。包含物极少。本层下叠压有 2 个坑或柱洞。为冯原文化时期堆积。

此层之下为红褐色铁锰生土层。

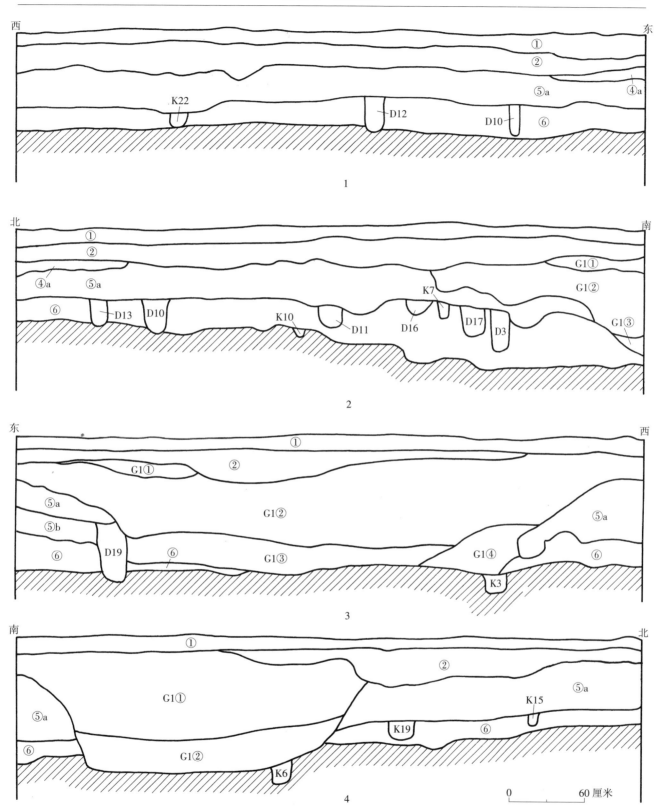

图五 T1 四壁剖面图
1. 北壁 2. 东壁 3. 南壁 4. 西壁

二 遗迹

本探方发现各类遗迹共78处，其中冯原时期的文化遗存77处，包括坑47个、柱洞30个（图六；彩版一七）。

坑

47个。开口于第⑤a层下的23个，开口于第⑤b层下的16个，叠压于G1下的6个，开

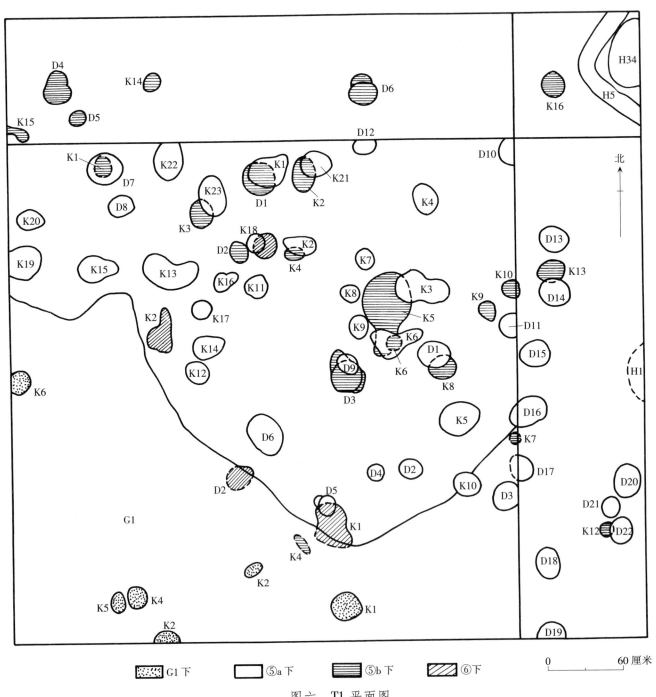

图六　T1平面图

口于第⑥层下的 2 个，平面基本呈不规则椭圆形或圆形，坑壁粗糙不平，坑底亦高低不平。部分可能系自然形成的坑窝，随后经人为填充，部分坑内出土少量的陶片。

柱洞

30 个。开口于第⑤a 层下的 22 个，开口于第⑤b 层下的 6 个，开口于第⑥层下的 2 个。平面基本呈圆形或椭圆形，较为规整，部分柱洞平面可见破损痕迹，表明其原应有柱子，填土为灰黑土或黑土，土质疏松，部分坑内包含少量的陶片。但这些柱洞和大量的坑在一起，很难将其作为一个完整的建筑分析。为准确地反映本探方的坑和柱洞情况，现将该探方的坑和柱洞列表如下。

表一 T1 各层下坑和柱洞统计表　　　　　　　　　　　　（单位：厘米）

序号	编号	层位	形制与结构			尺寸（直径－深）	填土	图号
			平面形制	坑壁	坑底			
1	K1	⑤a 下	不规则椭圆形	粗糙不平	锅底状	18～36－25	灰黑土	图七：23
2	K2	⑤a 下	椭圆形	较平整	平底	15～26－15	灰土	图七：24
3	K3	⑤a 下	不规则椭圆形	粗糙不平	锅底状	18～44－30	灰黑土	图七：25
4	K4	⑤a 下	不规则椭圆形	粗糙不平	锅底状	17×25－15	灰黑土	图七：26
5	K5	⑤a 下	椭圆形	较平整	平底	27～35－15	灰黑土	图七：27
6	K6	⑤a 下	不规则椭圆形	粗糙不平	高低不平	10～39－15	灰黑土	图七：28
7	K7	⑤a 下	圆形	较平整	锅底状	15－13	灰黑土	图七：29
8	K8	⑤a 下	近圆形	较平整	锅底状	14～18－13	灰黑土	图七：30
9	K9	⑤a 下	椭圆形	较平整	锅底状	15～19－18	黑土	图七：31
10	K10	⑤a 下	圆形	较平整	锅底状	22－20	灰黑土	图七：32
11	K11	⑤a 下	不规则圆形	较平整	锅底状	19－20	灰黑土	图七：33
12	K12	⑤a 下	圆形	平整	锅底状	20－27	黑土	图七：34
13	K13	⑤a 下	不规则椭圆形	粗糙不平	高低不平	24～47－20	灰黑土	图七：35
14	K14	⑤a 下	不规则椭圆形	粗糙不平	高低不平	18～27－18	灰黑土	图七：36
15	K15	⑤a 下	不规则椭圆形	粗糙不平	高低不平	13～32－17	灰黑土	图七：37
16	K16	⑤a 下	不规则椭圆形	粗糙不平	高低不平	10～25－10	黑土	图七：38
17	K17	⑤a	圆形	平整	锅底状	18－20	灰黑土	图七：39
18	K18	⑤a 下	圆形	平整	锅底状	14－14	灰黑土	图七：40
19	K19	⑤a 下	近圆形	平整	锅底状	20～25－13	灰黑土	图七：41
20	K20	⑤a 下	椭圆形	粗糙不平	高低不平	18～23－25	灰土	图七：42
21	K21	⑤a 下	椭圆形	平整	锅底状	20～25－25	灰黑土	图七：43
22	K22	⑤a 下	椭圆形	平整	平底	15～30－28	灰黑土	图七：44
23	K23	⑤a 下	椭圆形	平整	平底	22～33－25	黑土	图七：45
24	D1	⑤a 下	近圆形	平整	锅底状	23～25－38	灰黑土	图七：1

（续表一）

序号	编号	层位	形制与结构			尺寸（直径－深）	填土	图号
			平面形制	坑壁	坑底			
25	D2	⑤a 下	椭圆形	平整	锅底状	15～20－39	灰土	图七：2
26	D3	⑤a 下	圆形	平整	锅底状	23－35	灰黑土	图七：3
27	D4	⑤a 下	圆形	平整	锅底状	15－24	灰黑土	图七：4
28	D5	⑤a 下	椭圆形	不平	锅底状	10～20－23	灰黑土	图七：5
29	D6	⑤a 下	椭圆形	不平	高低不平	25～35－33	灰黑土	图七：6
30	D7	⑤a 下	圆形	不平	高低不平	28－30	灰黑土	图七：7
31	D8	⑤a 下	椭圆形	平整	锅底状	17～21－25	灰黑土	图七：8
32	D9	⑤a 下	椭圆形	平整	锅底状	14～20－23	灰黑土	图七：9
33	D10	⑤a 下	椭圆形	平整	锅底状	15～21－20	灰黑土	图七：10
34	D11	⑤a 下	椭圆形	平整	锅底状	15～20－25	灰黑土	图七：11
35	D12	⑤a 下	近圆形	平整	锅底状	12～18－15	灰黑土	图七：12
36	D13	⑤a 下	椭圆形	平整	锅底状	20～25－25	黑土	图七：13
37	D14	⑤a 下	圆形	平整	锅底状	25－26	灰黑土	图七：14
38	D15	⑤a 下	椭圆形	平整	平底	22～25－23	灰黑土	图七：15
39	D16	⑤a 下	椭圆形	平整	锅底状	22～34－38	黑土	图七：16
40	D17	⑤a 下	椭圆形	平整	锅底状	19～23－25	灰黑土	图七：17
41	D18	⑤a 下	椭圆形	不规整	平底	20～25－35	黑土	图七：18
42	D19	⑤a 下	椭圆形	不规整	高低不平	14～23－48	灰黑土	图七：19
43	D20	⑤a 下	圆形	不规整	平底	22－45	黑土	图七：20
44	D21	⑤a 下	圆形	平整	锅底状	15－32	灰黑土	图七：21
45	D22	⑤a 下	圆形	平整	锅底状	20－35	灰黑土	图七：22
46	K1	⑤b 下	椭圆形	平整	锅底状	13～18－8	黑土	图八：7
47	K2	⑤b 下	椭圆形	平整	锅底状	18～29－14	黑土	图八：8
48	K3	⑤b 下	椭圆形	平整	平底	18～22－13	灰土	图八：9
49	K4	⑤b 下	椭圆形	平整	锅底状	11～18－9	灰黑土	图八：10
50	K5	⑤b 下	葫芦形	粗糙不平	高低不平	16～71－18	黑土	图八：11
51	K6	⑤b 下	椭圆形	平整	锅底状	11～13－18	灰黑土	图八：12
52	K7	⑤b 下	圆形	平整	锅底状	8－13	灰黑土	图八：13
53	K8	⑤b 下	圆形	平整	锅底状	20－6	黑土	图八：14
54	K9	⑤b 下	圆形	平整	锅底状	16－9	灰黑土	图八：15

（续表一）

序号	编号	层位	形制与结构			尺寸（直径－深）	填土	图号
			平面形制	坑壁	坑底			
55	K10	⑤b 下	圆形	平整	锅底状	15－7	灰黑土	图八：16
56	K11	⑤b 下	椭圆形	平整	锅底状	9～20－9	黑土	图八：17
57	K12	⑤b 下	圆形	平整	锅底状	11－6	灰黑土	图八：18
58	K13	⑤b 下	椭圆形	平整	锅底状	18～24－6	黑土	图八：19
59	K14	⑤b 下	椭圆形	平整	锅底状	14－9	灰黑土	图八：20
60	K15	⑤b 下	不规则椭圆形	粗糙不平	平底	6～18－6	黑土	图八：21
61	K16	⑤b 下	近圆形	平整	锅底状	18～21－6	灰黑土	图八：22
62	D1	⑤b 下	椭圆形	平整	平底	27－22	黑土	图八：1
63	D2	⑤b 下	椭圆形	平整	锅底状	16－16	灰土	图八：2
64	D3	⑤b 下	不规则椭圆形	平整	锅底状	15～38－37	灰黑土	图八：3
65	D4	⑤b 下	不规则椭圆形	平整	锅底状	15～27－33	灰黑土	图八：4
66	D5	⑤b 下	圆形	平整	锅底状	16－9	黑土	图八：5
67	D6	⑤b 下	不规则椭圆形	平整	锅底状	17～27－20	灰黑土	图八：6
68	K1	G1 下	圆形	平整	锅底状	24－10	灰黑土	图八：23
69	K2	G1 下	椭圆形	平整	锅底状	10～17－9	黑土	图八：24
70	K3	G1 下	椭圆形	粗糙不平	高低不平	11～22－14	灰黑土	图八：25
71	K4	G1 下	圆形	平整	锅底状	17－9	黑土	图八：26
72	K5	G1 下	椭圆形	平整	锅底状	11～16－6	灰黑土	图八：27
73	K6	G1 下	椭圆形	平整	锅底状	16～18－13	黑土	图八：28
74	D1	⑥下	圆形	平整	锅底状	22－22	灰黑土	图八：29
75	D2	⑥下	椭圆形	平整	锅底状	18～26－20	黑土	图八：30
76	K1	⑥下	不规则形	不规整	高低不平	23～38－21	灰黑土	图八：32
77	K2	⑥下	不规则形	不规整	锅底状	9～37－29	黑土	图八：31

三 地层中出土遗物

（一）T1⑤a 层出土器物

T1 第⑤a 层出土器物以陶器为主，还有少量的石器和玉器，共挑选标本 341 件，包括石器 29 件、玉器 3 件、角器 1 件、陶器 308 件。

石器

29 件。以磨制石器为主，但残损严重，可能系在使用或二次利用过程中，致使石器表面

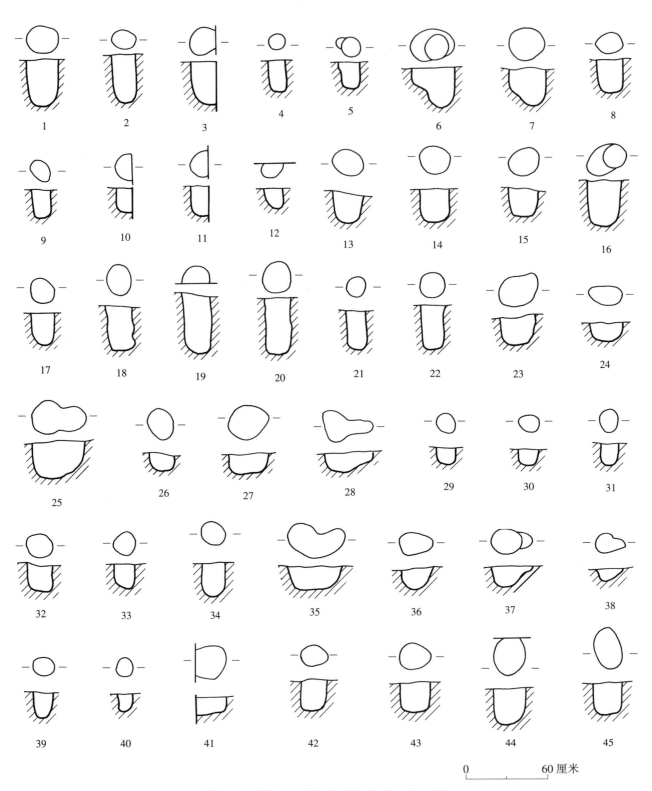

0   60 厘米

图七　T1⑤a 层下的柱洞和坑平、剖面图

1～22. D1～D22　23～45. K1～K23

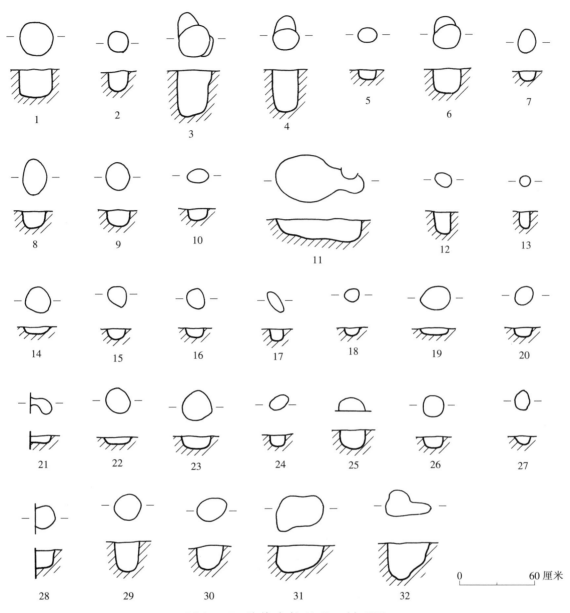

图八　T1 的坑和柱洞平、剖面图

1～6. D1～D6（T1⑤b 层下）　　7～22. K1～K16（T1⑤b 层下）　　23～28. K1～K6（G1 下）

29～32. D1、D2、K1、K2（T1⑥层下）

出现大量疤痕，疤痕主要集中在石器的顶部、一侧或器身表面。包括锛 12 件、凿 1 件、核 2件、刮削器 1 件、拍 1 件、残石器 12 件。

锛　12 件。依据形制的不同可分为两个类型。

第一类：3 件。体均呈长方形，双面弧刃。

标本 T1②：1，残，通体磨制，双面弧刃，顶部及其一侧可见打击后留下的打击点和放射线。长 6.8、残宽 4.6、厚 1.6 厘米（图九：1；彩版一八：1）。标本 T1⑤a：13，残，一面已被剥片，另一面可见剥片时留下的打击点和放射线，刃部可见磨制的痕迹。残长

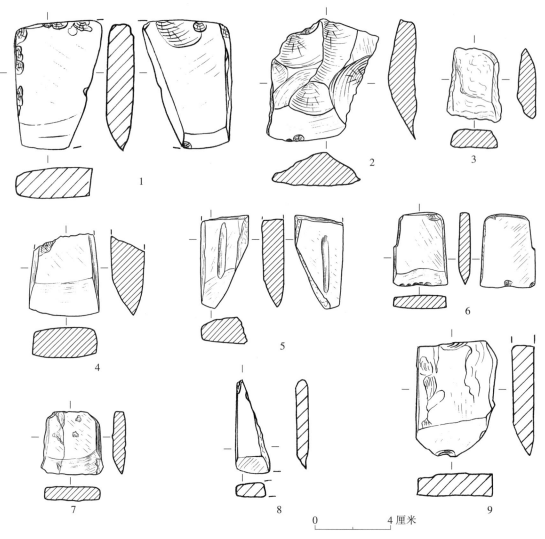

图九　T1 出土石锛

1. T1②:1　2. T1⑤a:13　3. T1⑤a:14　4. T1⑤a:7　5. T1⑤a:1　6. T1⑤a:2　7. T1⑤a:6
8. T1②:6　9. T1②:4

6.4、残宽4.9、厚1.8厘米（图九:2；彩版一八:2）。标本 T1⑤a:14，残损严重，一面可见磨制痕迹，另一面可见剥片时留下的打击点和放射线。残长4、残宽2.8、厚1厘米（图九:3）。

第二类：体均呈上窄下宽的梯形，通体磨制，单面弧刃。

标本 T1⑤a:7，上部残，一侧顶端可见打击点和放射线。残长4.4、宽3~3.7、厚1.7厘米（图九:4；彩版一八:3）。标本 T1⑤a:1，残甚，器身中部有一凹槽。残长4.8、残宽2.5、厚1.2厘米（图九:5）。标本 T1②:2，残，顶端一侧可见打击点和放射线。残长3.9、残宽2.8、厚0.7厘米（图九:6；彩版一八:4）。标本 T1⑤a:6，残，器身保留剥片后留下的疤痕。长3.3、宽3.2、厚0.7厘米（图九:7）。标本 T1②:6，仅存下部一小段。残长5、残宽1.9、厚0.8厘米（图九:8）。标本 T1②:4，残，刃部磨制，器表剥片痕迹明显，顶

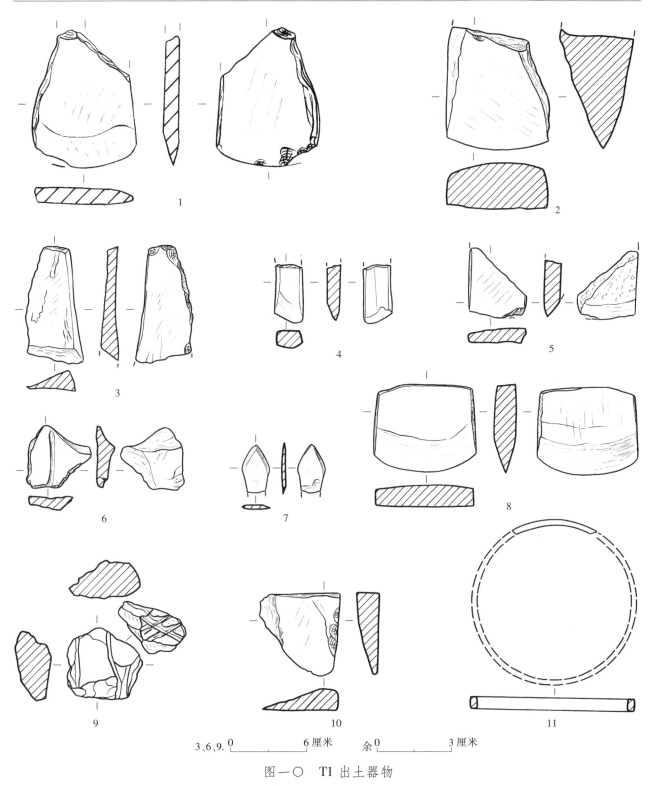

图一〇　T1 出土器物

1、2、5. 石锛（G1：1、T1⑤a：10、T1⑤a：25）　3、6. 石核（T1②：8、T1⑤a：23）　4. 石凿（G1：2）　7. 玉箭镞（T1⑤a：8）　8. 玉锛（T1⑤a：3）　9. 石拍（T1⑤a：373）　10. 石刮削器（T1⑤a：5）　11. 玉环（T1⑤a：20）

部和刃部可见打击后留下的打击点和放射线。残长 6、残宽 4.2、厚 1.3 厘米（图九：9）。标本 G1：1，一侧残，一面刃部使用痕迹明显。残长 5.1、宽 3.8、厚 0.7 厘米（图一〇：1；

彩版一九：1）。标本 T1⑤a：10，上部及一侧残。残长 4.8、残宽 3～3.8、厚 2.7 厘米（图一〇：2，彩版一九：2）。标本 T1⑤a：25，残，一面和刃部可见磨制痕迹，另一面可见打击后留下的疤痕。残长 2.4、宽 2.1、厚 0.6 厘米（图一〇：5；彩版一九：3）。

凿　1 件。

标本 G1：2，上部残，通体磨制，体呈长条形，双面弧刃。残长 2.2、宽 1、厚 0.7 厘米（图一〇：4）。

核　2 件。

标本 T1②：8，残，体呈不规则长方形，器表顶端和一侧可见剥片时留下的打击点和放射线。残长 8.6、残宽 4.2、厚 1.6 厘米（图一〇：3）。标本 T1⑤a：23，体呈不规则长方形，一面可见剥片后留下的疤痕。长 4.6、宽 4.6、厚 1.6 厘米（图一〇：6）。

刮削器　1 件。

标本 T1⑤a：5，体呈三角形，一面保持自然砺石面，另一面可见剥片后留下的疤痕，一侧可见打击后留下的打击点和放射线。长 3.1、宽 2.9、厚 0.9 厘米（图一〇：10）。

拍　1 件。

标本 T1⑤a：373，残，体呈长方形，器表剥片痕迹明显，一侧可见两道凹槽痕。残长 5.4、残宽 5.6、厚 2.9 厘米（图一〇：9）。

残石器　12 件。可能系石斧或石锛因使用后残断或剥片后形成的。

标本 T1②：2，残，体呈长方形，顶部和一侧可见磨制痕迹，刃部残缺，顶部、一侧及刃部可见打击后留下的打击点、放射线。残长 5.5、残宽 4.6、厚 1.6 厘米（图一一：1）。标本 T1②：3，残，仅存上部，磨制。残长 2.6、宽 2.5、厚 1.4～1.6 厘米（图一一：8）。标本 T1②：7，残，磨制，一面可见剥片后留下的疤痕，下端可见打击后留下的打击点、放射线。残长 2.2、宽 1.5、厚 0.6 厘米（图一一：2）。标本 T1⑤a：11，体呈不规则长方形，器表可见部分磨制的痕迹。残长 3.4、残宽 4、厚 1.5 厘米（图一一：10）。标本 T1⑤a：16，体呈不规则长方形，器表保留剥片留下的疤痕。残长 4.4、残宽 3.1、厚 1.8 厘米（图一一：11）。标本 T1⑤a：12，残，器表保留剥片留下的疤痕。残长 3.8、宽 2.8、厚 0.9 厘米（图一一：12）。标本 T1⑤a：21，残，体呈长方形，器表保留剥片时留下的疤痕。残长 9、宽 5.5、厚 0.6 厘米（图一一：3）。标本 T1⑤a：15，残损严重，一面和一侧保留有磨制的痕迹，另一面和一侧可见剥片后留下的打击点和放射线。残长 7.6、残宽 4.8、厚 3.2 厘米（图一一：7）。标本 T1⑤a：24，体呈长方形，残存少部分，器表剥片痕迹明显。残长 2.7、残宽 2、厚 0.7 厘米（图一一：6）。标本 T1⑤a：22，残损严重，器表两面保留有磨制的痕迹。残长 2.8、残宽 1.9、厚 0.5 厘米（图一一：5）。标本 T1⑤a：17，残，一面可见磨制痕迹。残长 4.6、残宽 4.6、厚 1.2 厘米（图一一：9）。标本 T1⑤a：19，残，体呈长方形，为剥片留下的残片。残长 5.8、残宽 2.8、厚 1.4 厘米（图一一：4）。

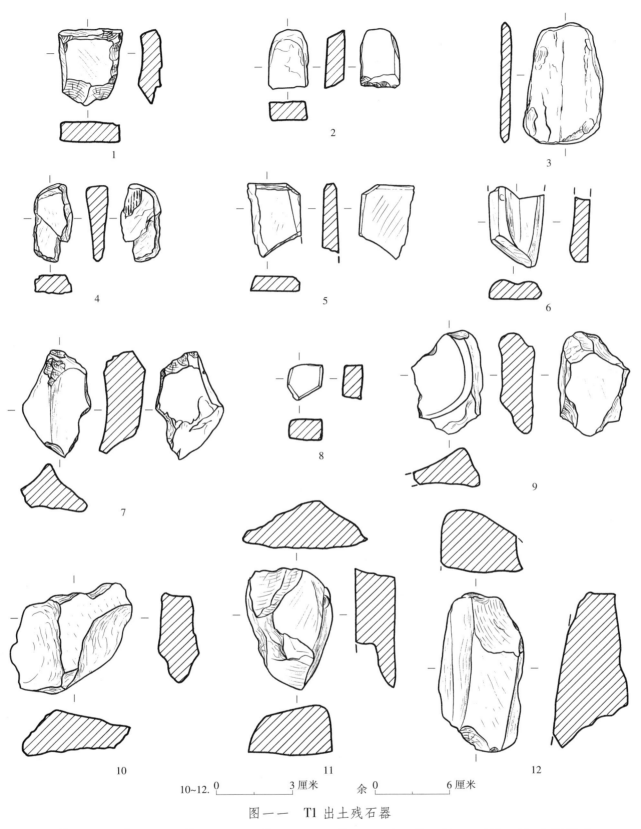

图一一　T1 出土残石器

1. T1②：2　2. T1②：7　3. T1⑤a：21　4. T1⑤a：19　5. T1⑤a：22　6. T1⑤a：24　7. T1⑤a：15　8. T1②：3
9. T1⑤a：17　10. T1⑤a：11　11. T1⑤a：16　12. T1⑤a：12

玉器

3 件。包括环 1 件、斧 1 件、箭镞 1 件。

环　1 件。

标本 T1⑤a：20，残，仅存三分之一，乳白色，体呈圆形。直径 6.1、宽 0.5、厚 0.2 厘米（图一〇：11）。

锛　1 件。

标本 T1⑤a：3，上部残，通体磨制，体呈长方形，双面弧刃。残长 3.3、宽 3.7、厚 0.9 厘米（图一〇：8；彩版二〇：1）。

箭镞　1 件。

标本 T1⑤a：8，仅存镞头部分，正视略呈三角形，通体磨制。残长 1.8、宽 1、厚 0.1 厘米（图一〇：7；彩版二〇：2）。

角器　1 件。为角环。

标本 T1⑤a：9，残，黑色，体呈环状。残长 2.5、宽 1.3、厚 0.1 厘米。

陶器

本探方第⑤a 地层共出土陶片 7052 片。从陶质来看，夹细砂陶比例约为 82.4%，粗砂陶约为 15.2%，泥质磨光陶比例约为 2.4%。从陶色上看，红陶、红褐陶、褐陶比例约为 84.7%，说明其陶色偏于红色。从纹饰上看，纹饰极其发达，约占陶片总数的 31.1%，部分陶器表面施陶衣。纹饰种类丰富，其中绳纹约占纹饰种类总数的 82%，其他纹饰有刻划纹、戳印纹、凹弦纹、凸棱纹、压印纹、梳刷纹、附加堆纹、篦点纹等，尤以在各种刻划纹带内填充篦齿状或篦点状戳印纹的装饰风格最具特点。集多种纹饰在单个陶器上的复合纹饰甚为流行，纹饰图案主要有云纹、S 形纹、几何形纹、圆圈纹、水波纹等（图一二～一八；彩版二一～二五）。陶器口部多为敛口和侈口，喇叭形口和直口次之，器类主要是圜底器和圈足器，器形包括侈口罐、钵、桶、支座、厚唇罐、纺轮、球等。

T1 第⑤a 层共挑选陶器标本 308 件。其中纹饰标本 151 件、器形标本 157 件，包括支座 5 件、纺轮 2 件、器鋬 5 件、器耳 1 件、圈足 32 件、喇叭口罐 12 件、厚唇罐 21 件、侈口罐 22 件、桶 1 件、敛口罐 1 件、钵 55 件。

支座　5 件。残损严重，仅 1 件可辨器形，体呈柱状，椭圆形底，器身弯曲，一侧饰弓形耳。

标本 T1⑤a：26，残，夹砂红褐陶。仅存底部，底面饰竖向绳纹。底径 6.2、残高 1.6 厘米（图一九：1）。标本 T1⑤a：28，残，夹细砂红褐陶。仅存支座底部，底面饰横向绳纹。底径 6.4、残高 4 厘米（图一九：3）。标本 T1⑤a：29，残，夹细砂红褐陶。仅存少量的底部，底面饰横向绳纹。底径 6、残高 3.4 厘米（图一九：2）。标本 T1⑤a：57，残，夹砂褐陶。体呈柱状，椭圆形底，器身弯曲，一侧饰弓形耳。器身饰经抹平的绳纹，底面饰竖向绳纹。残长 11、宽 5.6、底径 5.6 厘米（图一九：4；彩版二六：1）。标本 T1⑤a：58，两端残，夹砂褐陶。器身一端中部可见残留的泥条。素面。残长 8.8 厘米（图一九：5）。

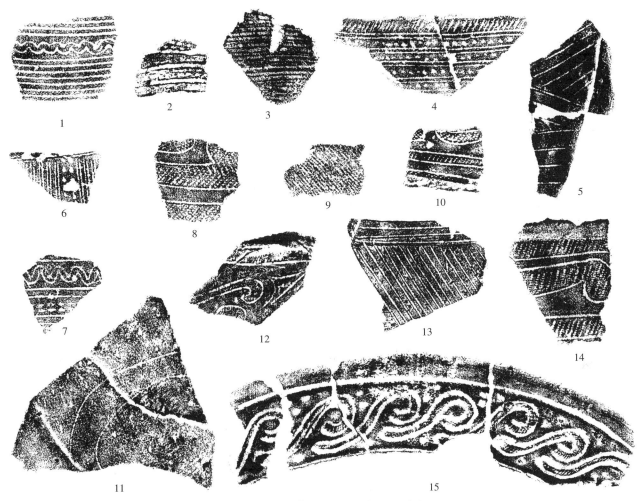

图一二　T1⑤a层出土陶器拓片*

1. 水波纹＋凹弦纹（T1⑤a：279）　2. 凹弦纹（T1⑤a：351）　3. 细绳纹（T1⑤a：21）　4. 短线＋凹弦纹＋坑点纹（T1⑤a：353）　5. 刻划线纹（T1⑤a：249）　6. 凹弦纹＋刻划线纹＋坑点纹（T1⑤a：357）　7. 水波纹＋凹弦纹（T1⑤a：379）　8. 刻划纹＋篦点纹（T1⑤a：301）　9. 细绳纹（T1⑤a：55）　10. 刻划纹＋篦点纹（T1⑤a：315）　11. 刻划纹（T1⑤a：257）　12. 凸棱＋刻划纹（T1⑤a：230）　13. 凹弦纹＋刻划线纹（T1⑤a：247）　14. 刻划纹＋篦点纹（T1⑤a：317）　15. 凹弦纹＋S形纹（T1⑤a：188）

纺轮　2件。依据形制的不同可分为两个类型。

第一类：1件。体呈塔形，中有一孔。

标本T1⑤a：4，残，夹砂红陶。直径1~3.7、孔径0.5、通高2.3厘米（图一九：7；彩版二六：2）。

第二类：1件。体呈饼状，中有一空。

标本T1⑤a：18，残，夹砂黑陶。器表刻划有四道凹弦纹，凹弦纹之间饰戳刺的坑点纹。直径4.5、厚0.7、孔径0.5厘米（图一九：6；彩版二六：3）。

---

* 本报告中所有陶器拓片均没有比例，另标明者除外。

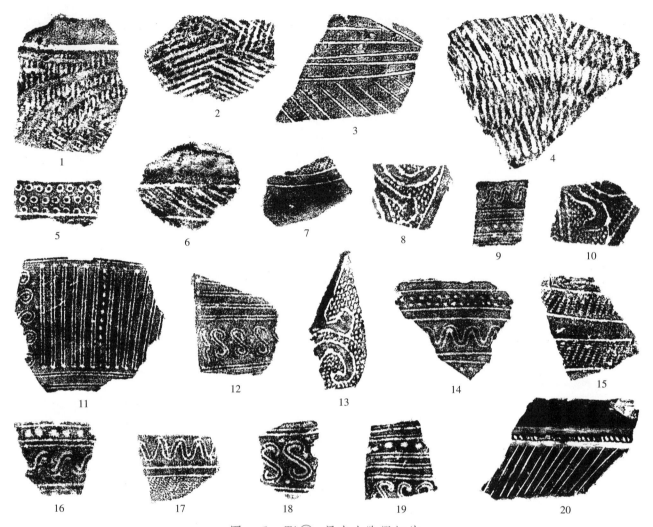

图一三　T1⑤a 层出土陶器拓片

1. 凹弦纹＋细绳纹（T1⑤a：98）　 2. 交错绳纹（T1⑤a：53）　 3. 刻划线纹（T1⑤a：248）　 4. 绳纹（T1⑤a：54）　 5. 圆圈纹＋凹弦纹（T1⑤a：18）　 6. 凹弦纹＋短线纹（T1⑤a：62）　 7. 刻划纹＋篦点纹（T1⑤a：293）　 8. 刻划纹＋篦点纹（T1⑤a：16）　 9. S 形纹＋凹弦纹（T1⑤a：275）　 10. 刻划纹＋篦点纹（T1⑤a：12）　 11. S 形纹＋刻划线纹＋凹弦纹（T1⑤a：283）12. 凹弦纹＋S 形纹（T1⑤a：284）　 13. 刻划纹＋篦点纹（T1⑤a：4）　 14. 凹弦纹＋水波纹（T1⑤a：278）　 15. 刻划纹＋篦点纹（T1⑤a：8）　 16. 点纹＋凹弦纹＋S 形纹（T1⑤a：276）　 17. 水波纹＋凹弦纹＋篦点纹（T1⑤a：282）　 18. 凹弦纹＋S 形纹（T1⑤a：288）　 19. 凹弦纹＋坑点纹＋S 形纹（T1⑤a：17）　 20. 凸棱＋坑点纹＋刻划线纹（T1⑤a：246）

器鋬　5 件。依据形制的不同可分为两型。

第一类：3 件。体呈舌状。

标本 T1⑤a：33，残，夹砂红褐陶。素面。长 3.6、宽 3.7、厚 1.5 厘米（图二〇：1）。标本 T1⑤a：34，残，夹砂红褐陶。素面。长 4.1、宽 3.8、厚 1.8 厘米（图二〇：2）。标本 T1⑤a：250，夹砂红褐陶。器表两面饰横向绳纹。残长 6、宽 2～6 厘米（图二〇：4）。

第二类：2 件。体呈柱状。

标本 T1⑤a：59，残，夹砂褐陶。器身略弯曲。素面。残长 2、宽 3.2 厘米（图二〇：5）。

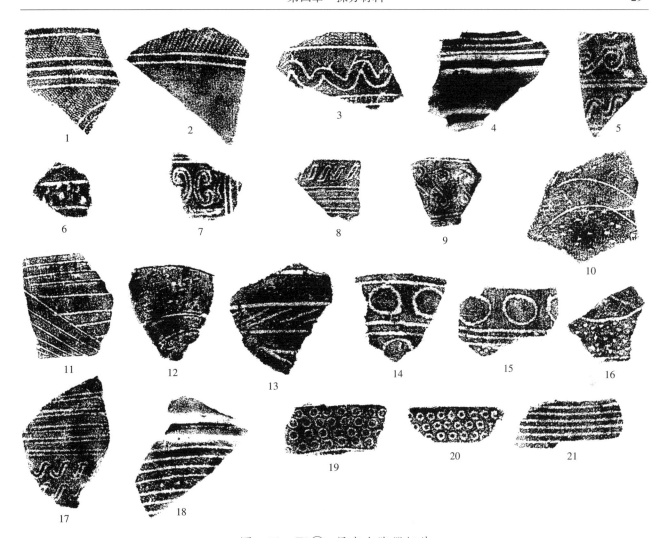

图一四 T1⑤a层出土陶器拓片

1. 刻划纹＋篦点纹（T1⑤a：332） 2. 凹弦纹＋绳纹（T1⑤a：334） 3. 凹弦纹＋水波纹＋绳纹（T1⑤a：280） 4. 凹弦纹＋凸棱（T1⑤a：209） 5. 凹弦纹＋S形纹（T1⑤a：289） 6. 凹弦纹＋坑点纹（T1⑤a：74） 7. 刻划线纹＋云纹（T1⑤a：291） 8. 凹弦纹＋S形纹（T1⑤a：290） 9. 凹弦纹＋S形纹（T1⑤a：332） 10. 刻划纹（T1⑤a：252） 11. 刻划线纹（T1⑤a：253） 12. 刻划纹（T1⑤a：250） 13. 刻划纹＋戳刺纹（T1⑤a：235） 14. 凹弦纹＋圆圈纹（T1⑤a：259） 15. 圆圈纹＋凹弦纹＋篦点纹（T1⑤a：257） 16. 刻划纹＋篦点纹（T1⑤a：251） 17. 凹弦纹＋S形纹（T1⑤a：273） 18. 凸棱＋凹弦纹＋坑点纹（T1⑤a：267） 19. 圆圈纹＋凹弦纹（T1⑤a：261） 20. 圆圈纹（T1⑤a：262） 21. 凹弦纹（T1⑤a：270）

标本T1⑤a：162，夹砂灰陶。体弯曲。素面。残长2.8厘米（图二〇：6）。

　　器耳 1件。

　　标本T1⑤a：200，夹砂褐陶，体呈弧状。器表饰经涂抹过的绳纹。残长7.4厘米（图二〇：3）。

　　圈足 32件。依据形制的不同可分为三个类型。

　　第一类：13件。呈桶状。

　　标本T1⑤a：43，圈足以上残，夹砂红褐陶。圈足底部和圈足部饰交错绳纹。底径

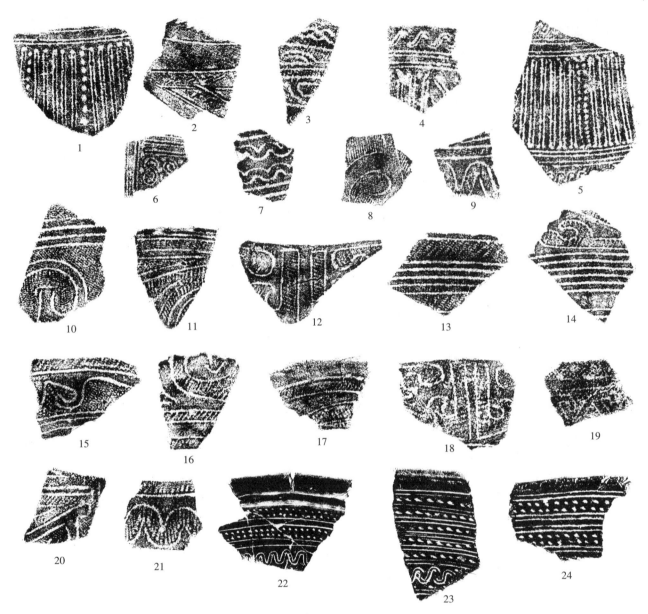

图一五　T1⑤a层出土陶器拓片

1. 凹弦纹＋刻划线纹＋坑点纹（T1⑤a：272）　　2. 刻划线纹（T1⑤a：256）　　3. 水波纹＋刻划纹（T1⑤a：309）　　4. S形纹＋凹弦纹＋刻划线纹（T1⑤a：274）　　5. 凹弦纹＋刻划线纹＋坑点纹＋S形纹（T1⑤a：271）　　6. S形纹＋刻划线纹（T1⑤a：286）　　7. 凹弦纹＋水波纹（T1⑤a：281）　　8. 刻划纹＋篦点纹（T1⑤a：292）　　9. 刻划纹＋水波纹（T1⑤a：300）　　10、11. 凹弦纹＋刻划纹（T1⑤a：320、322）　　12. 刻划纹（T1⑤a：319）　　13. 凹弦纹＋篦点纹（T1⑤a：294）　　14. 刻划纹＋凹弦纹（T1⑤a：318）　　15～17. 凹弦纹＋刻划纹（T1⑤a：321、323、313）　　18～20. 刻划纹＋篦点纹（T1⑤a：307、310、308）　　21. 刻划纹＋篦点纹＋水波纹（T1⑤a：299）　　22. 凹弦纹＋坑点纹＋水波纹（T1⑤a：277）　　23. 凹弦纹＋点纹＋S形纹（T1⑤a：287）　　24. 凹弦纹＋坑点纹（T1⑤a：343）

14.3、残高3.6厘米（图二一：1）。标本T1⑤a：41，足以上残，夹砂红褐陶。足部饰两道凹弦纹和竖向绳纹。底径14、足残高3.7厘米（图二一：9）。标本T1⑤a：182，夹砂红褐陶。底径17.7、残高3.9厘米（图二一：6；彩版二七：1）。标本T1⑤a：94，夹砂红褐陶。

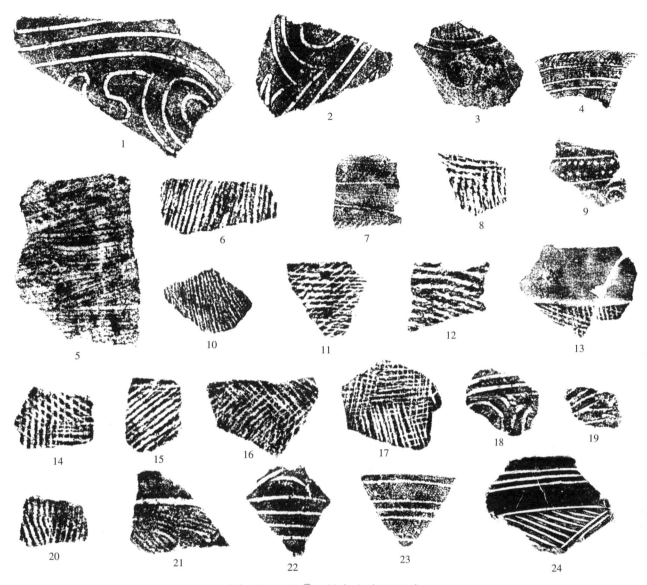

图一六 T1⑤a 层出土陶器拓片

1~3. 刻划纹（T1⑤a：215、216、375） 4. 凹弦纹＋篦点纹（T1⑤a：377） 5. 梳刷纹（T1⑤a：369） 6. 绳纹（T1⑤a：87） 7. 凹弦纹＋绳纹（T1⑤a：359） 8. 绳纹（T1⑤a：368） 9. 凹弦纹＋篦点纹（T1⑤a：349） 10. 绳纹（T1⑤a：107） 11. 交错绳纹（T1⑤a：39－1） 12. 绳纹（T1⑤a：88） 13. 凹弦纹＋交错绳纹（T1⑤a：108） 14. 交错绳纹（T1⑤a：83） 15. 绳纹（T1⑤a：39－3） 16. 交错绳纹（T1⑤a：39－2） 17. 交错绳纹（T1⑤a：82） 18、19. 刻划纹（T1⑤a：243、366） 20. 绳纹（T1⑤a：101） 21. 凹弦纹＋绳纹（T1⑤a：214） 22. 凹弦纹＋刻划纹（T1⑤a：232） 23. 凹弦纹＋篦点纹（T1⑤a：331） 24. 凹弦纹＋刻划纹（T1⑤a：245）

足部饰涂抹过的梳刷纹。底径10.8、残高3.9厘米（图二一：11）。标本T1⑤a：228，夹砂红褐陶。圈足上饰刻划的线纹和弦纹。底径13.4、残高2.7厘米（图二二：1）。标本T1⑤a：132，残，夹砂褐陶。底径16.3、残高3.8厘米（图二二：3）。标本T1⑤a：140，夹砂褐陶。底径18、残高4.1厘米（图二二：4）。标本T1⑤a：202，残，夹细砂红陶。底径14.7、残高3.7厘米（图二二：7）。标本T1⑤a：183，残，夹砂红陶。底径14.5、残高3.4厘米

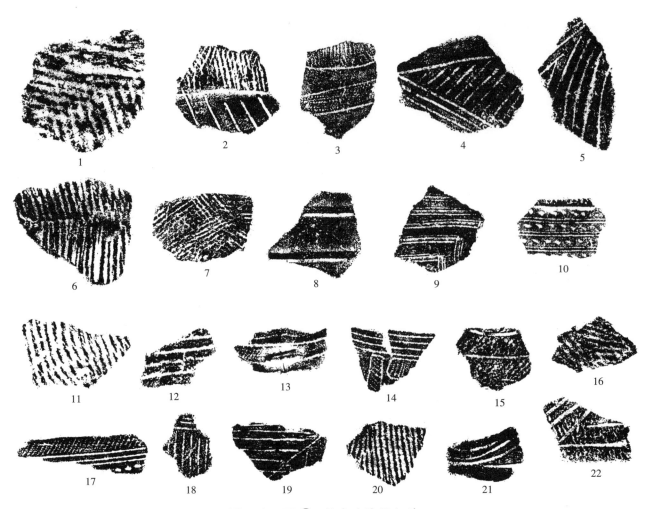

图一七　T1⑤a 层出土陶器拓片

1. 绳纹（T1⑤a：46）　2、3. 绳纹＋刻划线纹（T1⑤a：45、338）　4、5. 刻划线纹（T1⑤a：211、217）　6. 绳纹（T1⑤a：37）　7. 交错绳纹（T1⑤a：105）　8. 凸棱纹（T1⑤a：134）　9. 刻划纹（T1⑤a：224）　10. 凸棱纹＋凹弦纹＋坑点纹（T1⑤a：348）　11. 绳纹（T1⑤a：367）　12. 凹弦纹（T1⑤a：72）　13. 凹弦纹＋凸棱纹（T1⑤a：329）　14. 凹弦纹＋刻划纹（T1⑤a：357）　15. 凹弦纹＋绳纹（T1⑤a：90）　16. 绳纹（T1⑤a：106）　17. 坑点纹＋凹弦纹＋绳纹（T1⑤a：355）　18、19. 刻划线纹（T1⑤a：73、237）　20. 绳纹（T1⑤a：95）　21、22. 刻划纹（T1⑤a：219、96）

（图二二：8）。标本 T1⑤a：137，夹砂红褐陶。底径 14.6、残高 4.7 厘米（图二二：10）。标本 T1⑤a：31，残，夹砂红褐陶。足部饰竖向绳纹。圈足径 14.8、残高 3.4 厘米（图二二：12）。标本 T1⑤a：35，残，夹砂红褐陶。足部饰斜向绳纹。底径 10.5、足残高 3.9 厘米（图二二：13）。标本 T1⑤a：52，仅存圈足下部，夹砂褐陶。足部饰斜向绳纹。底径 13.5、残高 4 厘米（图二二：14）。

　　第二类：16 件。呈喇叭状，足尖外撇。

　　标本 T1⑤a：198，夹细砂红陶。底径 25.5、残高 2.4 厘米（图二一：4）。标本 T1⑤a：303，夹砂褐陶。足上饰两道凹弦纹和篦点纹。底径 12.8、残高 1.8 厘米（图二一：7）。标本

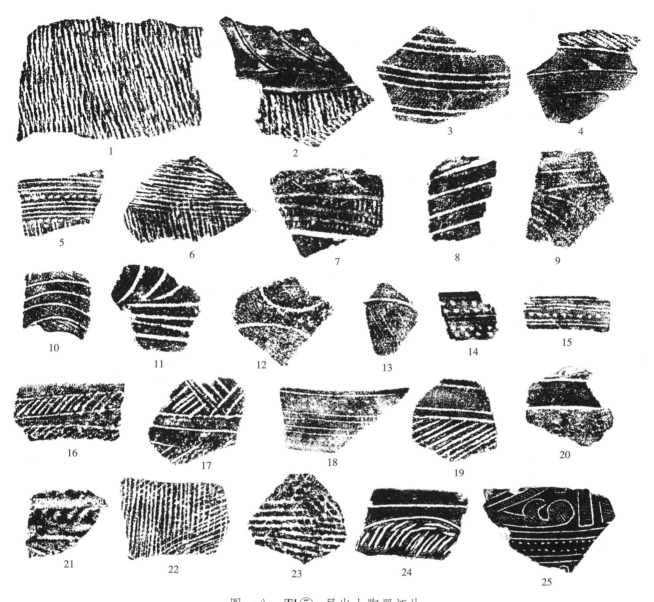

图一八 T1⑤a 层出土陶器拓片

1. 梳刷纹（T1⑤a：104） 2. 刻划纹＋绳纹（T1⑤a：244） 3. 凹弦纹＋篦点纹（T1⑤a：331） 4. 凹弦纹＋篦点纹＋绳纹（T1⑤a：333） 5. 凹弦纹＋刻划纹＋坑点纹（T1⑤a：347） 6. 绳纹（T1⑤a：93） 7. 凹弦纹＋刻划纹（T1⑤a：76） 8、9. 刻划线纹（T1⑤a：222、236） 10～13. 刻划纹（T1⑤a：233、68、218、213） 14、15. 凹弦纹＋坑点纹（T1⑤a：350、352） 16. 凹弦纹＋绳纹（T1⑤a：223） 17. 凹弦纹＋刻划纹（T1⑤a：221） 18. 凹弦纹＋坑点纹（T1⑤a：346） 19. 凹弦纹＋刻划线纹（T1⑤a：44） 20. 凹弦纹（T1⑤a：146） 21. 凸棱＋刻划纹（T1⑤a：159） 22、23. 交错绳纹（T1⑤a：92、89） 24. 凹弦纹＋刻划叶脉纹（T1⑤a：225） 25. 刻划纹＋凹弦纹＋坑点纹（T1⑤a：316）

T1⑤a：269，夹砂褐陶。底径 20.4、残高 1.4 厘米（图二一：8）。标本 T1⑤a：311，夹砂红褐陶。足下部饰两道凹弦纹，凹弦纹之间饰篦点纹，足上部刻划 S 形纹，S 形纹中饰篦点纹。底径 13.1、残高 2.4 厘米（图二一：10）。标本 T1⑤a：145，夹砂灰陶。底径 29.6、残高 2.8

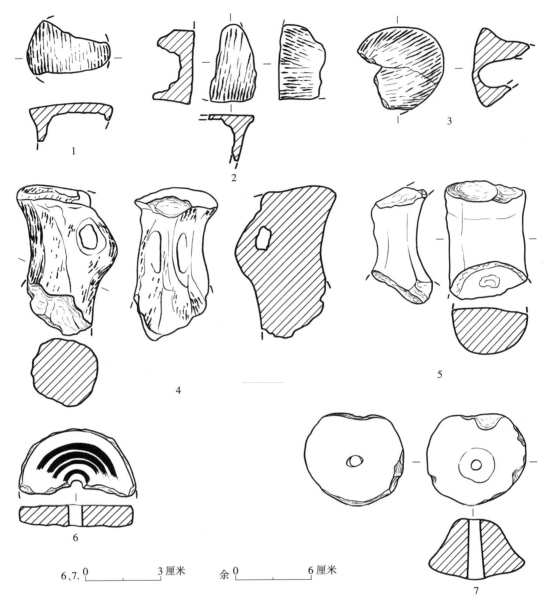

图一九　T1⑤a 层出土陶器

1~5. 支座（T1⑤a：26、29、28、57、58）　6、7. 纺轮（T1⑤a：18、4）

厘米（图二一：15）。标本 T1⑤a：337，夹砂灰黑陶。足上部饰两道凹弦纹，凹弦纹之间饰篦点纹。底径 20.7、残高 5.2 厘米（图二一：12）。标本 T1⑤a：188，夹砂黑陶。圈足上、下各饰一道凹弦纹，两道凹弦纹之间刻划有 S 形纹，S 形纹中戳刺有短线纹。底径 21.6、残高 4.4 厘米（图二一：13；彩版二七：4）。标本 T1⑤a：131，夹砂褐陶，足底饰绳纹。底径 9.1、残高 3.3 厘米（图二一：16）。标本 T1⑤a：99，仅存圈足下部，夹砂灰褐陶。足中部刻划有三角形纹，足下部饰两道凹弦纹。底径 18.5、残高 4.2 厘米（图二一：14）。标本 T1⑤a：111，夹砂褐陶。素面。底径 18.6、残高 4.6 厘米（图二二：2）。标本 T1⑤a：180，夹细砂红陶。圈足中部饰一道凸棱。底径 16.5、残高 4.5 厘米（图二二：5；图二七：2）。标

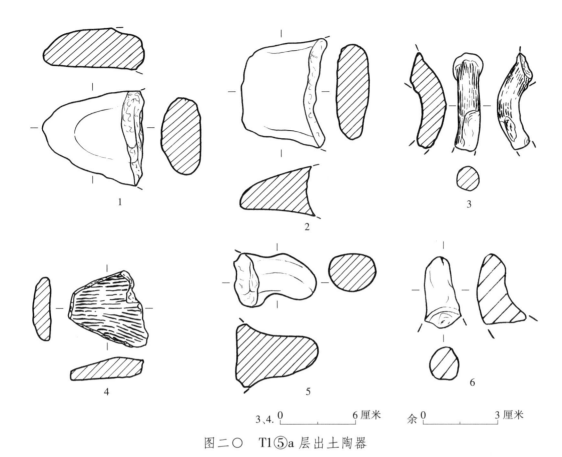

图二〇 T1⑤a 层出土陶器

1、2、4~6. 器鋬（T1⑤a：33、34、250、59、162） 3. 器耳（T1⑤a：200）

本 T1⑤a：129，夹砂褐陶。底径 10.7、残高 3.3 厘米（图二二：6）。标本 T1⑤a：121，夹砂红褐陶。底径 6.6、残高 3.4 厘米（图二二：9）。标本 T1⑤a：27，足以上残，夹砂红褐陶。足上部饰竖向绳纹。底径 12、残高 3.3 厘米（图二二：11）。标本 T1⑤a：181，夹细砂红褐陶。底径 20、残高 3.8 厘米（图二二：15；彩版二七：3）。标本 T1⑤a：371，夹砂褐陶。底径 20.8、残高 2.4 厘米（图二二：16）。

第三类：3 件。呈喇叭状，足尖内折。

标本 T1⑤a：345，夹砂红褐陶。足部饰三道凹弦纹，凹弦纹之间饰戳刺的坑点纹。底径 28.6、残高 1.3 厘米（图二一：3）。标本 T1⑤a：312，夹砂红褐陶。足下部饰两道凹弦纹，凹弦纹之间饰篦点纹，足上部刻划 S 形纹，S 形纹中饰篦点纹。底径 16.7、残高 2 厘米（图二一：2）。标本 T1⑤a：298，夹砂灰褐陶。圈足上饰 S 形纹，S 形纹内饰篦点纹。底径 18.6、残高 6.8 厘米（图二一：5）。

喇叭口罐 12 件。依据颈部的不同可分为两个类型。

第一类：4 件。颈部饰凸棱一周。

标本 T1⑤a：189，夹细砂红褐陶。圆唇，束颈。口径 25.4、残高 3.8 厘米（图二三：1）。标本 T1⑤a：190，夹砂红褐陶，表面磨光。圆唇。口径 28.7、残高 3.8 厘米（图二三：3）。标本 T1⑤a：186，夹砂红褐陶。圆唇，侈口，折肩，斜直腹。肩部饰一道凸棱。凸棱上戳刺

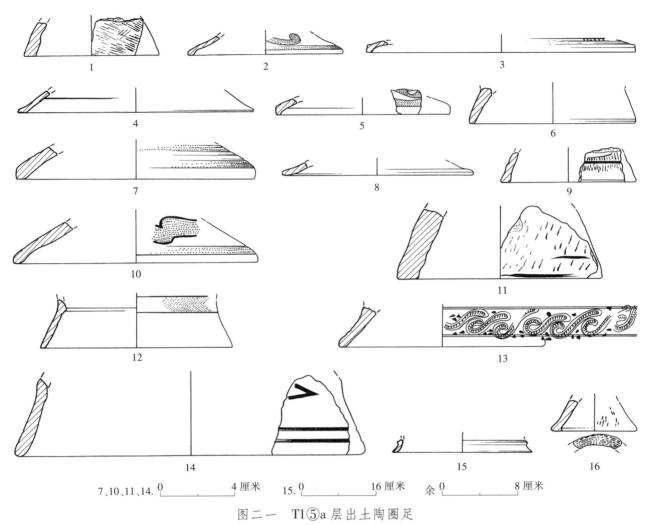

7、10、11、14. 0 ———— 4厘米　　15. 0 ———— 16厘米　　余 0 ———— 8厘米

图二一　T1⑤a层出土陶圈足

1. T1⑤a：43　2. T1⑤a：312　3. T1⑤a：345　4. T1⑤a：198　5. T1⑤a：298　6. T1⑤a：182　7. T1⑤a：303　8. T1⑤a：269　9.
T1⑤a：41　10. T1⑤a：311　11. T1⑤a：94　12. T1⑤a：337　13. T1⑤a：188　14. T1⑤a：99　15. T1⑤a：145　16. T1⑤a：131

有短线纹。口径 32.8、残高 4.6 厘米（图二三：11）。标本 T1⑤a：187，夹细砂红陶。圆唇，
束颈。颈中部饰一道凸棱。口径 29.5、残高 3.7 厘米（图二三：12）。

　　第二类：8 件。颈部无凸棱。

　　标本 T1⑤a：91，夹砂红褐陶。圆唇。口下部饰两道凹弦纹，其下饰斜向绳纹。口径
17.1、残高 4.1 厘米（图二三：5）。标本 T1⑤a：361，夹细砂红褐陶。厚圆唇，束颈。口径
17.2、残高 3.1 厘米（图二三：7）。标本 T1⑤a：147，夹砂红褐陶。圆唇。口径 40、残高 2.6
厘米（图二三：9）。标本 T1⑤a：260，夹砂褐陶。圆唇，侈口，口下部饰刻划的弧线纹。口
径 33、残高 1.6 厘米（图二三：2）。标本 T1⑤a：208，夹砂灰褐陶。圆唇。口径 30.5、残高
3.1 厘米（图二三：4）。标本 T1⑤a：231，夹砂灰褐陶。尖圆唇。口下部饰两道凹弦纹，其下
饰斜向绳纹。口径 22.9、残高 3.4 厘米（图二三：6）。标本 T1⑤a：77，夹砂褐陶。圆唇。口
下部饰两道凹弦纹，弦纹之间戳刺短线纹，其下有戳刺的变形 S 形纹，S 纹中饰戳刺短线纹。

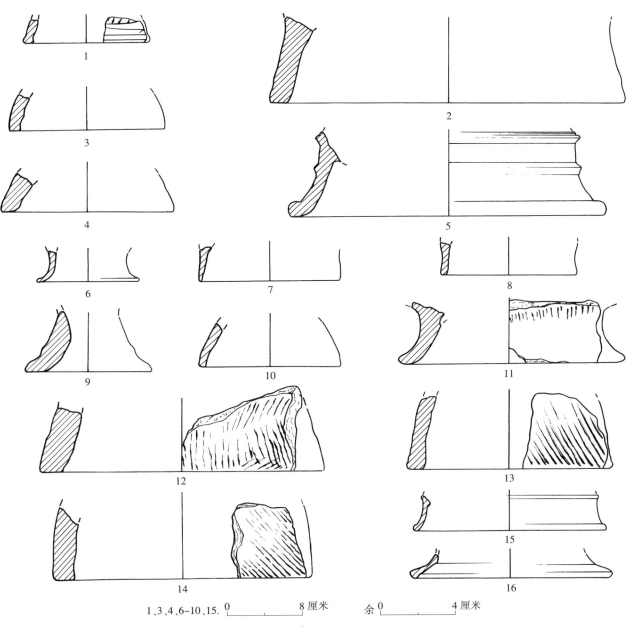

1、3、4、6~10、15. $\underline{0 \qquad\qquad 8}$ 厘米　　余 $\underline{0 \qquad\qquad 4}$ 厘米

图二二　T1⑤a 层出土陶圈足

1. T1⑤a：228　2. T1⑤a：111　3. T1⑤a：132　4. T1⑤a：140　5. T1⑤a：180　6. T1⑤a：129　7. T1⑤a：202

8. T1⑤a：183　9. T1⑤a：121　10. T1⑤a：137　11. T1⑤a：27　12. T1⑤a：31　13. T1⑤a：35　14. T1⑤a：52

15. T1⑤a：181　16. T1⑤a：371

口径 20.4、残高 2.4 厘米（图二三：10）。标本 T1⑤a：210，夹砂褐陶。圆唇。颈上部饰凹弦纹一周，颈中部饰刻划纹的三角形纹，三角形纹内饰刻划的短线纹。口径 22.5、残高 3.8 厘米（图二三：8）。

厚唇罐　21 件。均为厚方唇。依据口部的不同可分为三个类型。

第一类：10 件。直口。

标本 T1⑤a：66，夹砂褐陶。直腹。唇部饰斜向绳纹，口下部饰两道凹弦纹，腹上部戳刺

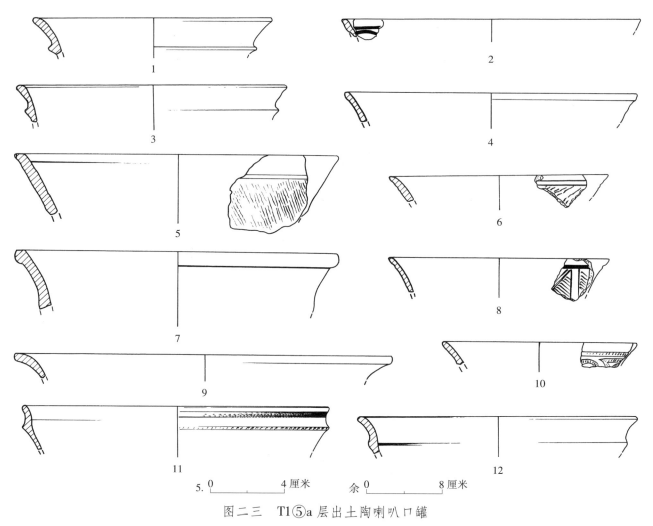

图二三　T1⑤a 层出土陶喇叭口罐

1. T1⑤a：189　2. T1⑤a：：260　3. T1⑤a：190　4. T1⑤a：208　5. T1⑤a：91　6. T1⑤a：231　7. T1⑤a：361
8. T1⑤a：210　9. T1⑤a：147　10. T1⑤a：77　11. T1⑤a：186　12. T1⑤a：187

短弧线纹和三角形纹。口径 49.4、残高 5.2 厘米（图二四：1）。标本 T1⑤a：100，夹砂褐陶。
唇部饰交错绳纹。口径 49.2、残高 4 厘米（图二四：2）。标本 T1⑤a：158，夹砂灰陶。口径
34.8、残高 3.4 厘米（图二四：11）。标本 T1⑤a：123，夹砂红褐陶。颈部饰一道凸棱。口径
33.2、残高 4 厘米（图二四：12）。标本 T1⑤a：141，夹砂褐陶。口径 34、残高 3.7 厘米（图
二四：13）。标本 T1⑤a：161，夹砂褐陶。唇部饰斜向绳纹。口径 38.5、残高 6.2 厘米（图
二四：4）。标本 T1⑤a：166，夹砂灰黑胎红衣陶。厚方唇。口径 48、残高 4.6 厘米（图
二五：1）。标本 T1⑤a：177，夹砂红陶。圆唇。口下部饰凹弦纹一周。口径 21.8、残高 3 厘
米（图二五：2）。标本 T1⑤a：61，夹砂褐陶。圆唇，直领。领上部饰凹弦纹两周，其下饰斜
向绳纹。口径 33.2、残高 3.8 厘米（图二五：7）。标本 T1⑤a：54，残，夹砂褐陶。圆唇，高
领，领以下残。口下部饰凹弦纹和斜向绳纹。口径 23、残高 3.1 厘米（图二五：4）。

第二类：10 件。侈口。

标本 T1⑤a：174，夹砂红陶。口下部饰刻划的线纹。口径 31.6、残高 3.2 厘米（图二四：7）。

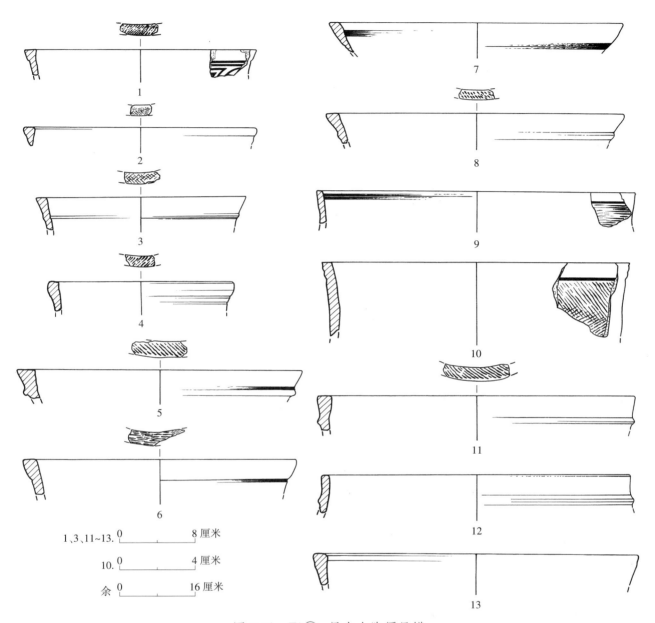

图二四　T1⑤a 层出土陶厚唇罐

1. T1⑤a：66　2. T1⑤a：100　3. T1⑤a：363　4. T1⑤a：161　5. T1⑤a：168　6. T1⑤a：112　7. T1⑤a：174
8. T1⑤a：117　9. T1⑤a：75　10. T1⑤a：97　11. T1⑤a：158　12. T1⑤a：123　13. T1⑤a：141

标本 T1⑤a：117，夹砂褐陶。唇部饰斜向绳纹，口下部饰一道凸棱。口径 32、残高 3.2 厘米（图二四：8）。标本 T1⑤a：168，夹砂灰黑陶。唇部饰斜向绳纹，口下部饰一道凸棱。口径 30.4、残高 6 厘米（图二四：5）。标本 T1⑤a：112，夹砂褐陶。唇部饰横向绳纹，口下部饰一道凹弦纹。口径 29.1、残高 3.8 厘米（图二四：6）。标本 T1⑤a：363，夹砂褐陶。唇部饰交错绳纹。口径 18.5、残高 2.6 厘米（图二四：3）。标本 T1⑤a：75，夹砂褐陶。口下部饰凹弦纹一周，其下饰横向刻划的线纹。口径 34.3、残高 3.6 厘米（图二四：9）。标本 T1⑤a：97，夹砂红褐陶。口下部饰一道凹弦纹，其下饰交错绳纹。口径 16.5、残高 3.9 厘米（图二四：10）。

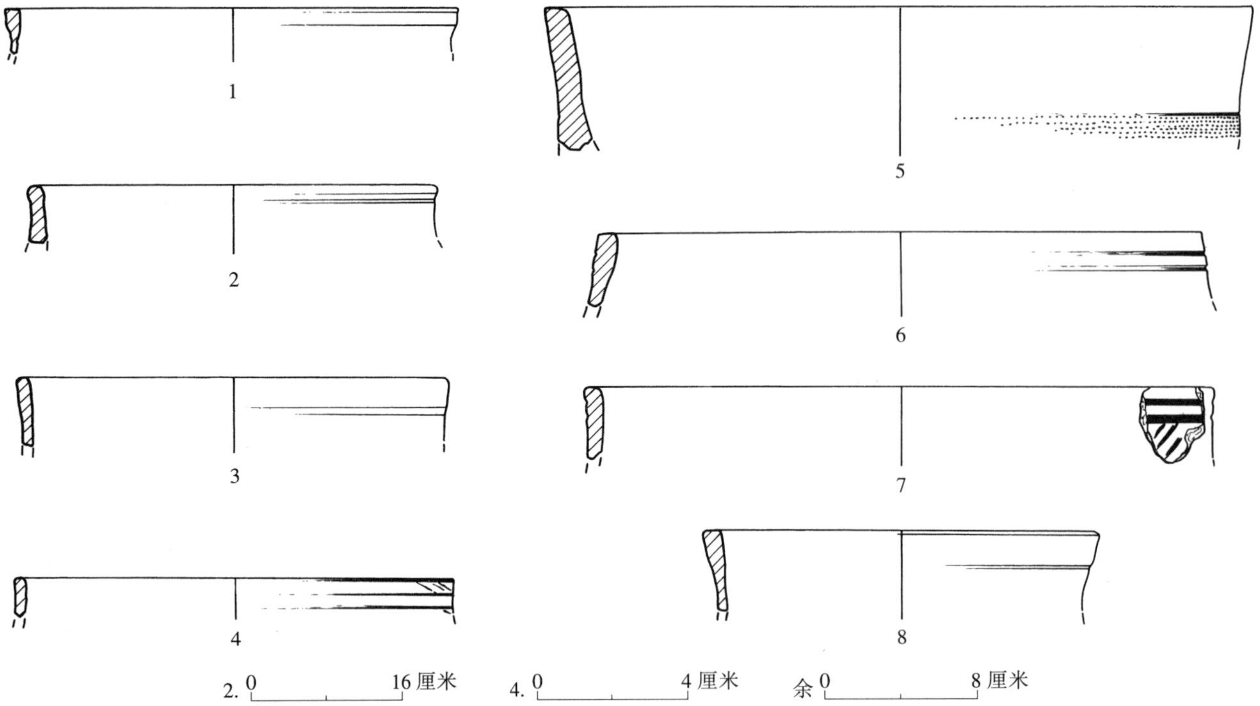

图二五　T1⑤a 层出土陶厚唇罐

1. T1⑤a：166　2. T1⑤a：177　3. T1⑤a：150　4. T1⑤a：54　5. T1⑤a：305　6. T1⑤a：67　7. T1⑤a：61　8. T1⑤a：169

标本 T1⑤a：150，夹砂红褐陶。方唇。颈部饰一道凸棱。口径 23、残高 3.6 厘米（图二五：3）。标本 T1⑤a：305，夹砂褐陶。方唇。口下部饰一道凹弦纹，其下饰篦点纹。口径 18.6、残高 3.8 厘米（图二五：5）。标本 T1⑤a：169，夹砂红褐陶。表面磨光，厚方唇。口径 41.6、残高 8.4 厘米（图二五：8）。

第三类：1 件。敛口。

标本 T1⑤a：67，夹砂红褐陶。圆唇，直领。领部戳刺凹弦纹两周。口径 46.4、残高 4 厘米（图二五：6）。

侈口罐　22 件。依据颈部的不同可分为两个类型。

第一类：15 件。颈部无凸棱。

标本 T1⑤a：133，夹砂褐陶。圆唇，口下部饰一周凹弦纹。口径 34、残高 2.4 厘米（图二六：1）。标本 T1⑤a：185，夹细砂红陶，表面磨光。圆唇。口径 29.8、残高 3.3 厘米（图二六：2）。标本 T1⑤a：239，夹砂红褐陶。尖圆唇。口下部饰刻划短线和弧线纹。口径 36.6、残高 2.8 厘米（图二六：3）。标本 T1⑤a：220，夹砂褐陶。圆唇。口下部饰两道凹弦纹，其下饰刻划的斜向短线纹。口径 26.8、残高 4.1 厘米（图二六：4）。标本 T1⑤a：79，夹砂红褐陶。尖圆唇。口下部饰梳刷纹。口径 14.9、残高 3.9 厘米（图二六：5）。标本 T1⑤a：263，夹砂褐陶。圆唇。口下部饰两道凹弦纹，其下饰刻划的短线纹。口径 18.4、残高 2.1 厘米（图二六：6）。标本 T1⑤a：47，残，夹砂褐陶。圆唇，高领，领以下残。口下部饰凹弦纹一周，颈部饰斜向绳纹。口径 14、残高 4 厘米（图二六：7）。标本 T1⑤a：152，夹细砂黑陶。

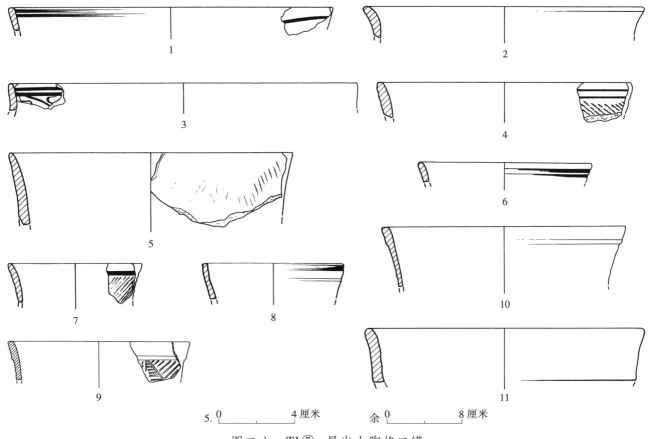

图二六　T1⑤a 层出土陶侈口罐

1. T1⑤a：133　2. T1⑤a：185　3. T1⑤a：239　4. T1⑤a：220　5. T1⑤a：79　6. T1⑤a：263　7. T1⑤a：47
8. T1⑤a：152　9. T1⑤a：69　10. T1⑤a：119　11. T1⑤a：378

方唇。口下部饰一周凹弦纹。口径 14.8、残高 3.8 厘米（图二八：8）。标本 T1⑤a：69，残，夹砂褐陶。方唇，颈微束。口下部饰凸棱一周，其下饰戳刺的叶脉纹。口径 19.1、残高 4 厘米（图二八：9）。标本 T1⑤a：119，夹砂褐陶。方唇。口下部饰一道凸棱。口径 26、残高 6.2 厘米（图二六：10）。标本 T1⑤a：378，夹砂红褐陶。圆唇，颈略束。口径 14.7、残高 2.8 厘米（图二六：11）。标本 T1⑤a：227，夹砂褐陶。圆唇。口下部饰两道凹弦纹。口径 18.5、残高 2.6 厘米（图二七：1）。标本 T1⑤a：78，夹砂褐陶。颈微束。口下部饰两道凹弦纹，其下饰梳刷纹。口径 24.6、残高 5.3 厘米（图二七：3）。标本 T1⑤a：71，夹砂褐陶。领部饰横向绳纹。口径 22.8、残高 3.2 厘米（图二七：11）。标本 T1⑤a：70，夹砂褐陶。圆唇。口下部饰两道凹弦纹，其下饰刻划的短线纹。口径 29.4、残高 4.7 厘米（图二七：12）。

第二类：7 件。颈部有凸棱。

标本 T1⑤a：255，夹细砂褐陶。圆唇，束颈。颈部饰刻划的弧线纹和戳刺的短线纹。口径 22.5、残高 4.9 厘米（图二七：8）。标本 T1⑤a：306，夹细砂红陶。方唇，颈略束。口径 23.4、残高 3.5 厘米（图二七：2）。标本 T1⑤a：110，夹砂红褐陶。圆唇。口径 50、残高 3.6 厘米（图二七：10）。标本 T1⑤a：193，夹细砂红陶。圆唇，凸棱上饰戳刺短线纹。口径 24.6、残高 3 厘米（图二七：4）。标本 T1⑤a：49，夹砂红褐陶。圆唇。颈部饰斜向绳纹。口径 30.8、

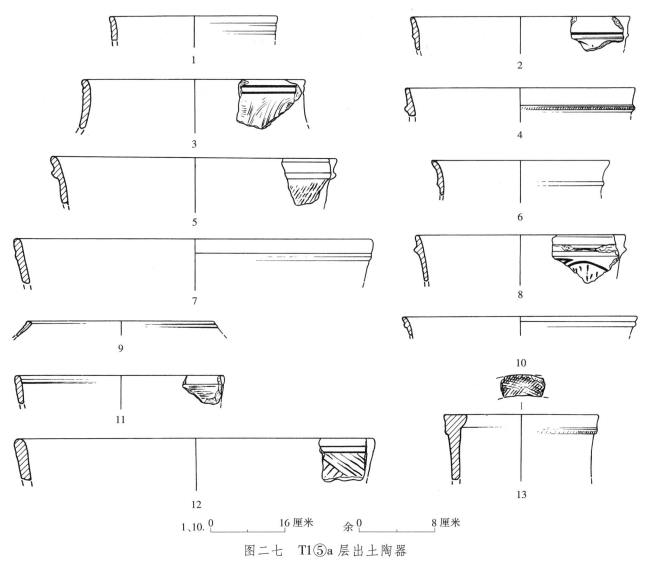

图二七　T1⑤a 层出土陶器

1~8、10~12. 侈口罐（T1⑤a：277、306、78、193、49、122、109、255、110、71、70）　9. 敛口罐（T1⑤a：135）　13. 桶（T1⑤a：60）

残高 4.7 厘米（图二七：5）。标本 T1⑤a：122，夹砂褐陶。尖圆唇。口径 19、残高 3.6 厘米（图二七：6）。标本 T1⑤a：109，夹砂红褐陶。口径 28.5、残高 4.8 厘米（图二七：7）。

桶　1 件。

标本 T1⑤a：60，夹砂褐陶。厚方唇，敛口，直腹。唇部饰交错绳纹，口下部饰凸棱一周，凸棱上戳刺短线纹。口径 16.6、残高 7 厘米（图二七：13）。

敛口罐　1 件。

标本 T1⑤a：135，夹砂褐陶。方唇，敛口。口下部饰两道凹弦纹。口径 20.4、残高 1.7 厘米（图二七：9）。

钵　55 件。依据形制的不同可分为五个类型。

第一类：14 件。敛口，腹上部饰一道凸棱。

标本 T1⑤a：295，夹砂褐陶。尖圆唇。腹上部饰戳刺的篦点纹。口径 31.2、残高 3.2 厘

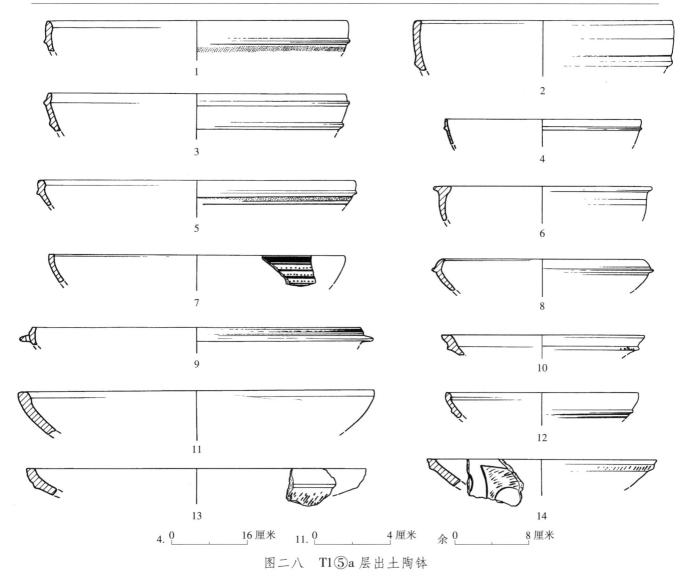

图二八 T1⑤a 层出土陶钵

1. T1⑤a：295 2. T1⑤a：128 3. T1⑤a：195 4. T1⑤a：205 5. T1⑤a：328 6. T1⑤a：365 7. T1⑤a：364

8. T1⑤a：203 9. T1⑤a：179 10. T1⑤a：360 11. T1⑤a：376 12. T1⑤a：265 13. T1⑤a：380 14. T1⑤a：65

米（图二八：1）。标本 T1⑤a：128，夹砂红褐陶。方唇。腹上部饰凹弦纹一周。口径 27、残高 5.2 厘米（图二八：2）。标本 T1⑤a：195，夹细砂红褐陶。圆唇。肩部和腹部分别饰两道凸棱。口径 30.8，残高 4 厘米（图二八：3）。标本 T1⑤a：328，夹砂红褐陶。圆唇。腹上部饰两道凹弦纹，两道凹弦纹中饰篦点纹。口径 32.8、残高 2.6 厘米（图二八：5）。标本 T1⑤a：265，夹砂红褐陶，表面磨光。圆唇，斜直腹。凸棱下饰两道凹弦纹。口径 20.2、残高 2.6 厘米（图二八：12）。标本 T1⑤a：179，夹砂红褐陶。方唇，凸棱较宽。口径 34.2、残高 1.8 厘米（图二八：9）。标本 T1⑤a：205，泥质红陶，表面磨光。口径 20.6、残高 2.6 厘米（图二八：4）。标本 T1⑤a：203，夹细砂红陶，器表磨光。尖圆唇。口径 21、残高 3.3 厘米（图二八：8）。标本 T1⑤a：264，夹细砂红褐陶。圆唇。腹上部饰两道凹弦纹和篦点纹。口径 28、残高 3 厘米（图二九：1）。标本 T1⑤a：266，夹砂褐陶。方唇。腹上部饰三道凹弦纹。口径23、残高2.9厘米（图二九：2）。标本T1⑤a：302，夹细砂红褐陶。圆唇。腹部饰篦点纹。口径22.2、残高2.6厘米（图二九：4）。标本T1⑤a：324，夹砂红褐陶。圆唇。凸棱上下各饰两道凹弦纹和篦点纹。口径25、残高4厘米（图二九：3）。标本T1⑤a：326，夹细砂红褐陶。圆唇。腹中部饰弦纹一周。口径23.3、残高3.4厘米（图二九：5）。标本T1⑤a：153，夹砂灰黑陶。圆唇。口径34.8、残高5.2厘米（图二九：14）。

　　第二类：15件。敛口，腹部无凸棱。

　　标本T1⑤a：364，夹细砂红褐陶。方唇。腹上部饰三组凹弦纹，每组凹弦纹中饰篦点纹。口径30.8、残高2.9厘米（图二八：7）。标本T1⑤a：376，夹砂灰褐陶。圆唇。口径18.5、残高2.2厘米（图二八：11）。标本T1⑤a：336，夹砂褐陶。尖圆唇。腹部饰戳刺的坑点纹。口径25.6、残高3.1厘米（图二九：7）。标本T1⑤a：342，夹砂红褐陶。圆唇。肩部戳刺有短线纹，腹上部饰三道凹弦纹和篦点纹。口径22.5、残高3.5厘米（图二九：12）。标本

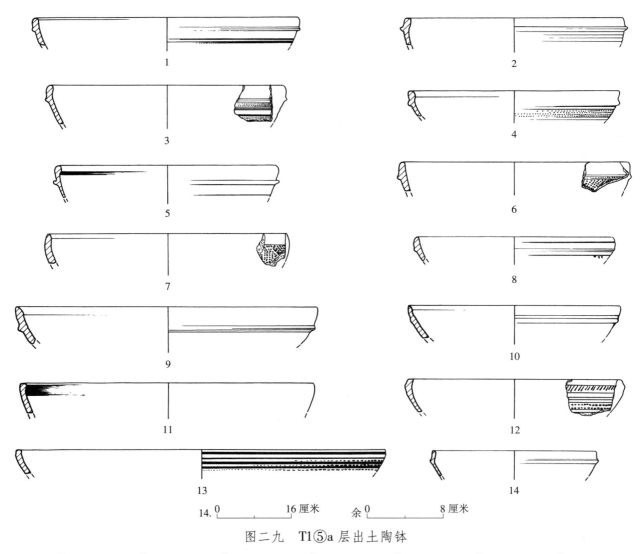

图二九　T1⑤a层出土陶钵

1. T1⑤a：264　2. T1⑤a：266　3. T1⑤a：：324　4. T1⑤a：302　5. T1⑤a：326　6. T1⑤a：327　7. T1⑤a：336

8. T1⑤a：335　9. T1⑤a：191　10. T1⑤a：206　11. T1⑤a：207　12. T1⑤a：342　13. T1⑤a：356　14. T1⑤a：153

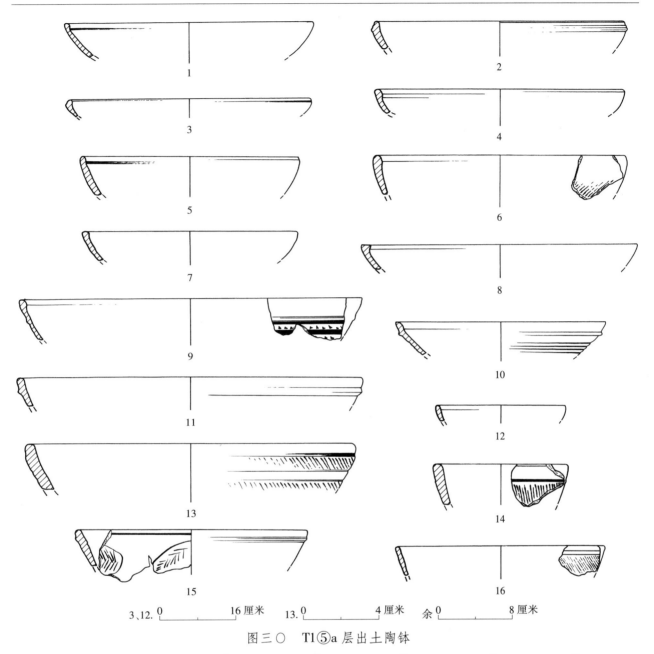

图三〇　T1⑤a层出土陶钵

1. T1⑤a：115　2. T1⑤a：116　3. T1⑤a：165　4. T1⑤a：175　5. T1⑤a：176　6. T1⑤a：30　7. T1⑤a：149
8. T1⑤a：143　9. T1⑤a：339　10. T1⑤a：238　11. T1⑤a：172　12. T1⑤a：146　13. T1⑤a：304　14. T1⑤a：38
15. T1⑤a：63　16. T1⑤a：212

T1⑤a：207，夹砂红褐陶。圆唇。口径31、残高3.2厘米（图二九：11）。标本T1⑤a：356，夹砂灰黑陶。方唇。腹上部饰凹弦纹和戳刺的坑点纹。口径39.2、残高2.5厘米（图二九：13）。标本T1⑤a：115，夹砂褐陶。圆唇，斜直腹。素面。口径26、残高3.7厘米（图三〇：1）。标本T1⑤a：165，夹细砂褐陶。圆唇，斜直腹。口径51.2、残高3.2厘米（图三〇：3）。标本T1⑤a：175，夹砂褐陶。圆唇，弧腹。口径26.5、残高2.5厘米（图三〇：4）。标本T1⑤a：176，夹细砂红陶。圆唇，弧腹。口下部饰凹弦纹一周。口径23.1、残高4.2厘米（图三〇：5）。标本 T1⑤a：30，夹砂褐陶。圆唇，弧腹。腹部饰斜向绳纹。口径 26.5、残高 4.1 厘米（图三〇：6）。标本 T1⑤a：149，夹砂褐陶。方唇，斜直腹。口径 22.6、残高 3 厘米（图三〇：7）。标本 T1⑤a：146，夹砂红褐陶。圆唇。口径 27.6、残高 3.2 厘米（图三〇：12）。标本 T1⑤a：330，夹细砂红陶。圆唇。腹部饰三道凹弦纹和篦点纹。口径 26.4、残高 3.4 厘米（图三一：1）。标本 T1⑤a：40，夹砂红褐陶。尖圆唇。腹上部饰一道凹弦纹，腹部饰纵向绳纹。口径 22.4、残高 4.1 厘米（图三一：7）。

第三类：13 件。侈口，弧腹，肩部饰一凸棱。

标本 T1⑤a：380，夹砂红褐陶。方唇，折肩。腹上部饰戳刺的坑点纹。口径 35.3、残高 2.6 厘米（图二八：13）。标本 T1⑤a：360，夹砂褐陶。凸棱上戳刺有坑点纹。口径 21.4、残高 2.1 厘米（图二八：10）。标本 T1⑤a：56，夹砂褐陶。方唇。凸棱上戳刺短线纹，唇部戳刺一周连续三角形纹，器身饰竖向绳纹。口径 36.6、残高 3.7 厘米（图三一：4）。标本 T1⑤a：65，夹砂红褐陶。口下部饰凸棱一周，凸棱上戳刺短线纹，腹部饰刻划纹和戳刺纹。口径 24、残高 4.8 厘米（图二八：14）。标本 T1⑤a：327，夹细砂红褐陶。圆唇，方唇。凸棱上戳刺有坑点纹，腹上部饰篦点纹和凹弦纹。口径 23.8、残高 3.1 厘米（图二九：6）。标本 T1⑤a：191，夹砂红陶。尖圆唇。口径 32.1、残高 4.1 厘米（图二九：9）。标本 T1⑤a：335，夹细砂灰褐陶。尖圆唇。腹上部饰弦纹一周，其下饰戳刺的篦点纹。口径 20.8、残高 2.4 厘米（图二九：8）。标本 T1⑤a：206，夹砂褐陶。圆唇。口径 2.3、残高 3.4 厘米（图二九：10）。标本 T1⑤a：116，夹砂褐陶。方唇。口径 26.4、残高 2.8 厘米（图三〇：2）。标本 T1⑤a：339，夹砂红褐陶。圆唇。腹上部饰两道凹弦纹和戳刺纹。口径 36、残高 4.2 厘米（图三〇：9）。标本 T1⑤a：172，夹砂红褐陶。圆唇。口径 36.3、残高 3 厘米（图三〇：11）。标本 T1⑤a：238，夹砂黑褐陶。腹部饰刻划的线纹。口径 22.4、残高 3.5 厘米（图三〇：10）。标本 T1⑤a：192，夹砂红褐陶。尖圆唇。口径 30.4、残高 2.4 厘米（图三一：8）。

第四类：8 件。侈口，弧腹，肩部无凸棱。

标本 T1⑤a：304，夹砂褐陶。圆唇。口下部饰三道凹弦纹，凹弦纹之间饰斜向绳纹。口径 17.4、残高 2.4 厘米（图三〇：13）。标本 T1⑤a：63，夹砂褐陶。圆唇，斜直腹。口下部饰凸棱一周，腹部饰刻划的叶脉纹。口径 24.4、残高 5.5 厘米（图三〇：15）。标本 T1⑤a：38，夹砂褐陶。圆唇。腹上部饰一道凹弦纹，腹部饰竖向绳纹。口径 14.2、残高 4.2 厘米（图三〇：14）。标本 T1⑤a：212，夹砂红褐陶。圆唇。口下部饰两道凹弦纹，其下饰刻划的竖线纹。口径 22.4、残高 3.1 厘米（图三〇：16）。标本 T1⑤a：64，夹砂褐陶。口下部饰一道凸棱，唇部饰绳纹，腹部饰戳刺的短线纹。口径 21.7、残高 3.9 厘米（图三一：5）。标本 T1⑤a：120，夹砂红褐陶。口下部饰两道凹弦纹。口径 30.4、残高 3.2 厘米（图三一：9）。标本 T1⑤a：125，夹砂红褐陶。口下部饰凹弦纹一周。口径 28、残高 2.6 厘米（图三一：10）。标本 T1⑤a：118，夹砂红褐陶。口下部饰凹弦纹一周。口径 29、残高 2.9 厘米（图三一：11）。

第五类：5 件。圆唇，窄平沿，敛口，深腹。

标本 T1⑤a：365，夹砂红褐陶。口径 23、残高 3.6 厘米（图二八：6）。标本 T1⑤a：226，

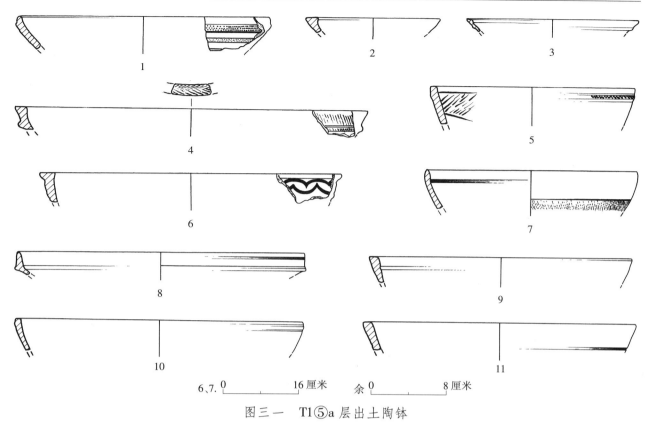

图三一　T1⑤a 层出土陶钵

1. T1⑤a：330　2. T1⑤a：48　3. T1⑤a：154　4. T1⑤a：56　5. T1⑤a：64　6. T1⑤a：226　7. T1⑤a：40
8. T1⑤a：192　9. T1⑤a：120　10. T1⑤a：125　11. T1⑤a：118

夹砂褐陶。沿上饰斜向绳纹，腹上部饰戳刺的连弧纹。口径 31.4、残高 3.1 厘米（图三一：6）。标本 T1⑤a：143，夹砂灰褐陶。斜直腹，唇部饰一周凹弦纹。口径 29.2、残高 2.8 厘米（图三〇：8）。标本 T1⑤a：154，夹砂灰陶。尖圆唇，口下部饰一道凸棱。口径 36.4、残高 2.6 厘米（图三一：3）。标本 T1⑤a：48，夹砂红褐陶。尖圆唇。口径 28.4、残高 3.5 厘米（图三一：2）。

（二）T1⑤b 层出土器物

T1 第⑤b 层出土器物极少，均为陶片，共出土 18 片。陶质中夹细砂陶的比例 88.9%，夹粗砂陶的比例为 11.1%，说明以夹细砂陶为主。从陶色来看，红和红褐色陶占多数，占比为 55.6%，其他还有黑褐和灰褐。纹饰主要有绳纹、凹弦纹和篦点纹。器形主要包括厚唇罐、钵、圈足、侈口罐等。本层共挑选陶器标本 14 件。

厚唇罐　4 件。依据形制的不同可分为两个类型。

第一类：3 件。厚方唇。

标本 T1⑤b：1，夹砂褐陶。唇部饰斜向绳纹。口径 32.3、残高 6 厘米（图三二：1）。标本 T1⑤b：2，夹砂红褐陶。唇部饰斜向绳纹，腹上部饰两道凹弦纹。口径 17.8、残高 4.8 厘米（图三二：2）。标本 T1⑤b：3，夹砂褐陶。唇部饰斜向绳纹，腹上部饰一道凹弦纹和刻划弧线纹。口径 19、残高 3.6 厘米（图三二：4）。

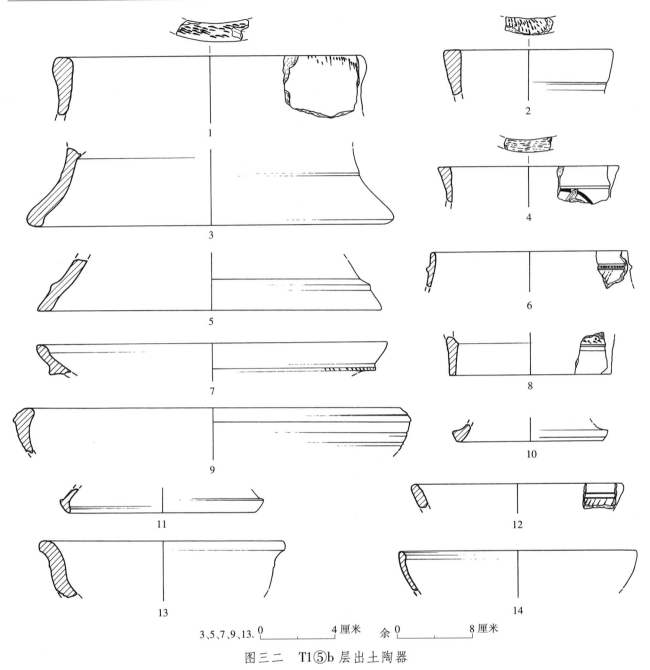

3、5、7、9、13. 0 ⊢——————⊣ 4厘米　　余 0 ⊢——————⊣ 8厘米

图三二　T1⑤b 层出土陶器

1、2、4、6. 厚唇罐（T1⑤b：1、2、3、15）　3、5、8、10、11. 圈足（T1⑤b：19、20、4、11、14）　7、9、13、

14. 钵（T1⑤b：5、6、9、13）　12. 侈口罐（T1⑤b：10）

第二类：1 件。圆唇。

标本 T1⑤b：15，夹砂红褐陶。弧肩。颈部饰一道凸棱，凸棱上戳刺有短线纹，其下刻划
有斜向的短线纹。口径 20.7、残高 3.7 厘米（图三二：6）。

圈足　5 件。依据形制的不同可分为三个类型。

第一类：1 件。直桶状。

标本 T1⑤b：4，夹砂红褐陶。圈足上饰两道凹弦纹和戳刺的坑点纹。底径 17、残高 4 厘米（图三二：8）。

第二类：3件。喇叭状，足尖外撇。

标本 T1⑤b：11，夹砂红褐陶。底径 15.4、残高 1.9 厘米（图三二：10）。标本 T1⑤b：20，夹砂褐陶。底径 18.4、残高 2.8 厘米（图三二：5）。标本 T1⑤b：19，夹砂红陶。足中部饰一道凹弦纹。底径 18.6、残高 4.2 厘米（图三二：3）。

第三类：1件。喇叭状，足尖内折。

标本 T1⑤b：14，夹砂褐陶。底径 20、残高 2.6 厘米（图三二：11）。

钵 4件。依据形制的不同可分为三个类型。

第一类：1件。侈口，斜直腹，肩部饰一道凸棱。

标本 T1⑤b：5，夹砂褐陶。尖圆唇，斜直腹，凸棱上戳刺有坑点纹。口径 18.5、残高 5 厘米（图三二：7）。

第二类：2件。敛口，弧腹。

标本 T1⑤b：6，夹砂红褐陶。圆唇，腹上部和肩部饰三道凹弦纹。口径 19.8、残高 6 厘米（图三二：9）。标本 T1⑤b：13，夹砂红褐陶。圆唇。口径 25、底径 4.2 厘米（图三二：14）。

第三类：1件。侈口，弧腹。

标本 T1⑤b：9，夹砂红褐陶。圆唇，束颈，弧腹。口径 13.2、残高 2.9 厘米（图三二：13）。

侈口罐　1件。

标本 T1⑤b：10，夹砂红褐陶。圆唇。口下部饰两道凹弦纹，其下饰刻划的短线纹。口径 22、残高 2.5 厘米（图三二：12）。

第二节　T2

位于发掘区的中部，2006 年 12 月 3 日开始布方发掘，于 2007 年 1 月 6 日清理完毕，陈卫东负责进行发掘、记录并绘图。

一　地层堆积

依据土质土色和包含物的不同，本探方的地层经统一后可分为 6 层（图三三；彩版二八）。

第①层：厚 10～15 厘米。黄灰色耕土层，土质疏松，包含有少量的瓷片、塑料、植物根茎等。

第②层：厚 0～10、深 10～15 厘米。黄红色土，土质较硬，包含有大量的红色砖块、少量的青花瓷片、白瓷片和极少量的石器。H34 开口于本层之下。为近现代堆积。

第③层：厚 10～24、深 10～20 厘米。浅灰色土，土质细密。包含有少量的砖块、瓷片等物。H1 开口于此层下。为近现代堆积。

第④层：依据土质土色的不同，本层可分为两个亚层。为丁朝至前黎朝堆积。

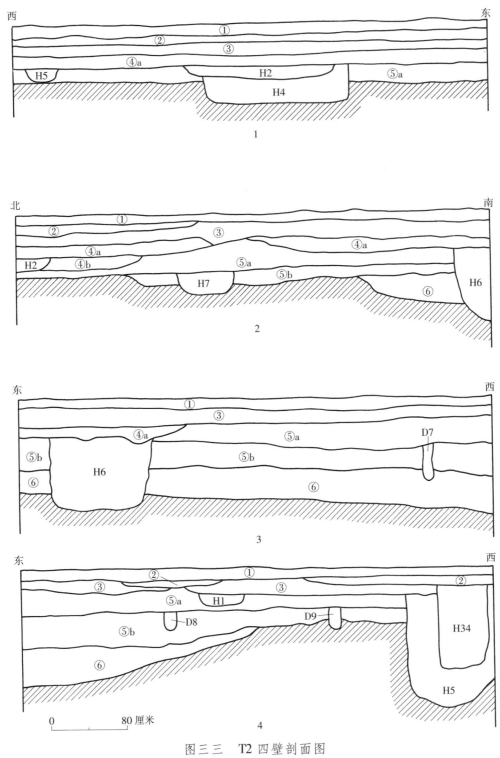

图三三　T2 四壁剖面图

1. 北壁　2. 东壁　3. 南壁　4. 西壁

　　第④a层：厚0～18、深28～34厘米。深褐色铁锰层，含有大量的铁锈，由东南角向北部倾斜。包含有极少量的瓷片、砖块等物。H3、H4、H5、H6开口于本层之下（灰坑开口区域未有第④b层堆积）。

第④b层：厚 0 ~ 12、深 42 厘米。灰褐色铁锰层，含有少量的铁锈，仅分布在东北部，包含有极少量的瓷片、砖块等物。H2 开口于本层之下。

第⑤层：依据土质土色的不同，本层可分为两个亚层。为冯原文化时期堆积。

第⑤a层：厚 0 ~ 44、深 26 ~ 44 厘米。黑灰色土，土质疏松，含有较多的红烧土颗粒。包括大量的陶器和少量的石器。H7、H8 开口于本层之下。

第⑤b层：厚 0 ~ 35、深 40 ~ 60 厘米。灰黄色土，土质较硬，从北向南分布，包含物较少。主要是陶器和石器。

第⑥层：厚 0 ~ 40、深 62 ~ 86 厘米。仅分布在探方西南部分，黄褐色土，夹杂有少量的灰土斑点，土质较硬。包含物极少。为冯原文化时期堆积。

此层之下为红褐色铁锰生土层。

二　遗迹

T2 内共清理各类遗迹 24 个，包括灰坑 8 座、柱洞 16 个（图三四；彩版二九）。

（一）灰坑

8 座。包括 H1 ~ H8，其中 H1、H2 为近现代灰坑。现将冯原文化时期灰坑的情况介绍如下。

H3

处于 T2 的东北部，开口于第④a 层下。被 H2 打破。

形制　平面呈上圆下方形，上部圆形，直径约 1.4 米；下部方形，边长 1 米；深 0.8 米。坑壁光滑，坑底平整。坑内堆积可分 3 层。第①层为灰黑色土，土质疏松，本层的北部堆积着大量的红烧土、炭屑。并包含有大量的陶片和少量的石器。厚 16 ~ 20 厘米。第②层为黄色黏土，土质较硬。包含有较多的铁锈。由东北向西南倾斜堆积。包含有少量的陶器。厚 24 ~ 30 厘米。第③层为灰色土，土质疏松，由东北向西南倾斜堆积。包含有少量的陶器。厚 21 ~ 27 厘米。此层之下为黄褐色生土（图三五；彩版三〇 ~ 三二）。

出土器物　H3 出土的器物包括陶器、石器和玉器。且以陶器为主，石器和玉器较少。共挑选标本 37 件[1]，包括陶器 32 件、石器 3 件、玉器 2 件。

石器

共 5 件。以磨制石器为主，包括锛 1 件、磨石 1 件、刮削器 1 件等。

锛　1 件。

标本 H3：3，残，体呈长方形，一面可见磨制的痕迹，另一面可见剥片留下的疤痕。残长 4.6、残宽 2.2 ~ 4、厚 1.3 厘米（图三六：1）。

磨石　1 件。

标本 H3：9，形制较小，体呈三棱状，三侧可见磨制的痕迹。长 3.9、宽 2.3、厚 2 厘米

---

〔1〕　从出土器物登记表上看，H3 共挑选标本 81 件，包括玉石器 5、陶器纹饰标本 23，陶器器形标本 53 件。部分器物因修复而销号，但部分器物的资料遗失，今只按资料完整的器物进行介绍和统计。

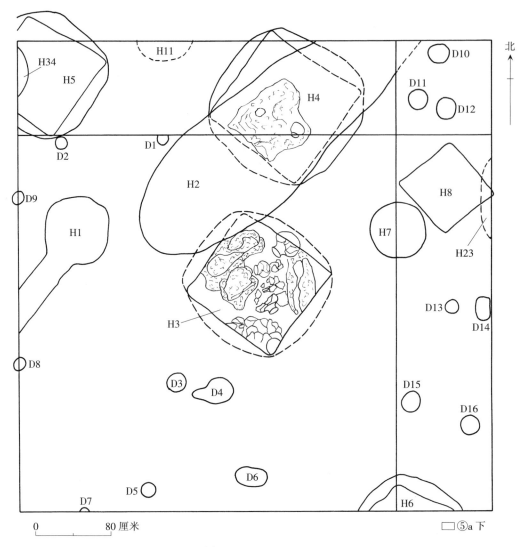

图三四　T2 平面图

（图三六：11）。

　　刮削器　1 件。

　　标本 H3：4，残，体呈弯弧状，平顶，弯弧刃，一面保持自然砺石面，一面可见剥片留下的疤痕。残长 5.8、宽 2、厚 0.1～1.5 厘米（图三六：2）。

玉器

2 件。均为环。

　　环　2 件。形制相似。

　　标本 H3：1，乳白色，残，环状。直径 6.7、宽 0.7、厚 0.3 厘米（图三六：3）。标本 H3：10，乳白色，残存四分之一，环状。直径 4.8、宽 0.7、厚 0.2 厘米（图三六：12）。

陶器

　　H3 共出土陶片 1720 片。从陶质来看，夹细砂陶比例约为 80%，夹粗砂陶约为 8.4%，泥质陶比例约为 10.6%。从陶色上看，红陶、红褐陶、褐陶比例约为 64.6%，说明其陶色偏于

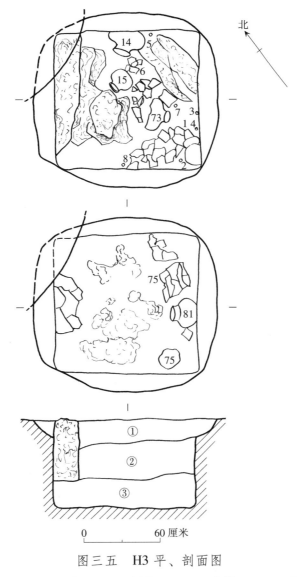

图三五 H3 平、剖面图

1. 石环 2、5~8. 陶球 3. 石锛 4. 石刮削器 14、15. 陶罐 73、81. 陶釜 75. 陶圜底器

红色。从纹饰上看，纹饰发达，约占陶片总数的 43%，部分施陶衣。纹饰种类丰富，其中绳纹居多，约占 64%，其他纹饰有刻划纹、戳印纹、凹弦纹、凸棱纹、压印纹、梳刷纹、附加堆纹等，尤以在各种刻划纹带内填充篦齿状或篦点状戳印纹的装饰风格最具特点，集多种纹饰在单个陶器上的复合纹饰甚为流行，纹饰图案主要有 S 形纹、几何形纹、圆圈纹、水波纹等（图三七；彩版三三、三四）。陶器口部多为敛口和侈口，器类主要是圜底器和圈足器，器形包括球、豆、钵、圈足、支座、釜等（彩版三五~三七）。

H3 共挑选陶器标本 32 件。其中纹饰标本 16 件、器形标本 16 件。器形包括球 7 件、豆 1 件、圈足 3 件、钵 1 件、釜 2 件、支座 1 件、圜底器 1 件。

球 7 件。形制相同，仅大小不同（彩版三八：1）。

标本 H3：2，夹细砂红褐陶，不规则球形。直径 2 厘米（图三六：4）。标本 H3：5，残，夹细砂红褐陶。直径 2 厘米（图三六：5）。标本 H3：6，残，夹细砂红褐陶。直径 1.7 厘米

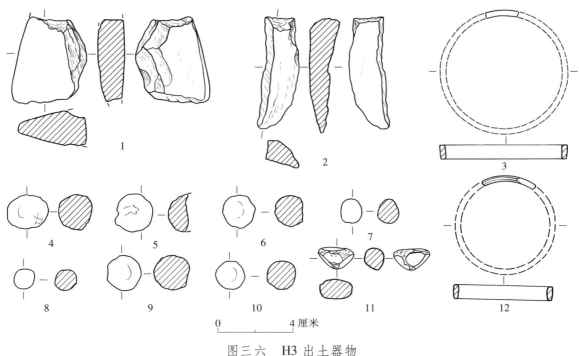

图三六 H3 出土器物

1. 石锛（H3:3） 2. 石刮削器（H3:4） 3、12. 玉环（H3:1、10） 4~10. 陶球（H3:2、5、6、
7、11、8、12） 11. 磨石（H3:9）

（图三六:6）。标本 H3:7，残，夹细砂红褐陶。不规则球形。直径1.1厘米（图三六:7）。
标本 H3:11，夹细砂红褐陶。直径1.1厘米（图三六:8）。标本 H3:8，夹细砂红褐陶。直
径1.7厘米（图三六:9）。标本 H3:12，夹细砂红褐陶。直径1.6厘米（图三六:10）。

豆 1件。

标本 H3:72，夹细砂红褐陶。尖圆唇，窄平沿，深盘，喇叭状圈足，器内可见明显的轮
制痕迹。口径17.2、底径11.6、通高10.4厘米（图三八:1）。

钵 1件。形制基本相似。

标本 H3:71，夹细砂红褐陶，表面磨光。厚圆唇，敛口，折肩，斜直腹，底部残。肩部
饰凹弦纹一周，肩部和腹部饰有宽、窄凸棱一周。口径28.5，残高5.7厘米（图三八:2；彩
版三八:2）。

圈足 3件。依据形制的不同可分为两个类型。

第一类：2件。喇叭状圈足，足尖外撇。

标本 H3:70，夹细砂红褐陶。喇叭状圈足，圈足以上残，圈足与器身一次性制作。盘下部
饰斜向绳纹，圈足内底部饰交错细绳纹。底径13.5、残高4.3厘米（图三八:3）。标本 H3:79，
夹细砂灰褐陶。肩部以上残，圆鼓腹，腹下部斜直，喇叭状圈足外撇。器身遍饰交错细绳纹。
底径18.8、残高33、最大腹径40厘米（图三九:1、3）。

第二类：1件。桶状圈足，足尖微外撇。

标本 H3:31，腹上部残，夹细砂红褐陶。器身腹部饰七组凹弦纹，上部两组中间戳印有

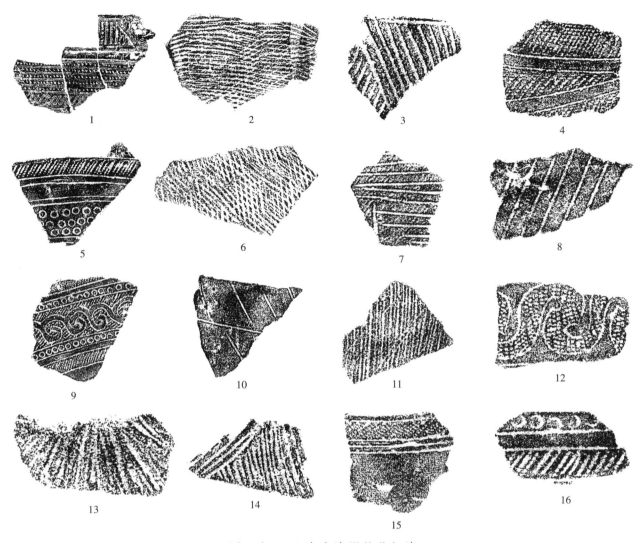

图三七　H3 出土陶器纹饰拓片

1. 刻划纹＋弦纹＋戳刺点纹＋S 纹（H3：31）　2. 交错绳纹（H3：42）　3. 刻划线纹（H3：49）　4. 绳纹＋刻划纹（H3：50）　5. 弦纹＋绳纹＋圆圈纹（H3：43）　6. 交错绳纹（H3：44）　7. 绳纹＋刻划线纹（H3：51）　8. 刻划线纹（H3：51）　9. 弦纹＋云纹＋绳纹（H3：45）　10. 刻划线纹（H3：46）　11. 交错绳纹（H3：53）　12. S 形纹＋戳刺点纹（H3：54）　13. 梳刷纹（H3：47）　14. 斜向绳纹（H3：48）　15. 弦纹＋戳刺点纹（H3：55）　16. 圆圈纹＋弦纹＋绳纹（H3：56）

S 形纹一周，其余五组凹弦纹之间饰戳印的篦点纹，圈足与器身之间饰有一道凸棱纹，凸棱纹上戳印有短线纹，圈足上饰有两道凹弦纹，弦纹中饰戳刺的长方形纹和篦点纹。底径 19.4、残高 11.3 厘米（图三八：4；彩版三八：3）。

支座　1 件。

标本 H3：13，残，夹细砂红褐陶。弯弧状，平顶。器身遍饰纵向细绳纹。顶部直径 5.2、残高 8.2 厘米（图三八：5）。

釜　2 件。依据形制不同可分为两个类型。

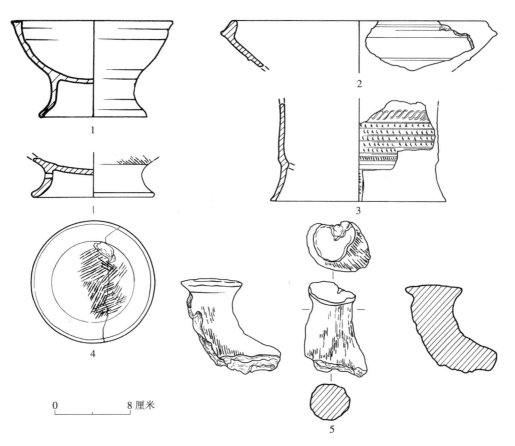

图三八　H3 出土陶器

1. 豆（H3：72）　　2. 钵（H3：71）　　3、4. 圈足（H3：70、31）　　5. 支座（H3：13）

第一类：1 件。圆鼓腹略垂。

标本 H3：81，夹砂红褐陶，表面因烧造原因致使部分区域呈现黑色。尖圆唇，窄平沿，高领，弧肩，圜底。领上部饰有凸棱一周，凸棱上戳印有短线纹，颈部饰有大云纹一周，云纹之间戳印有篦点纹，腹部及其底部饰有交错绳纹。口径 28、腹径 35.8、通高 36 厘米（图四〇：1、3；彩版三九、四〇）。

第二类：1 件。圆鼓腹。

标本 H3：73，夹砂红褐陶，表面因烧造原因致使部分区域呈现黑色。尖圆唇，窄平沿，高领，弧肩，圆鼓腹，腹下部残。领部饰有凹弦纹 14 道，上部和下部的两组凹弦纹中饰戳印的篦点纹，中部和肩部两组凹弦纹中饰小圆圈纹，腹上部饰有云纹一周，云纹之间戳印篦点纹。口径 20、残高 15.6 厘米（图四〇：2、4；彩版四一：1）。

圜底器　1 件。

标本 H3：75，夹细砂灰褐陶。肩部及其以上残，圆鼓腹略垂，圜底，器身遍饰交错细绳纹。残高 17.2、腹最大径 31.8 厘米（图三九：2、4；图四一：2、3）。

H4

处于 T2 的西北部，部分叠压在 T1 的北隔梁下，开口于第④层下，被 H2 打破。

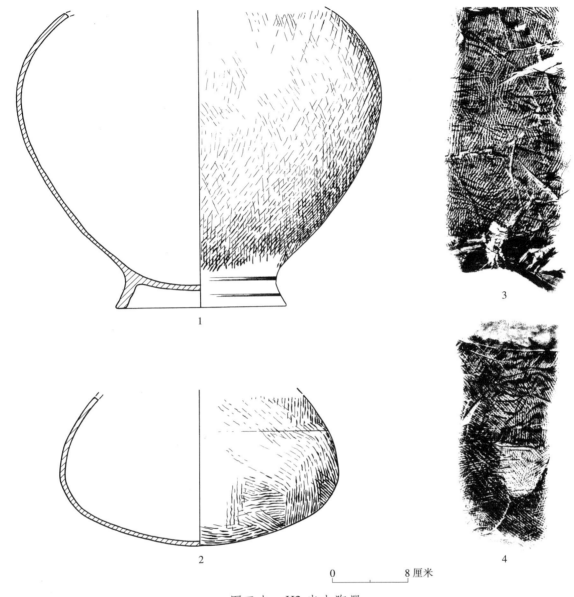

图三九 H3 出土陶器

1、3. 圈足（H3：79） 2、4. 圜底器（H3：75）

　　形制　平面呈长方形，长 1.4、宽 1.2、深 0.4 ~ 0.46 米。四壁较光滑，坑底较平。坑内堆积可分 3 层。第①层为分布在灰坑中间厚 0.06 米的红烧土堆积，并夹杂有大量的陶片，其中在红烧土的北部有一陶支座，东部有一陶钵。第②层为深灰黑色土，土质疏松，厚 0.1 ~ 0.2 米，包含有较多的陶片。第③层为黄褐色土，土质疏松，包含物较少，厚 0.1 ~ 0.24 米。此层之下为黄褐色生土（图四一；彩版四二）。

　　出土器物　H4 出土器物主要是陶器和石器，其中以陶器为主，石器数量较少。共挑选标本 34 件，其中石器 7 件、陶器 27 件。

石器

　　7 件。计有锛 4 件、球 1 件、范 1 件、核 1 件（彩版四三）。

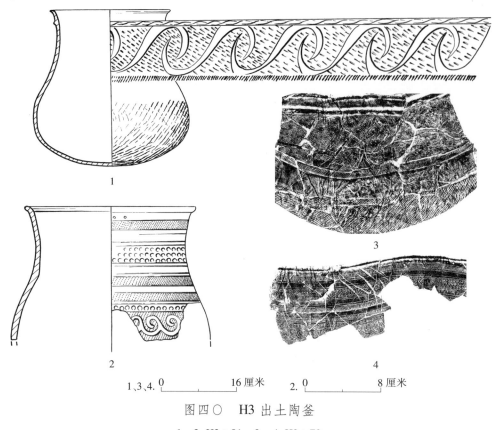

图四○　H3 出土陶釜

1、3. H3：81　2、4. H3：73

锛　4 件。形制相似。形体较小，磨制，均体呈长方形。

标本 H4：5，上部残缺，双面弧刃。残长 2.8、宽 3、厚 0.8 厘米（图四二：1；彩版四四：1）。
标本 H4：2，刃部残缺，仅存上部。残长 4.5、宽 4.6、厚 1.5 厘米（图四二：2）。标本 H4：1，
上部残，仅存刃部，双面弧刃。残长 4.5、宽 5.2、厚 1.4 厘米（图四二：4；彩版四四：2）。
标本 H4：3，刃部残缺，仅存上部。残长 4.2、宽 4.3、厚 1.3 厘米（图四二：5）。

球　1 件。

标本 H4：6，体呈椭圆形，表面光滑。长径 1.8、短径 1.4 厘米（图四二：6）。

范　1 件。

标本 H4：7，残。体呈长方形，器表因打击不平整，中有一长方形范痕，范痕磨光。残长
5.6、残宽 4.5、厚 1 厘米（图四二：3；彩版四四：3）。

核　1 件。

标本 H4：8，体呈不规则三角形，器身一面保持自然砺石面，一面可见剥片产生的打击点
放射线。长 11.2、宽 11.1、厚 3.3 厘米（图四二：8）。

陶器

H4 共出土陶片 595 片。从陶质来看，夹细砂陶比例约为 77%，粗砂陶约为 10%，泥质陶
比例约为 13%。从陶色上看，红陶、红褐陶、褐陶比例约为 78%，说明其陶色偏于红色。从

纹饰上看，纹饰发达，约占陶片总数的31%，部分施饰陶衣。纹饰种类丰富，其中绳纹居多，约占纹饰陶40%，其他纹饰有刻划纹、戳印纹、凹弦纹、凸棱纹、压印纹、梳刷纹、附加堆纹等，尤以在各种刻划纹带内填充篦齿状或篦点状戳印纹的装饰风格最具特点，集多种纹饰在单个陶器上的复合纹饰甚为流行，纹饰图案主要有云纹、S形纹、几何形纹等（图四三；彩版四五、四六）。陶器口部多为敛口和侈口，喇叭形口和直口次之，器类主要是圈足器，器形包括球、支座、侈口罐、喇叭口罐、钵、敛口罐、直口罐、圈足等（彩版四七、四八）。

共挑选陶器标本29件，其中器形标本19件、纹饰标本10件。器形标本计有侈口罐2件、喇叭口罐2件、钵4件、敛口罐1件、直口罐3件、圈足5件、球1件、支座1件。

喇叭口罐 2件。

标本H4∶13，夹砂红褐陶。方唇，凸棱上戳刺有坑点纹。口径39.5、残高8厘米（图四四∶1）。标本H4∶12，夹砂黑褐陶。圆唇。凸棱上戳刺有坑点纹。口径31.5、残高5.8厘米（图四四∶7）。

钵 4件。依据形制的不同可分为三个类型。

第一类：2件。敛口，弧腹。

标本H4∶17，残，夹砂红褐陶，器内呈灰褐色。圆唇，弧腹。口径29.8、残高6.7厘米（图四四∶3）。标本H4∶19，夹细砂红褐陶。圆唇。口下部饰两道凹弦纹。口径27.8、残高3.8厘米（图四四∶6）。

第二类：1件。敛口，口下部饰一凸棱。

标本H4∶14，夹细砂红褐陶，器表因烧造原因部分区域呈黑色。圆唇，敛口，斜直腹。凸棱下饰有三道凹弦纹，上部两道凹弦纹中饰篦点纹。口径29.5、残高3厘米（图四四∶5）。

第三类：1件。侈口，浅腹。

标本H4∶20，夹砂黑褐陶。圆唇。唇部有刻划的短线纹，余光素无纹。口径29.5、残高

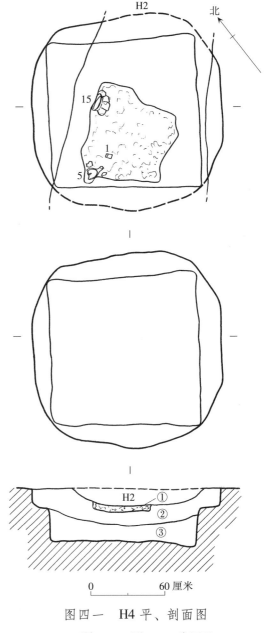

图四一 H4平、剖面图
1. 石锛 5. 石范 15. 陶圈足

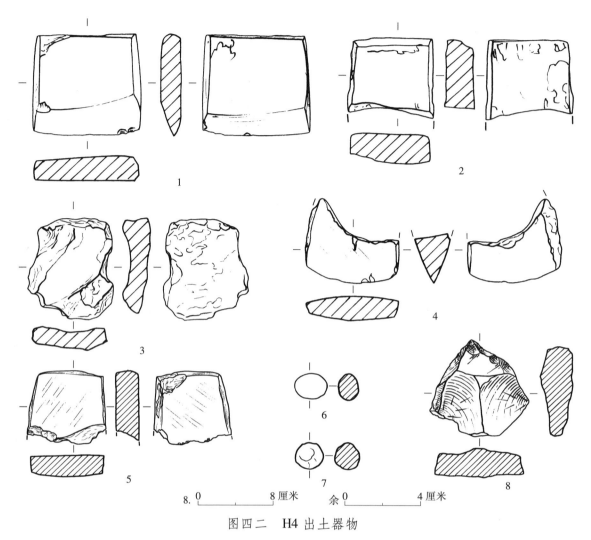

图四二　H4 出土器物

1、2、4、5. 石锛（H4：5、2、1、3）　3. 石范（H4：7）　6. 石球（H4：6）　7. 陶球（H4：4）
8. 石核（H4：8）

3.5 厘米（图四四：4）。

敛口罐　1 件。

标本 H4：18，夹粗砂红褐陶。圆唇，敛口，弧腹。口下部和腹上部分别饰两道凹弦纹，腹部饰纵向绳纹。口径 21.5、残高 7.2 厘米（图四五：1）。

侈口罐　2 件。依据形制的不同可分为两个类型。

第一类：1 件。形制相似，均为斜直腹，口下部饰一道凸棱。

标本 H4：25，夹砂红褐陶。方唇。口下部饰的凸棱上戳刺坑点纹，器内饰有两道凹弦纹，凹弦纹之间饰刻划的线纹。口径 35.2、残高 3.2 厘米（图四五：8）。

第二类：1 件。斜直腹，口下部无凸棱。

标本 H4：24，夹细砂灰褐陶。圆唇，窄平沿。口径 36、残高 4.8 厘米（图四五：3）。

厚唇罐　3 件。形制相似，均为厚方唇，直口微侈。

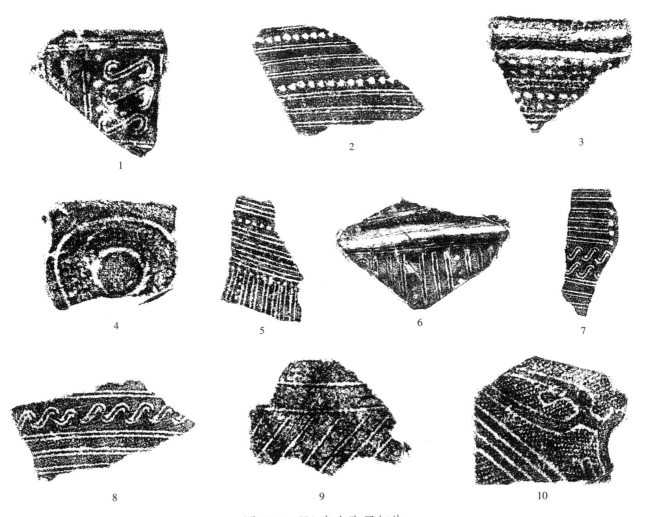

图四三 H4 出土陶器拓片

1. S 形纹 + 凹弦纹（H4：16） 2、3. 凹弦纹 + 篦点纹（H4：26、33） 4. 几何形纹 + 篦点纹（H4：34） 5. 凹弦纹 + 篦点纹 + 几何纹（H4：27） 6. 凸棱纹 + 凹弦纹（H4：28） 7、8. 凹弦纹 + S 形纹（H4：32、29） 9. 刻划纹 + 凹弦纹（H4：30） 10. 凹弦纹 + 篦点纹 + 云纹（H4：31）

标本 H4：21，夹细砂灰褐陶。唇部饰绳纹，腹上部饰有凹弦纹一周。口径 41.5、残高 4 厘米（图四五：7）。标本 H4：22，夹细砂红褐陶。口径 21、残高 5 厘米（图四五：2）。标本 H4：23，夹砂红褐。唇部饰绳纹，腹上部饰两道凹弦纹，凹弦纹之间饰刻划的短线纹。口径 32.8、残高 6 厘米（图四五：6）。

圈足 5 件。依据形制的不同可分为三个类型。

第一类：2 件。喇叭状圈足，足尖外撇。

标本 H4：10，夹细砂褐陶。圈足以上部分残，似豆的圈足。素面。底径 11.8、残高 5.1 厘米（图四五：9）。标本 H4：11，夹细砂褐陶。圈足以上部分残。素面。底径 12.2、残高 4.5 厘米（图四五：10）。

第二类：1 件。桶状。

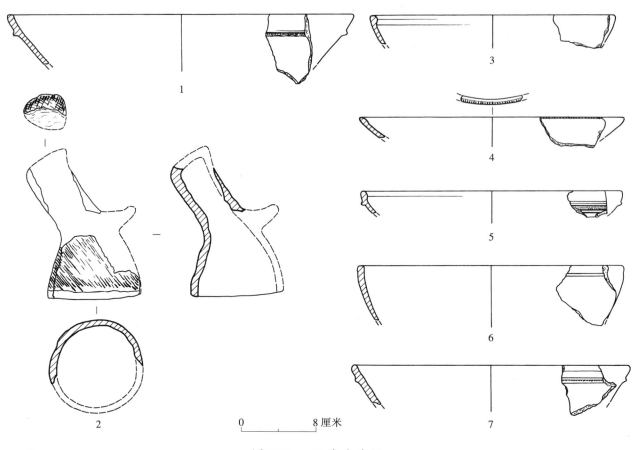

图四四　H4 出土陶器

1、7. 喇叭口罐（H4∶13、12）　2. 支座（H4∶31）　3~6. 钵（H4∶17、20、14、19）

标本 H4∶16，夹细砂红褐陶。圈足上上、下各饰一道凹弦纹，中饰竖向戳印的长方形纹和刻划的 S 形纹。底径 23.3、残高 4.5 厘米（图四五∶5）。

第三类：2 件。喇叭状圈足，足尖内折。

标本 H4∶9，夹细砂红褐陶。素面。口径 19.5、残高 3 厘米（图四五∶4）。标本 H4∶15，夹细砂红褐陶。圈足下部饰两道凹弦纹，凹弦纹之间饰篦点纹，上部饰刻划的云纹，云纹中饰篦点纹。口径 13.1、残高 1.6 厘米（图四五∶11；彩版四九∶1）。

球　1 件。

标本 H4∶4，夹细砂红褐陶。体呈球状。直径 1.5 厘米（图四二∶7）。

支座　1 件。形制相似。

标本 H4∶31，夹砂红褐陶。弧状，中空，平底，中部有一分支。器身遍饰纵向绳纹。底径 10.5、残高 17 厘米（图四四∶2；彩版四九∶2）。

H5

处于 T2 的西北部，部分叠压在 T1 的东隔梁下，开口于第④a 层下，被一近现代灰坑 H34 打破。

形制　平面呈上圆下方形，上部圆形的直径 1.6、深 0.2 米，下部方形边长 1.2、深 1.1

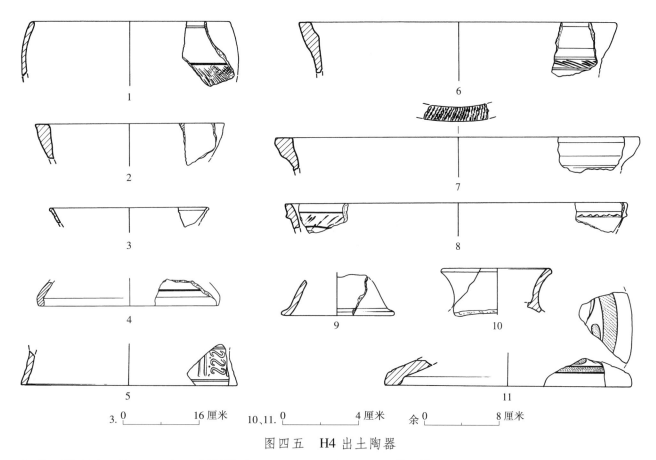

3. 0 ————————— 16厘米　　10、11. 0 ————————— 4厘米　　余 0 ————————— 8厘米

图四五　H4出土陶器

1. 敛口罐（H4：18）　2、6、7. 厚唇罐（H4：22、23、21）　3、8. 侈口罐（H4：24、25）　4、5、9～11. 圈足（H4：9、16、10、11、15）

米。四壁较光滑，坑底较平。坑内堆积可分3层。第①层为灰黑色土，土质疏松，由西南向东北倾斜堆积。包含有大量的陶片和少量的石器，厚0.7～0.85米。第②层黄色黏土，土质较硬，有较多的铁锈，由东北向西南倾斜堆积。包含有少量的陶器。厚0.1～0.15米。第③层为灰色土，土质疏松，由东北向西南倾斜堆积。包含有少量的陶器。厚0.2～0.3米。此层之下为黄褐色生土（图四六；彩版五〇）。

出土器物　主要是陶器和石器，其中以陶器为主，石器数量较少。共挑选39件标本，包括石器2件、陶器37件。

石器

2件。计有石核1件、刮削器1件。

核　1件。

标本H5：9，体呈长方形，一面保持自然砾石面，另一面可见剥片时留下的疤痕。长2.9、宽2.6、厚1.5厘米（图四七：1）。

刮削器　1件。

标本H5：14，体呈不规则长方形。平顶，器身经剥片形成。长1.7、宽0.5、厚0.4厘米（图四七：15）。

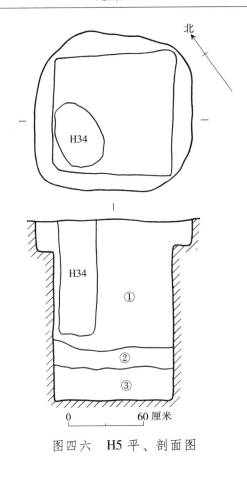

图四六　H5 平、剖面图

陶器

H5 共出土陶片 1081 片。从陶质来看，夹细砂陶比例约为 82%，粗砂陶约和泥质陶分别占 9%。从陶色上看，红陶和红褐陶比例约为 77%，说明其陶色偏于红色。从纹饰上看，纹饰发达，约占陶片总数的 44%。纹饰种类丰富，其中绳纹居多，约占纹饰陶 55%，其他纹饰有刻划线纹、凹弦纹、凸棱纹、压印纹、梳刷纹、坑点纹等（图四八；彩版五一、五二）。陶器口部多为敛口和侈口，喇叭形口和直口次之，器类主要是圈足器，器形包括球、支座、侈口罐、钵、敛口罐、直口罐、圈足等（彩版五三、五四）。

H5 共挑选陶器标本 37 件，其中 H5 器形标本 26 件，纹饰标本 11 件。器形标本计支座 2 件、球 12 件、器耳 2 件、侈口罐 4 件、喇叭口罐 1 件、钵 3 件、厚唇罐 2 件。

支座　2 件。形制相似，均呈上小下大，上端呈椭圆形外侈，曲身，实心。

标本 H5：37，夹细砂红褐陶。身一侧有一柱状凸起，身中设一圆形穿孔，器身遍饰竖向绳纹。上端长径 6、残高 10.4 厘米（图四九：1）。标本 H5：28，残损严重，夹砂红褐陶。器身遍饰竖向绳纹。顶部径 5.1、残高 6.8 厘米（图四七：16）。

球　12 件。形制相似，仅大小略有不同（彩版五五：1）。

标本 H5：3，夹细砂灰褐陶。直径 1.4~1.7 厘米（图四七：4）。标本 H5：13，夹细砂灰褐陶。直径 1.5 厘米（图四七：5）。标本 H5：8，夹砂红褐陶，残损严重。标本 H5：5，夹细砂灰褐陶，残存一半。直径 1.5 厘米（图四七：6）。标本 H5：12，夹细砂褐陶。直径 1.4 厘

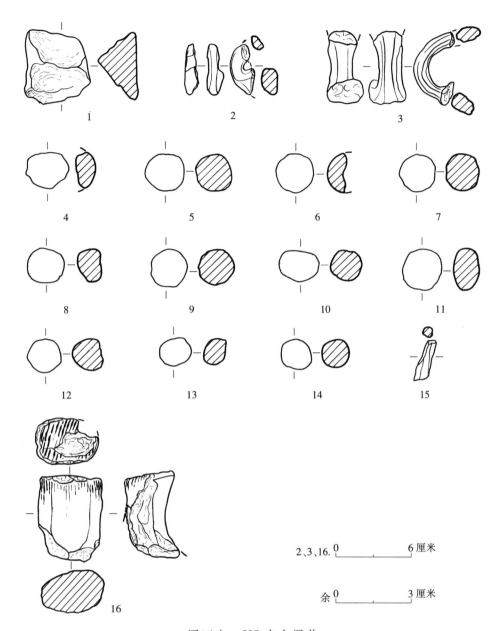

图四七　H5 出土器物

1. 石核（H5∶9）　　2、3. 陶器耳（H5∶17、18）　　4~14. 陶球（H5∶3、13、5、12、10、4、7、1、11、6、2）

15. 石刮削器（H5∶14）　　16. 陶支座（H5∶28）

米（图四七∶7）。标本 H5∶10，夹细砂褐陶。直径 1.4 厘米（图四七∶8）。标本 H5∶4，夹细砂灰褐陶。直径 1.4 厘米（图四七∶9）。标本 H5∶7，夹细砂灰褐陶。直径 1.2~1.6 厘米（图四七∶10）。标本 H5∶1，夹细砂红褐陶。直径 1.6 厘米（图四七∶11）。标本 H5∶11，夹细砂灰褐陶。直径 1.4 厘米（图四七∶12）。标本 H5∶6，夹细砂灰褐陶。直径 1.2 厘米（图四七∶13）。标本 H5∶2，夹细砂灰褐陶。直径 1.2 厘米（图四七∶14）。

　　器耳　2 件。形制相似，均为桥形耳。

　　标本 H5∶18，夹细砂褐陶。剖面呈柱状。残长 5.7、宽 2.9 厘米（图四七∶3；彩版五五∶2）。

图四八　H5 出土陶器拓片

1. 篦点纹＋戳刺纹（H5：32）　　2. 圆圈纹（H5：33）　　3. 短线纹＋凹弦纹（H5：15）　　4. 凸棱纹＋刻划线纹（H5：20）　　5. 刻划线纹（H5：34）　　6. 篦点纹＋几何形纹（H5：35）　　7. 凸棱纹＋刻划线纹（H5：21）　　8. 凹弦纹＋刻划线纹（H5：29）　　9. 篦点纹＋几何形纹（H5：36）　　10. 凹弦纹＋篦点纹＋水波纹（H5：30）　　11. 点纹＋凹弦纹（H5：31）

标本 H5：17，夹细砂红陶。饼状小耳。残长 4、宽 1.9 厘米（图四七：2；彩版五五：3）。

侈口罐　4 件。依据形制的不同可分为两个类型。

第一类：1 件。口沿下饰一道凸棱。

标本 H5：22，夹细砂褐陶。圆唇。口下部饰两道凹弦纹，颈部饰刻划的线纹。口径 23.1、残高 4.6 厘米（图四九：8）。

第二类：3 件。口沿下无凸棱。

标本 H5：20，夹细砂红陶。方唇，束颈。颈上部饰一凸棱，凸棱上戳刺有坑点纹，颈部饰刻划的线纹。口径 18.9、残高 7.5 厘米（图四九：3；彩版五六：1）。标本 H5：25，夹砂褐陶。圆唇。口内侧饰两道凹弦纹。口径 31.6、残高 4.2 厘米（图四九：10）。标本 H5：24，夹细砂褐陶。圆唇。口内侧饰两道凹弦纹。口径 31.6、残高 4.4 厘米（图四九：11）。

喇叭口罐　1 件。

标本 H5：15，夹细砂红褐陶。圆唇，斜直腹。口下部饰三道凹弦纹，上部两凹弦纹之间饰绳纹，腹部饰刻划纹。口径 14.5、残高 4.2 厘米（图四九：2）。

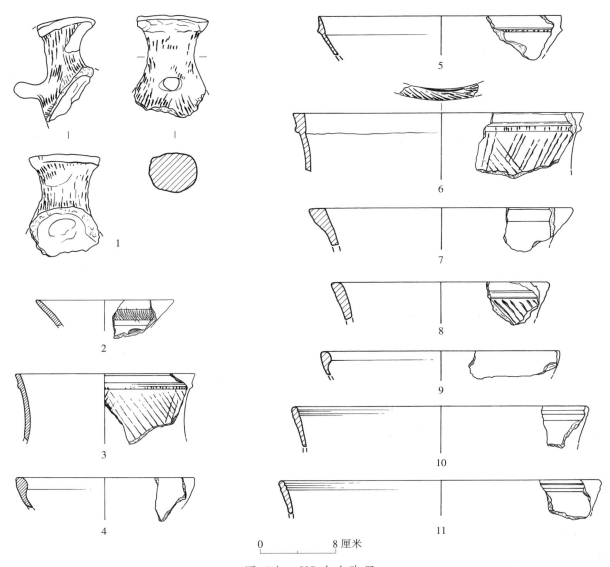

图四九　H5 出土陶器

1. 支座（H5：37）　2. 喇叭口罐（H5：15）　3、8、10、11. 侈口罐（H5：20、22、25、24）　4、5、9. 钵（H5：23、16、26）　6、7. 直口罐（H5：21、27）

钵　3 件。依据形制的不同可分为两个类型。

第一类：2 件。厚圆唇，敛口。

标本 H5：23，夹砂红褐陶。口径 18.8、残高 4.2 厘米（图四九：4）。标本 H5：26，夹砂红陶。口径 25.3、残高 3 厘米（图四九：9）。

第二类：1 件。侈口。

标本 H5：16，夹细砂褐陶。尖圆唇，斜直腹。口下部饰一道凸棱，凸棱上戳刺有坑点纹。口径 25.5、残高 4.7 厘米（图四九：5）。

厚唇罐　2 件。形制基本相似。均侈口。

标本 H5：21，夹细砂红褐陶。厚方唇。唇部饰斜向绳纹，口下部饰一凸棱，凸棱上戳刺

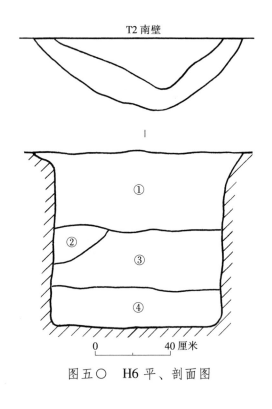

图五〇 H6 平、剖面图

有坑点纹，颈部饰刻划的线纹。口径30.7、残高7厘米（图四九：6；彩版五六：2）。标本 H5：27，夹砂红褐陶。厚方唇，口微侈。口径28、残高4.7厘米（图四九：7）。

H6

处于 T2 的东南角，部分叠压在该方的东隔梁和南部的探方下。开口于第④a层下。

形制　平面呈上圆下方形，上部圆形的直径1.1米，下部方形暴露的边长0.88米，深0.9米。坑内堆积可分为4层。第①层为灰黑色土，土质疏松。包含有大量红烧土块、炭屑、陶片和少量的石器。厚0.32～0.4米。第②层为黄色黏土，土质较纯，包含有较多的铁锈，仅存在于灰坑的东北角，包含有极少量的陶片。厚0～0.18米。第③层为灰色土，土质疏松，包含有少量的红烧土颗粒、炭屑和陶片。厚0.13～0.33米。第④层为灰褐色土，土质较硬，包含有少量的炭屑。厚0.18～0.21厘米。此层之下为黄褐色生土（图五〇）。

出土器物　主要是陶器，还有少量的石器，共挑选11件标本，包括石器1件、陶器10件。

石器

1件。为刮削器。

刮削器　1件。

标本 H6：1，体呈三棱状，一侧保留自然砾石面，另两侧可见打击点和放射线。长3.7、宽2.2、厚0.5厘米（图五一：1）。

陶器

H6 共出土陶片265片。从陶质来看，夹细砂陶比例约为67%，粗砂陶约为17%，泥质陶比例约为16%。从陶色上看，红陶和红褐陶比例约为66%，说明其陶色偏于红色。从纹饰上看，纹饰较发达，约占陶片总数的34%。纹饰种类丰富，其中绳纹居多，约占纹饰陶56%，其他纹饰有刻划线纹、凹弦纹、戳刺纹、梳刷纹等，以在各种刻划纹带内填充篦齿状或篦点状戳印纹的装饰风格最具特点；集多种纹饰在单个陶器上的复合纹饰甚为流行；纹饰图案主要有 S 形纹、几何形纹等（图五一：8～11；彩版五七）。陶器口部多为喇叭形口、直口，器形包括器鋬、支座、喇叭口罐、豆、钵、厚唇罐等（彩版五八）。

H6 共挑选陶器标本10件，包括器形标本6件、纹饰标本4件。器形标本计有器鋬1件、

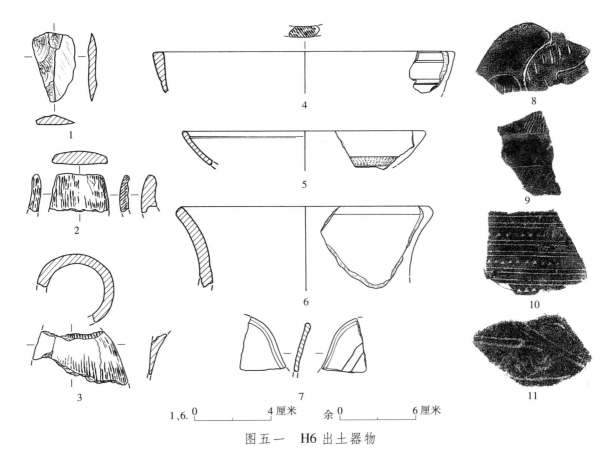

1、6. 0 ┣━━━━━━━┫ 4 厘米　　余 0 ┣━━━━━━━┫ 6 厘米

图五一　H6 出土器物

1. 石刮削器（H6：1）　2. 陶器鏊（H6：2）　3. 陶支座（H6：3）　4. 陶厚唇罐（H6：6）　5. 陶钵（H6：4）
6. 陶喇叭口罐（H6：7）　7. 陶豆（H6：5）　8. 戳刺纹＋几何形纹（H6：8）　9. 凹弦纹＋刻划线纹（H6：9）
10. 点纹＋凹弦纹（H6：10）　11. 几何形纹（H6：11）

支座 1 件、豆 1 件、喇叭口罐 1 件、钵 1 件、厚唇罐 1 件。

器鏊　1 件。

标本 H6：2，夹砂红褐陶。仅存底部，呈圆形，器身遍饰竖向绳纹。残高 3.9 厘米（图五一：2；彩版五九：1）。

支座　1 件。形制相似，残损严重。

标本 H6：3，夹砂褐陶。仅存下部，呈上大下小的柱状，空心。器身遍饰竖向绳纹。残高 5.4 厘米（图五一：3）。

豆　1 件。

标本 H6：5，夹砂红褐陶。呈六边形，推测可能为六边形豆的口沿，盘内饰两道凹弦纹。残长 4.8、残宽 5.8 厘米（图五一：7；彩版五九：2）。

喇叭口罐　1 件。

标本 H6：7，夹细砂红褐陶。圆唇，束颈。口径 13、残高 4.4 厘米（图五一：6）。

钵　1 件。

标本 H6：4，夹砂褐陶，器表因烧造原因部分呈黑色。圆唇，侈口，弧腹。腹部饰两道凹

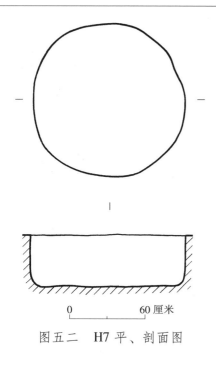

图五二　H7 平、剖面图

弦纹，凹弦纹中饰篦点纹。口径25.4、残高4.1厘米（图五一：5）。

厚唇罐　1件。

标本 H6：6，夹砂红褐陶。厚方唇，唇部饰斜向绳纹，口下部饰一道凹弦纹。口径31.6、残高4.4厘米（图五一：4）。

H7

处于 T2 的东部，部分叠压在该探方的东隔梁中，开口于第⑤层下。

形制　平面呈圆形，直径1.2、深0.4米。四壁光滑，坑底较平。坑内堆积为灰色土，土质疏松，包含有少量的陶片、红烧土颗粒和炭屑（图五二）。

出土器物　H7 出土器物极少，以陶器为主，仅有1件玉器。陶器陶质以夹细砂陶为主，还有少量的夹粗砂和泥质陶，陶色以红色和红褐色为主，纹饰主要为绳纹、刻划纹、戳印纹和几何形纹（图五三：4、5、6）。

H7 共挑选标本6件，其中陶器5件、玉器1件。陶器标本中纹饰标本3件、器形标本2件。器形标本计有喇叭口罐和圈足各1件。

陶喇叭口罐　1件。

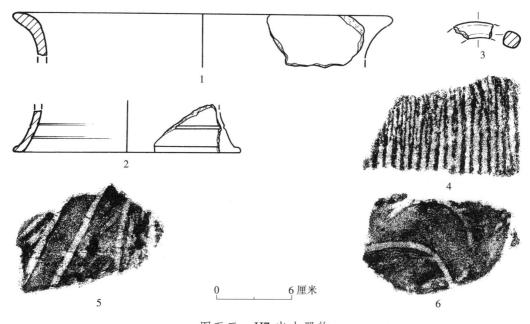

图五三　H7 出土器物

1. 陶喇叭口罐（H7：1）　2. 陶圈足（H7：2）　3. 玉璜（H7：3）　4. 绳纹（H7：4）　5. 戳刺纹（H7：6）
6. 几何形纹（H7：5）

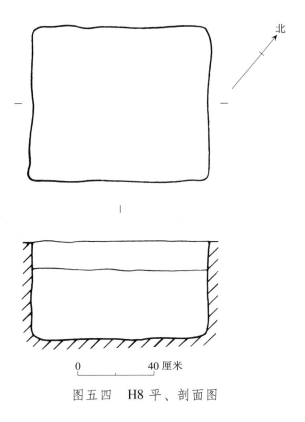

图五四 H8 平、剖面图

标本 H7：1，夹细砂红褐陶。圆唇，束颈。口径 29.8、残高 4 厘米（图五三：1）。

陶圈足 1 件。

标本 H7：2，夹细砂红陶。喇叭状圈足，足尖外撇。底径 17.7、残高 3.4 厘米（图五三：2）。

玉璜 1 件。标本 H7：3，残损严重，体呈圆形。残长 3 厘米（图五三：3）。

H8

处于该探方的东隔梁中，开口于第⑤a 层下。

形制 平面呈长方形，长 0.9、宽 0.78、深 0.5 米。坑内堆积可分为两层。上层为灰色土，土质疏松，包含少量的陶片和红烧土颗粒，厚 0.14 米。下层为黄褐色黏土，土质较硬，包含有少量的红烧土颗粒，厚 0.36 米（图五四；彩版六〇）。

出土器物 该灰坑仅出土陶片 29 件，以夹细砂陶为主，还有少量的泥质陶，陶色以红陶和红褐陶为主，纹饰主要为绳纹、凹弦纹、篦点纹、刻划纹等（图五五：3、4）。器形仅见圈足和钵。

H8 共挑选陶器标本 4 件，其中器形标本 3 件、纹饰标本 1 件。器形标本计有钵 1 件、圈足 1 件、釜 1 件。

圈足 1 件。

标本 H8：2，夹细砂褐陶。喇叭状圈足，足尖上翘。底径 12.4、残高 2.6 厘米（图五五：1）。

钵 1 件。

标本 H8：1，夹细砂红褐陶。圆唇，侈口。口下部饰刻划的线纹。口径 32.4、残高 4.7

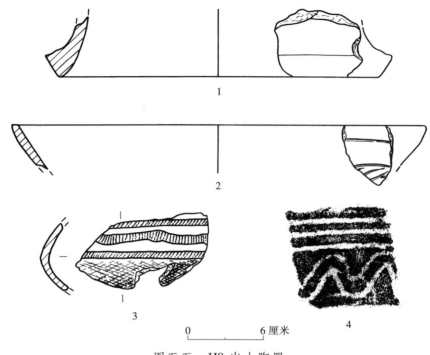

图五五　H8 出土陶器

1. 圈足（H8：2）　　2. 钵（H8：1）　　3. 凹弦纹＋绳纹＋篦点纹（H8：3）　　4. 凹弦纹＋刻划纹（H8：4）

厘米（图五五：2）。

釜　1 件。

标本 H8：3，夹砂灰褐陶。圆鼓腹。腹上部饰两两一组的凹弦纹，凹弦纹中饰戳刺的短线纹，腹下部饰交错绳纹。残高 5.2 厘米（图五五：3）。

（二）柱洞

16 个。主要分布在 H3、H4、H6 的旁边，但是无规律可循。平面基本呈圆形，壁面平整光滑，底部为锅底状（图五六）。现将本探方各柱洞的情况列表如下。

表二　T2 各层下坑和柱洞统计表　　　　　　　　　　　　　　　　　（单位：厘米）

序号	编号	层位	形制与结构			尺寸（直径－深）	填土	图号
			平面形制	坑壁	坑底			
1	D1	⑤a 下	圆形	平整	锅底状	12－16	灰黑土	图五六：1
2	D2	⑤a 下	圆形	平整	锅底状	14－20	黑土	图五六：2
3	D3	⑤a 下	圆形	平整	锅底状	22－20	灰黑土	图五六：3
4	D4	⑤a 下	葫芦形	平整	锅底状	4～46－21	黑土	图五六：4
5	D5	⑤a 下	圆形	平整	锅底状	18－26	灰黑土	图五六：5
6	D6	⑤a 下	椭圆形	平整	锅底状	20～34－26	灰黑土	图五六：6
7	D7	⑤a 下	圆形	平整	锅底状	11－16	黑土	图五六：7
8	D8	⑤a 下	圆形	平整	锅底状	13－20	灰黑土	图五六：8
9	D9	⑤a 下	圆形	平整	锅底状	14－22	灰黑土	图五六：9

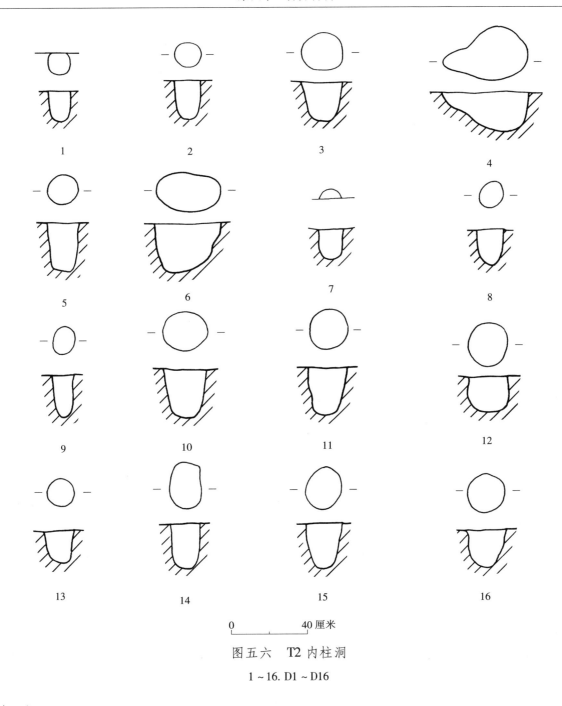

0 ⊢——————⊣ 40 厘米

图五六　T2 内柱洞

1～16. D1～D16

（续表二）

序号	编号	层位	形制与结构			尺寸（直径－深）	填土	图号
			平面形制	坑壁	坑底			
10	D10	⑤a下	圆形	平整	锅底状	24－26	灰黑土	图五六: 10
11	D11	⑤a下	圆形	平整	锅底状	20－25	灰黑土	图五六: 11
12	D12	⑤a下	圆形	平整	锅底状	21－18	灰黑土	图五六: 12
13	D13	⑤a下	圆形	平整	锅底状	15－18	灰黑土	图五六: 13
14	D14	⑤a下	不规则椭圆形	平整	锅底状	14～24－24	灰黑土	图五六: 14

（续表二）

序号	编号	层位	形制与结构			尺寸（直径－深）	填土	图号
			平面形制	坑壁	坑底			
15	D15	⑤a 下	近圆形	平整	锅底状	18～22－24	灰黑土	图五六：15
16	D16	⑤a 下	圆形	平整	锅底状	19－20	灰黑土	图五六：16

三　地层中出土遗物

（一）T2⑤a 层出土器物

以陶器为主，还有少量的石器。共挑选标本 88 件，包括石器 18 件、玉器 2 件、陶器 68 件。

石器

20 件。计锛 5 件、斧 5 件、璧形器 1 件、拍 2 件、网坠 1 件、核 4 件。

拍　2 件。

标本 T2⑤a：8，残，体呈长方形，器表剥片痕迹明显。一侧可见两道凹痕。残长 6、残宽 4.6、后 0.3～2.5 厘米（图五七：1）。标本 T2⑤a：4，残，体呈长方形，器表可见四个平行的凹槽。残长 6.1、残宽 2.6、厚 3.2 厘米（彩版六一：1）。

锛　5 件。形制基本相似，均体呈梯形或长方形，通体磨制。

标本 T2⑤a：6，通体磨制。体呈梯形，双面弧刃。长 2.7、宽 1.6～2.3、厚 0.8 厘米（图五七：2；彩版六一：2）。标本 T2⑤a：11，仅存下部，体呈长方形，双面弧刃。长 4.2、宽 5、厚 1.6 厘米（图五七：5；彩版六一：3）。标本 T2⑤a：10，仅存上端。体呈长方形。残长 2.8、宽 4.5、厚 1 厘米（图五七：6）。标本 T2⑤a：3，残，体呈长方形，双面弧刃。长 3.2、宽 2.8、厚 1.8 厘米（彩版六一：4）。标本 T2⑤a：5，刃部残缺，双面弧刃，长 4.5、宽 4.2、厚 2 厘米（彩版六二：1）。

璧形器　1 件。

标本 T2⑤a：2，残，黑色。体呈圆形，中间较厚，周边较薄。残长 3.3、残宽 4.5 厘米（彩版六二：2）。

斧　5 件。形制相似，体呈长方形，通体磨制。

标本 T2②：1，刃部略残。长 5.9、宽 2.6、厚 1 厘米（图五七：7）。标本 T2②：2，仅存上端。残长 4.3、残宽 3.1、后 1.4 厘米（图五七：8）。标本 T2⑤a：12，刃部残缺。残长 3.9、残宽 2.8、厚 1 厘米（图五八：1）。标本 T2⑤a：13，仅存下端，双面弧刃，刃部有明显的使用痕迹。残长 2.9、残宽 2.5、厚 1.2 厘米（图五八：3）。标本 T2⑤a：15，仅存上端。残长 2.7、宽 3.8、厚 0.6 厘米（图五八：8）。

网坠　1 件。

标本 T2⑤a：14，体呈亚腰形，上端较小，下端较大，中部有一挖槽。长 3.4、宽 5.5、

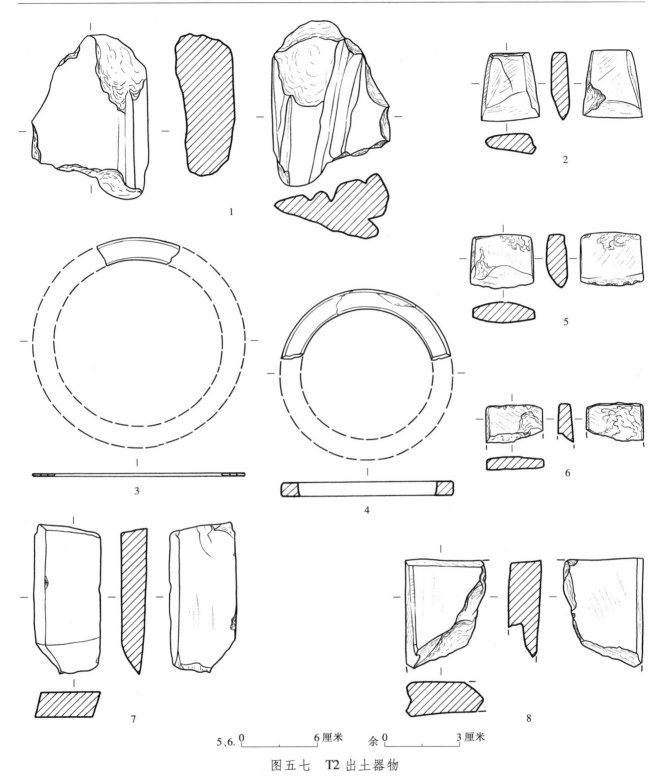

图五七　T2 出土器物

1. 石拍（T2⑤a：8）　　2、5、6. 石锛（T2⑤a：6、11、10）　　3、4. 玉环（T2⑤a：7、9）　　7、8. 石斧（T2②：1、2）

厚 1.9 厘米（图五八：7；彩版六二：3）。

核　4 件。

标本 T2⑤a：17，体呈不规则长方形，两侧可见剥片时留下的疤痕。长 6.6、宽 5.8、厚 3 厘

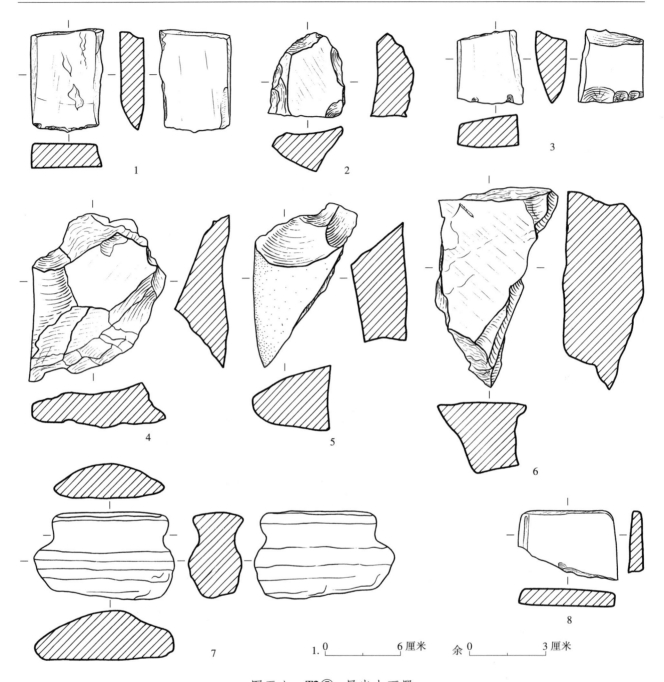

图五八　T2⑤a 层出土石器

1、3、8. 斧（T2⑤a：12、13、15）　2、4～6. 核（T2⑤a：17、18、19、20）　7. 网坠（T2⑤a：14）

米（图五八：2）。标本 T2⑤a：18，体呈不规则长方形，器表剥片痕迹明显，上端可见打击点和放射线。长 6.1、宽 5.1、厚 0.2～2 厘米（图五八：4）。标本 T2⑤a：19，体呈尖锥状，两面均保持自然砾石面，上端可见打击点和放射线。长 5.2、宽 3.6、厚 1.6～2.5 厘米（图五八：5）。标本 T2⑤a：20，体呈尖锥状，器表因剥片斑驳不清。长 7.8、宽 4.6、厚 0.1～3.2 厘米（图五八：6）。

玉器

2件。均为玉环。

环　2件。形制相似，均呈圆形，通体磨制。

标本T2⑤a：9，残存约一半，乳白色。直径6.8、宽1.5、厚0.6厘米（图五七：4；彩版六二：4）。标本T2⑤a：7，残存少量，乳白色。直径8.4、宽1.8、厚0.1厘米（图五七：3）。

陶器

探方T2第⑤a层共出土陶片2434片。从陶质来看，夹细砂陶比例约为73.5%，粗砂陶约为15.5%，泥质磨光陶比例约为11%。从陶色上看，红陶、红褐陶、褐陶比例约为64%，说明其陶色偏于红色。从纹饰上看，纹饰发达，约占陶片总数的33%，部分施饰陶衣。纹饰种类丰富，其中绳纹居多，约占纹饰种类总数的63%，其他纹饰有刻划纹、戳印纹、凹弦纹、凸棱纹、压印纹、梳刷纹、附加堆纹、篦点纹等，流行将多种纹饰施于单个陶器上，纹饰图案主要有云纹、S形纹、几何形纹、圆圈纹、水波纹等（图五九、六〇：1~9；彩版六三~六五）。陶器口部多为敛口和侈口，喇叭形口和直口次之，器类主要是圜底器和圈足器，器形包括钵、敛口罐、厚唇罐、侈口罐、喇叭口罐、器鋬、支座、圈足等。

T2第⑤a层共挑选陶器标本68件，其中纹饰标本21件、器形标本47件。器形标本包括钵8件、敛口罐5件、厚唇罐5件、侈口罐8件、喇叭口罐1件、圈足14件、器鋬4件、支座2件等。

钵　8件。依据口部和肩部的不同可分为四个类型。

第一类：3件。侈口，口下部无凸棱。

标本T2⑤a：54，夹砂褐陶。圆唇，斜直腹。腹部饰四道凹弦纹，上下两道凹弦纹之间饰戳刺的短线纹，上下两组凹弦纹之间饰刻划的水波纹，水波纹内饰刻划的短线纹。口径22、残高4.4厘米（图六一：1）。标本T2⑤a：52，夹砂灰褐陶。圆唇，斜直腹。腹部饰两道凹弦纹，凹弦纹之间饰刻划的水波纹。口径25.6、残高3.8厘米（图六一：3）。标本T2⑤a：53，夹砂褐陶。圆唇，侈口，弧腹。腹部饰两道凹弦纹，凹弦纹之间饰刻划的水波纹。口径24.5、残高4厘米（图六一：4）。

第二类：3件。侈口，肩部饰一道凸棱。

标本T2⑤a：66，夹砂红褐陶。圆唇，斜直腹。口径27.6、残高4.6厘米（图六一：2）。标本T2⑤a：60，夹砂黑褐陶。圆唇，弧腹。凸棱下饰刻划的短线纹。口径24.3、残高3.5厘米（图六一：5）。标本T2⑤a：33，夹砂褐陶。方唇，弧腹。素面。口径42、残高5.6厘米（图六一：6）。

第三类：1件。口微敛。

标本T2⑤a：27，夹细砂红陶。方唇，敛口。口下部饰舌状器鋬。口径20.4、残高2.8厘米（图六一：12）。

第四类：1件。敛口。

标本T2⑤a：49，夹砂红陶。圆唇，弧腹。腹部饰两道凹弦纹，凹弦纹之间饰戳刺一周小

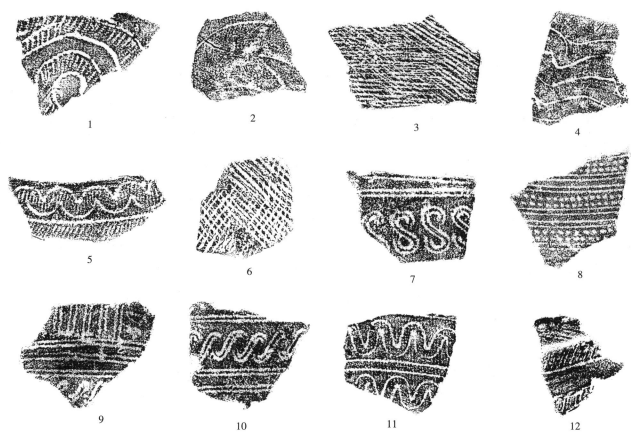

图五九　T2⑤a 层出土陶器拓片

1. 刻划纹＋绳纹（T2⑤a：70）　2. 刻划纹（T2⑤a：71）　3. 绳纹（T2⑤a：68）　4. 水波纹（T2⑤a：69）　5. 水波纹＋凹弦纹＋绳纹（T2⑤a：72）　6. 交错绳纹（T2⑤a：73）　7. 凹弦纹＋S 形纹（T2⑤a：76）　8. 凹弦纹＋戳刺点纹（T2⑤a：77）　9. 刻划纹＋凹弦纹＋S 形纹（T2⑤a：74）　10. 凹弦纹＋S 形纹（T2⑤a：75）　11. 凹弦纹＋水波纹（T2⑤a：78）　12. 叶脉纹＋凹弦纹＋绳纹（T2⑤a：79）

圆圈纹。残高 4.8 厘米（图六二：1）。

敛口罐　5 件。依据肩部的不同可分为两个类型。

第一类：3 件。鼓肩，肩部饰一道凸棱。

标本 T2⑤a：61，夹砂红褐陶。圆唇，弧腹。凸棱下饰弦纹和篦点纹。口径 33.4、残高 5 厘米（图六一：7；彩版六六：1）。标本 T2⑤a：67，夹砂红陶。圆唇，敛口，弧腹。凸棱上戳刺有坑点纹，凸棱下饰三道凹弦纹，凹弦纹之间饰刻划的线纹，腹部饰刻划的水波纹。口径 27、残高 3.4 厘米（图六一：9；彩版六六：2）。标本 T2⑤a：62，夹砂红褐陶。圆唇，敛口，弧腹。凸棱下是弦纹和戳刺的短线纹。腹上部饰连续 S 形纹，S 形纹中戳刺短线纹。口径 19.6、残高 3.3 厘米（图六一：10；彩版六六：3）。

第二类：2 件。弧肩，肩部无凸棱。

标本 T2⑤a：59，夹砂褐陶。圆唇，敛口，弧腹，肩部饰一道凹弦纹。腹上部饰刻划的弧线和三角纹组成的几何形纹。口径 29.6、残高 4.7 厘米（图六一：8）。标本 T2⑤a：58，夹砂红褐陶。圆唇，敛口，弧腹。口下部饰弦纹和戳刺的坑点纹。口径 22.2、残高 3.4 厘米（图六一：11）。

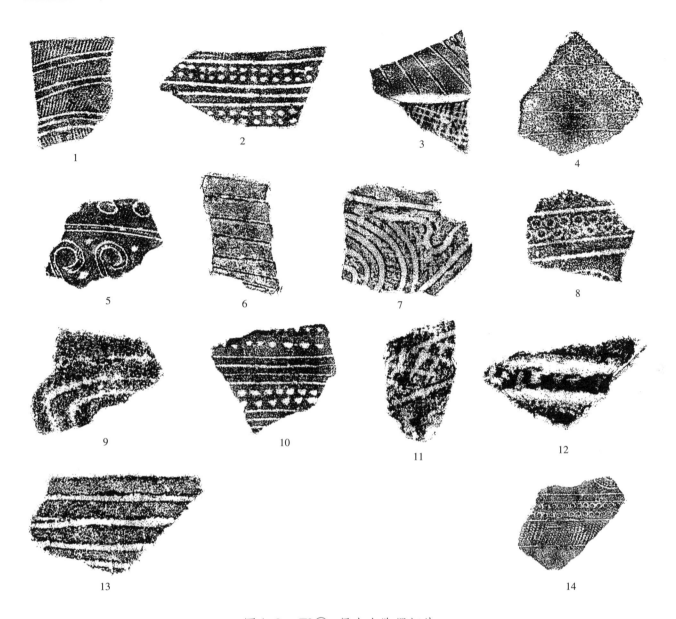

图六〇 T2⑤a 层出土陶器拓片

1. 刻划纹＋绳纹（T2⑤a：80） 2. 凹弦纹＋戳刺点纹（T2⑤a：81） 3. 刻划纹＋绳纹（T2⑤a：82） 4. 凹弦纹（T2⑤a：：83） 5. 圆圈纹＋凹弦纹＋S形纹（T2⑤a：84） 6. 凹弦纹（T2⑤a：85） 7. 刻划纹（T2⑤a：86） 8. 凹弦纹＋圆圈纹（T2⑤a：87） 9. 刻划纹（T2⑤a：88） 10. 凹弦纹＋戳刺点纹（T2⑤b：21） 11. 刻划纹（T2⑤b：22） 12. 凸棱纹（T2⑤b：23） 13. 凹弦纹（T2⑤b：24） 14. 凹弦纹＋圆圈纹＋篦点纹（T2⑤b：25）

厚唇罐 5 件。依据口部的不同可分为两个类型。

第一类：3 件。厚方唇，直口微侈。

标本 T2⑤a：42，夹砂红陶。束颈。唇部饰横向绳纹，口下部饰斜向绳纹，颈部饰一道凹弦纹。口径35、残高4.7厘米（图六二：4）。标本 T2⑤a：45，夹砂灰褐陶。唇部饰斜向绳纹，口下部饰两道凹弦纹。口径30.5、残高3.6厘米（图六二：6）。标本 T2⑤a：41，夹砂红

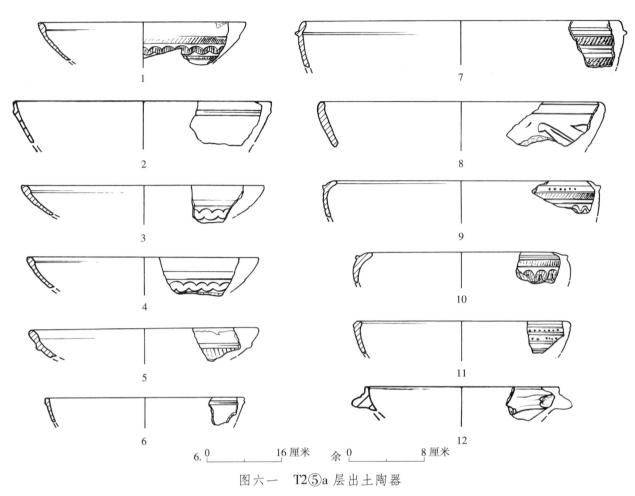

图六一　T2⑤a 层出土陶器

1~6.12. 钵（T2⑤a：54、66、52、53、60、33、27）　7~11. 敛口罐（T2⑤a：61、59、67、62、58）

陶。唇部饰斜向绳纹，口下部饰两道凹弦纹，凹弦纹之间饰刻划的水波纹。口径48、残高3.8厘米（图六二：5）。

第二类：2件。厚方唇，敛口。

标本 T2⑤a：43，夹砂褐陶。唇部饰斜向绳纹，口下部饰经涂抹的绳纹。口径54、残高4.8厘米（图六二：7）。标本 T2⑤a：44，夹砂红褐陶。唇部饰斜向绳纹。口径40.8、残高4.2厘米（图六二：8）。

侈口罐　8件。依据颈部的不同可分为两个类型。

第一类：7件。均侈口，长颈，颈部无凸棱。

标本 T2⑤a：64，夹砂红褐陶。圆唇。口径28.4、残高7.8厘米（图六二：9）。标本 T2⑤a：63，夹砂红陶。圆唇。口径28、残高4.2厘米（图六二：10）。标本 T2⑤a：65，夹砂红陶。圆唇。口径33、残高5.6厘米（图六二：11）。标本 T2⑤a：51，夹砂红褐陶。圆唇。口下部饰一道凹弦纹。口径29.2、残高5.3厘米（图六二：12）。标本 T2⑤a：35，夹砂红褐陶。尖圆唇。颈上部饰一道凹弦纹，颈部饰刻划的短线纹。口径20.5、残高5.8厘米（图六二：13）。标本 T2⑤a：34，夹细砂红褐陶。圆唇。口下部饰一道凹弦纹，颈部

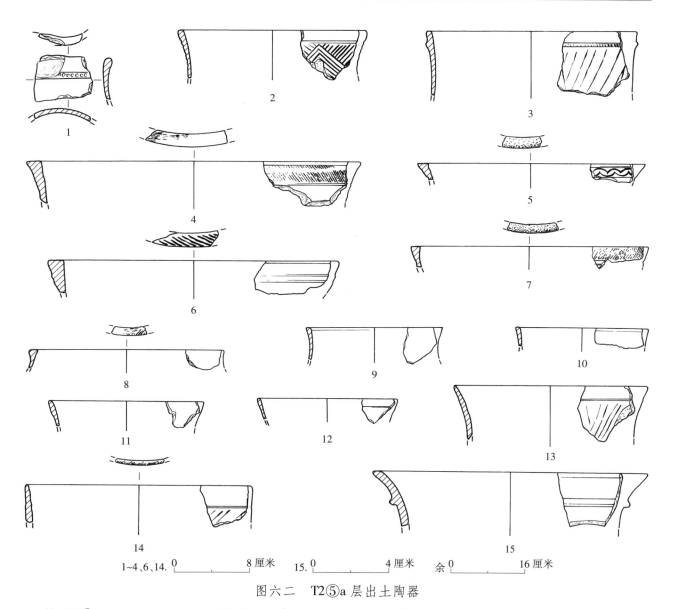

图六二　T2⑤a 层出土陶器

1. 钵（T2⑤a：49）　　2、3、9～14. 侈口罐（T2⑤a：34、32、64、63、65、51、35、36）　　4～8. 厚唇罐（T2⑤a：42、
41、45、43、44）　　15. 喇叭口罐（T2⑤a：30）

饰刻画的三角形纹和短线纹。口径 19.7、残高 5.1 厘米（图六二：2）。标本 T2⑤a：36，
夹砂红褐陶。尖圆唇。颈上部饰一道凹弦纹，其下饰刻划短线纹。口径 24、残高 4 厘米
（图六二：14）。

第二类：1 件。侈口，长颈，颈部有一道凸棱。

标本 T2⑤a：32，夹砂红褐陶。方唇。凸棱上戳刺有坑点纹，颈部饰刻划的线纹。口径
22.3、残高 6.6 厘米（图六二：3）。

喇叭口罐　1 件。

标本 T2⑤a：30，夹砂褐陶。尖圆唇，束颈。口径 14.6、残高 2.9 厘米（图六二：15）。

圈足　14 件。依据形制的不同可分为四个类型（彩版六七）。

第一类：6件。呈喇叭状，足尖内折。

标本 T2⑤a：57，夹细砂红褐陶。圈足上饰两两一组的凹弦纹，凹弦纹中饰篦点纹。底径 14.5、残高 1.7 厘米（图六三：1）。标本 T2⑤a：28，夹细砂红褐陶。圈足上饰三道凹弦纹。底径 18.3、残高 1.8 厘米（图六三：3）。标本 T2⑤a：29，夹细砂褐陶。足上饰两道凹弦纹。底径 18.3、残高 2.8 厘米（图六三：4）。标本 T2⑤a：48，夹砂红褐陶。底径 20.5、残高 5.6 厘米（图六三：5）。标本 T2⑤a：56，夹砂红褐陶。足部饰四道凹弦纹和篦点纹。底径 14.5、残高 1.6 厘米（图六三：10）。标本 T2⑤a：55，夹砂褐陶。足尖内折呈直角。足部饰四周凹弦纹。底径 14.3、残高 1.5 厘米（图六三：11）。

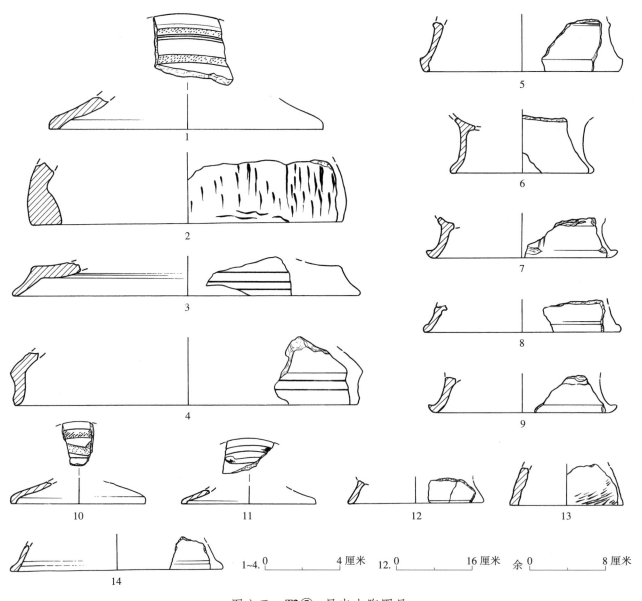

图六三　T2⑤a 层出土陶圈足

1. T2⑤a：57　2. T2⑤a：37　3. T2⑤a：28　4. T2⑤a：29　5. T2⑤a：48　6. T2⑤a：39　7. T2⑤a：46　8. T2⑤a：40
9. T2⑤a：47　10. T2⑤a：56　11. T2⑤a：55　12. T2⑤a：50　13. T2⑤a：25　14. T2⑤a：31

第二类：4 件。呈喇叭状，足尖外撇。

标本 T2⑤a：39，夹砂红陶。器内可见轮制的痕迹。底径 15、残高 5.9 厘米（图六三：6）。标本 T2⑤a：40，夹砂红褐陶。底径 40.8、残高 6.8 厘米（图六三：8）。标本 T2⑤a：50，夹砂红褐陶。底径 28.8、残高 5.2 厘米（图六三：12）。标本 T2⑤a：31，夹细砂褐陶。底径 22.6、残高 2.6 厘米（图六三：14）。

第三类：2 件。呈喇叭状，足尖上翘。

标本 T2⑤a：46，夹砂红褐陶。足部刻划有短线纹。底径 19、残高 4.1 厘米（图六三：7）。标本 T2⑤a：47，夹砂红陶。底径 18.5、残高 4 厘米（图六三：9）。

第四类：2 件。桶状。

标本 T2⑤a：37，夹砂红陶。足尖内收。器身遍饰绳纹。底径 16.5、残高 3.3 厘米（图六三：2）。标本 T2⑤a：25，夹细砂红褐陶。足尖外撇。足上饰斜向绳纹。底径 11.8、残高 4 厘米（图六三：13）。

器鋬　4 件。依据形制的不同可分为两个类型。

第一类：3 件。体呈舌状。

标本 T2⑤a：24，夹砂红褐陶。器表两侧饰横向绳纹。残长 6.2、宽 5、厚 2 厘米（图六四：1）。标本 T2⑤a：22，夹砂红陶。器表两侧饰横向绳纹。残长 4.5、宽 5.1、厚 2 厘米（图六四：5）。标本 T2⑤a：21，夹砂褐陶。器表两侧饰横向绳纹。长 3.6、宽 3.4、厚 1.6 厘

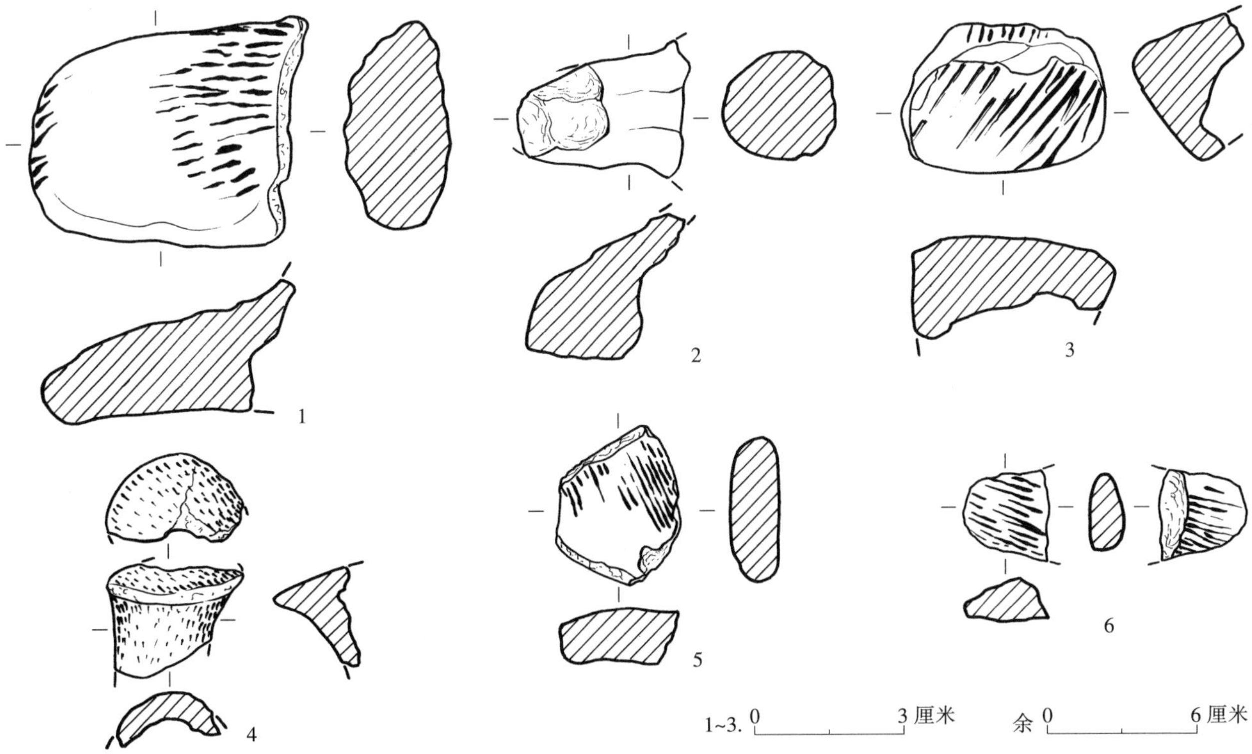

图六四　T2⑤a 层出土陶器

1、2、5、6. 器鋬（T2⑤a：24、23、22、21）　3、4. 支座（T2⑤a：38、26）

米（图六四：6）。

第二类：1件。体呈柱状。

标本 T2⑤a：23，残，夹砂红褐陶。体呈柱状，素面无纹。残长 2.6、宽 3.3、厚 2.3 厘米（图六四：2）。

支座　2件。形制相似，均体呈柱状，椭圆形底。

标本 T2⑤a：38，夹砂红褐陶。椭圆形底，器表和器底均饰绳纹。残高 2.9、宽 4 厘米（图六四：3）。标本 T2⑤a：26，夹砂红褐陶。器表和器底均饰绳纹。残高 4.5、宽 5.4 厘米（图六四：4）。

（二）T2⑤b 层出土器物

探方 T2 第⑤b 层出土器物主要是陶器，共出土陶片 950 片，石器仅 1 件。从陶质来看，夹细砂陶比例约为 87%，粗砂陶约为 3.2%，泥质磨光陶比例约为 9.8%。从陶色上看，红陶、红褐陶、褐陶比例约为 60%，说明其陶色偏于红色。从纹饰上看，纹饰发达，约占陶片总数的 36%，部分施陶衣。纹饰种类丰富，其中绳纹居多，约占纹饰种类总数的 44%，其他纹饰有刻划纹、戳印纹、凹弦纹、凸棱纹、压印纹、梳刷纹、附加堆纹、篦点纹等，流行将多种纹饰施于单个陶器上，纹饰图案主要有云纹、S 形纹、几何形纹、圆圈纹、水波纹等（图六〇：10～14，图六五；彩版六八）。器类主要是圜底器和圈足器，器形包括支座、纺轮、器耳、喇叭口罐、侈口罐、直口罐、钵等（彩版六九、七〇）。

T2 第⑤b 层共挑选标本 37 件，包括石器 1 件、陶器 36 件。

石器

1 件。为刮削器。

刮削器　1 件。

标本 T2⑤b：1，体呈尖锥状，器表可见剥片时留下的打击点和放射线。长 4.2、宽 2.4、厚 0.1～0.9 厘米（图六六：1）。

陶器

共挑选陶器标本 36 件，其中纹饰标本 17 件、器形标本 19 件。器形标本计支座 2 件、纺轮 1 件、器鋬 1 件、圈足 7 件、厚唇罐 2 件、侈口罐 2 件、喇叭口罐 4 件。

支座　2 件。形制相似。均体呈柱状，圆形底。

标本 T2⑤b：3，夹砂红陶。底部饰斜向绳纹。残高 4.3、底径 7.8 厘米（图六六：2）。标本 T2⑤b：4，夹砂红陶。素面。残高 4.1、底径 4.8 厘米（图六六：3）。

纺轮　1 件。

标本 T2⑤b：2，夹砂灰褐陶。饼状，器表饰四道凹弦纹和戳刺的坑点纹。直径 5.6、孔径 1.3、厚 0.6 厘米（图六六：5）。

器鋬　1 件。

标本 T2⑤b：7，夹细砂红褐陶。弧形，器表刻划出三道凸棱。残长 2.7、宽 1.2 厘米（图六六：6）。

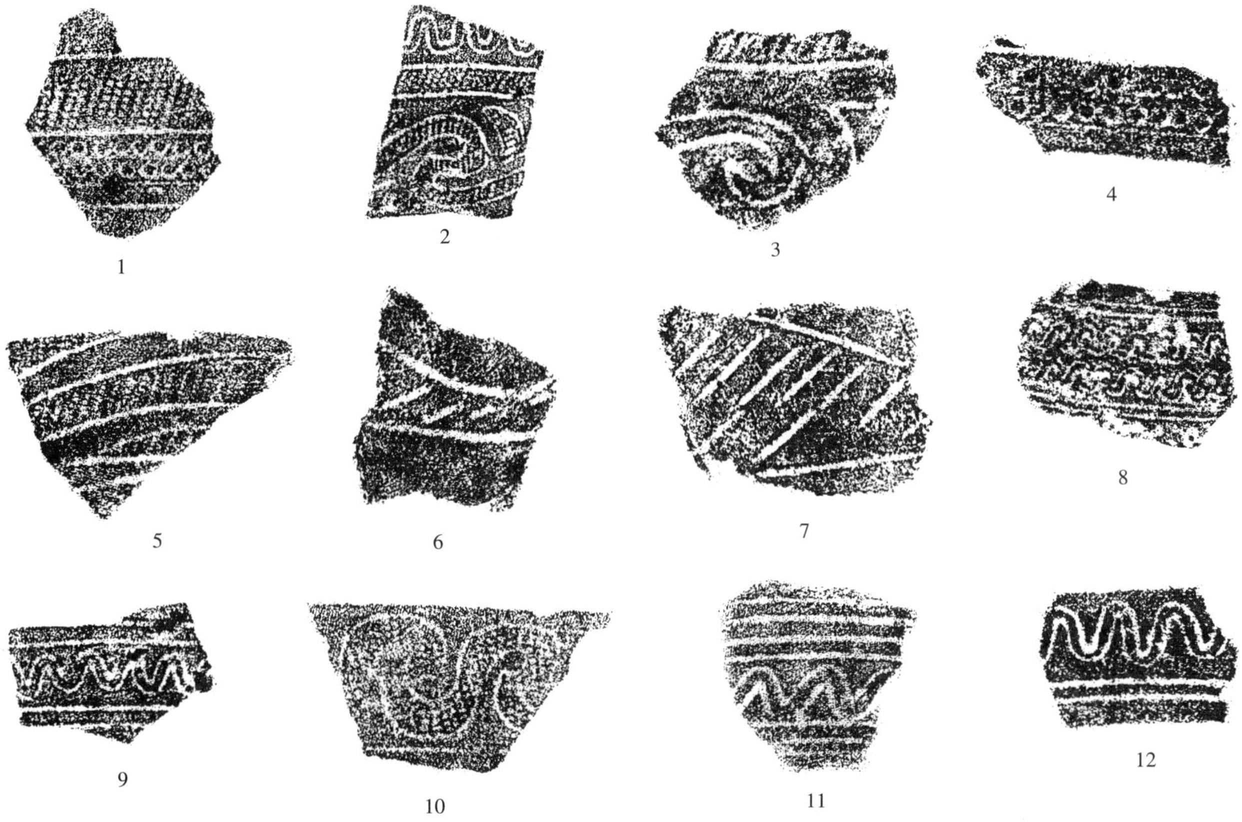

图六五　T2⑤b 层出土陶器拓片

1. 凹弦纹 + 篦点纹（T2⑤b：26）　2. 水波纹 + 凹弦纹 + 篦点纹 + 刻划纹（T2⑤b：27）　3. 刻划纹 + 凹弦纹（T2⑤b：28）　4. 凹弦纹 + 圆圈纹（T2⑤b：29）　5. 篦点纹 + 刻划纹（T2⑤b：30）　6. 刻划纹（T2⑤b：31）　7. 刻划纹（T2⑤b：32）　8. 凹弦纹 + S 形纹（T2⑤b：33）　9. 凹弦纹 + 水波纹（T2⑤b：34）　10. 刻划纹 + 篦点纹（T2⑤b：35）　11. 凹弦纹 + 水波纹（T2⑤b：36）　12. 水波纹 + 凹弦纹（T2⑤b：37）

圈足　7 件。依据形制的不同可分为三个类型。

第一类：2 件。喇叭状圈足，足尖上翘。

标本 T2⑤b：12，夹细砂红陶。底径 22.9、残高 4.2 厘米（图六六：7）。标本 T2⑤b：11，夹砂红褐陶。底径 24.7、残高 4.6 厘米（图六六：9）。

第二类：4 件。喇叭状圈足，足尖内折。

标本 T2⑤b：14，夹砂灰黑陶。圈足内折呈直角。足下端饰两道弦纹，弦纹之间饰绳纹，足中部饰刻划的 S 形纹，S 纹中饰篦点纹。底径 15.1、残高 1.6 厘米（图六六：4）。标本 T2⑤b：9，夹细砂红陶。足尖微外撇。足上饰四道凹弦纹。底径 22.8、残高 2.5 厘米（图六六：8）。标本 T2⑤b：8，夹细砂红陶。足尖微外撇。足上饰四道凹弦纹。底径 31.3、残高 4 厘米（图六六：11）。标本 T2⑤b：13，夹砂红褐陶。足尖内折呈直角。足上饰两道凹弦纹。底径 34.7、残高 2.8 厘米（图六六：12）。

第三类：1 件。桶状。

标本 T2⑤b：10，夹细砂红陶。足尖外撇。底径 18.8、残高 5.4 厘米（图六六：10）。

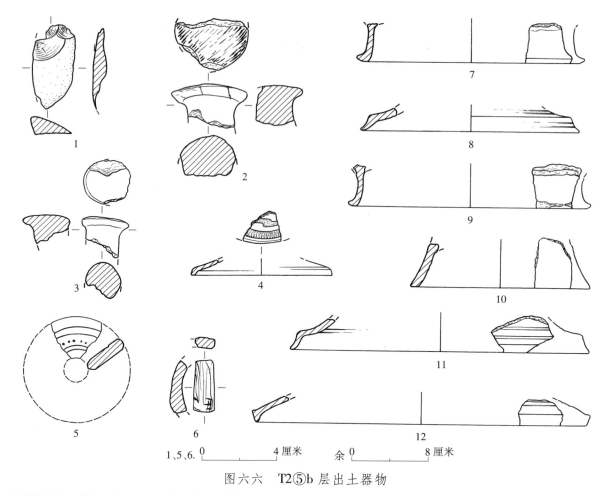

图六六　T2⑤b 层出土器物

1. 石刮削器（T2⑤b：1）　2.3. 陶支座（T2⑤b：3、4）　4、7～12. 陶圈足（T2⑤b：14、12、9、11、10、8、13）

5. 陶纺轮（T2⑤b：2）　6. 陶器鋬（T2⑤b：7）

　　厚唇罐　2 件。形制相似，均为厚方唇，直口微侈。

　　标本 T2⑤b：17，夹细砂灰褐陶。尖圆唇，窄平沿。沿上饰绳纹，腹部饰刻划的弧形纹，弧形纹中饰篦点纹。口径 44.2、残高 6 厘米（图六七：1）。标本 T2⑤b：15，夹砂红褐陶。唇上饰交错绳纹，颈上部饰刻划的水波纹。口径 48、残高 3.4 厘米（图六七：3）。

　　侈口罐　2 件。依据颈部的不同可分为两个类型。

　　第一类：1 件。颈部有凸棱。

　　标本 T2⑤b：20，夹细砂红褐陶。圆唇，颈略束。颈上部饰一道凸棱，下部饰刻划的短线纹。口径 14.5、残高 2.9 厘米（图六七：4）。

　　第二类：1 件。颈部无凸棱。

　　标本 T2⑤b：18，夹砂红褐陶。圆唇。口径 22.8、残高 4.7 厘米（图六七：2）。

　　喇叭口罐　4 件。依据唇部的不同可分为两个类型。

　　第一类：2 件。方唇，斜直腹。标本 T2⑤b：16，夹细砂红陶。口径 30.6、残高 3.9 厘米（图六七：5）。标本 T2⑤b：6，夹砂褐陶。腹上部刻划一半圆形，器内刻划短线纹。口径 37、

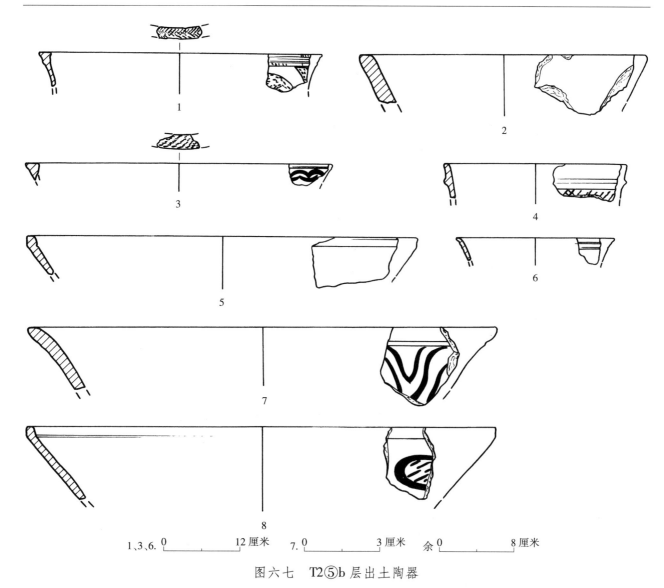

图六七　T2⑤b 层出土陶器

1.3. 厚唇罐（T2⑤b：17、15）　2、4. 侈口罐（T2⑤b：18、20）　5～8. 喇叭口罐（T2⑤b：16、19、5、6）

残高 5.7 厘米（图六七：8）。

第二类：2 件。圆唇，束颈。

标本 T2⑤b：19，夹砂褐陶。颈上部饰两道凹弦纹。口径 25.2、残高 4.2 厘米（图六七：6）。标本 T2⑤b：5，夹砂红褐陶。颈部饰刻划的水波纹。口径 18.4、残高 3.1 厘米（图六七：7）。

第三节　T3

T3 位于发掘区的西南角，2006 年 12 月 3 日布方发掘，于 2007 年 1 月 8 日清理完毕，雷雨负责进行发掘、记录并绘图。

一 地层堆积

依据土质土色和包含物的不同，本区域的地层经统一后可分为 5 层，本探方缺第②层（图六八；彩版七一：1）。

第①层：黄灰色耕土层，土质疏松，包含有少量的瓷片、塑料、植物根茎等。厚 10 ~ 15 厘米。近现代灰坑 H23 开口于本层下。

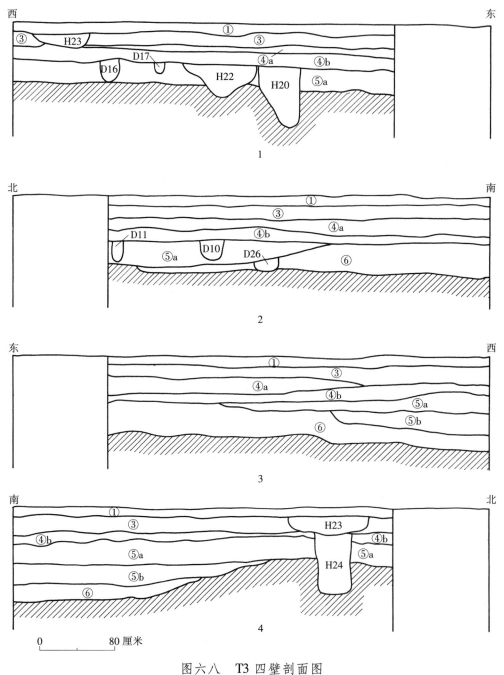

图六八 T3 四壁剖面图

1. 北壁　2. 东壁　3. 南壁　4. 西壁

第③层：浅灰色土，土质细密。包含有少量的砖块、瓷片等物。厚 10～16、深 10～15 厘米。近现代灰坑 H24 开口于本层下。

第④层：依据土质土色的不同，本层可分为两个亚层。

第④a 层：厚 0～20、深 20～30 厘米。深褐色铁锰层，土质疏松，由西向东呈坡状堆积，含有大量的铁锈，包含有极少量的瓷片、砖块等物。

第④b 层：灰褐色铁锰层，土质疏松，含有少量的铁锈，包含有极少量的瓷片、砖块等物。厚 2～18、深 28～44 厘米。H20、H22 开口于本层下。

第⑤层：依据土质土色的不同，本层可分为两个亚层。

第⑤a 层：黑灰色土，由东南向西北呈坡状堆积，土质疏松，含有较多的红烧土颗粒和炭屑，包括大量的陶器和少量的石器。厚 0～25、深 30～50 厘米。本层之下叠压有 H21 和 29 个柱洞。

第⑤b 层：灰黄色土，土质较硬，仅分布在探方的西南角，含有少量的红烧土颗粒和炭屑，包含物较少，主要是陶器和石器。厚 0～22、深 28～44 厘米。本层之下叠压有 21 个柱洞。

第⑥层：黄褐色土，夹杂有少量的灰土斑点，土质较硬，含有少量的炭屑，包含物极少，主要是陶器。厚 0～34、深 52～74 厘米。

此层之下为红褐色铁锰生土层。

二　遗迹

本探方共清理各类遗迹 45 座，包括灰坑 5 座、柱洞 40 个（图六九；彩版七一：2）。除 H23 和 H24 为近现代灰坑，H20、H21 和 H22 均为冯原文化时期，现将冯原文化时期的 3 座灰坑介绍如下。

（一）灰坑

3 座。主要为圆形和不规则圆形。

H20

处于 T3 的东北部，部分叠压于该探方的北隔梁下，开口于第④b 层下。

形制　平面呈不规则椭圆形，坑壁粗糙，坑底高低不平。长 1.2、宽 0.2～0.9、深 1.48～1.8 米（图七〇）。坑内堆积为灰黑色土，土质疏松，包含有少量的陶片。

出土器物　H20 出土的器物主要是陶器，共出土 49 件陶片。陶片以夹细砂陶为主，夹粗砂较少，陶色以红色和红褐色为主，黑褐次之，黄褐和褐色较少。纹饰以绳纹为主，还有少量的刻划纹、篦点纹、戳刺纹、弦纹等。器形主要是钵和罐[1]。

H21

处于 T3 的东北部，开口于第⑤a 层下，被 D1 和 D25 打破。

---

[1]　从出土器物登记表上看，H20 出土 1 件侈口罐口沿标本，但该标本原始图缺失。

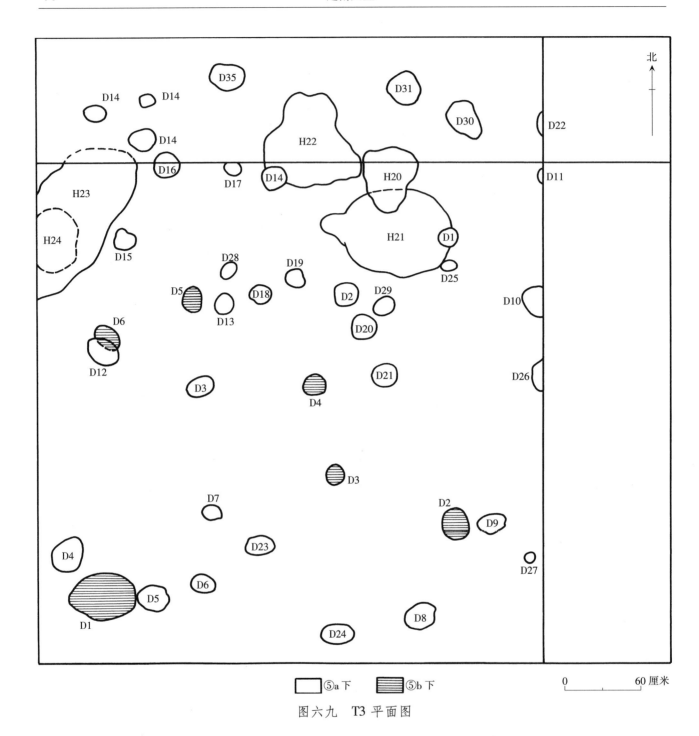

图六九　T3 平面图

形制　平面呈圆形，坑壁较光滑，坑底较平。直径 1.6、深 0.64 米（图七一）。坑内堆积为灰黑色土，土质疏松，包含有极少的陶片。

出土器物　仅出土少量的夹细砂红褐陶片。

H22

处于 T3 的北部，部分叠压于该探方的北隔梁下，开口于第④b 层下，被 D14 打破。

形制　平面呈不规则形，坑壁粗糙，坑底高低不平。长 0.7、宽 0.5～0.76、深 0.2～

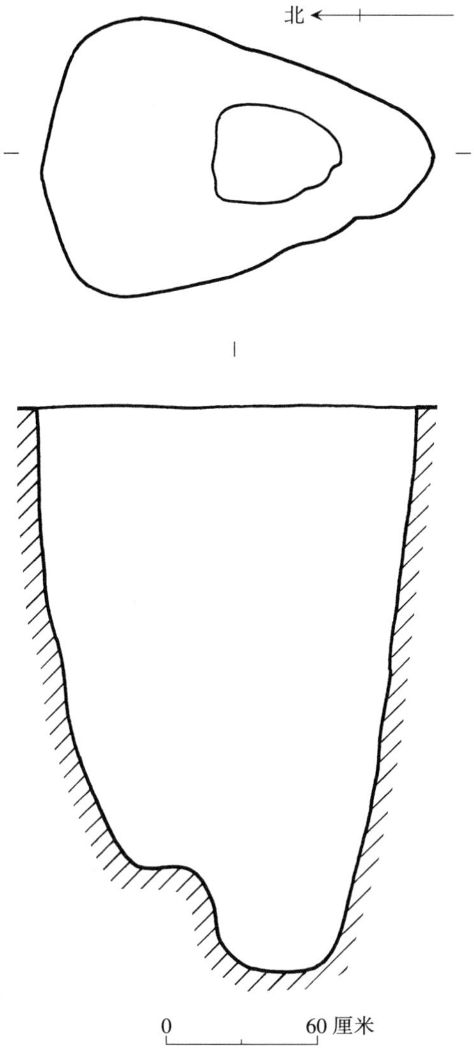

图七〇　H20平、剖面图

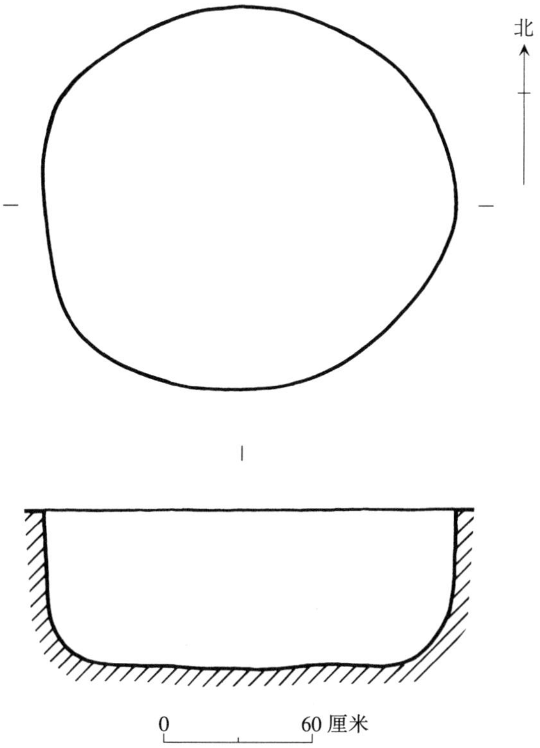

图七一　H21平、剖面图

0.44米（图七二）。坑内堆积为灰黑色土，土质疏松，包含有少量的陶片。

出土器物　H22出土的器物主要是陶器，共出土陶片225片。陶质以夹细砂红陶和红褐陶为主，还有少量的夹细砂黑褐陶、褐陶、泥质红褐陶等。纹饰以绳纹为主，戳印纹、圆圈纹、凹弦纹、凸棱纹、S形纹较少（图七三）。器形主要为钵、罐、支座、圈足器[1]。

（二）柱洞

本探方第⑤a和第⑤b层下发现各类柱洞40个，其中第⑤a层下发现34个，第⑤b层下发现6个（图七四）。分布无规律可循，但异常集中，说明其上部可能建有干栏式房屋，因后续的重修复建等原因，造成柱洞集中但无规律。为全面了解该探方的柱洞情况，现将本探方的柱洞列表如下。

〔1〕从出土器物登记表中看，H22共挑选标本13件，其中器形标本8件、纹饰标本5件。但器形标本原始图缺失。

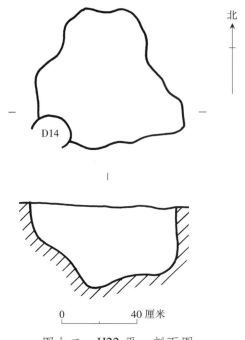

图七二　H22 平、剖面图

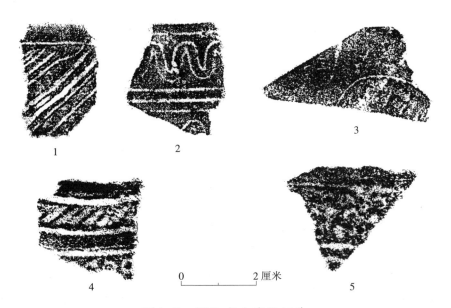

图七三　H22 出土陶器拓片

1. 凹弦纹 + 绳纹（H22∶9）　　2. 凹弦纹 + 水波纹（H22∶10）　　3. 刻划纹（H22∶11）

4. 凹弦纹 + 戳刺纹 + 圆圈纹（H22∶12）　　5. 凹弦纹 + 圆圈纹（H22∶13）

表三　T3 各层下坑和柱洞统计表　　　　　　　　　　　　　　　　（单位：厘米）

序号	编号	层位	形制与结构			尺寸 （直径 – 深）	填土	图号
			平面形制	坑壁	坑底			
1	D1	⑤a 下	圆形	平整	锅底状	18 – 38	灰黑土	图七四∶1
2	D2	⑤a 下	圆形	平整	锅底状	20 – 41	灰黑土	图七四∶2

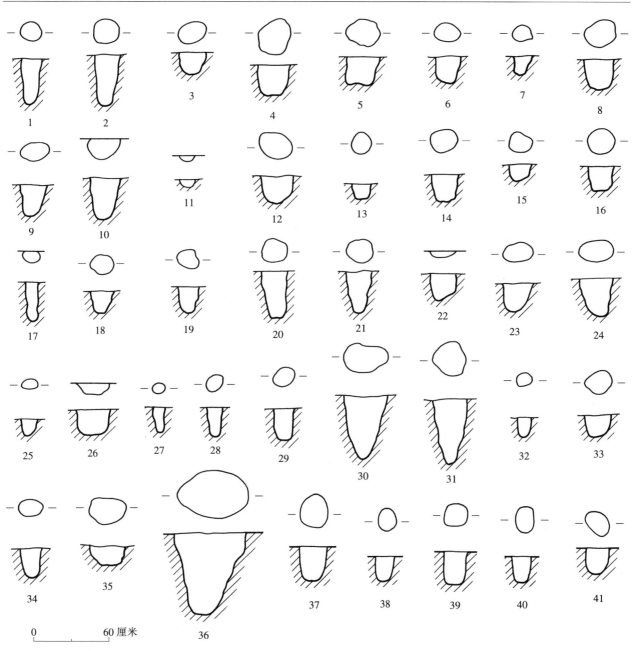

图七四　T3 内柱洞

1～34. T3⑤a 层下柱洞（D1～D34）　　35～40. T3⑤b 层下柱洞（D1～D6）

（续表三）

序号	编号	层位	形制与结构			尺寸（直径－深）	填土	图号
			平面形制	坑壁	坑底			
3	D3	⑤a 下	椭圆形	粗糙不平	平底	15～23－17	灰黑土	图七四: 3
4	D4	⑤a 下	椭圆形	粗糙不平	高低不平	20～31－25	黑土	图七四: 4
5	D5	⑤a 下	椭圆形	粗糙不平	平底	20×28－23	灰黑土	图七四: 5
6	D6	⑤a 下	近圆形	平整	锅底状	14～22－22	灰黑土	图七四: 6

（续表三）

序号	编号	层位	形制与结构			尺寸 （直径－深）	填土	图号
			平面形制	坑壁	坑底			
7	D7	⑤a 下	圆形	粗糙不平	高低不平	15－15	黑土	图七四：7
8	D8	⑤a 下	椭圆形	粗糙不平	高低不平	20～26－24	灰黑土	图七四：8
9	D9	⑤a 下	椭圆形	粗糙不平	锅底状	14～26－26	灰黑土	图七四：9
10	D10	⑤a 下	椭圆形	平整	锅底状	18～29－34	灰黑土	图七四：10
11	D11	⑤a 下	圆形	平整	锅底状	12－6	灰黑土	图七四：11
12	D12	⑤a 下	椭圆形	粗糙不平	锅底状	20～29－20	灰黑土	图七四：12
13	D13	⑤a 下	圆形	粗糙不平	高低不平	17－14	灰黑土	图七四：13
14	D14	⑤a 下	椭圆形	粗糙不平	高低不平	17～23－23	黑土	图七四：14
15	D15	⑤a 下	圆形	平整	锅底状	16－14	灰黑土	图七四：15
16	D16	⑤a 下	圆形	平整	平底	26－20	灰黑土	图七四：16
17	D17	⑤a 下	圆形	平整	平底	13－31	黑土	图七四：17
18	D18	⑤a 下	圆形	粗糙不平	高低不平	20－18	灰黑土	图七四：18
19	D19	⑤a 下	圆形	平整	锅底状	11～20－20	灰黑土	图七四：19
20	D20	⑤a 下	圆形	平整	平底	20－37	灰黑土	图七四：20
21	D21	⑤a 下	圆形	平整	平底	23－34	灰黑土	图七四：21
22	D22	⑤a 下	圆形	粗糙不平	高低不平	20－23	灰黑土	图七四：22
23	D23	⑤a 下	椭圆形	粗糙不平	高低不平	14～26－23	灰土	图七四：23
24	D24	⑤a 下	椭圆形	粗糙不平	高低不平	16～28－31	灰黑土	图七四：24
25	D25	⑤a 下	椭圆形	粗糙不平	高低不平	9～14－13	灰黑土	图七四：25
26	D26	⑤a 下	圆形	平整	锅底状	26－20	黑土	图七四：26
27	D27	⑤a 下	圆形	平整	锅底状	12－20	灰黑土	图七四：27
28	D28	⑤a 下	圆形	平整	平底	14－23	灰黑土	图七四：28
29	D29	⑤a 下	近圆形	平整	锅底状	14～20－26	灰黑土	图七四：29
30	D30	⑤b 下	椭圆形	平整	锅底状	20～37－52	灰黑土	图七四：30
31	D31	⑤a 下	椭圆形	平整	锅底状	20～29－52	灰黑土	图七四：31
32	D32	⑤a 下	圆形	较平整	锅底状	14－16	黑土	图七四：32
33	D33	⑤a 下	椭圆形	平整	锅底状	17～23－17	灰黑土	图七四：33
34	D34	⑤a 下	椭圆形	平整	锅底状	12～20－23	灰黑土	图七四：34
35	D35	⑤a 下	椭圆形	平整	高低不平	20～31－14	灰黑土	图七四：35
36	D1	⑤b 下	椭圆形	粗糙不平	高低不平	40～57－66	灰土	图七四：36
37	D2	⑤b 下	椭圆形	平整	锅底状	22～26－26	灰黑土	图七四：37
38	D3	⑤b 下	椭圆形	粗糙不平	锅底状	14～17－20	灰黑土	图七四：38
39	D4	⑤b 下	圆形	平整	锅底状	20－28	灰黑土	图七四：39
40	D5	⑤b 下	不规则椭圆形	较平整	锅底状	14～20－20	灰黑土	图七四：40
41	D6	⑤b 下	不规则椭圆形	较平整	锅底状	15～23－20	黑土	图七四：41

三　地层出土遗物

（一）T3⑤a 层出土遗物

出土器物主要是陶器，玉石器较少。共挑选标本 73 件，包括玉石器标本 8 件、陶器标本 65 件。

玉石器

8 件。计有石凿 1 件、石锛 4 件、石球 1 件、石核 1 件、玉璜 1 件。

石凿　1 件。

标本 T3⑤a：1，残，体呈长方形，通体磨制，双面弧刃。残长 3.6、残宽 1.3、厚 0.1～0.5 厘米（图七五：2）。

石球　1 件。

标本 T3⑤a：2，体呈椭圆球状，打磨光滑。长径 2.3、短径 1.8、厚 1.2 厘米（图七五：3；

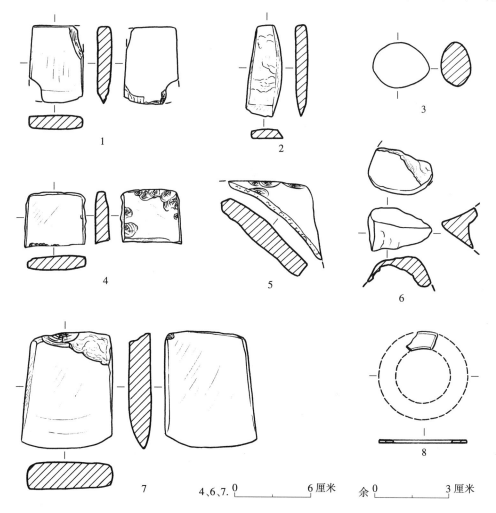

图七五　T3 出土器物

1、4、5、7. 石锛（T3⑤a：5、D1：8、T3⑤a：38、3）　2. 石凿（T3⑤a：1）　3. 石球（T3⑤a：2）

6. 石核（T3⑤a：22）　8. 玉璜（T3⑤a：7）

彩版七二：1）。

石锛　4件。形制基本相似，均体呈长方形，通体磨制。

标本T3⑤a：5，上部及一侧残，体呈长方形，通体磨制，双面弧刃。残长3、宽2.1、厚0.5厘米（图七五：1；彩版七二：2）。标本T3⑤a：3，上部残，双面弧刃。顶部有打击后留下的打击点和放射线。残长4.5、宽3.5、厚0.9厘米（图七五：7；彩版七二：3）。标本D1：8，仅存上部，一面保持磨制后的光滑表面，另一面则可见较多的打击后留下的打击点和放射线。残长4.2、宽4.8、厚1.2厘米（图七五：4）。标本T3⑤a：38，可能系石斧残件，仅存顶部和少量侧面，顶部可见打击后留下的四处打击点和放射线。残长3.2、残宽1.9、厚0.8厘米（图七五：5）。

石核　1件。

标本T3⑤a：22，体呈三棱状，两面可见剥片后留下的疤痕。长5.2、宽0.4～3.4厘米（图七五：6）。

玉璜　1件。

标本T3⑤a：7，仅存一小部分，白色，体呈圆形，宽缘。残长2.5、宽1.3、厚0.2厘米（图七五：8）。

陶器

T3第⑤a层共出土陶片3275片。从陶质来看，夹细砂陶比例约为83.6%，粗砂陶约为12.6%，泥质磨光陶比例约为3.8%。从陶色上看，红陶、红褐陶、褐陶比例约为62.7%，说明其陶色偏于红色。从纹饰上看，纹饰发达，约占陶片总数的42.1%，部分施陶衣。纹饰种类丰富，其中绳纹居多，约占54%，其他纹饰有刻划纹、戳印纹、凹弦纹、凸棱纹、压印纹、梳刷纹、附加堆纹等，尤以在各种刻划纹带内填充篦齿状或篦点状戳印纹的装饰风格最具特点，集多种纹饰在单个陶器上的复合纹饰甚为流行，纹饰图案主要有云纹、S形纹、几何形纹、圆圈纹、水波纹等（图七六、七七：1、2、5、6；彩版七三～七五）。陶器口部多为敛口和侈口，喇叭形口和直口次之。器类主要是圜底器和圈足器，器形包括器柄、支座、喇叭口罐、厚唇罐、圈足、钵等（彩版七六、七七）。

T3第⑤a层共挑选陶器标本65件，其中纹饰标本29件、器形标本36件。器形标本计有器柄1件、支座3件、喇叭口罐3件、侈口罐5件、厚唇罐3件、敛口罐1件、圈足12件、钵8件等。

器柄　1件。

标本T3⑤a：4，夹细砂红褐陶。呈柱状，柄端捏制成一陶狗头，并戳出眼睛和鼻孔，柄另一端下部饰有两周凹弦纹。残长6.4、柄径2.9厘米（图七八：1；彩版七二：4）。

支座　3件。形制基本相似。

标本T3⑤a：6，残，夹砂红褐陶。上端呈椭圆形，实心，下端残。残长6.8厘米（图七八：2）。标本T3⑤a：20，残，夹砂红褐陶。上端呈椭圆形外侈，下端呈桶状。上端长径5.2、残短径3.5、残高5.9厘米（图七八：3）。标本T3⑤a：22，残，夹砂红褐陶。仅存上

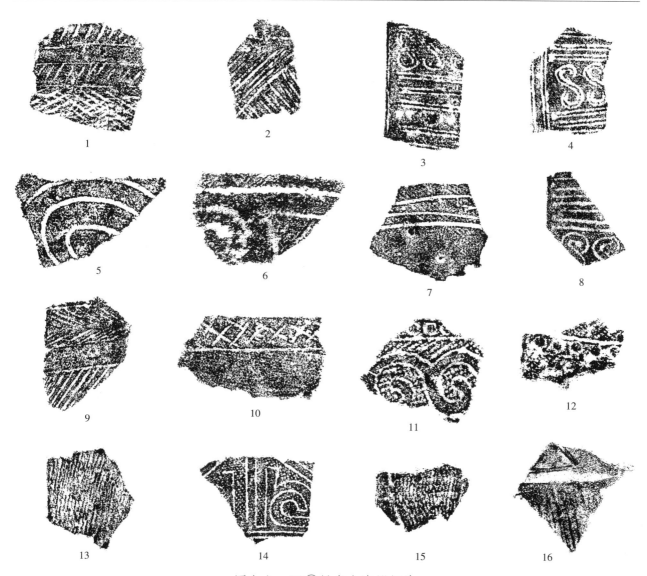

图七六　T3⑤层出土陶器拓片

1. 交错绳纹＋凹弦纹（T3⑤a：43）　　2. 交错绳纹（T3⑤a：44）　　3、4. S形纹＋刻划线纹（T3⑤a：51、52）　　5. 圆圈纹（T3⑤a：45）　　6. 凹弦纹＋圆圈纹（T3⑤a：46）　　7. 凹弦纹（T3⑤a：53）　　8. S形纹＋刻划短线纹（T3⑤a：54）　　9. 绳纹（T3⑤a：47）　　10. 戳刺纹（T3⑤a：48）　　11. 圆圈纹＋S形纹＋篦点纹（T3⑤a：55）　　12. 圆圈纹＋凹弦纹＋篦点纹（T3⑤a：56）　　13. 绳纹（T3⑤a：49）　　14. 几何形纹＋篦点纹（T3⑤a：50）　　15. 绳纹（T3⑤a：57）　　16. 凸棱纹＋绳纹（T3⑤a：62）

端，呈椭圆形。长径5.1、短径3.5、残高1.1厘米。

喇叭口罐　3件。依据颈部的不同可分为两个类型。

第一类：2件。颈部有一道凸棱。

标本T3⑤a：24，夹砂红褐陶。圆唇，束颈。口径22.2、残高2.9厘米（图七八：4）。标本T3⑤a：15，夹砂褐陶。圆唇，束颈。口径30.3、残高5.6厘米（图七八：5）。

第二类：1件。颈部无凸棱。

标本T3⑤a：10，泥质红褐陶。圆唇，束颈。颈上部饰一道凹弦纹，颈中部饰刻划线纹。

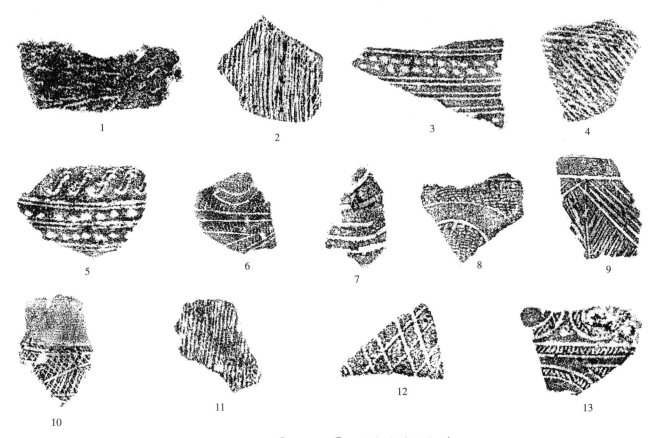

图七七　T3⑤a 和 T3⑤b 层出土陶器拓片

1. 戳刺纹（T3⑤a：63）　2. 梳刷纹（T3⑤a：65）　3. 点纹＋凹弦纹（T3⑤b：9）　4. 交错绳纹（T3⑤b：10）　5. S 形纹＋点纹＋凹弦纹（T3⑤a：66）　6. 几何形纹＋篦点纹（T3⑤a：68）　7. 刻划纹（T3⑤b：11）　8. 刻划纹＋篦点纹（T3⑤b：12）　9. 线纹＋刻划纹（T3⑤b：5）　10. 交错绳纹＋刻划纹（T3⑤b：6）　11. 绳纹（T3⑤b：8）　12. 刻划纹（T3⑤b：13）　13. 几何形纹＋戳刺纹（T3⑤b：7）

口径 19.2、残高 6.5 厘米（图七八：9）。

厚唇罐　3 件。形制基本相似，均为厚方唇，直口微侈。

标本 T3⑤a：61，夹砂灰褐陶。唇部饰斜向绳纹，口下部饰一道凸棱纹，凸棱纹上戳刺有坑点纹。口径 30、残高 4.3 厘米（图七八：6）。标本 T3⑤a：18，夹细砂红褐陶。唇部饰斜向绳纹，口下部饰一道凸棱，其下饰刻划的几何形纹。口径 34、残高 7.8 厘米（图七八：7）。标本 T3⑤a：19，夹细砂褐陶。口下部饰两道凹弦纹，颈部饰刻划的水波纹。口径 16.7、残高 4.7 厘米（图七八：8）。

侈口罐　5 件。依据唇部和颈部的不同可分为两个类型。

第一类：2 件。方唇，颈部饰一道凸棱。

标本 T3⑤a：17，夹细砂红褐陶。束颈。唇部饰交错绳纹，凸棱上戳刺有坑点纹，颈部饰刻划的线纹。口径 34、残高 7.4 厘米（图七九：1）。标本 T3⑤a：14，夹细砂红褐陶。颈略束。凸棱上戳刺有坑点纹，颈部饰刻划的线纹。口径 17.8、残高 4.9 厘米（图七九：3）。

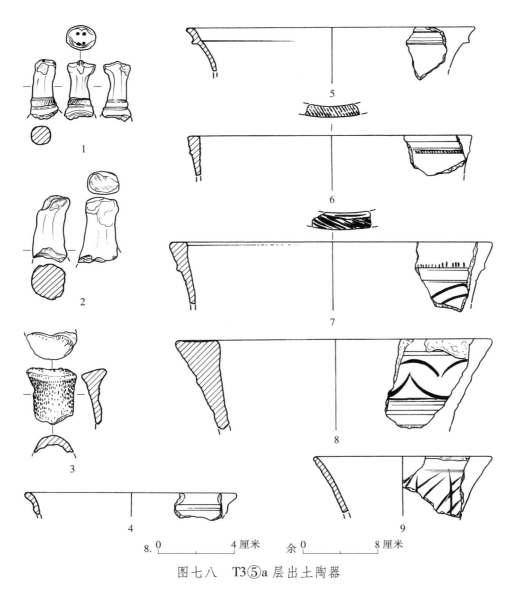

图七八 T3⑤a 层出土陶器

1. 器柄（T3⑤a：4） 2、3. 支座（T3⑤a：6、20） 4、5、9. 喇叭口罐（T3⑤a：24、15、10）

6～8. 厚唇罐（T3⑤a：61、18、18）

第二类：3 件。圆唇，颈部无凸棱。

标本 T3⑤a：13，夹细砂褐陶。口下部饰两道凹弦纹，其下饰刻划的叶脉纹。口径 25.6、残高 4.5 厘米（图七九：2）。标本 T3⑤a：9，泥质红陶。颈部饰刻划的弧线纹。口径 17.2、残高 7.3 厘米（图七九：4）。标本 T3⑤a：8，泥质红陶。颈部饰刻划的线纹。口径 16、残高 5.7 厘米（图七九：6）。

敛口罐 1 件。

标本 T3⑤a：57，夹细砂红褐陶。方唇，敛口，弧肩，鼓腹。口下部饰一道凹弦纹，腹部饰两道凹弦纹，其下饰纵向绳纹。口径 15.7、残高 5.2 厘米（图七九：5）。

圈足 12 件。依据形制的不同可分为三个类型。

第一类：6 件。呈喇叭形，足尖外撇。

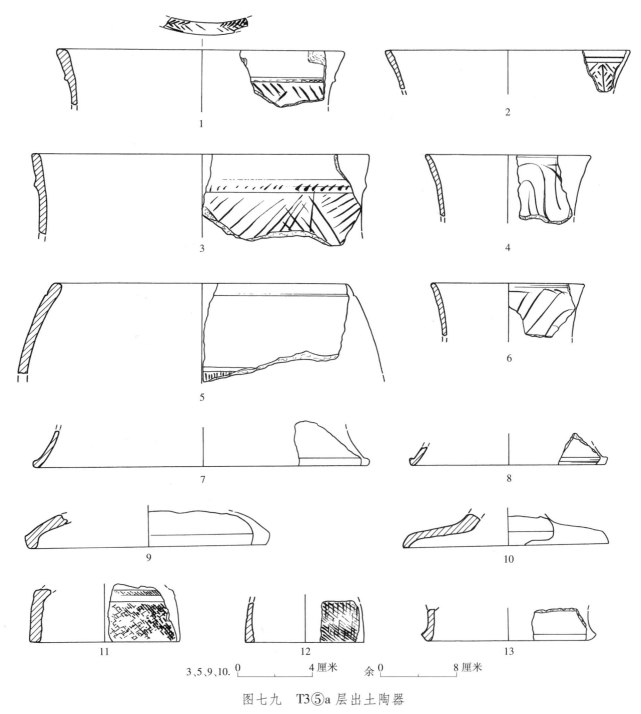

图七九 T3⑤a 层出土陶器

1~4、6. 侈口罐（T3⑤a：17、13、14、9、8） 5. 敛口罐（T3⑤a：57） 7~13. 圈足（T3⑤a：23、33、35、
34、21、60、32）

标本 T3⑤a：23，夹砂红褐陶。底径 35.6、残高 4.8 厘米（图七九：7）。标本 T3⑤a：33，
夹细砂褐陶。足尖上翘。底径 23、残高 3.3 厘米（图七九：8）。标本 T3⑤a：11，夹细砂红
陶。足部饰一道凸棱。底径 16.6、残高 4 厘米（图八○：1）。标本 T3⑤a：12，夹砂褐陶。足
部饰一道凸棱。底径 18.5、残高 4.3 厘米（图八○：9）。标本 T3⑤a：37，夹细砂红褐陶。底
径 27.6、残高 1.7 厘米（图八○：12）。标本 T3⑤a：36，夹砂红褐陶。仅存圈足中部，器身

饰戳刺的短线纹。残高 1.5 厘米（图八〇: 8）。

第二类：3 件。呈喇叭状，足尖内折。

标本 T3⑤a: 35，夹细砂灰褐陶。足尖内折呈直角。底径 12.6、残高 1.9 厘米（图七九: 9）。标本 T3⑤a: 34，夹砂褐陶。足尖内折。底径 10.8、残高 1.6 厘米（图七九: 10）。标本 T3⑤a: 58，夹细砂红陶。足尖内折呈直角。足部饰一道凹弦纹。底径 18.4、残高 2.7 厘米（图八〇: 11）。

第三类：3 件。呈桶状。

标本 T3⑤a: 21，夹砂红褐陶。足上部饰两道凹弦纹，器表饰经涂抹的绳纹。底径 16、残高 6.2 厘米（图七九: 11）。标本 T3⑤a: 60，夹砂褐陶。器身遍饰交错绳纹。底径 12.6、残高 4.4 厘米（图七九: 12）。标本 T3⑤a: 32，夹细砂褐陶。桶状圈足，足尖外撇。底径 18.2、

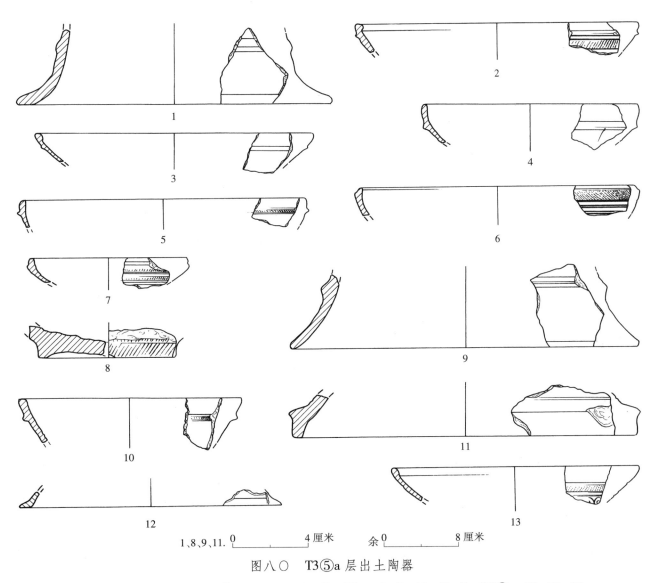

图八〇　T3⑤a 层出土陶器

1、8、9、11、12. 圈足（T3⑤a: 11、36、12、58、37）　2~7、10、13. 钵（T3⑤a: 25、27、28、26、29、31、16、30）

残高 3.4 厘米（图七九：13）。

钵　8 件。依据口部和肩部的不同可分为四个类型。

第一类：3 件。敛口，肩部饰一道凸棱。

标本 T3⑤a：26，夹细砂褐陶。方唇，弧腹。凸棱上饰刻划的短线纹。口径 30.2、残高 3 厘米（图八〇：5）。标本 T3⑤a：25，夹细砂红褐陶。圆唇，斜直腹。腹上部饰两道凹弦纹，凹弦纹之间饰篦点纹。口径 30、残高 3.5 厘米（图八〇：2）。标本 T3⑤a：28，夹砂红陶。圆唇，弧腹。腹部饰刻划的线纹。口径 23、残高 4.9 厘米（图八〇：4）。

第二类：2 件。敛口，肩部无凸棱。

标本 T3⑤a：29，夹细砂红陶。圆唇，弧腹。肩部饰篦点纹，腹部饰五道凹弦纹。口径 28.8、残高 3.2 厘米（图八〇：6）。标本 T3⑤a：31，夹砂红褐陶。弧腹。腹部饰凹弦纹和刻划的短线纹。口径 16.8、残高 3.2 厘米（图八〇：7）。

第三类：2 件。侈口，肩部饰一道凸棱。

标本 T3⑤a：27，夹砂褐陶。圆唇，斜直腹。口径 29.3、残高 4.2 厘米（图八〇：3）。标本 T3⑤a：16，泥质红陶。圆唇，斜直腹。凸棱上戳刺有坑点纹。口径 23.4、残高 5.6 厘米（图八〇：10）。

第四类：1 件。侈口，肩部无凸棱。

标本 T3⑤a：30，夹细砂红陶。圆唇，束颈。腹上部饰三道凹弦纹，上部两凹弦纹之间饰篦点纹，腹部饰刻划纹的云纹。口径 26.4、残高 4.1 厘米（图八〇：13）。

（二）T3⑤b 层出土遗物

本探方第⑤b 层共出土陶片 355 片。从陶质来看，夹细砂陶比例约为 87.9%，粗砂陶约为 5.4%，泥质磨光陶比例约为 6.7%。从陶色上看，红陶、红褐陶、褐陶比例约为 38%，说明其陶色偏于红色。从纹饰上看，纹饰较为发达，约占陶片总数的 36%。纹饰种类丰富，其中绳纹约占纹饰陶的 46%，其他纹饰有刻划纹、戳印纹、凹弦纹、凸棱纹、压印纹、梳刷纹、附加堆纹等。陶器器类主要是圜底器和圈足器，器形包括罐、钵、支座、圈足等。本层共挑选标本 13 件。陶器器形标本 4 件、纹饰标本 9 件（图七七：6～13；彩版七八、七九）[1]。

第四节　T4

T4 处于发掘区的西南角，2006 年 12 月 3 日布方发掘，于 2007 年 1 月 8 日清理完毕。孙伟刚负责进行发掘、记录并绘图。

一　地层堆积

依据土质土色和包含物的不同，本探方地层经统一后可分为 4 层，本探方缺第④、⑥层（图八一）。

---

〔1〕　本层器形标本原始图缺失。

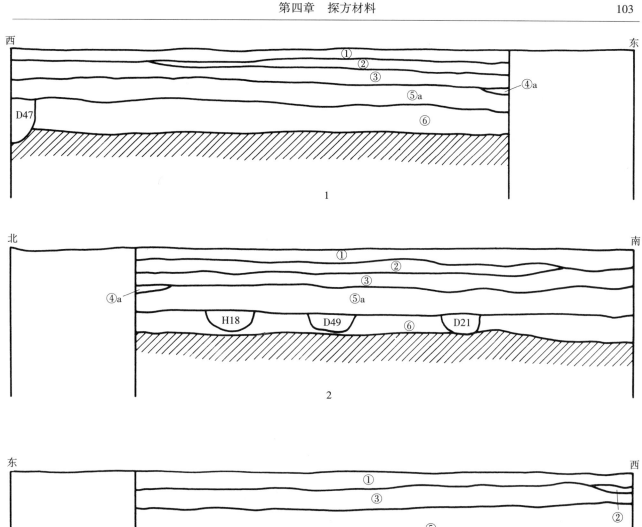

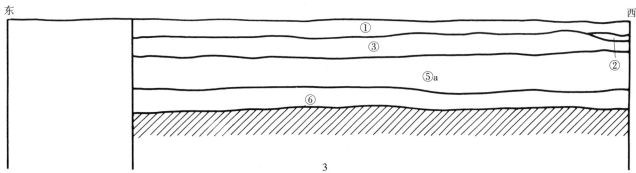

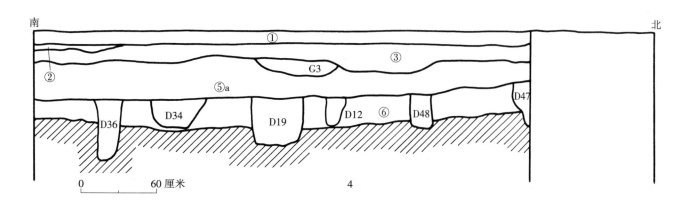

图八一 T4 四壁剖面图

1. 北壁 2. 东壁 3. 南壁 4. 西壁

第①层：耕土层。土质疏松，含砂量较大，土色黄灰。夹杂有一些红砖、瓦块、青瓷片等。厚 8~17 厘米。

第②层：扰土层。土质稍紧密，土色黄红。夹杂有大量的红色砖块、瓦片、青瓷片、青花瓷片等。深 8~17、厚 0~13 厘米。为近现代文化层。

第③层：扰土层。土质紧密，较为纯净，土色为浅灰色。夹杂有少量红色夹砂砖块、陶片、青瓷片等。H15、H26、H27、H28、H29、H30 开口于本层下。深 10~20、厚 8~22 厘米。为近现代文化层。

第⑤层：冯原文化层。可分为第⑤a、第⑤b 两小层。为冯原文化层。

第⑤a 层：土质松软，含有较多烧土点，土色黑灰。本层出土有大量夹砂红陶片及石楔、石锛、残玉环等遗物，可能为冯原文化时期的遗存。深 20~30、厚 14~30 厘米。M1 和 49 个柱洞开口于本层下。

第⑤b 层：土质较硬，土色为灰黄色。夹杂有极少量的夹砂红陶片。深 40~56、厚 12~20 厘米。H31 开口于本层下。

此层之下为红褐色铁锰生土层。

二 遗迹

T4 内共发现各类遗迹 58 座（图八二；彩版八〇），计有灰坑 7 座、沟 1 条、墓葬 1 座、柱洞 49 个。除 6 座灰坑（H15、H26、H27、H28、H29、H30）和沟（G3）为近现代灰坑外，H31、M1 和 49 个柱洞均为冯原文化时期的遗迹。现将本探方冯原文化时期的遗迹介绍如下。

（一）灰坑

1 座。

H31

处于 T4 的南部，开口于第⑤b 层下，被 G3 打破。

形制　平面为不规则长方形，上口很不规整，各侧壁面不甚平直。长 1.4、宽 0.56~0.7、深 0.42 米（图八三）。坑内填土为红褐色黏土，土质结构紧密。

出土器物　H31 仅出土一小片夹砂红陶片。

（二）墓葬

1 座。

M1

开口于第⑤a 层下，被 D1 和 D4 打破。为长方形竖穴土坑墓，方向为 99°，长 2.24、东侧宽 0.76 米，西侧因为坑壁坍塌，现宽 1.04、深 0.42 米（图八四；彩版八一）。墓内填土为灰黄色黏土，土质较硬。未发现葬具，亦未发现葬具朽痕。墓中人骨架保存较差，葬式为仰身直肢葬，头向东，面向上，双手平放于身体左右两侧，性别、年龄不详。随葬品仅 1 件陶豆，放置于墓主人的头端（彩版八二：1）。

为确保墓葬的完整性，并有利于今后的展示，越南国家历史博物馆派专业文物保护人员

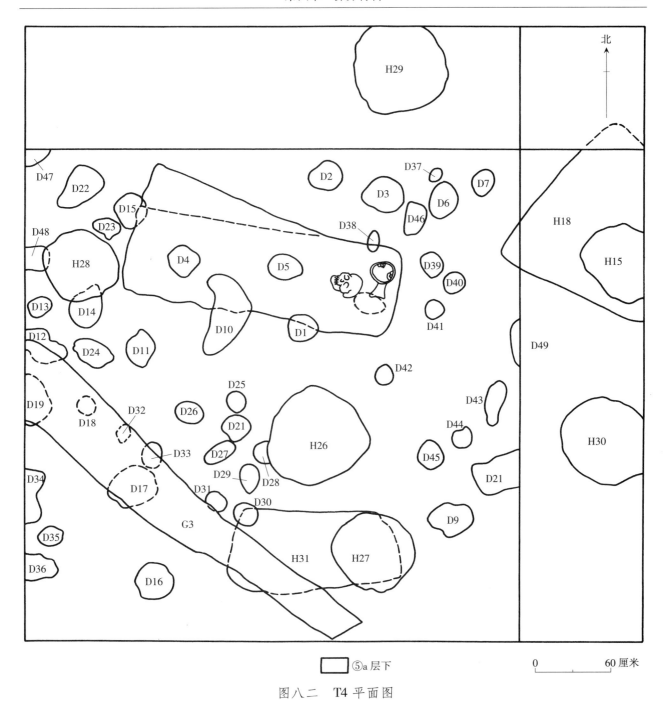

图八二 T4 平面图

对出土的人骨进行了加固（彩版八二：2），并打包运回越南永福省博物馆。同时，在墓葬刚被清理出来和被打包运走之前，越南国家历史博物馆的人员购买了香、蜡、水果、饼干、鲜花等物品，请当地的法师对墓主人进行了祭祀，这也是对古人的一种尊重（彩版八三）。

随葬器物 1件。陶豆。

陶豆 标本 M1：1，夹砂灰褐陶。圆唇，侈口，盘较深，中柄，喇叭状圈足，圈足内收。盘中部饰两周凹弦纹，凹弦纹中饰篦点纹，盘下部饰刻划的花卉纹，盘下端再饰两周凹弦纹，凹弦纹中饰刻划的短线纹。柄中部以戳刺的短线纹为四边，中饰刻划的S纹，S形纹中饰戳刺

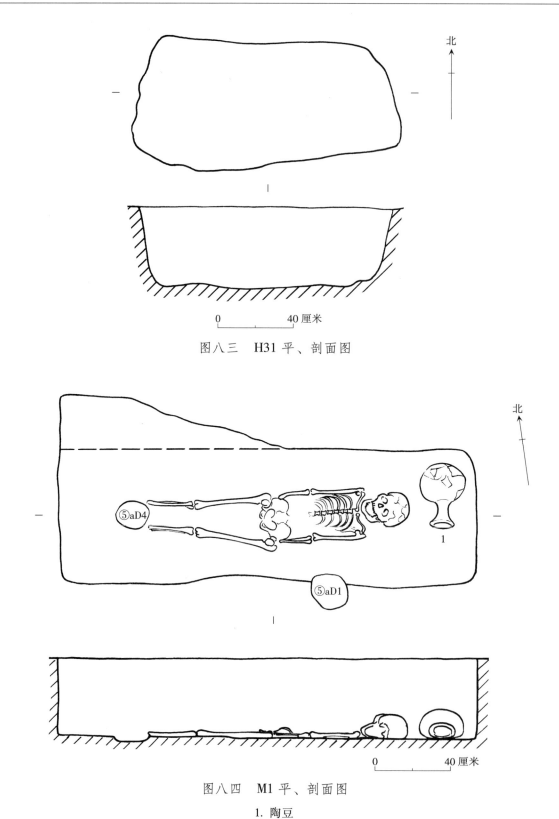

图八三　H31 平、剖面图

图八四　M1 平、剖面图

1. 陶豆

的短线纹。喇叭状圈足上饰连续的云纹，云纹中饰戳刺的短线纹。口径 21.2、底径 11.7、高 17.3 厘米（图八五、八六；彩版八四）。

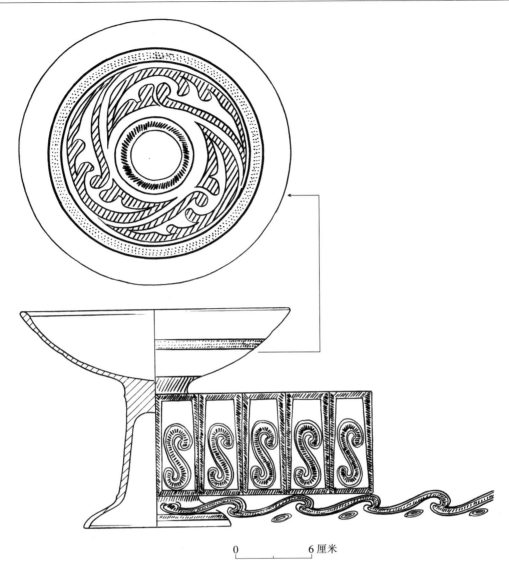

0   6厘米

图八五　M1 出土陶豆（M1∶1）

（三）柱洞

本探方共清理柱洞49个（图八七、八八），均开口于第⑤a层下，平面呈圆形或椭圆形，坑壁较平整光滑，坑底呈锅底状或平底，填土基本上为灰黑土，与周边土质明显区别，土质疏松。现将该探方柱洞情况列表如下。

表四　T4 各层下坑或柱洞统计表 （单位：厘米）

序号	编号	层位	形制与结构			尺寸（直径－深）	填土	图号
			平面形制	坑壁	坑底			
1	D1	⑤a下	近圆形	平整	平底	26－38	灰黑土	图八七：1
2	D2	⑤a下	圆形	平整	平底	26－33	灰黑土	图八七：2
3	D3	⑤a下	圆形	平整	平底	33－26	灰黑土	图八七：3

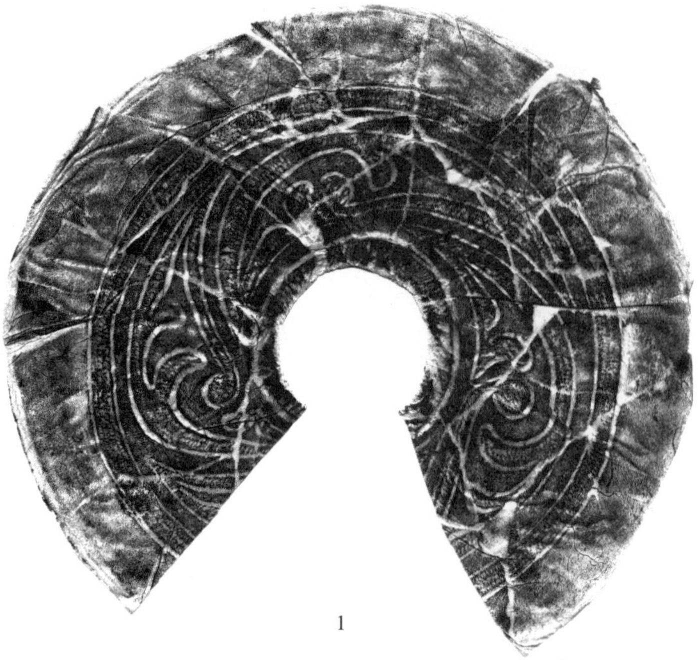

1

2

0 6厘米

图八六 M1出土陶豆（M1：1）拓片

1. 豆盘下部 2. 豆圈足上

（续表四）

序号	编号	层位	形制与结构			尺寸（直径－深）	填土	图号
			平面形制	坑壁	坑底			
4	D4	⑤a下	圆形	平整	平底	26－42	黑土	图八七：4
5	D5	⑤a下	椭圆形	平整	平底	5～28－23	灰黑土	图八七：5
6	D6	⑤a下	椭圆形	粗糙不平	圜底	17～33－15	黑土	图八七：6
7	D7	⑤a下	圆形	粗糙不平	圜底	16－10	灰黑土	图八七：7
8	D8	⑤a下	椭圆形	较平整	锅底状	12～25－10	灰黑土	图八七：8
9	D9	⑤a下	不规则椭圆形	粗糙不平	高低不平	17～38－19	黑土	图八七：9
10	D10	⑤a下	不规则椭圆形	粗糙不平	高低不平	12～63－21	灰黑土	图八七：10

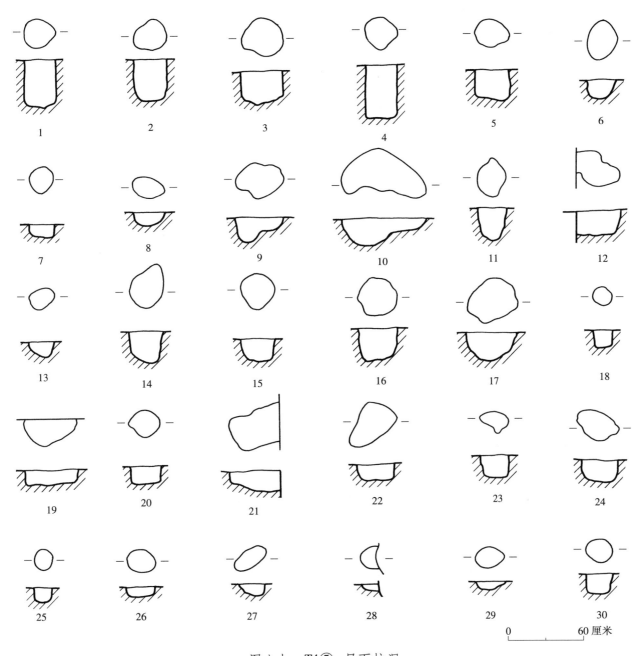

图八七 T4⑤a 层下柱洞

1~30. D1~D30

（续表四）

序号	编号	层位	形制与结构			尺寸（直径-深）	填土	图号
			平面形制	坑壁	坑底			
11	D11	⑤a 下	椭圆形	较平整	较平	7~31-26	黑土	图八七: 11
12	D12	⑤a 下	椭圆形	平整	平底	12~35-19	灰黑土	图八七: 12
13	D13	⑤a 下	椭圆形	平整	平底	10~21-12	灰黑土	图八七: 13

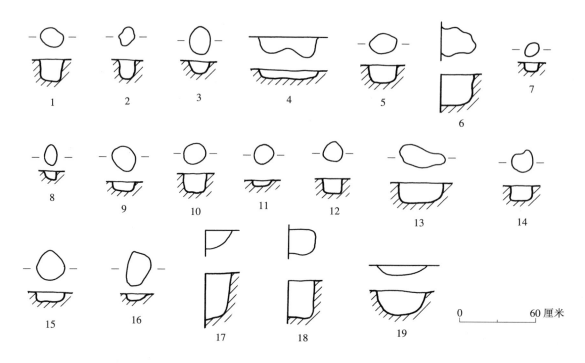

图八八　T4⑤a 层下柱洞

1～19. D31～D49

（续表四）

序号	编号	层位	形制与结构			尺寸 （直径 - 深）	填土	图号
			平面形制	坑壁	坑底			
14	D14	⑤a 下	椭圆形	平整	锅底状	11～35－25	灰黑土	图八七：14
15	D15	⑤a 下	圆形	平整	锅底状	26－18	黑土	图八七：15
16	D16	⑤a 下	圆形	较平整	锅底状	30－25	灰黑土	图八七：16
17	D17	⑤a 下	圆形	粗糙不平	高低不平	40－22	黑土	图八七：17
18	D18	⑤a 下	圆形	平整	平底	16－13	灰黑土	图八七：18
19	D19	⑤a 下	椭圆形	平整	平底	15～41－12	灰黑土	图八七：19
20	D20	⑤a 下	圆形	平整	平底	24－14	黑土	图八七：20
21	D21	⑤a 下	不规则椭圆形	粗糙不平	高低不平	19～40－16	灰黑土	图八七：21
22	D22	⑤a 下	不规则椭圆形	粗糙不平	高低不平	10～40－12	黑土	图八七：22
23	D23	⑤a 下	不规则椭圆形	粗糙不平	高低不平	5～23－18	灰黑土	图八七：23
24	D24	⑤a 下	椭圆形	较平整	较平	11～35－17	灰黑土	图八七：24
25	D25	⑤a 下	圆形	平整	锅底状	14－12	灰黑土	图八七：25
26	D26	⑤a 下	圆形	平整	锅底状	23－8	黑土	图八七：26
27	D27	⑤a 下	椭圆形	较平整	高低不平	10～28－10	灰黑土	图八七：27
28	D28	⑤a 下	椭圆形	较平整	锅底状	9～17－5	黑土	图八七：28

（续表四）

序号	编号	层位	形制与结构			尺寸（直径－深）	填土	图号
			平面形制	坑壁	坑底			
29	D29	⑤a 下	椭圆形	较平整	锅底状	11～24－7	灰黑土	图八七：29
30	D30	⑤a 下	圆形	平整	平底	21－17	灰黑土	图八七：30
31	D31	⑤a 下	椭圆形	平整	平底	13～17－18	灰黑土	图八八：1
32	D32	⑤a 下	椭圆形	较平整	底较平	9～16－16	灰黑土	图八八：2
33	D33	⑤a 下	椭圆形	较平整	锅底状	16～22－10	灰土	图八八：3
34	D34	⑤a 下	椭圆形	较平整	锅底状	8～45－7	灰黑土	图八八：4
35	D35	⑤a 下	椭圆形	平整	平底	10～21－14	灰黑土	图八八：5
36	D36	⑤a 下	椭圆形	平整	平底	11～28－25	灰土	图八八：6
37	D37	⑤a 下	近圆形	平整	平底	7～13－7	灰黑土	图八八：7
38	D38	⑤a 下	椭圆形	较平整	锅底状	11～17－7	灰黑土	图八八：8
39	D39	⑤a 下	近圆形	较平整	高低不平	17～21－7	灰黑土	图八八：9
40	D40	⑤a 下	圆形	平整	平底	16－14	黑土	图八八：10
41	D41	⑤a 下	圆形	粗糙不平	高低不平	16－5	灰黑土	图八八：11
42	D42	⑤a 下	圆形	平整	平底	16－12	黑土	图八八：12
43	D43	⑤a 下	不规则椭圆形	平整	平底	9～37－17	灰黑土	图八八：13
44	D44	⑤a 下	圆形	平整	平底	17－13	黑土	图八八：14
45	D45	⑤a 下	圆形	平整	平底	24－7	灰黑土	图八八：15
46	D46	⑤a 下	不规则椭圆形	粗糙不平	高低不平	12～27－5	灰土	图八八：16
47	D47	⑤a 下	圆形	平整	锅底状	21－37	灰黑土	图八八：17
48	D48	⑤a 下	椭圆形	平整	锅底状	18～21－30	灰黑土	图八八：18
49	D49	⑤a 下	圆形	平整	锅底状	38－19	灰黑土	图八八：19

三　出土遗物

（一）T4⑤a 出土器物

出土器物以陶器为主，还有少量的陶器。共挑选标本 67 件，其中石器 10 件、玉器 3 件、陶器 54 件。

石器

10 件。其中锛 6 件、核 2 件、凿 1 件、片 1 件。

锛　6 件。形制相似，均体呈长方形或梯形，通体磨制。

标本 T4⑤a：2，刃部残，体呈长方形，单面弧刃，刃部可见打击点和放射线。残长 3.5、宽 3.9、厚 0.8 厘米（图八九：1；彩版八五：1）。标本 T4⑤a：3，体呈长方形，单面弧刃，刃部使用痕迹明显。残长 3.3、宽 2.9、厚 0.6 厘米（图八九：2）。标本 T4③：1，体呈长方形，单面弧刃，刃部使用痕迹明显。残长 3、宽 1.6、厚 0.4 厘米（图八九：3）。标本 T4⑤a：6，

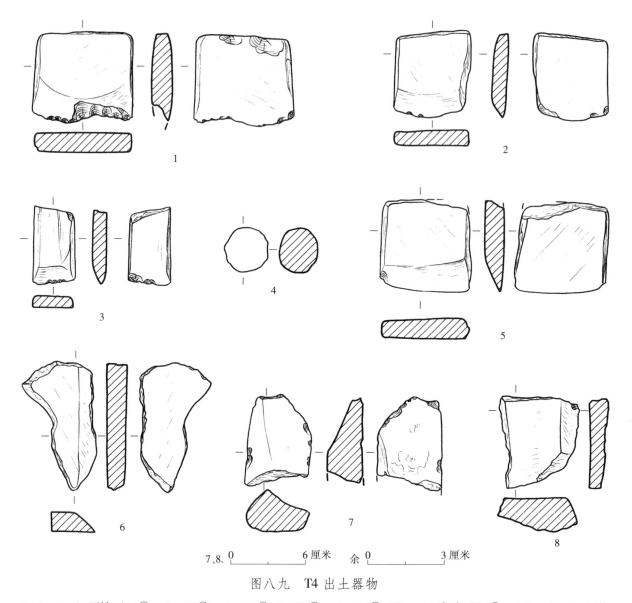

图八九　T4 出土器物

1~3、5、6. 石锛（T4⑤a：2、T4⑤a：3、T4③：1、T4⑤a：6、T4③：4）　4. 陶球（T4⑤a：7）　7、8. 石核
（T4③：2、T4③：3）

体呈长方形，单面弧刃。残长 3.6、宽 3.5、厚 0.8 厘米（图八九：5；彩版八六：1）。标本
T4③：4，仅存中间部分。残长 5、残宽 2.8、厚 0.7 厘米（图八九：6）。标本 T4⑤a：31，
体呈梯形，双面弧刃。残长 2.6、残宽 2、厚 0.2 厘米（图九〇：1；彩版八六：2）。

　　核　2 件。

　　标本 T4③：2，体呈长方形，器表可见剥片时留下的疤痕。残长 7、残宽 5、厚 3.2 厘米
（图八九：7）。标本 T4③：3，残，体呈长方形，一面可见剥片时留下的疤痕，另一面保持自然
砾石面。残长 7.2、残宽 6.2、厚 2.7 厘米（图八九：8）。

　　凿　1 件。

　　标本 T4⑤a：4，两端残，体呈狭长方形。残长 4.6、宽 0.4、厚 0.3 厘米（图九〇：5；

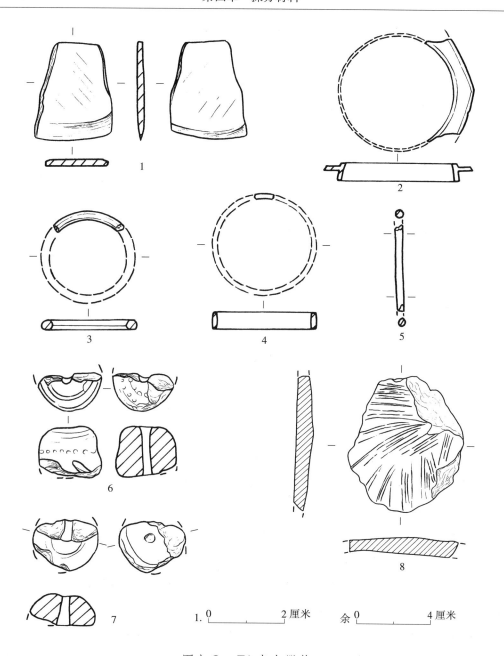

图九〇　T4 出土器物

1. 石锛（T4⑤a：31）　　2~4. 玉环（T4⑤a：5、T4⑤a：1、D36：1）　　5. 石凿（T4⑤a：4）

6、7. 陶纺轮（T4⑤a：8、T4⑤a：9）　　8. 石片（T4⑤a：30）

彩版八五：4）。

片　1件。

标本 T4⑤a：30，体呈椭圆形，一面保持自然砺石面，另一面可见打击点和放射线。长
7.2、最宽6.2、厚0.7厘米（图九〇：8）。

玉器

3件。包括 T 字形环 1 件、环 2 件。

T 字形环　1 件。

标本 T4⑤a：5，残，通体磨制，体呈菱形状，剖面呈 T 字形。直径 6.5、宽 1、厚 0.3 厘米（图九○：2；彩版八五：2）。

环　2 件。形制相似，均通体磨制，体呈圆形。

标本 D36：1，残。直径 5.5、厚 0.4 厘米（图九○：4）。标本 T4⑤a：1，残，通体磨制，体呈圆形。直径 5、厚 0.6 厘米（图九○：3；彩版八五：3）。

陶器

本探方第⑤a 层共出土陶片 1350 片。从陶质来看，夹细砂陶较多，粗砂陶次之，泥质磨光陶极少。从陶色上看，以红褐陶为主，还有少量的灰褐、黑褐。从纹饰上看，纹饰发达，约占陶片总数的 37%。纹饰种类丰富，其中绳纹居多，约占纹饰陶的 80%，其他纹饰有刻划纹、戳印纹、凹弦纹、凸棱纹、压印纹、梳刷纹、叶脉纹等（图九一）。陶器口部多为敛口和侈口，喇叭形口和直口次之，器类主要是圜底器和圈足器，器形包括球、纺轮、钵、圈足、侈口罐、厚唇罐等[1]。

本探方第⑤a 层共挑选陶器标本 54 件。其中器形 30 件、纹饰 24 件。器形标本计有球 1 件、纺轮 2 件、钵 8 件、圈足 10 件、侈口罐 2 件、喇叭口罐 4 件、厚唇罐 2 件。

球　1 件。

标本 T4⑤a：7，夹砂红褐陶。体呈球状。直径 1.7 厘米（图八九：4）。

纺轮　2 件。形制相似，均呈扁圆形。

标本 T4⑤a：8，夹砂褐陶。扁圆形，中有一穿孔。器身饰两组凹弦纹，每组凹弦纹中饰小圆圈纹。直径 3.3、厚 1.6 厘米（图九○：6）。标本 T4⑤a：9，夹砂灰褐陶。扁圆形，中有一孔。直径 3.5、厚 1.5 厘米（图九○：7）。

钵　9 件。依据口部和肩部的不同可分为三个类型。

第一类：5 件。敛口，鼓肩，肩部饰一道凸棱。

标本 T4⑤a：36，夹砂红褐陶。圆唇，斜直腹，腹部饰四道凹弦纹，上下两组凹弦纹之间饰篦点纹，腹中部饰刻划纹。口径 21、残高 2.9 厘米（图九二：1）。标本 T4⑤a：42，夹砂红陶。厚圆唇。口径 31.8、残高 3.7 厘米（图九二：9）。标本 T4⑤a：38，夹砂红陶。圆唇。腹部上下各饰三道凹弦纹，上下两组凹弦纹之间饰篦点纹。口径 23.2、残高 3.3 厘米（图九二：10）。标本 T4⑤a：41，夹细砂红陶。肩部饰一凸棱，腹部饰凹弦纹一周。口径 14.4、残高 1.7 厘米（图九二：6）。标本 T4⑤a：50，夹砂灰褐陶。尖圆唇。腹部饰刻划的半圆形纹，半圆形纹中饰刻划的叶脉纹。口径 34.4、残高 4.6 厘米（图九三：1）。

第二类：3 件。侈口，溜肩，肩部无凸棱。

标本 T4⑤a：53，夹砂红褐陶。圆唇，弧腹。腹部饰竖向绳纹。口径 30.2、残高 4.7 厘米（图九二：7）。标本 T4⑤a：40，夹砂红褐陶。圆唇。口径 25、残高 2.6 厘米（图九三：9）。标本 T4⑤a：61，夹细砂红褐陶。尖圆唇。口径 31.8、残高 4 厘米（图九三：3）。

---

[1]　本部分统计材料由越南国家历史博物馆提供。

图九一　T4⑤a 层出土陶器拓片

1. 刻划纹＋点纹（T4⑤a：32）　2. 刻划线纹（T4⑤a：33）　3. 水波纹＋凹弦纹（T4⑤a：10）　4. 梳刷纹（T4⑤a：11）　5. 凹弦纹＋绳纹（T4⑤a：12）　6. 几何形纹＋篦点纹（T4⑤a：13）　7. 几何形纹（T4⑤a：14）　8. 刻划纹（T4⑤a：15）　9. 凹弦纹＋点纹（T4⑤a：16）　10. 几何形纹（T4⑤a：17）　11. 水波纹＋凹弦纹（T4⑤a：18）　12. 几何形纹＋戳刺纹（T4⑤a：19）　13. 水波纹＋凹弦纹（T4⑤a：20）　14. 几何形纹＋篦点纹（T4⑤a：21）　15. S 形纹＋凹弦纹（T4⑤a：22）　16. 刻划纹（T4⑤a：23）　17. 几何形纹＋篦点纹（T4⑤a：24）　18. 水波纹＋篦点纹＋凹弦纹（T4⑤a：25）　19. 点纹＋几何形纹（T4⑤a：26）　20. 梳刷纹（T4⑤a：27）　21. 几何形纹＋篦点纹（T4⑤a：28）　22. 刻划纹（T4⑤a：29）　23. 点纹＋凹弦纹＋篦点纹（T4⑤a：34）　24. 点纹＋凹弦纹（T4⑤a：35）

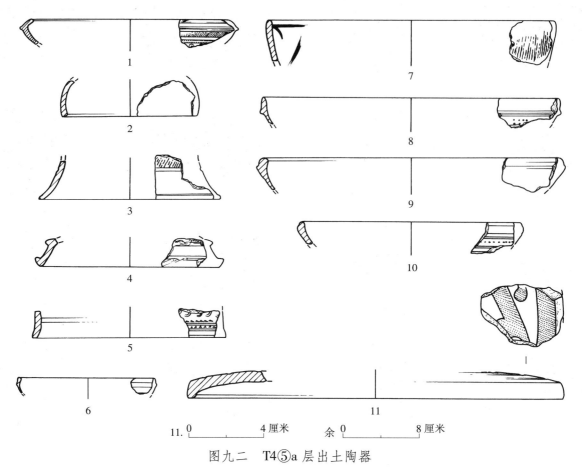

图九二　T4⑤a 层出土陶器

1、6~10. 钵（T4⑤a：36、41、53、37、42、38）　　2~5、11. 圈足（T4⑤a：39、51、54、62、60）

第三类：1 件。侈口，鼓肩，肩部饰一道凸棱。

标本 T4⑤a：37，夹细砂红褐陶。尖圆唇，弧腹。腹上部饰篦点纹。口径 31.2、残高 3.2 厘米（图九二：8）。

圈足　10 件。依据形制的不同可分为三个类型。

第一类：2 件。桶状。

标本 T4⑤a：39，夹砂褐陶。足尖内收。底径 14.4、残高 3.8 厘米（图九二：2）。标本 T4⑤a：62，夹细砂红陶。足尖外撇。足下部部饰两道凹弦纹和戳刺的点足上部刻划 S 形纹。底径 30.4、残高 3 厘米（图九二：5）。

第二类：5 件。喇叭状圈足，足尖外撇。

标本 T4⑤a：51，夹细砂红褐陶。足上饰两道凹弦纹，足上部饰刻划的线纹。底径 19.2、残高 4.8 厘米（图九二：3）。标本 T4⑤a：58，夹砂红褐陶。足中部饰两道凹弦纹，凹弦纹之间饰刻划的线纹，足上部饰小圆圈纹。底径 14.9、残高 4 厘米（图九四：1）。标本 T4⑤a：59，夹砂褐陶。足中部饰一道凹弦纹和一圆形孔，足上部饰篦点纹。底径 16.7、残高 3.7 厘米（图九四：3）。标本 T4⑤a：56，夹砂红褐陶。足部饰两道凹弦纹，足上部饰刻划的线纹。底径 16.6、残高 4.9 厘米（图九四：4）。标本 T4⑤a：57，夹砂褐陶。素面无纹。底径

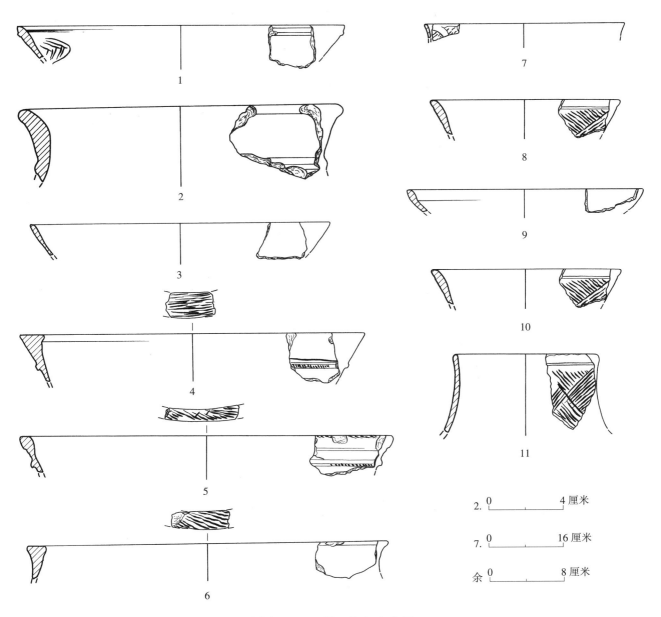

图九三　T4⑤a 层出土陶器

1、3、9. 钵（T4⑤a：50、61、40）　　2、5、8、10. 喇叭口罐（T4⑤a：52、44、43、48）　　4、6. 厚唇罐
（T4⑤a：45、46）　　7、11. 侈口罐（T4⑤a：49、47）

19.9、残高 4.1 厘米（图九四：5）。

第三类：2 件。喇叭状圈足，足尖上翘。

标本 T4⑤a：54，夹细砂褐陶。足中饰一道凸棱。底径 19.2、残高 3 厘米（图九二：4）。标本 T4⑤a：55，夹砂褐陶。底径 11.2、残高 3.8 厘米（图九四：2）。

第四类：1 件。喇叭状圈足，足尖内折。

标本 T4⑤a：60，夹砂红褐陶。足上饰有刻划的几何形纹和篦点纹。口径 19.8、残高 1.4 厘米（图九二：11）。

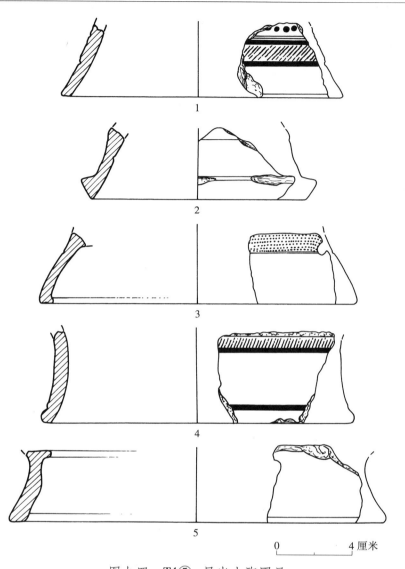

图九四　T4⑤a 层出土陶圈足

1. T4⑤a：58　2. T4⑤a：55　3. T4⑤a：59　4. T4⑤a：56　5. T4⑤a：57

侈口罐　2 件。形制相似，均侈口，束颈。

标本 T4⑤a：49，夹细砂红褐陶。圆唇，颈部饰刻划的弧线纹和线纹。口径 42.4、残高 4 厘米（图九三：7）。标本 T4⑤a：47，夹砂红褐陶。圆唇，直颈，弧肩。口下部饰一道凹弦纹，颈部饰刻划的线纹。口径 15.4、残高 8 厘米（图九三：11）。

喇叭口罐　4 件。依据颈部的不同可分为两个类型。

第一类：2 件。长颈，颈部饰一道凸棱。

标本 T4⑤a：43，夹砂红褐陶。尖圆唇，颈微束。凸棱上戳刺有短线纹，腹部饰刻划的线纹。口径 18.8、残高 4.1 厘米（图九三：8）。标本 T4⑤a：44，夹砂红褐陶。圆唇，窄平沿，弧腹。唇部饰斜向绳纹，凸棱上戳刺短线纹。口径 39.1、残高 4.3 厘米（图九三：5）。

第二类：2 件。短颈，颈部无凸棱。

标本 T4⑤a：48，夹砂红褐陶。圆唇。口下部饰一道凹弦纹，颈部饰戳刺的坑点纹。口径

20、残高 4 厘米（图九三：10）。标本 T4⑤a：52，夹砂红褐陶。厚圆唇，束颈。口径 17、残高 3.9 厘米（图九三：2）。

厚唇罐 2 件。形制相似，均为厚方唇，直口微敛。

标本 T4⑤a：45，夹砂褐陶。斜直腹。唇部饰斜向绳纹，口下部饰一道凸棱，凸棱上戳刺坑点纹。口径 36.2、残高 5.3 厘米（图九三：4）。标本 T4⑤a：46，夹砂褐陶。唇部饰斜向绳纹。口径 38、残高 3.9 厘米（图九三：6）。

（二）T4⑤b 层出土器物

本探方⑤b 层共出土陶片 115 片和 1 件石器。从陶质来看，夹细砂陶较多，粗砂陶次之，泥质磨光陶极少。从陶色上看，以红褐陶为主，还有少量的灰褐、黑褐。纹饰种类丰富，绳纹居多，其他纹饰有刻划纹、戳印纹、凹弦纹、凸棱纹、压印纹、梳刷纹、叶脉纹等。陶器口部多为侈口，器类主要是圜底器和圈足器。

本层共挑选标本 1 件，为石斧。

石斧 1 件。

标本 T4⑤b：1，残甚，体呈长方形，器表因剥片斑驳不清。残长 3.7、残宽 1.9、厚 1.1 厘米。

第五节 T5

T5 位于发掘区的西部，2006 年 12 月 3 日布方发掘，于 2007 年 1 月 8 日清理完毕。雷雨负责进行发掘、记录并绘图。

一 地层堆积

依据土质土色和包含物的不同，本区域的地层经统一后可分为 6 层，本探方大部区域缺第⑥层（图九五；彩版八七：1）。

第①层：黄灰色耕土层，土质疏松，包含有少量的瓷片、塑料、植物根茎等。厚 10～15 厘米。H9 开口于此层之下。

第②层：黄红色土，土质较硬，包含有大量的红色砖块、少量的青花瓷片、白瓷片和极少量的石器。厚 0～10、深 10～15 厘米。为近现代堆积。

第③层：浅灰色土，土质细密。包含有少量的砖块、瓷片等物。H10、H11、H12、H13、H14、H30 开口于此层下。厚 10～24、深 10～20 厘米。为近现代堆积。

第④层：依据土质土色的不同，本层可分为两个亚层。为丁朝至前黎朝堆积。

第④a 层：深褐色铁锰层，含有大量的铁锈，由东南角向北部倾斜。包含有极少量的瓷片、砖块等物。厚 0～18、深 28～34 厘米。H4、H5、H15、H16、H17 等灰坑开口于本层之下（灰坑开口区域层位缺少第④b 层）。

第④b 层：灰褐色铁锰层，含有少量的铁锈，仅分布在东北部，包含有极少量的瓷片、砖

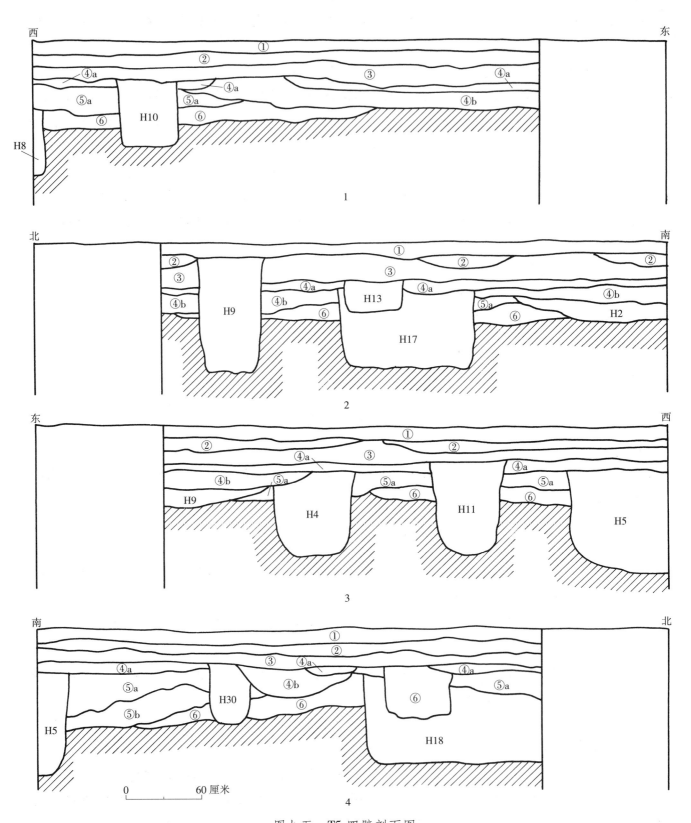

图九五　T5 四壁剖面图

1. 北壁　2. 东壁　3. 南壁　4. 西壁

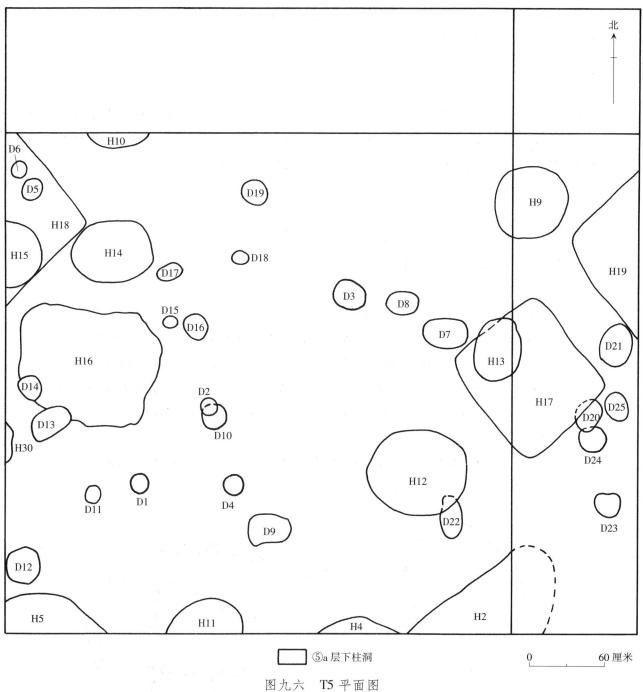

□ ⑤a 层下柱洞　　　0　　　　　60 厘米

图九六　T5 平面图

块等物。厚 0 ~ 12、深 42 厘米。H2 开口于本层之下。

第⑤层：依据土质土色的不同，本层可分为两个亚层。为冯原文化时期堆积。

第⑤a 层：黑灰色土，土质疏松，含有较多的红烧土颗粒。包括大量的陶器和少量的石器。厚 0 ~ 44、深 26 ~ 44 厘米。H18、H19 开口于本层之下。

第⑤b 层：灰黄色土，土质较硬，从北向南分布。包含物较少。厚 0 ~ 35、深 40 ~ 60 厘米。主要是陶器和石器。

第⑥层：仅分布在探方西南部分，黄褐色土，夹杂有少量的灰土斑点，土质较硬。包含物有少量的陶片。厚 0 ~ 40、深 62 ~ 86 厘米。为冯原文化时期堆积。

此层之下为红褐色铁锰生土层。

二　遗迹

本探方共清理各类遗迹 37 个，包括灰坑 12 座（不含与 T2 共有的 H2、H4、H5）、柱洞 25 个（彩版八七：2）。除 H9、H10、H11、H12、H13、H14、H30 等 7 个灰坑为近现代灰坑外，其余遗迹均为冯原文化时期，现将冯原文化时期的遗迹介绍如下。

（一）灰坑

5 座。

H15

处于 T5 的西北部，开口于第④a 层下（本区域缺少第④b 层），打破第⑤a、⑥层和 H18。

形制　平面呈不规则长方形，坑壁粗糙，坑底不平。长 0.8、宽 0.64、深 0.2 ~ 0.36 米（图九七：1）。坑内填土为灰黑色土，土质疏松，包含有少量的红烧土颗粒和炭屑。

出土器物　均为陶片，共出土陶片 29 件。陶片以夹细砂陶为主，夹粗砂陶较少，陶色以红褐、褐色为主，还有少量的红、灰褐、黑褐。纹饰以绳纹为主，还有少量的凹弦纹、篦点纹。器形主要是圈足器和圜底器。可辨器形有钵和釜。H15 挑选标本 1 件。

陶釜　1 件。

标本 H15：1，夹细砂灰褐陶。圆鼓腹。腹部饰刻划纹。残高 6.5 厘米（图九七：2）。

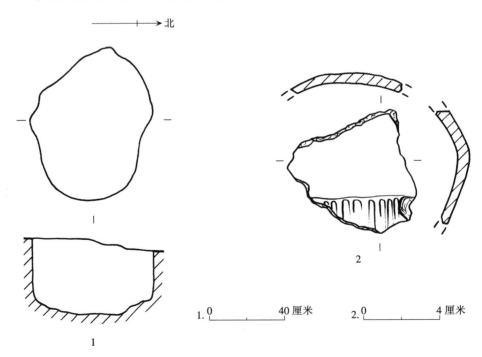

图九七　H15 平、剖面图及出土器物
1. 平、剖面图　2. 陶釜（H15：1）

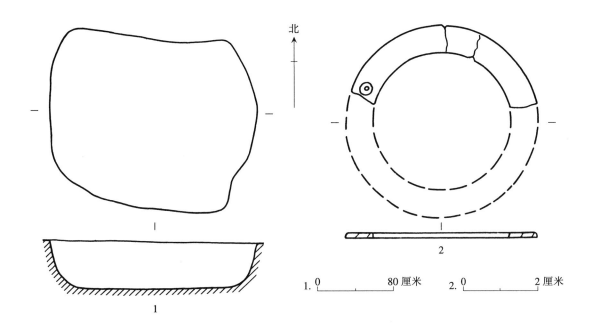

图九八　H16 平、剖面图及出土器物
1. 平、剖面图　2. 玉玦（H16：1）

H16

处于 T5 的西部，开口于第④a 层下（本区域缺少第④b 层），打破第⑤a、⑥层和 H18。

形制　平面呈不规则长方形，坑壁粗糙，坑底不平。长 2.14、宽 1.8、深 0.5 米（图九八：1）。坑内填土为灰黑色土，土质疏松，包含有少量的红烧土颗粒和炭屑（彩版八七：2）。

出土器物　除 1 件玉器外，均为陶片，共出土陶片 188 件。陶片均为夹细砂陶为主，陶色以红褐为主，还有一定数量的黄褐、灰褐、红、褐和黑褐。纹饰以绳纹为主，还有少量的凹弦纹、刻划纹、几何形纹、篦点纹等。器形主要是圈足器和圜底器，可辨器形有钵、釜、侈口罐等。H16 挑选标本 1 件。

玉玦　1 件。

标本 H16：1，残存一半，乳白色，体呈圆形，一端有一圆形穿孔。直径 5.1、宽 0.7、厚 0.1 厘米（图九八：2；彩版八八）。

H17

处于 T5 的东部，部分叠压于该探方的东隔梁，下开口于第④a 层下（本区域缺少第④b 层），被 H13 打破，打破第⑤a、⑥层和 D20。

形制　平面呈长方形，坑壁粗糙，坑底不平。长 1.14、宽 1、深 0.72 米（图九九：1）。坑内填土为灰黑色土，土质疏松，包含有少量的红烧土颗粒和炭屑。

出土器物　均为陶片，共出土陶片 94 件。陶片以夹细砂陶和夹粗砂陶为主，仅有少量的泥质陶，陶色以红褐为主，还有一定数量的黄褐、灰褐、红、褐和黑褐。纹饰以绳纹为主，还有少量的凹弦纹、刻划纹、篦点纹、几何形纹等（图九九：3、4）。器形主要是圈足器，可辨器形有钵、直口罐等。H17 挑选标本 3 件，其中器形标本 1 件、纹饰标本 2 件。

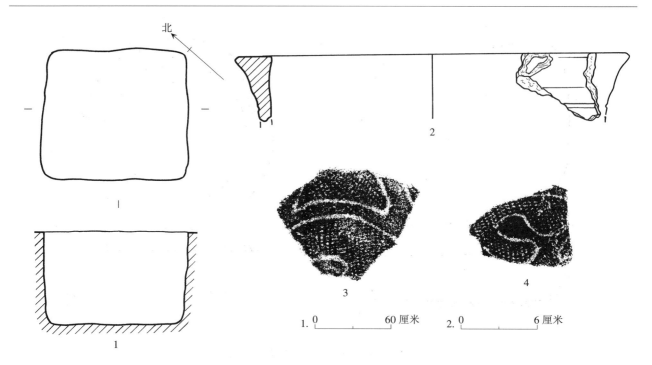

图九九　H17 平、剖面图及出土器物

1. 平、剖面图　2. 陶厚唇罐（H17∶1）　3、4. 几何形纹＋篦点纹（H17∶2、3）

厚唇罐　1 件。

标本 H17∶1，夹砂红陶。厚方唇。口下部饰一道凹弦纹。口径 30、残高 5.2 厘米（图九九∶2）。

H18

处于 T5 的西北角，部分叠压于该探方的西壁和北隔梁下，开口于第⑤a 层下，被 H15 和 D5、D6 打破，打破第⑥层和生土。

形制　平面呈不规则长方形，坑壁粗糙，坑底不平。长 1.3、宽 1～1.4、深 0.6 米（图一〇〇∶1）。坑内填土为灰黑色土，土质疏松，包含有少量的红烧土颗粒和炭屑。

出土器物　均为陶片，共出土陶片 43 件。陶片以夹细砂陶为主，还有少量的夹粗砂陶，陶色以红和红褐为主，还有一定数量的黄褐、灰褐、褐和黑褐。纹饰以凹弦纹和篦点纹为主，还有少量的绳纹、刻划纹、几何形纹等（图一〇〇∶2）。可辨器形有钵、侈口罐等。

H19

处于 T5 的东隔梁下，开口于第⑤a 层下，打破第⑥层和生土。

形制　平面呈不规则长方形，坑壁粗糙，坑底不平。残长 1.1、残宽 0.8、深 0.22 米（图一〇一∶1）。坑内填土为灰黑色土，土质疏松，包含有少量的红烧土颗粒和炭屑。

出土器物　共出土陶片 10 件。陶片以夹细砂陶和夹粗砂陶为主，陶色以红陶为主，还有一定数量的黄褐、灰褐、红褐和黑褐。纹饰以绳纹为主，还有少量的刻划纹和凹弦纹。可辨器形仅可见圈足器。H19 挑选标本 1 件。

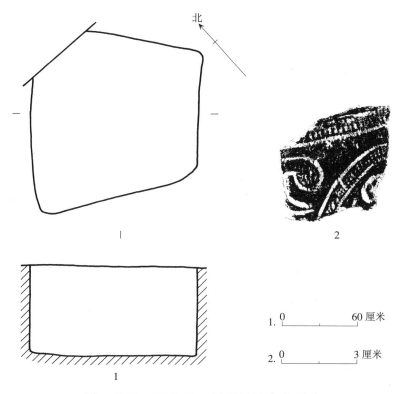

图一〇〇　H18 平、剖面图及出土器物

1. 平、剖面图　2. 几何形纹＋篦点纹陶器拓片（H18：1）

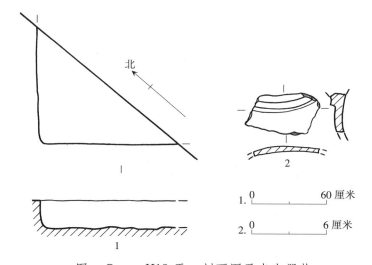

图一〇一　H19 平、剖面图及出土器物

1. 平、剖面图　2. 陶圈足（H19：1）

圈足　1 件。

标本 H19：1，夹砂红褐陶。仅存圈足与器底相连处。残高 3 厘米（图一〇一：2）。

（二）柱洞

本探方共清理柱洞 25 个（图一〇二），均开口于第⑤a 层下，平面呈圆形或椭圆形，坑壁较平整光滑，坑底呈锅底状或平底，填土基本上为灰黑土，与周边土质明显区别，土质疏松。

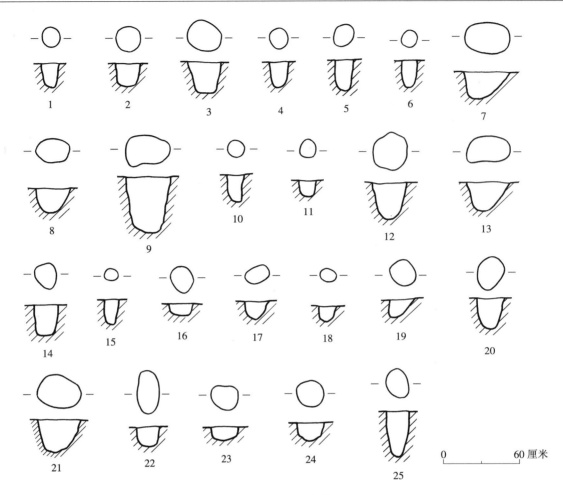

图一○二　T5 内柱洞

1～25. D1～D25

现将该探方柱洞情况列表如下。

表五　T5 各层下坑或柱洞统计表　　　　　　　　　　　　（单位：厘米）

序号	编号	层位	形制与结构			尺寸 （直径－深）	填土	图号
			平面形制	坑壁	坑底			
1	D1	⑤a	圆形	平整	锅底状	14－20	灰黑土	图一○二：1
2	D2	⑤a	圆形	平整	锅底状	20－18	灰黑土	图一○二：2
3	D3	⑤a	圆形	平整	锅底状	26－24	灰黑土	图一○二：3
4	D4	⑤a	圆形	平整	锅底状	15－20	黑土	图一○二：4
5	D5	⑤a	圆形	粗糙不平	圜底	17－24	灰黑土	图一○二：5
6	D6	⑤a	圆形	平整	圜底	13－22	灰黑土	图一○二：6
7	D7	⑤a	椭圆形	粗糙不平	圜底	24～36－22	黑土	图一○二：7
8	D8	⑤a	椭圆形	较平整	圜底	19～27－19	灰黑土	图一○二：8
9	D9	⑤a	近长方形	粗糙不平	圜底	18～36－44	黑土	图一○二：9

续表

序号	编号	层位	形制与结构			尺寸（直径－深）	填土	图号
			平面形制	坑壁	坑底			
10	D10	⑤a	圆形	粗糙不平	圜底	14－21	灰黑土	图一〇二：10
11	D11	⑤a	圆形	平整	平底	13－13	黑土	图一〇二：11
12	D12	⑤a	圆形	较平整	平底	28－29	灰黑土	图一〇二：12
13	D13	⑤a	椭圆形	粗糙不平	高低不平	20～35－23	黑土	图一〇二：13
14	D14	⑤a	圆形	较平整	底较平	18－25	灰黑土	图一〇二：14
15	D15	⑤a	圆形	平整	平底	11－20	灰黑土	图一〇二：15
16	D16	⑤a	圆形	平整	锅底状	19－10	黑土	图一〇二：16
17	D17	⑤a	椭圆形	粗糙不平	圜底	12～20－13	灰黑土	图一〇二：17
18	D18	⑤a	圆形	较平整	锅底状	14－12	黑土	图一〇二：18
19	D19	⑤a	圆形	粗糙不平	高低不平	20－15	灰黑土	图一〇二：19
20	D20	⑤a	椭圆形	粗糙不平	圜底	14～27－24	灰黑土	图一〇二：20
21	D21	⑤a	椭圆形	较平	圜底	26～34－27	灰黑土	图一〇二：21
22	D22	⑤a	椭圆形	粗糙不平	锅底状	18～35－16	灰黑土	图一〇二：22
23	D23	⑤a	不规则椭圆形	较平整	锅底状	19～22－11	灰黑土	图一〇二：23
24	D24	⑤a	圆形	粗糙不平	锅底状	22－14	黑土	图一〇二：24
25	D25	⑤a	椭圆形	较平整	圜底	13～18－37	灰黑土	图一〇二：25

三　地层中出土遗物

（一）T5⑤a层出土器物

T5第⑤a层出土器物以陶器为主，还有少量的石器。共挑选标本58件，其中石器4件、陶器54件。

石器

4件。均为石锛。

锛　依据形制的不同可分为两个类型。

第一类：3件。体呈长方形，通体磨制标本。

标本T5⑤a：2，残，双面弧刃，器身顶部可见打击点和放射线。长5.4、宽5、厚1厘米（图一〇三：1；彩版八九：1）。标本T5⑤a：3，残甚，仅存顶部一角。残长2.8、残宽2.5、厚2.5厘米（图一〇三：5）。标本T5⑤a：5，残，双面弧刃，器身可见多处打击点和放射线。长6、宽5.3、厚2.4厘米（图一〇三：4）。

第二类：体呈梯形，单面弧刃。

标本T5⑤a：1，刃部两端外撇，刃部使用痕迹明显。残长3.6、宽4.1、厚0.8厘米（图一〇三：2；彩版八九：2）。

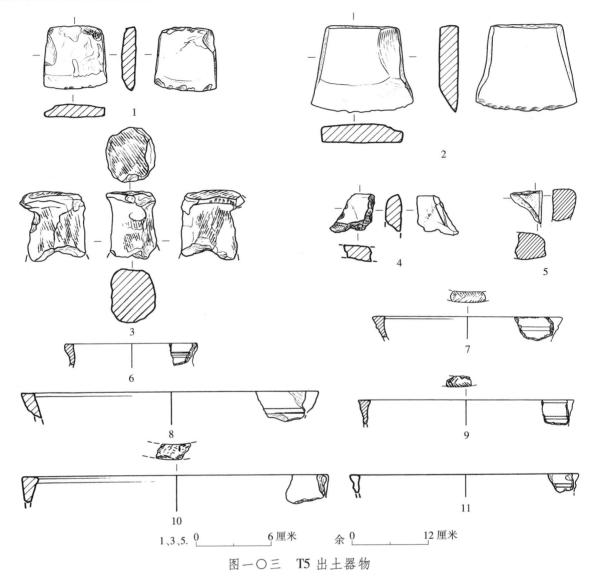

图一〇三　T5 出土器物

1、2、4、5. 石锛（T5⑤a：2、T5⑤a：1、T5⑤a：5、T5⑤a：3）　3. 陶支座（T5⑤a：4）　6~11. 陶厚唇罐（T5⑤a：9、T5⑤b：1、T5⑤a：6、T5⑤a：8、T5⑤a：7、T5⑤a：55）

陶器

本探方第⑤a层共出土陶片 958 片。从陶质来看，夹细砂陶比例约为 85%，粗砂陶约为 13%，泥质磨光陶比例约为 3%。从陶色上看，红陶、红褐陶比例约为 62%，说明其陶色偏于红色。从纹饰上看，纹饰发达，约占陶片总数的 42%。纹饰种类丰富，其中绳纹居多，约占纹饰陶的 54%，其他纹饰有刻划纹、戳印纹、凹弦纹、凸棱纹、压印纹、梳刷纹、附加堆纹等（图一〇四；彩版九〇、九一），尤以在各种刻划纹带内填充篦齿状或篦点状戳印纹的装饰风格最具特点，集多种纹饰在单个陶器上的复合纹饰甚为流行。纹饰图案主要有叶脉纹、云纹、S 形纹、几何形纹、圆圈纹、水波纹等等，但最普遍的是各种变形云纹、勾连云纹和 S 形纹。陶器口部多为敛口和侈口，喇叭形口和直口次之，器类主要是圜底器和圈足器，器形包括支座、厚唇罐、钵、圈足、喇叭口罐、侈口罐等（彩版九二、九三）。

本探方第⑤a 层共挑选标本 54 件，其中纹饰 24 件（含 3 件与器形标本重合的器物）、器形 29 件。器形标本计有支座 1 件、厚唇罐 5 件、钵 8 件、圈足 9 件、喇叭口罐 5 件、侈口罐 1 件等。

支座　1 件。

标本 T5⑤a：4，夹砂红陶。上端呈椭圆形外侈，实心。器身遍饰绳纹。上端长径 5.2、短径 4、残高 6 厘米（图一〇三：3）。

厚唇罐　5 件。形制基本相似，均厚方唇。

标本 T5⑤a：8，夹砂红陶。直口微敛，唇部饰斜向绳纹，颈部饰一道凹弦纹。口径 34.6、残高 4.2 厘米（图一〇三：9）。标本 T5⑤a：6，夹砂灰褐陶。直口微侈。口下部饰一道凹弦纹。口径 48.2、残高 5.4 厘米（图一〇三：8）。标本 T5⑤a：7，夹砂红陶。方唇。唇部饰斜向绳纹。口径 49.6、残高 4.8 厘米（图一〇三：10）。标本 T5⑤a：9，夹砂红陶。直口微侈，颈部饰三道凹弦纹。口径 21.6、残高 3.8 厘米（图一〇三：6）。标本 T5⑤a：55，夹砂褐陶。口下部饰一道凸棱。口径 36.8、残高 3 厘米（图一〇三：11）。

钵　8 件。依据形制的不同可分为三个类型。

第一类：3 件。侈口，肩部饰一凸棱。

标本 T5⑤a：28，夹细砂褐陶。圆唇，弧腹。口径 34.4、残高 3.5 厘米（图一〇五：1）。标本 T5⑤a：30，夹细砂灰陶。圆唇。口径 29.2、残高 3.4 厘米（图一〇五：4）。标本 T5⑤a：32，夹砂灰褐陶。圆唇。颈部饰一道凹弦纹。口径 28.2、残高 4 厘米（图一〇五：5）。标本 T5⑤a：27，夹砂黑褐陶。圆唇。口径 33.6、残高 2.8 厘米（图一〇六：1）。

第二类：4 件。敛口，肩部饰一凸棱。

标本 T5⑤a：20，夹细砂红陶。圆唇，弧腹。腹部饰四道凹弦纹，上下各两组凹弦纹中饰篦点纹。口径 32.4、残高 5.1 厘米（图一〇五：2；彩版九四：1）。标本 T5⑤a：31，夹细砂红褐陶。圆唇。腹部饰六道凹弦纹。口径 30.2、残高 3.4 厘米（图一〇五：3）。标本 T5⑤a：29，夹细砂红陶。圆唇。凸棱下部饰戳刺的线纹。口径 26、残高 2.8 厘米（图一〇五：6）。标本 T5⑤a：21，夹砂红褐陶。圆唇。唇部饰戳刺的三角形纹，肩部饰绳纹。口径 38.7、残高 3.3 厘米（图一〇五：16）。

第三类：1 件。敛口，肩部无凸棱。

标本 T5⑤a：10，夹砂红褐陶。圆唇，敛口。口径 30、残高 4.3 厘米（图一〇六：2）。

圈足　9 件。依据足部的不同可分为三个类型（彩版九四：2、3）。

第一类：7 件。喇叭状圈足，足尖外撇。

标本 T5⑤a：25，夹细砂红陶。足下端饰凹弦纹和篦点纹，上部饰刻划的线纹。底径 25.6、残高 2.7 厘米（图一〇五：7）。标本 T5⑤a：22，夹细砂灰褐陶。底径 8.7、残高 1.8 厘米（图一〇五：9）。标本 T5⑤a：23，夹细砂灰褐陶。底径 35.2、残高 3.2 厘米（图一〇五：10）。标本 T5⑤a：53，夹砂红褐陶。底径 19.8、残高 3.2 厘米（图一〇五：11）。标本 T5⑤a：12，夹砂红褐陶。圈足底部饰戳刺的三角形纹，足下部饰一道凸棱，上部饰斜向绳纹。口径 32.4、

1 2 3 4 5 6 7 8 9 10 11 12 13 14 15 16 17 18 19 20 21 22 23 24

图一〇四 T5⑤a层出土陶器拓片

1. 点纹+凹弦纹+S形纹（T5⑤a：11） 2、3. 几何形纹+篦点纹（T5⑤a：13、38） 4. 点纹+凹弦纹（T5⑤a：39） 5. 凹弦纹+篦点纹+水波纹（T5⑤a：46） 6. 凹弦纹+S形纹（T5⑤a：47） 7. 凸棱纹+篦点纹+凹弦纹（T5⑤a：20） 8. 绳纹（T5⑤a：33） 9. 几何形纹+篦点纹（T5⑤a：40） 10. 刻划纹+绳纹（T5⑤a：41） 11. 叶脉纹（T5⑤a：48） 12. 水波纹+凹弦纹（T5⑤a：49） 13. 绳纹（T5⑤a：34） 14. 凹弦纹+刻划纹（T5⑤a：35） 15. 几何形纹+篦点纹+刻划纹（T5⑤a：42） 16. 刻划纹（T5⑤a：43） 17. 绳纹（T5⑤a：50） 18. 刻划纹（T5⑤a：51） 19. 绳纹+刻划纹（T5⑤a：36） 20、21. 刻划纹（T5⑤a：37、44） 22. S形纹+刻划纹（T5⑤a：45） 23. 凹弦纹（T5⑤a：52） 24. 几何形纹+篦点纹（T5⑤a：54）

残高5.6厘米（图一〇五：12）。标本T5⑤a：24，夹砂灰褐陶。仅存圈足中部。残宽7.2厘米（图一〇五：13）。标本T5⑤a：16，夹砂红褐陶。底径21.6、残高3.8厘米（图一〇五：14）。

第二类：1件。喇叭状圈足，足尖上翘。

标本T5⑤a：26，夹细砂红陶。底径15.6、残高2.6厘米（图一〇五：8）。

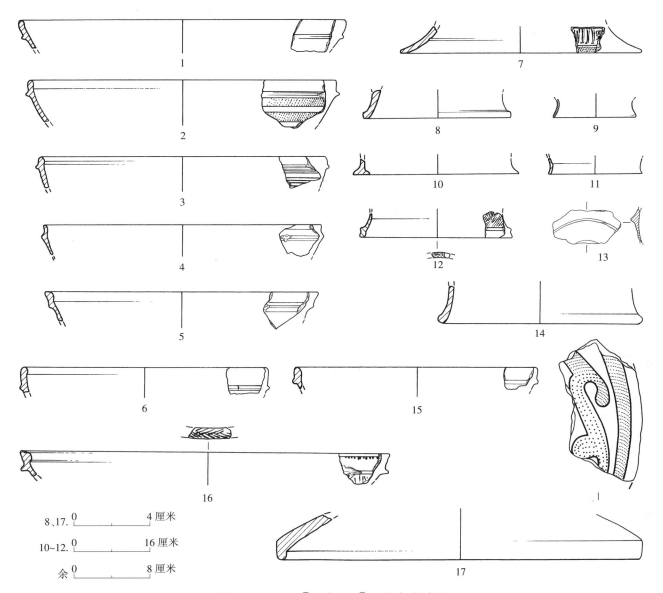

图一〇五　T5⑤a 和 T5⑤b 层出土陶器

1~6、15、16. 钵（T5⑤a：28、T5⑤a：20、T5⑤a：31、T5⑤a：30、T5⑤a：32、T5⑤a：29、T5⑤b：2、T5⑤a：21）

7~14、17. 圈足（T5⑤a：25、26、22、23、53、12、24、16、13）

第三类：1 件。喇叭状圈足，足尖内折。

标本 T5⑤a：13，夹砂红褐陶。足下部饰两道凹弦纹和篦点纹，足上部饰刻划的云纹，云纹中饰篦点纹。口径 19.3、残高 2.4 厘米（图一〇五：17）。

喇叭口罐　5 件。形制相似。均呈圆唇，喇叭口。

标本 T5⑤a：1，夹砂红褐陶。口下部饰一道凹弦纹和戳刺的坑点纹，颈下部有一圆孔。口径 14.5、残高 3.6 厘米（图一〇六：3）。标本 T5⑤a：19，夹细砂红陶。唇部戳刺有锯齿状短线纹，颈部饰经涂抹的竖向绳纹。口径 9.3、残高 3 厘米（图一〇六：4）。标本 T5⑤a：14，夹砂灰陶。颈上部饰一道凹弦纹。口径 36、残高 2.8 厘米（图一〇六：6）。标本 T5⑤a：15，

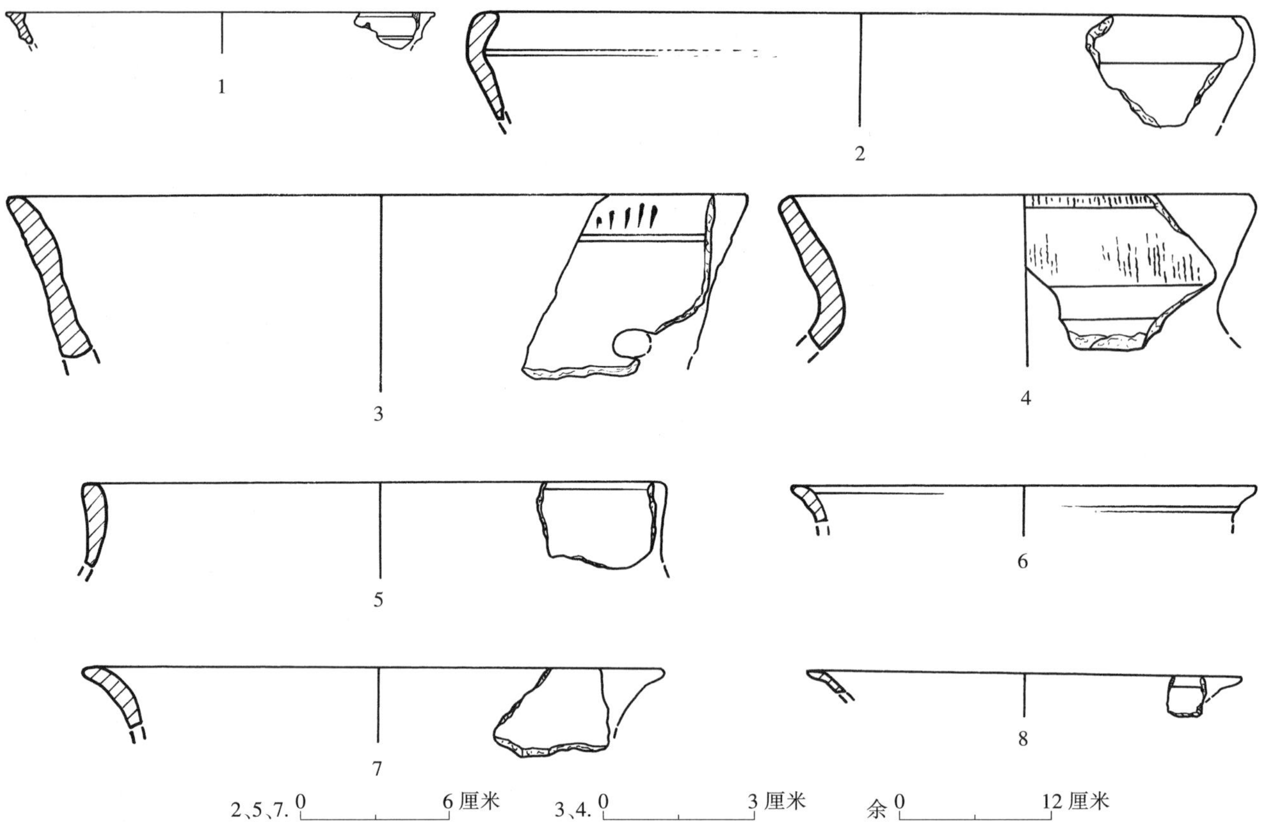
1
2
3
4
5
6
7
8
2、5、7. 0 6 厘米
3、4. 0 3 厘米
余 0 12 厘米

图一〇六 T5⑤a 层出土陶器

1、2. 钵（T5⑤a：27、10） 3、4、6～8. 喇叭口罐（T5⑤a：1、19、14、17、15） 5. 侈口罐（T5⑤a：18）

夹砂红褐陶。素面无纹。口径 34、残高 3.2 厘米（图一〇六：8）。标本 T5⑤a：17，夹砂红陶。素面无纹。口径 22.8、残高 3.5 厘米（图一〇六：7）。

侈口罐 1 件。

标本 T5⑤a：18，夹砂灰陶。圆唇。素面无纹。口径 23、残高 3.5 厘米（图一〇六：5）。

（二）T5⑤b 层出土器物

T5 第⑤b 层出土器物均为陶器，共出土陶片极少，仅 18 片。陶质以夹细砂陶为主，还有少量的夹粗砂陶，陶色以红和红褐色为主，还有少量的黄褐、灰褐和黑褐。纹饰以凹弦纹为主，还有少量的绳纹和篦点纹。可辨器形有钵、直口罐。本层挑选标本 2 件，为直口罐和钵各 1 件。

厚唇罐 1 件。

标本 T5⑤b：1，夹细砂红褐陶。方唇。唇部戳刺有三角形纹。口径 30.6、残高 4 厘米（图一〇三：7）。

钵 1 件。

标本 T5⑤b：2，夹细砂红陶。圆唇。口下部饰一道凸棱。口径 25.8、残高 2.4 厘米（图一〇五：15）。

第六节　T7

T7 位于发掘区的西部，2006 年 12 月 13 日布方发掘，于 2007 年 1 月 8 日清理完毕。孙伟刚、岳连建负责进行发掘、记录并绘图。

一　地层堆积

T7 内地层可分为 6 层，分别为第①、②、③、④、⑤、⑥层。这些地层在探方四壁堆积不太均匀，个别层位在探方西、南壁缺失（图一〇七）。

第①层：耕土层。土质疏松，含砂量较大，土色黄灰。夹杂有一些红砖、瓦块、青瓷片等。厚 10 厘米。

第②层：扰土层。土质稍紧密，土色黄红。夹杂有大量的红色砖块、瓦片、青瓷片、青花瓷片等。深 10、厚 5 ~ 10 厘米。为近现代堆积。G2 开口于本层下。

第③层：扰土层。土质紧密，较为纯净，土色为浅灰色。夹杂有少量红色夹砂砖块、陶片、青瓷片等。深 10 ~ 20、厚 0 ~ 15 厘米。为近现代堆积。H29 和 H32 开口于本层之下。

第④a 层，深褐色铁锰层。包含有大量颗粒状的铁砂质土，土质松散。为丁朝至前黎朝堆积。深 20 ~ 40、厚 0 ~ 15 厘米。26 个柱洞开口于本层之下。

第⑤a 层：土质松软，含有较多烧土点，土色黑灰。本层出土有大量夹砂红陶片及石楔、石锛、残玉环等遗物，可能为冯原文化时期的遗存。深 22 ~ 40、厚 0 ~ 18 厘米。冯原文化层。19 个柱洞开口于本层之下。

第⑥层：质地较硬，土色为黄褐色并夹杂有灰土斑点。包含有极少量的夹细砂红陶片。深 40 ~ 50、厚 20 ~ 36 厘米。H33 和 16 个柱洞开口于本层之下。

此层之下为红褐色铁锰生土层。

二　遗迹

本探方共发现各类遗迹 64 个，包括灰坑 2 座、沟 1 条、柱洞 61 个（图一〇八；彩版九五）。除 H32 和 G2 为近现代遗存外，其余 62 个遗迹均为冯原文化时期。

（一）灰坑

1 座。

H33

位于探方西端中部，开口于第⑥层下，打破生土。形制为近圆形，直桶状，壁面不甚平直。直径为 62、深 34 ~ 50 厘米（图一〇九）。其内土质、土色与第⑥层基本相同。其打破生土层，未发现任何遗物。

（二）柱洞

61 个。

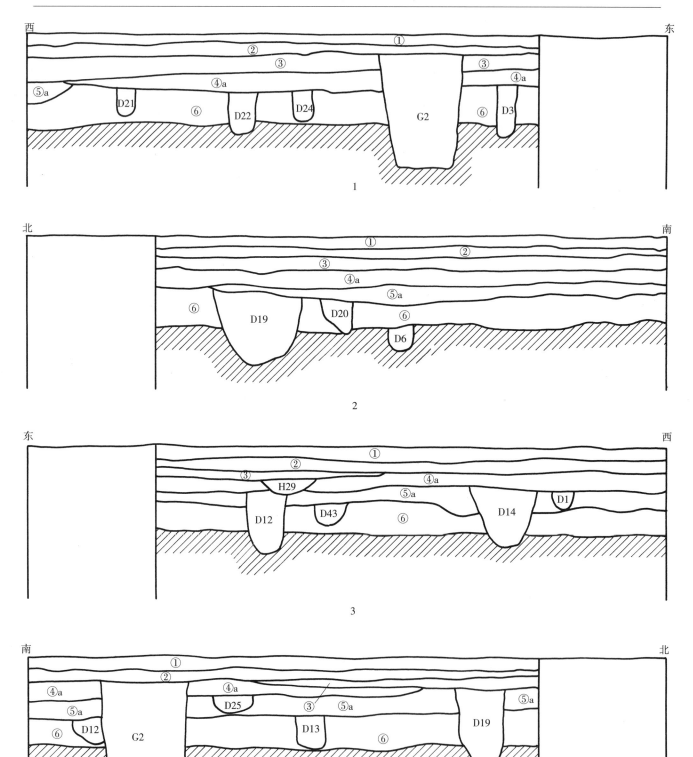

图一○七　T7 四壁剖面图

1. 北壁　2. 东壁　3. 南壁　4. 西壁

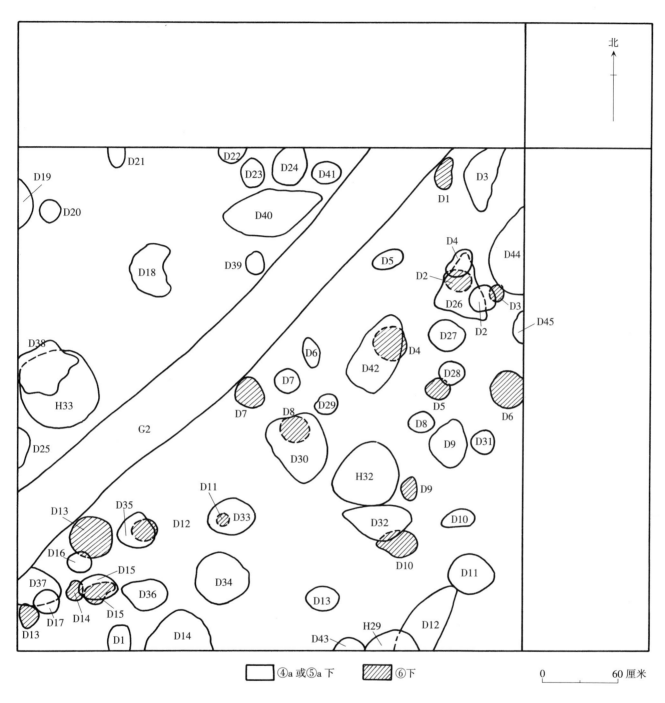

④a 或⑤a 下	⑥下

0　　　60 厘米

图一〇八　T7 平面图

开口于第④a 层下的 26 个，开口于第⑤a 层下的 19 个，开口于第⑥层下的 16 个。平面基本呈圆形或椭圆形，较为规整，部分柱洞平面可见破损痕迹，表明其原应有柱子，填土为灰黑土或黑土，土质疏松，部分坑内包含少量的陶片。但这些柱洞和大量的坑在一起，很难将其作为一个完整的建筑分析。为准确地反映本探方的坑和柱洞情况，现将该探方的柱洞列表如下。

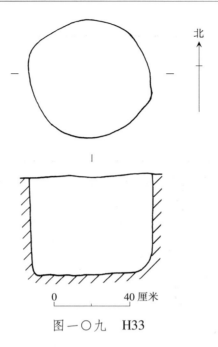

图一〇九　H33

表六　T7 各层下柱洞统计表

（单位：厘米）

序号	编号	层位	形制与结构			尺寸（直径－深）	填土	图号
			平面形制	坑壁	坑底			
1	D1	④a	圆形	平整	高低不平	22－24	灰黑土	图一一〇：1
2	D2	④a	圆形	较平整	较平	23－17	灰黑土	图一一〇：2
3	D3	④a	不规则椭圆形	粗糙不平	底较平	17～53－35	黑土	图一一〇：3
4	D4	④a	不规则椭圆形	粗糙不平	平底	17～28－41	灰黑土	图一一〇：4
5	D5	④a	椭圆形	粗糙不平	高低不平	15～27－28	灰黑土	图一一〇：5
6	D6	④a	不规则椭圆形	较平整	高低不平	15～23－13	黑土	图一一〇：6
7	D7	④a	圆形	平整	平底	22－43	灰黑土	图一一〇：7
8	D8	④a	圆形	平整	高低不平	23－20	黑土	图一一〇：8
9	D9	④a	不规则椭圆形	粗糙不平	高低不平	33～40－44	灰黑土	图一一〇：9
10	D10	④a	不规则椭圆形	粗糙不平	高低不平	15～30－12	灰黑土	图一一〇：10
11	D11	④a	圆形	粗糙不平	高低不平	37－40	灰黑土	图一一〇：11
12	D12	④a	圆形	较平整	平底	30～63－25	灰黑土	图一一〇：12
13	D13	④a	圆形	较平整	高低不平	27－24	黑土	图一一〇：13
14	D14	④a	圆形	平整	平底	56－20	灰黑土	图一一〇：14
15	D15	④a	椭圆形	粗糙不平	高低不平	20～33－17	灰黑土	图一一〇：15
16	D16	④a	圆形	粗糙不平	平底	20－20	黑土	图一一〇：16
17	D17	④a	圆形	平整	锅底状	24－13	灰黑土	图一一〇：17
18	D18	④a	不规则椭圆形	粗糙不平	高低不平	20～43－37	灰黑土	图一一〇：18

（续表六）

序号	编号	层位	形制与结构			尺寸（直径－深）	填土	图号
			平面形制	坑壁	坑底			
19	D19	④a	圆形	较平整	高低不平	38－19	灰黑土	图一一〇：19
20	D20	④a	圆形	较平整	底较平	17－13	灰黑土	图一一〇：20
21	D21	④a	椭圆形	平整	平底	13～17－33	灰土	图一一〇：21
22	D22	④a	不规则椭圆形	较平整	底较平	14～23－20	灰黑土	图一一〇：22
23	D23	④a	圆形	较平整	平底	24－28	灰黑土	图一一〇：23
24	D24	④a	圆形	较平整	底较平	30－23	灰黑土	图一一〇：24
25	D25	④a	圆形	较平整	平底	10－17	灰黑土	图一一〇：25
26	D26	⑤a	近三角形	粗糙不平	圜底	40～58－46	灰土	图一一〇：26
27	D27	⑤a	圆形	粗糙不平	尖圆底	30－15	灰黑土	图一一〇：27
28	D28	⑤a	圆形	较平整	圜底	23－13	黑土	图一一〇：28
29	D29	⑤a	圆形	平整	平底	20－12	灰黑土	图一一〇：29
30	D30	⑤a	椭圆形	粗糙不平	高低不平	43、56－20	灰黑土	图一一〇：30
31	D31	⑤a	圆形	平整	平底	20－14	灰黑土	图一一〇：31
32	D32	⑤a	椭圆形	粗糙不平	平底	30～56－7	灰黑土	图一一〇：32
33	D33	⑤a	椭圆形	平整	平底	30～40－15	灰黑土	图一一〇：33
34	D34	⑤a	圆形	粗糙不平	高低不平	43－13	灰黑土	图一一〇：34
35	D35	⑤a	不规则圆形	平整	平底	30－40	灰黑土	图一一〇：35
36	D36	⑤a	不规则椭圆形	较平整	高低不平	23～40－20	灰黑土	图一一〇：36
37	D37	⑤a	不规则椭圆形	粗糙不平	圜底	33～37－13	灰黑土	图一一〇：37
38	D38	⑤a	不规则长方形	粗糙不平	近平底	23～50－37	黑土	图一一〇：38
39	D39	⑤a	近圆形	平整	平底	17－43	灰黑土	图一一〇：39
40	D40	⑤a	不规则椭圆形	较平整	平底	40～83－32	灰黑土	图一一〇：40
41	D41	⑤a	圆形	平整	平底	26－17	黑土	图一一〇：41
42	D42	⑤a	不规则椭圆形	较平整	平底	35～67－25	灰黑土	图一一〇：42
43	D43	⑤a	圆形	平整	锅底状	27－17	灰黑土	图一一〇：43
44	D44	⑤a	不规则椭圆形	粗糙不平	圜底	27～73－60	灰黄土	图一一〇：44
45	D45	⑤a	不规则椭圆形	粗糙不平	高低不平	8～27－27	灰黑土	图一一〇：45
46	D1	⑥	不规则椭圆形	粗糙不平	圜底	13～27－28	黑土	图一一〇：46
47	D2	⑥	椭圆形	平整	平底	13～27－27	灰土	图一一〇：47
48	D3	⑥	圆形	平整	平底	13－13	黑土	图一一〇：48
49	D4	⑥	圆形	粗糙不平	高低不平	30－17	灰土	图一一〇：49
50	D5	⑥	圆形	平整	圜底	20－17	灰黄土	图一一〇：50

（续表六）

序号	编号	层位	形制与结构			尺寸 （直径－深）	填土	图号
			平面形制	坑壁	坑底			
51	D6	⑥	圆形	平整	圜底	30－28	灰褐土	图一一〇：51
52	D7	⑥	不规则椭圆形	平整	圜底	17～27－28	黄褐土	图一一〇：52
53	D8	⑥	圆形	平整	圜底	23－13	灰褐土	图一一〇：53
54	D9	⑥	不规则椭圆形	平整	圜底	13～18－9	灰黑土	图一一〇：54
55	D10	⑥	不规则椭圆形	粗糙不平	高低不平	26～33－10	黑土	图一一〇：55
56	D11	⑥	圆形	平整	平底	10－20	灰黑土	图一一〇：56
57	D12	⑥	圆形	平整	高低不平	20－23	褐土	图一一〇：57
58	D13	⑥	圆形	平整	圜底	35－17	灰褐土	图一一〇：58
59	D14	⑥	圆形	平整	圜底	15－17	黑土	图一一〇：59
60	D15	⑥	不规则椭圆形	粗糙不平	高低不平	10～27－20	灰黑土	图一一〇：60
61	D16	⑥	不规则椭圆形	粗糙不平	圜底	17～20－13	灰黑土	图一一〇：61

三　地层中出土遗物

本探方地层中出土器物较多，共挑选标本 19 件，主要是陶器和石器，其中石器 9 件、陶器 10 件。

石器

9 件。计拍 2 件、磨石 1 件、斧 4 件、锛 2 件。

拍　2 件。顶端可见凹槽，其他面磨光。

标本 T7④aD1：1，残损严重，体呈长方形。上端可见四条凹槽。残长 8.6、宽 6.8、厚 7 厘米（图一一一：1；彩版九六：1）。标本 T7④a：2，残损严重，仅存上部，呈不规则椭圆形，一面可见凹槽。残长 7、残宽 8.2、厚 5.9 厘米（图一一一：2）。

磨石　1 件。

标本 T7④a：3，体呈椭圆形，一面可见经磨制后留下的凹痕。长 6、宽 1.7、厚 2 厘米（图一一一：3）。

斧　4 件。形制基本相似。均体呈长方形。

标本 T7④b：3，残损严重，仅存上端，体呈长方形，上端可见打击点和放射线。残长 4.2、宽 8.8、厚 3.2 厘米（图一一一：4）。标本 T7④b：2，刃部残缺，体呈长方形，器表可见多处打击点和放射线。残长 14、宽 8、厚 4 厘米（图一一一：6）。标本 T7④b：4，残损严重，仅存上端一角，体呈长方形，器表可见多处打击点和放射线。残长 5.4、残宽 4、厚 1.6 厘米（图一一一：7）。标本 T7④aD1：2，残损严重，仅存中部，两面磨制痕迹明显。残长 2.9、残宽 2.5、厚 1.1 厘米（图一一一：8）。

锛　2 件。形制基本相似，均体呈长方形。

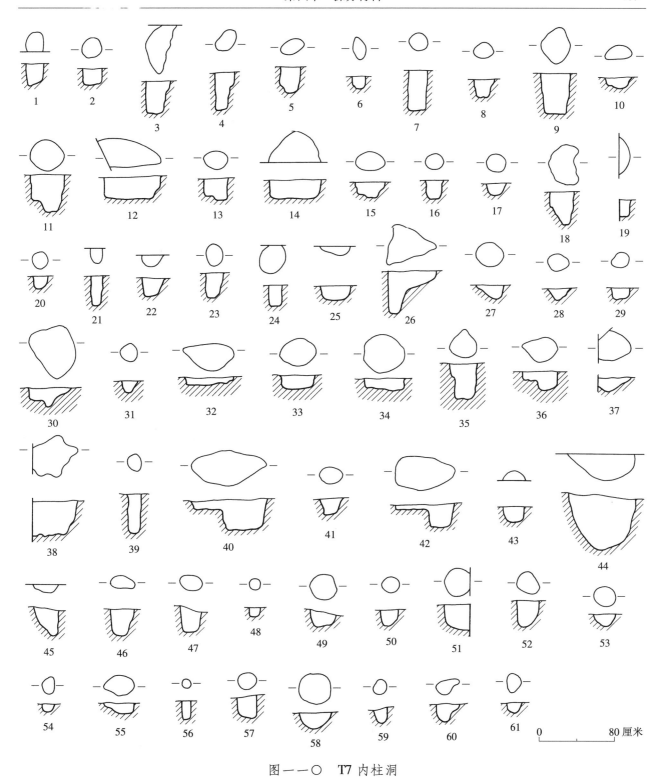

图一一〇　T7 内柱洞

1～25. ④a 层下柱洞（D1～D25）　　26～45. ⑤a 层下柱洞（D26～D45）　　46～61. ⑥层下柱洞（D1～D16）

标本 T7②：1，保存较好，双面弧刃，器表上端和一侧可见多处打击点和放射线。长 9.2、宽 8.6、厚 2.4 厘米（图一一一：5；彩版九六：2）。标本 T7④b：1，仅存刃部，为单面弧刃。残长 3.8、宽 4.2、厚 1 厘米（图一一一：9）。

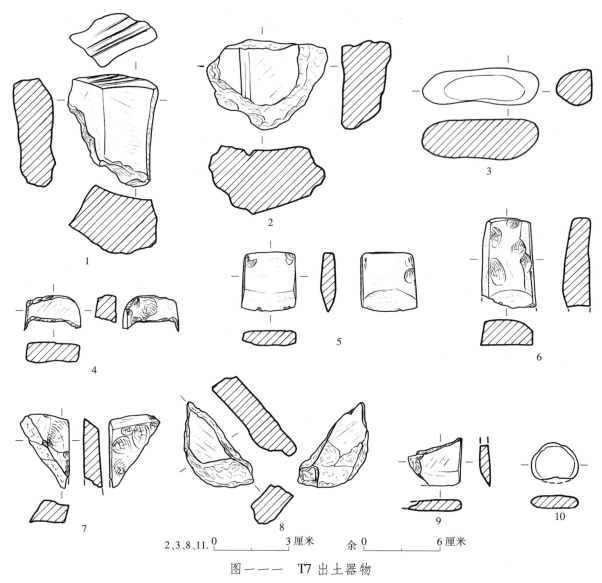

2、3、8、11. 0 ——— 3厘米   余 0 ——— 6厘米

图一一一   T7 出土器物

1、2. 石拍（T7④aD1：1、T7④a：2）   3. 磨石（T7④a：3）   4、6~8. 石斧（T7④b：3、T7④b：2、T7④b：4、
T7④aD1：2）   5、9. 石锛（T7②：1、T7④b：1）   10. 陶饼（T7④a：1）

陶器

本探方第⑤a层共出土陶片295片。从陶质来看，以夹细砂陶，夹粗砂陶次之，泥质磨光陶极少。从陶色上看，以红陶和红褐陶为主，还有少量的灰褐、黑褐陶。从纹饰上看，纹饰发达，且纹饰种类丰富，以绳纹为主，其他纹饰有刻划纹、戳印纹、凹弦纹、凸棱纹、压印纹、梳刷纹、附加堆纹等。陶器口部多为侈口，喇叭形口和直口次之。器类主要是圜底器和圈足器，器形包括饼、圈足、钵、喇叭口罐等[1]。

共挑选陶器标本10件，其中器形标本9件、纹饰标本1件。

---

〔1〕 本部分统计数据由越南国家博物馆提供。

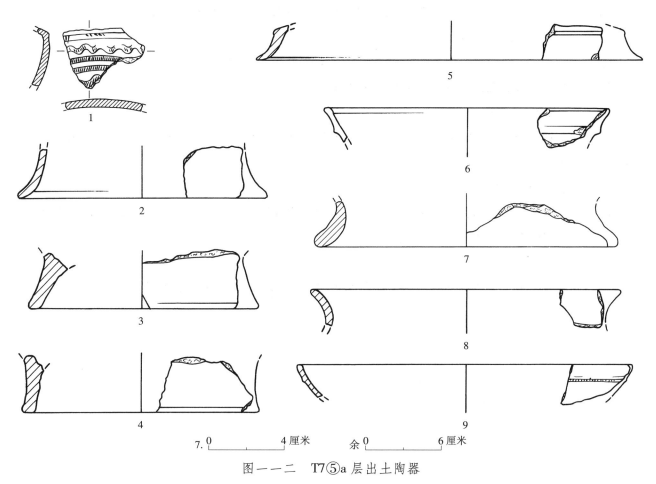

图一一二　T7⑤a 层出土陶器

1. 纹饰标本（T7⑤a：3）　　2～5、7. 圈足（T7⑤a：5、7、6、9、8）　　6、9. 钵（T7⑤a：10、11）

8. 喇叭口罐（T7⑤a：12）

纹饰标本　1 件。

标本 T7⑤a：3，夹砂红褐陶。肩部饰两道凹弦纹，腹上部饰戳刺的水波纹，水波纹中戳刺短线纹，腹下部饰两组凹弦纹，每组凹弦纹中戳刺短线纹。长 4.6、宽 6.1、厚 0.6 厘米（图一一二：1）。

器形标本　共挑选标本 9 件。计有圈足 5 件、钵 2 件、喇叭口罐 1 件、饼 1 件。

饼　1 件。

标本 T7④a：1，夹砂红褐陶。体呈圆形。直径 1.8、厚 0.5 厘米（图一一一：10）。

圈足　5 件。依据形制的不同可分为三个类型。

第一类：3 件。喇叭状圈足，足尖外撇。

标本 T7⑤a：5，夹砂红陶。底径 18、残高 4.6 厘米（图一一二：2）。标本 T7⑤a：7，夹砂褐陶。底径 19.6、残高 4.1 厘米（图一一二：3）。标本 T7⑤a：8，夹砂红褐陶。底径 15.8、残高 2.3 厘米（图一一二：7）。

第二类：1 件。喇叭状圈足，足尖内折。

标本 T7⑤a：9，夹细砂红褐陶。底径 30.3、残高 2.8 厘米（图一一二：5）。

第三类：1 件。桶状圈足。

标本 T7⑤a：6，夹砂红褐陶。底径 18.5、残高 4 厘米（图一一二：4）。

钵　2 件。依据形制的不同可分为两个类型。

第一类：1 件。侈口。

标本 T7⑤a：10，夹细砂红陶。圆唇。口下部饰一道凸棱。口径 22.3、残高 3.1 厘米（图一一二：6）。

第二类：1 件。敛口。

标本 T7⑤a：11，夹细砂红褐陶。方唇，侈口，弧腹。口下部饰一道凸棱，凸棱上戳刺有坑点纹。口径 26.2、残高 3.2 厘米（图一一二：9）。

喇叭口罐　1 件。

标本 T7⑤a：12，夹砂红陶。圆唇。素面无纹。口径 24.2、残高 3 厘米（图一一二：8）。

第五章　初步研究

第一节　义立遗址遗存的总体特征

一　生产工具

生产工具主要是石器。石器多通体磨制，偏于小型化，以锛、斧为主，另有少量的镞、凿、拍、范、球和打制石器（刮削器）等。锛的数量最多，石质较好，个别似玉质，一般呈梯形或长方形，单面或双面弧刃，且磨制精美，表明其技术可能已专门化。石斧比锛大，一般通体磨制，平面呈长方形，双面弧刃。作为制作树皮布的石拍，在义理遗址中首次发现，平面呈长方形，一端可见明显的凹槽，是中国东南沿海及东南亚地区最有特点的器物之一。石范的发现是冯原文化首次发现与青铜冶炼相关的器物，从其内部的痕迹推测是制作某些兵器的石范，同时考虑到义立遗址曾发现过一件铜矛[1]，推测可能是制作铜矛的石范。石球的数量较少，均呈球状，表面光滑。打制石器数量少，大部分为从磨制石器上剥片或利用砾石直接打制而成。另外还发现有少量的陶质纺轮和石质网坠。

二　生活用具

生活用具主要是陶器。陶器的制作方法以轮制为主，很多陶器的内壁上可见轮制的痕迹。陶系分夹砂陶和泥质陶两种，夹砂陶多羼白色石英砂，有粗细之分，以细砂为主。陶色以红色和红褐色为主，还有一定数量的灰褐、黄褐、黑褐等，少量的泥质陶表面施陶衣。陶器火候一般较高。

从纹饰上看，纹饰种类繁多，制作也非常精美，纹饰主要有绳纹、刻划纹、戳压纹、附加堆纹等。绳纹一般为细绳纹和中绳纹，纹样有竖向、斜向、交错和网状等，一般施于陶器的唇部、沿面、颈部、腹部和底部。刻划纹主要为水波纹、S形纹、平行线纹、弦纹、叶脉纹、几何形纹等，多施于陶器的颈部、腹部和圈足上。戳压纹主要为坑点纹、篦点纹、圆圈纹等，一般与刻划纹一起组成复杂的纹饰，多施于器物的腹部和圈足上。以篦点纹和刻划纹组成的水波纹、S形纹、云纹和几何形纹等陶器装饰风格最有特点。

---

[1] Nyuyen Van Hao（1968）：*Bao cao khai quat di chi Nghia Lap—Vinh Phu*，Tu lieu Vien Khao co hoc，Ha Noi。

从器类来看，主要盛行圜底器和圈足器，不见平底器和三足器。器形多侈口和敛口。喇叭口和直口次之，典型器物主要包括釜、豆、钵、罐等。

三 装饰品

义立遗址还出土少量的装饰品，均为玉器，磨制精细，主要包括环、T 字形环、玦等。环数量最多，多为乳白色，呈圆形，打磨光滑。玦的数量较少，呈半圆形，一端有孔。T 字形石环在中国至东南亚地区发现较多，但本次发掘出土的多领壁的 T 字形在越南系首次发现。这些装饰品一方面反映了其高超的制作水平，另一方面亦反映了义立遗址居民的精神生活。

四 建筑遗存和灰坑

义立遗址已发掘的 8 个探方（含河内国立大学发掘的 2 个探方）内均清理了大量的柱洞或小坑遗迹，这些柱洞分布并无规律，部分柱洞相互叠压打破，似乎表明遗址内曾存在干栏式建筑，而大量分布密集的柱洞表明这种建筑在短时间内可能存在毁坏重建现象。

义立遗址共清理灰坑 34 座，冯原文化时期的灰坑 16 座，这批灰坑可分为圆形、方形和不规则形。其中 11 个方形灰坑（含河内国立大学所发掘灰坑），可分为 A、B 两大类。

A 类为上圆下方形，口部直径约 1.2 米，底部边长约 1 米。坑内堆积可分为两种情形。第一种坑内堆积可分层，上层往往伴随着大量的红烧土颗粒或成片的红烧土堆积，中下层或下层均有黑烬层或黑灰土；上层堆积往往又放置有大量的大块陶片和玉石器，其中部分陶器可复原，推测原来放置的是完整或较完整的器物。第二种坑内无红烧土堆积，但有大量的灰烬或黑灰土堆积，出土大块陶片也不少。B 类为纯方形坑，边长约 1 米，出土陶片较少，填土为黄灰色土，包含有少量的红烧土颗粒。

两类方形灰坑形状和坑壁均十分规整，分布有序，方向基本上为东北——西南走向，显然不是一般意义的灰坑，且这类方形灰坑在越南分布范围较广，延续时间较长（从冯原文化到其后的铜荳文化都有发现，数量达数百个），因而推测包括义立遗址方形坑在内的这一大批方形坑可能与祭祀有关。

五 墓葬

义立遗址仅清理了一座墓葬，为长方形竖穴土坑墓，墓坑较浅，墓主人葬式为仰身直肢葬，头向东，面朝上，双手平放于身体的左右两侧，仅在墓主人头端放置一件陶豆。

总之，义立遗址冯原文化时期的居民过着定居的农业生活，兼有采集渔猎。建筑主要以干栏式建筑为主，并使用方形坑祭祀。义理遗址的轮制陶器较为发达，火候较高，器表纹饰丰富多彩，说明其制作工艺和技术都达到了很高的水平。石器多通体磨制，其中以磨制的锛和斧最为精致，说明其石器制作技术达到了相当高的水平。义立遗址的玉石装饰品亦较为发达，制作工艺较高，如环、玦、"T" 字形石环表面光滑，富有特征。

第二节　分期与年代

为弄清义立遗址的分期与年代，我们从遗址的地层关系、器物类型学和^{14}C测定三个方面来分析。

一　义立遗址的地层关系

义立遗址的地层经统一后可分为6层，第①、②、③为近现代层，第④层为丁朝至前黎朝文化层[1]，第⑤、⑥层为冯原文化层。涉及冯原文化时期的遗存包括第⑤a、⑤b、⑥层和第④、⑤a、⑤b层下的各遗迹。其从上向下的叠压打破关系如下。

第1组：④→H3、H4、H5、H6、H7、H8、H15、H16、H17[2]

第2组：⑤a→H18、H19、H20、H22、H23、M1

第3组：⑤b→H31

第4组：⑥→H33

以上的叠压打破关系，第4组中，第⑥层和H33出土器物极少，很难挑选出标本，故不能参与类型学分析工作。第3组中，H31仅出土1件夹砂红陶片，而第⑤a和⑤b层出土的器物基本相似，本身可以作为一个层处理。第⑤a层下的H18、H19、H20、H22、H23出土器物极少，很难发现代表性的器物参与类型学分析。这样我们将上述的4组关系重新梳理成如下两组叠压打破关系。

第1组：④→H3、H4、H5、H6、H7、H8、H15、H16、H17

第2组：⑤a→M1

二　器物的类型学分析

上述义立遗址的地层关系是进行类型学分析的基础，为全面的了解义立遗址的文化特征，并对其进行分期研究，就需要从器物类型学方面进行研究。而义立遗址出土器物中最典型的应属于陶器，故我们对义立遗址出土的陶器进行类型学研究。

义立遗址出土的陶器均为圜底器或圈足器，器形主要包括豆、圈足、支座、喇叭口罐、侈口罐、釜、钵、敛口罐、厚唇罐、球、器耳、器鋬等。

钵　依据口部的不同可分为3类型。

A型　敛微口。依据肩部有无凸棱可分为2亚型。

Aa型：口部饰凸棱。如标本T1⑤a：364（图一一三：1）。

Ab型：口部无凸棱。如标本T1⑤a：265（图一一三：3）。

---

〔1〕相当于中国的唐宋文化层。

〔2〕第④层的分布不是水平分布，部分区域缺少第④b层，为统一起见，这里仅用第④层说明。

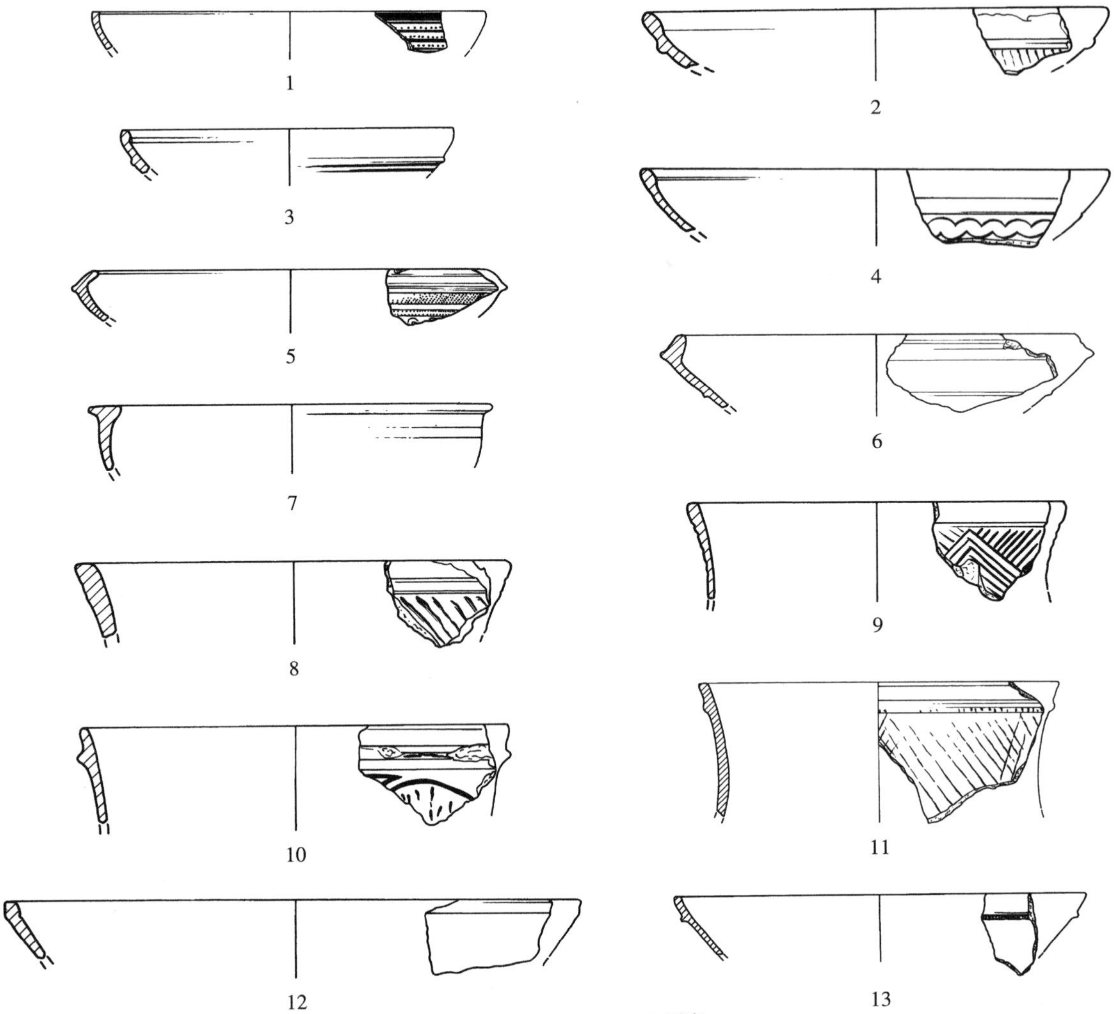

图一一三 陶钵和侈口罐的类型

1. Aa 型钵（T1⑤a：364） 2. Ba 型钵（T2⑤a：60） 3. Ab 型钵（T1⑤a：265） 4. Bb 型钵（T2⑤a：53） 5. CⅠ式钵（T4⑤a：36） 6. CⅡ式钵（H3：71） 7. D 型钵（T1⑤a：365） 8. AⅡ式侈口罐（H5：22） 9. AⅠ式侈口罐（T2⑤a：34） 10. BⅠ式侈口罐（T1⑤a：255） 11. BⅡ式侈口罐（H5：20） 12. CⅠ式侈口罐（T2⑤b：14） 13. CⅡ式侈口罐（H4：13）

B 型 侈口。依据肩部有无凸棱可分为 2 亚型。

Ba 型：口部饰凸棱。如标本 T2⑤a：60（图一一三：2）。

Bb 型：口部无凸棱。如标本 T2⑤a：53（图一一三：4）。

C 型 敛口，鼓肩。依据肩部的不同可分为 2 式。

Ⅰ式：肩部微弧。如标本 T4⑤a：62（图一一三：5）。

Ⅱ式：肩部略折。如标本 H3：71（图一一三：6）。

D 型 圆唇，窄平沿，敛口。如标本 T1⑤a：365（图一一三：7）。

侈口罐 依据形制的不同可分为 3 型。

A 型 颈部无凸棱。依据口部的不同可分为 2 式。

Ⅰ式：圆唇。如标本 T2⑤a：34（图一一三：9）。

Ⅱ式：圆唇近方。如标本 H5：22（图一一三：8）。

B 型　颈部饰凸棱。

Ⅰ式：圆唇。如标本 T1⑤a：255（图一一三：10）。

Ⅱ式：圆唇近方。如标本 H5：20（图一一三：11）。

C 型　方唇。依据口部的不同可分为 2 式。

Ⅰ式：口部微折。如标本 T2⑤b：14（图一一三：12）。

Ⅱ式：口部微敛。如标本 H4：13（图一一三：13）。

喇叭口罐　依据颈部的不同可分为 2 型。

A 型　颈部无凸棱。据口部的不同可分 2 式。

Ⅰ式：尖圆唇。如标本 T1⑤a：20（图一一四：1）。

Ⅱ式：圆唇。如标本 H6：7（图一一四：2）。

B 型　颈部饰一道凸棱。如标本 T1⑤a：189（图一一四：3）。

敛口罐　依据肩部的不同可分为 2 型。

A 型　肩部饰凸棱。如标本 T2⑤a：67（图一一四：5）。

B 型　肩部无凸棱。依据腹部的不同可分为 2 式。

Ⅰ式：斜直腹。如标本 T2⑤a：58（图一一四：4）。

Ⅱ式：鼓腹。如标本 H4：18（图一一四：6）。

厚唇罐　依据形制的不同可分为 2 型。

A 型　侈口。如标本 T3⑤a：19（图一一四：8）。

B 型　直口。如标本 T3⑤a：18（图一一四：7）。

釜　依据腹部的不同可分为 2 型。

A 型　圆鼓腹略垂。如标本 H3：81（图一一四：10）。

B 型　圆鼓腹。如标本 H3：73（图一一四：9）。

豆　依据形制的不同可分为 3 型。

A 型　高柄豆。如标本 M1：1。

B 型　矮柄豆。如标本 H3：72。

C 型　六边形豆。如标本 H6：5。

圈足　依据形制的不同可分为 3 型。

A 型　桶状，依据形制的不同可分为 2 式。

Aa Ⅰ式：覆盆状。如标本 T1⑤a：94（图一一五：1）。

Aa Ⅱ式：覆盆状，足尖外侈。如标本 H4：11（图一一五：2）。

Ab 型：直桶状。如标本 H3：31（图一一五：3）。

B 型　喇叭状圈足。依据形制的不同可分为 2 式。

Ⅰ式：足尖外折。如标本 T1⑤a：180（图一一五：4）。

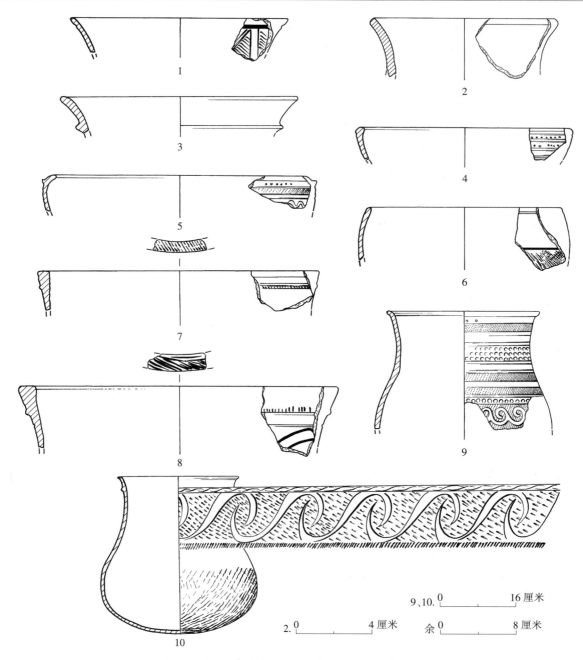

图一一四　陶喇叭口罐、敛口罐和釜的类型

1. A I 式喇叭口罐（T1⑤a：20）2. A II 式喇叭口罐（H6：7）　　3. B 型喇叭口罐（T1⑤a：189）　　4. B I 式敛口罐（T2⑤a：58）　　5. A 型敛口罐（T2⑤a：67）　　6. B II 式敛口罐（H4：18）　　7. B 型厚唇罐（T3⑤a：18）　　8. A 型厚唇罐（T3⑤a：19）　　9. B 型釜（H3：73）　　10. A 型釜（H3：81）

II 式：足尖外撇。如标本 H3：71（图一一五：6）。

C 型　浅盘状圈足。依据形制的不同可分为 2 亚型。

Ca 型：足尖内折呈直角。

I 式：圈足与足尖结合处呈弧状。如标本 T2⑤a：56（图一一五：8）。

II 式：圈足与足尖结合处呈直角状。如标本 H4：15（图一一五：7）。

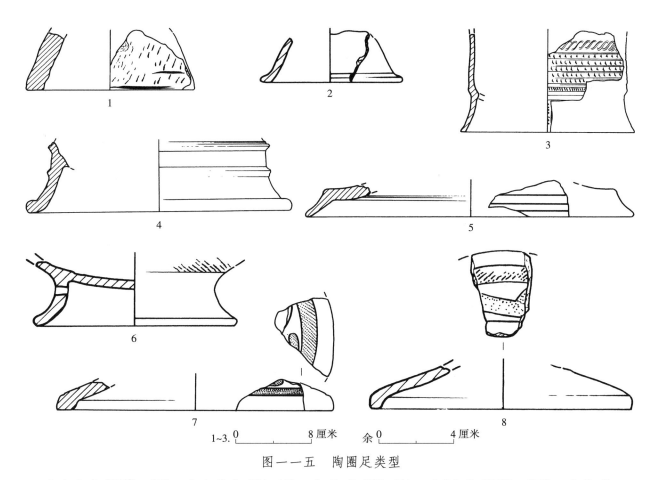

图一一五　陶圈足类型

1. AaⅠ式（T1⑤a：94）　　2. AaⅡ式（H4：11）　　3. Ab式（H3：31）　　4. BⅠ式（T1⑤a：180）　　5. Cb式
（T2⑤a：28）　　6. BⅡ式（H3：31）　　7. CaⅡ式（H4：15）　　8. CaⅠ式（T2⑤a：56）

Cb 型　足尖外折呈钝角。如标本 T2⑤a：28（图一一五：5）。

支座　均体呈柱状，椭圆形底，器身弯曲。依据形制的不同可分为 3 式。

Ⅰ式：一侧饰弓形耳。如标本 T1⑤a：57（图一一六：1）。

Ⅱ式：一侧饰柄状耳。如标本 H4：31（图一一六：2）。

Ⅲ式：无耳。如标本 H3：13（图一一六：3）。

纺轮　依据形制的不同可分为 2 型。

A 型　体呈塔状，中有一孔。如标本 T1⑤a：4（图一一六：4）。

B 型　体呈柄状，中有一孔。如标本 T1⑤a：18（图一一六：7）。

器耳　依据形制的不同可分为 2 型。

A 型　弓形耳较大。如标本 H5：18（图一一六：5）。

B 型　弓形耳较小。如标本 H5：17（图一一六：6）。

器鋬　依据形制的不同可分为 3 型。

A 型　呈舌状。如标本 T1⑤a：33（图一一六：8）。

B 型　呈柱状。如标本 T1⑤a：59（图一一六：10）。

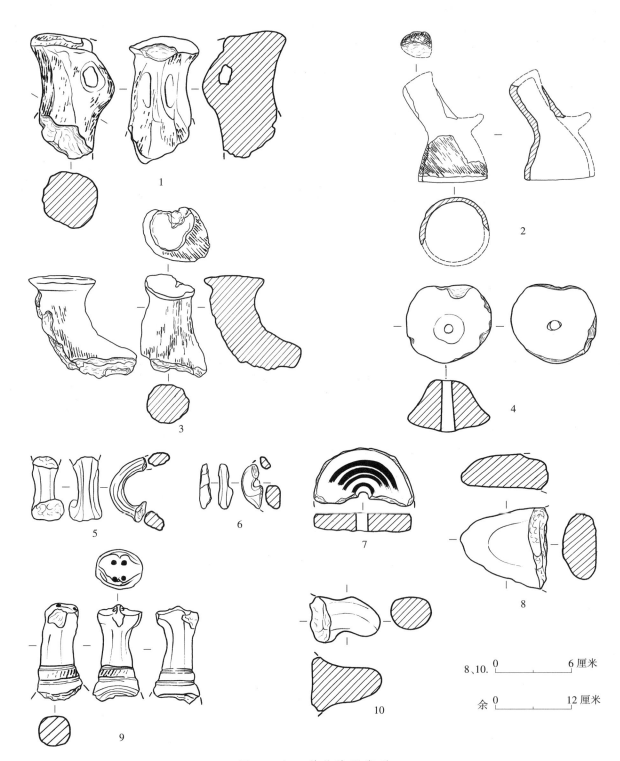

图一一六 其他陶器类型

1. Ⅰ式支座（T1⑤a：57）　2. Ⅱ式支座（H4：31）　3. Ⅲ式支座（H3：13）　4. A型纺轮（T1⑤a：4）　5. A型器耳（H5：18）　6. B型器耳（H5：17）　7. B型纺轮（T1⑤a：18）　8. A型器鋬（T1⑤a：33）　9. C型器鋬（T3⑤a：4）　10. B型器鋬（T1⑤a：59）

C 型　呈狗头状。如标本 T3⑤a：4（图一一六：9）。

球　均呈球状。

我们将上述的地层叠压打破关系和地层中出土器物组合放入附表一中，可以看出能够参与分期的器物共六类（圈足、支座、喇叭口罐、侈口罐、釜、钵）。再依据地层叠压打破关系和出土器物组合，将遗址分为前、后两段。前、后两段贯穿延续的器物占绝大多数，说明前、后两段是一脉相承、连续发展的。从整体上看，前段以第⑤a、第⑤b 层、M1 和第⑤层下的灰坑为代表，出土的陶器数量和器类最多，是该遗址的主要遗存。后段以第④层下的灰坑（H3、H4、H5、H6、H7、H8、H15、H16、H17、H18）为代表，出土的陶器器类数量和器类明显减少，是遗址的晚期阶段。

三　年代

要判断义立遗址的年代，可通过与周边区域的对比和^{14}C 检测来判断。从出土器物来看，前段中 M1 出土的陶豆与朋丘（Go Bong）遗址〔1〕出土的陶豆（02XRH1L7b4：321）相似，出土的 Aa 型、Ab 型、Ba 型、Bb 型、C Ⅰ式、D 型钵，A Ⅰ式喇叭口罐，Ⅰ式支座等与朋丘遗址出土的同类器物相似，但似乎要比朋丘遗址晚。后段中 H3 出土的釜（H3：81、73）、豆（H3：72）、六边形豆（H6：5）、支座（H4：31）、Aa Ⅱ式和 Ab 型圈足等与越南仁村〔2〕（Xom Ren）出土的同类器物相似。从出土器物与周边文化的对比上可以看出，其年代介于朋丘遗址至仁村遗址之间，但更接近于仁村遗址。而朋丘遗址和仁村遗址代表冯原文化的早、中期，故义立遗址的年代当在冯原文化的中期偏早阶段。

同时在本次发掘中，我们也采集了多个^{14}C 标本，分别在北京和河内进行了测试，中国社会科学院考古研究所碳十四实验室树轮校正年代：距今 3740～3520 年；北京大学碳十四实验室树轮校正年代：距今 3490～3770 年；越南考古学院实验室树轮校正年代为距今 3490～ 3890 年。因此，从出土器物的比较和^{14}C 来看，义立遗址的年代在冯原文化的中期偏早阶段，其绝对年代当在距今 3500～3700 年之间。

第三节　与周边文化或遗址之间的关系

一　与越南冯原文化诸遗址之间的关系

冯原文化因 1959 年冯原遗址的发掘而命名，迄今为止，已调查发现 100 余处冯原文化时期的遗址，其中 70 余处经过正式发掘。关于冯原文化的分期，以越南的何文瑨和韩

〔1〕 Pham Ly Huong：*Do Gom Go Bong*，Luan Van Tot Nghiep DHTHHN，tu lieu Khoa Lich su，1967；Han Van Tan，Han Van Khan：*Bao cao so bo hai lan khai quai di chi Go Bong*，*Thuong Nong*，*Phu Tho* trong TBKHDHTHHN tap Ⅴ，1970.

〔2〕 Nguyen Thi Kim Dung，Tang Chung：*Khai quat lan* Ⅱ *di chi Xom Ren*（*Phu Tho*）*Dang Hong Son*：*Bao cao*，*trong NPHMVKCH nam* 2003，2003；Ha Van Tan：*Thong bao ket qua khai quat di chi Xom Ren*，trong TBKH DHTHHN，1970.

文恩最有代表性。何文瑨将冯原文化分为朋丘（Go Bong）—仁村（Xom Ren）—铜荳（Dong Dao）的下层[1]，而韩文恩依据陶器纹饰的变化将其分为朋丘（Go Bong）—冯原（Phung Nguyen）—栾河（Lung Hoa）[2]。而义立遗址出土的器物与冯原文化的仁村遗址和冯原遗址较为接近，且该遗址处于冯原文化仁村阶段（或冯原阶段），属于一个大的文化系统。

二　与中国西南和华南地区各遗址或文化的关系

（一）与澜沧江流域新石器时代文化的关系

澜沧江流域的新石器时代文化主要集中在云南的大理州和保山市，主要包括大理州的新光、保山市蒲缥二台坡、蒲缥孔家山、道街里坝子和潞江旧城等遗址，其中以新光遗址最有代表性。1993 年，云南省文物考古研究所对该遗址进行了发掘，发掘面积 1000 平方米，清理的遗迹主要包括房址、灰坑、火塘和沟等；出土器物主要是石器和陶器，其中石器 642 件，主要包括锛、斧、矛、箭镞、凿、刀、镰、锥、纺轮等；其中锛数量最多，最具代表性。陶器以夹砂陶为主，还有一定数量的泥质陶。陶色以灰色为主，褐色次之，还有少量的红色。陶器纹饰复杂，主要包括附加堆纹、刻划网格纹、压印网格纹、波浪纹、水波纹、点线纹、三角形纹、回纹、乳丁纹等。器形主要包括罐、壶、钵、盘、缸、杯等[3]。其年代距今约 3700 年，比义立遗址的年代略早。该遗址流行的以锛为主要的生产工具，与义立遗址相似；同时陶器上丰富多彩的纹饰，特别是刻划纹和戳压纹组成的复合纹饰与义立遗址极为接近。作为连接成都平原与越南北部的云南地区，新光遗址无疑具有两种不同文化的特征，从出土陶器来看，其形制与成都平原地区较为接近，但纹饰更接近越南北部的冯原文化，而生产工具则接近越南北部的冯原文化。与此相近的遗存还包括云南永仁菜园子和磨盘地遗址[4]，这两个遗址出土的陶器纹饰和方形灰坑亦与义立遗址接近。

（二）与广西感驮岩遗址的关系

广西地区与越南北部接壤，两地山水相连，河海相同，自然地理和生态环境都十分相似。而广西南部诸河流域与越南的红河流域都位于北部湾沿岸地区，陆路和海路交通便利，史前时期无国界，史前时期的广西与越南红河流域的人类和文化的交往也十分便利，因此有必要将这两个相邻地区的考古学文化进行比较研究。广西地区目前发现与越南义立遗址接近的遗址为感驮岩遗址，该遗址位于广西那坡县县城北部，是一处洞穴遗址。1997～1998 年，广西壮族自治区文物工作队对该遗址进行了发掘，发掘面积 380 平方米。该遗址分为两期，其中第二期与义立遗址较为接近，出土的石器以斧、锛为主，出土的陶器纹饰丰富，以绳纹为主，还有一定数量的刻划纹和戳压纹，器形以圜底器和圈足器为主，流行罐、簋形器、釜、

〔1〕 ［越］何文晋著，［日］菊池诚一译：《ベトナムの考古文化》，（日）六兴出版社，1991 年。
〔2〕 Han Van Khan：*Van Hoa Phung Nguyen*，Nha Xuat Ban Dai Hoc Quoc Gia Ha Noi，2005。
〔3〕 云南省文物考古研究所等：《云南永平新光遗址发掘报告》，《考古学报》2002 年第 2 期。
〔4〕 云南省文物考古研究所等：《云南永仁菜园子、磨盘地遗址 2001 年发掘报告》，《考古学报》2003 年第 2 期。

钵等[1]。从其出土的石器和陶器看，其与义立遗址较为接近。这也说明，在冯原文化的中期，广西的感驮岩遗址和冯原文化并驾齐驱，相互影响，并不断地对周边区域特别是珠江流域产生重大影响。

（三）与三星堆文化的关系

三星堆文化以广汉三星堆遗址二、三期遗存命名，主要分布于成都平原至三峡内外这一狭长的区域，其典型遗址就是三星堆遗址。20 世纪 80 年代以来，四川省文物考古研究院对三星堆遗址进行了多次考古发掘，发现了夏商时期规模宏大的城址、宫殿性建筑基址群、祭祀礼仪性设施等重要文化遗存，特别是 1、2 号祭祀坑，出土了众多的青铜器、金器、玉器、石器、象牙、海贝和陶器，包括礼器如青铜尊、青铜罍、青铜盘、玉璧、玉瑗、玉璋，仪仗用具如青铜戈、玉戈等，宗教性用具如青铜神树、青铜人像、青铜面具等。三星堆遗址是夏商时期蜀国的政治、经济、宗教和文化中心[2]，以三星堆遗址为代表的三星堆文化对周边文化产生了重大影响，越南冯原文化亦受到其深刻影响，冯原文化中出土的玉戈、玉璋、T 字形玉环、玉璧等礼仪性用具就与三星堆遗址出土的同类器物非常相似。越南义立遗址出土的陶器虽多表现为土著文化因素，但一些玉石礼器和遗迹现象，如 T 字形玉环、石璧形器以及方形灰坑等则体现出与三星堆文化的某些相似性和一致性。

第四节　从三星堆到冯原

在张骞凿空西域、开通北方丝绸之路以前，南方丝绸之路一直是通往东南亚、西亚的唯一通道。这个通道所发挥的作用，可以追溯到商周时期，也就是越南的冯原文化时期。

商周时期，在南方丝绸之路南边的越南冯原文化发现的玉戈、玉璋、T 字形玉环、玉璧等与长江上游地区的三星堆遗址出土的同类器物，无论是器形、制造工艺、纹饰等均极为相似，这类器物在台湾、香港等地区亦有发现，传播远，影响深。同时三星堆和金沙遗址均出土大量的象牙、海贝，这些器物极有可能来源于西亚或东南亚地区。这也表明，从长江上游至东南亚地区的文化通道早在商周时期就已经形成。

从四川至越南的文化通道，较为快捷的当属南方丝绸之路。南方丝绸之路以成都为起点，向南分为东、西两路。西路沿牦牛道南下至大理，东路从成都平原南行经五尺道至大理。两道在大理汇为一道继续西行，经保山、腾冲，抵达缅甸密支那；或从保山出瑞丽进抵缅甸八莫，跨入外域。南方丝绸之路国外段有西线和东线两条：西线即"蜀身毒道"，从成都平原出云南至缅甸，西行至印度、巴基斯坦、阿富汗至中亚、西亚，这条纵贯亚洲的交通线，是古代欧亚大陆最长、历史最悠久的对外交通大动脉之一。南方丝绸之路国外段东线包括从四川经云南元江下红河至越南的红河道，和从蜀经夜郎至番禺（今广州）的牂牁道，经由此道发

---

〔1〕　广西壮族自治区文物工作队等：《广西那坡县感驮岩遗址发掘简报》，《考古》2003 年第 10 期。

〔2〕　四川省文物考古研究院：《四川考古 60 年》，《四川文物》2009 年第 6 期。

展了西南与东南沿海地区的关系[1]。如果我们将视野放得更广一些,就会发现在从四川成都至东南亚地区,特别是越南,沿线的遗址中有很多相似的文化因素,这些文化因素中又以刻划纹陶器最有代表性,从四川的凉山州安宁河流域,到云南大理的新光,再到云南的保山市,最后到广西的感驮岩和越南的冯原文化这样一个广大的地区,均存在大量的以刻划纹为主的陶器,就是这条线路存在的直接体现。同时也表明,在中国的商周时期,从长江上游至东南亚地区,出现了不同层次、不同规模的文化交流活动,这些交流活动增进了各个区域之间互动。

总之,本次发掘是中越两国之间进行的首次联合考古发掘,它对于研究越南北部青铜时代早期文化以及其与中国华南、西南地区青铜时代文化的关系和交流、了解三星堆文化的辐射范围、去向等具有重要意义。同时通过本次发掘,我们与越南文物及考古学界建立了广泛的联系,双方增进了了解和友谊,为今后进一步开展合作与交流打下了良好的基础。

---

[1] 段渝:《中国西南的对外交通——先秦两汉的南方丝绸之路》,《历史研究》2009 年第 1 期。

附　表

附表一　义立遗址出土陶器组合表

单位＼器类	豆	圈足	支座	喇叭口罐	侈口罐	厚唇罐	釜	敛口罐	钵	器耳	器鋬	球	纺轮
T1⑤a		AaⅠ，BⅠ，CaⅠ，Cb	Ⅰ	AⅠ，B	AⅠ，BⅠ	A，B		A，BⅠ	Aa，Ab，Ba，CⅠ，D	A，B	A，B		A，B
T1⑤b		AaⅠ，BⅠ，Ab，CaⅠ			AⅠ	A，B			Ab，CⅠ				
T2⑤a		AaⅠ，BⅠ，CaⅠ，Cb	Ⅰ	AⅠ，B	AⅠ，BⅠ	A，B		A，BⅠ	Aa，Ab，Ba		A，B		
T2⑤b		AaⅠ，BⅠ，Ab，CaⅠ	Ⅰ	AⅠ	AⅠ，BⅠ，CⅠ	A，B				B			B
T3⑤a		AaⅠ，BⅠ，CaⅠ	Ⅰ	AⅠ	AⅠ，BⅠ	A，B		BⅠ	Aa，Ab，Ba		C		
T4⑤a		AaⅠ，BⅠ，Ab，CaⅠ		AⅠ	AⅠ，BⅠ	A，B			Aa，Ab，Ba				A，B
T5⑤a		AaⅠ，BⅠ，Ab，CaⅠ	Ⅰ	AⅠ	AⅠ，BⅠ	A，B			Aa，Ab，Ba，CⅠ				
T7⑤a		AaⅠ，BⅠ，Ab，CaⅠ		AⅠ		B			Ab，Ba				
M1	A												
H3	B	Ab，BⅡ，	Ⅲ			A，B	√		CⅡ			√	
H4	C	AaⅡ，Ab，BⅡ，CaⅡ	Ⅱ		CⅡ	A，B		BⅡ	Aa，Ab，Bb			√	
H5			Ⅱ	AⅡ	BⅡ，CⅡ				Ab	A，B	B	√	
H6			Ⅱ	AⅡ		B			Aa		A		
H7		AaⅡ		AⅡ									
H8		BⅡ		AⅡ			√						
H15							√						
H17						B							
H19		√											

注：大写字母表示型，小写字母表示亚型，罗马字母表示式，√表示未参与分型分式。

附表二　义立遗址 ^{14}C 测定结果

样品编号	原编号	样品	^{14}碳年代	树轮校正后年代（BC）
Zk-3316	H3	木炭	3314±30	1680BC（3.7%）1670BC 1630BC（64.5%）1520BC
Zk-3317	H18	木炭	3394±30	1740BC（47.2%）1680BC 1670BC（21.0%）1630BC
BA0759	T7⑤a	木炭	3310±40	1630BC-1520BC（68.2%） 1690BC-1490BC（95.4%）
BA0760	T4⑤a	木炭	3375±45	1740BC-1610BC（68.2%） 1770BC-1520BC（95.4%）
HNK-330	H3	木炭	3320±50	1680BC-1520BC（68.2%） 1740BC-1490BC（95.4%）
HNK-331	H3	木炭	3410±70	1880BC-1610BC（68.2%） 1890BC-1520BC（95.4%）
HNK-333	T2⑤a	木炭	3560±105	2040BC-1740BC（68%） 2200BC-1600BC（95.4%）
HNK-334	T2⑤a 下 D7	木炭	3680±160	2300BC-1750BC（68%） 2600BC-1600BC（95.4%）

注：1. 编号为 Zk-3316 和 Zk-3317 的两个标本 ^{14}C 由中国社会科学院考古研究所碳十四实验室测定，所用 ^{14}C 半衰期为 5568 年，BP 为距 1950 年的年代。

2. 编号为 BA0759 和 BA0760 的两个标本 ^{14}C 由北京大学加速器质谱实验室测定，所用 ^{14}C 半衰期为 5568 年，BP 为距 1950 年的年代。

3. 编号为 HNK-330 和 HNK-331 的两个标本 ^{14}C 由越南国家博物馆测定，所用 ^{14}C 半衰期为 5570 年。

附表三　义立遗址灰坑和沟登记表

编号	位置	年代	开口层位	平面形制	坑壁	坑底	尺寸	土质土色及包含物	出土器物	备注
H1	T2西北部	近现代	①下	前方后圆	粗糙不平	平底	长1.67，宽0.28~70.2，深0.1米	灰黑色土，土质疏松	出土少量的瓷片	
H2	T3东北部	近现代	①下	椭圆形	较平整	锅底状	长1.86，宽1.54，深0.64米	灰黑色土，土质疏松	出土少量的陶片和瓷片、铁器等物	打破H3、H4
H3	T2东北部	冯原文化	④a下	上圆下方	平整较直	平底	上部圆形，直径约1.4米；下部方形，边长1，深0.8米	坑内堆积可分3层。第①层为灰黑色土，土质疏松，本层的北部堆积着大量的红烧土，炭屑，并含有大量的陶片和少量的石块，厚16~20厘米。第②层为黄色粘土，土质较硬，包含有较多的铁锈。由东北向西南倾斜堆积。厚24~30厘米。第③层为灰色土，土质疏松，包含有少量的陶器。由东北向西南倾斜堆积，厚21~27厘米	出土器物包括石器和陶器，以陶器为主，玉石器较少。玉石器主要是镯、石铲、磨石和刮削器。陶器以夹细砂红褐陶、红陶和褐陶为主，纹饰发达，以绳纹为主，还有刻划纹、戳引纹、回弦纹、压印纹、梳刷纹等。尤以在各种刻划纹带内填充篦齿状或篦点状戳印纹的装饰风格最具特点；集多种纹饰在单个陶器上的复合纹饰基为流行；纹饰图案主要有S形纹、几何形纹、圆圈纹、水波纹等。陶器口部多为敛口和侈口，器类主要是圆底器和圈足器，包括球、豆、钵、圈足、支座、釜等	被H2打破

（续附表三）

编号	位置	年代	开口层位	形制与结构				尺寸	土质土色及包含物	出土器物	备注
				平面形制	坑壁	坑底					
H4	T2 西北部	冯原文化	④a 下	长方形	平整较直	平底	长 1.4、宽 1.2、深 0.4～0.6 米	坑内堆积可分 3 层。第①层为分布在灰坑中间厚 0.06 米的红烧土堆积，并夹杂有大量陶片，东部有一陶钵。第②层为深灰黑色土，土质疏松，包含有较多的陶片；第③层为黄褐色土，土质疏松，包含物较少，厚 0.1～0.24 米	中在红烧土的北部有一陶支座。尤以 0.1～0.2 米，厚 0.1～0.2 米，土 其 出土器物主要是陶器和石器，其中以陶器为主，石器数量较少。石器主要是锛、球、范、砺石等。陶器以夹细砂红褐陶、红陶和褐陶为主，纹饰发达，以绳纹为主，还有刻划纹、截引文、回弦纹、压印纹、梳刷纹、附加堆纹等。尤以在各种刻划纹带内填充箆齿状或箆点状戳印纹的装饰风格最具特点；集多种纹饰在单个陶器上的复合纹饰甚为流行；纹饰图案主要有 S 形纹、几何形纹、圆圈纹、水波纹等。陶器口部多为敛口和侈口，器形包括球、支座、钵、移口罐、直口罐、圈足等	被 H2 打破
H5	T2 西北部和 T1 的东隔梁下	冯原文化	④a 下	上圆下方	平整较直	平底	上部圆形，直径 1.6、深 0.2 米；下部方形，边长 1.2、深 1 米	坑内堆积可分 3 层。第①层为灰黑色土，土质疏松，由西南向东北倾斜堆积。包含有大量的石器和少量的陶片。第②层黄色粘土，土质较硬，包含有较多的铁锈。由东北向西南倾斜堆积，厚 0.1～0.15 米。第③层为灰色土，土质疏松，包含有少量的陶器，由东北向西南倾斜堆积，厚 0.2～0.3 米	出土器物主要是陶器和石器，其中以陶器为主，石器数量较少。石器主要是刮削器和石核。陶器以夹细砂红褐和红陶为主，纹饰发达，以绳纹为主，还有刻划纹、截引文、回弦纹、压印纹、梳刷纹、附加堆纹	被 H34 打破

（续附表三）

编号	位置	年代	开口层位	形制与结构			尺寸	土质土色及包含物	出土器物	备注
				平面形制	坑壁	坑底				
									等。陶器口部多为敛口和侈口，喇叭形口和直口圈足器，器形主要是圈足器包括球、支座、侈口罐、钵、敛口罐、直口罐、圈足等	
H6	T2 西南角	冯原文化	④a 下	上圆下方	平整较直	平底	上部圆形，直径1.1米；下部方形，暴露的边长0.88，深0.9米	坑内堆积可分为4层。第①层为灰黑色土，土质疏松。包含有大量红烧土块、炭屑，陶片和少量的石器，厚0.32~0.4米。第②层黄色黏土，土质较纯，包含有较少量的铁锈、陶片的东北角，仅存在于灰坑的东北角，厚0~0.18米。第③层为灰色土，包含有极少量陶片，厚0.13~0.33米。第④层，灰褐色土，土质较硬，包含有少量的炭屑、炭屑和黄褐色颗粒，厚0.18~0.21厘米。此层之下为黄褐色生土	出土器物主要是陶器和石器，其中以陶器为主，石器数量极少，陶器以夹细砂红褐陶和红陶为主，纹饰发达，以绳纹为主。还有刻划文、戳引文、回弦纹、压印纹、梳刷纹，附加堆纹等。陶器口部多为敛口和侈口次之。陶器口部多较多，喇叭形口器、直口罐、喇叭口罐、厚唇罐等	
H7	T2 东部	冯原文化	⑤a 下	圆形	平整较直	平底	直径1.2，深0.4米	坑内堆积为灰色土，土质疏松，包含有少量的陶片，红烧土颗粒和炭屑	出土器物极少，以陶器为主，仅有1件玉器。陶质以夹细砂陶为主，还有少量的夹粗砂和泥质陶，陶色以红色和红褐色为主。纹饰以细纹、绳纹、刻划纹、戳印纹，器形主要是喇叭口罐和敛口罐。器形主要是喇叭口罐和圈足	

（续附表三）

编号	位置	年代	开口层位	形制与结构			尺寸	土质土色及包含物	出土器物	备注
				平面形制	坑壁	坑底				
H8	T2 东隔梁下	冯原文化	⑤a 下	长方形	平整较直	平底	长 0.9、宽 0.78、深 0.5 米	坑内堆积可分为两层。上层为灰色土，土质疏松，包含少量的陶片和红烧土颗粒，厚 0.14 米。下层为黄褐色黏土，土质较硬，包含有少量的红烧土颗粒，厚 0.36 米	出土陶片极少，以夹细砂陶为主，还有少量的泥质陶，陶色以红陶和红褐陶为主，纹饰主要为绳纹、凹弦纹、篦点纹、刻划纹等。器形仅见圈足和钵	
H9	T5 东北角，部分叠压于该探方的东隔梁下	近现代	③下	圆形	直桶状	平底	直径 0.59、深 0.9 米	灰黑色土，土质疏松	出土少量的陶片和瓷片	
H10	T5 西北角，部分叠压于该探方的北隔梁下	近现代	③下	椭圆形	直桶状	平底	长 0.48、宽 0.13、深 0.55 米	灰黑色土，土质疏松	出土少量的陶片和瓷片	
H11	T5 南壁下	近现代	③下	椭圆形	直桶状	平底	长 0.59、宽 0.28、深 0.73 米	灰色土，土质疏松	出土少量瓷片	
H12	T5 东南部	近现代	③下	椭圆形	直桶状	平底	径 0.68 ~ 0.8、深 0.55 米	灰色土，土质疏松	出土少量瓷片	
H13	T5 东部中，部分叠压该探方东隔梁下	近现代	③下	椭圆形	直桶状	平底	径 0.48 ~ 0.36、深 0.26 米	灰色土，土质疏松	出土少量瓷片	

（续附表三）

编号	位置	年代	开口层位	形制与结构 平面形制	坑壁	坑底	尺寸	土质土色及包含物	出土器物	备注
H14	T5西北部	近现代	③下	椭圆形	粗糙不平	高低不平	径0.36~0.48，深0.26米	浅灰色土，土质紧密	出土少量瓷片	
H15	T4东隔梁下	冯原文化	④a下	不规则长方形	直桶状	平底	长0.8、宽0.64、深0.2~0.36米	坑内填土为灰黑色土，土质疏松，包含有少量的红烧土颗粒和炭屑	共出土陶片较少。陶片以夹细砂陶为主，夹粗砂陶较少，陶色以红褐、褐色为主，还有少量的红、灰褐、黑褐。纹饰以绳纹为主，还有少量的回弦纹、篦点纹。器形主要是圈足器和圆底器，可辨器形有钵和釜	
H16	T5西部	冯原文化	④a下	不规则长方形	弧壁	锅底状	长2.14、宽1.8、深0.5米	坑内填土为灰黑色土，土质疏松，包含有少量的红烧土颗粒和炭屑	出土器物除1件玉器外，余者均为陶片。陶片以夹细砂陶为主，还有一定数量的黄褐、灰褐、红，以红褐和黑褐陶。纹饰以绳纹为主，还有少量的回弦纹、刻划纹、几何形纹、篦点纹等。器形主要是圈足器和圆底器，可辨器形有钵、釜、侈口罐等	

（续附表三）

编号	位置	年代	开口层位	形制与结构			尺寸	土质土色及包含物	出土器物	备注
				平面形制	坑壁	坑底				
H17	T5	冯原文化	④b 下	长方形	直桶状	平底	长 1.14、宽 1、深0.72 米	坑内填土为灰黑色土，土质疏松，包含有少量的红烧土颗粒和炭屑	出土器物均为陶片。陶片以夹细砂陶和夹粗砂陶为主，仅有少量的泥质陶，陶色以红褐为主，还有一定数量的黄褐、灰褐、红、褐和黑褐陶。纹饰以绳纹为主，还有少量的凹弦纹、刻划纹、篦点纹、几何形纹等。器形主要是圈足器，可辨器形有钵、直口罐等	被 H13 打破
H18	T5 西部和 T4 的东隔梁下	冯原文化	⑤a 下	不规则长方形	坑壁直	平底	长 1.3、宽 1 ~1.4、深0.6 米	坑内填土为灰黑色土，土质疏松，包含有少量的红烧土颗粒和炭屑	出土器物均为陶片。陶片以夹细砂陶为主，还有少量的夹粗砂陶，陶色以红和红褐为主，还有一定数量的黄褐、灰褐、褐和黑褐陶。纹饰以凹弦纹和篦点纹为主，还有少量的绳纹、刻划纹、几何形纹等。可辨器形有钵、侈口罐等	被 H15 和 D5、D6 打破
H19	T5 东部	冯原文化	⑤a 下	长方形	坑壁较直	平底	残长 1.1、残宽 0.8、深 0.22 米	坑内填土为灰黑色土，土质疏松，包含有少量的红烧土颗粒和炭屑	出土器物均为陶片。陶片以夹细砂陶和夹粗砂陶为主，陶色以红陶为主，还有一定数量的黄褐、灰褐、红褐和黑褐。纹饰以绳纹为主，还有少量的刻划纹和凹弦纹。可辨器形仅见圈足器	

（续附表三）

编号	位置	年代	开口层位	形制与结构			尺寸	土质土色及包含物	出土器物	备注
				平面形制	坑壁	坑底				
H20	T3 北隔梁下	冯原文化	⑤a 下	不规则椭圆形	粗糙不平整	高低不平	长 1.2、宽 0.2 ~ 0.9、深 1.48 ~ 1.8 米	坑内堆积为灰黑色土，土质疏松，包含有少量的陶片	出土器物主要是陶器，陶片以夹细砂陶为主，夹粗砂较少，陶色以红色和红褐色为主，黑褐次之，黄褐和褐色较少，纹饰以绳纹为主，还有少量的刻划纹、篦点纹、戳刺纹、弦纹等。器形主要是钵和罐	
H21	T3 东北部	冯原文化	⑤a 下	圆形	较平整	锅底状	直径 1.6、深 0.64 米	坑内堆积为灰黑色土，土质疏松，包含有极少量的陶片	出土少量的夹细砂红陶片	被 D1 和 D25 打破
H22	T3 东北部	冯原文化	⑤a 下	不规则长方形	粗糙不平	高低不平	长 0.7、宽 0.5 ~ 0.76、深 0.2 ~ 0.44 米	坑内堆积为灰黑色土，土质疏松，包含有少量的陶片	出土器物主要是陶器。以夹细砂红陶和红褐陶为主，还有少量的夹细砂黑褐陶、褐陶、泥质红褐陶等，纹饰以绳纹为主，戳印纹、圆圈纹、凹弦纹、凸棱纹、S 形纹较少。器形主要为钵、罐、支座、圈足器	被 D14 打破
H23	T3 西北部	现代	①下	长条形	粗糙不平	高低不平	长 1、宽 0.76、深 0.06 ~ 0.32 米	灰黑色土，土质疏松	包含少量的瓷片	打破 H24

（续附表三）

编号	位置	年代	开口层位	形制与结构			尺寸	土质土色及包含物	出土器物	备注
				平面形制	坑壁	坑底				
H24	T3 西北部	现代	①下	椭圆形	较平整	平底	长 0.5、宽 0.32、深 0.46～0.63 米	浅灰色土，土质紧密	包含少量瓷片	被 H23 打破
H26	T4 中部偏南	近现代	③下	近圆形	直桶状	平底	直径 0.8、深 0.57 米	浅灰色土，土质紧密	出土少量的瓷片	
H27	T4 东南部	近现代	③下	近圆形	直桶状	平底	直径 0.58、深 0.45 米	浅灰色土，土质紧密	出土少量的瓷片	
H28	T4 西北部	近现代	③下	近圆形	直桶状	平底	直径 0.54～0.58、深 0.58～0.66 米	浅灰色土，土质紧密	出土少量的瓷片	
H29	T4 北隔梁下	近现代	③下	近圆形	直桶状	平底	直径 0.8、深 0.74 米	浅灰色土，土质紧密	出土少量的瓷片	
H30	T4 东隔梁下	近现代	③下	近圆形	直桶状	平底	直径 0.72、深 0.52～0.56 米	浅灰色土，土质紧密	出土少量的瓷片	
H31	T4 南部	冯原文化	⑤b 下	不规则长方形	壁面不平整	平底	长 1.4、宽 0.56～0.7、深 0.42 米	坑内填土为红褐色黏土，土质结构紧密。	仅一小片夹砂红褐陶片	
H32	T7 东南部	近现代	③下	近圆形	直桶状	平底	直径 0.62、深 0.44～0.5 米	浅灰色土，土质紧密	少量的夹砂红褐陶片和瓷片	
H33	T7 西部中	冯原文化	⑥下	近圆形	直桶状	平底	直径 0.62、深 0.34～0.5 米	黄褐色土，土质紧密	未出土任何器物	

（续附表三）

编号	位置	年代	开口层位	形制与结构				土质土色及包含物	出土器物	备注
				平面形制	坑壁	坑底	尺寸			
H34	T2东隔梁下	近现代	①下	圆形	直筒状	锅底状	直径0.6、深0.68米	灰黑色土，土质疏松	出土少量的陶片、瓷片等物	打破H5
G1	T1南部	近现代	②下	不规则长条形	壁面不平整	高低不平	长4.9、宽1.7～2.8、深0.85米	沟内填土可分为三层。第①层，局部分布，灰褐色土，土质疏松，厚0～15厘米；第②层为灰黑色土，土质疏松，厚50厘米；第③层为黄褐色土，土质疏松，厚20厘米	出土少量的陶片、瓷片、瓦片、铁器、石器等	
G2	T7中部	近现代	②下	不规则长条形	壁面不平整	高低不平	长4.86、宽0.66、深0.9米	灰褐色土，土质疏松	出土少量的陶片、瓷片、瓦片、铁器、石器等	
G3	T4西南部	近现代	③下	不规则长条形	壁面不平整	高低不平	长3.67、宽0.3～0.73、深0.15米	灰色土，土质疏松	出土少量的陶片、瓷片、瓦片、铁器等物	

附表四　义立遗址出土陶器陶系统计表

陶质 / 陶色 / 数量 / 单位	细砂陶							粗砂陶							泥质磨光陶					总计	绳纹	弦纹	刻划纹	坑点纹	梳刷纹	圆圈纹	叶脉纹	复合纹饰	素面
	红	红褐	褐	黑褐	黄褐	灰褐	合计	红	红褐	褐	黑褐	黄褐	灰褐	合计	红	红褐	褐	黑褐	合计										
T1⑤a	475	5138	17		14	172	5816	104	139	393	42	325	75	1078		128	46		174	7068	1921	79	84	2	1	1	2	52	4926
T1⑤b		11				33	44	4				18		22	16	10	3	1	30	96	37	6	2			2		3	46
T2⑤a	901	260		373	243		1777	183		95		109		387	165	25		80	270	2434	513	37	81	16	10	18		136	1623
T2⑤b	397	80		183	165		825	9		7		15		31	76	13		4	93	949	148	29	41	11	1	15		94	610
T3⑤a	83	741	632	355	201	202	2214	11	158	25	17	87	32	330	11	46	21	10	88	2632	619	136	183	4	4	2		167	1517
T3⑤b	26	41	45	67	50	83	312	4		2		13		19	4	7	6	7	24	355	59	13	32	1				24	226
T5⑤a	302	234	122	37	89	29	813	43	8	35	10	24	4	124		6	12	3	21	958	214	52	28	1			1	103	559
T5⑤b	4	6			3	3	16				2			2						18	1	5		2					10
H3	599	440	301		39		1379	58		21		66		145		22	60	92	174	1698	360	14	65	22	7	8		82	1140
H4	305	46		50	59		460	25		8		24		57	78				78	595	72	12	35	8	3	1		53	411
H5	654	136		7	93		890	45			13	36		94	84	9		4	97	1081	352	14	55	7	1	4		38	610
H6	114	25		5	32		176	21		8		17		46	39			4	43	265	48	7	10	3	3	1		17	176
H7	12	20		17	7		56	6		2		9		17	17	10		4	31	104	19		1	1		3		13	67
H8	6	6		6	5		23								6					29	2		2					4	21
H15	1	8	10	2		2	23		4	1			1	6						29	8	1	1					5	14
H16	21	72	19	16	34	26	188													188	50	3	12	2				13	108
H17	5	32		5	6	2	50		17	4	7	11		39		2		3		94	12	9	3					18	52
H18	12	9	4	6		5	36		1		2	4		7						43	3	7	2					9	22
H19				1			1	4	1		1	1	1	9						10	3		1					1	5
H20	5	11		15	3		34	10		2	1	2		15						49	10	2	4					4	29
H22	19	46	35	48	15		163	8	8	6	2	15	6	45	2	8	6		16	225	55	14	16					19	121
总计	3941	7362	1185	1193	1058	557	15296	535	336	609	97	776	119	2473	498	286	154	212	1139	18920	4506	440	658	80	30	55	3	855	12293
百分比	21%	39%	6%	6%	6%	3%	81%	3%	2%	3%	1%	4%	1%	13%	3%	1%	1%	1%	6%	100%	24%	2%	3%	1%				5%	65%

注：本表不包含T4、T7和各探方各层下柱洞或坑的统计材料。

后　记

在秦代初平南越以前，中原地区对华南及东南亚地区的历史、文化、社会风俗完全不了解。即使到了两汉时期，从《淮南子》一书中，可以看出这种认识也仅局限于岭南地区。魏晋南北朝时期，特别是随着东晋王朝的南迁，并对岭南及越南北部地区进行大规模开发，岭南及越南北部的历史、地理、文化、经济、社会风俗等才开始出现在《水经注》、《华阳国志》等经典文献之中。其中，"蜀王子泮南迁，并建立瓯雒国"这段历史引人瞩目，但其中夹杂着大量的荒诞传说。究竟这一历史记载是否属实？在秦代初平南越以前，整个岭南和越南北部地区属于一种什么样的文化？

20世纪80年代以来，越南北部及中国香港、台湾等地陆续出土了几件形制与三星堆文化同类器极其相似的玉器，引起了学术界的广泛关注。而作为长江上游地区夏商时期最重要的遗址——三星堆遗址，是如何影响中国东南沿海及东南亚地区的，史书并未给出我们答案。因此，构筑从三星堆至东南亚的历史框架，剥茧抽丝，厘清宏大的历史脉络和文化传播线路，还原先秦时期宏大的文化交流背景，是本报告出版的目的。

本报告虽未完整地揭示出从三星堆至越南北部的宏大历史背景，但却为我们重新构筑"南方丝绸之路"提供了新的线索。我们相信，随着今后考古工作的持续开展，将能够清晰地呈现从三星堆到越南的宏大历史背景，为新时期"丝绸之路"的建设提供宝贵依据。

本次考古发掘领队为四川省文物考古研究院的雷雨和陕西省考古研究院的岳连建。参加发掘的中方人员为四川省文物考古研究院的陈卫东、陕西省考古研究院的孙伟刚，越方人员有越南国家历史博物馆的 Vu Quoc Hien（武国贤）、Vu Quoc Hien（吴世丰）、Nguyen Van Doan（阮文团）、Truong Dac Chien（张德战）、Le Hoai Anh（黎怀英）、Chu Van Ve（周文卫）、Le Ngoc Hung（黎玉雄）、Nguyen Quoc Binh（阮国平）和越南国家社会科学与人文中心考古学研究院的 Nyuyen Van Hao（阮文好），发掘过程中的翻译由阮文好（Nyuyen Van Hao）和武氏娟承担。

本报告由陈卫东、雷雨、岳连建、孙伟刚共同执笔完成。插图由越南的 Le Hoai Anh（黎怀英）绘制，四川省文物考古研究院的赵建清绘了部分插图。陶器修复由越南的 Chu Van Ve（周文卫）完成。英文翻译由刘伟负责。[14]C 测定由中国社会科学院考古研究所、北京大学、越南国家历史博物馆完成。

我们的工作得到了各方面的关心和支持。四川省文物局、陕西省文物局、越南国家历史博物馆、越南永福省博物馆、越南富寿省博物馆等单位给予了大力支持。四川省文物考古研究院的高大伦先生、周科华先生、陈显丹先生、唐飞先生，陕西省考古研究院的焦南峰先生、尹申平先生、王炜林先生、孙秉君先生等，在考古发掘和整理期间，也给予了很多关心和支持；他们也审阅了部分文稿，提出了许多很好的修改意见。特别是四川省文物考古研究院高大伦院长受陕西省考古研究院前任院长焦南峰先生和现任院长王炜林先生的委托，为本报告欣然作序，使本报告增色不少。越南国家社会科学与人文中心考古学研究院的阮文好先生和越南国家历史博物馆的阮国平先生在考古发掘和陪同考察的期间，不仅是很好的翻译，其专业知识亦令人钦佩。在此，对以上各单位和诸位先生表示深深的谢意。

由于发掘工作距今已有十年，加之后期编写时间紧迫，编者水平有限，报告中错漏之处在所难免，敬请专家学者批评指正。

编　者

2016 年 3 月

英文报告

Nghia Lap of Vietnam

Report on the Excavation of Remains
of Phung Nguyen Culture

Edited by

Institute of Cultural Relics and Archaeology of Sichuan Province
Institute of Archaeology of Shaanxi Province
Vietnam National Museum of History

Culture Relics Press
Beijing · 2016

Contents

Table of Figures

Table of Plates

Chapter I   Geographic Enviroment and Historical Development

Section One   Natural Enviroment, Geography and Climate

The Socialist Republic of Vietnam ("Vietnam") is located on the southeast part of Asia. It borders Yunnan and Guangxi Province of China to the north and Lao and Cambodia to the south. Its southeast part and southwest part are adjacent to the South China Sea and Gulf of Siam, respectively. Its south part controls the marine transport artery of the Pacific Ocean and the Indian Ocean. Since ancient times, Vietnam has occupied a very important strategic status. It covers an area of about 330,000 square meters and has about 73 million inhabitants (as of 1996). Vietnam is home to 54 ethnic groups, including the Kinh, Tay, Thai, Muong, Hmong, Khmer, and Hoa, and the dominant Kinh ethnic group constitutes 89% of the population. The official national language of Vietnam is Vietnamese. The long – established religions in Vietnam include Buddhism, Catholicism, Hoahaoism, and Caodaism. Vietnam is divided into 57 provinces and four municipalities which are administratively on the same level as provinces (Hanoi, Ho Chi Minh City, Haiphong, and Da Nang). Hanoi is the capital city of Vietnam.

Vietnam is on the east side of Indochina peninsula. The terrain is one sloping from northwest to southeast along a north – south strip bent in an "S" shape, with the northern and southern parts protruding and a narrow central area along a total length of 1,650 kilometers north – south, 650 kilometers wide at the east – west widest point, and short of 50 kilometers wide at the narrowest point (Figure 1). About a quarter of the total land area is mountains and plateaus, concentrated in the northern and central parts, which can be divided into three regions-mountains on the north of the Red River; mountains and the Truong Son Ra (Annamite Range) between Red River and Blue River; and Tay Nguyen region. The Annamite Range is in the west, winding throughout central Vietnam, obliquely across the north and south. It forms the natural boundaries between Vietnam and Laos. The largest plain is the Red River Delta in the north and the Mekong River Delta in the south. Plain area accounts for about a quarter of the total area of Vietnam, most of which was formed by alluvial silt from the river. The northern plains have the most fertile land in the north; and the southern plains are the most affluent ar-

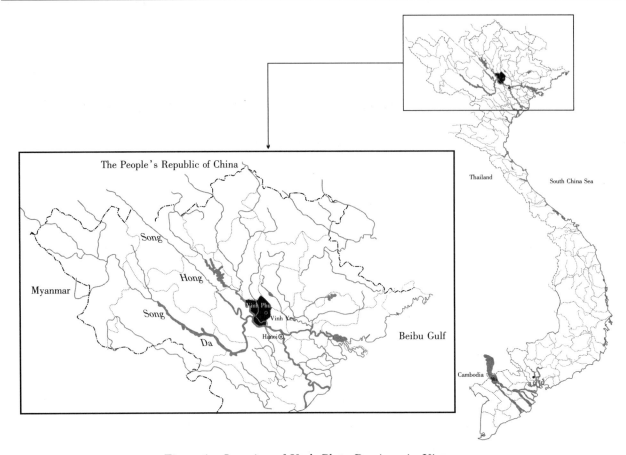

Figure 1   Location of Vĩnh Phúc Province in Vietnam

eas in the south. These two plains are the world famous rice production areas and natural food produce grannary of Vietnam. Meanwhile, they are also a major area where ancient Vietnamese culture was deliberated and developed.

Vietnam is hilly geographically with lots of rivers. There are more than a thousand large and small rivers in the country, of vertical length of over 41,000 kilometers. The rivers mostly enter the sea flowing from northwest to southeast. The main rivers, Red River (Song Hong) and the Mekong River (Song Kuu Long), are the largest rivers in Vietnam, originating in China's Yunnan province and the Tibet plateau. Vietnam has a vertical coastline of about 3,000 kilometers and enjoys abundant water resources.

Vietnam has a tropical monsoon climate. Due to terrain conditions and different distances from the equator, the climates in different regions vary. The south is close to the equator, and temperatures throughout the year are of no major difference; April is the hottest month and average temperature is 29℃. Northern climate vary more greatly; the hottest month is July, of monthly average temperature at 23℃, and the coldest month is January, of monthly average temperature at 15℃; northwestern mountainous regions can have winter night temperatures below zero. Vietnam has abundant rainfall, with average annual rainfall of 1800 – 2000ml. Vietnam's rainy and dry seasons divide the year. Monsoon rainfall accounts for 80% of annual rainfall. From May to October the northern part is in rainy season; from August to January the following year the central region is in rainy season; and from May to November is rainy season in southern regions. Similarly, from November to April is dry season in the northern region; from November to May is dry season in central region; and from February to July is dry season in the southern region. Annual sunshine time is not less than 1, 500 hours, the average annual humidity is at around 82%.[1]

Section Two   Historical Development

Discovery of Son Vi culture and Hoa Binh culture indicates human existence in the Sông Hồng floodplains in north Vietnam as far back as the Paleolithic Age.

Northern part of Vietnam in the Neolithic Age went through the Bac Son culture-Cai Beo culture, Da But culture, Quynh Van culture-Phung Nguyen culture, Ha Long culture and Bau Tro culture *etc*. There are many remains from that age, distributing across a large range, indicating the emergence of large number of settlements and frequent human activities in north Vietnam in the Neolithic Age. This is also the period known in history books of China and Vietnam as the "Văn Lang Kingdom" period.

Around 250BC, the Thục Phán tribe in northeast Vietnam defeated the Lạc Việt and Âu Việt tribes in the Red River floodplain and established the capital city in Thanh Loa of Kingdom of Âu Lạc. This became the first sovereign state in Vietnamese history.

After Qin unified China, the dynasty started territorial expansion southward. In 214BC, Qin set up governments in Guilin, Nanhai and Xiang County. Among them, Xiang County included today's northern Vietnam. In 207BC, the South China Sea general Zhao Tuo took the occasion of wars near the end of the Qin dynasty and annexated Guilin and Xiang County, declaring independence as the Nanyue King, establishing a separatist regime of Nanyue, which controlled the northern and central Vietnam.

In 111BC, Emperor Wudi of Han Dynasty sent general Lu Bode to pacification expedition to Nanyue, and established nine counties of Nanhai, Cangwu, Yulin, Hepu Jiaozhi, Jiuzhen, Rinan, Zhuya and Zhan'er, of which Jiaozhi, Jiuzhen and Rinan are in today's northern and central Vietnam. In 203AD, Han dynasty merged the three counties of Jiaozhi and the three of Nanhai and Guilin, referred to as Jiaozhou, i. e. Prefecture of Jiao.

As the Han dynasty fell and during the Three Kingdoms period, Jiaozhou was under Kingdom of Wu, and was re – divided into two administrative areas of Guangzhou (encompassing Guangdong and Guangxi) and Jiaozhou (the orginal three counties of Jiaozhi). In 280Ac, Jin defeated Wu, and

---

[1]   Guo Zhenduo, Zhang Xiaomei (Ed), *Vietnamese History*, Renmin University of China Publishing House, 2002.

Jiaozhou's Mu Taohuang surrendered to Jin.

In 544 AD, Lý Bí and Bing Shao staged an uprising and established the Van Xuân Quốc state, with capital city in Longbian and Lý Bí became the Emperor of Nanyue while Bing Shao became a minister. In 586 AD, Sui Kingdom defeated Chen Dynasty and unified China. In 602 AD Sui's general Liu Yu defeated the Van Xuân Quốc and again Jiaozhou was divided into the three counties of Jiaozhi, Jiuzhen and Rinan. In 618 AD, Tang dynasty defeated Sui and established the prefecture government. In 679 AD, due to poor military administration, uprisings frequented and the Jiaozhou prefecture government was changed to Annan military government.

In AD 938, the Vietnamese lord Ngô Quyền established the first dynasty of the feudal society of Vietnam, the Ngô dynasty, which later evolved as Đại Việt dynasty. In 980 AD, China's Song Dynasty sent troops to Vietnam on the ground of instability of the Đại Việt dynasty. Lê took over the throne and established the Lê dynasty. In 1010 AD, Lý Cong Uan established the Lý dynasty and in 1225 AD, Tran Thu Do established the Trần dynasty.

In 1400 AD, Hồ Dynasty was established. Following the 1406 Ming – Hồ War which the Ming Dynasty overthrew the Hồ dynasty in the name of resuming Hồ Dynasty and took over the entire country, Vietnamese independence was briefly interrupted. This was restored by Lê Loi's uprising in 1418. In 1427 the uprising force reached treaty with Ming dynasty and Ming military force withdrew from Vietnam. Lê Loi thus founded the Lê dynasty, with its capital city in Thaungdut (today's Hanoi).

In 1527, Mạc Đăng Dung overthrew the Lê emperor and established the Mạc dynasty. In 1530, general of the Lê dynasty Nguyễn helped descendant of the Lê to claim the throne and briefly resumed the Lê dynasty. Vietnam was divided with Lê dynasty in the south and the Mạc dynasty in the north. This is known as the Southern and Northern dynasties in Vietnam history. Intervention by Chinese Ming dynasty with troops resulted in Mạc Đăng Dung dividing the region of today's Cao Bang to Ming dynasty. Later on, the Mạc dynasty was conquered by Lê dynasty and retreated to Cao Bang with Ming dynasty's protection. Since then, war lords in Vietnam reshuffled the map and the country remained divided between Trịnh lords (north) and Nguyễn lords (south). In 1697 AD, Southern Ming's Yang Yandi retreated with remaining Ming forces to south of Vietnam and was driven to the south end of present day Vietnam. In 1733, the Nguyễn lords conquered the regions. This marks the substantial formation of territory of modern Vietnam. In 1771 AD, the three brothers from the village of Tây So'n to begin a revolt against Lord Nguyễn Phúc Thuân. They defeated the southern Trinh lords and northern Nguyễn in turn and established Lê Chiêu Thống as the emperor. Later, in a revolt by the descendants of Trịnh, Emperor Lê Chiêu Thống fled to the Qing Empire of China. Qing empire sent the governor of Guangxi and Guangdong Sun Shiyi to enter Vietnam with military forces based in Guangdong, Guangxi, Yunnan and Guizhou. In 1789, Nguyễn Huê's army defeated the Qing forces. He then took the title of Emperor under the reign name Quang Trung, but succumbed himself to the Qing Empire. In 1802, with support from the French, the southern Nguyễn lords ended the dynasty and Nguyễn dynasty took over the country. In 1862, French forces entered Vietnam and in 1844, Vietnam became a French colony.[1]

[1]   Jin Xudong, *Overview of Ancient Vietnamese History*, Southeast Asia, Vol. 2, 1986; (Vietnam) Tao Wei Ying, Liu Tong Wen, Zi Yue (translation), *Ancient Vietnam History*, Commercial Press, 1976; Guo Zhenduo, Zhang Xiaomei (Ed), *Vietnamese History*, Renmin University of China Publishing House, 2002.

Charpter II   Initiation of the Project and the Excavation Process

Section One   Project Background

Southeast Asia region has always been one of the focuses of attention in the international archaeology world. In particular, studies of pre – historic cultures of Southeast Asia have for many years been under heated discussions in the international academic world. These are also an important area of studies in China's archaeology and anthropology circles. In the past 20 years, along with a series of important archaeological discoveries made in the Southeast Asian region that offered new clues to studies in the universality and individualism of Southeast Asian cultures, the origin and dissemination of rice agriculture, migration of the Austronesian and metal smelting *etc.* , again bringing the Southeast Asian region into the spotlight in the academic world of archaeology. Chinese and foreign scholars have paid great attention to the region and conducted large amount of research studies.

In this project we cast our focus on the region of northern Vietnam in the studies. Throughout the entire Southeast Asian region, Vietnam has the closest bond with China. Vietnam has a recorded history of over 2,000 years, of which over a millennium was a county or prefecture directly under the reigns of China's feudal dynasties and for over another millennium it was a "vassal state" of independence under China. in 1884, Vietnam government was forced into the second *Treaty of Hue* with France and in 1885 France forced the Qing empire to enter the *Sino – French Treaty on Vietnam in Tianjin* by which the Qing government officially acknowledged Vietnam's status as a French protectorate, thus ending the "vassal state" relationship between China and Vietnam. Meanwhile Vietnam shares borders with China through mountains and rivers and is deeply and for a long time connected in history. Yet when did this connection begin, in what form and under what cultural dominance are some of the questions unanswered in the history books.

Since the 1980s, some jade pieces (jade tablets) were unearthed in turn in Vinh Phuc province and Phu Tho province in northern Vietnam, which are very similar to the same category of pieces unearthed in the Sanxingdui culture in shape and structure. The report on the excavation caused attention in China's academic world. Yet even earlier than that, a number of Chinese scholars who followed archaeological development in Southeast Asian region had already noticed the certain similarity or consistency between archaeological cultures from the Bronze Age to Iron Age in northern Vietnam and outlooks of those in the same period or earlier periods found in Sichuan areas.[1] Topped with the communications and exchanges between the ancient Shu kingdom and the ancient Văn Lang Kingdom that are more or less recorded and implied in the history literatures of China and Vietnam,[2] the understanding of relationship between archaeological cultures of the Sichuan Basin and Bronze Age of in northern Vietnam, particularly that of impact of the Sanxingdui culture on Southeast Asian cultures, becomes ever more necessary. This is also the intentions behind implementation of this project.

Section Two　Overview of Archaeological Excavation and Research

I. Overview of archaeological discoveries

Along the Sông Hồng river basin in northern Vietnam, to present several archaeological cultures including the Phung Nguyen culture, Dong Dau culture, Go Mun culture and Dong Son culture have been identified and established. However, the specific ranges of dates of above archaeological cultures are topic of different opinions and debates among scholars including those from Vietnam. However, the sequence of developments of of these archaeological cultures and general ranges of dates have been basically identified, i. e. Phung Nguyen culture→Dong Dau culture→Go Mun culture→Dong Son culture. General age is around the Chalcolithic period to early period of the Iron Age. There are many literatures on this. To general knowledge, the two important archaeological cultures are Phung Nguyen culture and Dong Son culture.[3]

---

[1]　That similarity or consistency are mainly represented in the remains of the two regions, e. g. boat funeral objects, bronze utensils and jade pieces etc. Please refer to "Discussions on Relationship between Civilizations of Ancient Sichuan and Southeast Asia", *Cultural Relics* Vol. 9, 1983.

[2]　It is recorded in literatures of both China and Vietnam that early history of Vietnam started with the Văn Lang Kingdom established by Xiong (or Luo) King. When the kingdom was under reign of the 18th generation king, it was conquered by Shu's prince Pan who established the Au Lac Kingdom and named himself the Anyang King. In Vietnamese literatures, relationship between the Shu's Anyang King and Văn Lang Kingdom was first seen in *Lingnan Zhi Guai-Jinguizhuan* (*Collection of Stories of Lingnan-Jingui Legend*), which states that Anyang King of Au Lac Kingdom is from Shu, in the surname of Shu and name of Pan. As his elderly asked for daughter of Xiong King for marriage and was refused, hatred harbored. Pan then started a conquest against the Xiong King and Văn Lang Kingdom. The kingdom was renamed as Au Lac and city was built in the place of Yueshang. " The later literatures including *Shiji Quanshu* (*Comprehensive Accounts of History*), *Annan Zhilue* (*Chronicles of Annam*) and *Yueshi Kao* (*Vietnam History*) etc. all recorded the events. The earliest history account in Chinese literature is seen in *Shuijingzhu-Yeyuhezhu* which says "Before prefecture was established in Jiaozhi, the land was under Luo's reign, which was along the river and people farmed the land, thus known as the Luo land. The Au Lac king reigned the county and had generals with bronze stamp empowered. Later the Shu prince brought a troop of 30,000 on a conquest over the king, prince and generals. Shu Prince was known as Anyang King. He was revolted against later by the Nanyue lords". Subsequent dynasties had literatures either recording or referring to this account. Refer to *Ancient History of Vietnam* by Tao Weiying (Vietnam) and translated by Liu Tongwen and Zi Yue, the Commercial Press, 1976; Men Wentong: *Studies of Vietnamese History*, People's Publishing House, 1983.

[3]　Guo Zhenduo, Zhang Xiaomei (ed.), *Vietnamese History*, Renmin University of China Publishing House, 2002.

To date, there have been over 100 sites of Phung Nguyen culture period found and excavated. O-ver 70 remains have been through formal excavation. These are mainly distributed in Phu Tho, Vinh Phuc, Hanoi, Ha Tay, Bac Ninh and other areas along the Sông Hồng river basin. The sites are mostly along the valleys, highlands and steppes by the river. Less were found along the coastline.[1] The are-as of distribution are coincidentally that recorded in Vietnam history and in legends of the Văn Lang Kingdom. The earlier Chalcolithic period is known in history as the pre – Van Lang period and middle to late periods are the period of the Văn Lang Kingdom, which links to the Dong Son culture in the lat-er period of Bronze Age. The Phung Nguyen sites were discovered in 1959 and were under large – scale archaeological excavations in 1961. As it was discovered the earliest and has abundant cultural impli-cations, it is named as "Phung Nguyen Culture".

II. Overview of studies by Vietnamese scholars

Excavation of remains of the Phung Nguyen culture started in 1959 with the archaeological excava-tion of Phung Nguyen site. Following that through 1969 to the 1970s, a number of important Phung Nguyen culture remains were found (Peng Qiu, Luan He, Jiang Dui and others), which prompted the Vietnamese scholars to rethink issues of the ancient Vietnamese history. This was also a period of great development in Vietnamese archaeology when lots of new ideas formulated.[2] Since the 1990s to date, some new important remains have been found, for instance the Xon Ren site (2002, 2003 and 2004). These have enriched the findings on Phung Nguyen culture. Based on the new materials, more and more Vietnamese scholars are starting to focus on Vietnam's own Phung Nguyen culture. Studies con-centrated on the dating, origin, cultural connotations, ethnology and civilization of the Phung Nguyen culture. The most representative work is Ha Van Tan's *Archaeological Cultures of Vietnam*[3] and Han Van Khan's *Phung Nguyen Culture*.[4] Mr. Ha Van Tan made a comprehensive account of ancient his-tory of Vietnam and reconstructed the age framework from the Paleolithic age to the Iron age, while conducting in – depth research into the Phung Nguyen Culture. And Mr. Han Van Khan's *Phung Nguyen Culture* offers comprehensive review of the discovery, research and excavation history of Phung Nguyen Culture and comprehensive overview of the dating, origin and cultural connotations of Phung Nguyen Culture. However, due to regional limitations, national psychology and other factors, it was difficult for Vietnamese scholars to engage in more extensive discussions on the relationships with cul-

---

[1]   Deng Cong, "Comparative Interpretations of Jade and Stone Artifacts from Phung Nguyen Remains of Vietnam and Dawan Remains of Hong Kong", *Study of Ancient Cultures of South China and Adjacent Regions*, Hong Kong Chinese University Publishing House, 1994.

[2]   *Ancient History of Vietnam* by Tao Weiying (Vietnam) and translated by Liu Tongwen and Zi Yue, the Commercial Press, 1976; *The First Remains from Bronze Age in Vietnam* edited by Li Wenlan, Fan Wengeng and Ruan Ling (Vietnam) and translated by Liang Zhim-ing, Hanoi Science Publishing House, 1963.

[3]   Ha Van Tan, translated by Kikuti Seiiti, 《ベトナムの考古文化》, Liuxing Publishing House, 1991.

[4]   Han Van Khan, *Van Hoa Phung Nguyen*, Nha Xuat Ban Dai Hoc Quoc Gia Ha Noi, 2005.

tures of surrounding regions. This is also a restraint on the more in – depth studies of Phung Nguyen culture by local Vietnamese scholars.

III. Overview of international studies

Archaeology in Vietnam since the contemporary times originated from the west. Particularly during the French colonization period, a number of scholars and collectors of Vietnamese bronze objects and stone tools casted their eyes on the entire Southeast Asian region in hope for comprehensive understanding of the ancient cultures of Southeast Asia. Western and Japanese scholars focus mainly on the overall Southeast Asian region. For instance, Professor Peter Bellwood in Australia discussed the role of Vietnam in Asia and Pacific regions in the perspective of agriculture and migration of the Austronesian.[1] New Zealand scholar Charles Higham focused more on the pre – historic cultures of Southeast Asian continent and interpreted the pre – historic cultures of mainland Southeast Asian region from a macroscopic perspective.[2] French scholar Solan [3] and Jeremy H. C. S. Davidson [4] from London University of the U. K. went into depth on analyzing the cultures in Vietnam region from the Neolithic Age to Chalcolithic Age, concluding the sequence of cultural developments in the region. And Japanese scholar Nishimura Masaya is the most representative figure in those studying ancient cultures of Vietnam. He made a comprehensive review of remains of ancient cultures of Vietnam and constructed the sequence of early cultures of Vietna.[5] Japanese scholar Yoshikai Masato followed the clue of T – shaped rings unearthed in China and Southeast Asia and discussed more extensively the relationship between China and Southeast Asia and particularly Vietnam.[6]

Generally speaking, visions taken by international scholars in the studies are broad and not limited within a certain country or region's cultures, but take the viewpoint of the entire Southeast Asian region for more extensive research covering lots of topics including the universality and individualism of cultures, origin and dissemination of rice agriculture, origin and dissemination of metal tools and migration of Austronesian among others. However, the limitations are that it is difficult for them to use the archaeological materials from China's southeast coast areas and southwest and south China regions. This affects the discussion of archaeological cultures in Southeast Asian region in a broader scope.

---

[1]   Peter Bellwood (U. S.), interview by Hong Xiaochun: "Interviews with Professor Peter Bellwood", *South Cultural Relics*, Vol. 3, 2001.

[2]   Charles Higham, *Early Culture of Mainlant southeast Asia*. Bangkok: River Book Ltd 2002.

[3]   Edmound Solan *et al.* (France), "Prehistoric Culture in Indo – China Peninsula", *Archaeology Reference* 2, Cultural Relics Publishing House, 1979.

[4]   Jeremy Davidson, "Archaeological Activities in Recent Years in Vietnam", *Archaeology Reference* 2, Cultural Relics Publishing House, 1979.

[5]   Nishimura Masaya (Japan), 《紅河平原とメコン・ドンナイ川平原の考古学的研究》, Tokyo University Social Science Department, doctorate dissertation 2006.

[6]   Yoshikai Masato (Japan), "T – Shaped Rings in China and Southeast Asia", translated by Chen De'an, *Sichuan Cultural Relics*, Vol. 2, 1999.

IV. Overview of studies conducted in China

Scholars in China started studies in the Vietnam region rather late. And studies concentrate on the relationship between China's southwest region and Vietnam and that between Yunnan and Vietnam or between the Guangxi and Guangdong region and Vietnam, relationship between Sichuan and Vietnam, origin of rice farming and origin of Austronesian.

In the 1980s, Mr. Tong Enzheng casted his focus on the communications and exchanges on archaeological cultures between China's southwest and Southeast Asian regions. In 1983 he published a paper titled "New Archaeological Discoveries in the Southeast Asian Region in the Recent Twenty Years and Studies on Ancient Civilizations in South China made by Foreign Scholars",[1] which discusses the issues of origin of agriculture in Southeast Asia and south China. Mr. Wu Chunming was dedicated to the studies of pre – historic cultures in Southeast Asia, their relationship with South China and origin of Austronesian, and the study of pre – historic cultures in northern Vietnam under the context of continental Southeast Asia. In the paper titled "Relationship between Cultures of the Lower Streams of Sông Hồng in the Neolithic Age and South China",[2] he reviewed studies made by predecessors on the ancestry of Neolithic Age cultures in northern Vietnam, analyzed in depth the development of cultural connotations in the Neolithic Age Age in lower streams of Sông Hồng and made a comparative study of the Neolithic cultures in northern Vietnam and South China. Since the 1980s, scholars in Hong Kong and Taiwan have also paid attention to the area, engaging in more extensive scopes of studies, not limiting themselves to the comparisons between northern Vietnam and South China. Mr. Zang Zhenhua from Taiwan includes Taiwan in the comparative studies of South China and Southeast Asian pre – historic cultures and published the paper titled "Relationship between Pre – historic Cultures of South China, Taiwan and Southeast Asia",[3] taking research perspective of origin and migration of the Austronesian. Professor Deng Cong from Hong Kong Chinese University looks at Hong Kong and the entire South Asian and Southeast Asian countries and jointly with Vietnamese scholars studied the cultural remains in northern Vietnam and published the paper "Archaeological Discoveries of Hai Phong Chang Qing Site of Vietnam"[4] in 2003.

In the 1980s, scholar of Yunnan Mr. Wang Dadao started to focus on the relationship between the Bronze Age culture in Yunnan and that in Vietnam, Thailand and other areas in Southeast Asia. His

[1]   Tong Enzheng, "New Archaeological Discoveries in Southeast Asian Regions in the Past 20 Years and Studies by Foreign Scholars on Origin of Ancient Civilizations of South China", *Southwest Minzu University Journal (Social Science Edition)* Vol. 3, 1983.

[2]   Lu Qinyi, Wu Chunming, "Cultures in the Neolithic Age of Lower Streams of Song Hong and South China", *Baiyue Studies*, Vol. 2, Anhui University Publishing House, 2011.

[3]   Zang Zhenhua, "Relationship of Pre – historic Cultures of South China, Taiwan and Southeast Asia: Ecological Position, Cultural Interactions and Historical Process", *Archaeology in the New Century-Diversified Interactive Academic Seminar on Culture, Position and Ecology*, 2003.

[4]   Deng Cong, Ruan Jinrong, "Archaeological Findings at Chang Qing Site of Hai Phong of Vietnam", *Southeast Archaeology Study*, Vol. 3, 2003.

papers "Relationship between Pottery Pieces of Yunnan's Bronze Age Culture, Vietnam's Dong Son Culture and Thailand's Ban Chiang Culture",[1] and "Relationship Between Pottery Pieces of Yunnan's Bronze Age Culture and Pottery Pieces of Vietnam's Dong Son Culture and Thailand's Ban Chiang Culture"[2] detail the relationships between factors of the Yunnan Bronze Age culture and Dong Son culture of Vietnam. In recent years, Li Kunsheng and Chen Guo's *Bronze Age Civilizations in Yunnan of China and Vietnam*[3] comprehensively accounts for the remains from the Neolithic Age to the Bronze Age in the two regions as well as comparative study of the cultural factors. Agriculture and bronze relics.

Guangdong and Guangxi provinces, particularly Guangxi, are connected with Vietnam across borders and share substantially similar geographical environment, climate conditions and ecological systems. The southern Guangxi and Sông Hồng river basin of Vietnam are all located on the coast of the Gulf of Tonkin with convenient water and land connections. Correspondingly there are many identical or similar cultural characteristics in pre − historic cultures.[4] The discovery of Gantuoyan Remains in Guangxi is the best proof of cultural exchanges between the two places. Of course there are relatively less studies on the early cultures of the two regions and relevant cross − nation studies are yet to be developed. This poses limitations on the studies of early cultures in the two regions.

Mr. Tong Enzheng was the first to cast academic interests on the relationship between Sichuan and Vietnam. In his paper "Discussions on the Relationship between Ancient Sichuan and Southeast Asian Civilizations",[5] he discussed in detail the relationship between cultural factors of ancient Sichuan and Vietnam. Following that more scholars have started to pay attention to the relationship between Sichuan and Vietnam. But these studies focus mainly on the routes taken by people of the Shu kingdom to the south and their influence on Vietnam.[6] In recent years, Sichuan's archeologists have started to pay attention to the communication between ancient cultures of Vietnam and Sichuan. Mr. Lei Yu's paper "Relationship between Sichuan and Vietnam in the Perspective of Archaeological Findings"[7]

[1]   Wang Dadao, "Yunnan's Bronze Age Culture and Relationship with Vietnam's Dong Son Culture and Thailand's Ban Chiang Culture", *Archaeology*, Vol. 6, 1990.

[2]   Wang Daodao, "Relationship of Pottery Pieces in Yunnan's Bronze Age Culture and Pottery Pieces of Vietnam's Dong Son Culture and Thailand's Ban Chiang Culture", *Southern Ethnological Archaeology*, Vol. 3, Sichuan University Publishing House, 1991.

[3]   Li Kunsheng, Chen Guo, *Bronze Age Cultures in Yunnan of China and Vietnam*, Social Science Literature Publishing House, 2013.

[4]   Guangxi Zhuang's Autonomous Region Cultural Relics Work Team, "Guangxi Napo Gantuoyan Site Excavation Report", *Archaeology*, Vol. 10, 2003.

[5]   Tong Enzheng, "Discussions of Relationship between Ancient Sichuan and Southeast Asian Civilizations", *Cultural Relics*, Vol. 9, 1983.

[6]   Wang Youpeng, "Excavation of Jianwei Bashu Tombs and Southern Migration of the Shu King", *Archaeology*, Vol. 12, 1984. Sun Hua, "Chronicles of Shu Kingdom Southern Migration", *Sichuan Basin's Bronze Age*, Science Publishing House, 2000.

[7]   Lei Yu, "Relationship between Sichuan and Vietnam from the Archaeological Perspective", *Sichuan Cultural Relics*, Vol. 6, 2006.

presents the communication of cultures between Sichuan and Vietnam from the Phung Nguyen culture period to the Qin and Han periods. And Mr. Peng Changlin made comparative study of the 8 ivory tablets unearthed in Vietnam with those ones unearthed from the Sanxingdui remains in Sichuan, demonstrating interactions between early cultures in the Sông Hồng plain and Sichuan basin.[1]

In general research and studies in China focus mainly on the communication and interactions between south China and Southeast Asia, in particular northern Vietnam, while the topics also reach over to the origin and dissemination of the Austronesin, dissemination of metal ware, origin and dissemination of high class jade pieces (such as jade tablets and jade dagger) *etc*. The perspectives taken are rather narrowed and many of the new materials have not been applied in the studies, lagging far behind the studies made in the west and by scholars in Taiwan and Hong Kong.

---

[1] Peng Changlin, "Studies of Ivory Tablets in Northern Vietnam", *China Archaeology*, Vol. 1, 2015.

Charpter Ⅲ   Working Processes

Section One   Archaeological Excavation Process

In July 2004, director of the Institute of Cultural Relics and Archaeology of Sichuan Province Gao Dalun visited Vietnam after attending a meeting in Nanning and indicated to the Vietnam National Museum of History during his visit intentions for cooperation between the two sides. The Vietnam National Museum of History actively responded to this. In February 2005, the Institute of Cultural Relics and Archaeology of Sichuan Province for the first time assigned research team consisting of Li Zhaohe, Chen De'an, Zhang Xiaoma, Hu Changyu, Lei Yu and Sun Zhibin to visit the Vietnam National Museum of history and the two parties reached memorandum of cooperation preliminarily. Considering the close relationship between archaeological cultures in the Bronze Age in Shaanxi's Hanzhong Basin and Chengdu Plain, the Institute of Cultural Relics and Archaeology of Sichuan Province invited Institute of Archaeology of Shaanxi Province to assign a joint research team consisting of Chen De'an, Lei Yu, Wang Zhangui, and Wang Weilin and made academic research in museums in Hanoi, Phu Tho, Vinh Phuc, Vang Tau and Ho Chi Minh and related remains and selected the location for excavation. In July 2006, Vietnam National Museum of History, Institute of Cultural Relics and Archaeology of Sichuan Province and Institute of Archaeology of Shaanxi Province entered a framework agreement on long – term cooperation in Chengdu and chose the excavation location for the first year (2006) at Nghia Lap site in Vinh Tuong of Vinh Phuc, Vietnam.

The Nghia Lap site is located in Nghia Lap village, Nghia Hing, Vinh Tuong of Vinh Phuc province in Vietnam, at the inter – junction of Sông Hồng and Song Lo, 1. 2 kilometers from the Song Lu in the west and around 1. 5 kilometers to the south from railway from Hanoi to Yen Bai, connected with Nghia Lap village in the east (Figure 2; Plate 1). In the center of the site is a temple. Geographic position of the central point of the site is 105°30′ east 21°18′ north, elevation of 11 meters above sea level and area of around 100,000 square meters. The site was under two rounds of investigations in 1963 and 1967. From December 1967 to February 1968 the Institute of Archaeology of Vietnamese Social Science Commission carried out an official excavation on

Figure 2   Location of Nghia Lap Remains in Vĩnh Phúc Province

the site.[1] In December 2006, at invitation of the Vietnam National Museum of History, Sichuan Province Institute of Archaeology, Institute of Archaeology of Shaanxi Province and Vietnam National Museum of History established a joint archaeological excavation team to conduct the second round of archaeological excavation of the Nghia Lap site.

Before the archaeological excavation started, the joint team zoned the site, with Nghia Lap Temple as the central point, dividing the site into Zone A and Zone B. Zone A is on the south of the Nghia Lap Temple and Zone B is on the south of the Nghia Lap Temple. Originally the Vietnam National Museum of History chose the location for archaeological excavation in that year in Zone B of the site. Following extensive investigation and surveying of the site by the joint team (Plate 2), as it was also the first time of archaeological investigation in Vietnam by using probing shovels, we found that Zone A of the site had more stratigraphic accumulation from the culture and was well preserved. The location for excavation was eventually chosen to be Zone A. After the selection, according to local traditions, staff of the Vietnam National Museum of History visited Nghia Lap for worship ritual (Plate 3 : 1) and invited priest of the Nghia Lap Temple to conduct a worship ritual on the site about to be excavated (Plate 3 : 2).

A total of 8 square units for exploration of the size of 5 × 5 meters were planned out in Zone A during the excavation (figure 3 : 1, 2; Plates 4 – 7), of which T1 – T5 and T7 were excavated by the joint archaeology team and T6 and T8 were excavated by the Vietnam Hanoi National University (meanwhile, Hanoi National University excavated a square unit in Zone A numbered T9). Excavation area was 200 square meters (materials of T6, T8 and T9 excavated by the Vietnam Hanoi National University are not included in this report). A total of 303 remains were excavated and sorted, including 34 pits, 1 tomb and 268 postholes or smaller pits related to buildings (Plates 8 – 10). Large number of pottery pieces and some jade and stone pieces were unearthed. A total of 834 specimens are selected (Figure 4; Plate 11 – 14).

Leader of the archaeological excavation team is Lei Yu from Institute of Cultural Relics and Archaeology of Sichuan Province and Yue Lianjian from Institute of Archaeology of Shaanxi Province. Chinese members of the team participating in the excavation are Chen Weidong from Institute of Cultural Relics and Archaeology of Sichuan Province, Yue Lianjian and Sun Weigang from Institute of Archaeology of Shaanxi Province. Vietnamese members are Vu Quoc Hien, Vu Quoc Hien, Nguyen Van Doan, Truong Dac Chien, Le Hoai Anh, Chu Van Ve, Le Ngoc Hung, Nguyen Quoc Binh Nyuyen Van Hao from Institute of Archaeology of the Vietnam National Centre for Social Sciences and Culture. Translation during the excavation works were undertaken by Nyuyen Van Hao and Wu Shi Juan (Plate 15 : 1).

---

[1]   Nyuyen Van Hao (1968), *Bao cao khai quat di chi Nghia Lap—Vinh Phu*, Tu lieu Vien Khao co hoc, Ha Noi.

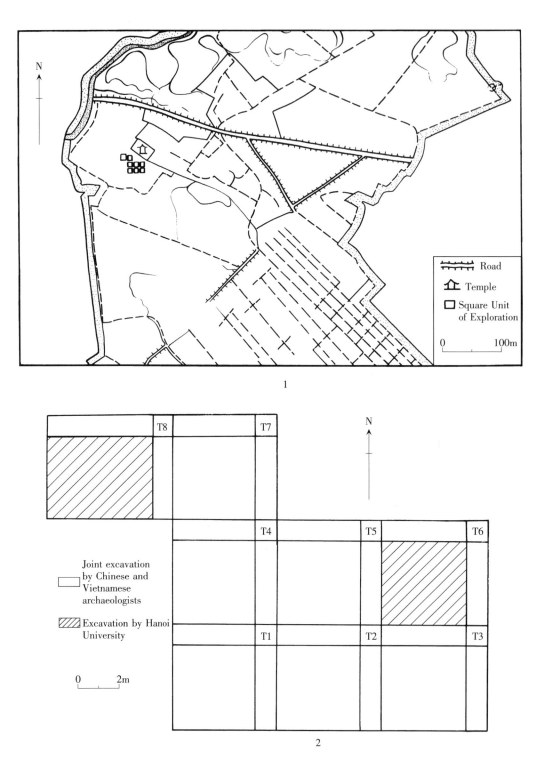

Figure 3   Topographic Map and Map of Excavation Square Units of the Nghia
Lap Remains Yu Gothic UI Light

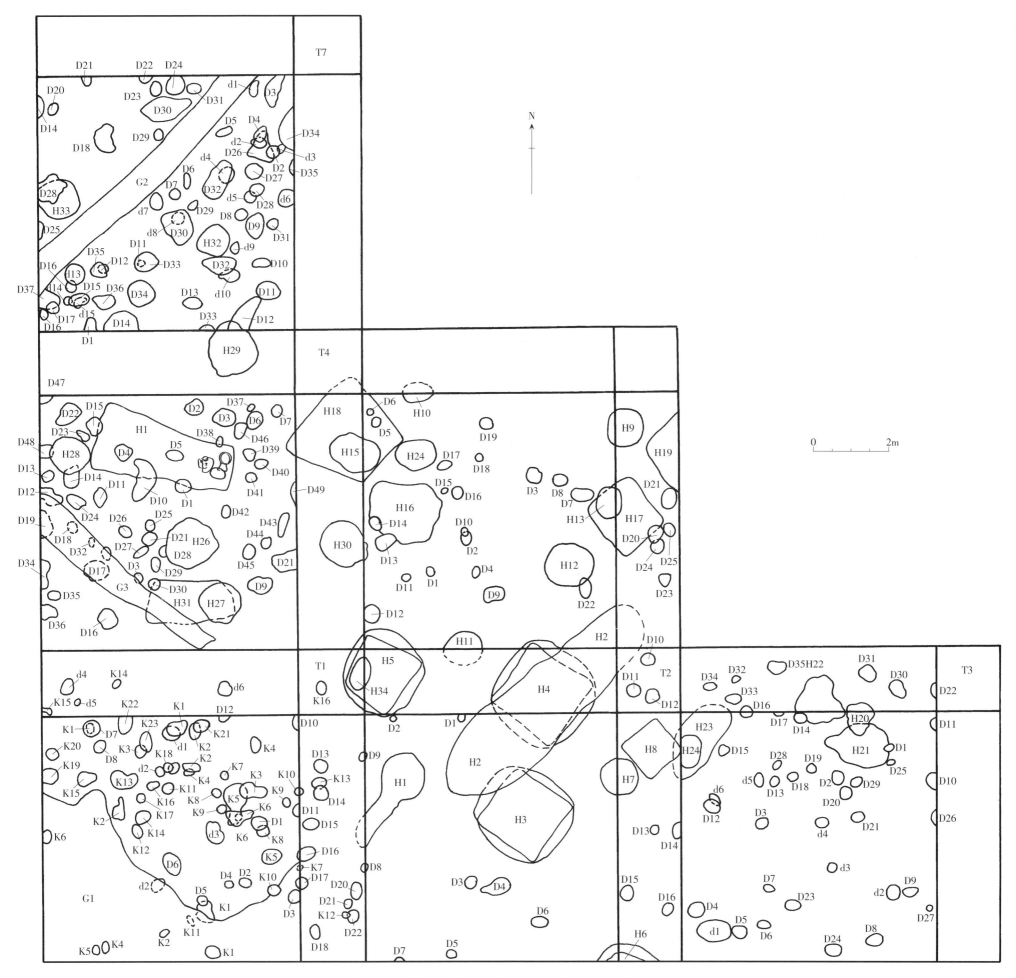

Figure 4　Master Plan of Sites at the Nghia Lap Remains

Notes：Pits（K）and gray pits（H）are all numbered according to the square unit of exploration．Capital letter denotes the area below the layer ⑤a，while lowercase letter denotes the area below the layer ⑤b or ⑥．

Section Two   Organization Process

As soon as the excavation works were completed, the excavation team members preliminarily organized the excavation materials and held a press conference at the Vinh Phuc Province Museum. Relevant members and staff of the China – Vietnam joint archaeological exploration team, Vietnam National Museum, Hanoi National University and Ho Chi Minh Mausoleum engaged in comprehensive discussions on the outcomes of the archaeological excavation, significance and treatment of the human skeleton (Plate 15:2). Major media in Vietnam also reported on the outcomes of the archaeological excavation.

In the second half of January, 2007, Lei Yu, Yue Lianjian and Chen Weidong completed the statistics summarization of all pottery pieces unearthed from all sites in the four square units of T1, T2, T3 and T5 and selected the specimens.[1] Following that, relevant staff of the Vietnam National Museum of History carried out drawing, restoration and photographing of the selected specimens. In 2011, relevant members of the Institute of Cultural Relics and Archaeology of Sichuan Province and Shaanxi Province Institute of Archaeology again visited Vietnam to check the unearthed specimens while researching into the remains and relics of Phung Nguyen Culture and asking for relevant staff of the Vietnam National Museum to help with statistics summarization and specimen selection of pottery pieces unearthed from T4 and T7. As staff from Sichuan and Shaanxi participating in the archaeological excavation were under heavy workload for excavation works in China, it took a long while to complete the archaeological excavation report. In 2015, the Institute of Cultural Relics and Archaeology of Sichuan Province reinitiated the organization works of the project, which comprehensive organization was under charge of Chen Weidong. Due to the fact that many of the original materials are missing and Chinese and Vietnamese sides disagree on some of the objects, the editors had to supplement and enhance all the original materials in the period from May to September 2015 and drafting of this report only started in October. The first draft was completed in March 2016.

This report has six chapters. Chapter One introduces the geographical environment and historical development of Vietnam. Chapter Two briefs on the project background and initiation. Chapter Three is on process of works undertaken. And Chapter Four details the excavation materials from the exploration square units. Chapter Five gives an outline of the preliminary studies conducted. Within the chapters, excavation materials are introduced by the stratigraphic accumulations, remains and artifacts unearthed from the strata. Focus is given to the remains from Phung Nguyen Culture period while those

---

[1]   T4 and T7 were excavated and sorted by Sun Weigang. However as he had to leave Vietnam due to affairs in China, the statistics and selection of specimens were undertaken by staff assigned by the Vietnam National Museum of History.

from contemporary and modern times are not discussed.

In order for the academic world to gain a comprehensive understanding of this archaeological excavation and in avoiding the personal bias in selection of materials by the authors, we offer full accounts of each of the square units, followed by discussions and conclusions made by the authors.

Large amount of remains and relics were unearthed in the archaeological excavation on Nghia Lap remains in 2006. Many related briefings or research papers have been published. In case of any inconsistency between published original materials and this report, this report should be considered the more authoritative.

Charpter IV Materials in the Excavation Square Units

Section One T1

T1 is located in the southwest corner of the overall excavation area. The square units for exploration were planned out and excavation works commenced on December 3, 2006 and exploration was completed on January 8, 2007. Yue Lianjian was in charge of conducting excavations, making records and plotting.

I. Stratigraphic accumulation

Based on differences in soil properties, colors and items contained within and through summarization, strata in present square unit for exploration can be divided into six strata (Figure 5; Plate 16). However, only stratums ①, ②, ⑤a and ⑥ are continuously distributed strata, and other stratums in the square units are not continuously distributed, reflecting by the fact that some stratums on the four walls are absent. For instance, on the east wall of T1, the stratums ③, ④b, and ⑤b are absent; on the west wall, the stratums ④ and ⑤b are absent; on the south wall, the stratums ③ and ④ are absent; on the north wall, the stratums ③ and ④ are absent. The details are stated as follows:

Stratum ①: 8 – 10 cm thick, yellow – gray color topsoil; loose soil, containing a small amount of ceramic, plastic and plant roots *etc*. Under this layer laminated G1.

Stratum ②: Thickness of 0 – 30, and 10 cm deep; yellow – red color soil; soil is hard, containing a large amount of red bricks, some blue and white porcelain pieces, white porcelain pieces and a very small amount of stone tools; accumulated over modern and contemporary times.

Stratum ③: Thickness from 0 – 16, 20 cm deep; light – gray color soil; soil is fine, containing a small amount of bricks, porcelain pieces and other items; accumulated over modern and contemporary times.

Stratum ④: It is distributed in the northeast part of the east beam of the square units for exploration, and only contains ④a layer, 0 – 12 cm thick, dark brown color topsoil; containing a high content of iron and manganese and a very small amount of ceramic and pottery chips; accumulated in the period from Nhà Đinh dynasty to pre Lê dynasty.

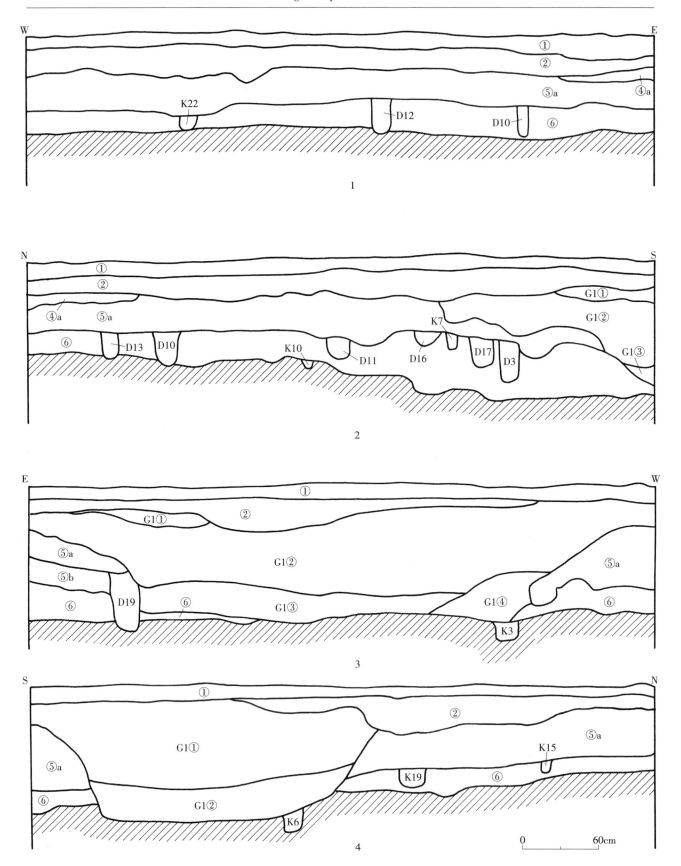

Figure 5   Sectional View of Four Walls of T1
1. North wall   2. East wall   3. South wall   4. West wall

Stratum ⑤: Based on different earth tones and soil, this layer can be divided into two sub – layers. It is accumulated from Phung Nguyen culture period.

⑤a: 20 – 52 thick, 34cm deep. Dark – gray color soil; soil is loose, containing more burnt soil particles. Including a large number of pottery and a small number of stone tools. Under this layer laminated with 23 pits or postholes.

⑤b: Thickness of 12 – 20, depth of 60 – 90cm. Pale yellow soil; the soil is hard, contain less materials, mainly pottery and stoneware. Under this layer laminated with 16 pits or postholes.

Stratum ⑥: Thickness of 12 – 24, 56 – 90 cm deep. Brown soil, mixed with a small amount of dust spots, hard soil. Very few inclusions. Under this layer lamination has two pits or postholes. It is accumulated from Phung Nguyen culture period.

Under this stratum is reddish – brown ferromanganese raw soil.

II. Remains

A total of 78 remains of various types were found in this square unit, including 77 cultural remains of the Phung Nguyen culture period, which consist of 47 pits and 30 postholes (Figure 6; Plate 17).

Pits: 47 in total; 23 opening under Stratum ⑤a and 16 opening under Stratum ⑤b, 6 laminated under G1, and 2 opening under Stratum ⑥. Plane shapes are substantially irregular oval or circular; pit walls are rough and bottoms are also uneven. Some are probably pit nests of natural formation, later filled by human. A small number of pottery pieces were unearthed in some of the pits.

Postholes: 30 in total; 22 opening under Stratum ⑤a, 6 opening under Stratum ⑤b, and 2 opening under Stratum ⑥. Plane shapes are substantially circular or oval, relatively structured, some postholes show signs of breakage in plain view, indicating where columns originally existed. Fillings are grayish black soil or black soil, loose soil. Some pits contain small number of pottery pieces. However, these postholes are together with a large number of pits, making it difficult to analyze it as a complete building. In order to accurately reflect the pits and postholes of this exploration square unit, pits and postholes in the square unit are listed below.

Table 1   Statistics of Pits and Postholes in Strata under T1   Unit: cm

S/N	Numbering	Horizon level	Shape and structure			Dimensions (diameter – depth)	Soil	Figure No.
			Plane form	Walls of the pit	Bottom of pit			
1	K1	Under ⑤a	Irregular oval	Uneven	Dome shaped	18 ~ 36 – 25	Grayish black soil	Figure 7:23
2	K2	Under ⑤a	Oval	Even	Flat	15 ~ 26 – 15	Gray soil	Figure 7:24
3	K3	Under ⑤a	Irregular oval	Uneven	Dome shaped	18 ~ 44 – 30	Grayish black soil	Figure 7:25

(continued 1)

S/N	Numbering	Horizon level	Shape and structure			Dimensions (diameter – depth)	Soil	Figure No.
			Plane form	Walls of the pit	Bottom of pit			
4	K4	Under ⑤a	Irregular oval	Uneven	Dome shaped	17 × 25 – 15	Grayish black soil	Figure 7 : 26
5	K5	Under ⑤a	Oval	Even	Flat	27 ~ 35 – 15	Grayish black soil	Figure 7 : 27
6	K6	Under ⑤a	Irregular oval	Uneven	Uneven	10 ~ 39 – 15	Grayish black soil	Figure 7 : 28
7	K7	Under ⑤a	Round	Even	Dome shaped	15 – 13	Grayish black soil	Figure 7 : 29
8	K8	Under ⑤a	Almost round	Even	Dome shaped	14 ~ 18 – 13	Grayish black soil	Figure 7 : 30
9	K9	Under ⑤a	Oval	Even	Dome shaped	15 ~ 19 – 18	Black soil	Figure 7 : 31
10	K10	Under ⑤a	Round	Even	Dome shaped	22 – 20	Grayish black soil	Figure 7 : 32
11	K11	Under ⑤a	Irregular round	Even	Dome shaped	19 – 20	Grayish black soil	Figure 7 : 33
12	K12	Under ⑤a	Round	Even	Dome shaped	20 – 27	Black soil	Figure 7 : 34
13	K13	Under ⑤a	Irregular oval	Uneven	Uneven	24 ~ 47 – 20	Grayish black soil	Figure 7 : 35
14	K14	Under ⑤a	Irregular oval	Uneven	Uneven	18 ~ 27 – 18	Grayish black soil	Figure 7 : 36
15	K15	Under ⑤a	Irregular oval	Uneven	Uneven	13 ~ 32 – 17	Grayish black soil	Figure 7 : 37
16	K16	Under ⑤a	Irregular oval	Uneven	Uneven	10 ~ 25 – 10	Black soil	Figure 7 : 38
17	K17	⑤a	Round	Even	Dome shaped	18 – 20	Grayish black soil	Figure 7 : 39
18	K18	Under ⑤a	Round	Even	Dome shaped	14 – 14	Grayish black soil	Figure 7 : 40
19	K19	Under ⑤a	Almost round	Even	Dome shaped	20 ~ 25 – 13	Grayish black soil	Figure 7 : 41
20	K20	Under ⑤a	Oval	Uneven	Uneven	18 ~ 23 – 25	Gray soil	Figure 7 : 42
21	K21	Under ⑤a	Oval	Even	Dome shaped	20 ~ 25 – 25	Grayish black soil	Figure 7 : 43
22	K22	Under ⑤a	Oval	Even	Flat	15 ~ 30 – 28	Grayish black soil	Figure 7 : 44
23	K23	Under ⑤a	Oval	Even	Flat	22 ~ 33 – 25	Black soil	Figure 7 : 45
24	D1	Under ⑤a	Almost round	Even	Dome shaped	23 ~ 25 – 38	Grayish black soil	Figure 7 : 1
25	D2	Under ⑤a	Oval	Even	Dome shaped	15 ~ 20 – 39	Gray soil	Figure 7 : 2
26	D3	Under ⑤a	Round	Even	Dome shaped	23 – 35	Grayish black soil	Figure 7 : 3
27	D4	Under ⑤a	Round	Even	Dome shaped	15 – 24	Grayish black soil	Figure 7 : 4
28	D5	Under ⑤a	Oval	Uneven	Dome shaped	10 ~ 20 – 23	Grayish black soil	Figure 7 : 5
29	D6	Under ⑤a	Oval	Uneven	Uneven	25 ~ 35 – 33	Grayish black soil	Figure 7 : 6
30	D7	Under ⑤a	Round	Uneven	Uneven	28 – 30	Grayish black soil	Figure 7 : 7
31	D8	Under ⑤a	Oval	Even	Dome shaped	17 ~ 21 – 25	Grayish black soil	Figure 7 : 8
32	D9	Under ⑤a	Oval	Even	Dome shaped	14 ~ 20 – 23	Grayish black soil	Figure 7 : 9
33	D10	Under ⑤a	Oval	Even	Dome shaped	15 ~ 21 – 20	Grayish black soil	Figure 7 : 10
34	D11	Under ⑤a	Oval	Even	Dome shaped	15 ~ 20 – 25	Grayish black soil	Figure 7 : 11
35	D12	Under ⑤a	Almost round	Even	Dome shaped	12 ~ 18 – 15	Grayish black soil	Figure 7 : 12

(continued 1)

S/N	Numbering	Horizon level	Shape and structure			Dimensions (diameter – depth)	Soil	Figure No.
			Plane form	Walls of the pit	Bottom of pit			
36	D13	Under ⑤a	Oval	Even	Dome shaped	20 ~ 25 – 25	Black soil	Figure 7 : 13
37	D14	Under ⑤a	Round	Even	Dome shaped	25 – 26	Grayish black soil	Figure 7 : 14
38	D15	Under ⑤a	Oval	Even	Flat	22 ~ 25 – 23	Grayish black soil	Figure 7 : 15
39	D16	Under ⑤a	Oval	Even	Dome shaped	22 ~ 34 – 38	Black soil	Figure 7 : 16
40	D17	Under ⑤a	Oval	Even	Dome shaped	19 ~ 23 – 25	Grayish black soil	Figure 7 : 17
41	D18	Under ⑤a	Oval	Uneven	Flat	20 ~ 25 – 35	Black soil	Figure 7 : 18
42	D19	Under ⑤a	Oval	Uneven	Uneven	14 ~ 23 – 48	Grayish black soil	Figure 7 : 19
43	D20	Under ⑤a	Round	Uneven	Flat	22 – 45	Black soil	Figure 7 : 20
44	D21	Under ⑤a	Round	Even	Dome shaped	15 – 32	Grayish black soil	Figure 7 : 21
45	D22	Under ⑤a	Round	Even	Dome shaped	20 – 35	Grayish black soil	Figure 7 : 22
46	K1	Under ⑤b	Oval	Even	Dome shaped	13 ~ 18 – 8	Black soil	Figure 8 : 7
47	K2	Under ⑤b	Oval	Even	Dome shaped	18 ~ 29 – 14	Black soil	Figure 8 : 8
48	K3	Under ⑤b	Oval	Even	Flat	18 ~ 22 – 13	Gray soil	Figure 8 : 9
49	K4	Under ⑤b	Oval	Even	Dome shaped	11 ~ 18 – 9	Grayish black soil	Figure 8 : 10
50	K5	Under ⑤b	Pear shaped	Uneven	Uneven	16 ~ 71 – 18	Black soil	Figure 8 : 11
51	K6	Under ⑤b	Oval	Uneven	Dome shaped	11 ~ 13 – 18	Grayish black soil	Figure 8 : 12
52	K7	Under ⑤b	Round	Uneven	Dome shaped	8 – 13	Grayish black soil	Figure 8 : 13
53	K8	Under ⑤b	Round	Uneven	Dome shaped	20 – 6	Black soil	Figure 8 : 14
54	K9	Under ⑤b	Round	Uneven	Dome shaped	16 – 9	Grayish black soil	Figure 8 : 15
55	K10	Under ⑤b	Round	Uneven	Dome shaped	15 – 7	Grayish black soil	Figure 8 : 16
56	K11	Under ⑤b	Oval	Uneven	Dome shaped	9 ~ 20 – 9	Black soil	Figure 8 : 17
57	K12	Under ⑤b	Round	Uneven	Dome shaped	11 – 6	Grayish black soil	Figure 8 : 18
58	K13	Under ⑤b	Oval	Uneven	Dome shaped	18 ~ 24 – 6	Black soil	Figure 8 : 19
59	K14	Under ⑤b	Oval	Uneven	Dome shaped	14 – 9	Grayish black soil	Figure 8 : 20
60	K15	Under ⑤b	Irregular oval	Uneven	Flat	6 ~ 18 – 6	Black soil	Figure 8 : 21
61	K16	Under ⑤b	Almost round	Even	Dome shaped	18 ~ 21 – 6	Grayish black soil	Figure 8 : 22
62	D1	Under ⑤b	Oval	Even	Flat	27 – 22	Black soil	Figure 8 : 1
63	D2	Under ⑤b	Oval	Even	Dome shaped	16 – 16	Gray soil	Figure 8 : 2
64	D3	Under ⑤b	Irregular oval	Even	Dome shaped	15 ~ 38 – 37	Grayish black soil	Figure 8 : 3
65	D4	Under ⑤b	Irregular oval	Even	Dome shaped	15 ~ 27 – 33	Grayish black soil	Figure 8 : 4
66	D5	Under ⑤b	Round	Even	Dome shaped	16 – 9	Black soil	Figure 8 : 5
67	D6	Under ⑤b	Irregular oval	Even	Dome shaped	17 ~ 27 – 20	Grayish black soil	Figure 8 : 6

(continued 1)

S/N	Numbering	Horizon level	Shape and structure			Dimensions (diameter – depth)	Soil	Figure No.
			Plane form	Walls of the pit	Bottom of pit			
68	K1	Under G1	Round	Even	Dome shaped	24 – 10	Grayish black soil	Figure 8 : 23
69	K2	Under G1	Oval	Even	Dome shaped	10 ~ 17 – 9	Black soil	Figure 8 : 24
70	K3	Under G1	Oval	Uneven	Uneven	11 ~ 22 – 14	Grayish black soil	Figure 8 : 25
71	K4	Under G1	Round	Even	Dome shaped	17 – 9	Black soil	Figure 8 : 26
72	K5	Under G1	Oval	Even	Dome shaped	11 ~ 16 – 6	Grayish black soil	Figure 8 : 27
73	K6	Under G1	Oval	Even	Dome shaped	16 ~ 18 – 13	Black soil	Figure 8 : 28
74	D1	Under ⑥	Round	Even	Dome shaped	22 – 22	Grayish black soil	Figure 8 : 29
75	D2	Under ⑥	Oval	Even	Dome shaped	18 ~ 26 – 20	Black soil	Figure 8 : 30
76	K1	Under ⑥	Irregular	Uneven	Uneven	23 ~ 38 – 21	Grayish black soil	Figure 8 : 32
77	K2	Under ⑥	Irregular	Uneven	Dome shaped	9 ~ 37 – 29	Black soil	Figure 8 : 31

III. Unearthed relics by stratum

1. Unearthed artifacts of stratum T1⑤a

Artifacts unearthed in stratum T1⑤a are mostly pottery objects, with a small number of stone tools and jade items. A total of 341 specimens were selected, including 29 stone tools, 3 jade pieces, 1 horn piece, and a total of 308 pottery pieces.

Stone tools： 29 pieces. These are mostly ground stone tools, but severely damaged. Possibly in the course of use or re – use, a large number of scars resulted on the surface of the stone tools. The scars are mainly concentrated at the top, one side or the body surface of the tool. These include 12 stone adzes, 1 stone chisel, 2 stone cores, 1 scraper, 1 stone flapper, and 12 residual stone tools.

Stone adzes： 12 pieces; according to the different shapes, these can be divided into two types.

Category 1：3 pieces; substantially rectangular, double – sided arc blade.

Specimens T1②：1, damaged, ground to shape, double arc edge, top and rear side have visible hit points and radiation rays. Length of 6.8, remaining part of width of 4.6, thickness of 1.6cm (Figure 9: 1; Plate 18: 1). Specimen T1⑤a: 13, damaged, one side has been flaked, visible on the other side are the hit points and radiation rays left from flaking, grinding traces visible on blade, remaining part of length of 6.4, width of 4.9 and thickness of 1.8cm (Figure 9: 2; Plate 18: 2). Specimen T1⑤a: 14, severely damaged, visible on one side grinding traces and visible on the other side the hit points and radiation rays from flaking, remaining part of length of 4, width of 2.8, and thickness of 1cm (Figure 9: 3).

Category 2：Presenting a trapezoid overall, ground to shape, single – sided arc blade. Specimen

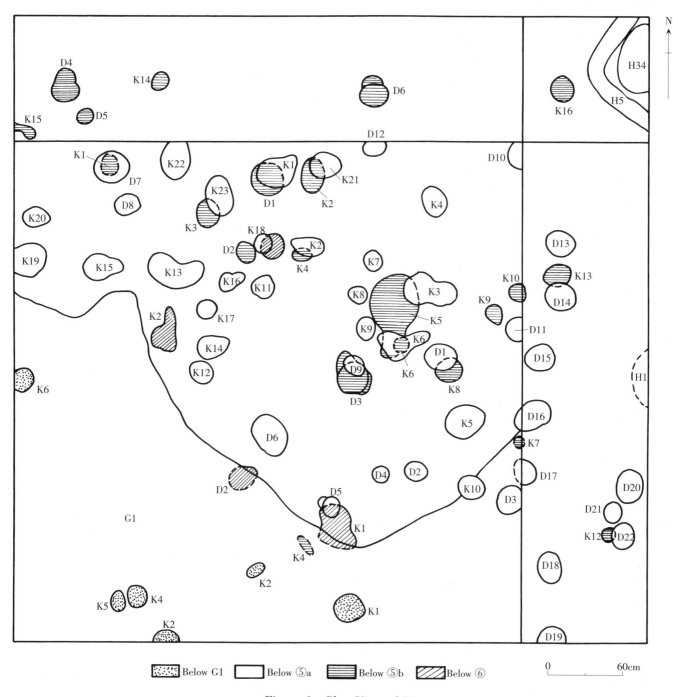

Below G1   Below ⑤a   Below ⑤b   Below ⑥

0   60cm

Figure 6   Plan View of T1

T1⑤a：7, damaged in the upper portion, impact points and radiation rays can be seen on top of one side, remaining part of length of 4.4, width of 3 − 3.7, thickness of 1.7cm（Figure 9：4; Plate 18：3）. Specimen T1⑤a：1, badly damaged, a slot in the middle of the tool; remaining part of length of 4.8; remaining part of width of 2.5, thickness of 1.2cm（Figure 9：5）. Specimen T1⑤a：2, damaged, impact points and radiation rays can be seen on top of one side; remaining part of length of 3.9; remaining part of width of 2.8, thickness of 0.7cm（Figure 9：6; Plate 18：4）. Specimen T1⑤a：6,

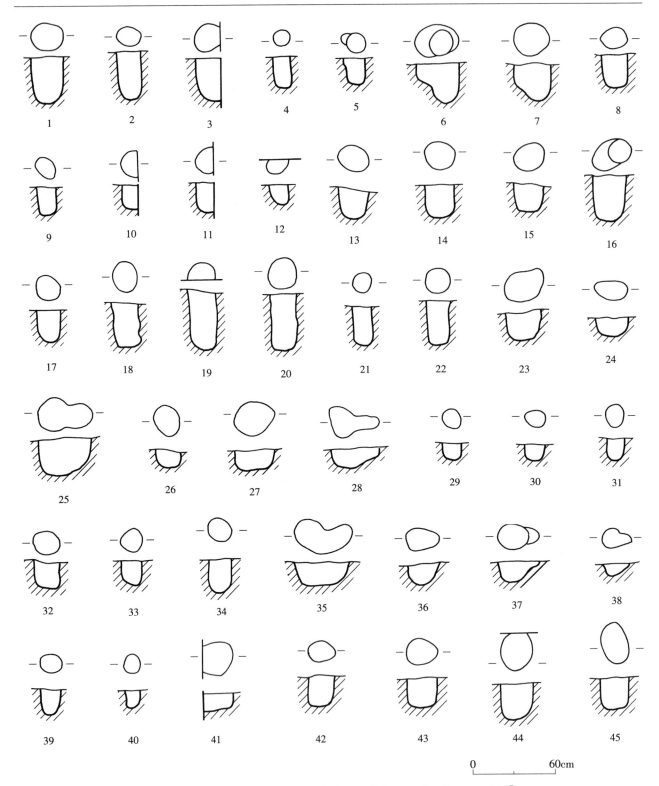

Figure 7   Sectional Plan of Postholes and Pits under Stratum T1⑤a
1 – 22. D1 – D22   23 – 45. K1 – K23

damaged, flaking marks remain on body of the tool; of length of 3.3, width of 3.2, thickness of

0.7cm (Figure 9:7). Specimen T1②:6, only small section in lower part remains; remaining part of

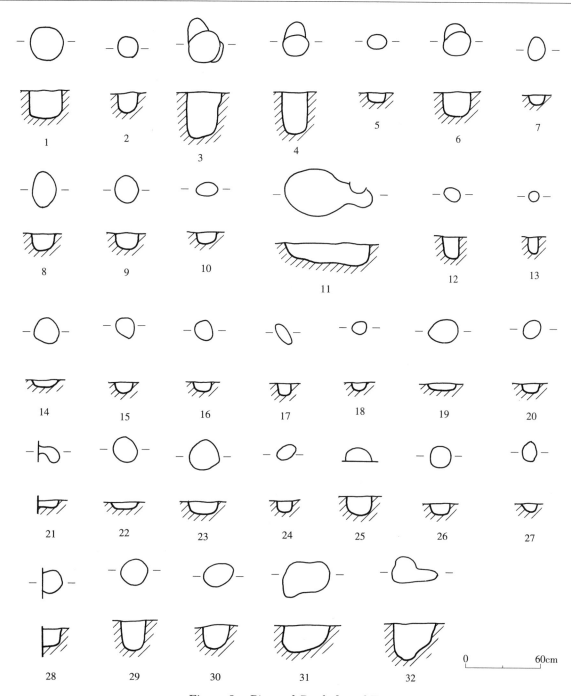

Figure 8   Pits and Postholes of T1
1 – 6. D1 – D6 (Below T1⑤b)   7 – 22. K1 – K16 (Below T1⑤b)   23 – 28. K1 – K6 (Below G1)
29 – 32. D1, D2, K1, K2 (Below T1⑥)

length of 5; remaining part of width of 1. 9, thickness of 0. 8cm (Figure 9 : 8). Specimen T1②: 4,
damaged, ground blade, apparent flaking traces on surface; on top and blade impact points and radiation rays from impact are visible; remaining part of length of 6; remaining part of width of 4. 2, thickness of 1. 3cm (Figure 9 : 9). Specimen G1 : 1, damaged on one side, apparent traces of use on one
side; remaining part of length of 5. 1, width of 3. 8, thickness of 0. 7cm (Figure 10 : 1; Plate 19 : 1).

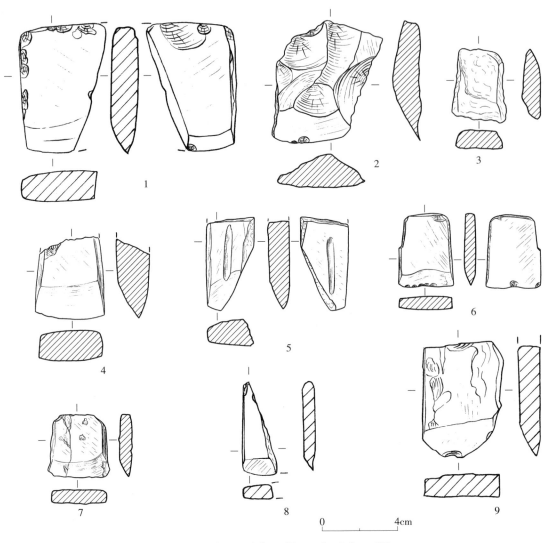

Figure 9   Stone Adzes Unearthed from T1

1. T1②: 1   2. T1⑤a: 13   3. T1⑤a: 14   4. T1⑤a: 7   5. T1⑤a: 1   6. T1⑤a: 2   7. T1⑤a: 6   8. T1②: 6   9. T1②: 4

Specimen T1⑤a: 10, damaged in upper part and on one side, remaining part of length of 4. 8; remaining part of width of 3 − 3. 8, thickness of 2. 7cm (Figure 10: 2; Plate 19: 2). Specimen T1⑤a: 25, damaged, grinding traces visible on one side and top, marks from impact visible on the other side; remaining part of length of 2. 4, width of 2. 1, thickness of 0. 6cm (Figure 10: 5; Plate 19: 3).

Stone chisel: 1 piece.

Specimen G1: 2; the upper portion damaged, ground to shape, in the shape of a long strip, double − sided arc blade, remaining part of length of 2. 2 width of 1, and thickness of 0. 7 cm (Figure 10: 4).

Stone cores: 2 pieces.

Specimen T1②: 8; damaged, body shape is of irregular rectangle, impact points and radiation rays from flaking visible on top part; remaining part of length of 8. 6; remaining part of width of 4. 2, thickness of 1. 6cm (Figure 10: 3). Specimen T1⑤a: 23; body shape is of irregular rectangle, marks from flaking visible on one side, length of 4. 6, width of 4. 6, thickness of 1. 6cm (Figure 10: 6).

Figure 10 Stone Tools Unearthed from T1

1, 2, 5. Stone adze (G1:1、T1⑤a:10、T1⑤a:25) 3, 6. Stone core (T1②:8、T1⑤a:23) 4. Stone chisel (G1:2) 7. Jade arrowhead (T1⑤a:8) 8. Jade adze (T1⑤a:3) 9. Stone flapper (T1⑤a:373) 10. Stone scraper (T1⑤a:5) 11. Jade ring (T1⑤a:20)

Scraper: 1 piece.

Specimen T1⑤a:5, body shape is of triangle, natural rock surface on one side, marks from flaking visible on the other side, impact points and radiation rays from impact visible on one side; length of 3. 1, width of 2. 9, thickness of 0. 9cm (Figure 10 : 10).

Stone flapper: 1 piece.

Specimen T1⑤a : 373, damaged, body shape is of rectangle, apparent flaking traces on surface; two concave slots visible on one side; remaining part of length of 5. 4; remaining part of width of 5. 6, thickness of 2. 9cm (Figure 10 : 9).

Stone tool residues: 12 pieces; possibly formed from broken or flaked stone axes or stone adzes.

Specimen T1②: 2, damaged, body shape is of rectangle, grinding traces visible on top and one side, blade damaged, impact points and radiation rays from impact are visible on one side, top and blade; remaining part of length of 5. 5; remaining part of width of 4. 6, thickness of 1. 6cm (Figure 11 : 1). Specimen T1②: 3, damaged, only upper part remains, ground to shape, remaining part of length of 2. 6, width of 2. 5, thickness of 1. 4 − 1. 6cm (Figure 11 : 8). Specimen T1②: 7, damaged, ground to shape, marks from flaking visible on one side, impact points and radiation rays from impact are visible on lower end; remaining part of length of 2. 2, width of 1. 5, thickness of 0. 6cm (Figure 11 : 2). Specimen T1⑤a: 11, body shape is of irregular rectangle, some grinding traces visible on surface, remaining part of length of 3. 4; remaining part of width of 4, thickness of 1. 5cm (Figure 11 : 10). Specimen T1⑤a: 16, body shape is of irregular rectangle, flaking marks remaining on surface; remaining part of length of 4. 4; remaining part of width of 3. 1, thickness of 1. 8cm (Figure 11 : 11). Specimen T1⑤a : 12, damaged, flaking marks remaining on surface; remaining part of length of 3. 8, width of 2. 8, thickness of 0. 9cm (Figure 11 : 12). Specimen T1⑤a : 21, damaged, body shape is of rectangle, flaking marks remaining on surface; remaining part of length of 9, width of 5. 5, thickness of 0. 6cm (Figure 11 : 3). Specimen T1⑤a : 15, severely damaged; grinding traces visible on one side and one angle, impact points and radiation rays from impact are visible on the other side and angle; remaining part of length of 7. 6; remaining part of width of 4. 8, thickness of 3. 2cm (Figure 11 : 7). Specimen T1⑤a : 24, body shape is of rectangle, small part remains, apparent flaking traces on surface; remaining part of length of 2. 7; remaining part of width of 2, thickness of 0. 7cm (Figure 11 : 6). Specimen T1⑤a: 22, severely damaged; grinding traces visible on both sides of surface; remaining part of length of 2. 8; remaining part of width of 1. 9, thickness of 0. 5cm (Figure 11 : 5). Specimen T1⑤a : 17, damaged, grinding traces visible on one side, remaining part of length of 4. 6; remaining part of width of 4. 6, thickness of 1. 2cm (Figure 11 : 9). Specimen T1⑤a: 19, damaged, body shape is of rectangle, residual from flaking, remaining part of length of 5. 8; remaining part of width of 2. 8, thickness of 1. 4cm (Figure 11 : 4).

Jade pieces: 3 pieces; including mainly 1 jade ring, 1 jade axe and 1 arrowhead.

Jade ring: 1 piece.

Specimen T1⑤a : 20, damaged, only 1/3 remains, beige color, of a round body; diameter of

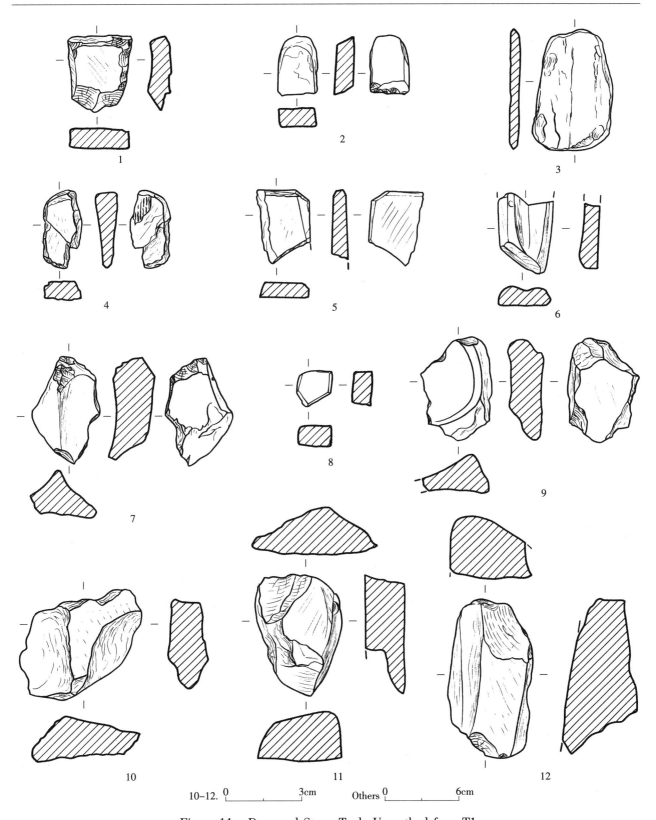

Figure 11   Damaged Stone Tools Unearthed from T1

1. T1②:2   2. T1②:7   3. T1⑤a:21   4. T1⑤a:19   5. T1⑤a:22   6. T1⑤a:24   7. T1⑤a:15   8. T1②:3
9. T1⑤a:17   10. T1⑤a:11   11. T1⑤a:16   12. T1⑤a:12

6. 1, width of 0. 5, thickness of 0. 2cm (Figure 10:11).

Jade adze: 1 piece.

Specimen T1⑤a:3, damaged in the upper portion, ground to shape, body shape is of rectangle, double – sided arc blade; remaining part of length of 3. 3, width of 3. 7, thickness of 0. 9cm (Figure 10:9; Plate 20:1).

Arrowhead: 1 piece.

Specimen T1⑤a:8, only head remains, triangular, ground to shape; remaining part of length of 1. 8, width of 1, thickness of 0. 1cm (Figure 10:10; Plate 20:2).

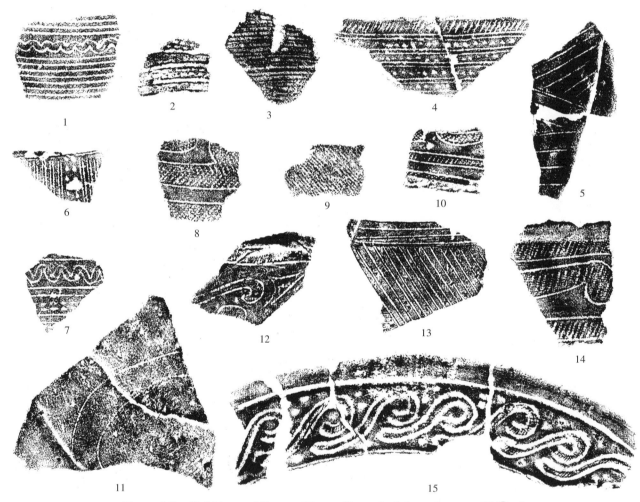

Figure 12   Rubbings of Pottery Pieces Unearthed from Stratum T1⑤a*

1. Water ripple pattern + concave string pattern (T1⑤a:279)   2. Concave string pattern (T1⑤a:351)   3. Thin rope pattern (T1⑤a:21)   4. Short line + concave string pattern + pit dot pattern (T1⑤a:353)   5. Engraved line pattern (T1⑤a:249) 6. Concave string pattern + engraved line pattern + pit dot pattern (T1⑤a:357)   7. Water ripple pattern + concave string pattern (T1⑤a:379)   8. Engraved pattern + combed dot pattern (T1⑤a:301)   9. Thin rope pattern (T1⑤a:55)   10. Engraved pattern + combed dot pattern (T1⑤a:315)   11. Engraved pattern (T1⑤a:257)   12. Protruding rim + engraved pattern (T1⑤a:230)   13. Concave string pattern + engraved line pattern (T1⑤a:247)   14. Engraved line pattern + combed dot pattern (T1⑤a:317)   15. Concave string pattern + S – shape pattern (T1⑤a:188)

* Unless otherwise indicated, all pottery rubbings herein do not have the scale.

Horn piece: 1 piece, 1 horn ring.

Specimen T1⑤a：9, damaged, black, body of circle shape, remaining part of length of 2.5, width of 1.3, thickness of 0.1cm.

Pottery pieces: A total of 7052 potter pieces were unearthed in Stratum ⑤a in this square unit. In terms of the earthenware materials, fine sand earthenware accounts for about 82.4%, coarse sand earthenware for about 15.2%, and clay polished earthenware for about 2.4%. In terms of colors of the pottery pieces, terracotta, reddish brown, and brown pottery pieces account

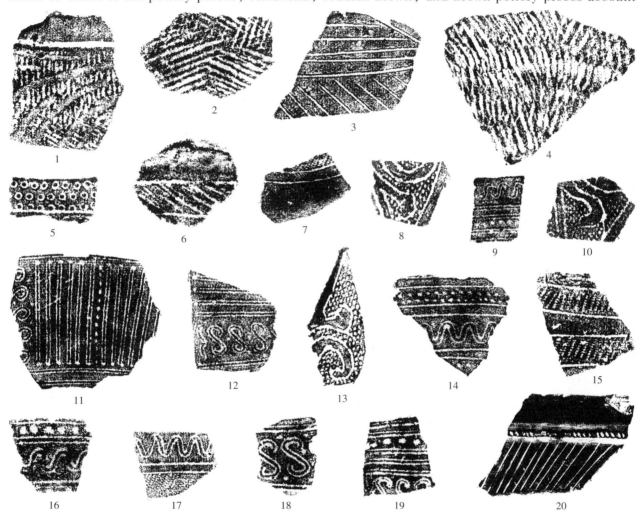

Figure 13   Rubbings of Pottery Pieces Unearthed from Stratum T1⑤a

1. Concave string pattern + thin rope pattern (T1⑤a：98)   2. Twist rope pattern (T1⑤a：53)   3. Engraved line pattern (T1⑤a：248)   4. Rope pattern (T1⑤a：54)   5. Circle pattern + concave string pattern (T1⑤a：18)   6. Concave string pattern + short line pattern (T1⑤a：62)   7. Engraved pattern + combed dot pattern (T1⑤a：293)   8. Engraved pattern + combed dot pattern (T1⑤a：16)   9. S－shape pattern + concave string pattern (T1⑤a：275)   10. Engraved pattern + combed dot pattern (T1⑤a：12)   11. S－shape pattern + engraved line pattern + concave string pattern (T1⑤a：283)   12. Concave string pattern + S－shape pattern (T1⑤a：284)   13. Engraved pattern + combed dot pattern (T1⑤a：4)   14. Water ripple pattern + concave string pattern (T1⑤a：278)   15. Engraved pattern + combed dot pattern (T1⑤a：8)   16. Dot pattern + concave string pattern + S－shape pattern (T1⑤a：276)   17. Water ripple pattern + concave string pattern + combed dot pattern (T1⑤a：282)   18. Concave string pattern + S－shape pattern (T1⑤a：288)   19. Concave string pattern + pit dot pattern + S－shape pattern (T1⑤a：17)   20. Protruding rim + pit dot pattern + engraved line pattern (T1⑤a：246)

for about 84. 7% , indicating that the pottery color is mostly reddish. In terms of pattern ornamentation, it was extremely well – developed, accounting for 31. 1% of the total number of pottery pieces. Some pieces have on the surface a thin ornamented coating. The decorations are of great variety, in which rope decorations account for about 82% of the total decorations. Other decorations include engraved line, stamp, concave string, protruding rim, pressure stamp, comb brushing, added mound and combed dots *etc*. Particularly, among all the engraved lines, the ones with comb teeth brushed or

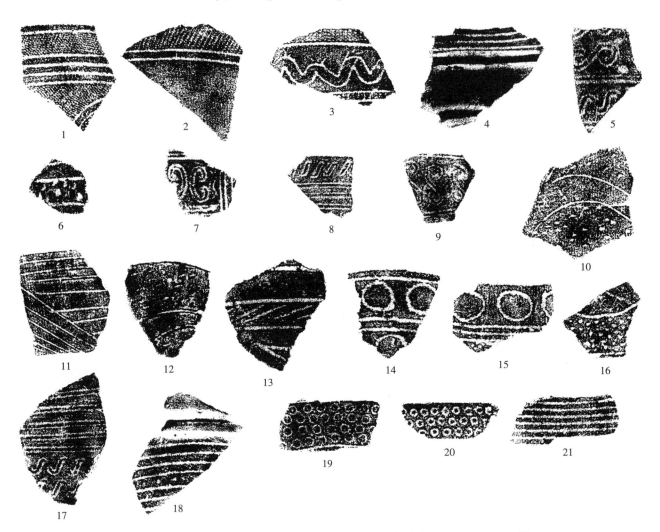

Figure 14   Rubbings of Pottery Pieces Unearthed from Stratum T1⑤a

1. Engraved pattern + combed dot pattern (T1⑤a : 332)   2. Concave string pattern + rope pattern (T1⑤a : 334)   3. Concave string pattern + water ripple pattern + rope pattern (T1⑤a : 280)   4. Concave string pattern + protruding rim (T1⑤a : 209)   5. Concave string pattern + S – shape pattern (T1⑤a : 289)   6. Concave string pattern + pit dot pattern (T1⑤a : 74)   7. Engraved line pattern + cloud pattern (T1⑤a : 291)   8. Concave string pattern + S – shape pattern (T1⑤a : 290)   9. Concave string pattern + S – shape pattern (T1 ⑤ a : 332)   10. Engraved pattern (T1 ⑤ a : 252)   11. Engraved line pattern (T1⑤a : 253)   12. Engraved pattern (T1⑤a : 250)   13. Engraved pattern + poked pattern (T1⑤a : 235)   14. Concave string pattern + circle pattern (T1⑤a : 259)   15. Circle pattern + concave string pattern + combed dot pattern (T1⑤a : 257)   16. Engraved pattern + combed dot pattern (T1⑤a : 251)   17. Concave string pattern + S – shape pattern (T1⑤a : 273)   18. Protruding rim + concave string pattern (T1⑤a : 267)   19. Circle pattern + concave string pattern (T1⑤a : 261)   20. Circle pattern (T1⑤a : 262)   21. Concave string pattern (T1⑤a : 270)

comb dotted stamps are the most characteristic. Compound ornamentations of multiple decorations on a

single pottery piece appear to have been very popular. The main ornamentation patterns are of clouds,

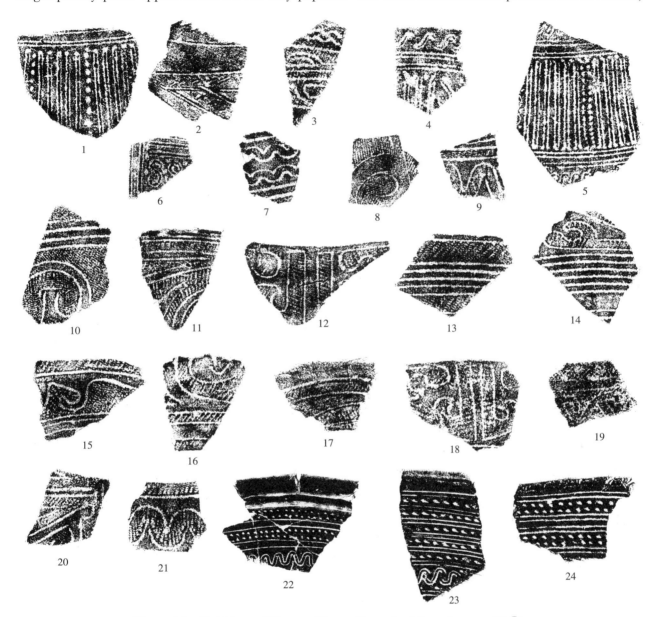

Figure 15   Rubbings of Pottery Pieces Unearthed from Stratum T1⑤a

1. Concave string pattern + engraved line pattern + pit dot pattern（T1⑤a：272）   2. Engraved line pattern（T1⑤a：256）   3. Water ripple pattern + engraved pattern（T1⑤a：309）   4. S – shape pattern + concave string pattern + engraved line pattern（T1⑤a：274）   5. Concave string pattern + engraved line pattern + pit dot pattern + S – shape pattern（T1⑤a：271）   6. S – shape pattern + engraved line pattern（T1⑤a：286）   7. Concave string pattern + water ripple pattern（T1⑤a：281）   8. Engraved pattern + combed dot pattern（T1⑤a：292）   9. Engraved pattern + water ripple pattern（T1⑤a：300）   10, 11. Concave string pattern + engraved pattern（T1⑤a：320, 322）   12. Engraved pattern（T1⑤a：319）   13. Concave string pattern + combed dot pattern（T1⑤a：294）   14. Engraved pattern + concave string pattern（T1⑤a：318）   15, 16, 17. Concave string pattern + engraved pattern（T1⑤a：321, 323, 313）   18, 19, 20. Engraved pattern + combed dot pattern（T1⑤a：307, 310, 308）   21. Engraved pattern + combed dot pattern + water ripple pattern（T1⑤a：299）   22. Concave string pattern + pit dot pattern + water ripple pattern（T1⑤a：277）   23. Concave string pattern + dot pattern + S – shape pattern（T1⑤a：287）   24. Concave string pattern + pit dot pattern（T1⑤a：343）

S – shape, geometric patterns, circles and water ripples (Figure 12 – 18; Plates 21 – 25) and the like. Pottery mouth parts are mostly contracted or flared; followed in number by trumpet – shaped and straight mouths. The artifacts are mostly with enclosure base and ring feet. Forms of the artifacts include flare – mouth jars, bowls, buckets, bases, thick lip jars, spinning wheels and pottery balls.

T1⑤a: A total of 308 specimens of pottery pieces are selected, of which 151 specimens are for

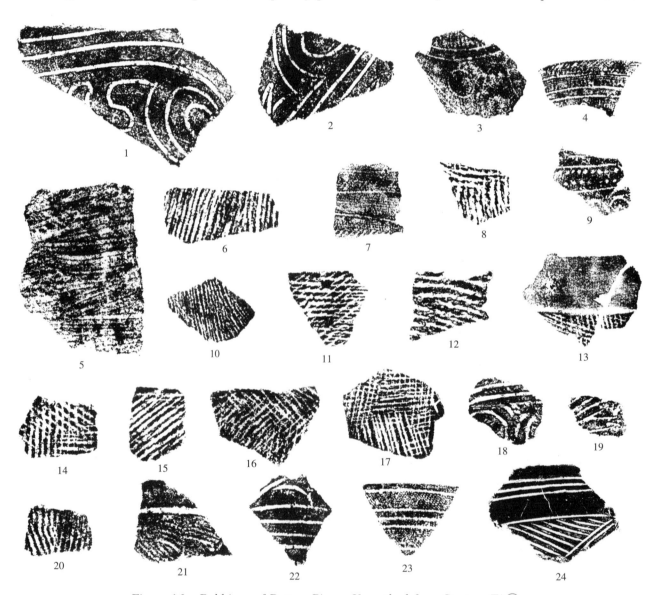

Figure 16   Rubbings of Pottery Pieces Unearthed from Stratum T1⑤a

1, 2, 3. Engraved pattern (T1⑤a: 215, 216, 375)   4. Concave string pattern + combed dot pattern (T1⑤a: 377)   5. Combing pattern (T1⑤a: 369)   6. Rope pattern (T1⑤a: 87)   7. Concave string pattern + rope pattern (T1⑤a: 359)   8. Rope pattern (T1⑤a: 368)   9. Concave string pattern + combed dot pattern (T1⑤a: 349)   10. Rope pattern (T1⑤a: 107)   11. Twist rope pattern (T1⑤a: 39 – 1)   12. Rope pattern (T1⑤a: 88)   13. Concave string pattern + twist rope pattern (T1⑤a: 108)   14. Twist rope pattern (T1⑤a: 83)   15. Rope pattern (T1⑤a: 39 – 3)   16. Twist rope pattern (T1⑤a: 39 – 2)   17. Twist rope pattern (T1⑤a: 82)   18, 19. Engraved pattern (T1⑤a: 243, 366)   20. Rope pattern (T1⑤a: 101)   21. Concave string pattern + rope pattern (T1⑤a: 214)   22. Concave string pattern + engraved pattern (T1⑤a: 232)   23. Concave string pattern + combed dot pattern (T1⑤a: 331)   24. Concave string pattern + engraved pattern (T1⑤a: 245)

ornamentations, 157 specimens are for forms, including 2 spinning wheel, 5 seats, 5 handles, 1 ear, 32 ring feet, 12 trumpet – mouth jars, 21 thick lip jars, 22 flare mouth jars, 1 bucket, 1 contracted mouth jar, and 55 bowls.

Spinning wheels: 2 pieces; based on shape and structure, these can be classified into two categories.

Category 1: 1 piece; in a tower shape, with a hole in the middle.

Specimen T1⑤a:4, damaged, terracotta; diameter of 1 – 3. 7, overall height of 2. 3, bore diameter of 0. 5cm (Figure 19:7; Plate 26:2).

Category 2: 1 piece; body presenting pie shape, with a hole in the middle.

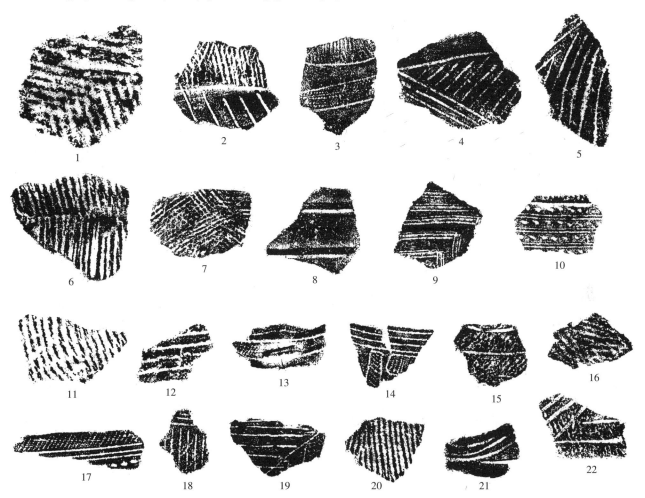

Figure 17   Rubbings of Pottery Pieces Unearthed from Stratum T1⑤a

1. Rope pattern (T1⑤a:46)   2, 3. Rope pattern + engraved line pattern (T1⑤a:45, 338)   4, 5. Engraved line pattern (T1⑤a:211, 217)   6. Rope pattern (T1⑤a:37)   7. Twist rope pattern (T1⑤a:105)   8. Protruding rim pattern (T1⑤a:134)   9. Engraved pattern (T1⑤a:224)   10. Protruding rim pattern + concave string pattern + pit dot pattern (T1⑤a:348)   11. Rope pattern (T1⑤a:367)   12. Concave string pattern (T1⑤a:72)   13. Concave string pattern + protruding rim pattern (T1⑤a:329)   14. Concave string pattern + engraved pattern (T1⑤a:357)   15. Concave string pattern + rope pattern (T1⑤a:90)   16. Rope pattern (T1⑤a:106)   17. Pit dot pattern + concave string pattern + rope pattern (T1⑤a:355)   18, 19. Engraved line pattern (T1⑤a:73, 237)   20. Rope pattern (T1⑤a:95)   21, 22. Engraved pattern (T1⑤a:219, 96)

Figure 18 Rubbings of Pottery Pieces Unearthed from Stratum T1⑤a

1. Combing pattern (T1⑤a: 104) 2. Engraved pattern + rope pattern (T1⑤a: 244) 3. Concave string pattern + combed dot pattern (T1⑤a: 331) 4. Concave string pattern + combed dot pattern + rope pattern (T1⑤a: 333) 5. Concave string pattern + engraved pattern + pit dot pattern (T1⑤a: 347) 6. Rope pattern (T1⑤a: 93) 7. Concave string pattern + engraved pattern (T1⑤a: 76) 8, 9. Engraved line pattern (T1⑤a: 222, 236) 10, 11, 12, 13. Engraved pattern (T1⑤a: 233, 68, 218, 213) 14, 15. Concave string pattern + pit dot pattern (T1⑤a: 350, 352) 16. Concave string pattern + rope pattern (T1⑤a: 223) 17. Concave string pattern + engraved pattern (T1⑤a: 221) 18. Concave string pattern + pit dot pattern (T1⑤a: 346) 19. Concave string pattern + engraved line dot pattern (T1⑤a: 44) 20. Concave string pattern (T1⑤a: 146) 21. Protruding rim + engraved pattern (T1⑤a: 159) 22. 23. Twist rope pattern (T1⑤a: 92, 89) 24. Concave string pattern + engraved leaf vein (T1⑤a: 225) 25. Engraved pattern + concave string pattern + pit dot pattern (T1⑤a: 316)

Specimen T1⑤a: 18, damaged, black earthenware, surface engraved with four concave string pattern, dot patterns poked between the concave strings; diameter of 4.5, thickness of 0.7, bore diameter of 0.5cm (Figure 19: 6; Plate 26: 3).

Bases: 5 pieces; severely damaged; only one identifiable, presenting a cylinder shape, oval base, bent, one side decorated with arch ear.

　　Specimen T1⑤a：26, damaged, reddish brown earthenware; only bottom remains, bottom decorated with vertical twist pattern; base diameter of 6.2, remaining part of height of 1.6cm (Figure 19：1). Specimen T1⑤a：28, damaged, fine reddish brown earthenware, only bottom of base remains, bottom decorated with horizontal twist line pattern; base diameter of 6.4, remaining part of height of 4cm (Figure 19：3). Specimen T1⑤a：29, damaged, fine reddish brown earthenware, only little bottom part remains, bottom decorated with horizontal twist line pattern; base diameter of 6, remaining part of height of 3.4cm (Figure 19：2). Specimen T1⑤a：57, damaged; brown earthenware, presenting a cylinder shape, oval base, bent, one side decorated with arch ear; body decorated

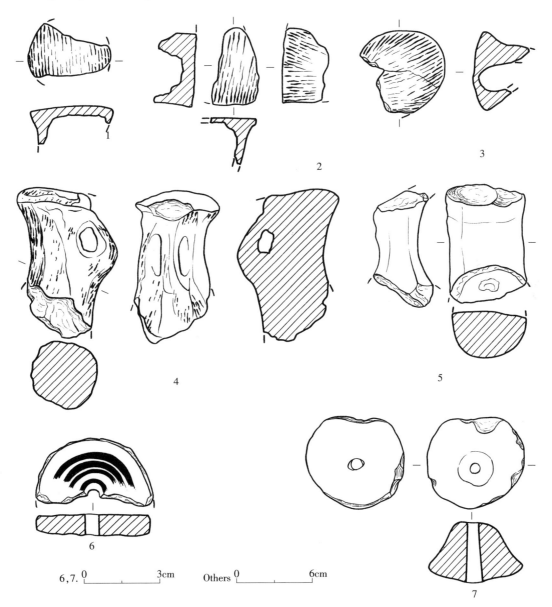

Figure 19   Pottery Bases and Spinning Wheels Unearthed from Stratum T1⑤a

1 – 5. Base （T1⑤a：26, 29, 28, 57, 58）   6, 7. Spinning wheel （T1⑤a：18, 4）

with flattened twist line pattern, bottom decorated with vertical twist pattern; remaining part of length of 11, width of 5.6, base diameter of 5.6cm (Figure 19:4; Plate 26:1). Specimen T1⑤a:58, damaged on two ends, brown earthenware, residual mud visible in middle of one end of the artifact; plain surface; remaining part of length of 8.8cm (Figure 19:5).

Handles: 5 pieces; based on shape and structure, these can be classified into two categories.

Category 1: 3 pieces; body presenting tongue shaped.

Specimen T1⑤a:33, damaged, reddish brown earthenware; plain surface; of length of 3.6, width of 3.7, thickness of 1.5cm (Figure 20:1). Specimen T1⑤a:34, damaged, reddish brown earthenware; plain surface; of length of 4.1, width of 3.8, thickness of 1.8cm (Figure 20:2). Specimen T1⑤a:250, reddish brown earthenware; surface two sides decorated with horizontal twist line pattern; remaining part of length of 6, width of 2 −6cm (Figure 20:4).

Category 2: 2 pieces; presenting a cylinder shape.

Specimen T1⑤a:59, damaged, brown earthenware, slightly bent, plain surface, remaining part of length of 2, width of 3.2cm (Figure 20:5). Specimen T1⑤a:162, gray earthenware, bent shape; remaining part of length of 2.8cm (Figure 20:6).

Ear: 1 piece.

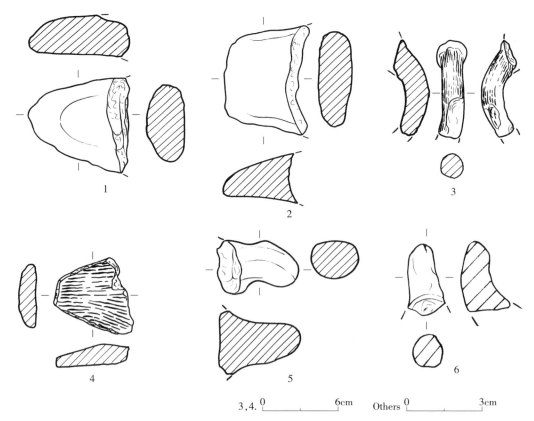

Figure 20   Pottery Utensil Handles and Ears Unearthed from Stratum T1⑤a
1, 2, 4, 5, 6. Handle (T1⑤a:33, 34, 250, 59, 162)   3. Utensil ear (T1⑤a:200)

Specimen T1⑤a：200, brown earthenware, of an arc－shaped body; surface decorated with twist line pattern; remaining part of length of 7. 4cm (Figure 20：3).

Ring feet: 32 pieces; can be classified into three categories based on shape and structure.

Category 1: 13 pieces; bucket shaped.

Specimen T1⑤a：43, damaged above ring foot; reddish brown earthenware; twist patterns decorated on base and body of ring foot; base diameter of 14. 3, remaining part of height of 3. 6cm (Figure 21：1). Specimen T1⑤a：41, part above foot is damaged, reddish brown earthenware; on the foot decorated with two concave string and vertical twist pattern; base diameter of 14, foot remaining part of height of 3. 7cm (Figure 21：9). Specimen T1⑤a：182, reddish brown earthenware; base diameter of 17. 7, remaining part of height of 3. 9cm (Figure 21：6; Plate 27：1). Specimen T1⑤a：94, reddish brown earthenware; on the foot decorated with comb brushing lines; base diameter of 10. 8, remaining part of height of 3. 9cm (Figure 21：11). Specimen T1⑤a：228, reddish brown earthenware; enclo-

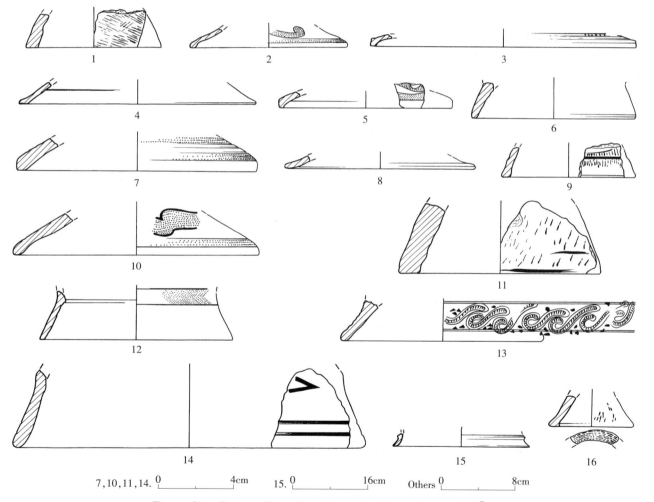

Figure 21   Pottery Ring Feet Unearthed from Stratum T1⑤a

1. T1⑤a：43   2. T1⑤a：312   3. T1⑤a：345   4. T1⑤a：198   5. T1⑤a：298   6. T1⑤a：182   7. T1⑤a：303   8. T1⑤a：269   9. T1⑤a：41   10. T1⑤a：311   11. T1⑤a：94   12. T1⑤a：337   13. T1⑤a：188   14. T1⑤a：99   15. T1⑤a：145   16. T1⑤a：131

sure on the foot decorated with engraved line and string patterns; base diameter of 13.4, remaining part of height of 2.7cm (Figure 22:1). Specimen T1⑤a:132, damaged, brown earthenware; base diameter of 16.3, remaining part of height of 3.8cm (Figure 22:3). Specimen T1⑤a:140, brown earthenware, base diameter of 18, remaining part of height of 4.1cm (Figure 22:4). Specimen T1⑤a:202, damaged, fine terracotta; base diameter of 14.7, remaining part of height of 3.7cm (Figure 22:7). Specimen T1⑤a:183, damaged, terracotta, base diameter of 14.5, remaining part of height of 3.4cm (Figure 22:8). Specimen T1⑤a:137, reddish brown earthenware; base diameter

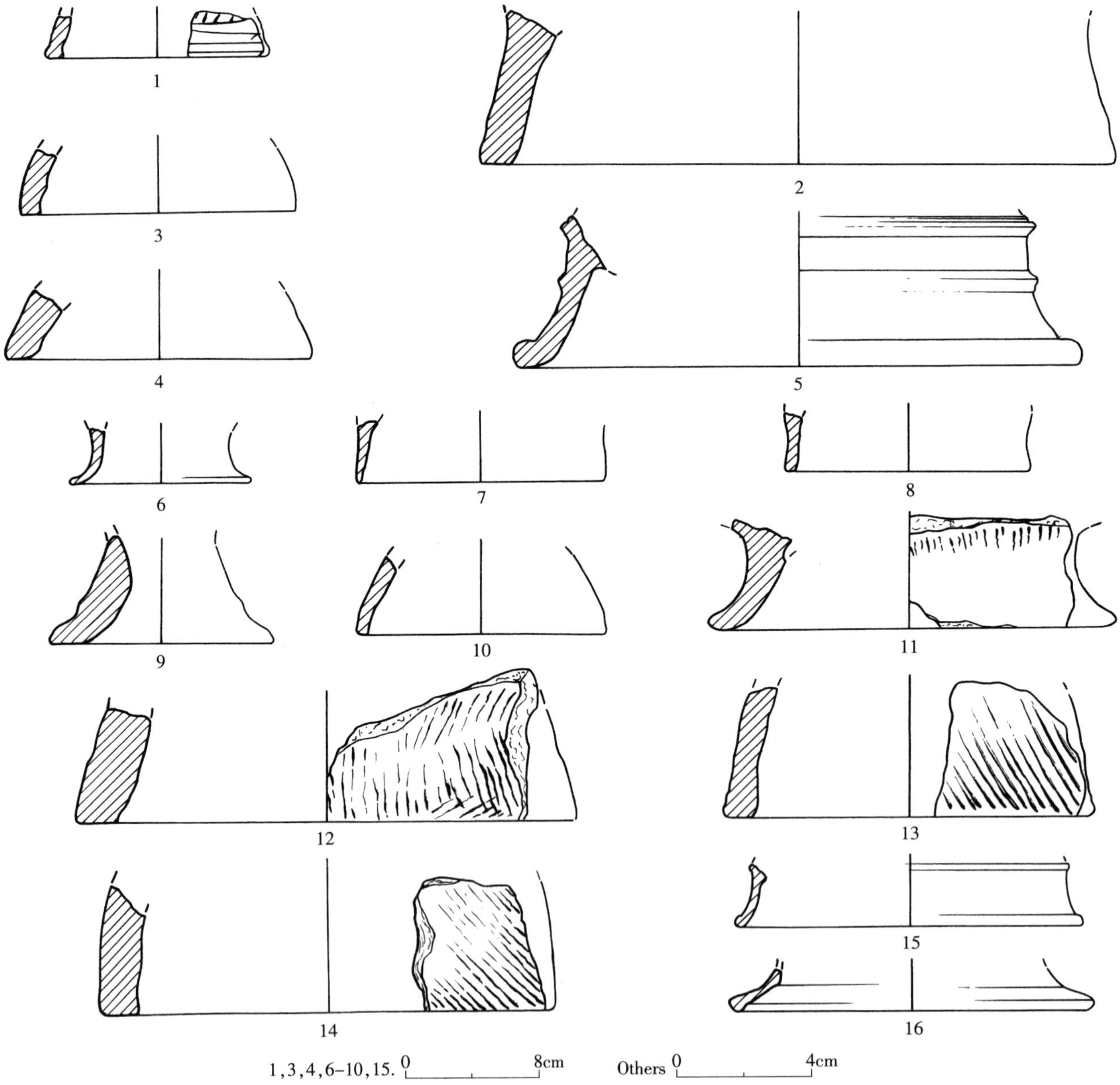
1
2
3
4
5
6
7
8
9
10
11
12
13
14
15
16
1,3,4,6–10,15. 0 8cm
Others 0 4cm

Figure 22 Pottery Ring Feet Unearthed from Stratum T1⑤a

1. T1⑤a:228 2. T1⑤a:111 3. T1⑤a:132 4. T1⑤a:140 5. T1⑤a:180 6. T1⑤a:129 7. T1⑤a:202 8. T1⑤a:183 9. T1⑤a:121 10. T1⑤a:137 11. T1⑤a:27 12. T1⑤a:31 13. T1⑤a:35 14. T1⑤a:52 15. T1⑤a:181 16. T1⑤a:371

of 14. 6, remaining part of height of 4. 7cm (Figure 22 : 10). Specimen T1⑤a : 31, damaged, reddish brown earthenware; on the foot decorated with vertical twist pattern; ring foot of diameter of 14. 8, remaining part of height of 3. 4cm (Figure 22 : 12). Specimen T1⑤a : 35, damaged, reddish brown earthenware; on the foot decorated with spiral twist pattern; base diameter of 10. 5, foot's remaining part of height of 3. 9cm (Figure 22 : 13). Specimen T1⑤a : 52, only lower part of ring foot remains, brown earthenware; on the foot decorated with spiral twist pattern, base diameter of 13. 5, remaining part of height of 4cm (Figure 22 : 14).

Category 2 : 16 pieces; presenting a trumpet shape, foot tip bent outward.

Specimen T1⑤a : 198, fine terracotta; base diameter of 25. 5, remaining part of height of 2. 4cm (Figure 21 : 4). Specimen T1⑤a : 303, brown earthenware, on the foot decorated with two concave string pattern and combed dots; base diameter of 12. 8, remaining part of height of 1. 8cm (Figure 21 : 7). Specimen T1⑤a : 269, brown earthenware; base diameter of 20. 4, remaining part of height of 1. 4cm (Figure 21 : 8). Specimen T1⑤a : 311, reddish brown earthenware; on the lower part of foot decorated with two concave strings, combed dots between concave string patterns, on upper part of foot engraved – shape lines, combed dots between the S – shape lines; base diameter of 13. 1, remaining part of height of 2. 4cm (Figure 21 : 10). Specimen T1⑤a : 145, gray earthenware; base diameter of 29. 6, remaining part of height of 2. 8cm (Figure 21 : 15). Specimen T1⑤a : 337, grayish black earthenware; upper part of foot decorated with two concave strings, combed dots between concave string patterns; base diameter of 20. 7, remaining part of height of 5. 2cm (Figure 21 : 12). Specimen T1⑤a : 188, black earthenware; a concave string decorated on each of upper and lower parts of ring foot, S – shape lines engraved between the two concave string lines, short lines poked between the S – shape patterns; base diameter of 21. 6, remaining part of height of 4. 4cm (Figure 21 : 13; Plate 27 : 4). Specimen T1⑤a : 131, brown earthenware, twist pattern decorated on bottom of foot; base diameter of 9. 1, remaining part of height of 3. 3cm (Figure 21 : 16). Specimen T1⑤a : 99, only lower part of ring foot remains, grayish brown earthenware; middle of foot engraved with triangular pattern, on the lower part of foot decorated with two concave strings; base diameter of 18. 5, remaining part of height of 4. 2cm (Figure 21 : 14). Specimen T1⑤a : 111, brown earthenware, plain surface; base diameter of 18. 6, remaining part of height of 4. 6cm (Figure 22 : 2). Specimen T1⑤a : 180, fine terracotta; center of ring foot decorated with a protruding rim; base diameter of 16. 5, remaining part of height of 4. 5cm (Figure 22 : 5; Figure 27 : 2). Specimen T1⑤a : 129, brown earthenware, base diameter of 10. 7, remaining part of height of 3. 3cm (Figure 22 : 6). Specimen T1⑤a : 121, reddish brown earthenware; base diameter of 6. 6, remaining part of height of 3. 4cm (Figure 22 : 9). Specimen T1⑤a : 27, part above foot is damaged, reddish brown earthenware; upper part of foot decorated with vertical twist pattern; base diameter of 12, remaining part of height of 3. 3cm (Figure 22 : 11). Specimen T1⑤a : 181, reddish brown fine earthenware; base diameter of 20, remaining part of height of

3. 8cm (Figure 22 : 15 ; Plate 27 : 3). Specimen T1 ⑤ a : 371 , brown earthenware; base diameter of 20. 8 , remaining part of height of 2. 4cm (Figure 22 : 16).

Category 3 : 3 pieces; presenting a trumpet shape, foot tip bent inward.

Specimen T1 ⑤ a : 345 , reddish brown earthenware; on the foot decorated with three concave strings, dot patterns poked between the concave strings; base diameter of 28. 6 , remaining part of height of 1. 3cm (Figure 21 : 3). Specimen T1⑤a: 312 , reddish brown earthenware; on the lower part of foot decorated with two concave strings, combed dots between concave string patterns, on upper part of foot engraved – shape lines, combed dots between the S – shape lines; base diameter of 16. 7 , remaining part of height of 2cm (Figure 21 : 2). Specimen T1⑤a: 298 , grayish brown earthenware; enclosure on the foot decorated withes – shape lines, combed dots between the S – shape patterns; base diameter of 18. 6 , remaining part of height of 6. 8cm (Figure 21 : 5).

Trumpet mouth jars: 12 pieces; classified into two categories based on the neck.

Category 1 : 4 pieces; neck decorated with protruding rim pattern.

Specimen T1 ⑤ a : 189 , fine reddish brown earthenware, round lip; contracted neck; mouth diameter of 25. 4 , remaining part of height of 3. 8cm (Figure 23 : 1). Specimen T1⑤a: 190 , reddish brown earthenware; polished surface, round lip; mouth diameter of 28. 7 , remaining part of height of 3. 8cm (Figure 23 : 3). Specimen T1⑤a: 186 , reddish brown earthenware; round lip and flared mouth, bent shoulder, inclined straight belly; decorated with a protruding rim on the shoulder. On the protruding rim poked short line pattern; mouth diameter of 32. 8 , remaining part of height of 4. 6cm (Figure 23 : 11). Specimen T1 ⑤ a : 187 , fine terracotta; round lip, contracted neck, middle of neck decorated with a protruding rim, mouth diameter of 29. 5 , remaining part of height of 3. 7cm (Figure 23 : 12).

Category 2 : 8 pieces; no protruding rim on the neck.

Specimen T1 ⑤ a : 91 , reddish brown earthenware; round lip; under mouth decorated with two concave strings, under which decorated with spiral twist pattern; mouth diameter of 17. 1 , remaining part of height of 4. 1cm (Figure 23 : 5). Specimen T1 ⑤ a : 361 , fine reddish brown earthenware, thickness of round lip and contracted neck; mouth diameter of 17. 2 , remaining part of height of 3. 1cm (Figure 23: 7). Specimen T1⑤a: 147 , reddish brown earthenware; round lip; mouth diameter of 40 , remaining part of height of 2. 6cm (Figure 23 : 9). Specimen T1⑤a: 260 , brown earthenware, round lip and flared mouth, under mouth decorated with engraved arc patterns; mouth diameter of 33 , remaining part of height of 1. 6cm (Figure 23 : 2). Specimen T1⑤a: 208 , grayish brown earthenware, round lip, mouth diameter of 30. 5 , remaining part of height of 3. 1cm (Figure 23 : 4). Specimen T1⑤a: 231 , grayish brown earthenware, sharp round lip, under mouth decorated with two concave strings, under which decorated with spiral twist pattern; mouth diameter of 22. 9 , remaining part of height of 3. 4cm (Figure 23 : 6). Specimen T1⑤a: 77 , brown earthenware, round lip; under mouth

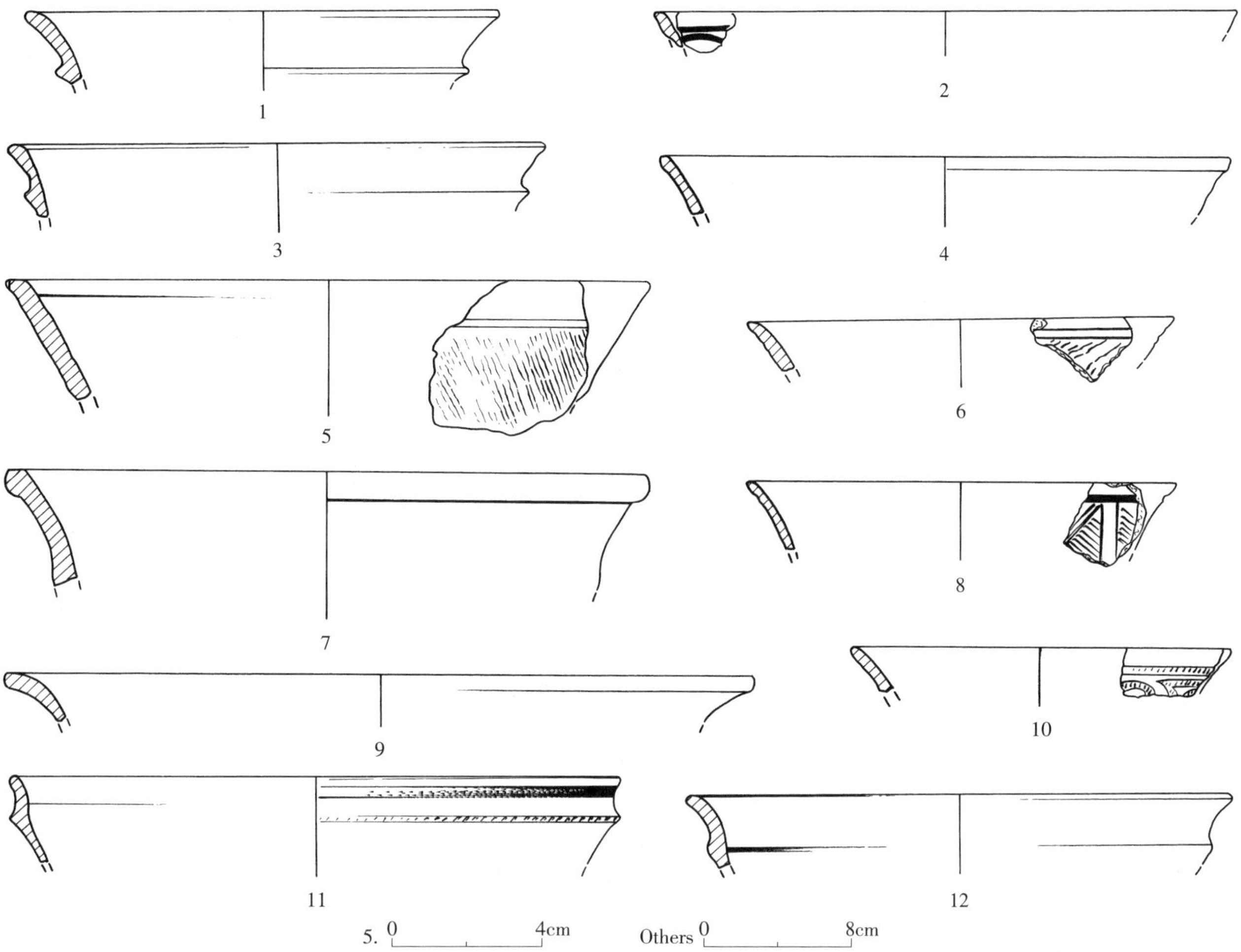

Figure 23 Pottery Trumpet – shape Mouth Jars Unearthed from Stratum T1⑤a

1. T1⑤a:189 2. T1⑤a:260 3. T1⑤a:190 4. T1⑤a:208 5. T1⑤a:91 6. T1⑤a:231 7. T1⑤a:361 8. T1⑤a:210 9. T1⑤a:147 10. T1⑤a:77 11. T1⑤a:186 12. T1⑤a:187

decorated with two concave strings, between strings poked short line pattern, under which are poked S – shape patterns decorated with poked short line pattern; mouth diameter of 20. 4, remaining part of height of 2. 4cm (Figure 23 : 10). Specimen T1⑤a:210, brown earthenware, round lip; upper neck decorated with concave string pattern circling, middle of neck decorated with engraved patterns of triangular pattern, in which decorated with engraved short lines; mouth diameter of 22. 5, remaining part of height of 3. 8cm (Figure 23 : 8).

Thick lip jars: 21 pieces; thick square lip; classified into three categories based on the lips.

Category 1: 10 pieces; straight mouth.

Specimen T1⑤a:66, brown earthenware, straight body; lip decorated with spiral twist pattern, under mouth decorated with two concave string pattern, belly upper part poked short arc line pattern and triangle patterns; mouth diameter of 49. 4, remaining part of height of 5. 2cm (Figure 24 : 1). Specimen T1⑤a : 100, brown earthenware; lip decorated with twist line pattern; mouth diameter of 49. 2, remaining part of height of 4cm (Figure 24 : 2). Specimen T1⑤a : 158, gray earthenware;

mouth diameter of 34. 8, remaining part of height of 3. 4cm (Figure 24 : 11). Specimen T1⑤a : 123, reddish brown earthenware; neck decorated with 1 protruding rim; mouth diameter of 33. 2, remaining part of height of 4cm (Figure 24 : 12). Specimen T1⑤a : 141, brown earthenware; mouth diameter of 34, remaining part of height of 3. 7cm (Figure 24 : 13). Specimen T1⑤a : 161, brown earthenware, lip decorated with spiral twist pattern, mouth diameter of 38. 5, remaining part of height of 6. 2cm (Figure 24 : 4). Specimen T1⑤a : 166, grayish black earthenware coated in red, thickness of square lip; mouth diameter of 48, remaining part of height of 4. 6cm (Figure 25 : 1). Specimen T1⑤a : 177, terracotta, round lip; under mouth decorated with concave string pattern; mouth diameter of 21. 8,

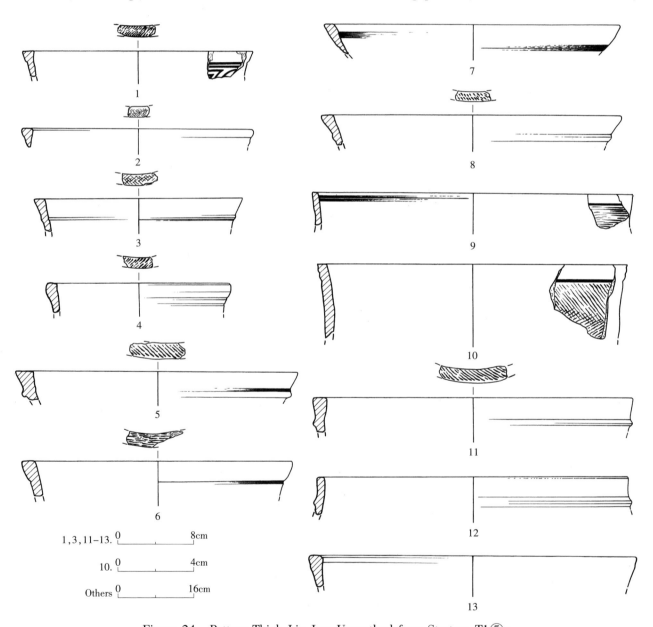

1,3,11–13. 0 ———— 8cm

10. 0 ———— 4cm

Others 0 ———— 16cm

Figure 24   Pottery Thick Lip Jars Unearthed from Stratum T1⑤a

1. T1⑤a : 66   2. T1⑤a : 100   3. T1⑤a : 363   4. T1⑤a : 161   5. T1⑤a : 168   6. T1⑤a : 112   7. T1⑤a : 174
8. T1⑤a : 117   9. T1⑤a : 75   10. T1⑤a : 97   11. T1⑤a : 158   12. T1⑤a : 123   13. T1⑤a : 141

remaining part of height of 3cm (Figure 25∶2). Specimen T1⑤a∶61, brown earthenware, round lip, straight collar; upper collar decorated with concave string pattern in 2 circles, under which decorated with spiral twist pattern; mouth diameter of 33.2, remaining part of height of 3.8cm (Figure 25∶7). Specimen T1⑤a∶54, damaged, brown earthenware, round lip, high collar, damaged below collar, under mouth decorated with concave string and spiral twist pattern, mouth diameter of 23, remaining part of height of 3.1cm (Figure 25∶4).

Category 2: 10 pieces; flare mouth.

Specimen T1⑤a∶174, terracotta; under mouth decorated with engraved line patterns; mouth diameter of 31.6, remaining part of height of 3.2cm (Figure 24∶7). Specimen T1⑤a∶117, brown earthenware, lip decorated with spiral twist pattern, with a protruding rim decorated under the mouth; mouth diameter of 32, remaining part of height of 3.2cm (Figure 24∶8). Specimen T1⑤a∶168, grayish black earthenware, lip decorated with spiral twist pattern, with a protruding rim decorated under the mouth. mouth diameter of 30.4, remaining part of height of 6cm (Figure 24∶5). Specimen T1⑤a∶112, brown earthenware, lip decorated with horizontal twist line pattern, under mouth decorated with one concave string; mouth diameter of 29.1, remaining part of height of 3.8cm (Figure 24∶6). Specimen T1⑤a∶363, brown earthenware, lip is of twist line pattern; mouth diameter of 18.5, remaining part of height of 2.6cm (Figure 24∶3). Specimen T1⑤a∶75, brown earthenware; under mouth decorated with concave string pattern circling, under which decorated with horizontal en-

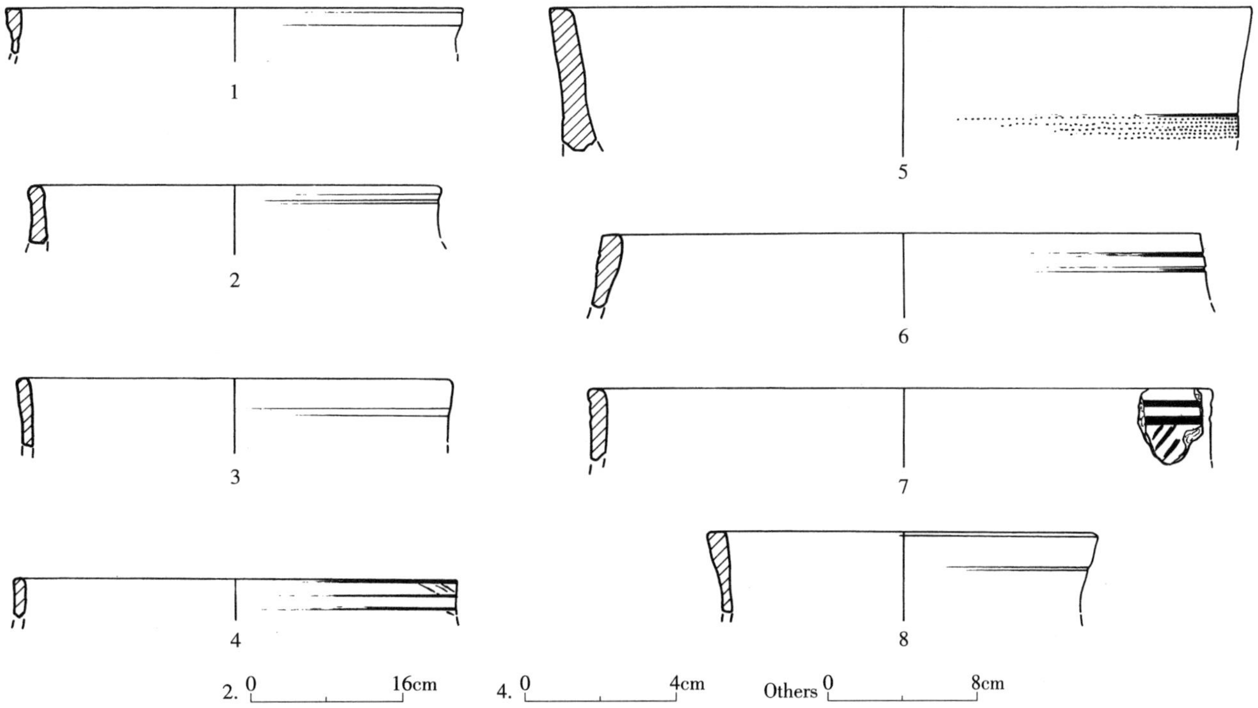
1
2
3
4
5
6
7
8
2. 0 16cm
4. 0 4cm
Others 0 8cm

Figure 25 Pottery Thick Lip Jars Unearthed from Stratum T1⑤a

1. T1⑤a∶166 2. T1⑤a∶177 3. T1⑤a∶150 4. T1⑤a∶54 5. T1⑤a∶305 6. T1⑤a∶67 7. T1⑤a∶61 8. T1⑤a∶169

graved line patterns; mouth diameter of 34. 3, remaining part of height of 3. 6cm (Figure 24 : 9). Specimen T1⑤a : 97, reddish brown earthenware; under mouth decorated with one concave string, under which decorated with twist line pattern; mouth diameter of 16. 5, remaining part of height of 3. 9cm (Figure 24 : 10). Specimen T1⑤a : 150, reddish brown earthenware; square lip; neck decorated with 1 protruding rim; mouth diameter of 23, remaining part of height of 3. 6cm (Figure 25 : 3). Specimen T1⑤a : 305, brown earthenware, square lip, under mouth decorated with one concave string, under which decorated with combed dots; mouth diameter of 18. 6, remaining part of height of 3. 8cm (Figure 25 : 5). Specimen T1⑤a : 169, reddish brown earthenware; polished surface, thickness of square lip; mouth diameter of 41. 6, remaining part of height of 8. 4cm (Figure 25 : 8).

Category 3 : 1 piece; contracted mouth.

Specimen T1⑤a : 67, reddish brown earthenware; round lip, straight collar; collar poked concave string pattern; mouth diameter of 46. 4, remaining part of height of 4cm (Figure 25 : 6).

Flare mouth jars : 22 pieces; classified into two categories based on the neck.

Category 1 : 15 pieces; no protruding rim on the neck.

Specimen T1⑤a : 133, brown earthenware, round lip, under mouth decorated with1 circle of concave string; mouth diameter of 34, remaining part of height of 2. 4cm (Figure 26 : 1). Specimen T1⑤a : 185, fine terracotta; polished surface, round lip; mouth diameter of 29. 8, remaining part of height of 3. 3cm (Figure 26 : 2). Specimen T1⑤a : 239, reddish brown earthenware; sharp round lip; under mouth decorated with engraved short lines and arc lines; mouth diameter of 36. 6, remaining part of height of 2. 8cm (Figure 26 : 3). Specimen T1⑤a : 220, brown earthenware, round lip, under mouth decorated with two concave strings, under which decorated with engraved inclined short lines; mouth diameter of 26. 8, remaining part of height of 4. 1cm (Figure 26 : 4). Specimen T1⑤a : 79, reddish brown earthenware; sharp round lip; under mouth decorated with comb brushing lines; mouth diameter of 14. 9, remaining part of height of 3. 9cm (Figure 26 : 5). Specimen T1⑤a : 263, brown earthenware, round lip, under mouth decorated with two concave strings, under which decorated with engraved short lines; mouth diameter of 18. 4, remaining part of height of 2. 1cm (Figure 26 : 6). Specimen T1⑤a : 47, damaged, brown earthenware, round lip, high collar, damaged below collar, under mouth decorated with concave string pattern circling, neck decorated with spiral twist pattern; mouth diameter of 14, remaining part of height of 4cm (Figure 26 : 7). Specimen T1⑤a : 152, fine black earthenware, square lip, under mouth decorated with1 circle of concave string; mouth diameter of 14. 8, remaining part of height of 3. 8cm (Figure 26 : 8). Specimen T1⑤a : 69, damaged, brown earthenware, square lip, neck slightly contracted, under mouth decorated with protruding rim pattern; under which decorated with poked leaf vein pattern; mouth diameter of 19. 1, remaining part of height of 4cm (Figure 26 : 9). Specimen T1⑤a : 119, brown earthenware, square lip, with a protruding rim decorated under the mouth. mouth diameter of 26, remaining part of height of 6. 2cm (Figure

26:10). Specimen T1⑤a:378, reddish brown earthenware; round lip, neck slightly contracted; mouth diameter of 14.7, remaining part of height of 2.8cm (Figure 26:11). Specimen T1⑤a:227, brown earthenware, round lip, under mouth decorated with two concave strings; mouth diameter of 18.5, remaining part of height of 2.6cm (Figure 27:1). Specimen T1⑤a:78, brown earthenware, neck slightly contracted; under mouth decorated with two concave strings, under which decorated with comb brushing lines; mouth diameter of 24.6, remaining part of height of 5.3cm (Figure 27:3). Specimen T1⑤a:71, brown earthenware, collar decorated with horizontal twist line pattern; mouth diameter of 22.8, remaining part of height of 3.2cm (Figure 27:11). Specimen T1⑤a:70, brown earthenware, round lip; under mouth decorated with two concave strings, under which decorated with engraved short lines; mouth diameter of 29.4, remaining part of height of 4.7cm (Figure 27:12).

Category 2: 7 pieces; with protruding rim on the neck.

Specimen T1⑤a:255, fine brown earthenware; round lip, contracted neck, neck decorated with engraved arc lines and poked short line pattern; mouth diameter of 22.5, remaining part of height of 4.9cm (Figure 27:8). Specimen T1⑤a:306, fine terracotta; square lip, neck slightly contracted;

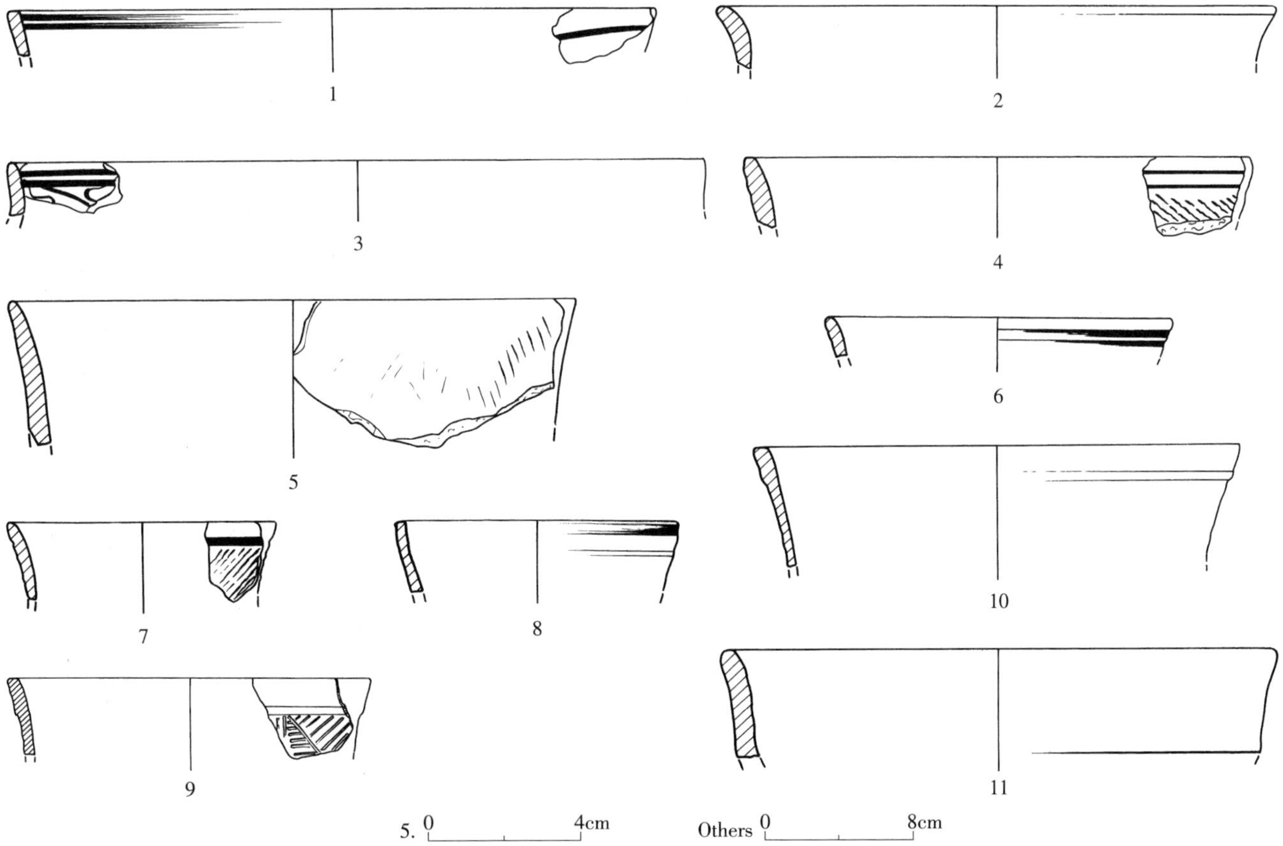
1
2
3
4
5
6
7
8
10
9
11
5. 0 4cm
Others 0 8cm

Figure 26 Pottery Flare Mouth Jars Unearthed from Stratum T1⑤a

1. T1⑤a:133 2. T1⑤a:185 3. T1⑤a:239 4. T1⑤a:220 5. T1⑤a:79 6. T1⑤a:263 7. T1⑤a:47 8. T1⑤a:152 9. T1⑤a:69 10. T1⑤a:119 11. T1⑤a:378

mouth diameter of 23. 4, remaining part of height of 3. 5cm (Figure 27:2). Specimen T1⑤a:110, reddish brown earthenware; round lip; mouth diameter of 50, remaining part of height of 3. 6cm (Figure 27:10). Specimen T1⑤a:193, fine terracotta; round lip, on the protruding rim decorated with poked short line pattern; mouth diameter of 24. 6, remaining part of height of 3cm (Figure 27:4). Specimen T1⑤a:49, reddish brown earthenware; round lip, neck decorated with spiral twist pattern; mouth diameter of 30. 8, remaining part of height of 4. 7cm (Figure 27:5). Specimen T1⑤a:122, brown earthenware, sharp round lip; mouth diameter of 19. remaining part of height of 3. 6cm (Figure 27:6). Specimen T1⑤a:109, reddish brown earthenware; mouth diameter of 28. 5, remaining part of height of 4. 8cm (Figure 27:7).

Bucket: 1 piece.

Specimen T1⑤a:60, brown earthenware, thickness of square lip, contracted mouth, straight

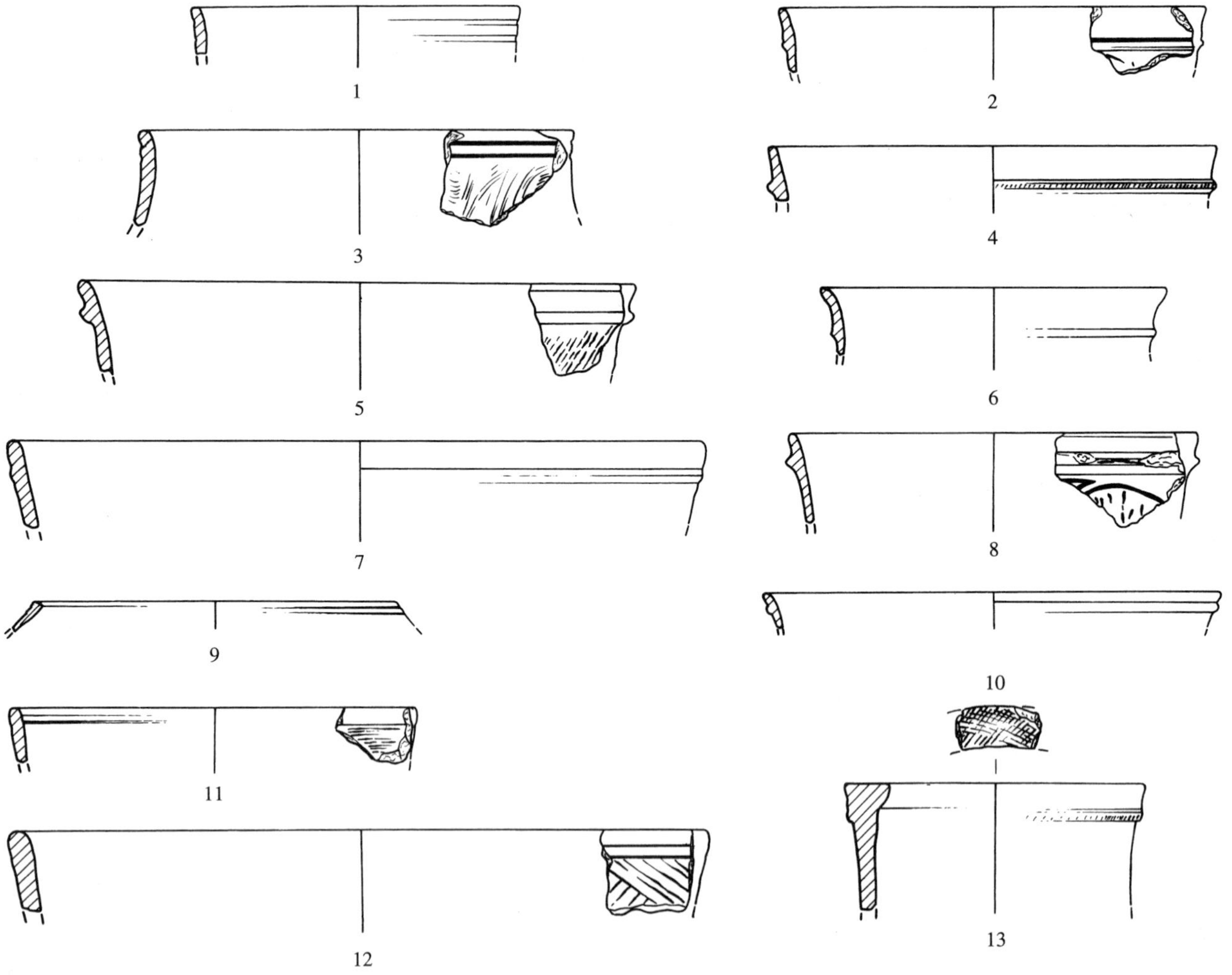

1, 10. 0 16cm Others 0 8cm

Figure 27 Pottery Artifacts Unearthed from Stratum T1⑤a

1-8, 10-12. Thick Lip Jars (T1⑤a:277, 306, 78, 193, 49, 122, 109, 255, 110, 71, 70) 9. Contracted mouth jar (T1⑤a:135) 13. Bucket (T1⑤a:60)

body; lip is of twist line pattern, under mouth decorated with protruding rim pattern; on the protruding rim poked short line pattern; mouth diameter of 16.6, remaining part of height of 7cm (Figure 27:13).

Contracted mouth jar: 1 piece.

Specimen T1⑤a:135, brown earthenware, square lip, contracted mouth, under mouth decorated with two concave strings; mouth diameter of 20.4, remaining part of height of 1.7cm (Figure 27:9).

Bowls: 55 pieces; classified into five categories based on shape and structure.

Category 1: 14 pieces; contracted mouth, upper belly decorated with 1 protruding rim.

Specimen T1⑤a:295, brown earthenware, sharp round lip, upper belly decorated with combed dots; mouth diameter of 31.2, remaining part of height of 3.2cm (Figure 28:1). Specimen T1⑤a: 128, reddish brown earthenware; square lip, upper belly decorated with concave string pattern; mouth diameter of 27, remaining part of height of 5.2cm (Figure 28:2). Specimen T1⑤a:195, fine reddish brown earthenware, round lip, shoulder and neck decorated with two protruding rims; mouth diameter of 30.8, remaining part of height of 4cm (Figure 28:3). Specimen T1⑤a:328, reddish brown earthenware; round lip, upper belly decorated with two concave strings, two concave string pattern decorated with combed dots; mouth diameter of 32.8, remaining part of height of 2.6cm (Figure 28:5). Specimen T1⑤a:265, reddish brown earthenware; polished surface; round lip, inclined straight belly; under the protruding rim decorated with two concave strings; mouth diameter of 20.2, remaining part of height of 2.6cm (Figure 28:12). Specimen T1⑤a:179, reddish brown earthenware; square lip, of wide protruding rim; mouth diameter of 34.2, remaining part of height of 1.8cm (Figure 28:9). Specimen T1⑤a:205, clay terracotta, polished surface; mouth diameter of 20.6, remaining part of height of 2.6cm (Figure 28:4). Specimen T1⑤a:203, fine terracotta; polished surface; sharp round lip; mouth diameter of 21, remaining part of height of 3.3cm (Figure 28:8). Specimen T1⑤a:264, fine reddish brown earthenware, round lip, upper belly decorated with two concave string pattern and combed dots; mouth diameter of 28, remaining part of height of 3cm (Figure 29:1). Specimen T1⑤a:266, brown earthenware, square lip, upper belly decorated with three concave strings; mouth diameter of 23, remaining part of height of 2.9cm (Figure 29:2). Specimen T1⑤a:302, fine reddish brown earthenware, round lip, belly decorated with combed dots; mouth diameter of 22.2, remaining part of height of 2.6cm (Figure 29:4). Specimen T1⑤a:324, reddish brown earthenware; round lip, on the protruding rim decorated with two concave string pattern and combed dots; mouth diameter of 25, remaining part of height of 4cm (Figure 29:3). Specimen T1⑤a:326, fine reddish brown earthenware, round lip, middle of belly decorated with string pattern, mouth diameter of 23.3, remaining part of height of 3.4cm (Figure 29:5). Specimen T1⑤a:153, grayish black earthenware, round lip; mouth diameter of 34.8, remaining part of height of 5.2cm (Figure 29:14).

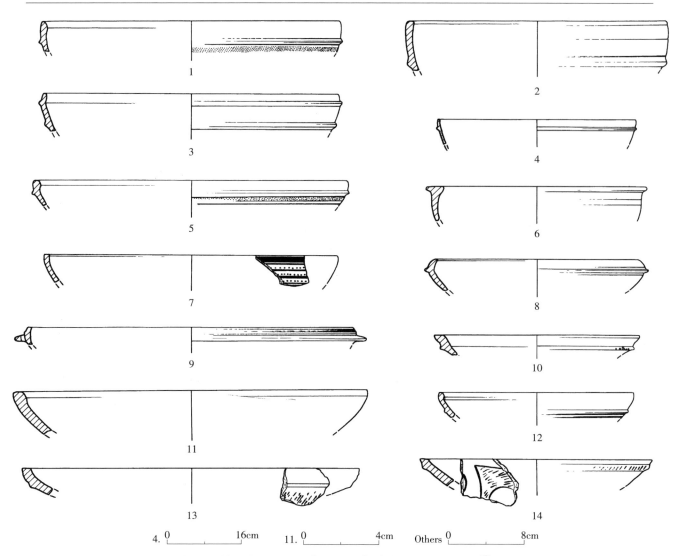

Figure 28   Pottery Bowls Unearthed from Stratum T1⑤a

1. T1⑤a:295   2. T1⑤a:128   3. T1⑤a:195   4. T1⑤a:205   5. T1⑤a:328   6. T1⑤a:365   7. T1⑤a:364
8. T1⑤a:203   9. T1⑤a:179   10. T1⑤a:360   11. T1⑤a:376   12. T1⑤a:265   13. T1⑤a:380   14. T1⑤a:65

Category 2: 15 pieces; contracted mouth, no protruding rim on the belly.

Specimen T1⑤a:364, fine reddish brown earthenware, square lip, upper belly decorated with 3 sets of concave string patterns, each concave string pattern decorated with combed dots; mouth diameter of 30.8, remaining part of height of 2.9cm (Figure 28:7). Specimen T1⑤a:376, grayish brown earthenware, round lip; mouth diameter of 18.5, remaining part of height of 2.2cm (Figure 28:11). Specimen T1⑤a:336, brown earthenware, sharp round lip, belly decorated with poked dot pattern; mouth diameter of 25.6, remaining part of height of 3.1cm (Figure 29:7). Specimen T1⑤a:342, reddish brown earthenware; round lip, shoulder with short line patterns, upper belly decorated with three concave strings pattern and combed dots; mouth diameter of 22.5, remaining part of height of 3.5cm (Figure 29:12). Specimen T1⑤a:40, reddish brown earthenware; sharp round lip; upper belly decorated with one concave string, belly decorated with vertical twist line pattern; mouth diame-

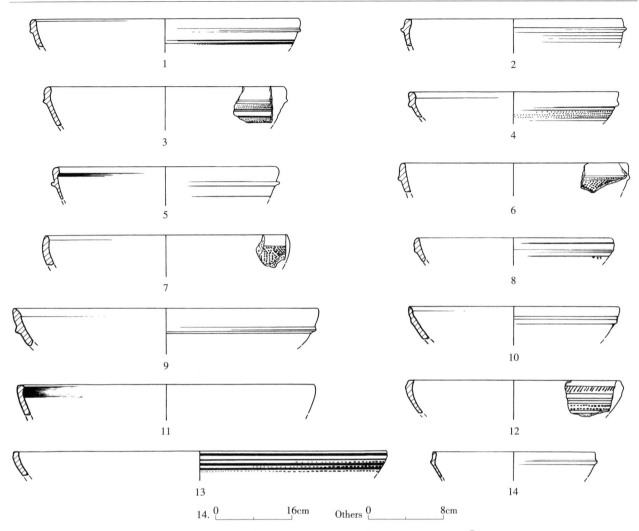

14. $\underset{0}{\llcorner}$_____$\underset{16cm}{\lrcorner}$ Others $\underset{0}{\llcorner}$_____$\underset{8cm}{\lrcorner}$

Figure 29   Pottery Bowls Unearthed from Stratum T1⑤a

1. T1⑤a：264   2. T1⑤a：266   3. T1⑤a：324   4. T1⑤a：302   5. T1⑤a：326   6. T1⑤a：327   7. T1⑤a：336

8. T1⑤a：335   9. T1⑤a：191   10. T1⑤a：206   11. T1⑤a：207   12. T1⑤a：342   13. T1⑤a：356   14. T1⑤a：153

ter of 22. 4, remaining part of height of 4. 1cm (Figure 31：7). Specimen T1⑤a：207, reddish brown earthenware；round lip；mouth diameter of 31, remaining part of height of 3. 2cm (Figure 29：11). Specimen T1⑤a：330, fine terracotta；round lip；belly decorated with three concave string pattern and combed dots；mouth diameter of 26. 4, remaining part of height of 3. 4cm (Figure 31：1). Specimen T1⑤a：356, grayish black earthenware, square lip；upper belly decorated with concave string patterns and poked dots；mouth diameter of 39. 2, remaining part of height of 2. 5cm (Figure 29：13). Specimen T1⑤a：115, brown earthenware, round lip, inclined straight belly；plain surface；mouth diameter of 26, remaining part of height of 3. 7cm (Figure 30：1). Specimen T1⑤a：165, fine brown earthenware；round lip, inclined straight belly；mouth diameter of 51. 2, remaining part of height of 3. 2cm (Figure 30：3). Specimen T1⑤a：175, brown earthenware, round lip, arc belly；mouth diameter of 26. 5, remaining part of height of 2. 5cm (Figure 30：4). Specimen T1⑤a：176, fine terracotta；round lip, arc belly；under mouth decorated with concave string pattern circling, mouth diameter of

23. 1, remaining part of height of 4. 2cm (Figure 30 : 5). Specimen T1⑤a : 30, brown earthenware, round lip, arc belly, belly decorated with spiral twist pattern; mouth diameter of 26. 5, remaining part of height of 4. 1cm (Figure 30 : 6). Specimen T1⑤a : 149, brown earthenware, square lip, inclined straight belly; mouth diameter of 22. 6, remaining part of height of 3cm (Figure 30 : 7). Specimen T1⑤a : 146, reddish brown earthenware; round lip; mouth diameter of 27. 6, remaining part of height of 3. 2cm (Figure 30 : 12).

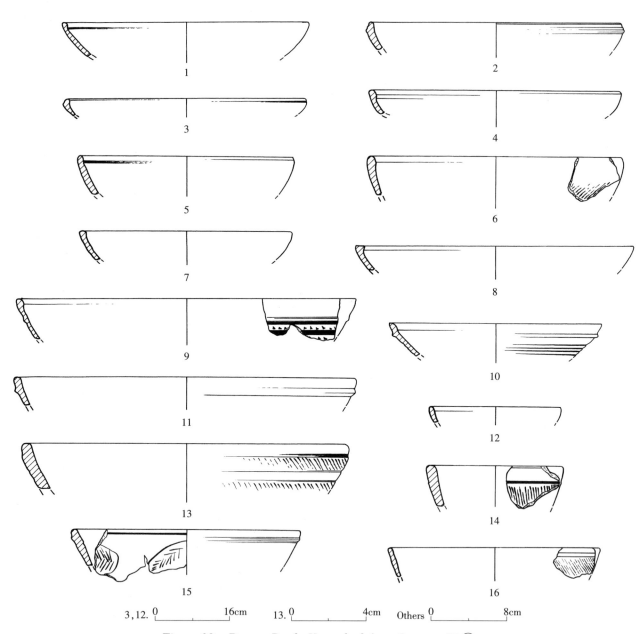

Figure 30   Pottery Bowls Unearthed from Stratum T1⑤a

1. T1⑤a : 115   2. T1⑤a : 116   3. T1⑤a : 165   4. T1⑤a : 175   5. T1⑤a : 176   6. T1⑤a : 30   7. T1⑤a : 149
8. T1⑤a : 143   9. T1⑤a : 339   10. T1⑤a : 238   11. T1⑤a : 172   12. T1⑤a : 146   13. T1⑤a : 304   14. T1⑤a : 38
15. T1⑤a : 63   16. T1⑤a : 212

Category 3: 13 pieces; flare mouth, arc belly, shoulder decorated with a protruding rim.

Specimen T1⑤a:380, reddish brown earthenware; square lip, bent shoulder; upper belly decorated with poked dot pattern; mouth diameter of 35.3, remaining part of height of 2.6cm (Figure 28:13). Specimen T1⑤a:360, brown earthenware, on the protruding rim are poked dots, mouth diameter of 21.4, remaining part of height of 2.1cm (Figure 28:10). Specimen T1⑤a:56, brown earthenware, square lip, on the protruding rim are short lines, lip decorated with a circle of continuous triangular pattern, body decorated with vertical twist pattern; mouth diameter of 36.6, remaining part of height of 3.7cm (Figure 31:4). Specimen T1⑤a:65, reddish brown earthenware; under mouth decorated with protruding rim pattern; on the protruding rim are short lines, belly decorated with engraved and poked patterns; mouth diameter of 24, remaining part of height of 4.8cm (Figure 28:14). Specimen T1⑤a:327, fine reddish brown earthenware, round lip, square lip, on the protruding rim are poked dots, upper belly decorated with combed dots and concave string patterns; mouth diameter of 23.8, remaining part of height of 3.1cm (Figure 29:6). Specimen T1⑤a:191, terracotta, sharp round lip; mouth diameter of 32.1, remaining part of height of 4.1cm (Figure 29:9). Specimen T1⑤a:335, fine grayish brown earthenware, sharp round lip, upper belly decorated with string pattern, under which decorated with combed dots, mouth diameter of 20.8, remaining part of height of 2.4cm (Figure 29:8). Specimen T1⑤a:206, brown earthenware, round lip; mouth diameter of 2.3, remaining part of height of 3.4cm (Figure 29:10). Specimen T1⑤a:116, brown earthenware, square lip; mouth diameter of 26.4, remaining part of height of 2.8cm (Figure 30:2). Specimen T1⑤a:339, reddish brown earthenware; round lip; upper belly decorated with two concave strings and poked lines; mouth diameter of 36, remaining part of height of 4.2cm (Figure 30:9). Specimen T1⑤a:172, reddish brown earthenware; round lip; mouth diameter of 36.3, remaining part of height of 3cm (Figure 30:11). Specimen T1⑤a:238, blackish brown earthenware; belly decorated with engraved line patterns; mouth diameter of 22.4, remaining part of height of 3.5cm (Figure 30:10). Specimen T1⑤a:192, reddish brown earthenware; sharp round lip; mouth diameter of 30.4, remaining part of height of 2.4cm (Figure 31:8).

Category 4: 8 pieces; flare mouth, arc belly, without protruding rim on the shoulder.

Specimen T1⑤a:304, brown earthenware; round lip; under mouth decorated with three concave strings, between concave strings decorated with spiral twist pattern; mouth diameter of 17.4, remaining part of height of 2.4cm (Figure 30:13). Specimen T1⑤a:63, brown earthenware, round lip, inclined straight belly; under mouth decorated with protruding rim pattern; belly decorated with engraved leaf vein pattern; mouth diameter of 24.4, remaining part of height of 5.5cm (Figure 30:15). Specimen T1⑤a:38, brown earthenware, round lip; upper belly decorated with one concave string, belly decorated with vertical twist pattern; mouth diameter of 14.2, remaining part of height of 4.2cm (Figure 30:14). Specimen T1⑤a:212, reddish brown earthenware; round lip, under mouth decora-

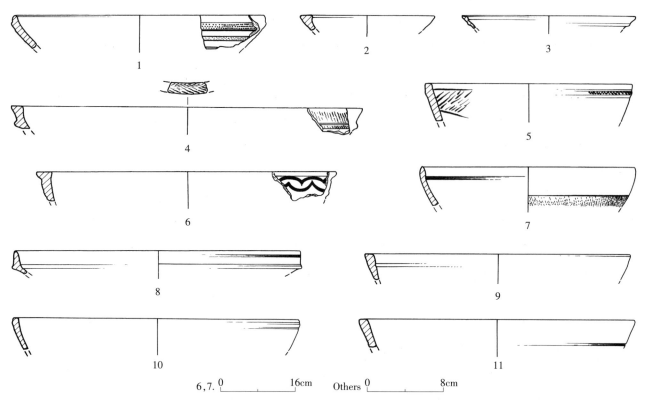

Figure 31   Pottery Bowls Unearthed from Stratum T1⑤a

1. T1⑤a：330   2. T1⑤a：48   3. T1⑤a：154   4. T1⑤a：56   5. T1⑤a：64   6. T1⑤a：226   7. T1⑤a：40   8. T1⑤a：192
9. T1⑤a：120   10. T1⑤a：125   11. T1⑤a：118

ted with two concave strings, under which decorated with engraved vertical lines; mouth diameter of 22. 4, remaining part of height of 3. 1cm (Figure 30：16). Specimen T1⑤a：64, brown earthenware; with a protruding rim decorated under the mouth; lip decorated with twist line pattern, belly decorated with poked short line pattern; mouth diameter of 21. 7, remaining part of height of 3. 9cm (Figure 31：5). Specimen T1⑤a：120, reddish brown earthenware; under mouth decorated with two concave strings; mouth diameter of 30. 4, remaining part of height of 3. 2cm (Figure 31 : 9). Specimen T1⑤a：125, reddish brown earthenware; under mouth decorated with concave string pattern; mouth diameter of 28, remaining part of height of 2. 6cm (Figure 31 : 10). Specimen T1⑤a：118, reddish brown earthenware; under mouth decorated with concave string pattern; mouth diameter of 29, remaining part of height of 2. 9cm (Figure 31：11).

Category 5：5 pieces; round lip, narrow flat edge, contracted mouth, deep belly.

Specimen T1⑤a：365, reddish brown earthenware; mouth diameter of 23, remaining part of height of 3. 6cm (Figure 28：6). Specimen T1⑤a：226, brown earthenware; edge decorated with spiral twist pattern, upper belly decorated with poked connected arc patterns; mouth diameter of 31. 4, remaining part of height of 3. 1cm (Figure 31：6). Specimen T1⑤a：143, grayish brown earthenware, inclined straight belly; lip decorated with 1 circle of concave string; mouth diameter of 29. 2, remaining part of height of 2. 8cm (Figure 30：8). Specimen T1⑤a：154, gray earthenware, sharp round lip; one protruding rim decorated under the mouth; mouth diameter of 36. 4, remaining part of height of 2. 6cm (Figure 31:3). Specimen T1⑤a:48, reddish brown earthenware; sharp round lip; mouth diameter of 28. 4, remaining part of height of 3. 5cm (Figure 31:2).

2. Unearthed artifacts of stratum T1⑤b

Very few artifacts were unearthed in Stratum T1⑤b. The ones unearthed are all pottery pieces. A total of 18 pottery pieces were unearthed, in which fine earthenware accounts for 88. 9% and coarse earthenware accounts for 11. 1% in terms of material, indicating dominance of fine earthenware; and terracotta and reddish brown earthenware are the most in terms of color, accounting for 55. 6%, supplemented by blackish brown and grayish brown; decorations are mostly twist line patter, concave strings and combed dots; forms are mainly thick lip jars, bowls, ring feet, flare mouth jars and the like. A total of 14 pottery specimens are selected from this stratum.

Thick lip jars: 4 pieces; based on shape and structure, these can be classified into two categories.

Category 1: 3 pieces; thick square lip.

Specimen T1⑤b:1, brown earthenware, lip decorated with spiral twist pattern; mouth diameter of 32. 3, remaining part of height of 6cm (Figure 32:1). Specimen T1⑤b:2, reddish brown earthenware; brown earthenware, lip decorated with spiral twist pattern, upper belly decorated with two concave strings; mouth diameter of 17. 8, remaining part of height of 4. 8cm (Figure 32:2). Specimen T1⑤b:3, brown earthenware, lip decorated with spiral twist pattern, upper belly decorated with one concave string and engraved lines; mouth diameter of 19, remaining part of height of 3. 6cm (Figure 32:4).

Category 2: 1 piece; round lip.

Specimen T1⑤b:15, reddish brown earthenware; arc shoulder; neck decorated with a protruding rim, on the protruding rim poked short line pattern, engraved with short line pattern; mouth diameter of 20. 7, remaining part of height of 3. 7cm (Figure 32:6).

Ring feet: 5 pieces; based on shape and structure, these can be classified into three categories.

Category 1: 1 piece; straight bucket shape.

Specimen T1⑤b:4, reddish brown earthenware; enclosure on the foot decorated with two concave string patterns and poked dots; base diameter of 17, remaining part of height of 4cm (Figure 32:8).

Category 2: 3 pieces, trumpet shape, foot tip bent outward.

Specimen T1⑤b:11, reddish brown earthenware; base diameter of 15. 4, remaining part of height of 1. 9cm (Figure 32:10). Specimen T1⑤b:20, brown earthenware; base diameter of 18. 4, remaining part of height of 2. 8cm (Figure 32:5). Specimen T1⑤b:19, terracotta, middle of foot decorated with one concave string; base diameter of 18. 6, remaining part of height of 4. 2cm (Figure

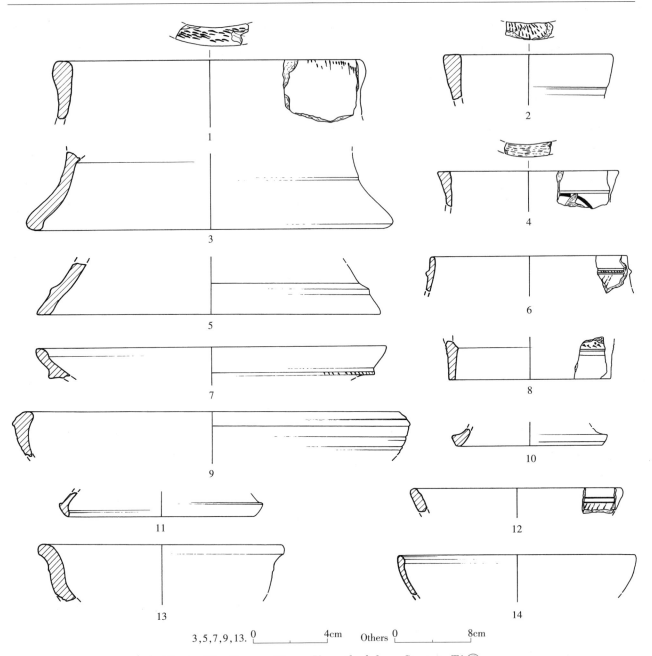

Figure 32　Pottery Pieces Unearthed from Stratum T1⑤a

1, 2, 4, 6. Thick lip jar (T1⑤b:1, 2, 3, 15)　3, 5, 8, 10, 11. Ring foot (T1⑤b:4, 11, 14, 19, 20)
7, 9, 13, 14. Bowl (T1⑤b:5, 6, 9, 13)　12. Flared mouth jar (T1⑤b:10)

32:3).

Category 3: 1 piece; trumpet shape, foot tip bent inward.

Specimen T1⑤b:14, brown earthenware; base diameter of 20, remaining part of height of 2.6cm (Figure 32:11).

Bowls: 4 pieces; based on shape and structure, these can be classified into three categories.

Category 1: 1 piece; flare mouth, tilted straight belly, decorated with a protruding rim on the shoulder.

Specimen T1⑤b：5, brown earthenware, sharp round lip, tilted straight belly, poked on the protruding rim are dotted patterns; mouth diameter of 18. 5, remaining part of height of 5cm (Figure 32：7).

Category 2：2 pieces; contracted mouth, arc belly.

Specimen T1⑤b：6, reddish brown earthenware; round lip; upper belly and shoulder decorated with three concave strings; mouth diameter of 19. 8, remaining part of height of 6cm (Figure 32：9). Specimen T1⑤b：13, reddish brown earthenware; round lip; mouth diameter of 25, base diameter of 4. 2cm (Figure 32：14).

Category 3：1 piece; flare mouth, arc belly.

Specimen T1⑤b：9, round lip, contracted neck, arc belly; mouth diameter of 13. 2, remaining part of height of 2. 9cm (Figure 32：13).

Flare mouth jar： 1 piece.

Specimen T1⑤b：10, reddish brown earthenware; round lip; under mouth decorated with two concave strings, under which decorated with engraved short lines; mouth diameter of 22, remaining part of height of 2. 5cm (Figure 32：12).

Section Two   T2

T2 is located in the center of the excavation area. The square units for exploration were planned out and excavation works commenced on December 3, 2006 and exploration was completed on January 6, 2007. Chen Weidong and Yue Lianjian were in charge of conducting excavations, making records and plotting.

I. Stratigraphic accumulation

Based on differences in soil properties, colors and items contained within and through summarization, strata in present square unit for exploration can be divided into six strata (Figure 33; Plate 28).

Stratum ①: Thickness of 10 – 15cm; yellow – gray color topsoil; loose soil, containing a small amount of ceramic, plastic and plant roots *etc*.

Stratum ②: Thickness of 0 – 10cm, depth of 10 – 15cm; yellowish red color soil; soil is hard, containing a large amount of red bricks, some blue and white porcelain pieces, white porcelain pieces and a very small amount of stone tools. H34 opening is under this stratum, accumulated over modern and contemporary times.

Stratum ③: Thickness of 10 – 24cm, depth of 10 – 20cm; light gray – color soil, of fine soil; containing small amount of bricks and porcelain pieces among other items. H1 opening is under this stratum, accumulated over modern and contemporary times.

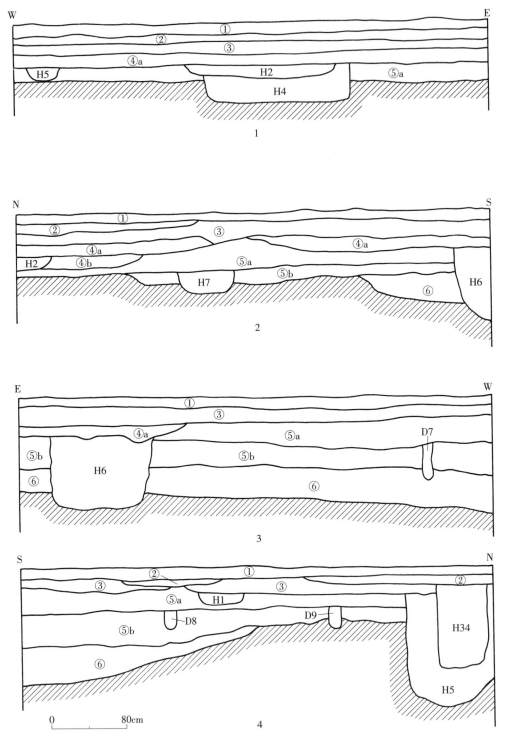

Figure 33   Sectional View of Four Walls of T2
1. North wall   2. East wall   3. South wall   4. West wall

Stratum ④: Based on differences in soil properties and colors, this stratum can be divided into two secondary strata, deposited in the Đại Việt dynasty and early Lê dynasty.

Stratum ④a: Thickness of 0 – 18cm, depth of 28 – 34cm; dark brown color ferromanganese soil stratum, containing large amount of iron rust, inclined from southeast corner towards north; containing very small amount of porcelain pieces, bricks and other items. H3, H4, H5 and H6 openings are under this stratum (no ④b deposit at opening of pit).

Stratum ④b: Thickness of 0 – 12cm, depth of 42cm, grayish brown ferromanganese, containing small amount of iron rust, distributing in northeast part only, containing very small amount of porcelain pieces, bricks and other items. H2 opening is under this stratum.

Stratum ⑤: Based on differences in soil properties and colors, this stratum can be divided into two secondary strata. Accumulated in the Phung Nguyen culture period.

⑤a: Thickness of 0 – 44cm, depth of 26 – 44cm. Dark – gray color soil; soil is loose, containing lots of burnt soil particles, including a large number of pottery pieces and a small number of stone tools. H7, H8 opening is under this stratum.

⑤b: Thickness of 0 – 35cm, depth of 40 – 60cm; gray yellow color soil; soil is hard; distributing southwards from north; containing little items. mainly are pottery pieces and stone tools.

Stratum ⑥: Thickness of 0 – 40cm, depth of 62 – 86cm; distributing only in southwest part of the square unit, yellowish brown soil, mixed with small amount of gray soil stains, hard soil; containing very little items; accumulated in the Phung Nguyen culture period.

Under this stratum is reddish – brown ferromanganese raw soil.

II. Remains

A total of 24 various remains was sorted within T2, including 8 pits and 16 postholes (Figure 34; Plate 29).

1. Pits

8 pits. Including H1 – H8, of which H1 and H2 are from contemporary and modern times. Information of pits from the Phung Nguyen culture period is presented below.

H3 is located in the northeast part of T2, opening under Stratum ④a, broken by H2.

Shape and structure: Plane shape of round upper part and square lower part, with upper part diameter of around 1. 4 meters and side length of the lower part square 1 meter, depth of 0. 8 meters. Walls of the pit are smooth and bottom is flat and even. Accumulations in the pit can be divided into three strata: Stratum ① being grayish black soil; loose soil; large amount of red burnt soil and charcoal found in the north of the stratum, also containing large amount of pottery pieces and small number of stone tools; thickness of 16 – 20cm. Stratum ② is of yellow clay soil, relatively hard, containing large amount of iron rust; depositing inclined from northeast to southwest; containing small number of pottery pieces; thickness of 24 – 30cm. Stratum ③ is gray soil; soil is loose, depositing inclined from northeast to southwest; containing small number of pottery pieces; thickness of 21 – 27cm. Below this stratum is yellowish brown raw soil (Figure 35; Figures 30 – 32).

Unearthed items: Artifacts unearthed in H3 include pottery pieces, stone tools and jade pieces,

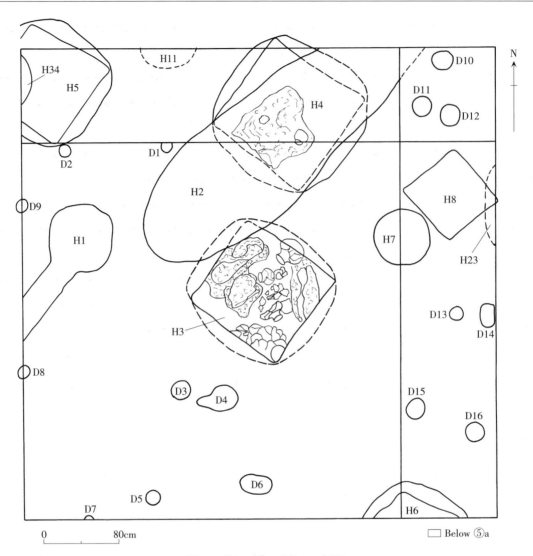

Figure 34   Plan View of T2

dominated by pottery pieces with relatively less stone tools and jade pieces. A total of 37 specimens are selected[1] , including 32 pottery pieces, 3 stone tools and 2 jade pieces.

Stone tools: 5 pieces; mostly ground to shape stone tools, including 1 stone adze, 1 grinding stone and 1 scraper.

Stone adze: 1 piece.

Specimen H3: 3, damaged, body shape is of rectangle, grinding traces visible on one side, marks from flaking visible on the other; remaining part of length of 4. 6; remaining part of width of 2. 2 − 4, thickness of 1. 3cm (Figure 36: 1).

Grinding stone: 1 piece.

---

[1] From registrar of unearthed artifacts, total of 81 specimens are selected from H3, including 5 jade pieces, 23 pottery ornamentation speci-
      mens, 53 pottery form specimens. Some items are cancelled numbers due to restoration. But information of some artifacts is missing and
      here we present information of complete materials only.

Specimen H3 : 9, of small form, body of triangle shape, grinding traces visible on three sides; of length of 3. 9, width of 2. 3, thickness of 2cm (Figure 36 : 11).

Scraper: 1 piece.

Specimen H3 : 4, damaged, body of arc shape, flat top, arc blade, natural rock on one side, marks from flaking visible on the other; remaining part of length of 5. 8, width of 2, thickness of 0. 1 − 1. 5cm (Figure 36 : 2).

Jade pieces: 2 pieces; all rings.

Rings: 2 pieces; of similar shape and structure.

Specimen H3 : 1, beige color, damaged, ring shaped; diameter of 6. 7, width of 0. 7, thickness of 0. 3cm (Figure 36 : 3). Specimen H3 : 10, beige color, remaining 1/4, ring shaped; diameter of 4. 8, width of 0. 7, thickness of 0. 2cm (Figure 36 : 12).

Pottery pieces: A total of 1, 720 potter pieces were unearthed in H3. In terms of the earthenware materials, fine sand earthenware accounts for about 80%, coarse sand earthenware for about 8. 4%, and clay polished earthenware for about 10. 6%. In terms of colors of the pottery pieces, terracotta, reddish brown, and brown pottery pieces account for about 64. 6%, indicating that the pottery color is mostly red-

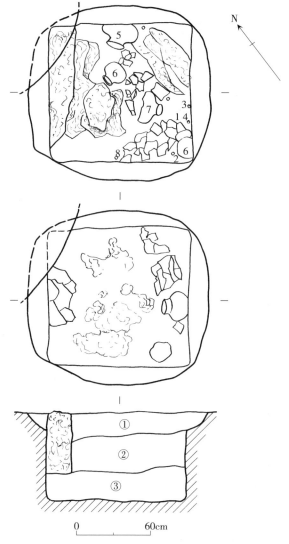

Figure 35   Sectional Plan of H3
1. Stone ring   2, 5 − 8. Pottery balls   3. Stone adez   4. Stone scraper   14, 15. Pottery jars   73, 81. Pottery kettles   75. Enclosure base

dish. In terms of pattern ornamentation, it was extremely well − developed, accounting for 43% of the total number of pottery pieces. Some pieces have on the surface a thin ornamented coating. The decorations are of great variety, in which rope decorations account for about 64% of the total decorations. Other decorations include engraved line, stamp, concave string, protruding rim, pressure stamp, comb brushing, and added mound *etc*. Particularly, among all the engraved lines, the ones with comb teeth brushed or comb dotted stamps are the most characteristic. Compound ornamentations of multiple decorations on a single pottery piece appear to have been very popular. The main ornamentation patterns are of clouds, S − shape, geometric patterns, circles and water ripples (Figure 37; Plate 33, 34) and the like. Pottery mouth parts are mostly contracted or flared. The artifacts are mostly with enclosure base and ring feet. Forms of the artifacts include pottery balls, stem dishes, bowls, ring feet, bases

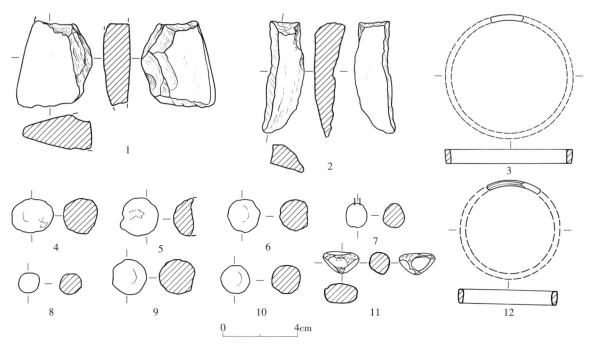

Figure 36   Unearthed Artifacts of H3
1. Stone adze (H3:3)   2. Stone scraper (H3:4)   3, 12. Jade ring (H3:1, 10)   4 – 10. Pottery ball (H3:2, 5, 6, 7, 11, 8, 12)   11. Grinding stone (H3:9)

and kettles *etc.* (Plates 35 – 37).

H3: A total of 32 specimens of pottery pieces are selected, of which 16 specimens are for orna-mentations, 16 specimens are for forms, including 7 pottery balls, 1 stem dish, 3 ring feet, 1 bowl, 2 kettles, 1 base and 1 enclosure base.

Pottery balls: 7 pieces; sphere, similar size, different forms (Plate 38:1).

Specimen H3:2, reddish brown fine sand earthenware, irregular sphere shaped, diameter of 2cm (Fig-ure 36:4). Specimen H3:5, damaged, reddish brown fine sand earthenware, diameter of 2cm (Figure 36:5). Specimen H3:6, damaged, reddish brown fine sand earthenware, diameter of 1.7cm (Figure 36:6). Specimen H3:7, damaged, reddish brown fine sand earthenware, irregular sphere shaped, diameter of 1.1cm (Figure 36:7). Specimen H3:11, reddish brown fine sand earthenware, diameter of 1.1cm (Fig-ure 36:8). Specimen H3:8, reddish brown fine sand earthenware, diameter of 1.7cm (Figure 36:9). Spec-imen H3:12, reddish brown fine sand earthenware, diameter of 1.6cm (Figure 36:10).

Stem dish: 1 piece.

Specimen H3:72, reddish brown fine sand earthenware, sharp round lip, narrow flat edge, depth of dish, horn – shaped ring foot, apparent traces from rotation making visible inside the artifact; bore diameter of 17.2, diameter at bottom of 11.6, overall height of 10.4cm (Figure 38:1).

Bowl: 1 piece; of basically similar shape and structure.

Specimen H3:71, reddish brown fine sand earthenware, polished surface, thickness of round lip, contracted mouth, bent shoulder, tilted straight belly, bottom damaged; shoulder decorated with con-

Figure 37   Rubbings of Ornamentations of Pottery Pieces Unearthed from H3

1. Engraved pattern + string pattern + poked dot pattern (H3:31)   2. Twist rope pattern (H3:42)   3. Engraved line pattern (H3:49)   4. Rope pattern + engraved pattern (H3:50)   5. String pattern + rope pattern + circle pattern (H3:43)   6. Twist rope pattern (H3:44)   7. Rope pattern + engraved line pattern (H3:51)   8. Engraved line pattern (H3:51)   9. String pattern + cloud pattern + Rope pattern (H3:45)   10. Engraved line pattern (H3:46)   11. Twist rope pattern (H3:53)   12. S-shape pattern + poked dot pattern (H3:54)   13. Combing pattern (H3:47)   14. Diagonal rope pattern (H3:48)   15. String pattern + poked dot pattern (H3:55)   16. Circle pattern + string pattern + rope pattern (H3:56)

cave string pattern, shoulder and belly decorated with broad and narrow protruding rim pattern; bore diameter of 28.5, remaining part of height of 5.7cm (Figure 38:2; Plate 38:2).

Ring feet: 3 pieces; can be classified into two categories based on shape and structure.

Category 1: 2 pieces; horn-shaped ring foot, foot tip bent outward.

Specimen H3:70, reddish brown fine sand earthenware, horn-shaped ring foot, damaged above ring foot; ring foot made with utensil, lower part decorated with spiral twist pattern, ring foot inner bottom decorated with twist line pattern; diameter at bottom of 13.5, remaining part of height of 4.3cm (Figure 38:3). Specimen H3:79, grayish brown fine sand earthenware, damaged above shoulder,

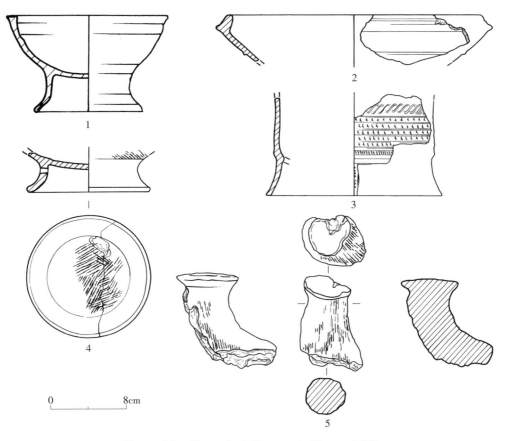

Figure 38   Unearthed Pottery Artifacts of H3
1. Stem dish（H3：72） 2. Bowl（H3：71） 3, 4. Ring foot（H3：70, 31） 5. Base（H3：13）

drum belly, belly straight, trumpet shape ring foot reaching outward; decorated with twist line pattern; diameter at bottom of 18. 8, remaining part of height of 33, maximum diameter at belly of 40cm（Figure 39：1, 3）.

Category 2: 1 piece; bucket shape ring foot, foot tip reaching outward.

Specimen H3：31, belly upper part damaged, reddish brown fine earthenware; belly decorated with seven sets of concave string pattern, upper part with two sets of S – shape lines, the other five sets between concave strings decorated with stamped combed dots, ring foot decorated with a protruding rim, stamped with short line pattern, enclosure on the foot decorated with two concave string pattern, in the strings decorated with poked rectangular patterns and combed dots; diameter at bottom of 19. 4, remaining part of height of 11. 3cm（Figure 38：4; Plate 38：3）.

Pottery base: 1 piece.

Specimen H3：13, damaged, reddish brown fine sand earthenware, arc shaped, flat top; decorated with vertical twist line pattern; top diameter of 5. 2, remaining part of height of 8. 2cm（Figure 38：5）.

Kettles: 2 pieces; categorized into two based on shape.

Category 1: 1 piece; drum belly slightly hanging.

Specimen H3 : 81, reddish brown sand earthenware, some parts blackened due to burning in making, sharp round lip, narrow flat edge, high collar, arc shoulder, enclosure base; upper collar decorated with protruding rim pattern; on the protruding rim stamp short line pattern, neck decorated with cloud pattern, cloud pattern with stamp combed dots, belly and bottom decorated with twist line pattern; bore diameter of 28, diameter at belly of 35. 8, overall height of 36cm (Figure 40:1, 3; Plates 39, 40).

Category 2: 1 piece; drum belly.

Specimen H3 : 73, reddish brown sand earthenware, blackened due to burning in making, sharp round lip, narrow flat edge, high collar, arc shoulder, drum belly, belly lower part damaged; collar

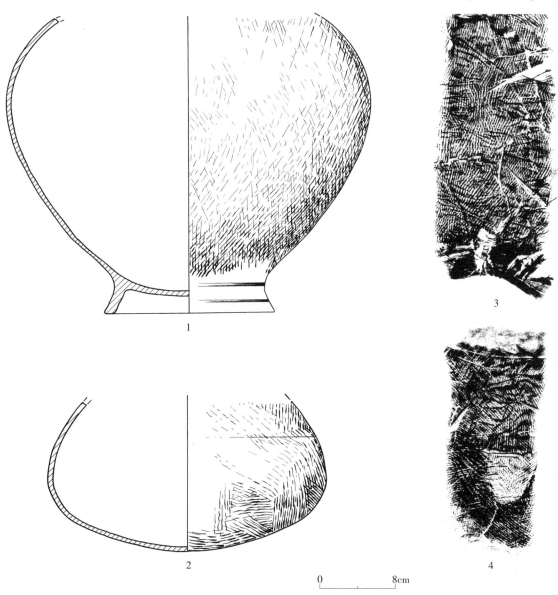

0   8cm

Figure 39 Pottery Pieces Unearthed from H3
1. Ring foot (H3 : 79) 2. Enclosure base (H3 : 75) 3. Rubbings of patterns on pottery (H3 : 79)
4. Rubbings of patterns on pottery (H3 : 75)

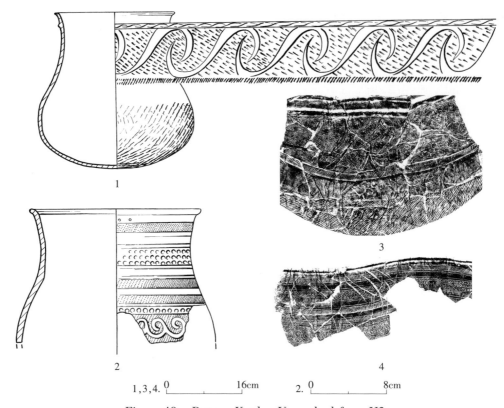

Figure 40   Pottery Kettles Unearthed from H3

1. H3:81   2. H3:73   3. Rubbings of patterns on pottery kettle (H3:81)   4. Rubbings of patterns on pottery kettle (H3:73)

decorated with 14 concave string patterns, upper part and lower part two sets of concave string pattern decorated with stamped combed dots, middle and should have two sets of concave string pattern decorated with circles, upper belly decorated with cloud pattern, cloud pattern with stamp combed dots; bore diameter of 20, remaining part of height of 15. 6cm (Figure 40:2, 4; Plate 41:1).

Enclosure base: 1 piece.

Specimen H3:75, grayish brown fine sand earthenware, shoulder and above damaged, drum belly, enclosure base, decorated with twist line pattern, remaining part of height of 17. 2, belly diameter 31. 8cm (Figure 39:2, 4; Plate 41:2, 3).

H4 is located in the northwest part of T2, partly laminated under north beam of T1, opening under Stratum, broken by H2.

Shape and structure: rectangular in plane view, length of 1. 4, width of 1. 2, depth of 0. 4 − 0. 46 meters. Walls of the pit are smooth and bottom is flat and even. Accumulations in the pit can be divided into three strata. Stratum ① is in the middle of the pit; thickness of 0. 06 meters; red burnt soil with large amount of pottery pieces, among which a pottery base was found in the north of the red burnt soil and a pottery bowl found in the east; Stratum ② is of dark grayish black color soil, soil is loose, thickness of 0. 1 − 0. 2 meters; containing lots of pottery pieces; Stratum ③ is yellowish brown color soil; soil is loose, containing little items, thickness of 0. 1 – 0. 24 meters. Below this stratum is yellowish brown raw soil (Figure 41; Plate 42).

Unearthed items: Artifacts unearthed in H4 include pottery pieces and stone tools, dominated by pottery pieces with relatively less stone tools. A total of 34 specimens are selected, including 27 pottery pieces and 7 stone tools.

Stone tools: 7 pieces, including 4 stone adzes, 1 stone ball, 1 stone mold and 1 stone core (Plate 43).

Stone adzes: 4 pieces, of similar shape and structure, small, ground to shape, body presenting length of square shape.

Specimen H4 : 5, upper part damaged, double – sided arc blade, remaining part of length of 2. 8, width of 3, thickness of 0. 8cm (Figure 42 : 1; Plate 44 : 1). Specimen H4 : 2, blade damaged, only upper part remains, remaining part of length of 4. 5, width of 4. 6, thickness of 1. 5cm (Figure 42 : 2). Specimen H4 : 1, damaged in the upper portion, only blade remains, double – sided arc blade, remaining part of length of 4. 5, width of 5. 2, thickness of 1. 4cm (Figure 42 : 4; Plate 44 : 2). Specimen H4 : 3, blade damaged, only upper part remains, remaining part of length of 4. 2, width of 4. 3, thickness of 1. 3cm (Figure 42 : 5).

Stone ball: 1 piece.

Specimen H4 : 6, oval shape, smooth surface; of longer diameter of 1. 8, shorter diameter of 1. 4cm (Figure 42 : 6).

Stone flapper: 1 piece.

Specimen H4 : 7, damaged; body shape is of rectangle, uneven surface due to impact, with mold trace of rectangular shape in the middle, which is polished; remaining part of length of 5. 6; remaining part of width of 4. 5, thickness of 1cm (Figure 42 : 3; Plate 44 : 3).

Stone core: 1 piece.

Specimen H4 : 8, irregular triangle, natural rock on one side, impact points and radiation rays from impact visible on the other side; of length of 11. 2, width of 11. 1, thickness of 3. 3cm (Figure

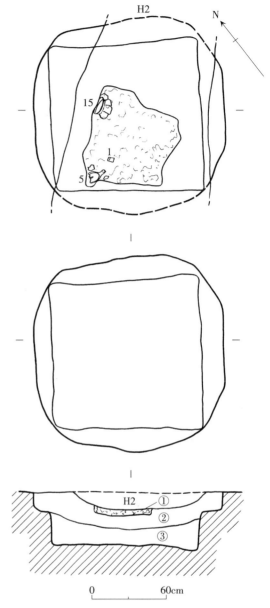

Figure 41   Sectional Plan of H4
1. Stone adze   5. Stone flapper
15. Pottery ring feet

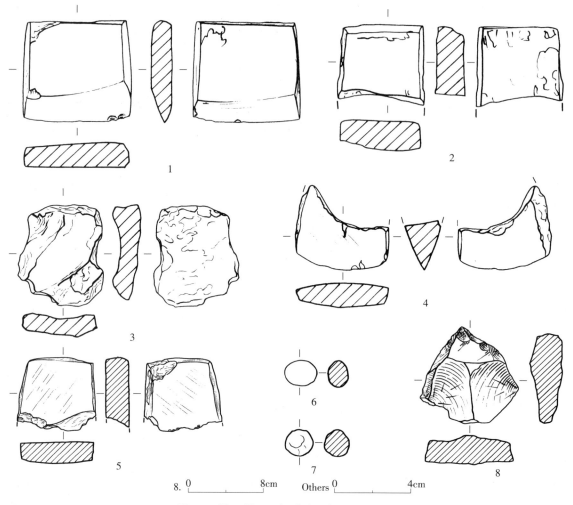

Figure 42   Unearthed Artifacts of H4

1, 2, 4, 5. Stone adze （H4：5, 2, 1, 3） 3. Stone mold （H4：7） 6. Stone ball （H4：6） 7. Pottery ball
（H4：4） 8. Stone core （H4：8）

42：8）.

Pottery pieces：A total of 595 potter pieces were unearthed in H4. In terms of the earthenware
materials, fine sand earthenware accounts for about 77%, coarse sand earthenware for about 10%,
and clay polished earthenware for about 13%. In terms of colors of the pottery pieces, terracotta, reddish brown, and brown pottery pieces account for about 78%, indicating that the pottery color is mostly
reddish. In terms of pattern ornamentation, it was extremely well – developed, accounting for 31% of
the total number of pottery pieces. Some pieces have on the surface a thin ornamented coating. The
decorations are of great variety, in which rope decorations account for about 40% of the total decorations. Other decorations include engraved line, stamp, concave string, protruding rim, pressure
stamp, comb brushing, added mound and combed dots *etc*. Particularly, among all the engraved lines,
the ones with comb teeth brushed or comb dotted stamps are the most characteristic. Compound ornamentations of multiple decorations on a single pottery piece appear to have been very popular. The

main ornamentation patterns are of clouds, S – shape, geometric patterns (Figure 43; Plates 45, 46) and the like. Pottery mouth parts are mostly contracted or flared; followed in number by trumpet – shaped and straight mouths. The artifacts are mostly with enclosure base. Forms of the artifacts include pottery balls, bases, flare mouth jars, trumpet – shape mouth jars, bowls, contracted mouth jars, straight – mouth jars and ring feet *etc.* (Plates 47, 48).

A total of 29 specimens of pottery pieces are selected, of which 19 specimens are for forms, 10 specimens are for ornamentations. Form specimens include 1 pottery ball, 1 base, 2 flare mouth jars, 2 trumpet – shape mouth jars, 4 bowls, 1 contracted mouth jar, 3 straight – mouth jars and 5 ring feet.

Pottery ball: 1 piece.

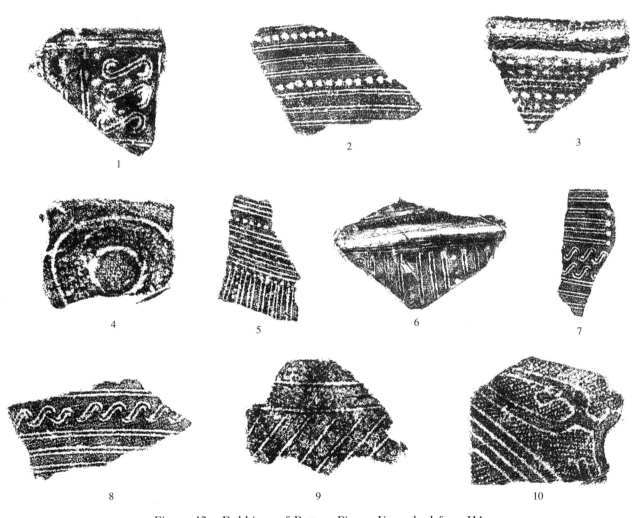

Figure 43   Rubbings of Pottery Pieces Unearthed from H4

1. S – shape pattern + concave string pattern (H4 : 16)   2, 3. Concave string pattern + combed dot pattern (H4 : 26, 33)
4. Geometrical form pattern + combed dot pattern (H4 : 34)   5. Concave string pattern + combed dot pattern + geometrical form pattern (H4 : 27)   6. Protruding rim pattern + concave string pattern (H4 : 28)   7, 8. Concave string pattern + S – shape pattern (H4 : 32, 29)   9. Engraved pattern + concave string pattern (H4 : 30)   10. Concave string pattern + combed dot pattern + cloud pattern (H4 : 31)

Specimen H4 : 4, reddish brown fine sand earthenware, sphere shaped; diameter of 1. 5cm (Figure 42 : 7).

Base: 1 piece; of similar shape and structure.

Specimen H4 : 31, reddish brown sand earthenware, arc shaped, hollow in the middle, flat bottom, one branch in the middle, decorated with vertical twist line pattern; diameter at bottom of 10. 5, remaining part of height of 17cm (Figure 44 : 2; Plate 49 : 2).

Flare mouth jars: 2 pieces.

Specimen H4 : 13, reddish brown sand earthenware, square lip, poked on the protruding rim are dotted patterns; bore diameter of 39. 5, remaining part of height of 8cm (Figure 44 : 1). Specimen H4 : 12, blackish brown earthenware, round lip, poked on the protruding rim are dotted patterns; bore diameter of 31. 5, remaining part of height of 5. 8cm (Figure 44 : 7).

Bowls: 4 pieces; can be classified into three categories based on shape and structure.

Category 1: 2 pieces; contracted mouth, arc belly.

Specimen H4 : 17, damaged, reddish brown earthenware, grayish brown inside, round lip, arc belly; bore diameter of 29. 8, remaining part of height of 6. 7cm (Figure 44 : 3). Specimen H4 : 19,

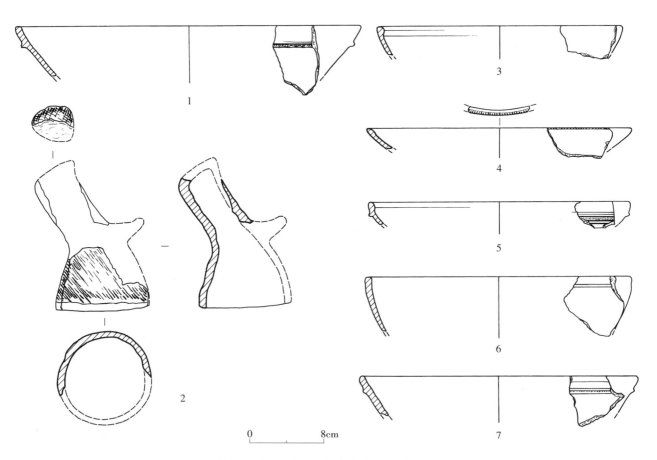

Figure 44   Unearthed Artifacts of H4
1, 7. Flared mouth jar (H4 : 13, 12)   2. Base (H4 : 31)   3 – 6. Bowl (H4 : 17, 20, 14, 19)

reddish brown fine sand earthenware, round lip, under mouth decorated with two concave strings; bore diameter of 27. 8, remaining part of height of 3. 8cm (Figure 44:6).

　　Category 2: 1 piece; contracted mouth, under mouth decorated with a protruding rim.

　　Specimen H4:14, reddish brown fine sand earthenware, part of surface blackened due to burning in making, round lip, contracted mouth, tilted straight belly, under the protruding rim decorated with three concave strings, in upper part are 2 concave string pattern decorated with combed dots; bore diameter of 29. 5, remaining part of height of 3cm (Figure 44:5).

　　Category 3: 1 piece; flare mouth, shallow belly.

　　Specimen H4:20, blackish brown earthenware, round lip; lip engraved short lines; bore diameter of 29. 5, remaining part of height of 3. 5cm (Figure 44:4).

Contracted mouth jar: 1 piece.

　　Specimen H4:18, coarse reddish brown earthenware, round lip, contracted mouth, arc belly; lower part of mouth and belly upper part separately decorated with two concave strings, belly decorated with vertical twist line pattern; bore diameter of 21. 5, remaining part of height of 7. 2cm (Figure 45:1).

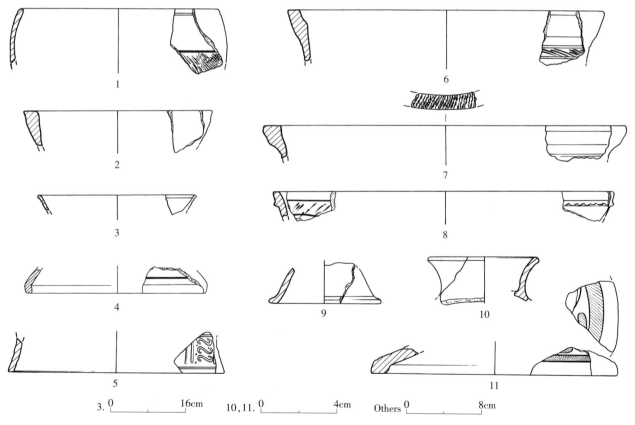

Figure 45　Pottery Artifacts Unearthed from H4

1. Contracted mouth jar (H4:18)　2, 6, 7. Thick lip jar (H4:22, 23, 21)　3, 8. Flared mouth jar (H4:24, 25)
4, 5, 9 – 11. Ring foot (H4:9, 16, 10, 11, 15)

Flare mouth jars: 2 pieces; can be classified into two categories based on shape and structure.

Category 1: 1 piece; of similar shape and structure, all tilted straight belly, with a protruding rim decorated under the mouth.

Specimen H4:25, reddish brown sand earthenware, square lip; under mouth decorated with dotting pattern on the protruding rim poked, inside decorated with two concave strings, between concave strings decorated with engraved line patterns; bore diameter of 35.2, remaining part of height of 3.2cm (Figure 45:8).

Category 2: 1 piece; tilted straight belly, lower part no protruding rim.

Specimen H4:24, grayish brown fine sand earthenware, round lip, narrow flat edge; bore diameter of 36, remaining part of height of 4.8cm (Figure 45:3).

Thick lip jars: 3 pieces; of similar shape and structure, all of thick square lip, straight mouth slightly flared.

Specimen H4:21, grayish brown fine sand earthenware, lip decorated with twist line pattern, upper belly decorated with concave string pattern; bore diameter of 41.5, remaining part of height of 4cm (Figure 45:7). Specimen H4:22, reddish brown fine sand earthenware, bore diameter of 21, remaining part of height of 5cm (Figure 45:2). Specimen H4:23, reddish brown earthenware, lip decorated with twist line pattern, upper belly decorated with two concave string pattern, between concave strings decorated with engraved short lines; bore diameter of 32.8, remaining part of height of 6cm (Figure 45:6).

Ring feet: 5 pieces; can be classified into three categories based on shape and structure.

Category 1: 2 pieces; horn – shaped ring foot, foot tip bent outward.

Specimen H4:10, fine brown earthenware; ring foot upper part damaged, ring foot, plain surface; diameter at bottom of 11.8, remaining part of height of 5.1cm (Figure 45:9). Specimen H4:11, fine brown earthenware; ring foot upper part damaged, plain surface; diameter at bottom of 12.2, remaining part of height of 4.5cm (Figure 45:10).

Category 2: 1 piece; bucket shaped.

Specimen H4:16, reddish brown fine sand earthenware, ring foot decorated with one concave string, decorated with vertical stamped rectangular patterns and engraved S – shape pattern; diameter at bottom of 23.3, remaining part of height of 4.5cm (Figure 45:5).

Category 3: 2 pieces; horn – shaped ring foot, foot tip bent inward.

Specimen H4:9, reddish brown fine sand earthenware, plain surface; bore diameter of 19.5, remaining part of height of 3cm (Figure 45:4). Specimen H4:15, reddish brown fine sand earthenware, ring on the lower part of foot decorated with two concave string pattern, combed dots between concave string patterns, upper part decorated with engraved cloud pattern, cloud pattern decorated with combed dots; bore diameter of 13.1, remaining part of height of 1.6cm (Figure 45:11; Plate

49 : 1).

H5 is located in the northwest part of T2, partly laminated under east beam of T1, opening under Stratum ④a, broken by a pit of contemporary and modern times H34.

Shape and structure: plane shape of round upper part and square lower part, with upper part diameter of around 1.6 meters, depth of 0.2 meters, side length of the lower part square 1.2 meters, depth of 1.1 meters. Walls of the pit are smooth and bottom is flat and even. Accumulations in the pit can be divided into three strata. Stratum ① is grayish black soil, soil is loose, depositing inclined from southwest to northeast; containing large amount of pottery pieces and small number of stone tools; thickness of 0.7 - 0.85 meters. stratum ② yellow clay soil, relatively hard, containing large amount of iron rust' depositing inclined from northeast to southwest; containing small number of pottery pieces; thickness of 0.1 - 0.15 meters. stratum ③ is gray soil, soil is loose, depositing inclined from northeast to southwest; containing small number of pottery

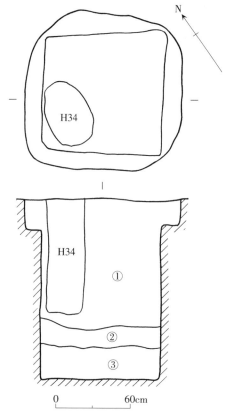

Figure 46   Sectional Plan of H5

pieces; thickness of 0.2 - 0.3 meters. Below this stratum is yellowish brown raw soil (Figure 46; Plate 50).

Unearthed items: Mainly are pottery pieces and stone tools; most are pottery pieces; with a small number of stone tools. A total of 39 specimens are selected, including 37 pottery pieces and 2 stone tools.

Stone tools: 2 pieces, including 1 scraper and 1 stone core.

Scraper: 1 piece.

Specimen H5 : 14, body shape is of irregular rectangle, flat top, made by flaking; of length of 1.7, width of 0.5, thickness of 0.4cm (Figure 47 : 15).

Stone core: 1 piece.

Specimen H5 : 9, body shape is of rectangle, natural rock on one side, impact points and radiation rays from impact visible on the other side; of length of 2.9, width of 2.6, thickness of 1.5cm (Figure 47 : 1).

Pottery pieces: A total of 1, 081 potter pieces were unearthed in H5. In terms of the earthenware materials, fine sand earthenware accounts for about 82%, coarse sand earthenware and clay polished earthenware both for about 9%. In terms of colors of the pottery pieces, terracotta, reddish brown, and brown pottery pieces account for about 77%, indicating that the pottery color is mostly reddish. In terms of pattern ornamentation, it was extremely well – developed, accounting for 44% of the total number of pottery pieces. The decorations are of great variety, in which rope decorations account for about 55% of the total decorations. Other decorations include engraved line, stamp, concave string, protruding rim, pressure stamp, comb brushing, and dotting *etc*. (Figure 48; Plates 51, 52) Pottery mouth parts are mostly contracted or flared, followed by trumpet – shaped and straight mouths. Artifacts are mostly with enclosure base. Forms of the artifacts include pottery balls, bases, flare mouth jars, bowls, contracted mouth jar s, straight – mouth jars and ring feet *etc*. (Plate 53, 54).

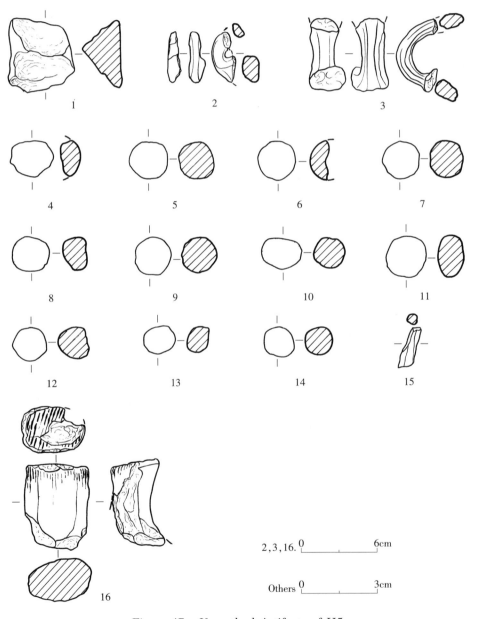

Figure 47   Unearthed Artifacts of H5

1. Stone core (H5:9)   2, 3. Pottery utensil ear (H5:18, 17)   4 – 14. Pottery ball (H5:3, 13, 5, 12, 10, 4, 7, 1, 11, 6, 2)   15. Stone scraper (H5:14)   16. Pottery base (H5:28)

A total of 37 specimens of pottery pieces are selected, of which 26 specimens are for forms and 11 are for ornamentations, including 2 bases, 12 pottery balls, 2 ears, 4 flare mouth jars, 1 trumpet − shape mouth jar, 3 bowls and 2 thick lip jars.

Bases: 2 pieces; of similar shape and structure, small lower part and big upper part, oval upper part, bent, filled.

Specimen H5:37, reddish brown fine sand earthenware, protruding on one side, with a hole, decorated with vertical twist pattern; top long diameter of 6, remaining part of height of 10. 4cm (Figure 49:1). Specimen H5:28, severely damaged; reddish brown sand earthenware, decorated with vertical twist pattern; top diameter of 5. 1, remaining part of height of 6. 8cm (Figure 47:16).

Pottery balls: 12 pieces; of similar shape and structure, of sphere shape (Plate 55:1).

Specimen H5:3, grayish brown fine sand earthenware, diameter of 1. 4 − 1. 7cm (Figure 47:4). Specimen H5:13, grayish brown fine sand earthenware, diameter of 1. 5cm. Specimen H5:8, reddish brown sand earthenware, severely damaged (Figure 47:5). Specimen H5:5, remaining half, grayish brown fine sand earthenware, diameter of 1. 5cm (Figure 47:6). Specimen H5:12, fine brown earth-

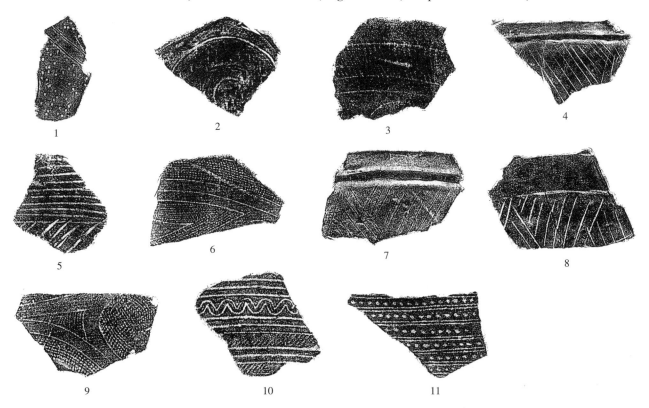

Figure 48   Rubbings of Pottery Pieces Unearthed from Stratum H5

1. Combed dot pattern + poked pattern (H5:32)   2. Circle pattern (H5:33)   3. Short line pattern + concave string pattern (H5:15)   4. Protruding rim pattern + engraved line pattern (H5:20)   5. Engraved line pattern (H5:34)   6. Combed dot pattern + geometrical form pattern (H5:35)   7. Protruding rim pattern + engraved line pattern (H5:21)   8. Concave string pattern + engraved line pattern (H5:29)   9. Combed dot pattern + geometrical form pattern (H5:36)   10. Concave string pattern + combed dot pattern + water ripple pattern (H5:30)   11. Dot pattern + concave string pattern (H5:31)

enware; diameter of 1. 4cm (Figure 47 : 7). Specimen H5 : 10, fine brown earthenware; diameter of 1. 4cm (Figure 47 : 8). Specimen H5 : 4, grayish brown fine sand earthenware, diameter of 1. 4cm (Figure 48 : 9). Specimen H5 : 7, grayish brown fine sand earthenware, diameter of 1. 2 – 1. 6cm (Figure 47 : 10). Specimen H5 : 1, reddish brown fine sand earthenware, diameter of 1. 6cm (Figure 47 : 11). Specimen H5 : 11, grayish brown fine sand earthenware, diameter of 1. 4cm (Figure 47 : 12). Specimen H5 : 6, grayish brown fine sand earthenware, diameter of 1. 2cm (Figure 47 : 13). Specimen H5 : 2, grayish brown fine sand earthenware, diameter of 1. 2cm (Figure 47 : 14).

Ears: 2 pieces; of similar shape and structure, all bridge ears.

Specimen H3 : 18, fine brown earthenware; cylinder by section; remaining part of length of 5. 7, width of 2. 9cm (Figure 47 : 3; Plate 55 : 2). Specimen H3 : 17, fine terracotta, pie shape small ear; remaining part of length of 4, width of 1. 9cm (Figure 47 : 2; Plate 55 : 3).

Flare mouth jars: 4 pieces; can be classified into two categories based on shape and structure.

Category 1: 1 piece, below mouth edge decorated with 1 protruding rim.

Specimen H5 : 22, fine brown earthenware; round lip, under mouth decorated with two concave strings, neck decorated with engraved line patterns; bore diameter of 23. 1, remaining part of height of 4. 6cm (Figure 49 : 8).

Category 2: 3 pieces; below mouth edge no protruding rim.

Specimen H5 : 20, fine terracotta, square lip, contracted neck, upper neck decorated with a protruding rim, on the protruding rim are poked dots, neck decorated with engraved line patterns; bore diameter of 18. 9, remaining part of height of 7. 5cm (Figure 49 : 3; Plate 56 : 1). Specimen H5 : 25, brown sand earthenware, round lip, inside decorated with two concave strings; bore diameter of 31. 6, remaining part of height of 4. 2cm (Figure 49 : 10). Specimen H5 : 24, fine brown earthenware; round lip, inside decorated with two concave strings; bore diameter of 31. 6, remaining part of height of 4. 4cm (Figure 49 : 11).

Trumpet - shape mouth jar: 1 piece.

Specimen H5 : 15, reddish brown fine sand earthenware, round lip, inclined straight belly; under mouth decorated with three concave strings, upper part between concave strings decorated with twist line pattern, belly decorated with engraved patterns; bore diameter of 14. 5, remaining part of height of 4. 2cm (Figure 49 : 2).

Bowls: 3 pieces; can be classified into two categories based on shape and structure.

Category 1: 2 pieces; thickness of round lip, contracted mouth.

Specimen H5 : 23, reddish brown sand earthenware; bore diameter of 18. 8, remaining part of height of 4. 2cm (Figure 49 : 4). Specimen H5 : 26, terracotta, bore diameter of 25. 3, remaining part of height of 3cm (Figure 49 : 9).

Category 2: 1 piece; flare mouth.

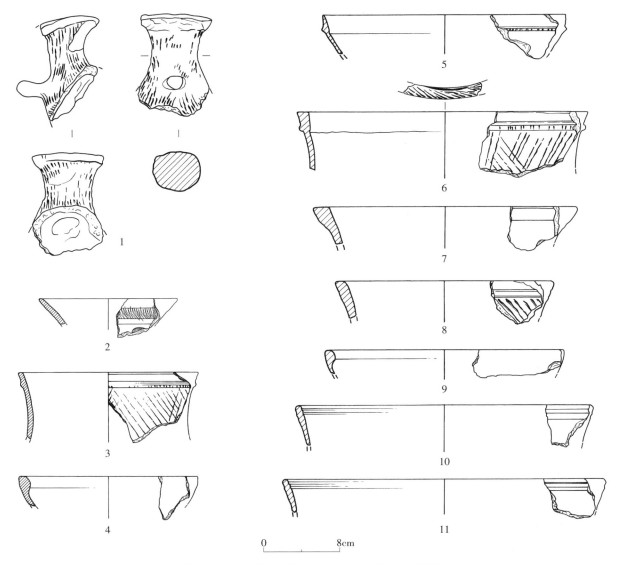

Figure 49　Unearthed Pottery Artifacts of H5

1. Base（H5：37）　2. Trumpet – shape mouth jar（H5：15）　3, 8, 10, 11. Flared mouth jar（H5：20, 22, 25, 24）
4, 5, 9. Bowl（H5：23, 16, 26）　6, 7. Thick lip jar（H5：21, 27）

Specimen H5：16, fine brown earthenware; sharp round lip, tilted straight belly, one protruding rim decorated under the mouth; poked on the protruding rim are dotted patterns; bore diameter of 25.5, remaining part of height of 4.7cm（Figure 49：5）.

Thick lip jars: 2 pieces; of basically similar shape and structure; flare mouth.

Specimen H5：21, reddish brown fine sand earthenware, of thick square lip, lip decorated with spiral twist pattern, under mouth decorated with a protruding rim, on the protruding rim are poked dots, neck decorated with engraved line patterns; bore diameter of 30.7, remaining part of height of 7cm（Figure 49：6; Plate 56：2）. Specimen H5：27, reddish brown sand earthenware, of thick square lip, slightly flared; bore diameter of 28, remaining part of height of 4.7cm（Figure 49：7）.

H6 is located at southeast corner of T2, partly laminated under east beam of the unit and the

T2 南壁

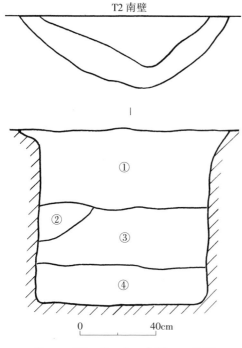

Figure 50   Sectional Plan of H6

southern unit; opening under stratum ④a.

Shape and structure: Plane shape of round upper part and square lower part, with upper part diameter of around 1.1 meters, side length exposed of the lower square part is of 0.88 meters, depth of 0.9 meters. Accumulations in the pit can be divided into 4 strata: stratum ① is grayish black soil, loose soil; containing large amount of burnt soil clots, charcoal, pottery pieces and a small number of stone tools, thickness of 0.32 – 0.4 meters; stratum ② is yellow clay soil, soil is pure, containing large amount of iron rust, existing only in northeast corner of pit, containing very small number of pottery pieces; thickness of 0 – 0.18 meters; stratum ③ is gray soil, soil is loose, containing a small number of burnt soil particles, charcoal and pottery pieces; thickness of 0.13 – 0.33 meters; stratum ④ is grayish brown soil, hard soil, containing a small number of charcoal, thickness of 0.18 – 0.21 meters. Below this stratum is yellowish brown raw soil (Figure 50).

Unearthed items: Mostly pottery pieces, with a small number of stone tools. A total of 11 specimens are selected, including 1 stone tool and 10 pottery pieces.

Stone tools: 1 piece, including 1 scraper.

Scraper: 1 piece.

Specimen H6:1, body of triangle shape, natural rock on one side and impact points and radiation ray visible on the other side; of length of 3.7, width of 2.2, thickness of 0.5cm (Figure 51:1).

Pottery pieces: A total of 265 potter pieces were unearthed in H6. In terms of the earthenware materials, fine sand earthenware accounts for about 67%, coarse sand earthenware for about 17%, and clay polished earthenware for about 16%. In terms of colors of the pottery pieces, terracotta, reddish brown, and brown pottery pieces account for about 66%, indicating that the pottery color is mostly reddish. In terms of pattern ornamentation, it was extremely well – developed, accounting for 34% of the total number of pottery pieces. Some pieces have on the surface a thin ornamented coating. The decorations are of great variety, in which rope decorations account for about 56% of the total decorations. Other decorations include engraved line, concave string, poking and comb brushing *etc*. Particularly, among all the engraved lines, the ones with comb teeth brushed or comb dotted stamps are the most characteristic. Compound ornamentations of multiple decorations on a single pottery piece appear to have been very popular. The main ornamentation patterns are of clouds, S – shape and geometric patterns (Figure 51 : 8 – 11; Plate 57) and the like. Pottery mouth parts are mostly trumpet – shaped and straight mouths. Forms of the artifacts include handles, bases, trumpet – shape mouth jars, stem dishes, bowls and thick lip jars *etc.* (Plate 58).

H6: A total of 10 specimens of pottery pieces are selected, of which 4 specimens are for ornamentations and 6 specimens are for forms, including 1 handle, 1 base, 1 stem dish, 1 trumpet – shape mouth jar, 1 bowl and 1 thick lip jar.

Handle: 1 piece.

Specimen H6 : 2, reddish brown sand earthenware, only bottom remains, round shaped, decorated with vertical twist pattern; remaining part of height of 3.9cm (Figure 51 : 2; Plate 59 : 1).

Base: 1 piece; of similar shape and structure, severely damaged.

Specimen H6 : 3, brown sand earthenware, only remaining lower part, cylinder shaped; hollow; decorated with vertical twist pattern; remaining part of height of 5.4cm (Figure 51 : 3).

Stem dish: 1 piece.

Specimen H6 : 5, reddish brown sand earthenware, of hexagon, deduced to be edge of a stem

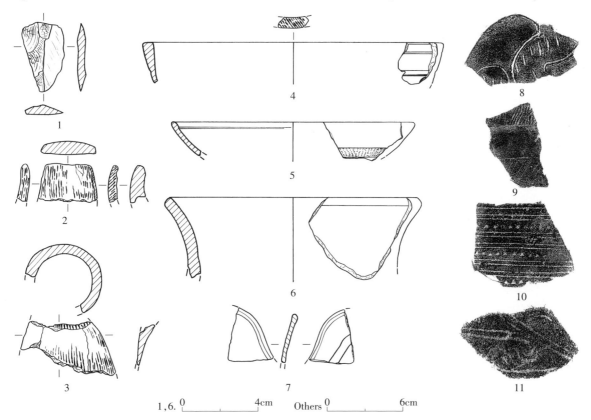

Figure 51   Unearthed Artifacts of H6

(Note: The scales of rubbings vary)

1. Stone scraper (H6 : 1)   2. Pottery handle (H6 : 2)   3. Pottery base (H6 : 3)   4. Thick lip jar (H6 : 6)   5. Bowl (H6 : 4)   6. Trumpet – shape mouth jar (H6 : 7)   7. Hexagonal stem dish (H6 : 5)   8. Poked pattern + geometrical form pattern (H6 : 8)   9. Concave string pattern + engraved line pattern (H6 : 9)   10. Dot pattern + concave string pattern (H6 : 10)   11. Geometrical form pattern (H6 : 11)

dish, inside decorated with two concave strings; remaining part of length of 4. 8; remaining part of width of 5. 8cm (Figure 51:7; Plate 59:2).

Trumpet - shape mouth jar: 1 piece.

Specimen H6:7, reddish brown fine sand earthenware, round lip, contracted neck; bore diameter of 13, remaining part of height of 4. 4cm (Figure 51:6).

Bowl: 1 piece.

Specimen H6:4, brown sand earthenware, part of surface blackened due to burning in making, , round lip, flare mouth, arc belly; belly decorated with two concave strings, concave string pattern decorated with combed dots; bore diameter of 25. 4, remaining part of height of 4. 1cm (Figure 51:5).

Thick lip jar: 1 piece.

Specimen H6:6, reddish brown sand earthenware, of thick square lip, lip decorated with spiral twist pattern, under mouth decorated with one concave string; bore diameter of 31. 6, remaining part of height of 4. 4cm (Figure 51:4).

H7 is located in the east part of T2, partly laminated under the east beam of the square unit, opening under Stratum ⑤.

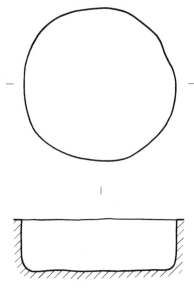

Figure 52   Sectional Plan of H7

Shape and structure: round shaped, diameter of 1. 2, depth of 0. 4 meters, Walls of the pit are smooth and bottom is flat and even. Deposit in the pit is gray soil, soil is loose, containing a small number of pottery pieces, burnt soil particles and charcoal (Figure 52).

Unearthed items: Very few artifacts were unearthed in H7. The ones unearthed are mostly pottery pieces and there is only 1 jade piece. Fine earthenware accounts for the most, with some coarse earthenware and clay earthenware; and terracotta and reddish brown earthenware are the most in terms of color; decorations are mostly twist line pattern, concave patterns, stamp and geometrical ones (Figure 53:4 − 6).

A total of 6 specimens are selected from H7, including 5 pottery specimens, 1 jade piece. In the pottery specimens 3 are for decoration and 2 for forms. Form specimens include one each of trumpet mouth jar and ring foot.

Trumpet - shape mouth jar: 1 piece.

Specimen H7:1, reddish brown fine sand earthenware, round lip, contracted neck; bore diameter of 29. 8, remaining part of height of 4cm (Figure 53:1).

Ring foot: 1 piece.

Specimen H7:2, fine terracotta, horn − shaped ring foot, foot tip bent outward, diameter at bot-

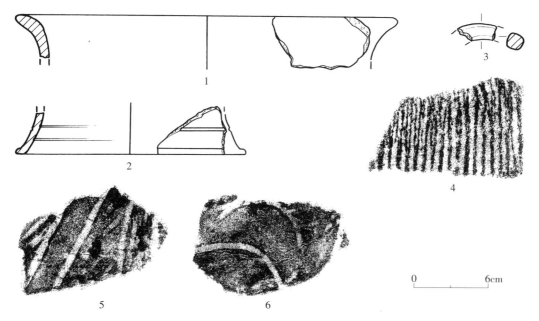

Figure 53   Unearthed Artifacts of H7

(Note: The scales of rubbings vary)

1. Pottery trumpet – shape mouth jar (H7:1)   2. Pottery ring foot (H7:2)   3. Jade pendant (H7:3)
4. Rope pattern (H7:4)   5. Poked pattern (H7:6)   6. Geometrical form pattern (H7:5)

tom of 17. 7, remaining part of height of 3. 4cm (Figure 53 : 2).

Jade pendant: 1 piece. Specimen H7 : 3, severely damaged; of a round body; remaining part of length of 3cm (Figure 53 : 3).

H8 is in the east beam of the square unit, opening under Stratum ⑤a (Plate 60).

Shape and structure: rectangular in plane view, length of 0. 9, width of 0. 78, depth of 0. 5 meters. Accumulations in the pit can be divided into two strata. Upper one is gray soil, soil is loose, containing a small number of pottery pieces and burnt soil particles, thickness of 0. 14 meters; lower layer of yellowish brown clay soil, hard soil, containing a small number of burnt soil particles, thickness of 0. 36 meters (Figure 54).

Unearthed item: only 29 pottery pieces were unearthed from this pit. Most are fine earthenware, with small number of clay earthenware. Colors are most terracotta and reddish brown earthenware. Decorations are mostly twist line pattern, concave string pattern,

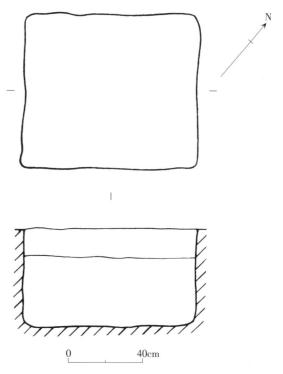

Figure 54   Sectional Plan of H8

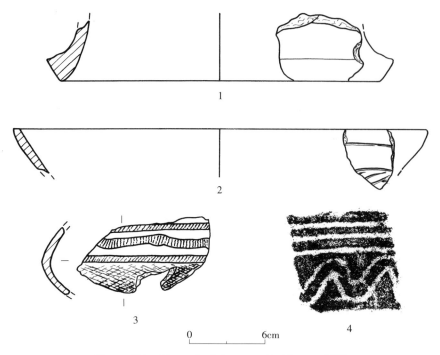

Figure 55   Unearthed Pottery Artifacts of H8
1. Ring feet (H8:2)   2. Trumpet – shape mouth jar (H8:1)   3. Concave string pattern + rope
pattern + combed dot pattern (H8:3)   4. Concave string pattern + engraved pattern (H8:4)

combed dots and engraved patterns. (Figure 55:3, 4). Forms are only ring feet and bowls.

Total of 8 pottery specimens are selected from H8, of which 3 are form specimens and 1 is ornamentation specimen. Forms include 1 bowl, 1 ring foot and 1 kettle.

Ring foot: 1 piece.

Specimen H8:2, fine brown earthenware; horn – shaped ring foot, foot tip bent upward; diameter
at bottom of 12.4, remaining height of 2.6cm (Figure 55:1).

Bowl: 1 piece.

Specimen H8:1, reddish brown fine sand earthenware, round lip, flare mouth; under mouth decorated with engraved line patterns; bore diameter of 32.4, remaining part of height of 4.7cm (Figure
55:2).

Kettle: 1 piece.

Specimen H8:3, grayish brown sand earthenware, drum belly; upper belly decorated with concave string pattern, concave string pattern decorated with poked short line pattern; belly lower part
decorated with twist line pattern; remaining part of height of 5.2cm (Figure 55:3).

2. Postholes

16 postholes, mainly distributed by H3, H4 and H6 but without a certain rule. Plane of ground
shape; walls are smooth, bottom is dome shaped (Figure 56). Information of postholes in the unit is
presented below.

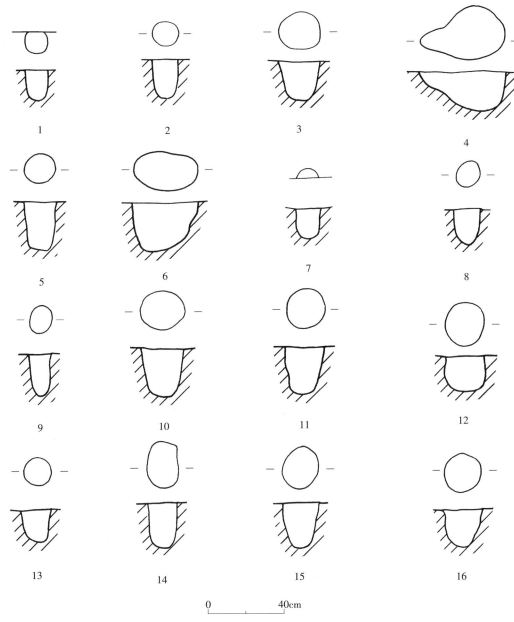

Figure 56   Postholes in T2

1 – 16. Posthole

Table 2   Statistics of Pits and Postholes in T2   Unit: cm

S/N	Numbering	Horizon level	Shape and structure			Dimensions (diameter – depth)	Soil	Figure No.
			Plane form	Walls of the pit	Bottom of pit			
1	D1	Under ⑤a	Round	Smooth	Dome shaped	12 – 16	Grayish black soil	Figure 56 : 1
2	D2	Under ⑤a	Round	Smooth	Dome shaped	14 – 20	Black soil	Figure 56 : 2
3	D3	Under ⑤a	Round	Smooth	Dome shaped	22 – 20	Grayish black soil	Figure 56 : 3

(continued 2)

S/N	Numbering	Horizon level	Shape and structure			Dimensions (diameter – depth)	Soil	Figure No.
			Plane form	Walls of the pit	Bottom of pit			
4	D4	Under ⑤a	Pear shaped	Smooth	Dome shaped	4 ~ 46 – 21	Black soil	Figure 56 : 4
5	D5	Under ⑤a	Round	Smooth	Dome shaped	18 – 26	Grayish black soil	Figure 56 : 5
6	D6	Under ⑤a	Oval	Smooth	Dome shaped	20 ~ 34 – 26	Grayish black soil	Figure 56 : 6
7	D7	Under ⑤a	Round	Smooth	Dome shaped	11 – 16	Black soil	Figure 56 : 7
8	D8	Under ⑤a	Round	Smooth	Dome shaped	13 – 20	Grayish black soil	Figure 56 : 8
9	D9	Under ⑤a	Round	Smooth	Dome shaped	14 – 22	Grayish black soil	Figure 56 : 9
10	D10	Under ⑤a	Round	Smooth	Dome shaped	24 – 26	Grayish black soil	Figure 56 : 10
11	D11	Under ⑤a	Round	Smooth	Dome shaped	20 – 25	Grayish black soil	Figure 56 : 11
12	D12	Under ⑤a	Round	Smooth	Dome shaped	21 – 18	Grayish black soil	Figure 56 : 12
13	D13	Under ⑤a	Round	Smooth	Dome shaped	15 – 18	Grayish black soil	Figure 56 : 13
14	D14	Under ⑤a	Irregular oval	Smooth	Dome shaped	14 ~ 24 – 24	Grayish black soil	Figure 56 : 14
15	D15	Under ⑤a	Almost round	Smooth	Dome shaped	18 ~ 22 – 24	Grayish black soil	Figure 56 : 15
16	D16	Under ⑤a	Round	Smooth	Dome shaped	19 – 20	Grayish black soil	Figure 56 : 16

III. Unearthed artifacts of the strata

1. Unearthed items of T2⑤a

Mostly pottery pieces, with a small number of stone tools. A total of 88 specimens are selected, including 18 stone tool, 2 jade pieces and 68 pottery pieces.

Stone tools: 20 pieces, including 5 stone adzes, 5 stone axes, 1 stone plate, 2 stone flappers, 1 net sinker and 4 stone cores.

Stone flappers: 2 pieces.

Specimen T2⑤a : 8, damaged, body shape is of rectangle, marks from flaking visible on surface; two slots on one side; remaining part of length of 6; remaining part of width of 4. 6, 0. 3 – 2. 5cm (Figure 57 : 1). Specimen T2⑤a : 4, damaged, body shape is of rectangle, 4 parallel slots seen on surface; remaining part of length of 6. 1; remaining part of width of 2. 6, thickness of 3. 2cm (Plate 61 : 1).

Stone adzes: 5 pieces; shape and structure are substantially similar; trapezoid or rectangle shape, ground to shape.

Specimen T2⑤a : 6, ground to shape, trapezoid, double – sided arc blade; of length of 2. 7, width of 1. 6 – 2. 3, thickness of 0. 8cm (Figure 57 : 2; Plate 61 : 2). Specimen T2⑤a : 11, only lower part remains, body shape is of rectangle, double – sided arc blade; of length of 4. 2, width of 5,

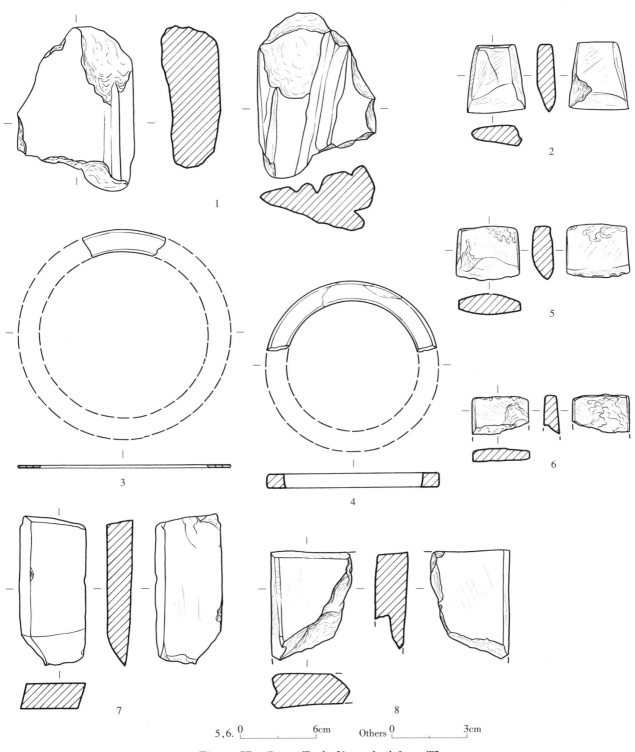

Figure 57　Stone Tools Unearthed from T2

1. Stone flapper（T2⑤a：8）　2, 5, 6. Stone adze（T2⑤a：6, 11, 10）　3, 4. Jade ring（T2⑤a：7, 9）
7, 8. Stone axe（T2②：1, 2）

thickness of 1. 6cm（Figure 57：5； Plate 61：3）. Specimen T2⑤a：10, only upper part remains, rectangular body； remaining part of length of 2. 8, width of 4. 5, thickness of 1cm（Figure 57：6）. Specimen T2⑤a：3, damaged, body shape is of rectangle, double – sided arc blade； of length of 3. 2, width of 2. 8, thickness of 1. 8cm (Plate 61 : 4). Specimen T2⑤a : 5, blade damaged, double – sided arc blade, length of 4. 5, width of 4. 2, thickness of 2cm (Plate 62 : 1).

Stone piece: 1 piece.

Specimen T2⑤a : 2, damaged, black, body of round shape, thin on edges; remaining part of length of 3. 3; remaining part of width of 4. 5cm (Plate 62 : 2).

Stone axes: 5 pieces; of similar shape and structure, body shape is of rectangle, ground to shape.

Specimen T2②: 1, damaged; of length of 5. 9, width of 2. 6, thickness of 1cm (Figure 57 : 7). Specimen T2②: 2, only remaining top; remaining part of length of 4. 3; remaining part of width of 3. 1, with thickness of 1. 4cm (Figure 57 : 8). Specimen T2⑤a : 12, blade damaged, remaining part of length of 3. 9; remaining part of width of 2. 8, thickness of 1cm (Figure 58 : 1). Specimen T2⑤a : 13, only remaining lower end, double – sided arc blade; remaining part of length of 2. 9; remaining part of width of 2. 5, thickness of 1. 2cm (Figure 58 : 3). Specimen T2⑤a : 15, only remaining top, remaining part of length of 2. 7, width of 3. 8, thickness of 0. 6cm (Figure 58 : 8).

Net sinker: 1 piece.

Specimen T2⑤a : 14, body presenting vase shape, top smaller, lower end bigger; of length of 3. 4, width of 5. 5, thickness of 1. 9cm (Figure 58 : 7; Plate 62 : 3).

Stone cores: 4 pieces.

Specimen T2⑤a : 17, body shape is of irregular rectangle, marks from flaking visible on two sides; of length of 6. 6, width of 5. 8, thickness of 3cm (Figure 58 : 2). Specimen T2⑤a : 18, body shape is of irregular rectangle, apparent flaking traces on surface; impact points and radiation rays from impact are visible in upper part; of length of 6. 1, width of 5. 1, thickness of 0. 2 – 2cm (Figure 58 : 4). Specimen T2⑤a : 19, pricked shaped, natural rock on both sides, impact points and radiation rays from impact visible on the top; of length of 5. 2, width of 3. 6, thickness of 1. 6 – 2. 5cm (Figure 58 : 5). Specimen T2⑤a : 20, pricked shaped, surfaced ragged due to flaking; of length of 7. 8, width of 4. 6, thickness of 0. 1 – 3. 2cm (Figure 58 : 6).

Jade pieces: 2 pieces, all rings.

Jade rings: 2 pieces; of similar shape and structure, round shaped, ground to shape.

Specimen T2⑤a : 9, remaining half, beige color, diameter of 6. 8, width of 1. 5, thickness of 0. 6cm (Figure 57 : 5; Plate 62 : 4). Specimen T2⑤a : 7, remaining in small amount, beige color, diameter of 8. 4, width of 1. 8, thickness of 0. 1cm (Figure 57 : 3).

Pottery pieces: A total of 2, 434 potter pieces were unearthed in Stratum ⑤a in this square unit. In terms of the earthenware materials, fine sand earthenware accounts for about 73. 5%, coarse sand earthenware for about 15. 5%, and clay polished earthenware for about 11%. In terms of colors of the pottery pieces, terracotta, reddish brown, and brown pottery pieces account for about 64%, in-

Figure 58 Stone Tools Unearthed from Stratum T2⑤a

1, 3, 8. Axe (T2⑤a:12, 13, 15) 2, 4-6. Core (T2⑤a:17, 18, 19, 20) 7. Net sinker (T2⑤a:14)

dicating that the pottery color is mostly reddish. In terms of pattern ornamentation, it was extremely well-developed, accounting for 33% of the total number of pottery pieces. Some pieces have on the surface a thin ornamented coating. The decorations are of great variety, in which rope decorations account for about 63% of the total decorations. Other decorations include engraved line, stamp, concave string, protruding rim, pressure stamp, comb brushing, added mound and comb dotting *etc*. Multiple decorations on a single pottery piece appear to have been very popular. The main ornamentation patterns are of clouds, S – shape, geometric patterns, circles and water ripples (Figure 59, 60 : 1 – 9; Plates 63 – 65) and the like. Pottery mouth parts are mostly contracted or flared, followed by trumpet – shape mouth and straight mouth. The artifacts are mostly enclosure bases and ring feet. Forms of the artifacts include bowls, contracted mouth jars, thick lip jars, flare mouth jars, trumpet – shape mouth jars, handles, bases and ring feet *etc.*

T2⑤a: A total of 68 specimens of pottery pieces are selected, of which 21 specimens are for ornamentations and 47 specimens are for forms, including 8 bowls, 5 contracted mouth jars, 5 thick lip jars, 8 flare mouth jars, 1 trumpet – shape mouth jar, 14 ring feet, 4 handles and 2 bases *etc.*

Bowls: 8 pieces; classified into four categories based on the mouth and shoulder.

Category 1: 3 pieces; flare mouth, no protruding rim on the lower part of the mouth.

Specimen T2⑤a: 54, brown sand earthenware, round lip, inclined straight belly; belly decorated with four concave string pattern, two between concave strings decorated with poked short line pattern,

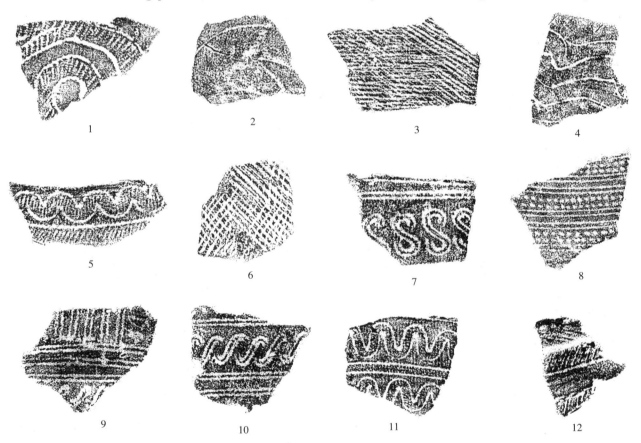

Figure 59   Rubbings of Pottery Pieces Unearthed from Stratum T2⑤a

1. Engraved pattern + rope pattern (T2⑤a: 70)   2. Engraved pattern (T2⑤a: 71)   3. Rope pattern (T2⑤a: 68)   4. Water ripple pattern (T2⑤a: 69)   5. Water ripple pattern + concave string pattern + rope pattern (T2⑤a: 72)   6. Twist rope pattern (T2⑤a: 73)   7. Concave string pattern + S – shape pattern (T2⑤a: 76)   8. Concave string pattern + poked dot pattern (T2⑤ a: 77)   9. Engraved pattern + concave string pattern + S – shape pattern (T2⑤a: 74)   10. Concave string pattern + S – shape pattern (T2⑤a: 75)   11. Concave string pattern + water ripple pattern (T2⑤a: 78)   12. Leaf vein pattern + concave string pattern + rope pattern (T2⑤a: 79)

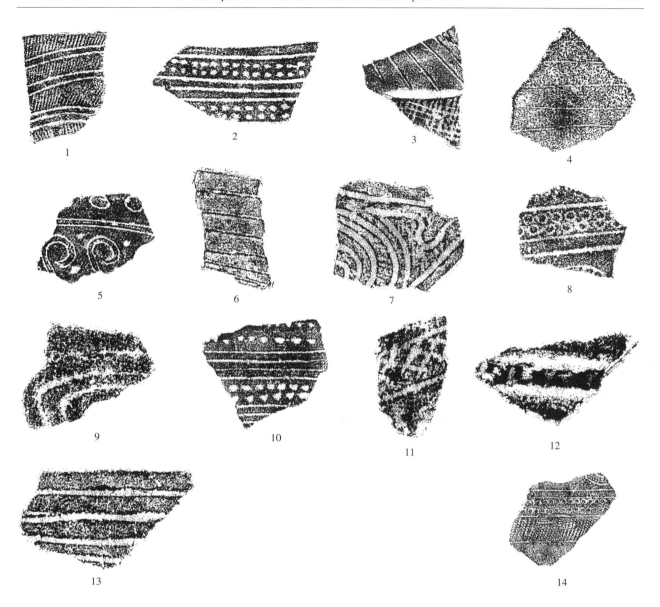

Figure 60   Rubbings of Pottery Pieces Unearthed from Stratum T2⑤a

1. Engraved pattern + rope pattern (T2⑤a：80)   2. Concave string pattern + poked dot pattern (T2⑤a：81)   3. Engraved pattern + rope pattern (T2⑤a：82)   4. Concave string pattern (T2⑤a：83)   5. Circle pattern + concave string pattern + S – shape pattern (T2⑤a：84)   6. Concave string pattern (T2⑤a：85)   7. Engraved pattern (T2⑤a：86)   8. Concave string pattern + circle pattern (T2⑤a：87)   9. Engraved pattern (T2⑤a：88)   10. Concave string pattern + poked dot pattern (T2⑤b：21)   11. Engraved pattern (T2⑤b：22)   12. Protruding rim pattern (T2⑤b：23)   13. Concave string pattern (T2⑤b：24)   14. Concave string pattern + circle pattern + combed dot pattern (T2⑤b：25)

upper and lower between concave strings decorated with engraved water ripple patterns, water ripple patterns decorated with engraved short lines; bore diameter of 22, remaining part of height of 4. 4cm (Figure 61：1). Specimen T2⑤a：52, grayish brown sand earthenware, round lip, inclined straight belly; belly decorated with two concave strings, between concave strings decorated with engraved water ripple patterns; bore diameter of 25. 6, remaining part of height of 3. 8cm (Figure 61：3). Specimen T2⑤a：53, brown sand earthenware, round lip, flare mouth, arc belly; belly decorated with two concave strings, between concave strings decorated with engraved water ripple patterns; bore diameter of 24. 5, remaining part of height of 4cm (Figure 61 : 4).

Category 2 : 3 pieces; flare mouth, decorated with a protruding rim on the shoulder.

Specimen T2⑤a : 66, reddish brown sand earthenware, round lip, inclined straight belly; bore diameter of 27. 6, remaining part of height of 4. 6cm (Figure 61 : 2). Specimen T2⑤a : 60, blackish brown earthenware, round lip, arc belly; under the protruding rim decorated with engraved short lines; bore diameter of 24. 3, remaining part of height of 3. 5cm (Figure 61 : 5). Specimen T2⑤a : 33, brown sand earthenware, square lip, arc belly; bore diameter of 42, remaining part of height of 5. 6cm (Figure 61 : 6).

Category 3 : 1 piece; mouth slightly contracted.

Specimen T2⑤a : 27, fine terracotta, square lip, contracted mouth, under mouth decorated with tongue shaped handle; bore diameter of 20. 4, remaining part of height of 2. 8cm (Figure 61 : 12).

Category 4 : 1 piece; contracted mouth.

Specimen T2 ⑤ a : 49, terracotta, round lip, arc belly; belly decorated with two concave

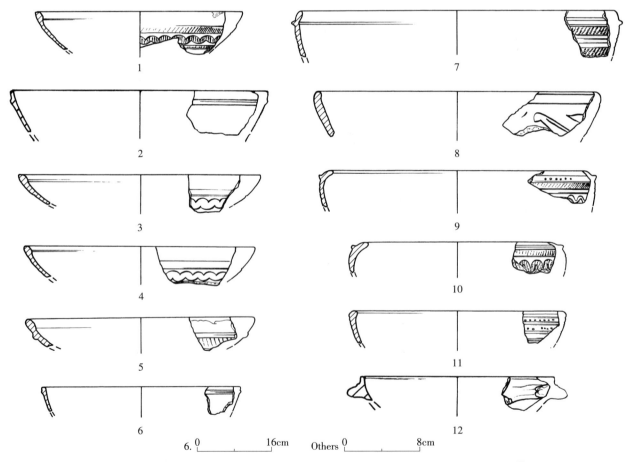

Figure 61   Pottery Bowls and Contracted Jars Unearthed from Stratum T2⑤a
1 – 6, 12. Pottery bowl (T2⑤a : 54, 66, 52, 53, 60, 33, 27)   7 – 11. Contracted mouth jar
(T2⑤a : 61, 59, 67, 62, 58)

strings, between concave strings decorated with poked circles; remaining part of height of 4. 8 cm (Figure 62 : 1).

Contracted mouth jars: 5 pieces; classified into two categories based on the neck.

Category 1: 3 pieces; drum shoulder, decorated with a protruding rim on the shoulder.

Specimen T2⑤a: 61, reddish brown sand earthenware, round lip, arc belly; under the protruding rim decorated with strings and combed dots; bore diameter of 33. 4, remaining part of height of 5 cm (Figure 61 : 7; Plate 66 : 1). Specimen T2⑤a: 67, terracotta, round lip, contracted mouth, arc belly; on the protruding rim are poked dots, under the protruding rim decorated with three concave strings, between concave strings decorated with engraved lines, belly decorated with engraved water ripple patterns; bore diameter of 27, remaining part of height of 3. 4 cm (Figure 61 : 9; Plate

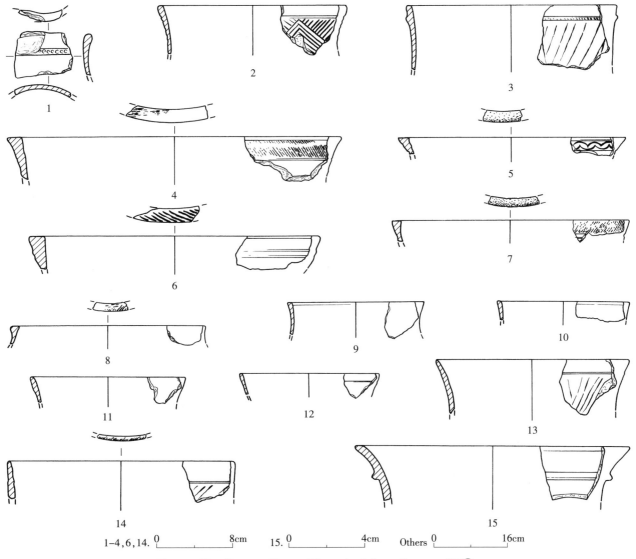

Figure 62   Pottery Pieces Unearthed from Stratum T2⑤a

1. Bowl (T2⑤a: 49)   2, 3, 9 – 14. Straight mouth jar (T2⑤a: 34, 32, 64, 63, 65, 51, 35, 36)   4 – 8. Thick lip jar (T2⑤a: 42, 41, 45, 43, 44)   15. Trumpet – shape mouth jar (T2⑤a: 30)

66 : 2). Specimen T2⑤a : 62 , reddish brown sand earthenware, round lip, contracted mouth, arc belly; under the protruding rim are strings and poked short line pattern; upper belly decorated with S – shape pattern, S – shape pattern poked short line pattern; bore diameter of 19. 6 , remaining part of height of 3. 3cm (Figure 61 : 10; Plate 66 : 3).

Category 2 : 2 pieces; arc shoulder, without protruding rim on the shoulder.

Specimen T2⑤a : 59 , brown sand earthenware, round lip, contracted mouth, arc belly, shoulder decorated with one concave string; upper belly decorated with engraved arc and geometrical patterns; bore diameter of 29. 6 , remaining part of height of 4. 7cm (Figure 61 : 8). Specimen T2⑤a : 58 , reddish brown sand earthenware, round lip, contracted mouth, arc belly; under mouth decorated with strings and poked dot pattern; bore diameter of 22. 2 , remaining part of height of 3. 4cm (Figure 61 : 11).

Thick lip jars: 5 pieces; classified into two categories based on mouth.

Category 1 : 3 pieces; of thick square lip, straight mouth slightly flared.

Specimen T2⑤a : 42 , terracotta, contracted neck; lip decorated with horizontal twist line pattern, under mouth decorated with spiral twist pattern, neck decorated with one concave string; bore diameter of 35 , remaining part of height of 4. 7cm (Figure 62 : 4). Specimen T2⑤a : 45 , grayish brown sand earthenware, lip decorated with spiral twist pattern, under mouth decorated with two concave strings; bore diameter of 30. 5 , remaining part of height of 3. 6cm (Figure 62 : 6). Specimen T2⑤a : 41 , terracotta, lip decorated with spiral twist pattern, under mouth decorated with two concave strings, between concave strings decorated with engraved water ripple patterns; bore diameter of 48 , remaining part of height of 3. 8cm (Figure 62 : 5).

Category 2 : 2 pieces; of thick square lip, contracted mouth.

Specimen T2⑤a : 43 , brown sand earthenware, lip decorated with spiral twist pattern, under mouth decorated with twist line pattern; bore diameter of 54 , remaining part of height of 4. 8cm (Figure 62 : 7). Specimen T2⑤a : 44 , reddish brown sand earthenware, lip decorated with spiral twist pattern; bore diameter of 40. 8 , remaining part of height of 4. 2cm (Figure 62 : 8).

Flare mouth jars: 8 pieces; classified into two categories based on the neck shape.

Category 1 : 7 pieces; flare mouth, long neck, no protruded ledge on the neck.

Specimen T2⑤a : 64 , reddish brown sand earthenware, round lip; bore diameter of 28. 4 , remaining part of height of 7. 8cm (Figure 62 : 9). Specimen T2⑤a : 63 , terracotta, round lip; bore diameter of 28 , remaining part of height of 4. 2cm (Figure 62 : 10). Specimen T2⑤a : 65 , terracotta, round lip; bore diameter of 33 , remaining part of height of 5. 6cm (Figure 62 : 11). Specimen T2⑤a : 51 , reddish brown sand earthenware, round lip; under mouth decorated with one concave string; bore diameter of 29. 2 , remaining part of height of 5. 3cm (Figure 62 : 12). Specimen T2⑤a : 35 , reddish brown sand earthenware, sharp round lip, upper neck decorated with one concave string, neck decorated with engraved short lines; bore diameter of 20.5, remaining part of height of 5.8cm (Figure 62:13). Specimen T2⑤a:34, reddish brown fine sand earthenware, round lip, under mouth decorated with one concave string, neck decorated with triangle and short line pattern; bore diameter of 19.7, remaining part of height of 5.1cm (Figure 62:2). Specimen T2⑤a:36, reddish brown sand earthenware, sharp round lip; upper neck decorated with one concave string, under which decorated with short line pattern; bore diameter of 24, remaining part of height of 4cm (Figure 62:14).

Category 2: 1 piece; flare mouth, long neck, a protruding rim on the neck.

Specimen T2⑤a:32, reddish brown sand earthenware, square lip, on the protruding rim are poked dots, neck decorated with engraved line patterns; bore diameter of 22.3, remaining part of height of 6.6cm (Figure62:3).

Trumpet - shape mouth jar: 1 piece.

Specimen T2⑤a:30, brown sand earthenware, sharp round lip, contracted neck; bore diameter of 14.6, remaining part of height of 2.9cm (Figure 62:15).

Ring feet: 4 pieces; classified into four categories based on shape and structure (Plate 67).

Category 1: 6 pieces; presenting a trumpet shape, foot tip bent inward.

Specimen T2⑤a:57, reddish brown fine sand earthenware, enclosure on the foot decorated with concave string pattern, concave string pattern decorated with combed dots; diameter at bottom of 14.5, remaining part of height of 1.7cm (Figure 63:1). Specimen T2⑤a:28, reddish brown fine sand earthenware, enclosure on the foot decorated with three concave strings; diameter at bottom of 18.3, remaining part of height of 1.8cm (Figure 63:3). Specimen T2⑤a:29, fine brown earthenware; on the foot decorated with two concave string pattern; diameter at bottom of 18.3, remaining part of height of 2.8cm (Figure 63:4). Specimen T2⑤a:48, reddish brown sand earthenware, diameter at bottom of 20.5, remaining part of height of 5.6cm (Figure 63:5). Specimen T2⑤a:56, reddish brown sand earthenware, on the foot decorated with four concave string pattern and combed dots; diameter at bottom of 14.5, remaining part of height of 1.6cm (Figure 63:10). Specimen T2⑤a:55, brown sand earthenware, foot tip bent inward; on the foot decorated with 4concave string pattern; diameter at bottom of 14.3, remaining part of height of 1.5cm (Figure 63:11).

Category 2: 4 pieces; presenting a trumpet shape, foot tip bent outward.

Specimen T2⑤a:39, terracotta; rotational making traces; diameter at bottom of 15, remaining part of height of 5.9cm (Figure 63:6). Specimen T2⑤a:40, reddish brown sand earthenware; diameter at bottom of 40.8, remaining part of height of 6.8cm (Figure 63:8). Specimen T2⑤a:50, reddish brown sand earthenware; diameter at bottom of 28.8, remaining part of height of 5.2cm (Figure 63:12). Specimen T2⑤a:31, brown fine sand earthenware; diameter at bottom of 22.6, remaining part of height of 2.6cm (Figure 63:14).

Category 3: 2 pieces; presenting a trumpet shape with foot tip bending upward.

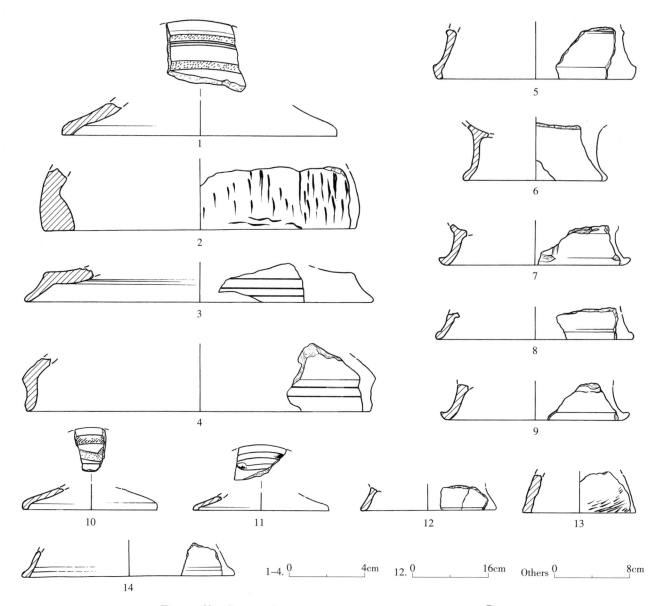

Figure 63   Pottery Ring Feet Unearthed from Stratum T2⑤a

1. T2⑤a:57   2. T2⑤a:37   3. T2⑤a:28   4. T2⑤a:29   5. T2⑤a:48   6. T2⑤a:39   7. T2⑤a:46   8. T2⑤a:40
9. T2⑤a:47   10. T2⑤a:56   11. T2⑤a:55   12. T2⑤a:50   13. T2⑤a:25   14. T2⑤a:31

Specimen T2⑤a:46, reddish brown sand earthenware, foot engraved with short line pattern; diameter at bottom of 19, remaining part of height of 4.1cm (Figure 63:7) Specimen T2⑤a:47, terracotta; diameter at bottom of 18.5, remaining part of height of 4cm (Figure 63:9).

Category 4: 2 pieces; bucket shaped.

Specimen T2⑤a:37, terracotta, foot tip inward, decorated with twist line pattern; diameter at bottom of 16.5, remaining part of height of 3.3cm (Figure 63:2). Specimen T2⑤a:25, reddish brown fine sand earthenware, foot tip reaching outward, on the foot decorated with spiral twist pattern; diameter at bottom of 11.8, remaining part of height of 4cm (Figure 63:13).

Handles: 4 pieces; can be classified into two categories based on shape and structure.

Category 1: 3 pieces; body presenting tongue shaped.

Specimen T2⑤a : 24, reddish brown sand earthenware, surface decorated with horizontal twist line pattern; remaining part of length of 6.2, width of 5, thickness of 2cm (Figure 64 : 1). Specimen T2⑤a : 22, terracotta; surface decorated with horizontal twist line pattern; remaining part of length of 4.5, width of 5.1, thickness of 2cm (Figure 64 : 5). Specimen T2⑤a : 21, brown earthenware; surface decorated with horizontal twist line pattern; of length of 3.6, width of 3.4, thickness of 1.6cm (Figure 64 : 6).

Category 2: 1 piece; presenting a cylinder shape.

Specimen T2⑤a : 23, damaged, reddish brown sand earthenware, presenting a cylinder shape, remaining part of length of 2.6, width of 3.3, thickness of 2.3cm (Figure 64 : 2).

Bases: 2 pieces; of similar shape and structure, presenting a cylinder shape, oval base.

Specimen T2⑤a : 38, reddish brown sand earthenware, oval base, surface and bottom decorated with twist line pattern; remaining part of height of 2.9, width of 4cm (Figure 64 : 3). Specimen T2⑤a : 26, reddish brown sand earthenware, surface and bottom decorated with twist line pattern; remaining part of height of 4.5, width of 5.4cm (Figure 64 : 4).

2. Unearthed artifacts of stratum T2⑤b

Unearthed artifacts from Stratum T2⑤b are mostly pottery pieces and only 1 stone tool. A total of

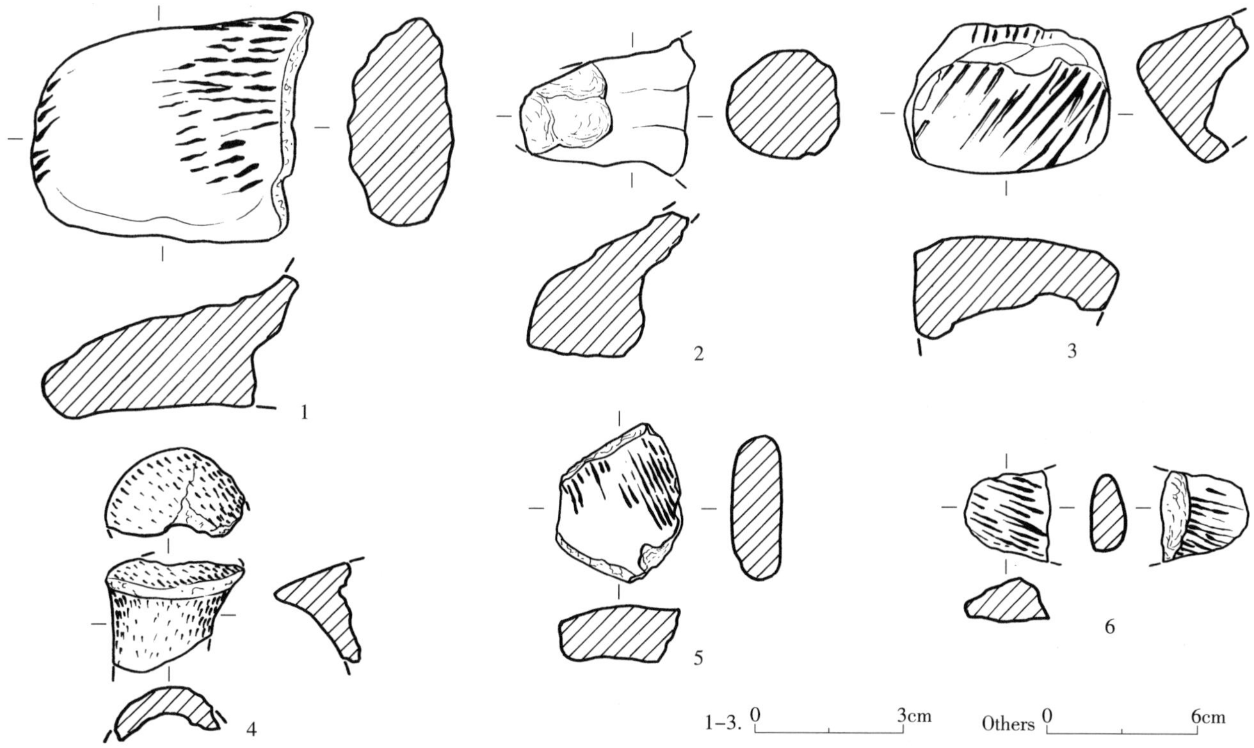
1
2
3
4
5
6
1-3. 0 3cm
Others 0 6cm

Figure 64 Pottery Bases and Handles Unearthed from Stratum T2⑤a
1, 2, 5, 6. Handle (T2⑤a : 24, 23, 22, 21) 3, 4. Bases (T2⑤a : 38, 26)

950 potter pieces were unearthed. In terms of the earthenware materials, fine sand earthenware accounts for about 87%, coarse sand earthenware for about 3.2%, and clay polished earthenware for about 9.8%. In terms of colors of the pottery pieces, terracotta, reddish brown, and brown pottery pieces account for about 60%, indicating that the pottery color is mostly reddish. In terms of pattern ornamentation, it was extremely well – developed, accounting for 346% of the total number of pottery pieces. Some pieces have on the surface a thin ornamented coating. The decorations are of great variety, in which rope decorations account for about 44% of the total decorations. Other decorations include engraved line, stamp, concave string, protruding rim, pressure stamp, comb brushing, added mound and comb dotting *etc*. Multiple decorations on a single pottery piece appear to have been very popular. The main ornamentation patterns are of clouds, S – shape, geometric patterns, circles, water ripples (Figure 60: 10 – 14; Figure 61; Plate 68) and the like. The artifacts are mostly with enclosure base and ring feet. Forms of the artifacts include bases, spinning wheels, ears, trumpet – shape mouth jars, flare mouth jars, straight – mouth jars and bowls *etc*. (Plates 69, 70).

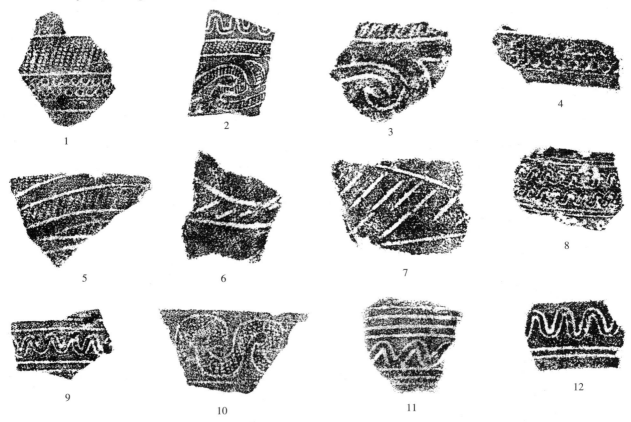

Figure 65   Rubbings of Pottery Pieces Unearthed from Stratum T2⑤a

1. Concave string pattern + combed dot pattern (T2⑤b: 26)   2. Water ripple pattern + concave string pattern + combed dot pattern + engraved pattern (T2⑤b: 27)   3. Engraved pattern + concave string pattern (T2⑤b: 28)   4. Concave string pattern + circle pattern (T2⑤b: 29)   5. Combed dot pattern + engraved pattern (T2⑤b: 30)   6. Engraved pattern (T2⑤b: 31)   7. Engraved pattern (T2⑤b: 32)   8. Concave string pattern + S – shape pattern (T2⑤b: 33)   9. Concave string pattern + water ripple pattern (T2⑤b: 34)   10. Engraved pattern + combed dot pattern (T2⑤b: 35)   11. Concave string pattern + water ripple pattern (T2⑤b: 36)   12. Water ripple pattern + concave string pattern (T2⑤b: 37)

T2⑤b: A total of 37 specimens of pottery pieces are selected, including 1 stone tool and 36 pottery pieces.

Stone tool: 1 piece, 1 scraper.

Scraper: 1 piece.

Specimen T2⑤b:1, body presenting scone shape, surface visible are impact points and radiation rays; of length of 4.2, width of 2.4, thickness of 0.1 - 0.9cm (Figure 66:1).

Pottery pieces: A total of 36 specimen, including 17 ornamentation specimens and 19 form specimens, 2 bases, 1 spinning wheel, 1 handle, 7 ring foot, 2 thick lip jars, 2 flare mouth jars, and 4 trumpet mouth jars.

Bases: 2 pieces; of similar shape and structure; presenting a cylinder shape.

Specimen T2⑤b:3, terracotta; bottom decorated with spiral twist pattern; remaining part of height of 4.3, diameter at bottom of 7.8cm (Figure 66:2). Specimen T2⑤b:4, terracotta, plain surface; remaining part of height of 4.1, diameter at bottom of 4.8cm (Figure 66:3).

Spinning wheel: 1 piece.

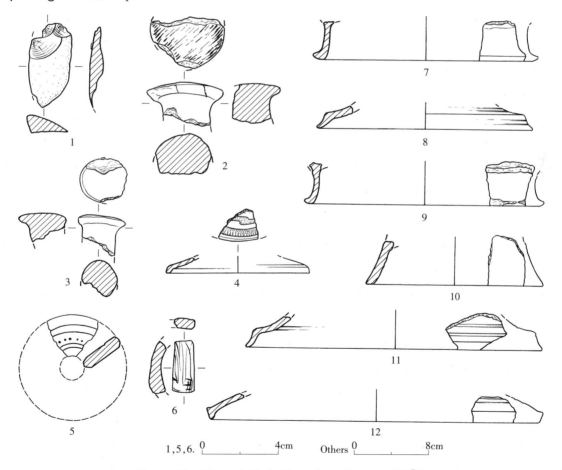

Figure 66   Unearthed Artifacts from Stratum T2⑤b

1. Stone scraper (T2⑤b:1)   2. 3. Pottery base (T2⑤b:3, 4)   4 - 7, 13. Pottery ring foot (T2⑤b:14, 12, 9, 11, 10, 8, 13)   5. Pottery spinning wheel (T2⑤b:2)   6. Pottery handle (T2⑤b:7)

Specimen T2⑤b : 2 , grayish brown sand earthenware, pie shape, surface decorated with four concave string patterns and poked dots; diameter of 5. 6 , aperture of 1. 3 , thickness of 0. 6cm (Figure 66 : 5).

Handle: 1 piece.

Specimen T2⑤b : 7 , reddish brown fine sand earthenware, arc, surface with three protruding rims; remaining part of length of 2. 7 , width of 1. 2cm (Figure 66 : 6).

Ring feet: 7 pieces; can be classified into three categories based on shape and structure.

Category 1 : 2 pieces; horn – shaped ring foot, foot tip bent upward.

Specimen T2⑤b : 12 , fine terracotta, diameter at bottom of 22. 9 , remaining part of height of 4. 2cm (Figure 66 : 7). Specimen T2⑤b : 11 , reddish brown sand earthenware. diameter at bottom of 24. 7 , remaining part of height of 4. 6cm (Figure 66 : 9).

Category 2 : 4 pieces; horn – shaped ring foot, foot tip bent inward.

Specimen T2⑤b : 14 , grayish black sand earthenware, ring foot bent inward, lower foot decorated with two string patterns, string patterns with decorated with twist line pattern, middle of foot decorated with engraved S – shape pattern, S – shaped patterns decorated with combed dots; diameter at bottom of 15. 1 , remaining part of height of 1. 6cm (Figure 66 : 4). Specimen T2⑤b : 9 , fine terracotta, foot tip reaching outward, on the foot decorated with four concave string pattern; diameter at bottom of 22. 8 , remaining part of height of 2. 5cm (Figure 66 : 8). Specimen T2⑤b : 8 , fine terracotta, foot tip reaching outward; on the foot decorated with four concave string pattern; diameter at bottom of 31. 3 , remaining part of height of 4cm (Figure 66 : 11). Specimen T2⑤b : 13 , reddish brown sand earthenware, foot tip bent inward; on the foot decorated with two concave string pattern; diameter at bottom of 34. 7 , remaining part of height of 2. 8cm (Figure 66 : 12).

Category 3 : 1 piece; bucket shaped.

Specimen T2⑤b : 10 , fine terracotta, foot tip bent outward; diameter at bottom of 18. 8 , remaining part of height of 5. 4cm (Figure 66 : 10).

Thick lip jars: 2 pieces; of similar shape and structure, all of thick square lip, straight mouth slightly flared.

Specimen T2⑤b : 17 , grayish brown fine sand earthenware, sharp round lip, narrow flat edge; edge decorated with twist line pattern, belly decorated with engraved decorated with combed dots; bore diameter of 44. 2 , remaining part of height of 6cm (Figure 67 : 1). Specimen T2⑤b : 15 , reddish brown sand earthenware; decorated with twist line pattern, upper neck decorated with engraved water ripple patterns; bore diameter of 48 , remaining part of height of 3. 4cm (Figure 67 : 3).

Flare mouth jars: 2 pieces; classified into two categories based on the neck.

Category 1 : 1 piece, with protruded ledge on the neck.

Specimen T2⑤b : 20 , reddish brown fine sand earthenware, round lip, neck slightly contracted,

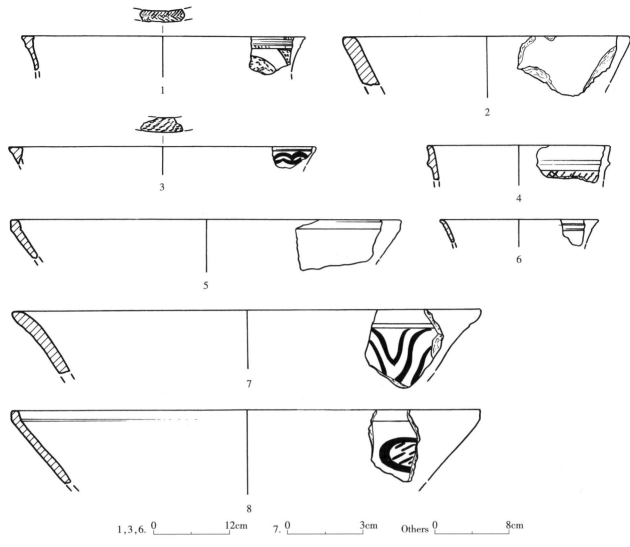

Figure 67   Unearthed Artifacts from Stratum T2⑤b

1, 3. Thick lip jar (T2⑤b:17, 15)   2, 4. Flared mouth jar (T2⑤b:18, 20)   5 – 8. Trumpet – shape mouth jar (T2⑤b:16, 19, 5, 6)

upper neck decorated with a protruding rim, lower part decorated with engraved short lines; bore diameter of 14.5, remaining part of height of 2.9cm (Figure 67:4).

Category 2: 1 piece, no protruded ledge on the neck.

Specimen T2⑤b:18, reddish brown sand earthenware, round lip; bore diameter of 22.8, remaining part of height of 4.7cm (Figure 67:2).

Flare mouth jars: 4 pieces; can be classified into two categories based on lip part.

Category 1: 2 pieces. square lip, inclined straight belly. Specimen T2⑤b:16, fine terracotta, bore diameter of 30.6, remaining part of height of 3.9cm (Figure 67:5). Specimen T2⑤b:6, brown earthenware; belly upper part, short line pattern; bore diameter of 37, remaining part of height of 5.7cm (Figure 67:8).

Category 2: 2 pieces; round lip, contracted neck.

Specimen T2⑤b:19, brown earthenware; upper neck decorated with two concave strings; bore diameter of 25.2, remaining part of height of 4.2cm (Figure 67:6). Specimen T2⑤b:5, reddish brown sand earthenware, neck engraved with water ripple patterns; bore diameter of 18.4, remaining part of height of 3.1cm (Figure 67:7).

<h1 style="text-align:center">Section Three   T3</h1>

T3 is located in the southwest corner of the excavation area. The square units for exploration were planned out and excavation works commenced on December 3, 2006 and exploration was completed on January 8, 2007. Lei Yu was in charge of conducting excavations, making records and plotting.

I. Stratigraphic accumulation

Based on soil properties, colors and items contained, strata in this area are summarized and classified into 5; Stratum ② is missing in this unit (Figure 68; Plate 71:1).

Stratum ①: Thickness of 10-15cm; yellow-gray color topsoil; loose soil, containing a small amount of ceramic, plastic and plant roots etc. pit from modern and contemporary times H23 opening is under this stratum.

Stratum ③: Thickness of 10-16, depth of 10-15cm; light gray-color soil, of fine soil. containing small amount of bricks and porcelain pieces among other items; pit from modern and contemporary times H24 opening is under this stratum.

Stratum ④: Based on differences in soil properties and colors, this stratum can be divided into two secondary strata.

④a: Thickness of 0-20, depth of 20-30cm; dark brown ferromanganese layer, soil is loose, depositing from west to east, containing large amount of iron rust, containing very small amount of porcelain pieces, bricks and other items.

④b: Thickness of 2-18, depth of 28-44cm; grayish brown ferromanganese, soil is loose, containing small amount of iron rust, containing very small amount of porcelain pieces, bricks and other items. H20, H22 opening is under this stratum.

Stratum ⑤: Based on differences in soil properties and colors, this stratum can be divided into two secondary strata.

⑤a: Thickness of 0-25, depth of 30-50cm; blackish gray soil, depositing from southeast to northwest; soil is loose, containing many burnt soil particles and charcoal, including large number of pottery pieces and a small number of stone tools; H21 and 29 are laminated below this stratum;

⑤b: Thickness of 0-22, depth of 28-44cm; gray yellow color soil; soil is hard; distributing

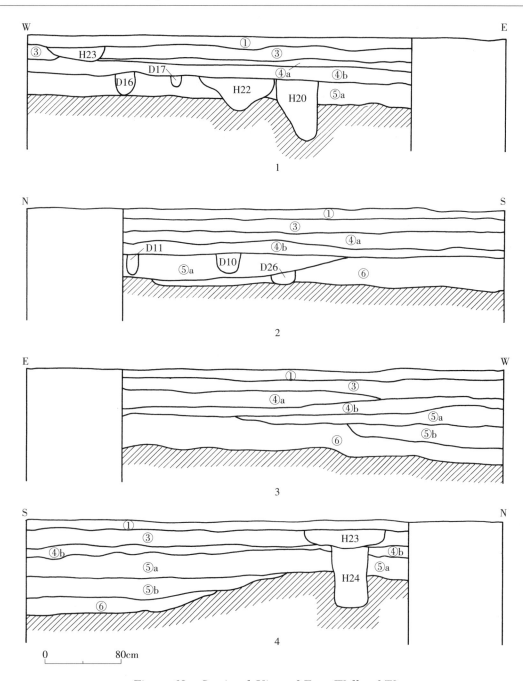

Figure 68   Sectional View of Four Walls of T3
1. North wall   2. East wall   3. South wall   4. West wall

only in southwest corner of unit, containing a small number of burnt soil particles and charcoal, containing little items, mainly pottery pieces and stone tools; 21 postholes are laminated below this stratum;

Stratum ⑥: Thickness of 0 – 34, depth of 52 – 74cm; yellowish brown soil, mixed with small amount of gray soil stains, hard soil, containing a small number of charcoal, containing very little items, mainly pottery pieces.

Under this stratum is reddish – brown ferromanganese raw soil.

II. Remains

A total of 45 remains of various types were found in this square unit, including 5 pits and 40 postholes (Figure 69; Plate 71:2), of which H1 and H2 are from contemporary and modern times and
H20, H21 and H22 are from Phung Nguyen culture period. Information of pits from the Phung Nguyen
culture period is presented below.

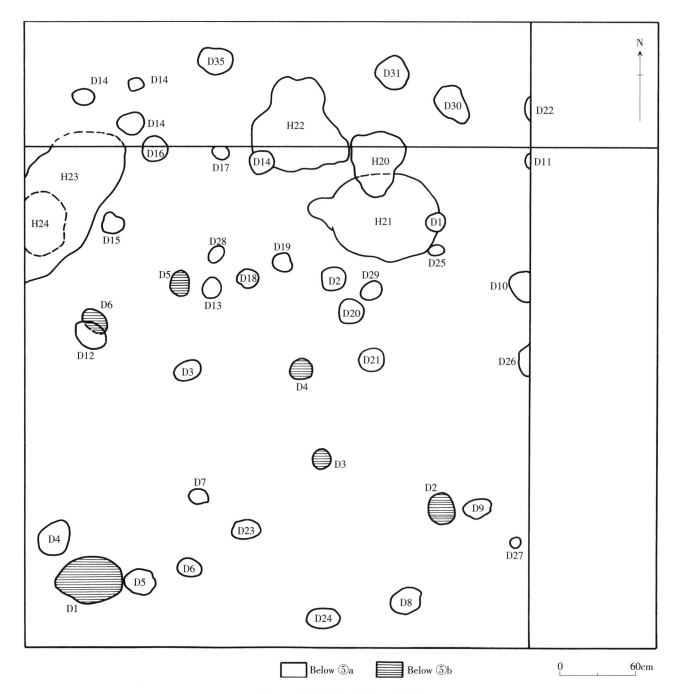

Figure 69   Plan View of T3

1. Pits: 3 pits

H20 is located in northeast part of T3, partly laminated under north beam of the unit, opening under stratum ④b.

Shape and structure: Plane shape of irregular oval, uneven walls, uneven bottom; of length of 1.2, width of 0.2 − 0.9, depth of 1.48 − 1.8 meters (Figure 70); deposit in the pit is grayish black soil, soil is loose, containing a small number of pottery pieces.

Unearthed items: Unearthed artifacts of H20 are mostly pottery pieces. A total of 49 pottery pieces were unearthed, mostly fine earthenware, with small number of coarse earthenware. Colors are dominated by terracotta and reddish brown earthenware, followed by blackish brown and less yellowish brown and brown. Decorations are mostly twist line pattern, with small number of engraved patterns, combed dots, poked patterns and string patterns *etc*. Forms are mostly bowls and jars.[1]

H21 is located in northeast part of T3, opening under stratum ⑤a, broken by D1 and D25.

Shape and structure: Plane round shaped, smooth walls, even bottom; diameter of 1.6, depth of 0.64 meters (Figure 71). Deposit in the pit is grayish black soil, soil is loose, containing very few pottery pieces.

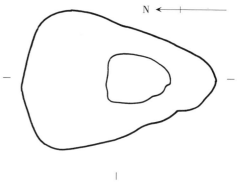

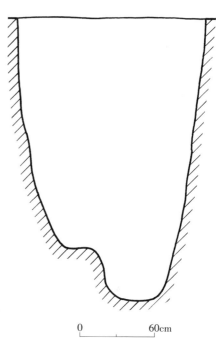

Figure 70   Sectional Plan of H20

Unearthed items: Only a small number of fine reddish brown earthenware.

H22 is located in the north part of T3, partly laminated under north beam of the unit, opening under stratum ④b, broken by D14.

Shape and structure: Irregular plane shape, uneven walls, uneven bottom; of length of 0.7, width of 0.5 − 0.76, depth of 0.2 − 0.44 meters (Figure 72). Deposit in the pit is grayish black soil; soil is loose, containing a small number of pottery pieces.

Unearthed items: Artifacts unearthed in H22 are mostly pottery pieces, total of 225 pieces, mostly terracotta and reddish brown earthenware, with a small number of fine blackish brown earthenware, brown earthenware and red clay earthenware *etc*. decorations are mostly twist line patterns, less stamp, circle, concave string, protruding rim and S − shape patterns (Figure 73). Forms are mostly

---

[1]   From registrar of unearthed artifacts, 1 flare mouth jar is unearthed in H20. However original figures of form specimens are missing.

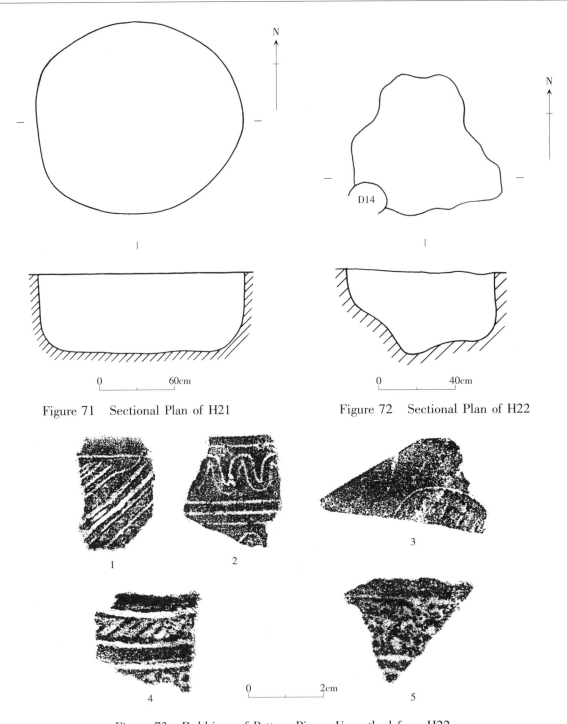

Figure 71   Sectional Plan of H21   Figure 72   Sectional Plan of H22

Figure 73   Rubbings of Pottery Pieces Unearthed from H22

1. Concave string pattern + rope pattern（H22：9） 2. Concave string pattern + water ripple pattern（H22：10） 3. Engraved pattern（H22：11） 4. Concave string pattern + poked pattern + circle pattern（H22：12） 5. Concave string pattern + circle pattern（H22：13）

bowls, jars, bases and ring feet.[1]

_____

[1] From registrar of unearthed artifacts, total of 13 specimens are selected from H22, including 8 form specimens and 5 ornamentation speci-
    mens. However original figures of form specimens are missing.

2. Postholes

40 in total was found under strata ⑤a and⑤b; 34 found under Stratum ⑤a, and 6 found under Stratum ⑤b (Figure 74). There is no rule in the distribution but these are abnormally concentrated, indicating possibility of column houses above previously and the postholes are concentrated without a certain rule due to subsequent reconstruction and restoration. To comprehensively understand information of postholes of this exploration square unit, postholes in the square unit are listed below.

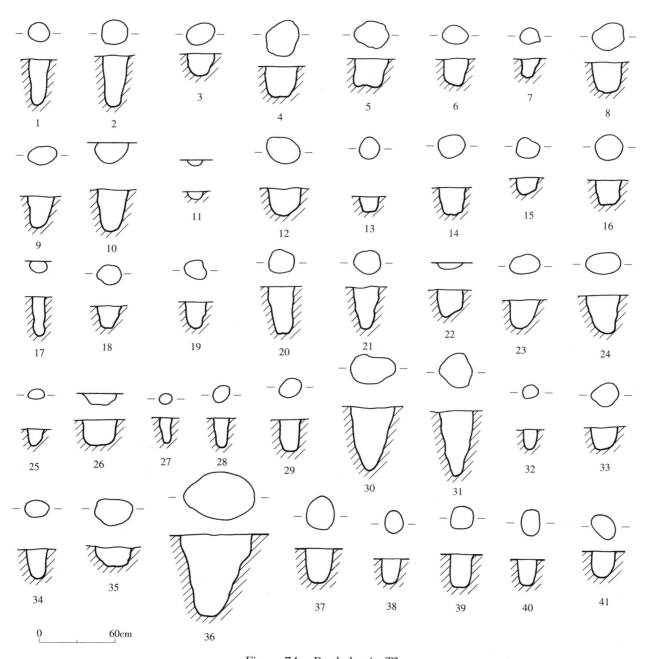

Figure 74   Postholes in T3

1 – 35. Postholes below T3⑤a layer (D1 – D34)   36 – 41. Postholes below T3⑤b layer (D1 – D6)

Table 3　Statistics of Pits and Postholes in Strata under T3　　　　Unit：cm

S/N	Numbering	Horizon level	Shape and structure			Dimensions (diameter – depth)	Soil	Figure No.
			Plane form	Walls of the pit	Bottom of pit			
1	D1	Under ⑤a	Round	Smooth	Dome shaped	18 – 38	Grayish black soil	Figure 74：1
2	D2	Under ⑤a	Round	Smooth	Dome shaped	20 – 41	Grayish black soil	Figure 74：2
3	D3	Under ⑤a	Oval	Rough	Flat	15 ~ 23 – 17	Grayish black soil	Figure 74：3
4	D4	Under ⑤a	Oval	Rough	Uneven	20 ~ 31 – 25	Black soil	Figure 74：4
5	D5	Under ⑤a	Oval	Rough	Flat	20 × 28 – 23	Grayish black soil	Figure 74：5
6	D6	Under ⑤a	Almost round	Smooth	Dome shaped	14 ~ 22 – 22	Grayish black soil	Figure 74：6
7	D7	Under ⑤a	Round	Rough	Uneven	15 – 15	Black soil	Figure 74：7
8	D8	Under ⑤a	Oval	Rough	Uneven	20 ~ 26 – 24	Grayish black soil	Figure 74：8
9	D9	Under ⑤a	Oval	Rough	Dome shaped	14 ~ 26 – 26	Grayish black soil	Figure 74：9
10	D10	Under ⑤a	Oval	Smooth	Dome shaped	18 ~ 29 – 34	Grayish black soil	Figure 74：10
11	D11	Under ⑤a	Round	Smooth	Dome shaped	12 – 6	Grayish black soil	Figure 74：11
12	D12	Under ⑤a	Oval	Rough	Dome shaped	20 ~ 29 – 20	Grayish black soil	Figure 74：12
13	D13	Under ⑤a	Round	Rough	Uneven	17 – 14	Grayish black soil	Figure 74：13
14	D14	Under ⑤a	Oval	Rough	Uneven	17 ~ 23 – 23	Black soil	Figure 74：14
15	D15	Under ⑤a	Round	Smooth	Dome shaped	16 – 14	Grayish black soil	Figure 74：15
16	D16	Under ⑤a	Round	Smooth	Flat	26 – 20	Grayish black soil	Figure 74：16
17	D17	Under ⑤a	Round	Smooth	Flat	13 – 31	Black soil	Figure 74：17
18	D18	Under ⑤a	Round	Rough	Uneven	20 – 18	Grayish black soil	Figure 74：18
19	D19	Under ⑤a	Round	Smooth	Dome shaped	11 ~ 20 – 20	Grayish black soil	Figure 74：19
20	D20	Under ⑤a	Round	Smooth	Flat	20 – 37	Grayish black soil	Figure 74：20
21	D21	Under ⑤a	Round	Smooth	Flat	23 – 34	Grayish black soil	Figure 74：21
22	D22	Under ⑤a	Round	Rough	Uneven	20 – 23	Grayish black soil	Figure 74：22
23	D23	Under ⑤a	Oval	Rough	Uneven	14 ~ 26 – 23	Gray soil	Figure 74：23
24	D24	Under ⑤a	Oval	Rough	Uneven	16 ~ 28 – 31	Grayish black soil	Figure 74：24
25	D25	Under ⑤a	Oval	Rough	Uneven	9 ~ 14 – 13	Grayish black soil	Figure 74：25
26	D26	Under ⑤a	Round	Smooth	Dome shaped	26 – 20	Black soil	Figure 74：26
27	D27	Under ⑤a	Round	Smooth	Dome shaped	12 – 20	Grayish black soil	Figure 74：27
28	D28	Under ⑤a	Round	Smooth	Flat	14 – 23	Grayish black soil	Figure 74：28
29	D29	Under ⑤a	Almost round	Smooth	Dome shaped	14 ~ 20 – 26	Grayish black soil	Figure 74：29
30	D30	Under ⑤a	Oval	Smooth	Dome shaped	20 ~ 37 – 52	Grayish black soil	Figure 74：30
31	D31	Under ⑤a	Oval	Smooth	Dome shaped	20 ~ 29 – 52	Grayish black soil	Figure 74：31

(continued 3)

S/N	Numbering	Horizon level	Shape and structure			Dimensions (diameter – depth)	Soil	Figure No.
			Plane form	Walls of the pit	Bottom of pit			
32	D32	Under ⑤a	Round	Relatively smooth	Dome shaped	14 – 16	Black soil	Figure 74 : 32
33	D33	Under ⑤a	Oval	Smooth	Dome shaped	17 ~ 23 – 17	Grayish black soil	Figure 74 : 33
34	D34	Under ⑤a	Oval	Smooth	Dome shaped	12 ~ 20 – 23	Grayish black soil	Figure 74 : 34
35	D35	Under ⑤a	Oval	Smooth	Uneven	20 ~ 31 – 14	Grayish black soil	Figure 74 : 35
36	D1	Under ⑤a	Oval	Rough	Uneven	40 ~ 57 – 66	gray soil	Figure 74 : 36
37	D2	Under ⑤a	Oval	Smooth	Dome shaped	22 ~ 26 – 26	Grayish black soil	Figure 74 : 37
38	D3	Under ⑤a	Oval	Rough	Dome shaped	14 ~ 17 – 20	Grayish black soil	Figure 74 : 38
39	D4	Under ⑤a	Round	Smooth	Dome shaped	20 – 28	Grayish black soil	Figure 74 : 39
40	D5	Under ⑤a	Irregular oval	Relatively smooth	Dome shaped	14 ~ 20 – 20	Grayish black soil	Figure 74 : 40
41	D6	Under ⑤a	Irregular oval	Relatively smooth	Dome shaped	15 ~ 23 – 20	Black soil	Figure 74 : 41

III. Unearthed artifacts of the stratum

1. Unearthed artifacts of stratum ⑤a

Artifacts unearthed are mainly pottery pieces with a small number of jade and stone objects. A total of 73 specimens are selected, including 8 jade pieces, 65 pottery pieces.

Jade tools: 8 piece, 1 stone chisel, 4 stone adzes, 1 stone ball, 1 stone core and 1 stone pendant.

Stone chisel: 1 piece.

Specimen T3②: 1, damaged, body shape is of rectangle, ground to shape, double – sided arc blade; remaining part of length of 3. 6; remaining part of width of 1. 3, thickness of 0. 1 – 0. 5cm (Figure 75 : 2).

Stone ball: 1 piece.

Specimen T3②: 2, body of oval shape, finely ground and polished; of longer diameter of 2. 3, shorter diameter of 1. 8, thickness of 1. 2cm (Figure 75 : 3 ; Plate 72 : 1).

Stone adzes: 4 pieces; shape and structure are substantially similar; body shape is of rectangle, ground to shape.

Specimen T3⑤a: 5, damaged in upper part and on one side, body shape is of rectangle, ground to shape, double – sided arc blade; remaining part of length of 3, width of 2. 1, thickness of 0. 5cm (Figure 75 : 1 ; Plate 72 : 2). Specimen T3⑤a : 3, damaged in the upper portion, double – sided arc

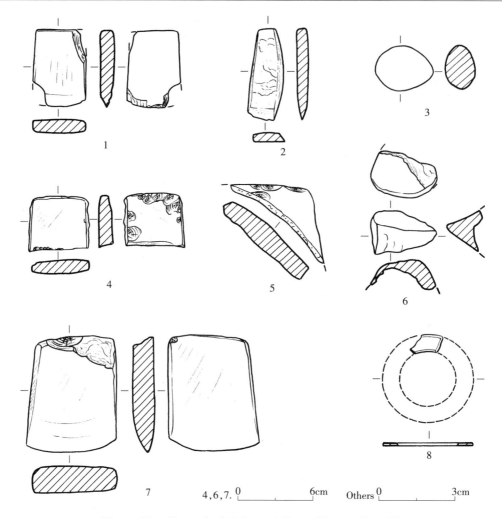

Figure 75   Unearthed Jade and Stone Pieces from T3
1, 4, 5, 7. Stone adze (T3⑤a：5, D1：8, T3⑤a：38, T3⑤a：3)   2. Stone chisel (T3⑤a：1)
3. Stone ball (T3⑤a：2)   6. Stone core (T3⑤a：22)   8. Jade pendant (T3⑤a：7)

blade; on the top are impact points and radiation rays from impact, remaining part of length of 4. 5,
width of 3. 5, thickness of 0. 9cm (Figure 75：7; Plate 72：3). Specimen D1：8, only upper part remains, smooth surface remains on one side, more impact points and radiation rays from impact visible
on the other side; remaining part of length of 4. 2, width of 4. 8, thickness of 1. 2cm (Figure 75：4).
Specimen T3⑤a：38, possibly residual piece of stone ax, only top part and some side remain, on the
top 4 impact points and radiation rays from impact are visible; remaining part of length of 3. 2; remaining part of width of 1. 9, thickness of 0. 8cm (Figure 75：5).

Stone core: 1 piece.

Specimen T3⑤a：22, body of triangle shape, flaking mark visible on both sides; of length of
5. 2, width of 0. 4 – 3. 4cm (Figure 75：6).

Jade pendant: 1 piece.

Specimen T3⑤a：7, only a small part remains, white, body of round shape, wide edge, remaining part of length of 2. 5, width of 1. 3, thickness of 0. 2cm (Figure 75 : 8).

Pottery pieces: A total of 3, 275 potter pieces were unearthed in T3⑤a. In terms of the earthenware materials, fine sand earthenware accounts for about 83. 6%, coarse sand earthenware for about 12. 6%, and clay polished earthenware for about 3. 8%. In terms of colors of the pottery pieces, terracotta, reddish brown, and brown pottery pieces account for about 62. 7%, indicating that the pottery color is mostly reddish. In terms of pattern ornamentation, it was extremely well – developed, accounting for 42. 1% of the total number of pottery pieces. Some pieces have on the surface a thin ornamen-

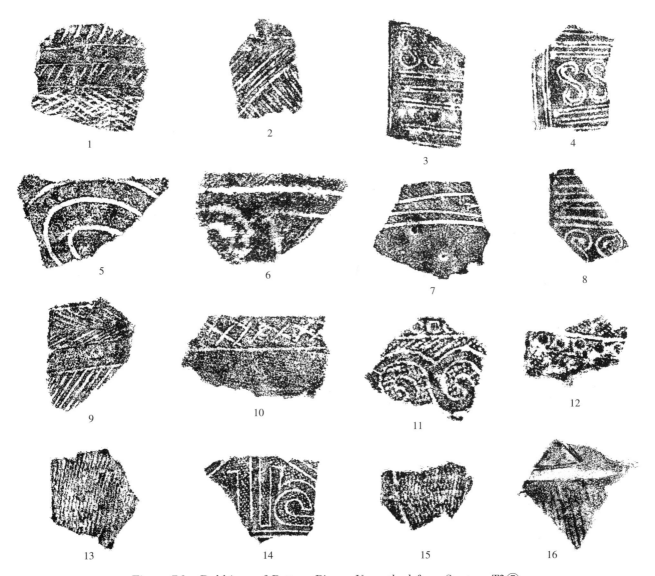

Figure 76   Rubbings of Pottery Pieces Unearthed from Stratum T3⑤a

1. Twist rope pattern + concave string pattern (T3⑤a : 43)   2. Twist rope pattern (T3⑤a : 44)   3, 4. S – shape pattern + engraved line pattern (T3⑤a : 51, 52)   5. Circle pattern (T3⑤a : 45)   6. Concave string pattern + circle pattern (T3⑤a : 46)   7. Concave string pattern (T3⑤a : 53)   8. S – shape pattern + engraved short line pattern (T3⑤a : 54)   9. Rope pattern (T3⑤ a : 47)   10. Poked pattern (T3⑤a : 48)   11. Circle pattern + S – shape pattern + combed dot pattern (T3⑤a : 55)   12. Circle pattern + concave string pattern + combed dot pattern (T3⑤a : 56)   13. Rope pattern (T3⑤a : 49)   14. Geometrical form pattern + combed dot pattern (T3⑤a : 50)   15. Rope pattern (T3⑤a : 57)   16. Protruding rim pattern + rope pattern (T3⑤a : 62)

ted coating. The decorations are of great variety, in which rope decorations account for about 54% of the total decorations. Other decorations include engraved line, stamp, concave string, protruding rim, pressure stamp, comb brushing and added mound *etc*. Particularly, among all the engraved lines, the ones with comb teeth brushed or comb dotted stamps are the most characteristic. Compound ornamentations of multiple decorations on a single pottery piece appear to have been very popular. The main ornamentation patterns are of clouds, S – shape, geometric patterns, circles and water ripples (Figure 76; figure 77: 1, 2, 5, 6; Plates 73 – 75) and the like. Pottery mouth parts are mostly contracted or flared, followed in number by trumpet – shaped and straight mouths. The artifacts are mostly with enclosure base and ring feet. Forms of the artifacts include handles, bases, trumpet – shape mouth jars, thick lip jars, ring feet and bowls *etc*. (Plates 76, 77).

T3⑤a: A total of 65 specimens of pottery pieces are selected, of which 29 specimens are for ornamentations and 36 specimens are for forms, including 1 handle, 1 base, 3 trumpet – shape mouth jars, 5 flare mouth jars, 3 thick lip jars, 1 contracted mouth jar, 12 ring feet and 8 bowls.

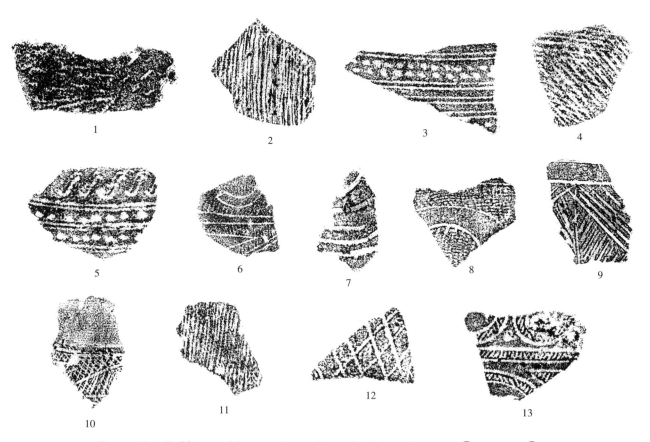

Figure 77   Rubbings of Pottery Pieces Unearthed from Strata T3⑤a and T3⑤b

1. Poked pattern (T3⑤a: 63)   2. Combing pattern (T3⑤a: 65)   3. Dot pattern + concave string pattern (T3⑤b: 9)   4. Twist rope pattern (T3⑤b: 10)   5. S – shape pattern + dot pattern + concave string pattern (T3⑤a: 66)   6. Geometrical form pattern + combed dot pattern (T3⑤a: 68)   7. Engraved pattern (T3⑤b: 11)   8. Engraved pattern + combed dot pattern (T3⑤b: 12)   9. Line pattern + engraved pattern (T3⑤b: 5)   10. Twist rope pattern + engraved pattern (T3⑤b: 6)   11. Rope pattern (T3⑤b: 8)   12. Engraved pattern (T3⑤b: 13)   13. Protruding rim pattern + poked pattern (T3⑤b: 7)

Handle: 1 piece.

Specimen T3⑤a: 4, reddish brown fine sand earthenware, of cylinder shape, with a dog head made at the end, with eyes and nostril, the other end of the handle on the lower part decorated with concave string pattern; remaining part of length of 6. 4, diameter of 2. 9cm (Figure 78: 1; Plate 72: 4).

Bases: 3 pieces; of basically similar shape and structure.

Specimen T3⑤a: 6, damaged, reddish brown sand earthenware, top oval shape, filled, lower end damaged; remaining part of length of 6. 8cm (Figure 78: 2). Specimen T3⑤a: 20, damaged, reddish brown sand earthenware, top oval shape flared, bucket shape in lower part; top long diameter of 5. 2, damaged short diameter of 3. 5, remaining part of height of 5. 9cm (Figure 78: 3). Specimen T3⑤a: 22, damaged, reddish brown sand earthenware, only remaining top, oval shape; of longer diameter of 5. 1, shorter diameter of 3. 5, remaining part of height of 1. 1cm.

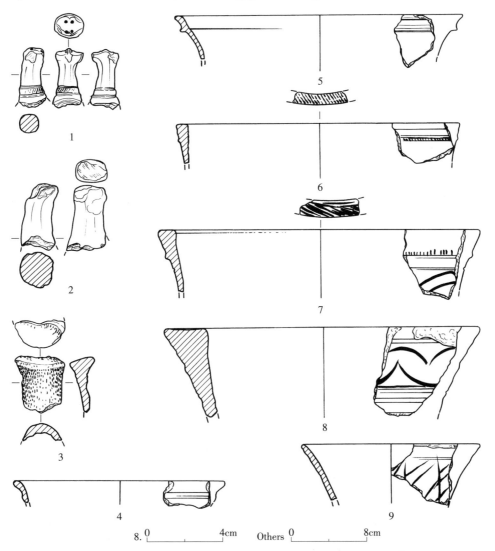

Figure 78   Unearthed Pottery Artifacts from Stratum T3⑤a

1. Handle (T3⑤a: 4)   2, 3. Base (T3⑤a: 6, 20)   4, 5, 9. Trumpet – shape mouth jar (T3⑤a: 24, 15, 10)   6 – 8. Thick lip jar (T3⑤a: 61, 18, 19)

Trumpet - shape mouth jars: 3 pieces; classified into two categories based on the neck.

Category 1: 2 pieces; with a protruding rim on the neck.

Specimen T3⑤a:24, reddish brown sand earthenware, round lip, contracted neck; bore diameter of 22. 2, remaining part of height of 2. 9cm (Figure 78:4). Specimen T3⑤a:15, brown sand earthenware, round lip, contracted neck; bore diameter of 30. 3, remaining part of height of 5. 6cm (Figure 78:5).

Category 2: 1 piece; no protruded ledge on the neck.

Specimen T3⑤a:10, reddish brown clay earthenware, round lip, contracted neck; upper neck decorated with one concave string, middle of neck decorated with engraved line patterns; bore diameter of 19. 2, remaining part of height of 6. 5cm (Figure 78:9).

Thick lip jars: 3 pieces; shape and structure are substantially similar; all of thick square lip, straight mouth slightly flared.

Specimen T3⑤a:61, grayish brown earthenware; lip decorated with spiral twist pattern, under mouth decorated with a protruding rim, poked with dots; bore diameter of 30, remaining part of height of 4. 3cm (Figure 78:6). Specimen T3⑤a:18, reddish brown fine sand earthenware, lip decorated with spiral twist pattern, one protruding rim decorated under the mouth; under which decorated with engraved geometrical patterns; bore diameter of 34, remaining part of height of 7. 8cm (Figure 78:6). Specimen T3⑤a:19, brown fine sand earthenware. under mouth decorated with two concave strings, neck decorated with engraved water ripple patterns; bore diameter of 16. 7, remaining part of height of 4. 7cm (Figure 78:8).

Flare mouth jars: 5 pieces; classified into two categories based on the mouth and neck.

Category 1: 2 pieces; square lip, neck decorated with 1 protruding rim.

Specimen T3⑤a:17, reddish brown fine sand earthenware, contracted neck, lip decorated with twist line pattern, on the protruding rim are poked dots, neck decorated with engraved line patterns; bore diameter of 34, remaining part of height of 7. 4cm (Figure 79:1). Specimen T3⑤a:14, reddish brown fine sand earthenware, neck slightly contracted, on the protruding rim are poked dots, neck decorated with engraved line patterns; bore diameter of 17. 8, remaining part of height of 4. 9cm (Figure 79:3).

Category 2: 3 pieces; round lip, no protruded ledge on the neck.

Specimen T3⑤a:13, fine brown earthenware; under mouth decorated with two concave strings, under which decorated with engraved leaf vein pattern; bore diameter of 25. 6, remaining part of height of 4. 5cm (Figure 79:2). Specimen T3⑤a:9, clay terracotta, neck decorated with engraved arc patterns; bore diameter of 17. 2, remaining part of height of 7. 3cm (Figure 79:4). Specimen T3⑤a:8, terracotta; neck decorated with engraved line patterns; bore diameter of 16, remaining part of height of 5. 7cm (Figure 79:6).

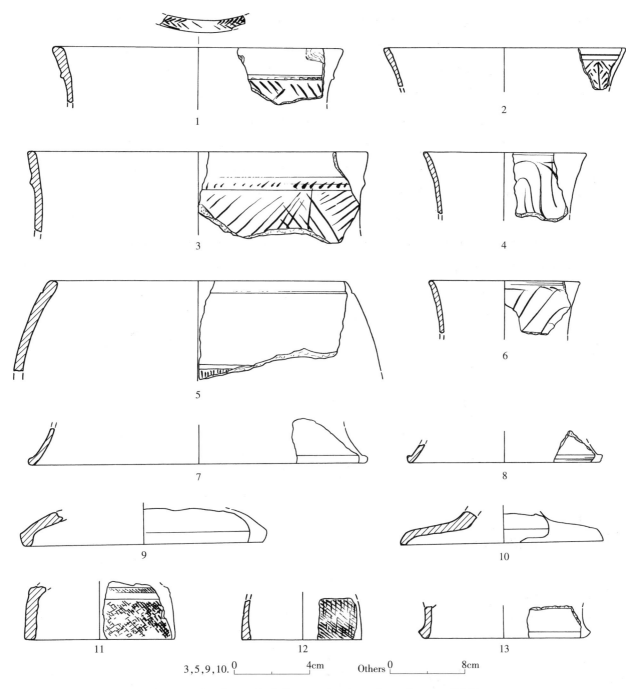

Figure 79   Unearthed Pottery Artifacts from Stratum T3⑤a

1–4, 6. Flared mouth jar (T3⑤a：17, 13, 14, 9, 8)   5. Contracted mouth jar (T3⑤a：57)   7–13. Ring foot
(T3⑤a：23, 33, 35, 34, 21, 60, 32)

Contracted mouth jar: 1 piece.

Specimen T3⑤a：57, reddish brown fine sand earthenware, square lip, contracted mouth, arc
shoulder, drum belly; under mouth decorated with one concave string, belly decorated with two concave strings, under which decorated with vertical twist line pattern; bore diameter of 15.7, remaining
part of height of 5.2cm (Figure 79：5).

Ring feet: 12 pieces; can be classified into three categories based on shape and structure.

Category 1: 6 pieces; trumpet shaped, foot tip bent outward.

Specimen T3⑤a:23, reddish brown sand earthenware. diameter at bottom of 35.6, remaining part of height of 4.8cm (Figure 79:7); Specimen T3⑤a:33, brown fine sand earthenware. foot tip bent upward; diameter at bottom of 23, remaining part of height of 3.3cm (Figure 79:8). Specimen T3⑤a:11, fine terracotta, a protruding rim decorated on foot; diameter at bottom of 16.6, remaining part of height of 4cm (Figure 80:1). Specimen T3⑤a:12, brown sand earthenware, a protruding rim decorated on foot; diameter at bottom of 18.5, remaining part of height of 4.3cm (Figure 80:9). Specimen T3⑤a:37, reddish brown fine earthenware; diameter at bottom of 27.6, remaining part of height of 1.7cm (Figure 80:12). Specimen T3⑤a:36, reddish brown sand earthenware, only middle part of ring foot remains; body decorated with poked short line pattern; remaining part of height of

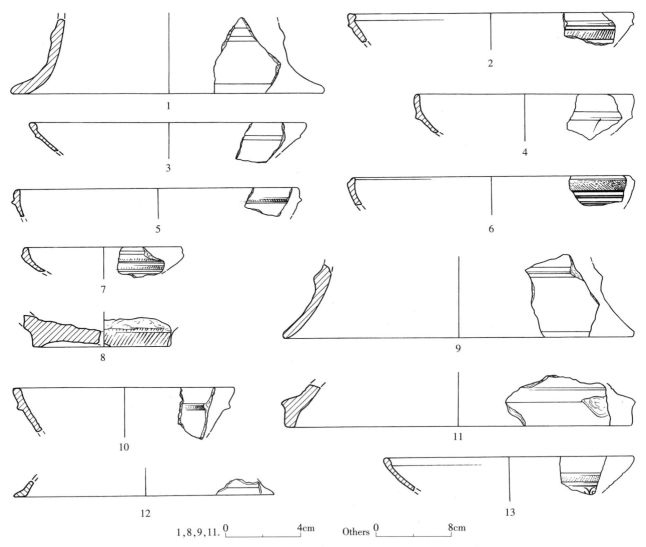

Figure 80   Unearthed Pottery Artifacts from Stratum T3⑤a
1, 8, 9, 11, 12. Ring foot (T3⑤a:11, 36, 12, 58, 37)   2–7, 10, 13. Bowl (T3⑤a:25, 27, 28, 26, 29, 31, 16, 30)

1. 5cm (Figure 80 : 8).

Category 2 : 3 pieces ; presenting a trumpet shape, foot tip bent inward.

Specimen T3⑤a : 35, grayish brown fine sand earthenware, foot tip bent inward ; diameter at bottom of 12. 6, remaining part of height of 1. 9cm (Figure 79 : 9). Specimen T3⑤a : 34, brown sand earthenware, foot tip bent inward ; diameter at bottom of 10. 8, remaining part of height of 1. 6cm (Figure 79 : 10). Specimen T3⑤a : 58, fine terracotta, foot tip bent inward, on the foot decorated with one concave string ; diameter at bottom of 18. 43, remaining part of height of 2. 7cm (Figure 80 : 11).

Category 3 : 3 pieces ; bucket shaped.

Specimen T3⑤a : 21, reddish brown sand earthenware. upper part of foot decorated with two concave strings, surface decorated with painted twist line pattern ; diameter at bottom of 16, remaining part of height of 6. 2cm (Figure 79 : 11). Specimen T3⑤a : 60, brown earthenware ; decorated with twist line pattern, diameter at bottom of 12. 6, remaining part of height of 4. 4cm (Figure 79 : 12). Specimen T3⑤a : 32, fine brown earthenware ; bucket shape ring foot, foot tip bent outward. diameter at bottom of 18. 2, remaining part of height of 3. 4cm (Figure 79 : 13).

Bowls : 8 pieces ; classified into three categories based on mouth and shoulder.

Category 1 : 3 pieces ; contracted mouth, decorated with a protruding rim on the shoulder.

Specimen T3⑤a : 26, fine brown earthenware ; square lip, arc belly ; on the protruding rim decorated with engraved short lines ; bore diameter of 30. 2, remaining part of height of 3cm (Figure 80 : 5). Specimen T3⑤a : 25, reddish brown fine sand earthenware, round lip, inclined straight belly ; upper belly decorated with two concave strings, two combed dots between concave string patterns ; bore diameter of 30, remaining part of height of 3. 5cm (Figure 80 : 2). Specimen T3⑤a : 28, terracotta, round lip, arc belly ; belly decorated with engraved line patterns ; bore diameter of 23, remaining part of height of 4. 9cm (Figure 80 : 4).

Category 2 : 2 pieces ; contracted mouth, without protruding rim on the shoulder.

Specimen T3⑤a : 29, fine terracotta, round lip, arc belly ; shoulder decorated with combed dots, belly decorated with five concave string patterns ; bore diameter of 28. 8, remaining part of height of 3. 2cm (Figure 80 : 6). Specimen T3⑤a : 31, reddish brown sand earthenware, arc belly ; belly decorated with concave string and engraved short lines ; bore diameter of 16. 8, remaining part of height of 3. 2cm (Figure 80 : 7).

Category 3 : 2 pieces ; flare mouth, decorated with a protruding rim on the shoulder.

Specimen T3⑤a : 27, brown sand earthenware, round lip, inclined straight belly ; bore diameter of 29. 3, remaining part of height of 4. 2cm (Figure 80 : 3). Specimen T3⑤a : 16, clay terracotta, round lip, tilted straight belly, poked on the protruding rim are dotted patterns ; bore diameter of 23. 4, remaining part of height of 5. 6cm (Figure 80 : 10).

Category 4: 1 piece; flare mouth, without protruding rim on the shoulder.

Specimen T3⑤a: 30, fine terracotta, round lip, contracted neck; upper belly decorated with three concave strings, upper part with combed dots between concave string patterns, and cloud pattern with belly decorated with engraved patterns; bore diameter of 26. 4, remaining part of height of 4. 1cm (Figure 80:13).

2. Unearthed artifacts of stratum T3⑤b

A total of 355 potter pieces were unearthed in Stratum ⑤b in this square unit. In terms of the earthenware materials, fine sand earthenware accounts for about 87. 9%, coarse sand earthenware for about 5. 4%, and clay polished earthenware for about 6. 7%. In terms of colors of the pottery pieces, terracotta, reddish brown, and brown pottery pieces account for about 38%, indicating that the pottery color is mostly reddish. In terms of pattern ornamentation, it was rather well – developed, accounting for 36% of the total number of pottery pieces. The decorations are of great variety, in which rope decorations account for about 46% of the total decorations. Other decorations include engraved line, stamp, concave string, protruding rim, pressure stamp, comb brushing, and added mound *etc*. The pottery artifacts are mostly with enclosure base and ring feet. Forms of the artifacts include jars, bowls, bases and ring feet *etc*. A total of 13 specimens of pottery pieces are selected from this stratum, of which 9 specimens are for ornamentations and 4 specimens are for forms (Figure 77:6 – 13; Plates 78, 79).[1]

Section Four   T4

T4 is located in the southwest corner of the excavation area. The square units for exploration were planned out and excavation works commenced on December 3, 2006 and exploration was completed on January 8, 2007. Sun Weigang was in charge of conducting excavations, making records and plotting.

I. Stratigraphic accumulation

Based on soil properties, colors and items contained, strata in this area are summarized and classified into 4 strata. Strata ④ and ⑥ are missing (Figure 81).

Stratum ①: Thickness of 8 – 17cm; top soil; soil is loose, with sand; yellowish gray; with some bricks, tiles and porcelain pieces.

Stratum ②: Depth of 8 – 17cm, thickness of 0 – 13cm; disturbed soil; compacted soil; yellowish red; large number of bricks, tiles and porcelain pieces; from contemporary cultures.

Stratum ③: Depth of 10 – 20, thickness of 8 – 22cm; disturbed soil; compacted soil, pure, with some bricks, tiles and porcelain pieces; H15, H26, H27, H28, H29, H30 opening is under this stra-

---

[1]   Original figure of the form specimen is missing.

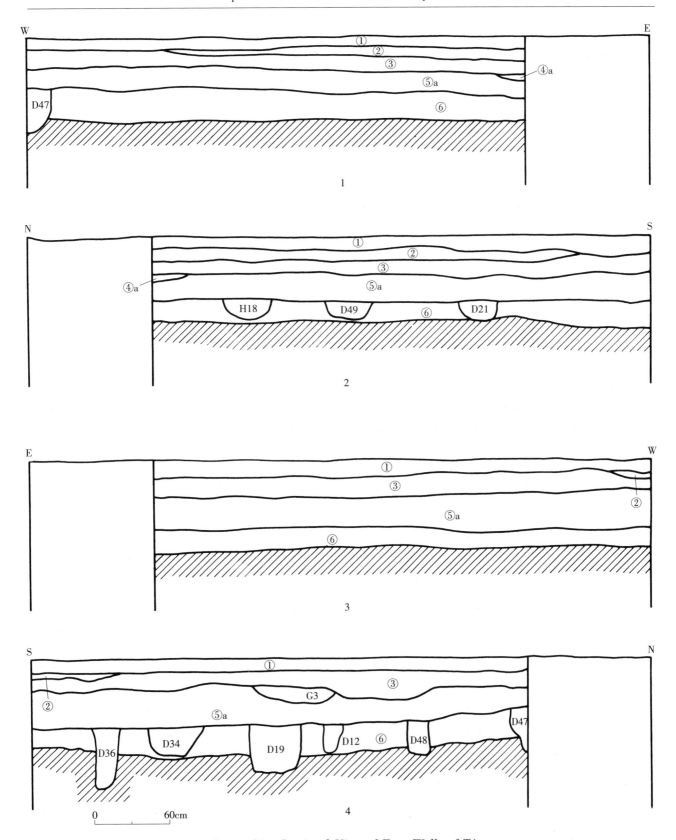

Figure 81   Sectional View of Four Walls of T4
1. North wall   2. East wall   3. South wall   4. West wall

tum. from contemporary cultures;

Stratum ⑤: Of Phung Nguyen culture; divided to strata ⑤a, ⑤b; of Phung Nguyen culture.

Stratum ⑤a: Depth of 20 – 30, thickness of 14 – 30cm; loose soil, with some pottery piece, stone pieces, damaged jade and other relics, possibly from Phung Nguyen culture; M1 and 49 opening is under this stratum.

Stratum ⑤b: Depth of 40 – 56, thickness of 12 – 20cm; hard soil; grayish yellow; mixed with a small number of pottery pieces; H31 opening is under this stratum.

Under this stratum is reddish – brown ferromanganese raw soil.

II. Remains

A total of 58 remains of various types were found in T4 (Figure 82; Plate 80), including 7 pits, 1 ditch, 1 tomb and 49 postholes. 6 pits (H15, H26, H27, H28, H29, H30) and ditch (G3) are from contemporary times. Remains from the Phung Nguyen culture period are presented below.

1. Pit: 1 pit

H31 is located in the south of T4, opening under stratum ⑤b, broken by G3.

Shape and structure: Irregular length of square shape, uneven and unsmooth walls; of length of 1. 4, width of 0. 56 – 0. 7, depth of 0. 42 meters (Figure 83), filled with reddish brown clay soil, compacted.

Unearthed items: Only a small piece of terracotta unearthed in H31.

2. Tomb: 1 tomb

M1: opening under stratum ⑤a, broken by D1 and D4; rectangular shape vertical tomb, in the direction of 99°, length of 2. 24 meters, east side width of 0. 76 meters, due to collapse, west side width now is 1. 04 meters, depth of 0. 42 meters (Figure 84; Plate 81). Filling in the tomb is yellow clay soil, of hard soil; no funeral items found nor remains; bone structure of corpse inside badly preserved; facing up and limbs straight, head to the east and both hands on left and right sides of the body; gender and age unknown; only one burial item found, a stem dish, placed at the head of the owner (Plate 82:1).

To ensure integrity of tomb and for future display, the Vietnam National Museum assigned specialist relic protection staff to reinforce the human skeleton (Plate 82:2) and packed for storage at Vinh Phuc museum. Meanwhile, before burial items are sorted and packaged, staff of Vietnam National Museum bought incense, candles, fruits, biscuits and flowers *etc.* and asked local priest for a worship ritual for the tomb owner. This is respect for the ancient people and shows humanistic concerns of the archeologists (Plate 83).

Burial item: 1 piece of stem dish.

Specimen M1:1, grayish brown sand earthenware, round lip, flare mouth, deep dish, medium

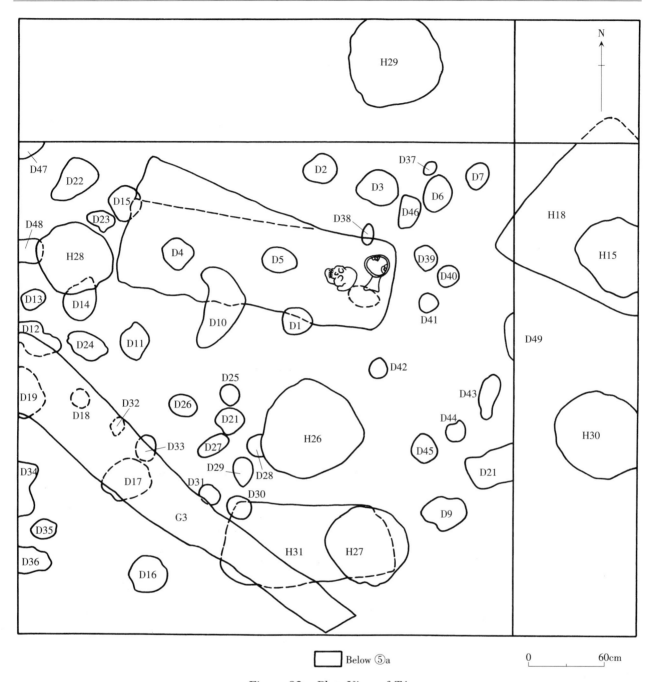

Below ⑤a

0 _____ 60cm

Figure 82   Plan View of T4

stem, horn – shaped ring foot, ring foot inwards; center of dish decorated with two concave string patterns, concave string pattern decorated with combed dots, lower part decorated with engraved flowers,
lower end decorated with two concave string patterns, concave string pattern decorated with engraved
short lines; center of handle poked short line pattern on four sides, decorated with engraved S – shape
pattern which is decorated with poked short line pattern; trumpet shape enclosure on the foot decorated
with continuous cloud pattern, cloud pattern decorated with poked short line pattern; bore diameter of
21. 2, diameter at bottom of 11. 7, height of 17. 3cm (Figure 85, 86; Plate 84).

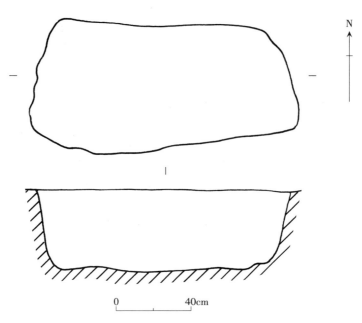

Figure 83   Sectional Plan of H31

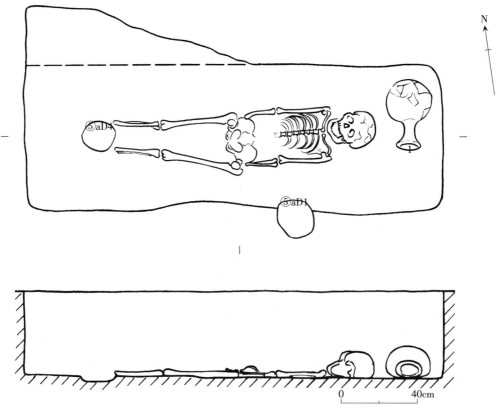

Figure 84   Sectional Plan of M1

1. Pottery stem dish

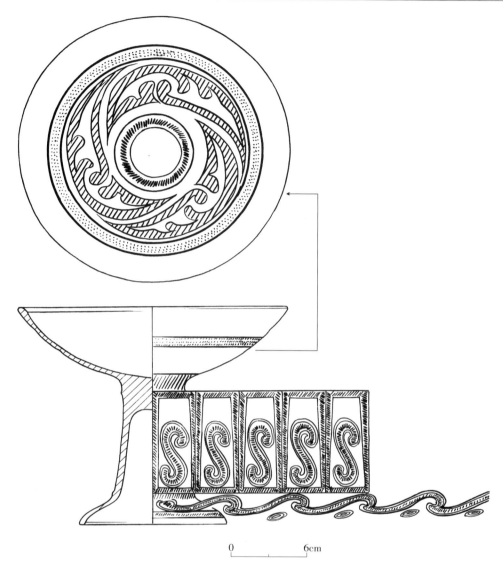

0 _____ 6cm

Figure 85   Pottery Stem Dish (M1 : 1) Unearthed from M1

3. Postholes

Postholes: 49 in total (Figure 87 , 88) , all opening under Stratum ⑤a. Plane shapes are substantially circular or oval. Walls are smooth. Bottoms are bell shaped or flat. Fillings are grayish black soil, distinct from surrounding soils, loose soil. Postholes of this exploration square unit are listed below.

Table 4   Statistics of Pits and Postholes in Strata under T4   Unit: cm

S/N	Numbering	Horizon level	Shape and structure			Dimensions (diameter – depth)	Soil	Figure No.
			Plane form	Walls of the pit	Bottom of pit			
1	D1	Below ⑤a	Almost round	Smooth	Flat	26 – 38	Grayish black soil	Figure 87 : 1
2	D2	Below ⑤a	Round	Smooth	Flat	26 – 33	Grayish black soil	Figure 87 : 2

(continued 4)

S/N	Numbering	Horizon level	Shape and structure			Dimensions (diameter – depth)	Soil	Figure No.
			Plane form	Walls of the pit	Bottom of pit			
3	D3	Below ⑤a	Round	Smooth	Flat	33 – 26	Grayish black soil	Figure 87 : 3
4	D4	Below ⑤a	Round	Smooth	Flat	26 – 42	Black soil	Figure 87 : 4
5	D5	Below ⑤a	Oval	Smooth	Flat	5 ~ 28 – 23	Grayish black soil	Figure 87 : 5
6	D6	Below ⑤a	Oval	Rough	Round bottom	17 ~ 33 – 15	Black soil	Figure 87 : 6
7	D7	Below ⑤a	Round	Rough	Round bottom	16 – 10	Grayish black soil	Figure 87 : 7
8	D8	Below ⑤a	Oval	Relatively smooth	Dome shaped	12 ~ 25 – 10	Grayish black soil	Figure 87 : 8
9	D9	Below ⑤a	Irregular oval	Rough	Uneven	17 ~ 38 – 19	Black soil	Figure 87 : 9
10	D10	Below ⑤a	Irregular oval	Rough	Uneven	12 ~ 63 – 21	Grayish black soil	Figure 87 : 10
11	D11	Below ⑤a	Oval	Relatively smooth	Relatively even	7 ~ 31 – 26	Black soil	Figure 87 : 11
12	D12	Below ⑤a	Oval	Smooth	Flat	12 ~ 35 – 19	Grayish black soil	Figure 87 : 12
13	D13	Below ⑤a	Oval	Smooth	Flat	10 ~ 21 – 12	Grayish black soil	Figure 87 : 13
14	D14	Below ⑤a	Oval	Smooth	Dome shaped	11 ~ 35 – 25	Grayish black soil	Figure 87 : 14
15	D15	Below ⑤a	Round	Smooth	Dome shaped	26 – 18	Black soil	Figure 87 : 15
16	D16	Below ⑤a	Round	Relatively smooth	Dome shaped	30 – 25	Grayish black soil	Figure 87 : 16
17	D17	Below ⑤a	Round	Rough	Uneven	40 – 22	Black soil	Figure 87 : 17
18	D18	Below ⑤a	Round	Smooth	Flat	16 – 13	Grayish black soil	Figure 87 : 18
19	D19	Below ⑤a	Oval	Smooth	Flat	15 ~ 41 – 12	Grayish black soil	Figure 87 : 19
20	D20	Below ⑤a	Round	Smooth	Flat	24 – 14	Black soil	Figure 87 : 20
21	D21	Below ⑤a	Irregular oval	Rough	Uneven	19 ~ 40 – 16	Grayish black soil	Figure 87 : 21
22	D22	Below ⑤a	Irregular oval	Rough	Uneven	10 ~ 40 – 12	Black soil	Figure 87 : 22
23	D23	Below ⑤a	Irregular oval	Rough	Uneven	5 ~ 23 – 18	Grayish black soil	Figure 87 : 23
24	D24	Below ⑤a	Oval	Relatively smooth	Relatively even	11 ~ 35 – 17	Grayish black soil	Figure 87 : 24
25	D25	Below ⑤a	Round	Smooth	Dome shaped	14 – 12	Grayish black soil	Figure 87 : 25
26	D26	Below ⑤a	Round	Smooth	Dome shaped	23 – 8	Black soil	Figure 87 : 26
27	D27	Below ⑤a	Oval	Relatively smooth	Uneven	10 ~ 28 – 10	Grayish black soil	Figure 87 : 27

(continued 4)

S/N	Numbering	Horizon level	Shape and structure			Dimensions (diameter – depth)	Soil	Figure No.
			Plane form	Walls of the pit	Bottom of pit			
28	D28	Below ⑤a	Oval	Relatively smooth	Dome shaped	9 ~ 17 – 5	Black soil	Figure 87 : 28
29	D29	Below ⑤a	Oval	Relatively smooth	Dome shaped	11 ~ 24 – 7	Grayish black soil	Figure 87 : 29
30	D30	Below ⑤a	Round	Smooth	Flat	21 – 17	Grayish black soil	Figure 87 : 30
31	D31	Below ⑤a	Oval	Smooth	Flat	13 ~ 17 – 18	Grayish black soil	Figure 88 : 1
32	D32	Below ⑤a	Oval	Relatively smooth	Relatively even	9 ~ 16 – 16	Grayish black soil	Figure 88 : 2
33	D33	Below ⑤a	Oval	Relatively smooth	Dome shaped	16 ~ 22 – 10	Gray soil	Figure 88 : 3
34	D34	Below ⑤a	Oval	Relatively smooth	Dome shaped	8 ~ 45 – 7	Grayish black soil	Figure 88 : 4
35	D35	Below ⑤a	Oval	Smooth	Flat	10 ~ 21 – 14	Grayish black soil	Figure 88 : 5
36	D36	Below ⑤a	Oval	Smooth	Flat	11 ~ 28 – 25	Gray soil	Figure 88 : 6
37	D37	Below ⑤a	Almost round	Smooth	Flat	7 ~ 13 – 7	Grayish black soil	Figure 88 : 7
38	D38	Below ⑤a	Oval	Relatively smooth	Dome shaped	11 ~ 17 – 7	Grayish black soil	Figure 88 : 8
39	D39	Below ⑤a	Almost round	Relatively smooth	Uneven	17 ~ 21 – 7	Grayish black soil	Figure 88 : 9
40	D40	Below ⑤a	Round	Smooth	Flat	16 – 14	Black soil	Figure 88 : 10
41	D41	Below ⑤a	Round	Rough	Uneven	16 – 5	Grayish black soil	Figure 88 : 11
42	D42	Below ⑤a	Round	Smooth	Flat	16 – 12	Black soil	Figure 88 : 12
43	D43	Below ⑤a	Irregular oval	Smooth	Flat	9 ~ 37 – 17	Grayish black soil	Figure 88 : 13
44	D44	Below ⑤a	Round	Smooth	Flat	17 – 13	Black soil	Figure 88 : 14
45	D45	Below ⑤a	Round	Smooth	Flat	24 – 7	Grayish black soil	Figure 88 : 15
46	D46	Below ⑤a	Irregular oval	Rough	Uneven	12 ~ 27 – 5	Gray soil	Figure 88 : 16
47	D47	Below ⑤a	Round	Smooth	Dome shaped	21 – 37	Grayish black soil	Figure 88 : 17
48	D48	Below ⑤a	Oval	Smooth	Dome shaped	18 ~ 21 – 30	Grayish black soil	Figure 88 : 18
49	D49	Below ⑤a	Round	Smooth	Dome shaped	38 – 19	Grayish black soil	Figure 88 : 19

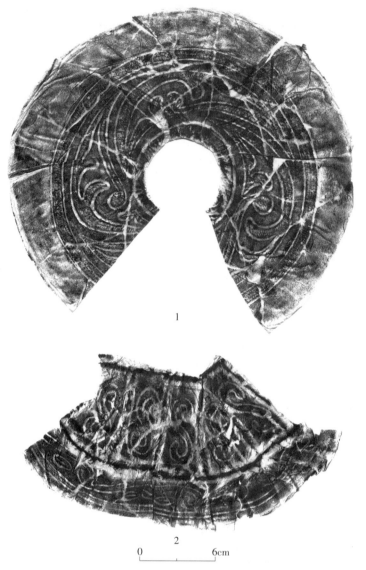

1

2

0 _____ 6cm

Figure 86   Rubbings of Pottery Stem Dish (M1 : 1) Unearthed from M1
1. Lower part   2. Ring feet

III. Unearthed artifacts

1. Unearthed artifacts of stratum T4⑤a

Mostly pottery pieces, with a small number of stone tools. A total of 67 specimens are selected, including 10 stone tool, 3 jade pieces and 54 pottery pieces.

Stone tools: 10 pieces, including 6 stone adzes, 2stone cores, 1 stone chisel and 1 stone plate.

Stone adzes: 6 pieces; of similar shape and structure, rectangular or trapezoid, ground to shape.

Specimen T4⑤a:2, blade damaged, body shape is of rectangle, single – sided arc blade, impact points and radiation rays from impact are visible on blade; remaining part of length of 3. 5, width of 3. 9, thickness of 0. 8cm (Figure 89 : 1 ; Plate 85 : 1). Specimen T4⑤a : 3, body shape is of rectan-

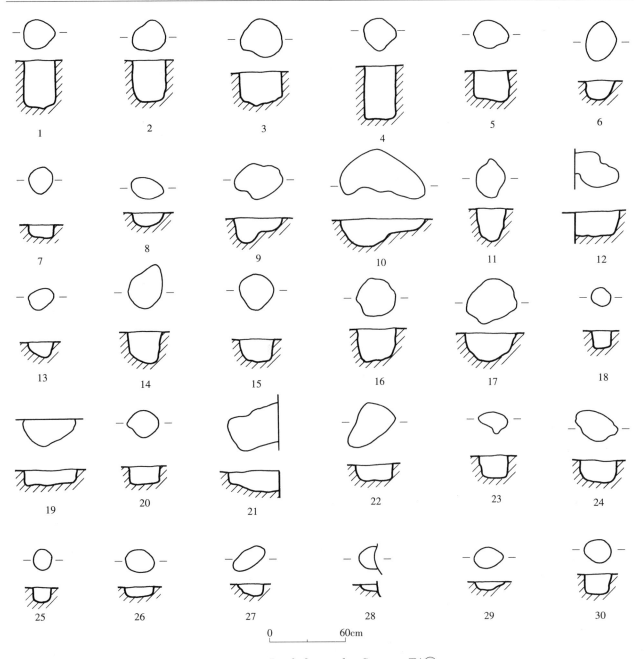

Figure 87   Postholes under Stratum T4⑤a
1 – 30. Posthole (D1 – D30)

gle, single – sided arc blade, apparent traces of use on blade; remaining part of length of 3. 3, width of 2. 9, thickness of 0. 6cm (Figure 89 : 2). Specimen T4③ : 1, body shape is of rectangle, single – sided arc blade, apparent traces of use on blade; remaining part of length of 3, width of 1. 6, thickness of 0. 4cm (Figure 89 : 3). Specimen T4⑤a : 6, body shape is of rectangle, single – sided arc blade. remaining part of length of 3. 6, width of 3. 5, thickness of 0. 8cm (Figure 89 : 5; Plate 86 : 1). Specimen T4③ : 4, only middle part remains, remaining part of length of 5; remaining part of width of 2. 8, thickness of 0. 7cm (Figure 89 : 6). Specimen T4⑤a : 31, trapezoid, double – si-

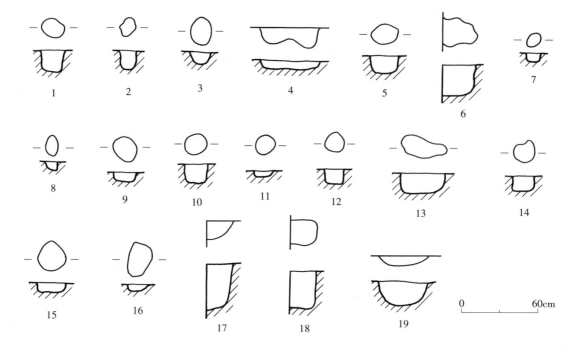

Figure 88   Postholes under Stratum T4⑤a
1 – 19. Posthole (D31 – D49)

ded arc blade, remaining part of length of 2. 6; remaining part of width of 2, thickness of 0. 2cm (Figure 90 : 1; Plate 86 : 2).

Stone cores: 2 pieces.

Specimen T4③:2, body shape is of rectangle, marks from flaking visible on surface, remaining part of length of 7; remaining part of width of 5, thickness of 3. 2cm (Figure 89 : 7). Specimen T4③:3, damaged, body shape is of rectangle, natural rock on one side, impact points and radiation rays from impact visible on the other side; remaining part of length of 7. 2; remaining part of width of 6. 2, thickness of 2. 7cm (Figure 89 : 8).

Stone chisel: 1 piece.

Specimen T4⑤a : 4, damaged on both ends, rectangular in shape, remaining part of length of 4. 6, width of 0. 4, thickness of 0. 3cm (Figure 90 : 5; Plate 85 : 4).

Stone flake: 1 piece.

Specimen T4⑤a : 30, oval shaped, natural rock on one side, impact points and radiation rays from impact visible on the other side, length of 7. 2, maximum width of 6. 2, thickness of 0. 7cm (Figure 90 : 8).

Jade pieces: 3 pieces, including 1 T – shaped ring and 2 rings.

T - shaped ring: 1 piece.

Specimen T4⑤a:5, damaged, ground to shape, diamond shaped, T – shape in section view; diameter of 6. 5, width of 1, thickness of 0. 3cm (Figure 90:2; Plate 85:2).

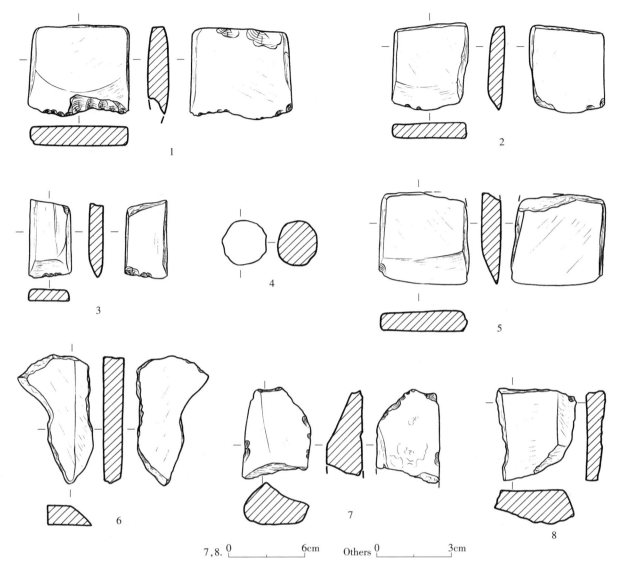

Figure 89   Stone Tools and Pottery Balls Unearthed from T4

1 – 3, 5, 6. Stone adze (T4⑤a : 2, T4⑤a : 3, T4③ : 1, T4⑤a : 6, T4③ : 4)   4. Pottery ball (T4⑤a : 7)

7, 8. Stone core (T4③ : 2, T4③ : 3)

Rings: 2 pieces; of similar shape and structure, ground to shape, of a round body.

Specimen D36 : 1, damaged, diameter of 5. 5, thickness of 0. 4cm (Figure 90 : 4). Specimen T4⑤a : 1, damaged, ground to shape, of a round body; diameter of 5, thickness of 0. 6cm (Figure 90 : 3; Plate 85 : 3).

Pottery pieces: A total of 1350 potter pieces were unearthed in Stratum ⑤a in this square unit. In terms of the earthenware materials, fine sand earthenware accounts for the most, followed by coarse sand earthenware, and clay polished earthenware is rare. In terms of colors of the pottery pieces, terra-cotta, reddish brown, and brown pottery pieces account for the most, with small number of grayish brown and blackish brown ones. In terms of pattern ornamentation, it was extremely well – developed, accounting for 37% of the total number of pottery pieces. The decorations are of great variety, in which

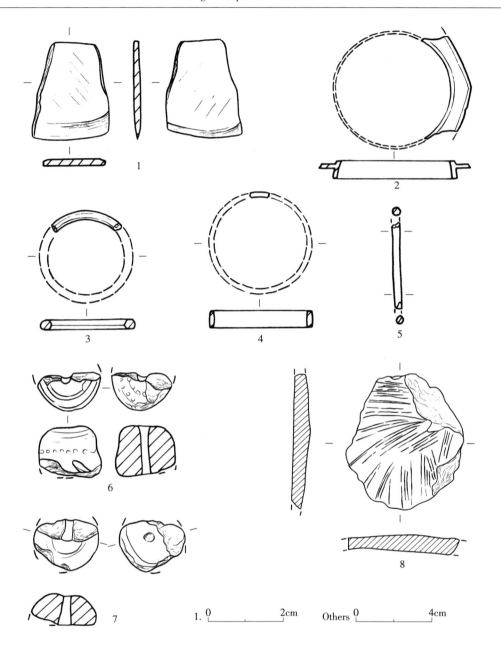

Figure 90   Stone Tools and Pottery Spinning Wheels Unearthed from T4
1. Stone adze（T4⑤a：31） 2-4. Jade ring（T4⑤a：5，T4⑤a：1，D36：1） 5. Stone chisel（T4⑤a：4）
6，7. Pottery spinning wheel（T4⑤a：8，T4⑤a：9） 8. Stone chip（T4⑤a：30）

rope decorations account for about 80% of the total decorations. Other decorations include engraved line, stamp, concave string, protruding rim, pressure stamp, comb brushing and leaf vein *etc*. （Figure 91）. Pottery mouth parts are mostly contracted or flared, followed by trumpet shape and straight mouths. Artifacts are mostly with enclosure base and ring feet. Forms of the artifacts include pottery balls, spinning wheels, bowls, ring feet, flare mouth jar, thick lip jars *etc*.[1]

---

〔1〕 Statistical data in this section was provided by Vietnam National Museum of History.

Figure 91 Rubbings of Pottery Pieces Unearthed from Stratum T4⑤a

1. Engraved pattern + dot pattern (T4⑤a: 32) 2. Engraved line pattern (T4⑤a: 33) 3. Water ripple pattern + concave string pattern (T4⑤a: 10) 4. Combing pattern (T4⑤a: 11) 5. Concave string pattern + rope pattern (T4⑤a: 12) 6. Geometrical form pattern + combed dot pattern (T4⑤a: 13) 7. Geometrical form pattern (T4⑤a: 14) 8. Engraved pattern (T4⑤a: 15) 9. Concave string pattern + pit dot pattern (T4⑤a: 16) 10. Geometrical form pattern (T4⑤a: 17) 11. Water ripple pattern + concave string pattern (T4⑤a: 18) 12. Geometrical form pattern + poked pattern (T4⑤a: 19) 13. Water ripple pattern + concave string pattern (T4⑤a: 20) 14. Geometrical form pattern + combed dot pattern (T4⑤a: 21) 15. S – shape pattern + concave string pattern (T4⑤a: 22) 16. Engraved pattern (T4⑤a: 23) 17. Geometrical form pattern + combed dot pattern (T4⑤a: 24) 18. Water ripple pattern + combed dot pattern + concave string pattern (T4⑤a: 25) 19. Pit dot pattern + geometrical form pattern (T4⑤a: 26) 20. Combing pattern (T4⑤a: 27) 21. Geometrical form pattern + combed dot pattern (T4⑤a: 28) 22. Engraved pattern (T4⑤a: 29) 23. Pit dot pattern + concave string pattern + combed dot pattern (T4⑤a: 34) 24. Pit dot pattern + concave string pattern (T4⑤a: 35)

⑤a in this square unit: a total of 54 specimens of pottery pieces are selected, of which 24 specimens are for ornamentations and 30 specimens are for forms, including 1 pottery ball, 1 spinning wheel, 8 bowls, 10 ring feet, 2 flare mouth jars, 4 trumpet – shape mouth jars and 2thick lip jars.

Pottery ball: 1 piece.

Specimen T4⑤a: 7, reddish brown sand earthenware, sphere shaped; diameter of 1.7cm (Figure 89:4).

Spinning wheels: 2 pieces; of similar shape and structure, oval shaped.

Specimen T4⑤a: 8, brown sand earthenware, oval shaped, 1 hole ; body decorated with concave string pattern, each concave string pattern decorated with circles; diameter of 3.3, thickness of 1.6cm (Figure 90:6). Specimen T4⑤a:9, grayish brown sand earthenware, oval shaped, 1, diameter of 3.5, thickness of 1.5cm (Figure 90:7).

Bowls: 9 pieces; classified into three categories based on shoulder and mouth.

Category 1: 5 pieces. contracted mouth, drum shoulder, decorated with a protruding rim on the shoulder.

Specimen T4⑤a: 36, reddish brown sand earthenware, round lip, tilted straight belly, belly decorated with four concave string pattern, upper and lower combed dots between concave string patterns, middle of belly decorated with engraved patterns; bore diameter of 21, remaining part of height of 2.9cm (Figure 92 : 5). Specimen T4⑤a : 42, terracotta, thickness of round lip; bore diameter of 31.8, remaining part of height of 3.7cm (Figure 92:9). Specimen T4⑤a:38, terracotta, round lip; belly decorated with 3 concave string pattern, upper and lower combed dots between concave string patterns; bore diameter of 23.2, remaining part of height of 3.3cm (Figure 92 : 10). Specimen T4⑤a:41, fine terracotta, shoulder decorated with a protruding rim, belly decorated with concave string pattern; bore diameter of 14.4, remaining part of height of 1.7cm (Figure 92 : 6). Specimen T4⑤a:50, grayish brown sand earthenware, sharp round lip, belly decorated with engraved semi – circle, semi – circle decorated with engraved leaf vein pattern; bore diameter of 34.4, remaining part of height of 4.6cm (Figure 93:1).

Category 2: 3 pieces; flare mouth, slim shoulder, without protruding rim on the shoulder.

Specimen T4⑤a: 53, reddish brown sand earthenware, round lip, arc belly, belly decorated with vertical twist pattern; bore diameter of 30.2, remaining part of height of 4.7cm (Figure 92:7). Specimen T4⑤a:40, reddish brown sand earthenware, round lip; bore diameter of 25, remaining part of height of 2.6cm (Figure 93:9). Specimen T4⑤a:61, reddish brown fine sand earthenware, sharp round lip; bore diameter of 31.8, remaining part of height of 4cm (Figure 93:3).

Category 3: 1 piece; flare mouth, drum shoulder, decorated with a protruding rim on the shoulder.

Specimen T4⑤a : 37, reddish brown fine sand earthenware, sharp round lip, arc belly; upper

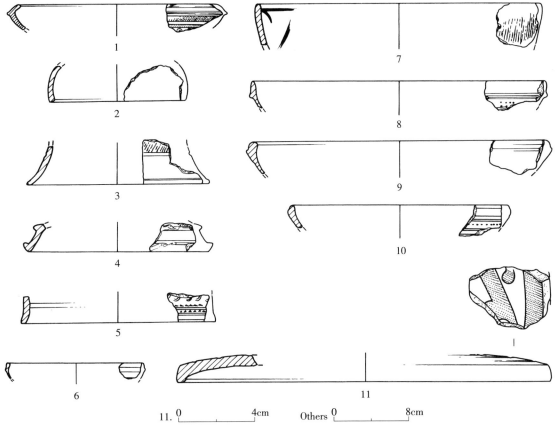

Figure 92   Pottery Pieces Unearthed from Stratum T4⑤a

1, 6－10. Ring foot（T4⑤a：36, 41, 53, 37, 42, 38） 2－5, 11. Bowl（T4⑤a：39, 51, 54, 62, 60）

belly decorated with combed dots；bore diameter of 31. 2，remaining part of height of 3. 2cm（Figure 92：8）.

Ring feet：10 pieces；can be classified into three categories based on shape and structure.

Category 1：2 pieces；bucket shaped.

Specimen T4⑤a：39，brown sand earthenware，foot tips contracted inward；diameter at bottom of 14. 4，remaining part of height of 3. 8cm（Figure 92：1）. Specimen T4⑤a：62，fine terracotta，foot tip bent outward. Bottom of foot decorated with two concave string and poked dots on upper part of foot engraved－shape lines，diameter at bottom of 30. 4，remaining part of height of 3cm（Figure 92：5）.

Category 2：5 pieces；horn－shaped ring foot，foot tip bent outward.

Specimen T4⑤a：51，reddish brown fine earthenware；two concave string patterns decorated on foot，engraved patterns on upper part of foot；diameter at bottom of 19. 2，remaining part of height of 4. 8cm（Figure 92：3）. Specimen T4⑤a：58，reddish brown sand earthenware. middle of foot decorated with two concave strings，between concave strings decorated with engraved line pattern，upper part of foot decorated with circles；diameter at bottom of 14. 9，remaining part of height of 4cm（Figure 94：1）. Specimen T4⑤a：59，brown earthenware；middle of foot decorated with one concave string and a hole，upper part of foot decorated with combed dots；diameter at bottom of 16. 7，remaining part

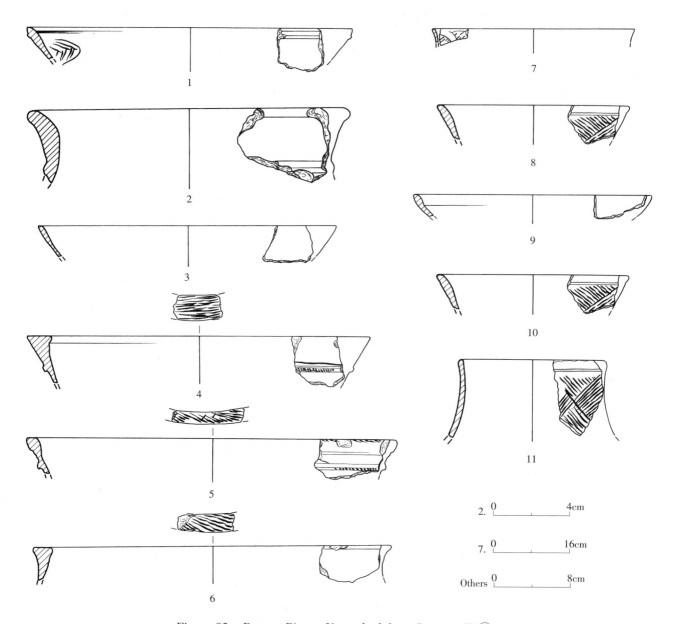

Figure 93   Pottery Pieces Unearthed from Stratum T4⑤a
1, 3, 9. Bowl (T4⑤a:50, 61, 40)   2, 5, 8, 10. Trumpet–shape mouth jar (T4⑤a:52, 44, 43, 48)
4, 6. Thick lip jar (T4⑤a:45, 46)   7, 11. Flared mouth jar (T4⑤a:49, 47)

of height of 3.7cm (Figure 94:3). Specimen T4⑤a:56, reddish brown sand earthenware; two concave string patterns decorated on foot, engraved patterns on upper part of foot; diameter at bottom of 16.6, remaining part of height of 4.9cm (Figure 94:4). Specimen T4⑤a:57, brown earthenware; diameter at bottom of 19.9, remaining part of height of 4.1cm (Figure 94:5).

Category 3: 2 pieces; horn–shaped ring foot, foot tip bent upward.

Specimen T4⑤a:54, brown fine sand earthenware; foot decorated with 1 protruding rim; diameter at bottom of 19.2, remaining part of height of 3cm (Figure 92:4). Specimen T4⑤a:55, brown earthenware; diameter at bottom of 11.2, remaining part of height of 3.8cm (Figure 94:2).

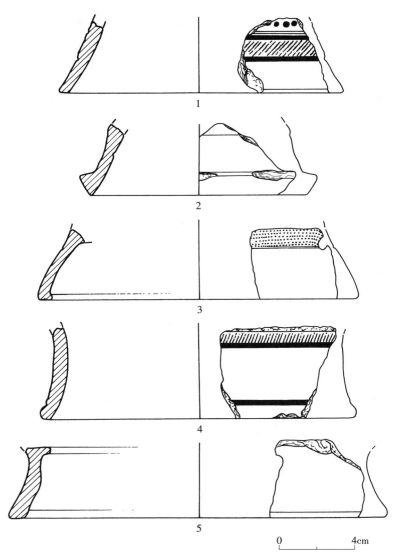

Figure 94   Pottery Ring Feet Unearthed from Stratum T4⑤a
1. T4⑤a：58   2. T4⑤a：55   3. T4⑤a：59   4. T4⑤a：56   5. T4⑤a：57

Category 4：1 piece；horn – shaped ring foot, foot tip bent inward.

Specimen T4⑤a：60, reddish brown sand earthenware, on the foot decorated with engraved geometrical patterns and combed dots；bore diameter of 19. 8, remaining part of height of 1. 4cm (Figure 92：11).

Flare mouth jars：2 pieces；of similar shape and structure, flare mouth, contracted neck.

Specimen T4⑤a：49, reddish brown fine sand earthenware, round lip, neck decorated with engraved arc lines and lines；bore diameter of 42. 4, remaining part of height of 4cm (Figure 93：7).
Specimen T4⑤a：47, reddish brown sand earthenware, round lip, straight neck, arc shoulder；under mouth decorated with one concave string, neck decorated with engraved line patterns；bore diameter of 15. 4, remaining part of height of 8cm (Figure 93：11).

Trumpet - shape mouth jars：4 pieces；classified into two categories based on the neck.

Category 1: 2 pieces; long neck, neck decorated with 1 protruding rim.

Specimen T4⑤a:43, reddish brown sand earthenware, sharp round lip, neck slightly contracted, on the protruding rim poked short line pattern, belly decorated with engraved line patterns; bore diameter of 18.8, remaining part of height of 4.1cm (Figure 94:2). Specimen T4⑤a:44, reddish brown sand earthenware, round lip, narrow flat edge, arc belly; lip decorated with spiral twist pattern, on the protruding rim poked short line pattern; bore diameter of 39.1, remaining part of height of 4.3cm (Figure 93:5).

Category 2: 2 pieces; short neck, no protruded ledge on the neck.

Specimen T4⑤a:48, reddish brown sand earthenware, round lip; under mouth decorated with one concave string, neck decorated with poked dot pattern; bore diameter of 20, remaining part of height of 4cm (Figure 93:10). Specimen T4⑤a:52, thickness of round lip, contracted neck; bore diameter of 17, remaining part of height of 3.9cm (Figure 93:2).

Thick lip jars: 2 pieces; of similar shape and structure, all of thick square lip, straight mouth slightly contracted.

Specimen T4⑤a:45, brown sand earthenware, inclined straight belly; lip decorated with spiral twist pattern, one protruding rim decorated under the mouth; on the protruding rim poked pit dot pattern; bore diameter of 36.2, remaining part of height of 5.3cm (Figure 93:4). Specimen T4⑤a:46, brown sand earthenware, lip decorated with spiral twist pattern; bore diameter of 38, remaining part of height of 3.9cm (Figure 93:6).

2. Unearthed artifacts of stratum T4⑤b

A total of 115 pottery pieces and 1 stone tool were unearthed from this stratum. In terms of materials, there are more fine earthenware, followed by coarse earthenware and very few polished clay earthenware. In terms of color, reddish brown earthenware is the most with small number of grayish brown, blackish brown. Decorations are of great variety, mostly twist line pattern, stamp, concave string, protruding rim, pressure stamp, comb brushing and leaf vein patterns. Mouths of the pottery pieces are mostly flared. Forms are mostly enclosure bases and ring feet.

1 specimen is selected from this stratum, i.e. the 1 stone ax.

Stone axes: 1 piece.

Specimen T4⑤b:1, severely damaged; body shape is of rectangle, surface ragged; remaining part of length of 3.7; remaining part of width of 1.9, thickness of 1.1cm.

Section Five   T5

T5 is located in the western part of the excavation area. The square units for exploration were planned out and excavation works commenced on December 3, 2006 and exploration was completed on

January 8, 2007. Lei Yu was in charge of conducting excavations, making records and plotting.

I. Stratigraphic accumulation

Based on soil properties, colors and items contained, strata in this area are summarized and classified into 6 strata, number ⑥ is missing in the large part of this unit (Figure 95; Plate 87∶1).

Stratum ①: Thickness of 10 – 15cm; yellow – gray color topsoil; loose soil, containing a small amount of ceramic, plastic and plant roots *etc.*; H9 opening is under this stratum.

Stratum ②: Thickness of 0 – 10cm, depth of 10 – 15cm; yellowish red color soil, soil is hard, containing a large amount of red bricks, some blue and white porcelain pieces, white porcelain pieces and a very small amount of stone tools; accumulated over modern and contemporary times.

Stratum ③: Thickness of 10 – 24cm, depth of 10 – 20cm; light gray – color soil, of fine soil. containing small amount of bricks and porcelain pieces among other items. Opening of H10, H11, H12, H13, H14, and H30 pits is under this stratum; accumulated over modern and contemporary times.

Stratum ④: Based on differences in soil properties and colors, this stratum can be divided into two secondary strata, deposited in the Đại Việt dynasty and early Lê dynasty.

Stratum ④a: Thickness of 0 – 18cm, depth of 28 – 34cm; dark brown color ferromanganese soil stratum, containing large amount of iron rust, inclined from southeast corner towards north; containing very small amount of porcelain pieces, bricks and other items. Opening of H4, H5, H15, H16, and H17 pits is under this stratum (④b missing at opening of pit).

Stratum ④b: Thickness of 0 – 12cm, depth of 42cm; grayish brown ferromanganese, containing small amount of iron rust, distributing in northeast part only, containing very small amount of porcelain pieces, bricks and other items. H2 opening is under this stratum.

Stratum ⑤: Based on differences in soil properties and colors, this stratum can be divided into two secondary strata, accumulated in the Phung Nguyen culture period.

⑤a: Thickness of 0 – 44cm, depth of 26 – 44cm; Dark – gray color soil; soil is loose, containing lots of burnt soil particles, including a large number of pottery pieces and a small number of stone tools. H18, H19 opening is under this stratum.

⑤b: Thickness of 0 – 35cm, depth of 40 – 60cm; gray yellow color soil; soil is hard; distributing southwards from north; containing little items, mainly pottery pieces and stone tools.

Stratum ⑥: Thickness of 0 – 40cm, depth of 62 – 86cm; distributing only in southwest part of the square unit, yellowish brown soil, mixed with small amount of gray soil stains, hard soil; containing a small number of pottery pieces; accumulated in the Phung Nguyen culture period.

Under this stratum is reddish – brown ferromanganese raw soil.

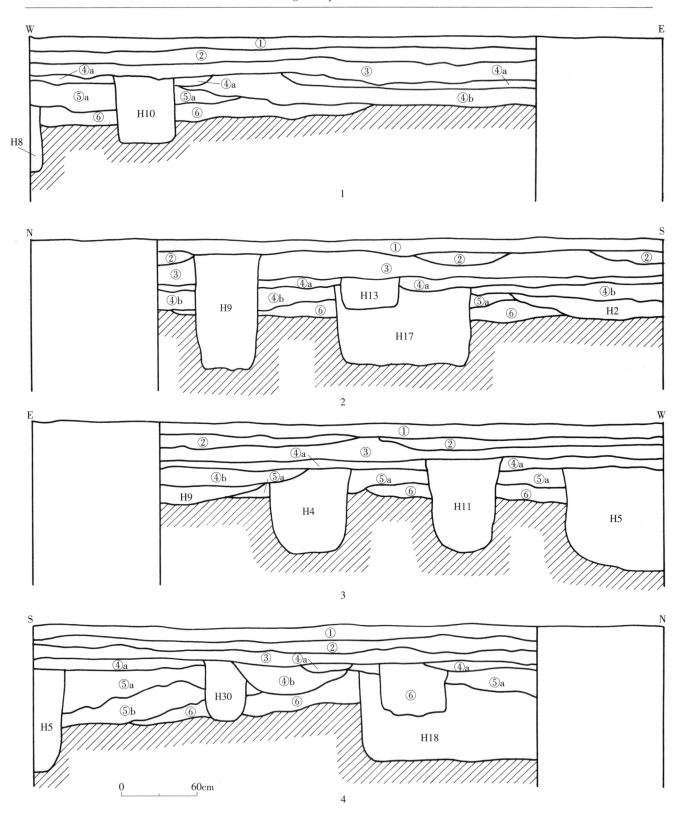

Figure 95　Sectional View of Four Walls of T5
1.　North wall　2.　East wall　3.　South wall　4.　West wall

II. Remains

A total of 37 remains of various types were found in this square unit, including 12 pits (excluding H2, H4 and H5 shared with T2) and 25 postholes. Except for 7 pits of H9, H10, H11, H12, H13, H14 and H30 which are from modern and contemporary times, the remaining ones are from Phung Nguyen culture period and these are presented below.

1. Pits: 5 pits

H15 is located in northwest of T5, opening under stratum ④a (④b missing in this area), breaking⑤a, ⑥ and H18.

Shape and structure: Irregular rectangle, uneven walls, uneven bottom; of length of 0.8, width of 0.64, depth of 0.2 – 0.36 meters (Figure 97:1); filing is grayish black soil, soil is loose, containing a small number of burnt soil particles and charcoal.

Unearthed items: All are pottery pieces, 29 pieces in total, mostly fine earthenware, less coarse earthenware, mostly reddish brown earthenware and brown ones, with small number of terracotta, grayish brown and blackish brown ones. Decorations are mostly twist line pattern, with some concave string pattern and combed dots. Forms are mostly ring feet and enclosure bases. Identified forms are bowls and kettles. 1 specimen is selected for H15.

Pottery kettle: 1 piece.

Specimen H15:1, grayish brown fine sand earthenware, drum belly, belly decorated with engraved patterns; remaining part of height of 6.5cm (Figure 97:2).

H16 is located in the west part of T5, opening under stratum ④a (④b missing), breaking ⑤a, ⑥ and H18.

Shape and structure: Irregular rectangle, uneven walls, uneven bottom; of length of 2.14, width of 1.8, depth of 0.5m (Figure 98:1). Filling is grayish black soil; soil is loose, containing a small number of burnt soil particles and charcoal (Plate 87:2).

Unearthed items: Except for 1 jade piece, the others are pottery pieces, 188 in total, mostly fine earthenware, of reddish brown earthenware, some number of yellowish brown, grayish brown, terracotta, brown and blackish brown. Decorations are mostly twist line pattern, with some concave string pattern, engraved patterns, geometrical patterns and combed dots etc. Forms are mostly ring feet and enclosure bases. Identified are bowls, kettles, flare mouth jars.

Jade pendant: 1 piece.

Specimen H16:1, remaining half, beige color, body of round shape, with a hole; diameter of 5.1, width of 0.7, thickness of 0.1cm (Figure 98:2; Plate 88).

H17 is located in east of T5, partly laminated under east beam of the unit, opening under stratum ④a (④b missing), broken by H13, breaking ⑤a, ⑥ and D20.

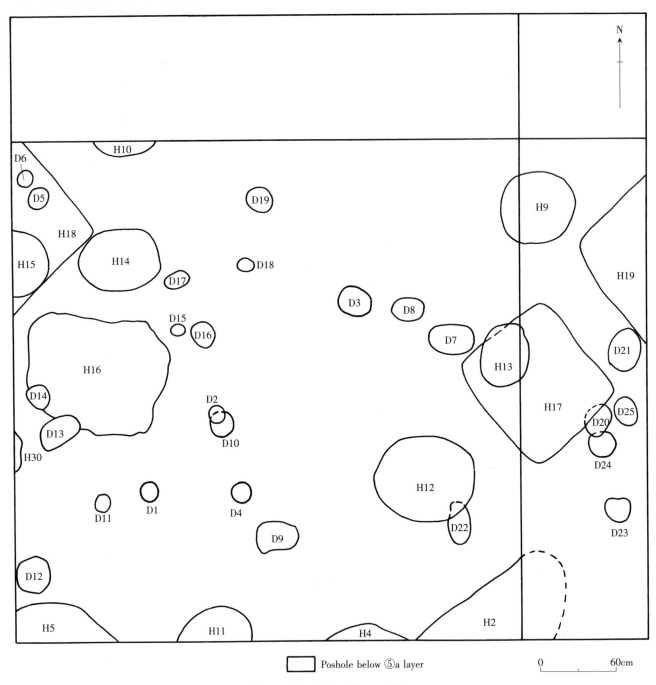

Figure 96   Plan View of T5

Shape and structure: Rectangular in plane view, uneven walls, uneven bottom; of length of 1. 14, width of 1, depth of 0. 72 m (Figure 99:1). Filling is grayish black soil, soil is loose, containing a small number of burnt soil particles and charcoal.

Unearthed items: All are pottery pieces, 188 in total, mostly fine earthenware and coarse earthenware, with some clay earthenware, of reddish brown earthenware, some number of yellowish brown, grayish brown, terracotta, brown and blackish brown. Decorations are mostly twist line pattern, with some concave string pattern, engraved patterns, geometrical patterns and combed dots *etc.* (Figure

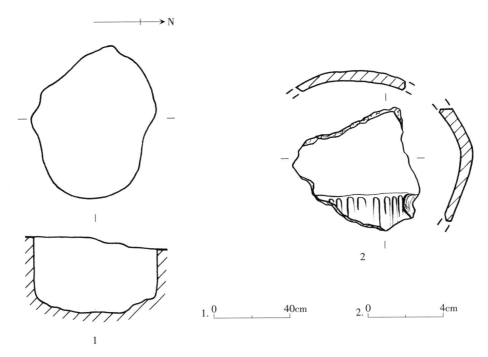

Figure 97   Sectional Plan and Unearthed Artifacts of H15
1. Sectional plan   2. Pottery kettle（H15：1）

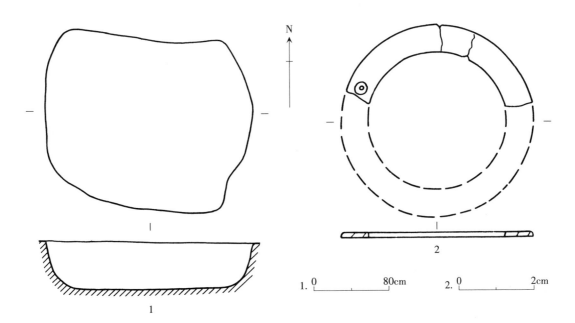

Figure 98   Sectional Plan and Unearthed Artifacts of H16
1. Sectional plan   2. Jade *jue*（H16：1）

99：3，4）. Forms are mostly ring feet. Identified are bowls, straight mouth jars. 3 specimens are selected from H17, of which 1 is form specimen and 2 are ornamentation specimens.

Thick lip jar： 1 piece.

Specimen H17：1, terracotta, of thick square lip, under mouth decorated with one concave string；

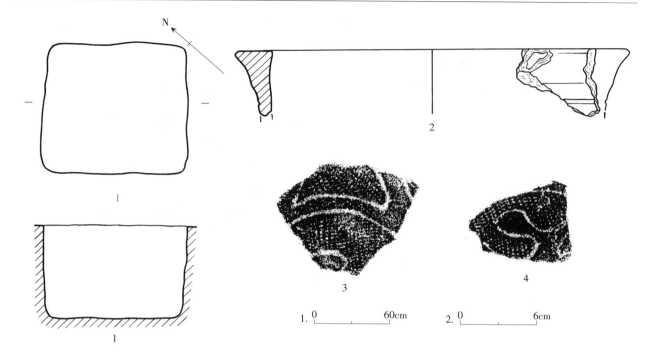

Figure 99   Sectional Plan and Unearthed Artifacts of H17
1. Sectional plan   2. Pottery thick lip jar (H17:1)   3, 4. Geometrical form pattern + combed
dot pattern (H17:2, 3)

bore diameter of 30, remaining part of height of 5. 2cm (Figure 99:2).

H18 is located in the northwest corner of T5, partly laminated under west wall and north beam, opening under stratum ⑤a, broken by H15 and D5, D6, breaking ⑥ and raw soil.

Shape and structure: Irregular rectangle, uneven walls, uneven bottom; of length of 1. 3, width of 1 − 1. 4, depth of 0. 6 meters (Figure 100:1). Filling is grayish black soil, soil is loose, containing a small number of burnt soil particles and charcoal.

Unearthed items: All are pottery pieces, 43 in total, mostly fine earthenware and coarse earthenware, with some clay earthenware, of reddish brown earthenware, some number of yellowish brown, grayish brown, terracotta, brown and blackish brown. Decorations are mostly concave string pattern, with some twist line pattern, engraved patterns, geometrical patterns and combed dots *etc.* (Figure 100:2). Identified are bowls, flare mouth jars.

H19: Under east beam of T5, opening under stratum ⑤a, breaking ⑥ and raw soil.

Shape and structure: Irregular rectangle, uneven walls, uneven bottom; remaining part of length of 1. 1; remaining part of width of 0. 8, depth of 0. 22 meters (Figure 101:1). Filling is grayish black soil, soil is loose, containing a small number of burnt soil particles and charcoal.

Unearthed items: All are pottery pieces, 10 in total, mostly fine earthenware and coarse earthenware, of terracotta, some number of yellowish brown, grayish brown, reddish brown and blackish brown. Decorations are mostly twist line pattern, with some engraved patterns and concave string pat-

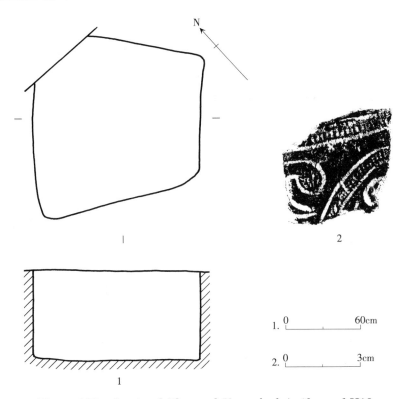

Figure 100   Sectional Plan and Unearthed Artifacts of H18
1. Sectional plan   2. Geometrical form pattern + combed dot pattern（H18:1）

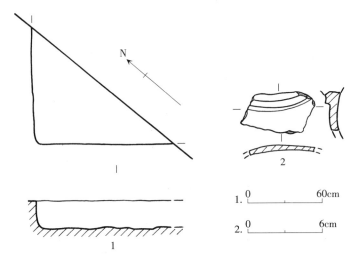

Figure 101   Sectional Plan and Unearthed Artifacts of H19
1. Sectional plan   2. Ring foot（H19:1）

tern. Identified are ring feet. 1 specimen is selected from H19.

Ring foot: 1 piece.

Specimen H19:1, reddish brown sand earthenware, only remaining ring foot; remaining part of height of 3cm（Figure 101:2）.

2. Postholes: 25

Postholes: 25 in total (Figure 102), all opening under Stratum ⑤a. Plane shapes are substantially circular or oval. Walls are smooth. Bottoms are bell shaped or flat. Fillings are grayish black soil, distinct from surrounding soils, loose soil. Postholes of this exploration square unit are listed below.

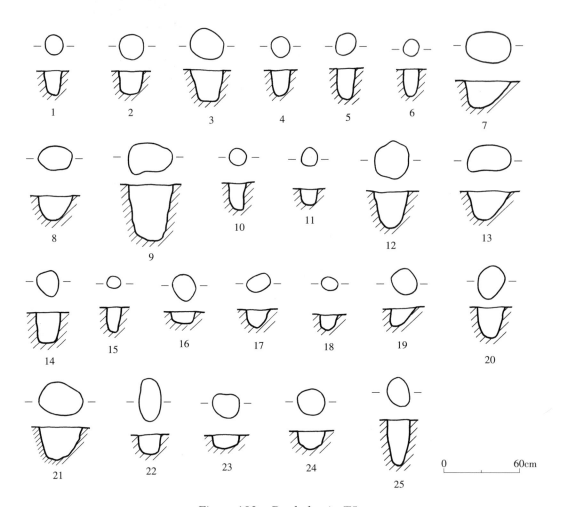

Figure 102   Postholes in T5
1 – 25. Posthole (D1 – D25)

Table 5   Statistics of Pits and Postholes in Strata under T5   Unit: cm

S/N	Numbering	Horizon level	Shape and structure			Dimensions (diameter – depth)	Soil	Figure No.
			Plane form	Walls of the pit	Bottom of pit			
1	D1	⑤a	Round	Smooth	Dome shaped	14 – 20	Grayish black soil	Figure 102 : 1
2	D2	⑤a	Round	Smooth	Dome shaped	20 – 18	Grayish black soil	Figure 102 : 2
3	D3	⑤a	Round	Smooth	Dome shaped	26 – 24	Grayish black soil	Figure 102 : 3
4	D4	⑤a	Round	Smooth	Dome shaped	15 – 20	Black soil	Figure 102 : 4

(continued 5)

S/N	Numbering	Horizon level	Shape and structure			Dimensions (diameter – depth)	Soil	Figure No.
			Plane form	Walls of the pit	Bottom of pit			
5	D5	⑤a	Round	Rough	Round bottom	17 – 24	Grayish black soil	Figure 102:5
6	D6	⑤a	Round	Smooth	Round bottom	13 – 22	Grayish black soil	Figure 102:6
7	D7	⑤a	Oval	Rough	Round bottom	24 ~ 36 – 22	Black soil	Figure 102:7
8	D8	⑤a	Oval	Relatively smooth	Round bottom	19 ~ 27 – 19	Grayish black soil	Figure 102:8
9	D9	⑤a	Almost rectangular	Rough	Round bottom	18 ~ 36 – 44	Black soil	Figure 102:9
10	D10	⑤a	Round	Rough	Round bottom	14 – 21	Grayish black soil	Figure 102:10
11	D11	⑤a	Round	Smooth	Flat	13 – 13	Black soil	Figure 102:11
12	D12	⑤a	Round	Relatively smooth	Flat	28 – 29	Grayish black soil	Figure 102:12
13	D13	⑤a	Oval	Rough	Uneven	20 ~ 35 – 23	Black soil	Figure 102:13
14	D14	⑤a	Round	Relatively smooth	Relatively even	18 – 25	Grayish black soil	Figure 102:14
15	D15	⑤a	Round	Smooth	Flat	11 – 20	Grayish black soil	Figure 102:15
16	D16	⑤a	Round	Smooth	Dome shaped	19 – 10	Black soil	Figure 102:16
17	D17	⑤a	Oval	Rough	Round bottom	12 ~ 20 – 13	Grayish black soil	Figure 102:17
18	D18	⑤a	Round	Relatively smooth	Dome shaped	14 – 12	Black soil	Figure 102:18
19	D19	⑤a	Round	Rough	Uneven	20 – 15	Grayish black soil	Figure 102:19
20	D20	⑤a	Oval	Rough	Round bottom	14 ~ 27 – 24	Grayish black soil	Figure 102:20
21	D21	⑤a	Oval	Relatively even	Round bottom	26 ~ 34 – 27	Grayish black soil	Figure 102:21
22	D22	⑤a	Oval	Rough	Dome shaped	18 ~ 35 – 16	Grayish black soil	Figure 102:22
23	D23	⑤a	Irregular oval	Relatively smooth	Dome shaped	19 ~ 22 – 11	Grayish black soil	Figure 102:23
24	D24	⑤a	Round	Rough	Dome shaped	22 – 14	Black soil	Figure 102:24
25	D25	⑤a	Oval	Relatively smooth	Round bottom	13 ~ 18 – 37	Grayish black soil	Figure 102:25

III. Unearthed artifacts

1. Unearthed artifacts of stratum T5⑤a

Mostly pottery pieces, with a small number of stone tools. A total of 58 specimens are selected, including 4 stone tool and 54 pottery pieces.

Stone tools: 4 pieces; all adzes; based on shape and structure, these can be classified into two categories.

Adze: 4 pieces.

Category 1: 3 pieces; body shape is of rectangle, ground to shape.

Specimen T5⑤a:2, damaged, double – sided arc blade, impact points and radiation rays from

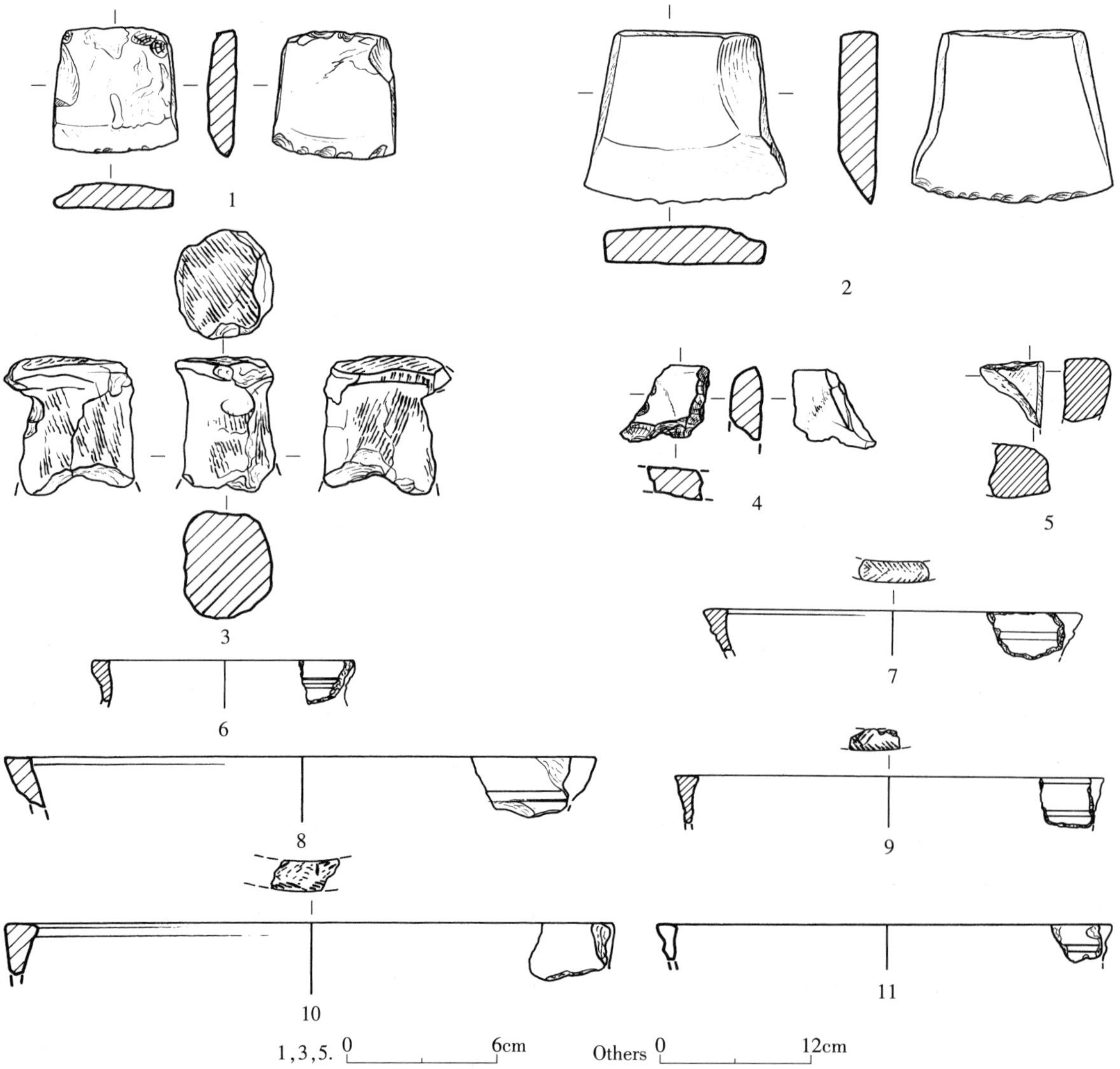
1
2
3
4
5
6
7
8
9
10
11
1,3,5. 0 6cm
Others 0 12cm

Figure 103 Stone Tools and Pottery Pieces Unearthed from T5

1, 2, 4, 5. Stone adze (T5⑤a:2, 1, 5, 3) 3. Pottery base (T5⑤a:4) 6 – 11. Pottery thick lip jar (T5⑤a:9, T5⑤b:1, T5⑤a:6, T5⑤a:8, T5⑤a:7, T5⑤a:55)

impact are visible on top; of length of 5. 4, width of 5, thickness of 1cm (Figure 103 : 1; Plate 89 : 1). Specimen T5⑤a : 3, badly damaged, only a corner on top remains, remaining part of length of 2. 8; remaining part of width of 2. 5, thickness of 2. 5cm (Figure 103 : 5). Specimen T5⑤a : 5, damaged, double – sided arc blade, impact points and radiation rays from impact are visible; of length of 6, width of 5. 3, thickness of 2. 4cm (Figure 103 : 4).

Category 2: Trapezoid, single – sided arc blade.

Specimen T5⑤a : 1, blade bent outward, apparent traces of use on blade; remaining part of length of 3. 6, width of 4. 1, thickness of 0. 8cm (Figure 103 : 2; Plate 89 : 2).

Pottery pieces: A total of 958 potter pieces were unearthed in Stratum ⑤a in this square unit. In terms of the earthenware materials, fine sand earthenware accounts for about 85%, coarse sand earthenware for about 13%, and clay polished earthenware for about 3%. In terms of colors of the pottery pieces, terracotta, reddish brown, and brown pottery pieces account for about 862%, indicating that the pottery color is mostly reddish. In terms of pattern ornamentation, it was extremely well – developed, accounting for 42% of the total number of pottery pieces. The decorations are of great variety, in which rope decorations account for about 54% of the total decorations. Other decorations include engraved line, stamp, concave string, protruding rim, pressure stamp, comb brushing and added mound etc. (Figure 104; Plates 90, 91). Particularly among all the engraved lines, the ones with comb teeth brushed or comb dotted stamps are the most characteristic. Compound ornamentations of multiple decorations on a single pottery piece appear to have been very popular. The main ornamentation patterns are of leaf veins, clouds, S – shape, geometric patterns, circles and water ripples, of which various shapes of cloud patterns, connected cloud patterns and S – shapes are most common. Pottery mouth parts are mostly contracted or flared; followed in number by trumpet – shaped and straight mouths. The artifacts are mostly with enclosure base and ring feet. Forms of the artifacts include bases, thick lip jars, bowls, ring feet, trumpet – shape mouth jar and flare mouth jars (Plates 92, 93).

In Stratum ⑤a within the square unit: a total of 54 specimens of pottery pieces are selected, of which 24 specimens are for ornamentations (including 3 coinciding with form specimens), 29 specimens are for forms, including 1 base, 5 thick lip jars, 8 bowls, 9 ring feet, 5 trumpet – shape mouth jars and 1 flare mouth jar.

Base: 1 piece.

Specimen T5⑤a : 4, terracotta, top oval shape flared, filled, decorated with twist line pattern; top long diameter of 5. 2, shorter diameter of 4, remaining part of height of 6cm (Figure 103 : 3).

Thick lip jars: 5 pieces; shape and structure are substantially similar; thickness of square lip.

Specimen T5⑤a : 8, terracotta, straight mouth slightly contracted, lip decorated with spiral twist pattern, neck decorated with one concave string; bore diameter of 34. 6, remaining part of height of 4. 2cm (Figure 103 : 9). Specimen T5⑤a : 6, grayish brown sand earthenware, straight mouth slightly

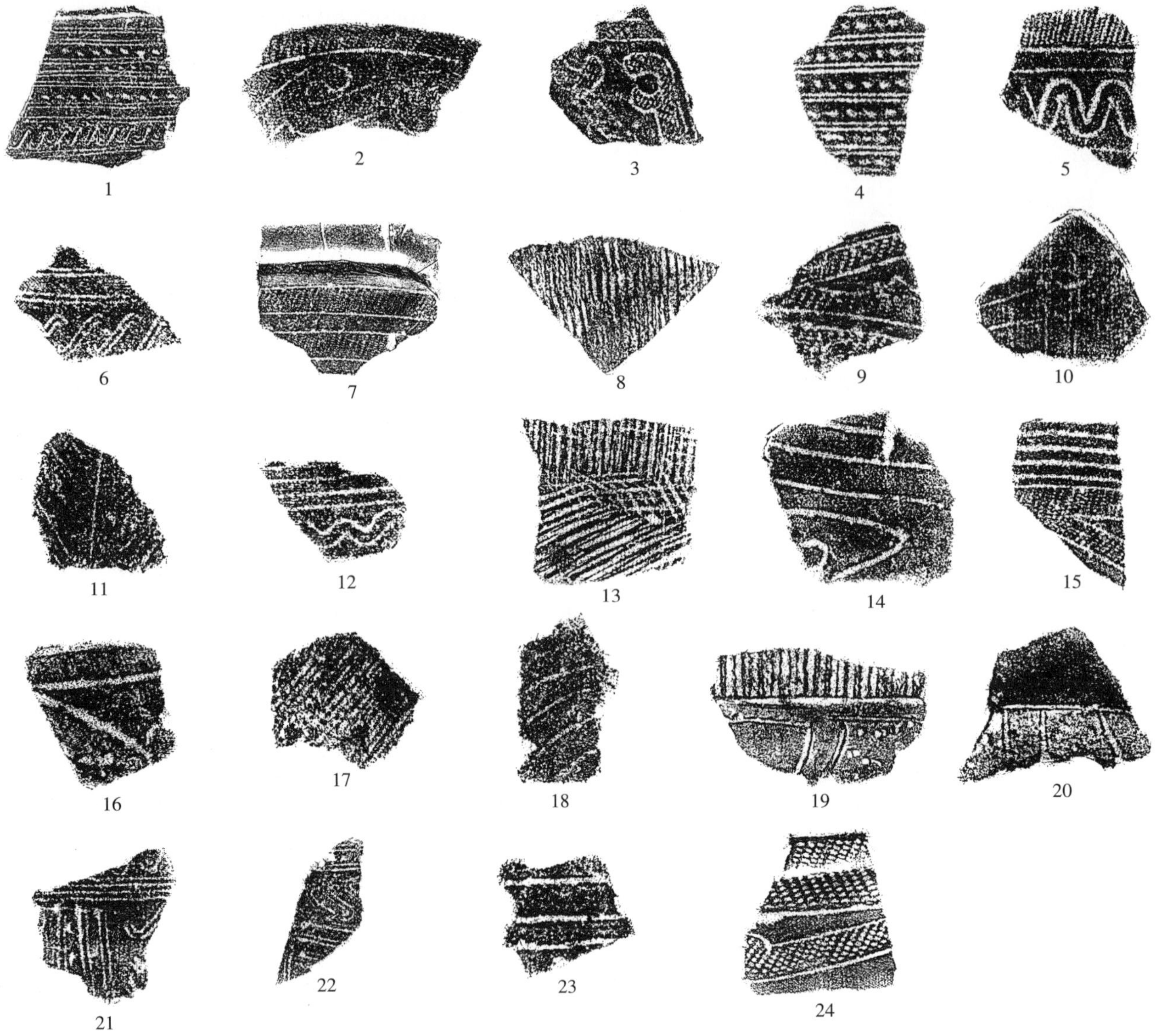

Figure 104 Rubbings of Pottery Pieces Unearthed from Stratum T5⑤a

1. Pit dot pattern + concave string pattern + S – shape pattern (T5⑤a: 11) 2, 3. Geometrical form pattern + combed dot pattern (T5⑤a: 13, 38) 4. Pit dot pattern + concave string pattern (T5⑤a: 39) 5. Concave string pattern + combed dot pattern + water ripple pattern (T5⑤a: 46) 6. Concave string pattern + S – shape pattern (T5⑤a: 47) 7. Protruding rim pattern + combed dot pattern + concave string pattern (T5⑤a: 20) 8. Rope pattern (T5⑤a: 33) 9. Geometrical form pattern + combed dot pattern (T5⑤a: 40) 10. Engraved pattern + rope pattern (T5⑤a: 41) 11. Leaf vein pattern (T5⑤a: 48) 12. Water ripple pattern + concave string pattern (T5⑤a: 49) 13. Rope pattern (T5⑤a: 34) 14. Concave string pattern + engraved pattern (T5⑤a: 35) 15. Geometrical form pattern + combed dot pattern + engraved pattern (T5⑤a: 42) 16. Engraved pattern (T5⑤a: 43) 17. Rope pattern (T5⑤a: 50) 18. Engraved pattern (T5⑤a: 51) 19. Rope pattern + engraved pattern (T5⑤a: 36) 20. 21. Engraved pattern (T5⑤a: 37, 44) 22. S – shape pattern + engraved pattern (T5⑤a: 45) 23. Concave string pattern (T5⑤a: 52) 24. Geometrical form pattern + combed dot pattern (T5⑤a: 54)

flared, under mouth decorated with one concave string; bore diameter of 48. 2, remaining part of height of 5. 4cm (Figure 103: 8). Specimen T5⑤a: 7, terracotta, square lip, lip decorated with spiral twist pattern; bore diameter of 49. 6, remaining part of height of 4. 8cm (Figure 103: 10). Specimen T5⑤a: 9, terracotta, straight mouth slightly flared, neck decorated with three concave strings; bore diameter of 21. 6, remaining part of height of 3. 8cm (Figure 103 : 6). Specimen T5⑤a : 55, brown sand earthenware, one protruding rim decorated under the mouth ; bore diameter of 36. 8, remaining part of height of 3cm (Figure 103 : 11).

Bowls: 8 pieces ; can be classified into three categories based on shape and structure.

Category 1 : 3 pieces ; flare mouth, shoulder decorated with a protruding rim.

Specimen T5⑤a : 28, fine brown earthenware ; round lip, arc belly ; bore diameter of 34. 4, remaining part of height of 3. 5cm (Figure 105 : 1). Specimen T5⑤a : 30, fine gray earthenware, round lip ; bore diameter of 29. 2, remaining part of height of 3. 4cm (Figure 105 : 4). Specimen T5⑤a : 32, grayish brown sand earthenware, round lip, neck decorated with one concave string ; bore diameter of

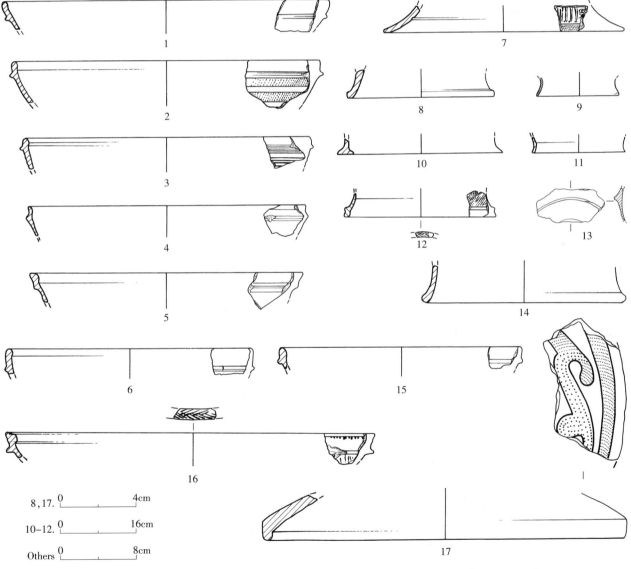

Figure 105   Pottery Bowls and Ring Feet Unearthed from Strata T5⑤a and T5⑤b
1 – 6, 15, 16. Bowl (T5⑤a : 28, T5⑤a : 20, T5⑤a : 31, T5⑤a : 30, T5⑤a : 32, T5⑤a : 29, T5⑤b : 2, T5⑤a : 21)
7 – 14, 17. Ring foot (T5⑤a : 25, 26, 22, 23, 53, 12, 24, 16, 13)

28. 2, remaining part of height of 4cm (Figure 105 : 5). Specimen T5⑤a : 27, blackish brown earthenware, round lip; bore diameter of 33. 6, remaining part of height of 2. 8cm (Figure 106 : 1).

Category 2: 4 pieces; contracted mouth, shoulder decorated with a protruding rim.

Specimen T5⑤a : 20, fine terracotta, round lip, arc belly, belly decorated with 4 concave string pattern, two sets of concave string pattern with combed dots; bore diameter of 32. 4, remaining part of height of 5. 1cm (Figure 105 : 2; Plate 94 : 1). Specimen T5⑤a : 31, reddish brown fine sand earthenware, round lip, belly decorated with 6 concave string pattern; bore diameter of 30. 2, remaining part of height of 3. 4cm (Figure 105 : 3). Specimen T5⑤a : 29, fine terracotta, round lip, under the protruding rim decorated with poked lines; bore diameter of 26, remaining part of height of 2. 8cm (Figure 105 : 6). Specimen T5⑤a : 21, reddish brown sand earthenware, round lip, lip decorated with poked triangular pattern, shoulder decorated with twist line pattern; bore diameter of 38. 7, remaining part of height of 3. 3cm (Figure 105 : 16).

Category 3: 1 piece; contracted mouth, without protruding rim on the shoulder.

Specimen T5⑤a : 10, reddish brown sand earthenware, round lip, contracted mouth; bore diameter of 30, remaining part of height of 4. 3cm (Figure 106 : 2).

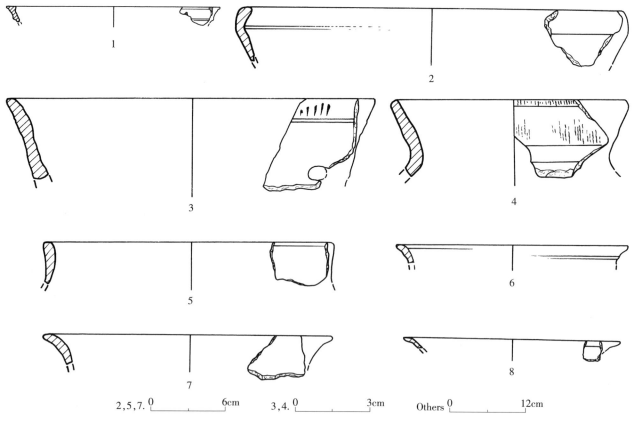

Figure 106   Pottery Pieces Unearthed from Stratum T5⑤a

1, 2. Bowl (T5⑤a : 27, 10)   3, 4, 6 - 8. Trumpet - shape mouth jar (T5⑤a : 1, 19, 14, 17, 15)   6. Flared mouth jar (T5⑤a : 18)

Ring feet: 9 pieces; classified into three categories based on the foot (Plate 94:2, 3).

Category 1: 7 pieces; horn – shaped ring foot, foot tip bent outward.

Specimen T5⑤a:25, fine terracotta, lower foot decorated with concave string and combed dots, upper part decorated with engraved line patterns; diameter at bottom of 25.6, remaining part of height of 2.7cm (Figure 105:7). Specimen T5⑤a:22, fine grayish brown earthenware; diameter at bottom of 8.7, remaining part of height of 1.8cm (Figure 105:9). Specimen T5⑤a:23, fine grayish brown earthenware; diameter at bottom of 35.2, remaining part of height of 3.2cm (Figure 105:10). Specimen T5⑤a:53, reddish brown sand earthenware, diameter at bottom of 19.8, remaining part of height of 3.2cm (Figure 105:11). Specimen T5⑤a:12, reddish brown sand earthenware, ring foot bottom decorated with poked triangular pattern, on the lower part of foot decorated with a protruding rim, upper part decorated with spiral twist pattern; bore diameter of 32.4, remaining part of height of 5.6cm (Figure 105:12). Specimen T5⑤a:24, grayish brown sand earthenware, only middle part of ring foot remains; remaining part of width of 7.2cm (Figure 105:13). Specimen T5⑤a:16, reddish brown sand earthenware. diameter at bottom of 21.6, remaining part of height of 3.8cm (Figure 105:14).

Category 2: 1 piece; horn – shaped ring foot, foot tip bent upward.

Specimen T5⑤a:26, fine terracotta, diameter at bottom of 15.6, remaining part of height of 2.6cm (Figure 105:8).

Category 3: 1 piece; horn – shaped ring foot, foot tip bent inward.

Specimen T5⑤a:13, reddish brown sand earthenware, on the lower part of foot decorated with two concave string and combed dots, upper part of foot decorated with engraved cloud pattern, cloud pattern decorated with combed dots; bore diameter of 19.3, remaining part of height of 2.4cm (Figure 105:17).

Trumpet - shape mouth jars: 5 pieces; of similar shape and structure, round lip, trumpet mouth.

Specimen T5⑤a:1, reddish brown sand earthenware, under mouth decorated with one concave string patterns and poked dots; lower neck has a bore diameter; bore diameter of 14.5, remaining part of height of 3.6cm (Figure 106:3). Specimen T5⑤a:19, fine terracotta, lip poked seesaw pattern, neck decorated with vertical twist pattern; bore diameter of 9.3, remaining part of height of 3cm (Figure 106:4). Specimen T5⑤a:14, gray earthenware, upper neck decorated with one concave string; bore diameter of 36, remaining part of height of 2.8cm (Figure 106:6). Specimen T5⑤a:15, reddish brown sand earthenware. bore diameter of 34, remaining part of height of 3.2cm (Figure 106:8). Specimen T5⑤a:17, terracotta; bore diameter of 22.8, remaining part of height of 3.5cm (Figure 106:7).

Flare mouth jar: 1 piece.

Specimen T5⑤a:18, gray earthenware, round lip; bore diameter of 23, remaining part of height of 3.5cm (Figure 106:5).

2. Unearthed artifacts of stratum T5⑤b

Artifacts are all pottery pieces, 18 in total, mostly fine earthenware and coarse earthenware, with some clay earthenware, of reddish brown earthenware, some number of yellowish brown, grayish brown, terracotta, brown and blackish brown. Decorations are mostly concave string pattern, with some twist line pattern and combed dots *etc*. Identified are bowls and straight mouth jars. 2 specimens are selected from this stratum, 1 straight mouth jar and 1 bowl.

Thick lip jar: 1 piece.

Specimen T5⑤b : 1, reddish brown fine sand earthenware, square lip, lip poked triangle patterns; bore diameter of 30. 6, remaining part of height of 4cm (Figure 103 : 7).

Bowl: 1 piece.

Specimen T5⑤b : 2, fine terracotta, round lip, with a protruding rim decorated under the mouth; bore diameter of 25. 8, remaining part of height of 2. 4cm (Figure 105 : 15).

Section Six T7

T7 is located in western part of the excavation area. The square units for exploration were planned out and excavation works commenced on December 13, 2006 and exploration was completed on January 8, 2007. Sun Weigang and Yue Lianjian were in charge of conducting excavations, making records and plotting.

I. Stratigraphic accumulation

7 strata in T4, namely ①, ②, ③, ④, ⑤, ⑥; unevenly deposited along the four walls of unit, some on west of unit, south wall missing (Figure 107).

Stratum ①: Thickness of 10cm; top soil; soil is loose, with large amount of sands; yellowish gray; with some bricks, tiles and porcelain pieces.

Stratum ②: Depth of 10, thickness of 5 – 10cm; disturbed soil; compacted soil; yellowish red; with many bricks, tiles and porcelain pieces; accumulated over modern and contemporary times. G2 opening is under this stratum.

Stratum ③: Depth of 10 – 20, thickness of 0 – 15cm; disturbed soil; compacted, pure, with many bricks, pottery pieces and porcelain pieces; accumulated over modern and contemporary times. H29 and H32 opening is under this stratum.

Stratum ④a: Depth of 20 – 40, thickness of 0 – 15cm; dark brown ferromanganese layer; containing iron sand soil, loose soil; deposited in the Đại Việt dynasty and early Lê dynasty. Posthole 26 opening is under this stratum.

Stratum ⑤a: Depth of 22 – 40, thickness of 0 – 18cm; of Phung Nguyen culture; loose, burnt and blackish soil; found pottery pieces, stone tools, damaged jade rings and other relics, possibly from Phung Nguyen culture; 19 postholes opening is under this stratum.

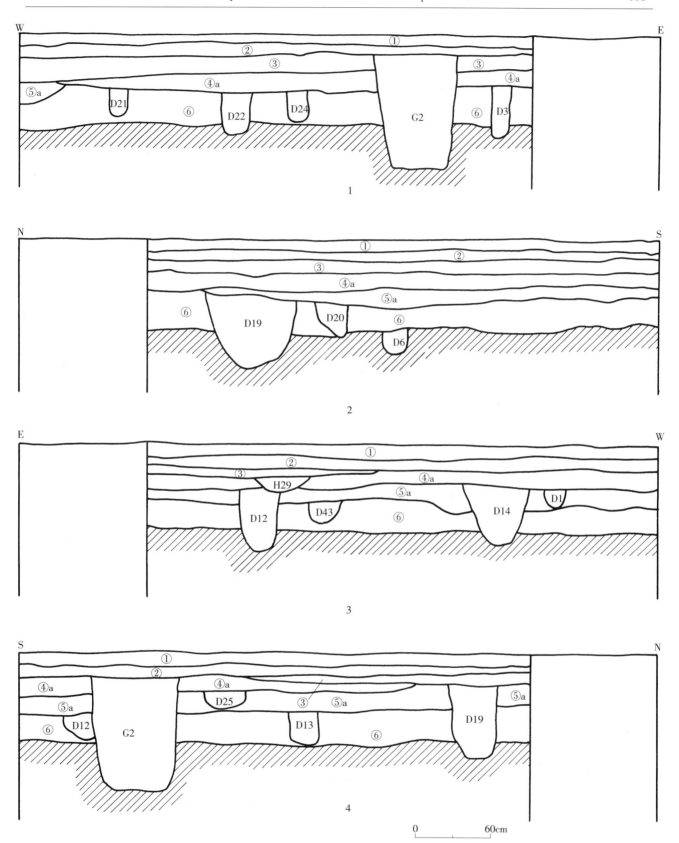

Figure 107   Sectional View of Four Walls of T7
1. North wall   2. East wall   3. South wall   4. West wall

Stratum ⑥: Depth of 40 – 50, thickness of 20 – 36cm; hard, yellowish brown soil mixed with gray soil stains; a small number of pottery pieces; H33 and 16 postholes opening is under this stratum.

Under this stratum is reddish – brown ferromanganese raw soil.

II. Remains

64 sites found in the unit, including 2 pits, 1 ditch, and 61 postholes (Figure 108; Plate 95). Other than H32 and G2 are from contemporary and modern times, the 62 sites are all from Phung

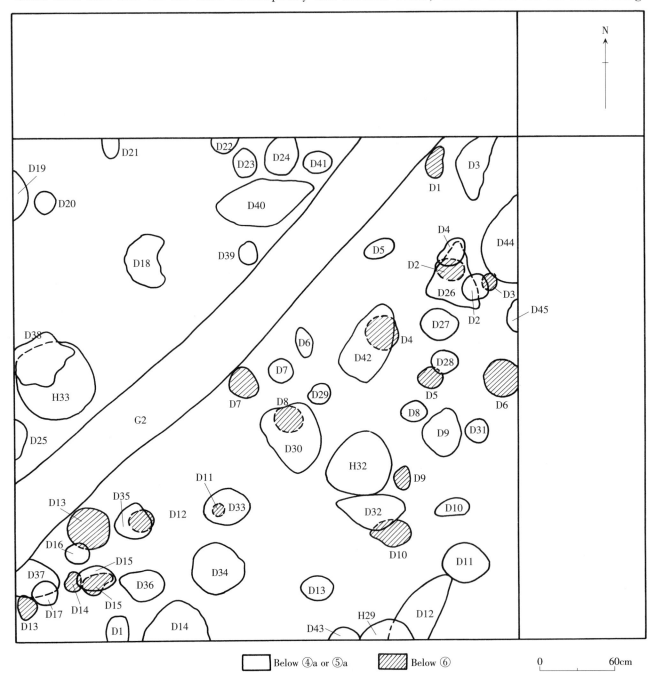

Figure 108   Plan View of T7

Nguyen culture period.

1. Pit: 1, H33

H33 is located in center of west side of unit, opening under stratum ⑥, breaking raw soil.

Shape and structure: Near round shape of bucket form, not even, diameter of 0. 62, depth of 0. 34 – 0. 5 meters (Figure 109). Properties and color of soil basically the same as ⑥; breaking through raw soil. No relic is found.

2. Postholes: 61

26 have opening under stratum ④, 19 opening under stratum ⑤a, 16 opening under stratum ⑥; plane of round shape or oval, regular, some damage seen, indicating original columns, filling of grayish black soil or black soil, soil is loose, containing a small number of pottery pieces. However, these postholes are together with large number of pits, making it difficult to analyze the building as a whole.

To accurately reflect pits and postholes in this unit, these are listed below.

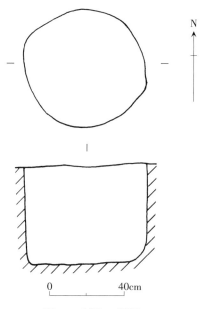

Figure 109   H33

Table 6   Statistics of Postholes in T7   Unit: cm

S/N	Numbering	Horizon level	Shape and structure			Dimensions (diameter – depth)	Soil	Figure No.
			Plane form	Walls of the pit	Bottom of pit			
1	D1	④a	Round	Smooth	Uneven	22 – 24	Grayish black soil	Figure 110：1
2	D2	④a	Round	Relatively smooth	Relatively even	23 – 17	Grayish black soil	Figure 110：2
3	D3	④a	Irregular oval	Rough	Relatively even	17 ~ 53 – 35	Black soil	Figure 110：3
4	D4	④a	Irregular oval	Rough	Flat	17 ~ 28 – 41	Grayish black soil	Figure 110：4
5	D5	④a	Oval	Rough	Uneven	15 ~ 27 – 28	Grayish black soil	Figure 110：5
6	D6	④a	Irregular oval	Relatively smooth	Uneven	15 ~ 23 – 13	Black soil	Figure 110：6
7	D7	④a	Round	Smooth	Flat	22 – 43	Grayish black soil	Figure 110：7
8	D8	④a	Round	Smooth	Uneven	23 – 20	Black soil	Figure 110：8
9	D9	④a	Irregular oval	Rough	Uneven	33 ~ 40 – 44	Grayish black soil	Figure 110：9
10	D10	④a	Irregular oval	Rough	Uneven	15 ~ 30 – 12	Grayish black soil	Figure 110：10
11	D11	④a	Round	Rough	Uneven	37 – 40	Grayish black soil	Figure 110：11

(continued 6)

S/N	Numbering	Horizon level	Shape and structure			Dimensions (diameter – depth)	Soil	Figure No.
			Plane form	Walls of the pit	Bottom of pit			
12	D12	④a	Round	Relatively smooth	Flat	30 ~ 63 – 25	Grayish black soil	Figure 110 : 12
13	D13	④a	Round	Relatively smooth	Uneven	27 – 24	Black soil	Figure 110 : 13
14	D14	④a	Round	Smooth	Flat	56 – 20	Grayish black soil	Figure 110 : 14
15	D15	④a	Oval	Rough	Uneven	20 ~ 33 – 17	Grayish black soil	Figure 110 : 15
16	D16	④a	Round	Rough	Flat	20 – 20	Black soil	Figure 110 : 16
17	D17	④a	Round	Smooth	Dome shaped	24 – 13	Grayish black soil	Figure 110 : 17
18	D18	④a	Irregular oval	Rough	Uneven	20 ~ 43 – 37	Grayish black soil	Figure 110 : 18
19	D19	④a	Round	Relatively smooth	Uneven	38 – 19	Grayish black soil	Figure 110 : 19
20	D20	④a	Round	Relatively smooth	Relatively even	17 – 13	Grayish black soil	Figure 110 : 20
21	D21	④a	Oval	Smooth	Flat	13 ~ 17 – 33	Gray soil	Figure 110 : 21
22	D22	④a	Irregular oval	Relatively smooth	Relatively even	14 ~ 23 – 20	Grayish black soil	Figure 110 : 22
23	D23	④a	Round	Relatively smooth	Flat	24 – 28	Grayish black soil	Figure 110 : 23
24	D24	④a	Round	Relatively smooth	Relatively even	30 – 23	Grayish black soil	Figure 110 : 24
25	D25	④a	Round	Relatively smooth	Flat	10 – 17	Grayish black soil	Figure 110 : 25
26	D26	⑤a	Almost triangular	Rough	Round bottom	40 ~ 58 – 46	Gray soil	Figure 110 : 26
27	D27	⑤a	Round	Rough	Sharp circle	30 – 15	Grayish black soil	Figure 110 : 27
28	D28	⑤a	Round	Relatively smooth	Round bottom	23 – 13	Black soil	Figure 110 : 28
29	D29	⑤a	Round	Smooth	Flat	20 – 12	Grayish black soil	Figure 110 : 29
30	D30	⑤a	Oval	Rough	Uneven	43`56 – 20	Grayish black soil	Figure 110 : 30
31	D31	⑤a	Round	Smooth	Flat	20 – 14	Grayish black soil	Figure 110 : 31
32	D32	⑤a	Oval	Rough	Flat	30 ~ 56 – 7	Grayish black soil	Figure 110 : 32
33	D33	⑤a	Oval	Smooth	Flat	30 ~ 40 – 15	Grayish black soil	Figure 110 : 33
34	D34	⑤a	Round	Rough	Uneven	43 – 13	Grayish black soil	Figure 110 : 34

(continued 6)

S/N	Numbering	Horizon level	Shape and structure			Dimensions (diameter – depth)	Soil	Figure No.
			Plane form	Walls of the pit	Bottom of pit			
35	D35	⑤a	Irregular round	Smooth	Flat	30 – 40	Grayish black soil	Figure 110 : 35
36	D36	⑤a	Irregular oval	Relatively smooth	Uneven	23 ~ 40 – 20	Grayish black soil	Figure 110 : 36
37	D37	⑤a	Irregular oval	Rough	Round bottom	33 ~ 37 – 13	Grayish black soil	Figure 110 : 37
38	D38	⑤a	Irregular rectangle	Rough	Almost flat	23 ~ 50 – 37	Black soil	Figure 110 : 38
39	D39	⑤a	Almost round	Smooth	Flat	17 – 43	Grayish black soil	Figure 110 : 39
40	D40	⑤a	Irregular oval	Relatively smooth	Flat	40 ~ 83 – 32	Grayish black soil	Figure 110 : 40
41	D41	⑤a	Round	Smooth	Flat	26 – 17	Black soil	Figure 110 : 41
42	D42	⑤a	Irregular oval	Relatively smooth	Flat	35 ~ 67 – 25	Grayish black soil	Figure 110 : 42
43	D43	⑤a	Round	Smooth	Dome shaped	27 – 17	Grayish black soil	Figure 110 : 43
44	D44	⑤a	Irregular oval	Rough	Round bottom	27 ~ 73 – 60	Grayish yellow soil	Figure 110 : 44
45	D45	⑤a	Irregular oval	Rough	Uneven	8 ~ 27 – 27	Grayish black soil	Figure 110 : 45
46	D1	⑥	Irregular oval	Rough	Round bottom	13 ~ 27 – 28	Black soil	Figure 110 : 46
47	D2	⑥	Oval	Smooth	Flat	13 ~ 27 – 27	Gray soil	Figure 110 : 47
48	D3	⑥	Round	Smooth	Flat	13 – 13	Black soil	Figure 110 : 48
49	D4	⑥	Round	Rough	Uneven	30 – 17	Gray soil	Figure 110 : 49
50	D5	⑥	Round	Smooth	Round bottom	20 – 17	Grayish yellow	Figure 110 : 50
51	D6	⑥	Round	Smooth	Round bottom	30 – 28	Grayish brown	Figure 110 : 51
52	D7	⑥	Irregular oval	Smooth	Round bottom	17 ~ 27 – 28	Yellowish brown	Figure 110 : 52
53	D8	⑥	Round	Smooth	Round bottom	23 – 13	Grayish brown	Figure 110 : 53
54	D9	⑥	Irregular oval	Smooth	Round bottom	13 ~ 18 – 9	Grayish black soil	Figure 110 : 54
55	D10	⑥	Irregular oval	Rough	Uneven	26 ~ 33 – 10	Black soil	Figure 110 : 55
56	D11	⑥	Round	Smooth	Flat	10 – 20	Grayish black soil	Figure 110 : 56
57	D12	⑥	Round	Smooth	Uneven	20 – 23	Brown soil	Figure 110 : 57
58	D13	⑥	Round	Smooth	Round bottom	35 – 17	Grayish brown	Figure 110 : 58
59	D14	⑥	Round	Smooth	Round bottom	15 – 17	Black soil	Figure 110 : 59
60	D15	⑥	Irregular oval	Rough	Uneven	10 ~ 27 – 20	Grayish black soil	Figure 110 : 60
61	D16	⑥	Irregular oval	Rough	Round bottom	17 ~ 20 – 13	Grayish black soil	Figure 110 : 61

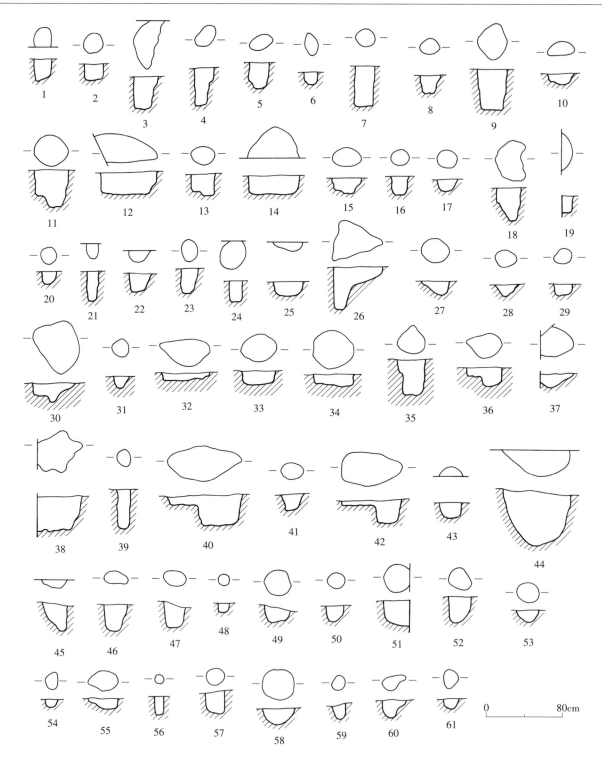

Figure 110   Postholes in T7

1 – 25. Postholes below ④a layer（D1 – D25）   26 – 45. Postholes below ⑤a layer（D26 – D45）

46 – 61. Postholes below ⑥（D1 – D16）

III. Unearthed artifacts

Many artifacts were unearthed in this stratum, mostly pottery pieces and stone tools. A total of 19 specimens are selected, including 9 stone tool and 10 pottery pieces.

Stone tools: 9 pieces; including 2 flappers, 1 grinding stone, 4 stone axes, 2 adzes.

Stone flappers: 2 pieces; slots seen on top; other parts polished.

Specimen T7④aD1：1, severely damaged; rectangular; 4 slots seen on top; remaining part of length of 8.6, width of 6.8, thickness of 7cm (Figure 111：1; Plate 96：1). Specimen T7④a：2, severely damaged; only upper part remains, irregular oval, slot on one side; remaining part of length of 7; remaining part of width of 8.2, thickness of 5.9cm (Figure 111：2).

Grinding stone: 1 piece.

Specimen T7④a：3, oval, grinding traces visible on one side; of length of 6, width of 1.7, thickness of 2cm (Figure 111：3).

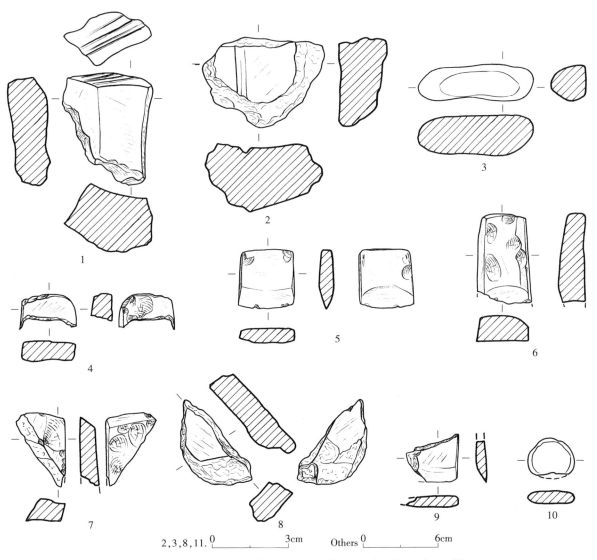

2,3,8,11. |0_____3cm| Others |0_____6cm|

Figure 111　Unearthed Stone and Pottery Artifacts from T7

1, 2. Stone flapper (T7④aD1：1, T7④a：2)　3. Grinding stone (T7④a：3)　4, 6–8. Stone axe (T7④b：3, T7④b：2, T7④b：4, T7④aD1：2)　5, 9. Stone adze (T7②：1, T7④b：1)　10. Pottery tablet (T7④a：1)

Stone axes: 4 pieces; of basically similar shape and structure; rectangular.

Specimen T7④b: 3, severely damaged; only upper part remains, body shape is of rectangle, impact points and radiation rays from impact are visible on top; remaining part of length of 4.2, width of 8.8, thickness of 3.2cm (Figure 111: 4). Specimen T7④b: 2, blade damaged, body shape is of rectangle, multiple impact points and radiation rays from impact are visible; remaining part of length of 14, width of 8, thickness of 4cm (Figure 111: 6). Specimen T7④b: 4, severely damaged; only an upper corner remains, body shape is of rectangle, multiple impact points and radiation rays from impact are visible; remaining part of length of 5.4; remaining part of width of 4, thickness of 1.6cm (Figure 111: 7). Specimen T7④aD1: 2, severely damaged; only middle section remains, both sides ground to shape with traces; remaining part of length of 2.9; remaining part of width of 2.5, thickness of 1.1cm (Figure 111: 8).

Stone adzes: 2 pieces; shape and structure are substantially similar; rectangular.

Specimen T7②: 1, well preserved, double – sided arc blade, impact points and radiation rays from impact are visible on top and one side; of length of 9.2, width of 8.6, thickness of 2.4cm (Figure 111: 5; Plate 96: 2). Specimen T7④b: 1, only blade remains, single – sided arc blade; remaining part of length of 3.8, width of 4.2, thickness of 1cm (Figure 111: 9).

Pottery pieces: A total of 295 potter pieces were unearthed in Stratum ⑤a in this square unit. In terms of the earthenware materials, fine sand earthenware accounts for the most, followed by coarse sand earthenware, and clay polished earthenware is very rare. In terms of colors of the pottery pieces, terracotta and reddish brown pieces account for the most, with small numbers in grayish brown and blackish brown. In terms of pattern ornamentation, it was extremely well – developed. The decorations are of great variety, in which rope decorations account for the most. Other decorations include engraved line, stamp, concave string, protruding rim, pressure stamp, comb brushing and added mound *etc*. Pottery mouth parts are mostly flared, followed in numbers by trumpet – shaped and straight mouths. Artifacts are mostly with enclosure base and ring feet. Forms of the artifacts include ring feet, bowls, trumpet – shape mouth jars and Pottery pies *etc*.[1]

A total of 10 specimens of pottery pieces are selected, of which 9 specimens are for forms and 1 is for ornamentations.

Ornamentation specimen: 1 piece.

Specimen T7⑤a: 3, reddish brown sand earthenware, shoulder decorated with two concave strings, upper belly decorated with poked water ripple patterns, water ripple patterns poked short line pattern, belly lower part decorated with two sets of concave string pattern, each concave string pattern poked short line pattern, length of 4.6, width of 6.1, thickness of 0.6cm (Figure 112: 1).

---

[1] Statistical data in this section was provided by Vietnam National Museum of History.

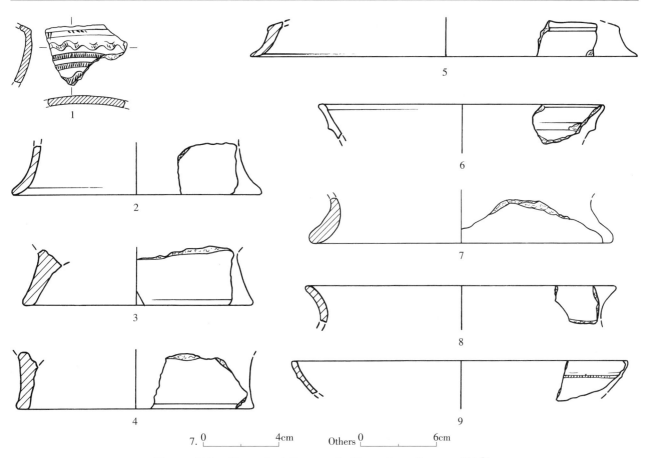

Figure 112   Unearthed Pottery Artifacts from Stratum T7⑤a

1. Sample patterns （T7⑤a：3） 2－5, 7. Ring feet （T7⑤a：5, 7, 6, 9, 8） 6, 9. Bowl （T7⑤a：10, 11）
8. Trumpet－shape mouth jar （T7⑤a：12）

Forms：9 specimens selected in total, including 5 ring feet, 2 bowls, 1 trumpet mouth jar, 1 pottery pie.

Pottery pie：1 piece.

Specimen T7④a：1, reddish brown sand earthenware, of a round body; diameter of 1.8, thickness of 0.5cm （Figure 111：10）.

Ring feet：5 pieces; can be classified into three categories based on shape and structure.

Category 1：3 pieces; horn－shaped ring foot, foot tip bent outward.

Specimen T7⑤a：5, terracotta; diameter at bottom of 18, remaining part of height of 4.6cm （Figure 112：2）. Specimen T7⑤a：7, brown earthenware; diameter at bottom of 19.6, remaining part of height of 4.1cm （Figure 112：3）. Specimen T7⑤a：8, reddish brown sand earthenware. diameter at bottom of 15.8, remaining part of height of 2.3cm （Figure 112：7）.

Category 2：1 piece; horn－shaped ring foot, foot tip bent inward.

Specimen T7⑤a：9, reddish brown fine earthenware; diameter at bottom of 30.3, remaining part of height of 2.8cm （Figure 112：5）.

Category 3: 1 piece; bucket shape ring foot.

Specimen T7⑤a: 6, reddish brown sand earthenware. diameter at bottom of 18. 5, remaining part of height of 4cm (Figure 112:4).

Bowls: 2 pieces; can be classified into two categories based on shape and structure.

Category 1: 1 piece; flare mouth.

Specimen T7 ⑤ a : 10, fine terracotta, round lip, with a protruding rim decorated under the mouth; bore diameter of 22. 3, remaining part of height of 3. 1cm (Figure 112:6).

Category 2: 1 piece; contracted mouth.

Specimen T7⑤a:11, fine sand reddish brown earthenware of square lip; flare mouth, arc belly; one protruding rim decorated under the mouth; poked on the protruding rim are dotted patterns; bore diameter of 26. 2, remaining part of height of 3. 2cm (Figure 112:9).

Trumpet - shape mouth jars: 1 piece.

Specimen T7⑤a: 12, terracotta, round lip; bore diameter of 24. 2, remaining part of height of 3cm (Figure 112:8).

Chapter V   Preliminary Study

Section One   General Characteristics of the Nghia Lap Remains

I. Production tools

Production tools are mainly stone tools. The stone tools are mostly ground to the overall shape and are rather small, most are adzes and axes, along with a small number of arrowheads, chisels, flappers, stone molds, stone balls and chipped stone tools (scrapers) and the like. Adzes are of the largest number, of better stone quality, some are jade – like, generally trapezoidal or rectangular, with single or double – sided arc edge and finely ground. This indicates the possibility of technical specialization. The stone axes are bigger than the adzes, mostly ground to shape throughout, rectangular on the flat side, with double – sided arc edge. Stone flappers used for production of bark cloth were discovered in the ruins of Nghia Lap for the first time. There are rectangular on the flat side, with a groove that can be seen clearly on one end. It is one of the artifacts the southeast coast of China and Southeast Asia that is the most characteristic. The discovery of stone mold marks the first discovery of artifacts related to bronze smelting in the Phung Nguyen culture. Presuming from the inside marks it was used to pro-duce some of the weapons. Taking into account the discovery of a copper spear at the Nghia Lap ruins, presumably this was used to produce the copper spears. Stone balls are of a smaller number. There are spherical with a smooth surface. The number of chipped stone tools is small. Most of these were made by flaking off the ground stone tools or chipping using a grinder stone. A small number of pottery spin-ning wheels and stone net sinkers were also found.

II. Household utensils

Household utensils are mostly pottery pieces, which were made mainly by rotational making. Inte-rior of many pottery pieces have traces of rotational making. The pottery system includes earthenware and clay pottery. The earthenware pieces are mostly of white quartz sands, both coarse and fine, most-ly fine. Colors are mostly that of terracotta and reddish brown, with certain numbers in grayish brown, yellowish brown and blackish brown *etc*. Some clay pottery pieces have thin coating. These were usually made in high – temperature fire.

In terms of decorations, there is a great variety and delicately made. The decorations include twist line, engraved, stamp, and added mound lines. The twist lines are usually thin twist to medium twist lines of vertical, diagonal, crossing and net patterns, normally applied on the lip, surface, neck, belly and bottom of pottery pieces. The engraved lines are normally water ripple, S – shape, parallel, strong, leaf vein and geometrical patterns, mostly on the neck, belly or ring feet of the artifacts. Stamped decorations are mostly dotted, combed dots and circle patterns, normally composing into complex decorations with engraved patterns on the belly and ring feet of artifacts. The most characteristics are the water ripple, S – shape, cloud and geometrical patterns comprised of combed dots and engraved lines.

In terms of forms, enclosure base utensils and ring foot utensils were popular. Flat base or three – foot utensils were not found. Most of the utensils are of flared or contracted mouth, followed by trumpet – shape mouth and straight mouth. Typical artifacts include kettle, stem dish, bowl and jars *etc*.

III. Ornaments

A small number of ornaments were also unearthed at Nghia Lap remains. These are all jade pieces that were finely made, including mainly rings, T – shaped rings and pendants *etc*. The rings are the most in number, mostly of beige color, round and smoothly shaped. There are less pendants, normally of semi – circle shape with a ring on an end. Many T – shape stone rings were found in China and Southeast Asia. But the multi – material T – shape rings unearthed in this excavation are the first ones discovered in Vietnam. These ornaments reflect the advanced level of making as well as the spiritual life of people in Nghia Lap remains.

IV. Remains of buildings and pits

Large number of postholes or smaller pit remains was found in all 8 square units excavated in the Nghia Lap remains (including the 2 excavated by Hanoi National University). They are randomly distributed, some laminating and breaking over each other, indicating the existence of column buildings in the site. And large number of densely distributed postholes indicates that these buildings were destroyed and rebuilt within a short period of time.

A total of 34 pits were sorted in the Nghia Lap remains, of which 16 are from Phung Nguyen culture period and can be divided into round, square and irregular shapes. 11 of the square pits (including those excavated by Hanoi National University) can be classified into category A and category B.

Category A pits are in the shape of round in upper part and square in lower part of diameter at the mouth of 1. 2 meters, and side length at bottom of around 1 meter. Deposits in the pits are in two cases; firstly the deposits are by strata with upper ones accompanied with large amount of red burnt soil particles or piles of red burnt soil, middle and lower ones with black ashes or blackish gray soil and in the upper layers placed with large number of large pottery pieces and jade and stone tools, which pottery pieces can be restored. The deduction is that originally complete or relatively complete objects were placed here. The second type is that there is no red burnt soil deposit in the pit, but large amount of ashes and blackish gray soil and many large pottery pieces. Category B is square pits of around 1 meter in side length, unearthing less pottery pieces, filled with yellowish gray soil containing some red burnt soil particles.

Shape and walls of the two categories of square pits are regular and orderly distributed along basically the northeast-southwest orientation. These are obviously not ordinary pits. Such pits are widely distributed in Vietnam and for a long time (found in Phung Nguyen and later Dong Dau culture for hundreds in number). Therefore the deduction is that these square pits including ones at Nghia Lap remains are related to worship rituals.

V. Tomb

Only one tomb was sorted in the Nghia Lap remains. It is rectangular in shape, rather shallow. The owner lied facing up and limbs straight, head to the east and facing up, both hands on the two sides of the body. There was only one pottery stem dish at the head of the owner.

In summary, people in the Phung Nguyen culture period at Nghia Lap remains lived in agricultural settlement, along with gathering, fishing and hunting. The buildings were mainly column buildings and square pits were used for worship rituals. The rotational making of pottery pieces in Nghia Lap remains was highly developed. Pottery was made in high temperature burning. Surfaces have great variety of decorations, indicating very high level of craftsmanship and technology. Most of the stone tools were ground to shape. The ground adzes and axes are most delicately made, indicating advancement of stone tool making technologies. There were also well developed jade and stone ornaments in the Nghia Lap remains such as rings, pendants, T – shaped rings of smooth surface and great features.

Section Two   Staging and Dating

To clarify the stage and dates of the Nghia Lap remains, we make analyses from the three aspects of stratigraphic relationship in the remains, topology of the artifacts and ^{14}C dating.

I. Stratigraphic relationships in the Nghia Lap remains

After summarization, strata at the Nghia Lap site can be classified into six strata; strata ①, ② and ③ are from contemporary and modern times, stratum ④ is one from cultures in the Dinh dynasty to early Ly dynasty[1] and strata ⑤ and ⑥ are from Phung Nguyen culture period. Remains concerning the Phung Nguyen culture period include strata ⑤a, ⑤b, ⑥ and ④, ⑤a, ⑤b. The laminating and breaking relations from top to bottom are as follows:

Group 1: ④ → H3, H4, H5, H6, H7, H8, H15, H16, H17[2]

Group 2: ⑤a → H18, H19, H20, H22, H23, M1

Group 3: ⑤b → H31

Group 4: ⑥ → H33

Among above lamination and breaking relations, in group 4, stratum ⑥ and H33 have very few artifacts unearthed, making it difficult to pick out specimens, and therefore cannot be included in the typology analysis; in group 3, H31 only unearthed a coarse terracotta tablet, and unearthed artifacts of stratum⑤ and stratum ⑤b are substantially similar, so they can be treated as one stratum. H18, H19, H20, H22 and H23 under stratum ⑤a had very few artifacts unearthed. It is difficult to identify representative objects to be included in typology analysis. In that logic, we have re – grouped the above 4 groups into below two groups by relations of lamination and breaking.

Group 1: ④ → H3, H4, H5, H6, H7, H8, H15, H16, H17

Group 2: ⑤a → M1

II. Topology analysis of the artifacts

The stratigraphic relationship in the Nghia Lap remains described above serves as the basis of topology analysis. To gain a comprehensive understanding of the cultural characteristics of the Nghia Lap remains and study these by historical stages, we need to study the topology of the artifacts. The most typical artifacts unearthed from the Nghia Lap are pottery pieces. Therefore our topology study is on the pottery pieces unearthed from the Nghia Lap remains.

Pottery pieces unearthed from Nghia Lap are all with enclosure bases or ring feet. The forms include mainly stem dish, ring feet, base, trumpet – shaped mouth jars, flare mouth jars, kettles, bowls, contracted mouth jars, thick lip jars, pottery balls, ears (of utensils) and handles (of utensils) etc.

Bowls: based on the shape of mouth these can be divided into three categories.

Category A: slightly contracted mouth. Based on whether there is protruding rim on the shoulder these can be divided into two sub – categories.

Sub – category Aa: mouth decorated with protruding rim, e. g. Specimen T1⑤a:364 (Figure 113:1).

---

[1]   Equivalent to the culture stratum in Tang Dynasty and Song Dynasty in Chinese history.

[2]   The stratum distribution in ④is not the horizontal distribution, and in some areas the ④b stratum is absent. To maintain uniformity, here only ④ is used as illustration.

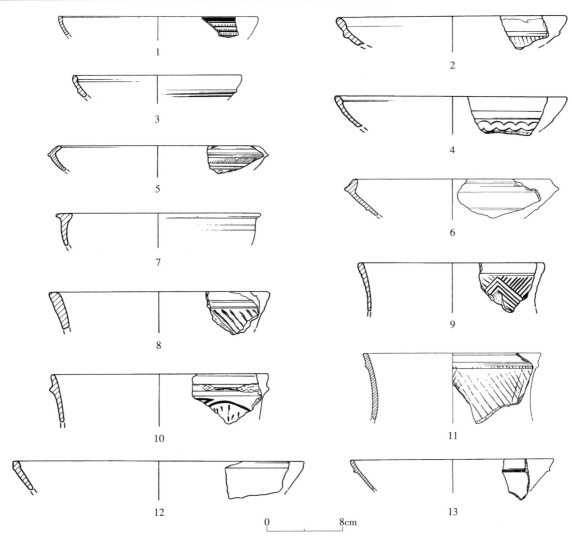

Figure 113   Categories of Pottery Bowls and Flare Mouth Jars

1. Aa category bowl (T4⑤a:36)   2. Ba category bowl (T2⑤a:53)   3. Ab category bowl (T1⑤a:365)   4. Bb category bowl (T2⑤a:60)   5. C I category bowl (T1⑤a:265)   6. C II category bowl (H3:71)   7. D category bowl (T1⑤a:364)   8. A II category flared mouth jar (H5:20)   9. A I category flared mouth jar (T2⑤b:14)   10. B I category flared mouth jar (H5:22)   11. B II category flared mouth jar (T2⑤a:34)   12. C I category flared mouth jar (H4:13)   13. C II category flared mouth jar (T1⑤a:255)

Sub – category Ab: mouth without protruding rim, e. g. Specimen T1⑤a:265 (Figure 113:3).

Category B: flare mouth. Based on whether there is protruding rim on the shoulder these can be divided into two subtypes.

Sub – category Ba: mouth decorated with protruding rim, e. g. Specimen T2⑤a:60 Figure 113:2).

Sub – category Bb: mouth without protruding rim, e. g. Specimen T2⑤a:53 (Figure 113:4).

Category C: contracted mouth, drum shoulder. Based on shape of the shoulder, these can be divided into two styles.

Style I: shoulder slightly arced, e. g. Specimen T4⑤a:62 (Figure 113:5).

Style II: shoulder slightly bent, e. g. Specimen H3:71 (Figure 113:6).

Category D: round lip, narrow and flat edge, contracted mouth, e. g. Specimen T1 ⑤a : 365 (Figure 113 : 7).

Flared mouth jars: based shape and structure, these can be divided into three categories.

Category A: without protruding rim on the neck. based on the shape of mouth these can be divided into two styles.

Style I: round lip. Such as Specimen T2⑤a: 34 (Figure 113 : 9).

Style II: round but approximating to square lip. Such as Specimen H5 : 22 (Figure 113 : 8).

Category B: protruded rim decoration on the neck.

Style I: round lip. Such as Specimen T1⑤a: 255 (Figure 113 : 10).

Style II: round approximating to square lip. Such as Specimen H5 : 20 (Figure 113 : 11).

Category C: square lips. Based on the shape of mouth these can be divided into two styles.

Style I: mouth slightly bent, e. g. Specimen T2⑤b: 14 (Figure 113 : 12).

Style II: mouth slightly contracted, e. g. Specimen H4 : 13 (Figure 113 : 13).

Trumpet - shape mouth jars: Based on shape of the shoulder, these can be divided into two categories.

Category A: without protruding rim on the neck. based on the shape of mouth these can be divided into two styles.

Style I: sharp round lip. e. g. Specimen T1⑤a: 20 (Figure 114 : 1).

Style II: round lip. e. g. Specimen H6 : 7 (Figure 114 : 2)

Category B: protruded rim decoration on the neck. e. g. Specimen T1⑤a: 189 (Figure 114 : 3).

Contracted mouth jar: based on the shape of shoulder, these can be divided into two categories.

Category A: protruding rim on the shoulder. Specimens T2⑤a: 67 (Figure 114 : 5).

Type B: without protruding rim on the shoulder. And based on shape of belly, these can be divided into two styles.

Style I: slant belly, e. g. Specimen T2⑤a: 58 (Figure 114 : 4).

Style II: drum belly, e. g. Specimen H4 : 18 (Figure 114 : 6).

Thick lip jars: based on shape and structure, these can be divided into two categories.

Category A: flare mouth, e. g. Specimen T3⑤ a: 19 (Figure 114 : 8).

Category B: straight mouth, e. g. Specimen T3⑤ a: 18 (Figure 114 : 7).

Kettles: based on shape of the belly, these can be divided into two categories.

Category A: drum belly slightly hanging, e. g. Specimen H3 : 81 (Figure 114 : 10).

Category B: drum belly, e. g. Specimen H3 : 73 (Figure 114 : 9).

Stem dishes: based on the shape and structure these can be divided into three categories.

Category A: high stem dish, e. g. Specimen M1 : 1.

Category B: short stem dish, e. g. Specimen H3 : 72.

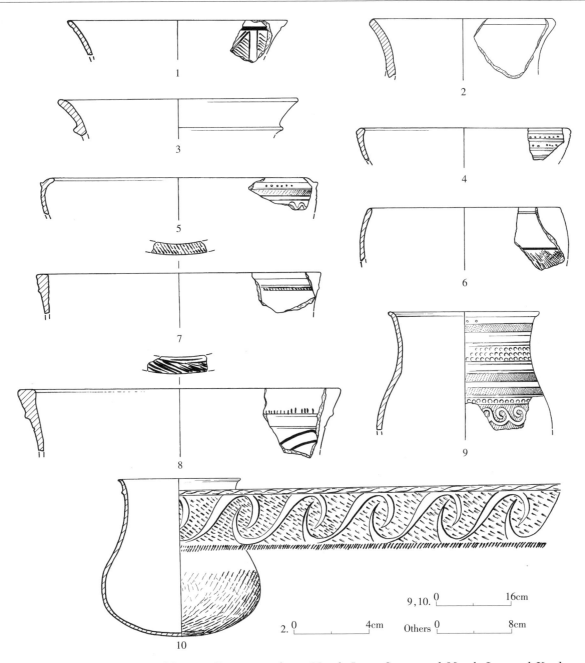

Figure 114　Categories of Pottery Trumpet – shape Mouth Jars, Contracted Mouth Jars and Kettles

1. A I category trumpet – shape mouth jar （T1⑤a：20）　2. A II category trumpet – shape mouth jar （H6：7）　3. B category trumpet – shape mouth jar （T1⑤a：189）　4. B I category contracted mouth jar （T2⑤a：58）　5. A category contracted mouth jar （T2⑤a：67）　6. B II category contracted mouth jar （H4：18）　7. B category thick lip jar （T3⑤a：18）　8. A category thick lip jar （T3⑤a：19）　9. B category kettle （H3：73）　10. A category kettle （H3：81）

Category C：hexagon dish, e. g. Specimen H6：5.

Ring feet： based on the shape and structure these can be divided into three categories.

Category A：bucket shaped. based on the shape and structure these can be divided into two styles.

Style Aa I：dome shaped. e. g. Specimen T1⑤a：94 （Figure 115：1）.

Style Aa II：dome shaped with foot tip flared outward. e. g. Specimen H4：11 （Figure 115：2）.

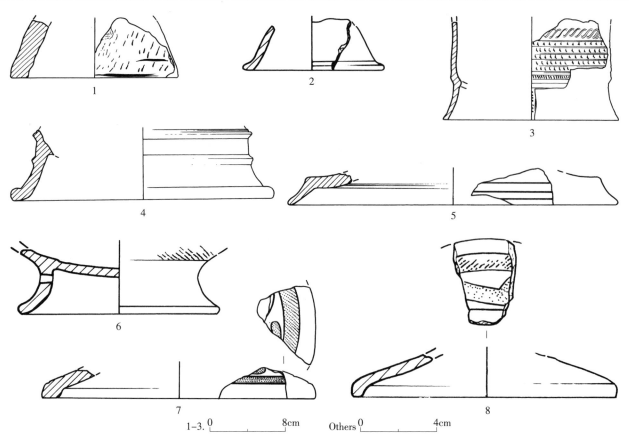

Figure 115   Categories of Pottery Ring Feet

1. Aa I category (T1⑤a:94)   2. Aa II category (H4:11)   3. Ab category (H3:31)   4. B I category (T1⑤a:180)
5. Cb category (T2⑤a:28)   6. B II category (H3:31)   7. Ca II category (H4:15)   8. Ca I category (T2⑤a:56)

Style Ab: bucket shaped, e. g. Specimen H3:31 (Figure 115:3).

Category B: trumpet shaped ring feet. Based on the shape and structure these can be divided into two styles.

Style I: foot tip outward bent. e. g. Specimen T1⑤a:180 (Figure 115:4).

Style II: foot tip outward tipped. e. g. Specimen H3:71 (Figure 115:6).

Category C: shallow dish shaped ring feet. Based on the shape and structure these can be divided into two sub – categories.

Sub – category Ca: foot tip inward bent to straight angle.

Style I: connection between ring foot and tip in an arc shape. e. g. Specimen T2⑤a:56 (Figure 115:8).

Style II: connection between ring foot and tip in an straight angle. e. g. Specimen H4:15 (Figure 115:7).

Sub – category Cb: foot tip bent outward into a blunt angle. e. g. Specimen T2⑤a:28 (Figure 115:5).

Bases: cylinder shaped with oval bottom, bent. Based on the shape and structure these can be divided into three styles.

Style I: arc – shaped ear decorated on one side. e. g. Specimen T1⑤a：57 (Figure 116：1).

Style II: handle – shaped ear decorated on one side. e. g. Specimen H4：31 (Figure 116：2).

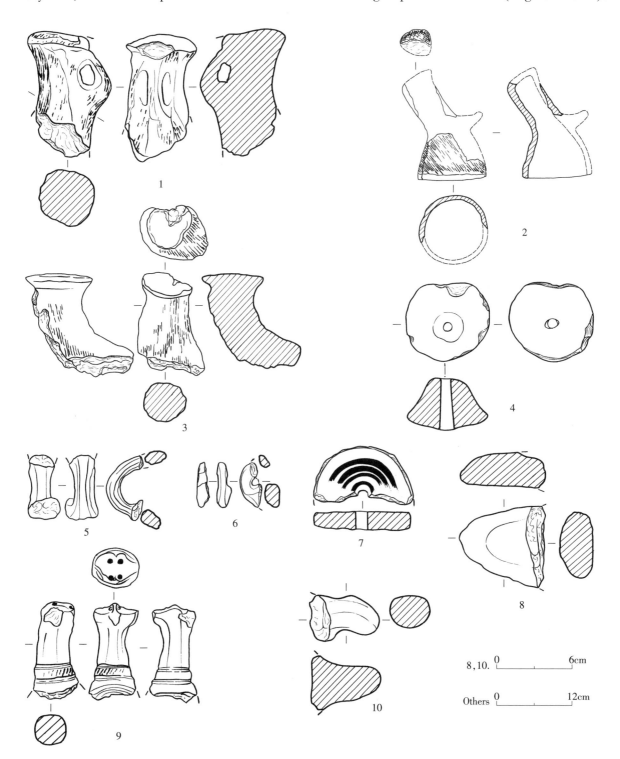

Figure 116   Other Pottery Categories

1. I category base (T1⑤a：57)   2. II category base (H4：31)   3. III category base (H3：13)   4. A category spinning wheel (T1⑤a：4)   5. A category utensil ear (H5：18)   6. B category utensil ear (H5：17)   7. B category spinning wheel (T1⑤a：18)   8. A category handle (T1⑤a：33)   9. C category handle (T3⑤a：4)   10. B category handle (T1⑤a：59)

Style III: without ear. e. g. Specimen H3:13 (Figure 116:3).

Spinning wheels: based on the shape and structure these can be divided into two categories.

Category A: tower shaped with a hole in the middle. e. g. Specimen T1⑤a:4 (Figure 116:4).

Category B: handle shaped with a hole in the middle. e. g. Specimen T1⑤a:18 (Figure 116:7).

Ears: based on the shape and structure these can be divided into two categories.

Category A: large arc – shaped ear. e. g. Specimen H5:18 (Figure 116:5).

Category B: small arc – shaped ear. e. g. Specimen H5:17 (Figure 116:6).

Handles: based on the shape and structure these can be divided into three categories.

Category A: tongue shaped. e. g. Specimen T1⑤a:33 (Figure 116:8).

Category B: cylinder shaped. e. g. Specimen T1⑤a:59 (Figure 116:10).

Category C: dog head style. e. g. Specimen T3⑤a:4 (Figure 116:9).

Pottery balls: sphere shaped.

Placing above stratigraphic laminating and breaking relations and the portfolios of unearthed artifacts from the strata into Annex 1, we can see that there are six categories of artifacts that can be used in staging (ring feet, bases, trumpet – shaped jars, flare mouth jars, kettles and bowls). And based on the laminating and breaking relations and the portfolios of unearthed artifacts, the entire site is divided into front and back sections. A majority of the artifacts run through both sections, indicating that they are of the same heritage through continuous development. Overall, the front section is represented by pits under strata ⑤a, ⑤b, M1 and ⑤ with the most number and types of pottery pieces unearthed and is therefore considered to include the key remains of the site. The back section is represented by pits under stratum ④ (H3, H4, H5, H6, H7, H8, H15, H16, H17 and H18) with significantly reduced number and categories of pottery pieces unearthed. This is the later period of the site.

III. Dating

Date of the Nghia Lap remains can be determined by comparisons with surrounding areas and ^{14}C dating. By the unearthed artifacts, pottery stem dishes unearthed from M1 in the front section are similar to those unearthed from the Go Bong remains[1] (02XRH1L7b4:321) and bowls of Category Aa, Ab, Ba, Bb, CI and D, trumpet – shape mouth jars of AI and bases of I are similar to those unearthed in Go Bong remains, but appear to be from later time than the Go Bong remains. The kettles (H3:81, 73), stem dishes (H3:72), hexagon stem dishes (H6:5), bases (H4:31) and ring feet of AaII and Ab unearthed from the back section appear to be similar to those from the Xom Ren remains. [2] By

[1]   Pham Ly Huong, *Do Gom Go Bong*, Luan Van Tot Nghiep DHTHHN, tu lieu Khoa Lich su, 1967. Han Van Tan, Han Van Khan, *Bao cao so bo hai lan khai quai di chi Go Bong*, *Thuong Nong, Phu Tho* trong TBKHDHTHHN tap V, 1970.

[2]   Nguyen Thi Kim Dung, Tang Chung, *Khai quat lan* II *di chi Xom Ren* (*Phu Tho*) *Dang Hong Son: Bao cao*, trong NPHMVKCH nam 2003, 2003. Ha Van Tan, *Thong bao ket qua khai quat di chi Xom Ren*, trong TBKH DHTHHN, 1970.

comparing the unearthed artifacts with those from the surrounding culture remains we can see that the dates are between the Go Bong remains and Xom Ren remains, closure to the Xom Ren remains. The Go Bong remains and Xom Ren remains represent the early and middle periods of Phung Nguyen culture. Therefore, dates of the Nghia Lap remains should be around earlier times of middle of the Phung Nguyen culture period.

Also, during the excavation, we collected many ^{14}C specimens and had these tested in Beijing and Hanoi. Chinese Academy of Social Sciences Archaeology Institute ^{14}C Laboratory made tree ring correction on the dates to be 3740 – 3520 from present days. Tree ring corrected year estimated by Peking University AMS Laboratory is 3490 – 3770 from present days; and that by Vietnam Archaeology College Laboratory is 3490 – 3890 from present. Therefore based on comparisons of unearthed artifacts and ^{14}C dating, time of Nghia Lap remains is around the earlier days of middle of the Phung Nguyen culture period, in absolute terms, around 3500 – 3700 before present days.

Section Three   Relationships with Surrounding Cultures and Remains

I. Relationship with the sites of Phung Nguyen culture of Vietnam

The Phung Nguyen culture received the name due to excavation of the Phung Nguyen site in 1959. To date, over 100 Phung Nguyen culture period sites have been discovered and over 70 of these have been officially excavated. The staging of Phung Nguyen culture is best presented by Ha Van Tan and Han Van Khan in Vietnam. Mr. Ha Van Tan stages the Phung Nguyen culture to the lower stratum under Go Bong-Xom Ren and Dong Dau,[1] while Mr. Han Van Khan stages that to Go Bong – Phung Nguyen-Lung Hoa based on variations of decorations of the pottery pieces.[2] Artifacts unearthed from Nghia Lap remains are similar to the Xom Ren remains and the Phung Nguyen remains. And it is located in the Xom Ren stage of Phung Nguyen culture (or the Phung Nguyen stage), belonging to a larger culture system.

II. Relationship with sites or cultures in southwest China and south China regions

(1) Relationship with the Neolithic Age cultures in the Lantsang River basin

Cultures in the Neolithic Age along the Lantsang River basin concentrated mainly in Dali Prefecture and Baoshan City of Yunnan, covering the sites in Xinguang of Dali, Pupiao Ertaipo, Pupiao Kongjiashan, Daojieli Bazi and Lujiang of Baoshan City. Among these the Xinguang Remains is the

[1]   Ha Van Tan, translated by Kikuti Seiiti, 《ベトナムの考古文化》, Liuxing Publishing House, 1991.
[2]   Han Van Khan, 《Van Hoa Phung Nguyen》, Nha Xuat Ban Dai Hoc Quoc Gia Ha Noi, 2005.

most representative. In 1993, the Yunnan Province Institute of Cultural Relics and Archaeology excavated the site. Excavation area is 1,000 square meters. The sorted sites include mainly that of buildings, pits, fire pit and ditches *etc*. The unearthed artifacts are mainly stone tools and pottery pieces,
including 642 stone tools of mainly stone adzes, axes, spears, arrowheads, chisels, knives, sickles,
awls and spinning wheels *etc*., of which the adzes are of the greatest number and the most representative. The pottery pieces are mainly earthenware with decorations of added mound, engraved cells,
stamped cells, wave, water ripple, dotted line, triangular, maze and nail patterns. Forms are mainly
jars, kettles, bowls, dishes, vases, and cups *etc*.[1] The dates are around 3, 700 before present
days, a little earlier than the Nghia Lap remains. At the remains the adzes appear to be a key production tool, similar to Nghia Lap remains. As a region in Yunnan connecting the Chengdu Plain and
northern Vietnam, Xinguang Remains undoubtedly have characteristics of both cultures. Seen from the
unearthed pottery pieces, the forms are similar to those from Chengdu Plain, but decorations are similar to that of the Phung Nguyen culture in northern Vietnam. The production tools are close to that of
the Phung Nguyen culture in northern Vietnam. Similar sites include the Caiyuanzi and Mopandi sites
[2] in Yongren of Yunnan which pottery decorations and square pits are very similar to those of the Nghia Lap remains.

(II) Relationship with Guangxi's Gantuoyan site

Guangxi borders with northern Vietnam and the two places share the waters and mountains, similar natural, geographical and ecological environments. Rivers in south Guangxi and Song Hong of Vietnam are all located along coast of the Tonkin Gulf of convenient land and maritime transport. There was
no border in the pre – historic period when human and cultural exchanges in Guangxi and Song Hong
basin of Vietnam were very convenient. Therefore it is necessary to compare the studies of archaeological cultures in these two adjacent regions. So far the Gantuoyan Remains in Guangxi is the one discovered to be similar to Nghia Lap remains of Vietnam. The site is located in the north of Napo county of
Guangxi. It is a cave remain. From 1997 to 1998, the Guangxi Zhuang's Autonomous Region Cultural
Relics Work Team excavated the site in an area of 380 square meters. The site is in two stages, which
second stage is close to that of the Nghia Lap remains. Unearthed stone tools are mainly axes and adzes. Unearthed pottery pieces are of great variety of decorations, mostly twist lines along with some engraved and stamped patterns. Forms are mostly enclosure bases and ring feet ones. Jars, round mouth
utensils, kettles and bowls were popular.[3] Seen from the unearthed stone tools and pottery pieces,

---

[1]   Yunnan Province Institute of Cultural Relics and Archaeology, "Report of Excavation of Xinguang Remains in Yongping of Yunnan", *Ar-
       chaeology Journal*, Vol. 2, 2002.

[2]   Yunnan Province Institute of Cultural Relics and Archaeology, "Report of Excavation of Caiyuanzi and Mopandi sites in Yongren of Yun-
       nan in 2001", *Archaeology*, Vol. 10, 2003.

[3]   Guangxi Zhuang's Autonomous Region Cultural Relics Work Team, "Guangxi Napo Gantuoyan Site Excavation Report", *Archaeology*,
       Vol. 10, 2003.

these are very close to that of the Nghia Lap remains. It also indicates that in the middle period of Phung Nguyen culture, Guangxi's Gantuoyan remains and Phung Nguyen culture were paralleled and influenced each other, casting significant influence on surrounding regions, in particular the Pearl River basin.

(Ⅲ) Relationship with Sanxingdui culture

Sanxingdui Culture is named after the remains of Phase Ⅱ and Phase Ⅲ of Sanxingdui site in Guanghan, mainly distributing through the stripe shaped area from Chengdu Plain to the Three Gorges. The typical site is the Sanxingdui Site. Since the 1980s, Institute of Cultural Relics and Archaeology of Sichuan Province made many archaeological excavations at the site and discovered large scale city site, palace building foundations, and ritual facility remains in Xia and Shang periods. Particularly, the excavation of No. 1 and No. 2 ritual pits found many bronze, jade, gold, pottery and stone pieces, and ivories and seashells, including ritual utensils such as wine vessel, urn – shaped wine vessel, dish, jade pendant, ornament and ivory tablets, parade tools such as bronze spears and jade spears, religious tools such as bronze tree, bronze sculpture and masks *etc*. These indicate that the Sanxingdui Remains was once the political, economic, religious and cultural center of Shu Kingdom.[1] Meanwhile, the Sanxingdui Remains casted significant influence on surrounding cultures including the Phung Nguyen culture of Vietnam. Jade spears, pendant, T – shaped rings and ornaments along with other ritual tools unearthed in Phung Nguyen culture sites are very similar to those unearthed at Sanxingdui Remains. The pottery pieces of Nghia Lap remains in Vietnam are mostly of aboriginal culture factors. But some jade ritual utensils and phenomena at the site such as the T – shaped rings, stone ornaments and square pits present some similarity and consistency with the Sanxingdui Culture.

Section Four   From Sanxingdui to Phung Nguyen

Before Zhang Qian headed the expedition to the west and opened up the northern Silk Road, the southern Silk Road had been the only channel to Southeast Asia and West Asia. Its role can be traced back to the Shang and Zhou periods, i. e. the Phung Nguyen culture period in Vietnam.

In the Shang and Zhou periods, i. e. the Phung Nguyen culture periods in Vietnam along the south of the southern Silk Road, jade spears, jade pendants, T – shaped rings and ornaments found here are very similar to those unearthed in Sanxingdui Remain in the upper streams of Yangtze River in terms of form, manufacturing and decorations. These artifacts were also found in Taiwan and Hong Kong. The far – reaching dissemination and influence are impressive. Meanwhile, in both Sanxingdui

[1]   Institute of Cultural Relics and Archaeology of Sichuan Province, "60 Years of Archaeology in Sichuan", *Sichuan Cultural Relics*, Vol. 6, 2009.

and Nghia Lap remains, large amount of ivory and shell pieces were discovered. These are very likely to originate from West Asia or Southeast Asia regions. It also indicates that the cultural channel from upper streams of Yangtze River to Southeast Asia emerged in as early as the Shang and Zhou periods.

That cultural channel from Sichuan to Vietnam is along the fast and convenient southern Silk Road, which originated from Chengdu towards south and stems to eastern and western routes, which western one was along the Yak Road to Dali in the south and eastern route reaches Dali from the Chengdu Plain through the Wuchi Roads. The two roads converge into one at Dali extending further west through Baoshan and Tengchong to Myitkyina or Bhamo in Myanmar through Baoshan and Ruili at the border, thus reaching through the border. The southern Silk Road has on the section outside China western and eastern routes, the western route being the "Shu's toxic road", from Chengdu Plain to Yunnan, reaching Myanmar and to India, Pakistan, Afghanistan to Central Asia and West Asia. This transportation route through Asia was one of the key routes of the longest distance and history in the ancient Eurasian continent. The eastern route of the section outside border of the southern Silk Road includes the Red River channel from Sichuan to Yuanjiang in Yunnan and to Song Hong in Vietnam and the Zangke Road from Sichuan to Panyu (today's Guangzhou) through Yelang, along which the southwest region and southeast coastal region developed their relationships.[1] If we look further afar, we can see many similar cultural factors in remains from Chengdu of Sichuan to the Southeast Asian regions especially Vietnam. Among these factors the most representative is engraved decoration pottery. Across the vast areas of Anning River basin in Liangshan Prefecture in Sichuan, Xinguang of Dali in Yunnan, Baoshan of Yunnan, Gantuoyan in Guangxi and Phung Nguyen culture in Vietnam, pottery pieces of engraved line decorations existed in great numbers. This is the direct presentation of existence of the route. It also suggests the cultural exchange activities of different levels and different scales throughout upper streams of Yangtze River and Southeast Asian regions in Shang and Zhou periods in China, which enhanced the interactions between the regions.

In conclusion, this excavation is the first joint archaeological excavation between China and Vietnam. It has significant meanings for the studies in early cultures of Bronze Age in northern Vietnam, relationship and communications with Bronze Age cultures in south China and southwest China, understanding of the radius of influence of Sanxingdui Culture and direction *etc*. Also through the excavation works, we established extensive connections with Vietnam's cultural relics and archaeology circles. Understanding and friendship between the two sides have been enhanced, forming excellent foundation for further cooperation and communication.

---

[1]   Duan Yu, "External Transport of Southwest China-the Southern Silk Road in the Early Qin and Two Han Dynasties Periods", *Historical Study*, Vol. 1, 2009.

Annex

Annex 1 Table of Profiles of Unearthed Pottery Pieces of Nghia Lap Remains

Utensil / Unit	Stem Dish	Ring Feet	Base	Trumpet-shape Mouth Jars	Flare Mouth Jars	Thick Lip Jars	Kettles	Contracted Mouth Jars	Bowls	Ears	Handles	Pottery Balls	Spinning Wheels
T1⑤a		Aa Ⅰ, B Ⅰ, Ca Ⅰ, Cb	Ⅰ	A Ⅰ, B	A Ⅰ, B Ⅰ	A, B		A, B Ⅰ	Aa, Ab, Ba, C Ⅰ, D	A, B	A, B		A, B
T1⑤b		Aa Ⅰ, B Ⅰ, Ab, Ca Ⅰ			A Ⅰ	A, B			Ab, C Ⅰ				
T2⑤a		Aa Ⅰ, B Ⅰ, Ca Ⅰ, Cb	Ⅰ	A Ⅰ, B	A Ⅰ, B Ⅰ	A, B		A, B Ⅰ	Aa, Ab, Ba		A, B		
T2⑤b		Aa Ⅰ, B Ⅰ, Ab, Ca Ⅰ	Ⅰ	A Ⅰ	AⅠ, BⅠ, CⅠ	A, B				B			B
T3⑤a		Aa Ⅰ, B Ⅰ, Ca Ⅰ	Ⅰ	A Ⅰ	A Ⅰ, B Ⅰ	A, B		B Ⅰ	Aa, Ab, Ba		C		
T4⑤a		Aa Ⅰ, B Ⅰ, Ab, Ca Ⅰ		A Ⅰ	A Ⅰ, B Ⅰ	A, B			Aa, Ab, Ba				A, B
T5⑤a		Aa Ⅰ, B Ⅰ, Ab, Ca Ⅰ	Ⅰ	A Ⅰ	A Ⅰ, B Ⅰ	A, B			Aa, Ab, Ba, C Ⅰ				
T7⑤a		Aa Ⅰ, B Ⅰ, Ab, Ca Ⅰ		A Ⅰ		B			Ab, Ba				
M1	A												
H3	B	Ab, B Ⅱ,	Ⅲ			A, B	√		C Ⅱ			√	
H4	C	Aa Ⅱ, Ab, B Ⅱ, Ca Ⅱ	Ⅱ		C Ⅱ	A, B		B Ⅱ	Aa, Ab, Bb			√	
H5			Ⅱ	A Ⅱ	B Ⅱ, C Ⅱ				Ab	A, B	B	√	
H6			Ⅱ	A Ⅱ		B			Aa		A		
H7		Aa Ⅱ		A Ⅱ									
H8		B Ⅱ		A Ⅱ			√						
H15							√						
H17						B							
H19		√											

Note: The upper – case letters indicate the form and lower – case letters indicate sub – form; Roman numbers indicate the style and a tick "√" indicates that the item was not classified.

Annex 2   Table of Carbon – 14 Dating of Nghia Lap Remains in Vietnam

Sample	Original Number	Sample	Carbon – 14 Dating	Tree – ring Corrected Date (BC)
Zk – 3316	H3	Charcoal	3314 ± 30	1680BC (3.7%) 1670BC 1630BC (64.5%) 1520BC
Zk – 3317	H18	Charcoal	3394 ± 30	1740BC (47.2%) 1680BC 1670BC (21.0%) 1630BC
BA0759	T7⑤a	Charcoal	3310 ± 40	1630BC – 1520BC (68.2%) 1690BC – 1490BC (95.4%)
BA0760	T4⑤a	Charcoal	3375 ± 45	1740BC – 1610BC (68.2%) 1770BC – 1520BC (95.4%)
HNK – 330	H3	Charcoal	3320 ± 50	1680BC – 1520BC (68.2%) 1740BC – 1490BC (95.4%)
HNK – 331	H3	Charcoal	3410 ± 70	1880BC – 1610BC (68.2%) 1890BC – 1520BC (95.4%)
HNK – 333	T2⑤a	Charcoal	3560 ± 105	2040BC – 1740BC (68%) 2200BC – 1600BC (95.4%)
HNK – 334	D7 below T2⑤a	Charcoal	3680 ± 160	2300BC – 1750BC (68%) 2600BC – 1600BC (95.4%)

Notes:

1. The Carbon – 14 dating of samples numbered Zk – 3316 and Zk – 3317 was carried out by the Carbon – 14 Laboratory of the Archaeology Institute of the Chinese Academy of Social Sciences. The half – life period used is 5, 568 years. BP indicates years dating back from 1950.

2. The Carbon – 14 dating of samples numbered BA0759 and BA0760 was carried out by the AMS Laboratory of the Peking University. The half – life period used is 5, 568 years. BP indicates years dating back from 1950.

3. The Carbon – 14 dating of samples numbered HNK – 330 and HNK – 331 was carried out by the Vietnam National Museum. The half – life period used is 5, 570 years.

Annex 3   Registration Table of Pits at Nghia Lap Remains

| Number | Location | Date | Opening to | Shape and Structure | | | Dimensions | Soil Properties, Color and Inclusions | Unearthed Artifacts | Remarks |
				Plane Shape	Walls	Bottom				
H1	Northwest of T2	Modern and contemporary times	Under ①	Square in the front and round in the rear	Uneven	Flat	Length of 1.67, Width of 0.28 ~ 70.2, Depth of 0.1m	Grayish black loose soil	Small number of porcelain pieces unearthed	
H2	Northeast of T3	Modern and contemporary times	Under ①	Oval	Relatively even	Dome shape	Length of 1.86, Width of 1.54, Depth of 0.64m	Grayish black loose soil	A small number of pottery and porcelain pieces along with iron items unearthed	Breaking H3, H4
H3	Northeast of T2	Phung Nguyen culture	Under ④a	Round in upper part and square in lower part	Relatively straight and even	Flat	Upper round part of diameter of around 1.4m, lower square side length of 1m, Depth of 0.8m	Accumulations in the pit can be divided into three strata: Stratum ① being grayish black soil; loose soil; large amount of red burnt soil and charcoal found in the north of the stratum, also containing large amount of pottery pieces and small number of stone tools; thickness of 16–20cm. Stratum ② is of yellow clay soil, relatively hard, containing large amount of iron rust; depositing inclined from northeast to southwest; containing small number of pottery pieces; thickness of 24–30cm. Stratum ③ is gray soil;	Artifacts unearthed in H3 include pottery pieces, stone tools and jade pieces, dominated by pottery pieces with relatively less stone tools and jade pieces. Stone tools are mostly ground to shape stone tools, including stone adze, grinding stone and scraper. Pottery pieces are mostly fine reddish brown earthenware, terracotta and brown earthenware. Pattern ornamentation was extremely well – developed, The decorations are mostly rope decorations. Other decorations include engraved line, stamp, concave string, protruded rim, pressure stamp, comb brushing, and added mound etc. Particularly, among all the engraved lines, the ones with comb teeth brushed or comb dotted stamps are the most characteristic. Compound ornamentations of multiple decorations on a single pottery piece appear to have been very popular. The	Broken by H2

(continued schedule 3)

Number	Location	Date	Opening to	Shape and Structure			Dimensions	Soil Properties, Color and Inclusions	Unearthed Artifacts	Remarks
				Plane Shape	Walls	Bottom				
								soil is loose, depositing inclined from northeast to southwest; containing small number of pottery pieces; thickness of 21 – 27cm. Below this stratum is yellowish brown raw soil	main ornamentation patterns are of clouds, S – shape, geometric patterns, circles and water ripples and the like. Pottery mouth parts are mostly contracted or flared. The artifacts are mostly with enclosure base and ring feet. Forms of the artifacts include ceramic balls, stem dishes, bowls, ring feet, bases and kettles *etc.*	
H4	Northwest of T2	Phung Nguyen culture	Under ④a	Round in upper part and square in lower part	Relatively straight and even	Flat	Length of 1.4, Width of 1.2, Depth of 0.4 – 0.6m	Accumulations in the pit can be divided into three strata. Stratum ① is in the middle of the pit; thickness of 0.06 meters; red burnt soil with large amount of pottery pieces, among which a pottery base was found in the north of the red burnt soil and a pottery bowl found in the east; Stratum ② is of dark grayish black color soil, soil is loose, thickness of 0.1 – 0.2 meters; containing lots of pottery pieces; stratum ③ is yellowish brown color soil, soil is loose, containing little	Unearthed artifacts are mostly pottery pieces and stone tools, dominated by pottery and less stone tools. Stone tools are mostly adze, balls, mold and grinding stone. Pottery pieces are mostly fine reddish brown earthenware, terracotta and brown earthenware. Pattern ornamentation was extremely well – developed. The decorations are mostly rope decorations. Other decorations include engraved line, stamp, concave string, protruded rim, pressure stamp, comb brushing, and added mound *etc.* Particularly, among all the engraved lines, the ones with comb teeth brushed or comb dotted stamps are the most characteristic. Compound ornamentations of multiple decorations on a single pottery piece appear to have been very popular. The main ornam-	Broken by H2

(continued schedule 3)

Number	Location	Date	Opening to	Shape and Structure			Dimensions	Soil Properties, Color and Inclusions	Unearthed Artifacts	Remarks
				Plane Shape	Walls	Bottom				
								items, thickness of 0.1 – 0.24 meters. Below this stratum is yellowish brown raw soil	entation patterns are of clouds, S – shape, geometric patterns and the like. Pottery mouth parts are mostly contracted or flared; followed in number by trumpet – shaped and straight mouths. The artifacts are mostly with enclosure base. Forms of the artifacts include ceramic balls, bases, flare mouth jars, trumpet – shape mouth jars, bowls, contracted mouth jars, straight – mouth jars and ring feet *etc.*	
H5	Northwest of T1 and west beam of T2	Phung Nguyen culture	Under ④a	Round in upper part and square in lower part	Relatively straight and even	Flat	Upper part diameter of 1.6m, Depth of 0.2m, lower square side length of 1.2, Depth of 1m	Accumulations in the pit can be divided into three strata. Stratum ① is grayish black soil, soil is loose, depositing inclined from southwest to northeast; containing large amount of pottery pieces and small number of stone tools; thickness of 0.7 – 0.85 meters. stratum ② yellow clay soil, relatively hard, containing large amount of iron rust' depositing inclined from northeast to southwest; containing small number of pottery pieces; thickness of 0.1 –	Unearthed mainly are pottery pieces and stone tools; most are pottery pieces; with a small number of stone tools. Stone tools are mostly scrapers and stone core. Pottery pieces are mostly fine reddish brown earthenware, terracotta and brown earthenware. Pattern ornamentation was extremely well – developed. The decorations are mostly rope decorations. Other decorations include engraved line, stamp, concave string, protruded rim, pressure stamp, comb brushing, and dotting *etc.* Pottery mouth parts are mostly contracted or flared, followed by trumpet – shaped and straight mouths. Artifacts are mostly with enclosure base. Forms of the artifacts include ceramic	Broken by H34

(continued schedule 3)

Number	Location	Date	Opening to	Shape and Structure			Dimensions	Soil Properties, Color and Inclusions	Unearthed Artifacts	Remarks
				Plane Shape	Walls	Bottom				
								0.15 meters. stratum ③ is gray soil, soil is loose, depositing inclined from northeast to southwest; containing small number of pottery pieces; thickness of 0.2 – 0.3 meters. Below this stratum is yellowish brown raw soil	balls, bases, flare mouth jar s, contracted mouth jar s, straight – mouth jar s and ring feet *etc.*	
H6	Southwest of T2	Phung Nguyen culture	Under ④a	Round in upper part and square in lower part	Relatively straight and even	Flat	Upper part diameter of 1. 1m, exposed length of lower square part of 0. 88m, Depth of 0.9m	Accumulations in the pit can be divided into 4 strata: stratum ① is grayish black soil, loose; containing large amount of burnt soil clots, charcoal, pottery pieces and a small number of stone tools, thickness of 0.32 – 0.4 meters; stratum ② is yellow clay soil, soil is pure, containing large amount of iron rust, existing only in northeast corner of pit, containing very small number of pottery pieces; thickness of pottery pieces; 0 – 0.18 meters; stratum ③ is gray soil, soil is loose, containing	Unearthed mostly pottery pieces, with a small number of stone tools. Stone tool is only a scraper. Pottery pieces are mostly fine reddish brown earthenware, terracotta and brown earthenware. Pattern ornamentation was extremely well – developed. The decorations are mostly rope decorations. Other decorations include engraved line, concave string, poking and comb brushing etc. Particularly, among all the engraved lines, the ones with comb teeth brushed or comb dotted stamps are the most characteristic. Compound ornamentations of multiple decorations on a single pottery piece appear to have been very popular. The main ornamentation patterns are of clouds, S – shape and geometric patterns and the like. Pottery mouth parts are mostly trumpet – shaped and	

(continued schedule 3)

Number	Location	Date	Opening to	Shape and Structure			Dimensions	Soil Properties, Color and Inclusions	Unearthed Artifacts	Remarks
				Plane Shape	Walls	Bottom				
								a small number of burnt soil particles, charcoal and pottery pieces; thickness of 0.13 – 0.33 meters; stratum ④, grayish brown soil, hard soil, containing a small number of charcoal, thickness of 0.18 – 0.21cm; Below this stratum is yellowish brown raw soil	straight mouths. Forms of the artifacts include handles, bases, trumpet – shape mouth jars, stem dishes, bowls and thick lip jars *etc.*	
H7	East of T2	Phung Nguyen culture	Under ⑤a	Round	Relatively straight and even	Flat	Diameter of 1.2, Depth of 0.4m	Gray soil deposit in the pit, loose soil, containing small amount of pottery pieces, red burnt soil particles and charcoal	Very few artifacts were unearthed in H7. The ones unearthed are mostly pottery pieces and there is only 1 jade piece. Fine earthenware accounts for the most, with some coarse earthenware and clay earthenware; and terracotta and reddish brown earthenware are the most in terms of color; decorations are mostly twist line pattern, concave patterns, stamp and geometrical ones	

(continued schedule 3)

Number	Location	Date	Opening to	Shape and Structure			Dimensions	Soil Properties, Color and Inclusions	Unearthed Artifacts	Remarks
				Plane Shape	Walls	Bottom				
H8	Below east beam of T2	Phung Nguyen culture	Under ⑤a	Rectangular	Relatively straight and even	Flat	Length of 0.9, Width of 0.78, Depth of 0.5m	Accumulations in the pit can be divided into two strata. Upper one is gray soil, soil is loose, containing a small number of pottery pieces and burnt soil particles, thickness of 0.14 meters; lower layer of yellowish brown clay soil, hard soil, containing a small number of burnt soil particles, thickness of 0.36 meters	Very few artifacts were unearthed. Most are fine earthenware, with small number of clay earthenware. Colors are most terracotta and reddish brown earthenware. Decorations are mostly twist line pattern, concave string pattern, combed dots and engraved patterns. Forms are only ring feet and bowls	
H9	Northeast corner of T5, partly laminated under east beam of the unit	Modern and contemporary times	Under ③	Round	Bucket shape	Flat	Diameter of 0.59, Depth of 0.9m	Reddish brown clay soil filling, compacted structure	Only one piece of reddish brown earthenware	
H10	Northwest corner of T5, partly laminated under north beam of the unit	Modern and contemporary times	Under ③	Oval	Bucket shape	Flat	Length of 0.48, Width of 0.13, Depth of 0.55m	Grayish black loose soil	A small number of pottery and porcelain pieces unearthed	

(continued schedule 3)

Number	Location	Date	Opening to	Shape and Structure			Dimensions	Soil Properties, Color and Inclusions	Unearthed Artifacts	Remarks
				Plane Shape	Walls	Bottom				
H11	Under south wall of T5	Modern and contemporary times	Under ③	Oval	Bucket shape	Flat	Length of 0.59, Width of 0.28, Depth of 0.73m	Grayish black loose soil	A small number of pottery and porcelain pieces unearthed	
H12	Southeast of T5	Modern and contemporary times	Under ③	Oval	Bucket shape	Flat	Diameter of 0.68 – 0.8, Depth of 0.55m	Loose gray soil	A small number of porcelain pieces unearthed	
H13	In east part of T5, partly laminated under east beam of the unit	Modern and contemporary times	Under ③	Oval	Bucket shape	Flat	Diameter of 0.48 – 0.36, Depth of 0.26m	Loose gray soil	A small number of porcelain pieces unearthed	
H14	Northwest of T5	Modern and contemporary times	Under ③	Oval	Uneven	Uneven	Diameter of 0.36 – 0.48, Depth of 0.26m	Loose gray soil	A small number of porcelain pieces unearthed	
H15	Below east beam of T4	Phung Nguyen culture	Under ④a	Irregular rectangular	Bucket shape	Flat	Length of 0.8, Width of 0.64, Depth of 0.2 – 0.36m	Filing is grayish black soil, soil is loose, containing a small number of burnt soil particles and charcoal	Very few pottery pieces unearthed, mostly fine earthenware, less coarse earthenware, mostly reddish brown earthenware and brown ones, with small number of terracotta, grayish brown and blackish brown ones. Decorations are mostly twist line pattern, with some concave string pattern and combed dots. Forms are mostly ring feet and enclosure bases. Identified forms are bowls and kettles	

(continued schedule 3)

| Number | Location | Date | Opening to | Shape and Structure | | | Dimensions | Soil Properties, Color and Inclusions | Unearthed Artifacts | Remarks |
				Plane Shape	Walls	Bottom				
H16	West of T5	Phung Nguyen culture	Under ④a	Irregular rectangular	Arc walls	Dome shape	Length of 2.14, Width of 1.8, Depth of 0.5m	Filing is grayish black soil, soil is loose, containing a small number of burnt soil particles and charcoal	Except for 1 jade piece, all are pottery pieces, mostly fine earthenware, of reddish brown earthenware, some number of yellowish brown, grayish brown, terracotta, brown and blackish brown. Decorations are mostly twist line pattern, with some concave string pattern, engraved patterns, geometrical patterns and combed dots etc. Forms are mostly ring feet and enclosure bases. Identified are bowls, kettles, flare mouth jars	
H17	T5	Phung Nguyen culture	Under ④b	Rectangular	Bucket shape	Flat	Length of 1.14, Width of 1, Depth of 0.72m	Filing is grayish black soil, soil is loose, containing a small number of burnt soil particles and charcoal	Mostly fine earthenware and coarse earthenware, with some clay earthenware, of reddish brown earthenware, some number of yellowish brown, grayish brown, terracotta, brown and blackish brown. Decorations are mostly twist line pattern, with some concave string pattern, engraved patterns, geometrical patterns and combed dots etc. Forms are mostly ring feet. Identified are bowls, straight mouth jars	Broken by H34

(continued schedule 3)

Number	Location	Date	Opening to	Shape and Structure			Dimensions	Soil Properties, Color and Inclusions	Unearthed Artifacts	Remarks
				Plane Shape	Walls	Bottom				
H18	West of T5 and under east beam of T4	Phung Nguyen culture	Under ⑤a	Irregular rectangular	Straight walls	Flat	Length of 1.3, Width of 1 – 1.4, Depth of 0.6m	Filing is grayish black soil, soil is loose, containing a small number of burnt soil particles and charcoal	Mostly fine earthenware and coarse earthenware, with some clay earthenware, of reddish brown earthenware, some number of yellowish brown, grayish brown, terracotta, brown and blackish brown. Decorations are mostly concave string pattern, with some twist line pattern, engraved patterns, geometrical patterns and combed dots etc. Identified are bowls, flare mouth jars	Broken by H15, D5, D6
H19	East of T5	Phung Nguyen culture	Under ⑤a	Rectangular	Relatively straight walls	Flat	Remaining part length of 1.1, remaining part width of 0.8, Depth of 0.22m	Filing is grayish black soil, soil is loose, containing a small number of burnt soil particles and charcoal	Mostly fine earthenware and coarse earthenware, of terracotta, some number of yellowish brown, grayish brown, reddish brown and blackish brown. Decorations are mostly twist line pattern, with some engraved patterns and concave string pattern. Identified are ring feet	
H20	Below north beam of T3	Phung Nguyen culture	Under ⑤a	Irregular oval	Uneven	Uneven	Length of 1.2, Width of 0.2 – 0.9, Depth of 1.48 – 1.8m	Deposit in the pit is grayish black soil, soil is loose, containing a small number of pottery pieces	Mostly fine earthenware, with small number of coarse earthenware. Colors are dominated by terracotta and reddish brown earthenware, followed by blackish brown and less yellowish brown and brown. Decorations are mostly twist line pattern, with small number of engraved patterns, combed dots, poked patterns and string patterns *etc.* Forms are mostly bowls and jars	

(continued schedule 3)

Number	Location	Date	Opening to	Shape and Structure			Dimensions	Soil Properties, Color and Inclusions	Unearthed Artifacts	Remarks
				Plane Shape	Walls	Bottom				
H21	Northeast of T3	Phung Nguyen culture	Under ⑤a	Round	Relatively even	Dome shape	Diameter of 1.6, Depth of 0.64m	Deposit in the pit is grayish black soil, soil is loose, containing very few pottery pieces	Only a small number of fine reddish brown earthenware	Broken by D1, D25
H22	Northeast of T3	Phung Nguyen culture	Under ⑤a	Irregular rectangular	Uneven	Uneven	Length of 0.7, Width of 0.5 – 0.76, Depth of 0.2 – 0.44m	Deposit in the pit is grayish black soil, soil is loose, containing a small number of pottery pieces	Mostly terracotta and reddish brown earthenware, with a small number of fine blackish brown earthenware, brown earthenware and red clay earthenware etc. decorations are mostly twist line patterns, less stamp, circle, concave string, protruding rim and S – shape patterns. Forms are mostly bowls, jars, bases and ring feet	Broken by D14
H23	Northwest of T3	Modern times	Under ①	Stripe	Uneven	Uneven	Length of 1, Width of 0.76, Depth of 0.06 – 0.32m	Grayish black loose soil	Containing small amount of porcelain pieces	Breaking H24
H24	Northwest of T3	Modern times	Under ①	Oval	Relatively even	Flat	Length of 0.5, Width of 0.32, Depth of 0.46 – 0.63m	Compacted pale gray soil	Containing small amount of porcelain pieces	Breaking H23
H26	Center to south of T4	Modern and contemporary times	Under ③	Almost round	Bucket shape	Flat	Diameter of 0.8, Depth of 0.57m	Compacted pale gray soil	Small number of porcelain pieces unearthed	

(continued schedule 3)

Number	Location	Date	Opening to	Shape and Structure			Dimensions	Soil Properties, Color and Inclusions	Unearthed Artifacts	Remarks
				Plane Shape	Walls	Bottom				
H27	Southeast of T4	Modern and contemporary times	Under ③	Almost round	Bucket shape	Flat	Diameter of 0.58, Depth of 0.45m	Compacted pale gray soil	Small number of porcelain pieces unearthed	
H28	Northwest of T4	Modern and contemporary times	Under ③	Almost round	Bucket shape	Flat	Diameter of 0.54 – 0.58, Depth of 0.58 – 0.66m	Compacted pale gray soil	Small number of porcelain pieces unearthed	
H29	Below north beam of T4	Modern and contemporary times	Under ③	Almost round	Bucket shape	Flat	Diameter of 0.8, Depth of 0.74m	Compacted pale gray soil	Small number of porcelain pieces unearthed	
H30	Below east beam of T4	Modern and contemporary times	Under ③	Almost round	Bucket shape	Flat	Diameter of 0.72, Depth of 0.52 – 0.56m	Compacted pale gray soil	Small number of porcelain pieces unearthed	
H31	South of T4	Phung Nguyen culture	Under ⑤b	Irregular rectangular	Uneven walls	Flat	Length of 1.4, Width of 0.56 – 0.7, Depth of 0.42m	Reddish brown clay soil filling, compacted structure	Only one piece of reddish brown earthenware	
H32	Southeast of T7	Modern and contemporary times	Under③	Almost round	Bucket shape	Flat	Diameter of 0.62, Depth of 0.44 – 0.5m	Compacted pale gray soil	Small number of reddish brown earthenware and porcelain pieces	
H33	West of T7	Phung Nguyen culture	Under ⑥	Almost round	Bucket shape	Flat	Diameter of 0.62, Depth of 0.34 – 0.5m	Compacted yellowish brown soil	No artifacts unearthed	
H34	Below east beam of T2	Modern and contemporary times	Under ①	Round	Bucket shape	Dome shape	Diameter of 0.6, Depth of 0.68m	Grayish black loose soil	Small number of pottery and porcelain pieces	Breaking H5

(continued schedule 3)

Number	Location	Date	Opening to	Shape and Structure			Dimensions	Soil Properties, Color and Inclusions	Unearthed Artifacts	Remarks
				Plane Shape	Walls	Bottom				
G1	South of T1	Modern and contemporary times	Under ②	Irregular stripe	Uneven walls	Uneven	Length of 4.9, Width of 1.7 - 2.8, Depth of 0.85m	3 strata in the ditch: stratum ①: partially distributed, loose grayish brown soil, thickness of 0 - 0.15; stratum ②, grayish black soil, thickness of 0.5 meters; and stratum ③, loose yellowish brown soil, thickness of 0.2 meters	Small number of pottery, porcelain, tile, iron and stone pieces unearthed	
G2	Center of T7	Modern and contemporary times	Under ②	Irregular stripe	Uneven walls	Uneven	Length of 4.86, Width of 0.66, Depth of 0.9m	Loose grayish brown soil	Small number of pottery, porcelain, tile, iron and stone pieces unearthed	
G3	Southwest of T4	Modern and contemporary times	Under ②	Irregular stripe	Uneven walls	Uneven	Length of 3.67, Width of 0.3 - 0.73, Depth of 0.15m	Loose gray soil	Small number of pottery, porcelain, tile and iron pieces unearthed	

Annex 4 Table of Statistics of Pottery Systems of Pottery Pieces Unearthed at Nghia Lap Remains

Material / Color / Quantity / Unit	Fine earthenware							Coarse earthenware							Polished clay earthenware					Total	Twist line decor-ation	String	Engr-aved	Dots	Comb brus-hing	Circle	Leaf vein	Com-pound decor-ation	Plain
	Terra-cotta	Red-dish brown	Brown	Blac-kish brown	Yello-wish brown	Gray-ish brown	Total	Terr-acotta	Red-dish brown	Brown	Blac-kish brown	Blac-kish brown	Yello-wish brown	Total	Terr-acotta	Red-dish brown	Brown	Blac-kish brown	Total										
T1⑤a	475	5138	17		14	172	5816	104	139	393	42	325	75	1078		128	46		174	7068	1921	79	84	2	1	1	2	52	4926
T1⑤b		11				33	44	4				18		22	16	10	3	1	30	96	37	6	2			2		3	46
T2⑤a	901	260		373	243		1777	183		95		109		387	165	25		80	270	2434	513	37	81	16	10	18		136	1623
T2⑤b	397	80		183	165		825	9		7		15		31	76	13		4	93	949	148	29	41	11	1	15		94	610
T3⑤a	83	741	632	355	201	202	2214	11	158	25	17	87	32	330	11	46	21	10	88	2632	619	136	183	4	4	2		167	1517
T3⑤b	26	41	45	67	50	83	312	4		2		13		19	4	7	6	7	24	355	59	13	32	1				24	226
T5⑤a	302	234	122	37	89	29	813	43	8	35	10	24	4	124		6	12	3	21	958	214	52	28	1			1	103	559
T5⑤b	4	6			3	3	16				2			2						18	1	5		2					10
H3	599	440	301		39		1379	58		21		66		145		22	60	92	174	1698	360	14	65	22	7	8		82	1140
H4	305	46		50	59		460	25		8		24		57	78				78	595	72	12	35	8	3	1		53	411
H5	654	136		7	93		890	45			13	36		94	84	9		4	97	1081	352	14	55	7	1	4		38	610
H6	114	25		5	32		176	21		8		17		46	39			4	43	265	48	7	10	3	3	1		17	176
H7	12	20		17	7		56	6		2		9		17	17	10		4	31	104	19		1	1		3		13	67
H8	6	6		6	5		23								6					29	2		2					4	21
H15	1	8	10	2		2	23		4	1			1	6						29	8	1	1					5	14
H16	21	72	19	16	34	26	188													188	50	3	12	2				13	108
H17	5	32		5	6	2	50		17	4	7	11		39		2		3		94	12	9	3					18	52
H18	12	9	4	6		5	36		1		2	4		7						43	3	7	2					9	22
H19				1			1	4	1		1	1	1	9						10	3		1					1	5
H20	5	11		15	3		34	10		2	1	2		15						49	10	2	4					4	29
H22	19	46	35	48	15		163	8	8	6	2	15	6	45	2	8	6		16	225	55	14	16					19	121
Total	3941	7362	1185	1193	1058	557	15296	535	336	609	97	776	119	2473	498	286	154	212	1139	18920	4506	440	658	80	30	55	3	855	12293
Percentage	21%	39%	6%	6%	6%	3%	81%	3%	2%	3%	1%	4%	1%	13%	3%	1%	1%	1%	6%	100%	24%	2%	3%	1%				5%	65%

Note: The statistical data of postholes or pits in T4, T7 and the strata in various exploration square units are not included in this Table.

Postscript

Before Nanyue was conquered for the first time by the Qin dynasty, almost nothing about the history, culture and social custom of the South China and the Southeast Asian region was known to the central regions of China. Even by the two Han dynasties period, as we learn from *Huangnanzi*, on south of Huai River, any knowledge about the region was limited to the Lingnan areas. In Wei, Jin and the Southern and Northern dynasties period, particularly with the southward migration of the East Jin dynasty and large – scale development of Lingnan and northern region of Vietnam, information about the history, geography, culture, economy and social custom started to emerge in some of the classical literatures including *Shuijingzhu* (*Notes on Waters*) and *Huayang Guozhi* (*Huayang State Chronicles*). Among these classical narratives, the most notable is the history told of the "southern migration of Shu King Zipan and establishment of Au Lac Kingdom". Yet the historical account is mingled with many absurd folktales. Is this history true? What culture prevailed the Lingnan and northern Vietnam regions before Qin's first conquer of Nanyue?

Since the 1980s, several jade pieces were unearthed in northern Vietnam, Hong Kong and Taiwan that are very similar to those discovered in the Sanxingdui culture. This aroused extensive attention in the academic world. But the history books indicate nothing as to how the Sanxingdui remains, as the most important one in the Xia and Shang periods in upper streams of Yangtze River, influenced China's southeast coastal regions and the Southeast Asian regions. Therefore, objectives of implementation of this project are to construct a historical framework spanning from Sanxingdui to Southeast Asia, and to sort the timelines in history as well as the cultural routes taken to reconstruct the grand cultural exchange context in early Qin period.

Though this report does not reveal in full picture the grand historical background from Sanxingdui to Vietnam, it offers us new clues to reconstruct the "Southern Silk Road". We believe with the continued implementation of the archaeological work, a full picture of the grand history from Sanxingdui to Vietnam will be presented and serve as a basis for the development of "Silk Road" in the new era.

Leader of the archaeological excavation team is Lei Yu from Institute of Cultural Relics and Archaeology of Sichuan Province and Yue Lianjian from Institute of Archaeology of Shaanxi Province. Chinese members of the team participating in the excavation are Chen Weidong from Institute of Cultural Relics and Archaeology of Sichuan Province, Yue Lianjian and Sun Weigang from Institute of Archaeology of Shaanxi Province. Vietnamese members are Vu Quoc Hien, Vu Quoc Hien, Nguyen Van Doan, Truong Dac Chien, Le Hoai Anh, Chu Van Ve, Le Ngoc Hung, Nguyen Quoc Binh Nyuyen Van Hao from Institute of Archaeology of the Vietnam National Centre for Social Sciences and Culture. Translation during the excavation works were undertaken by Nyuyen Van Hao and Wu Shi Juan.

This report is co – authored by Chen Weidong, Lei Yu, Yue Lianjian and Sun Weigang. Illustrations are made by Le Hoai Anh. Zhao Jianqing from Institute of Cultural Relics and Archaeology of Sichuan Province drew some of the illustrations. Liu Wei is responsible for translating the Report into English. Restoration of pottery pieces was undertaken by Chu Van Ve. C – 14 dating was carried out by Chinese Academy of Social Sciences Archaeology Institute, Peking University and Vietnam National Museum of History.

Our works received care and support from all sides including the great support from Sichuan Province Cultural Relics Bureau, Shaanxi Province Cultural Relics Bureau, Vietnam National Museum of History, Vietnam Vinh Phuc Province Museum, Vietnam Phu Tho Province Museum and other organisations and departments. Mr. Gao Dalun, Mr. Zhou Kehua, Mr. Chen Xiandan and Mr. Tang Fei fro Institute of Cultural Relics and Archaeology of Sichuan Province, Mr. Jiao Nanfeng, Mr. Yin Shenping, Mr. Wang Weilin and Mr. Sun Bingjun from Institute of Archaeology of Shaanxi Province provided much care and support throughout the archaeological excavation and data sorting. They also reviewed some of the texts and offered excellent suggestions for revision. In particular, Mr. Gao Dalun, director of the Institute of Cultural Relics and Archaeology of Sichuan Province, wrote an insightful foreword for this Report, with the entrustment of Mr. Jiao Nanfeng and Mr. Wang Weilin, the former and current directors of Institute of Archaeology of Shaanxi Province, which provided further insights for the future work. Mr. Nyuyen Van Hao from Institute of Archaeology of the Vietnam National Centre for Social Sciences and Culture and Mr. Nguyen Quoc Binh from Vietnam National Museum of History not only helped as excellent translators during the archaeological excavation and in accompanying us on the research tours, but also impressed us with their expertise. We would like to express our sincere gratitude to above organizations and gentlemen.

As the excavation was carried out a long time ago, and the editors of this report have their limitations and had to work under a tight timetable, mistakes and omissions are inevitable. We appreciate comments and suggestions from relevant experts and scholars.

Authors and Compilers

March 2016

彩版

彩版一　遗址远景

彩版一　遗址远景
Plate 1　Panoramic View of Nghia Lap Site in Vietnam

彩版二　遗址勘探
Plate 2　Archeological Exploration

1. 越南国家历史博物馆工作人员前往义立寺祭拜

1. Vietnam National Museum of History Staff at Worship Ritual at Nghia Lap Temple

2. 义立寺法师在工地上祭祀

2. Nghia Lap Temple priest at Ritual Carried out at the Site

彩版三　发掘前准备

Plate 3　Priest before Excavation

彩版四　发掘场景

Plate 4　Excavation in Progress

彩版五 发掘场景

Plate 5 Excavation in Progress

彩版六　发掘场景

Plate 6　Excavation in Progress

彩版七　发掘场景

Plate 7　Excavation in Progress

彩版八　发掘区全景（未打隔梁）

Plate 8　Panoramic View of the Excavation Area (Before Partitions set up)

彩版九　发掘区全景（打隔梁后）

Plate 9　Panoramic View of the Excavation Area (After Partitions set up)

彩版一〇　发掘区局部

Plate 10　Distribution of the Square Pits

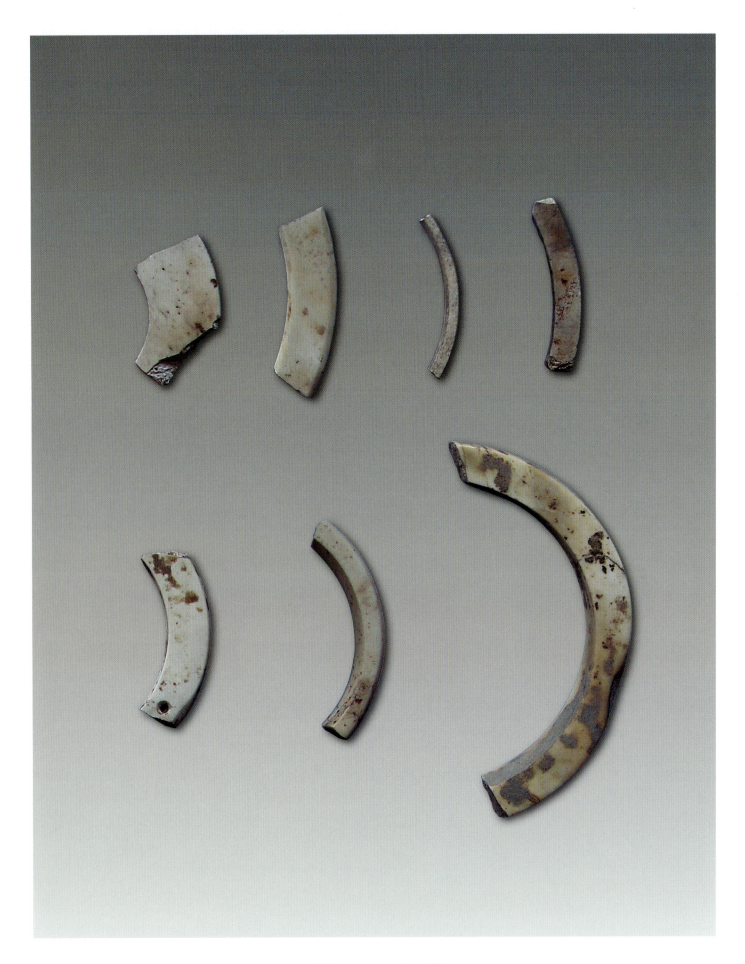

彩版一一　出土玉器

Plate 11　Unearthed Jade Pieces

彩版一二　出土石器

Plate 12　Unearthed Stone Pieces

彩版一三　出土石器

Plate 13　Unearthed Stone Pieces

彩版一四　出土石器

Plate 14　Unearthed Stone Pieces

1. 发掘人员合影（从右向左：陈卫东、雷雨、阮文好、岳连建、孙伟刚）
1. Chinese Staff and Nyuyen Van Hao (Right to Left: Chen Weidong, Lei Yu, Nyuyen Van Hao, Yue Lianjian and Sun Weigang)

2. 新闻发布会现场
2. Press Conference

彩版一五　发掘人员合影及召开新闻发布会
Plate 15　Excavation Staff and Press Conference

彩版一六　T1 南壁剖面

Plate 16　Section of South Wall of T1

彩版一七　T1⑤a层下柱洞

Plate 17　Distribution of Postholes under T1⑤a

1. T1 ⑤ a :1

2. T1 ⑤ a:13

3. T1 ⑤ a:7

4. T1 ⑤ a:2

彩版一八　T1 出土石锛
Plate 18　Stone Adzes from T1

2. T1 ⑤ a:10

1. G1:1

3. T1 ⑤ a:25

彩版一九　T1 出土石锛

Plate 19　Stone Adzes from T1

1. 锛（T1 ⑤ a:3）
1. Adze (T1 ⑤ a: 3)

2. 箭镞（T1 ⑤ a:8）
2. Arrowhead (T1 ⑤ a: 8)

彩版二〇　T1 出土玉器
Plate 20　Jade Pieces from T1

彩版二一　T1⑤a层出土刻划纹陶片

Plate 21　Pottery Pieces with Engraved Pattern Unearthed from T1⑤a

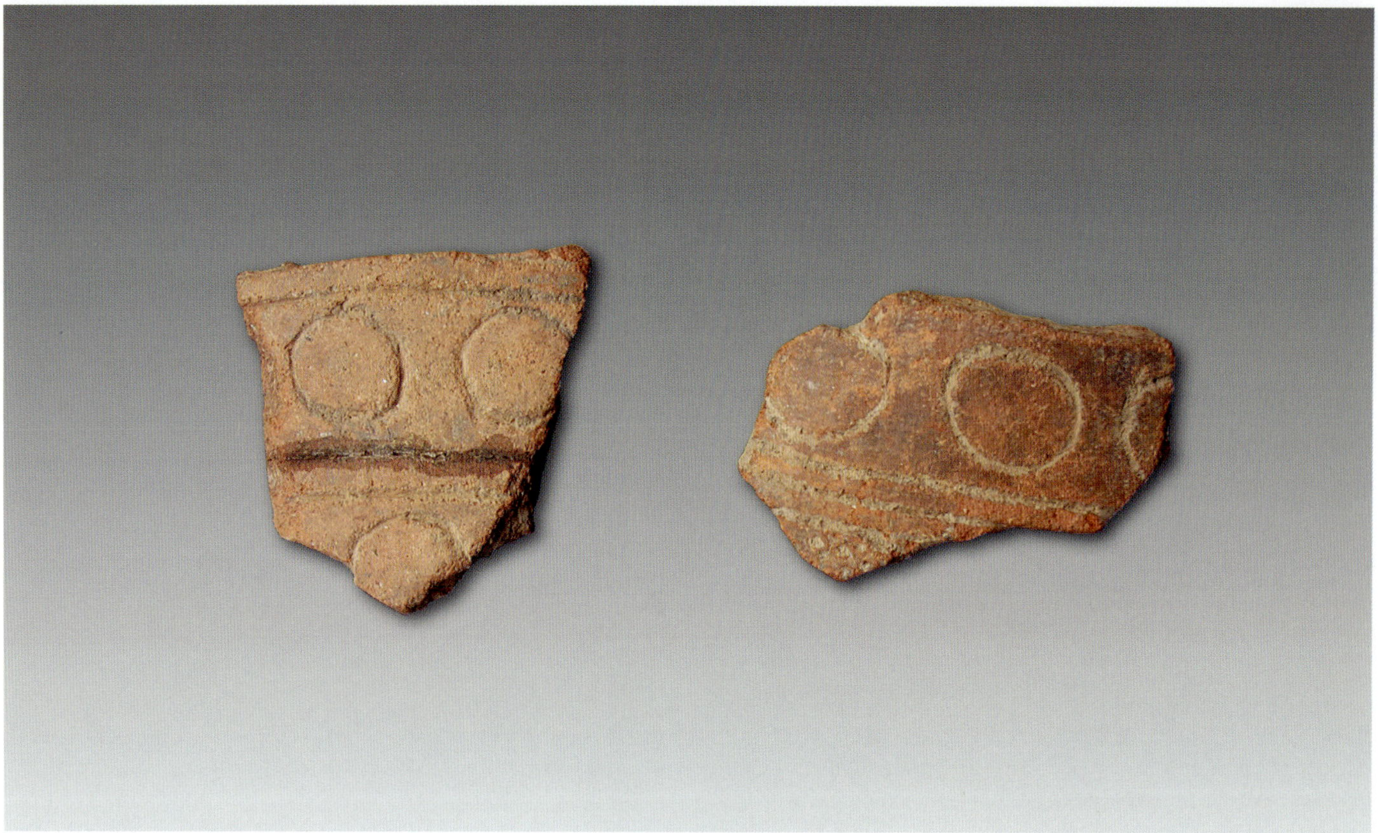

1. 圆圈纹陶片
1. Pottery Pieces with Circle Pattern

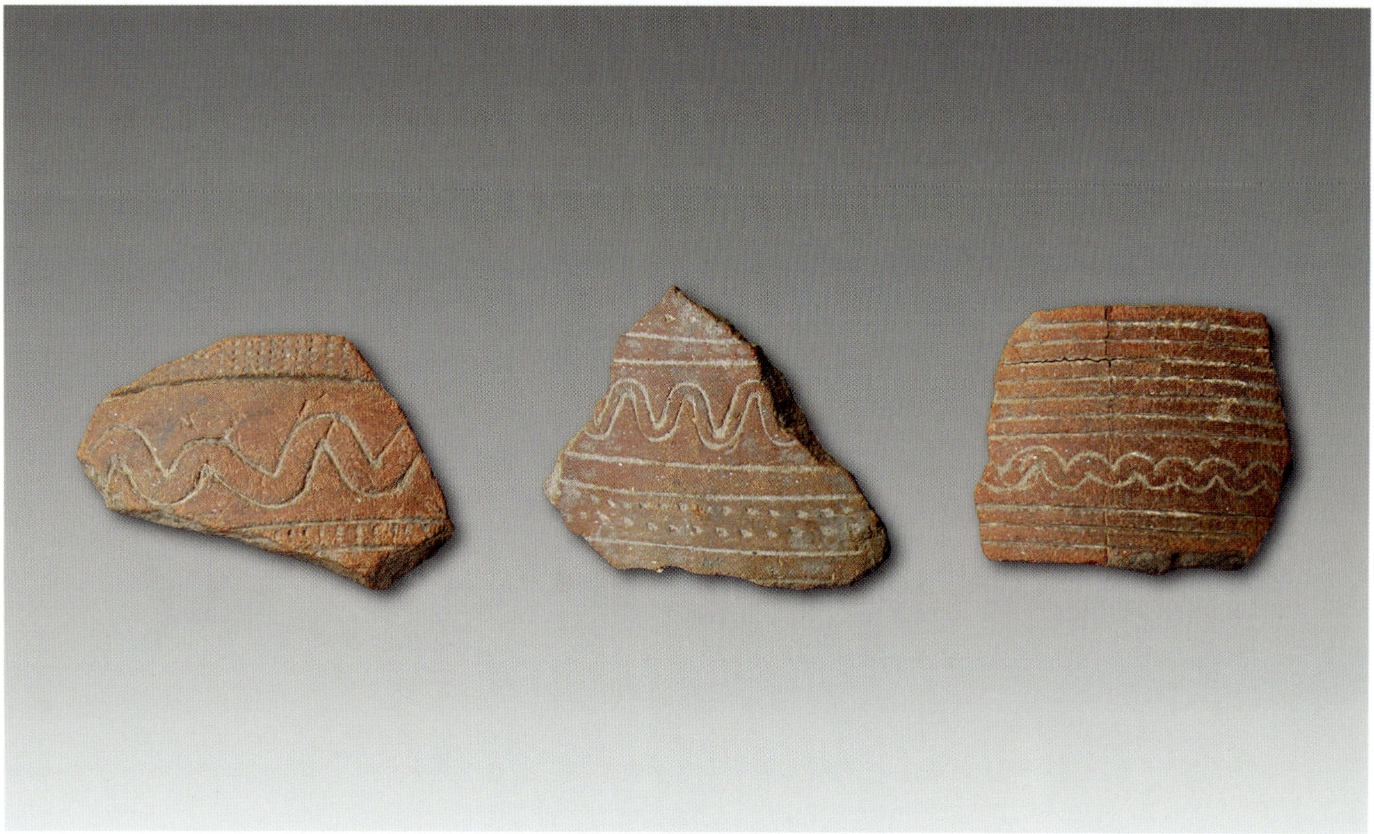

2. 水波纹陶片
2. Pottery Pieces with Water Ripple Pattern

彩版二二　T1 ⑤ a 层出土圆圈纹、水波纹陶片
Plate 22　Pottery Pieces Unearthed from T1⑤a

彩版二三　T1⑤a层出土 S 形纹陶片

Plate 23　Pottery Pieces with S-shape Pattern and Water Ripple Pattern Unearthed from T1⑤a

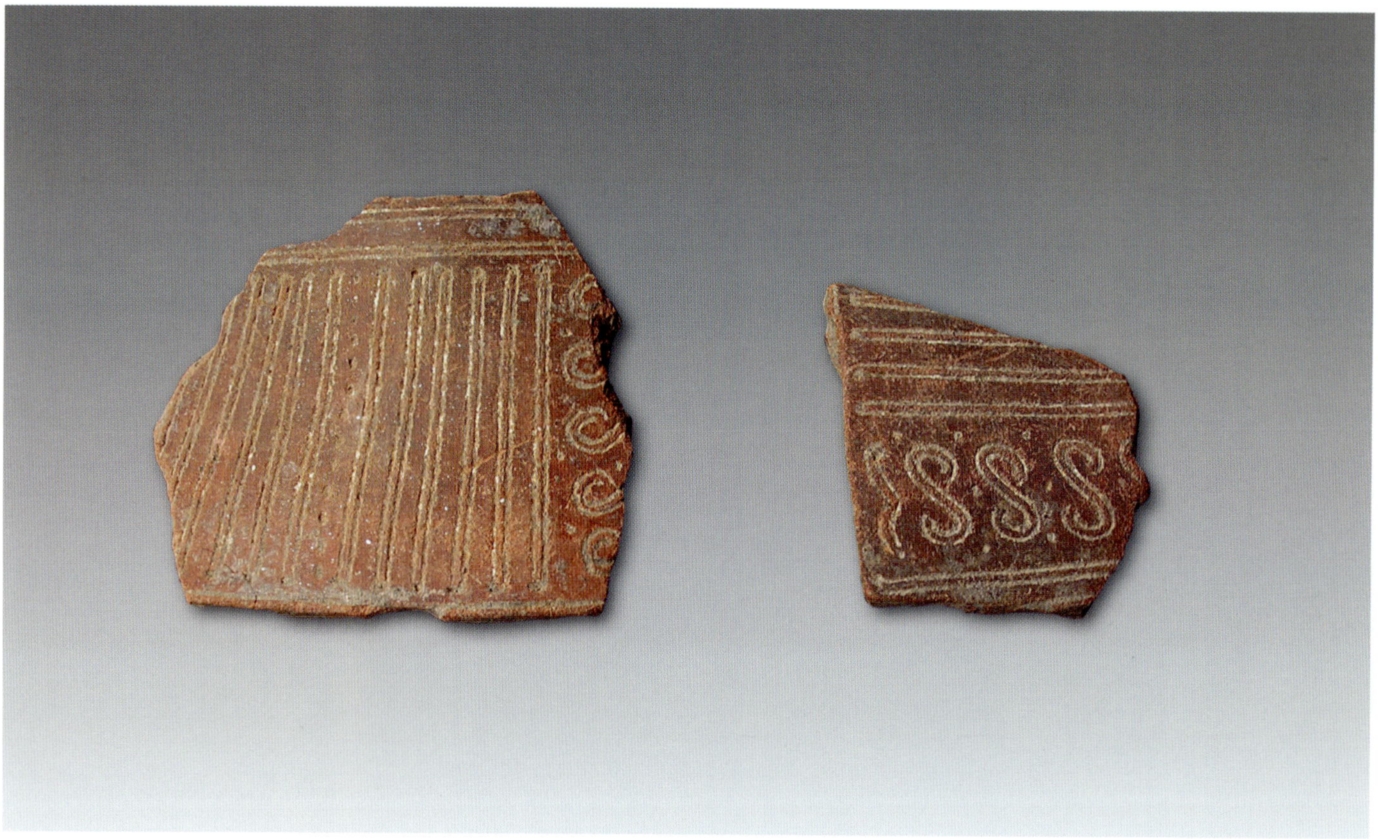

1. S 形纹陶片
1. Pottery Pieces with S-shape Pattern

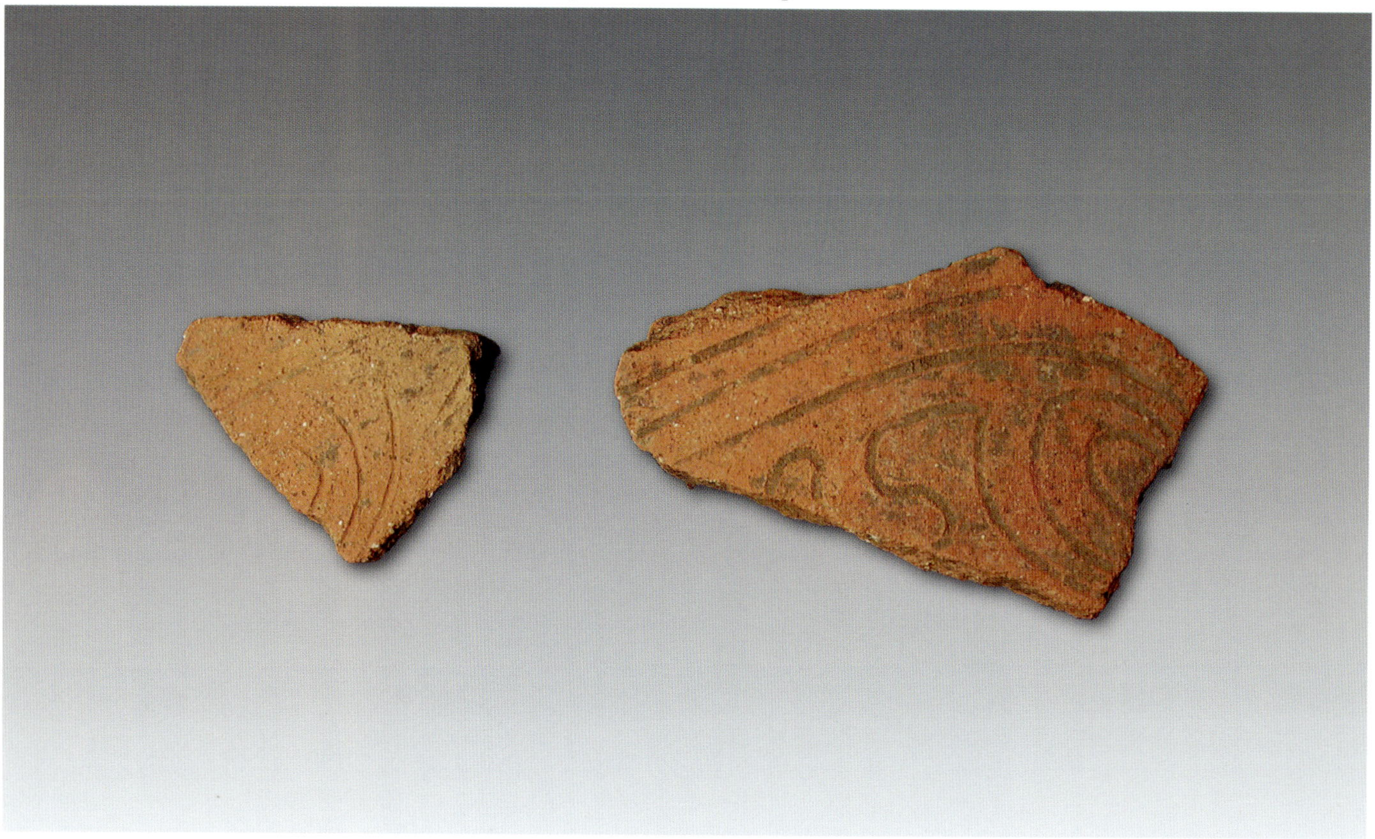

2. 刻划纹陶片
2. Pottery Pieces with Engraved Pattern

彩版二四　T1 ⑤ a 层出土 S 形纹、刻划纹陶片
Plate 24　Pottery Pieces with S–shape Pattern and Engraved Pattern Unearthed from T1⑤a

彩版二五 T1⑤a层出土刻划纹陶片
Plate 25 Pottery Pieces with Engraved Pattern Unearthed from T1⑤a

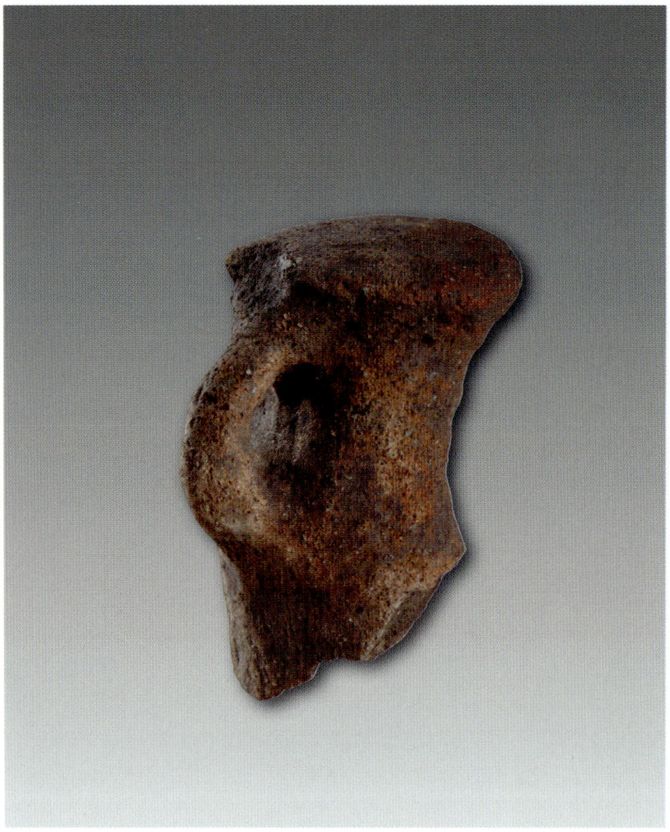

1. 支座（T1 ⑤ a:57）
1. Bases (T1 ⑤ a: 57)

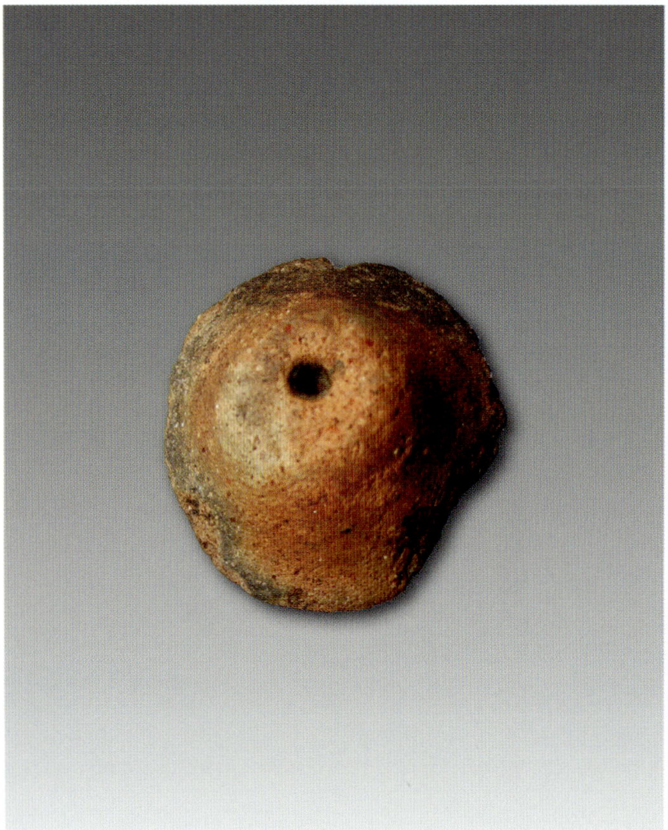

2. 纺轮（T1 ⑤ a:4）
2. Spinning Wheel (T1 ⑤ a: 4)

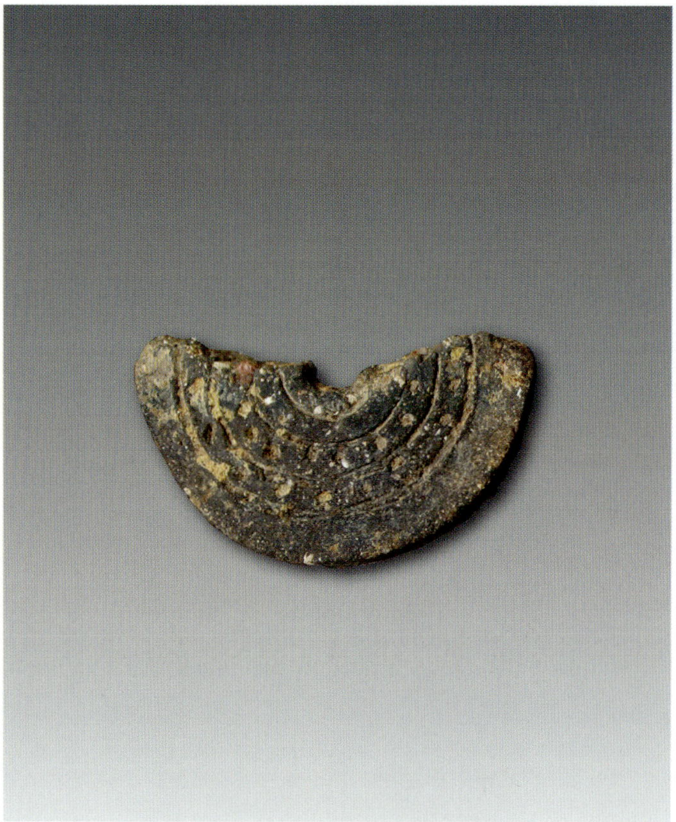

3. 纺轮（T1 ⑤ a:18）
3. Spinning Wheel (T1 ⑤ a: 18)

彩版二六　T1 出土陶器
Plate 26　Pottery Pieces Unearthed from T1

1. T1 ⑤ a:182

2. T1 ⑤ a:180

3. T1 ⑤ a:181

4. T1 ⑤ a:188

彩版二七　T1 出土陶圈足

Plate 27　Pottery Ring Feet Unearthed from T1

彩版二八　T2 东壁剖面

Plate 28　Section of East Wall of T2

彩版二九　T2 内灰坑

Plate 29　Distribution of Pits in T2

彩版三〇　H3 第①层陶器出土情况

Plate 30　Pottery Pieces Unearthed from H3 Stratum ①

彩版三一　H3 第②层陶器出土情况
Plate 31　Pottery Pieces Unearthed from H3 Stratum ②

彩版三二　H3 第③层陶器出土情况

Plate 32　Pottery Pieces Unearthed from H3 Stratum ③

彩版三三　H3 出土陶器纹饰组合

Plate 33　Portfolio of Pottery Patterns of Pieces Unearthed from H3

彩版三四　H3 出土陶器纹饰组合

Plate 34　Portfolio of Pottery Patterns of Pieces Unearthed from H3

彩版三五　H3 出土陶器组合
Plate 35　Portfolio of Pottery Pieces Unearthed from H3

彩版三六　H3 出土陶器组合

Plate 36　Portfolio of Pottery Pieces Unearthed from H3

彩版三七　H3 出土陶器组合
Plate 37　Portfolio of Pottery Pieces Unearthed from H3

1. 球
1. Pottery Balls

2. 钵（H3:71）
2. Pottery Bowl (H3:71)

3. 圈足（H3:31）
3. Ring Foot (H3:31)

彩版三八　H3 出土陶器
Plate 38　Pottery Artifacts Unearthed from H3

彩版三九　H3 出土陶釜（H3:81）

Plate 39　Pottery Kettle (H3:81) Unearthed from H3

1. 颈部纹饰
1. Pattern on the kettle

2. 底部纹饰
2. Ornamentation on bottom of kettle

彩版四〇　H3 出土陶釜（H3:81）局部
Plate 40　Part of Pottery Kettle (H3:81) Unearthed from H3

1. 釜（H3:73）
1. Pottery Kettle (H3:73)

2. 圜底器（H3:75）
2. Enclosure Base (H3:75)

3. 圜底器（H3:75）
3. Enclosure Base (H3:75)

彩版四一　H3 出土陶器
Plate 41　Pottery Artifacts Unearthed from H3

彩版四二　H4

Plate 42　H4

彩版四三　H4 出土器物组合
Plate 43　Portfolio of Stone Tools Unearthed from H4

1. 锛（H4:5）
1. Stone Adze (H4:5)

3. 范（H4:7）
3. Stone Mold (H4:7)

2. 锛（H4:1）
2. Stone Adze (H4: 1)

彩版四四　H4 出土石器
Plate 44　Stone Tools Unearthed from H4

彩版四五　H4 出土陶器纹饰组合

Plate 45　Portfolio of Pottery Patterns of Pieces Unearthed from H4

彩版四六　H4 出土陶器纹饰组合

Plate 46　Portfolio of Pottery Patterns of Pieces Unearthed from H4

彩版四七　H4 出土陶器组合
Plate 47　Portfolio of Pottery Pieces Unearthed from H4

彩版四八　H4 出土陶器组合

Plate 48　Portfolio of Pottery Pieces Unearthed from H4

1. 圈足（H4:15）
1. Bases (H4:31)

2. 支座（H4:31）
2. Ring Feet (H4:15)

彩版四九　H4 出土陶器
Plate 49　Pottery Artifacts Unearthed from H4

彩版五〇　H5

Plate 50　H5

彩版五一　H5 出土陶器纹饰组合

Plate 51　Portfolio of Pottery Patterns of Pieces Unearthed from H5

彩版五二　H5 出土陶器纹饰组合

Plate 52　Portfolio of Pottery Patterns of Pieces Unearthed from H5

彩版五三　H5 出土陶器组合
Plate 53　Portfolio of Pottery Pieces Unearthed from H5

彩版五四　H5 出土陶器组合

Plate 54　Portfolio of Pottery Pieces Unearthed from H5

1. 球
1. Balls

2. 器耳（H5:18）
2. Utensil Ear (H5:18)

3. 器耳（H5:17）
3. Utensil Ear (H5:17)

彩版五五　H5 出土陶器
Plate 55　Pottery Artifacts Unearthed from H5

1. 侈口罐（H5:20）
1. Flare mouth jar (H5: 20)

2. 厚唇罐（H5:21）
2. Thick lip jar（H5:21）

彩版五六　H5 出土陶罐
Plate 56　Pottery Thick Lip Jars and Flare Mouth Jars Unearthed from H5

彩版五七　H6出土陶器纹饰组合

Plate 57　Portfolio of Pottery Patterns of Pieces Unearthed from H6

彩版五八　H6 出土陶器组合

Plate 58　Portfolio of Pottery Pieces Unearthed from H6

1. 器鋬（H6:2）
1. Handle (H6:2)

2. 豆（H6:5）
2. Hexagon Stem Dish(H6:5)

彩版五九　H6 出土陶器
Plate 59　Stone Tools Unearthed from H6

1. 拍（T2 ⑤ a:4）
1. Flapper (T2 ⑤ a: 4)

2. 锛（T2 ⑤ a:6）
2. Adze (T2 ⑤ a: 6)

3. 锛（T2 ⑤ a:11）
3. Adze (T2 ⑤ a: 11)

4. 锛（T2 ⑤ a:3）
4. Adze (T2 ⑤ a: 3)

彩版六一　T2 出土石器
Plate 61　Stone Tools Unearthed from T2

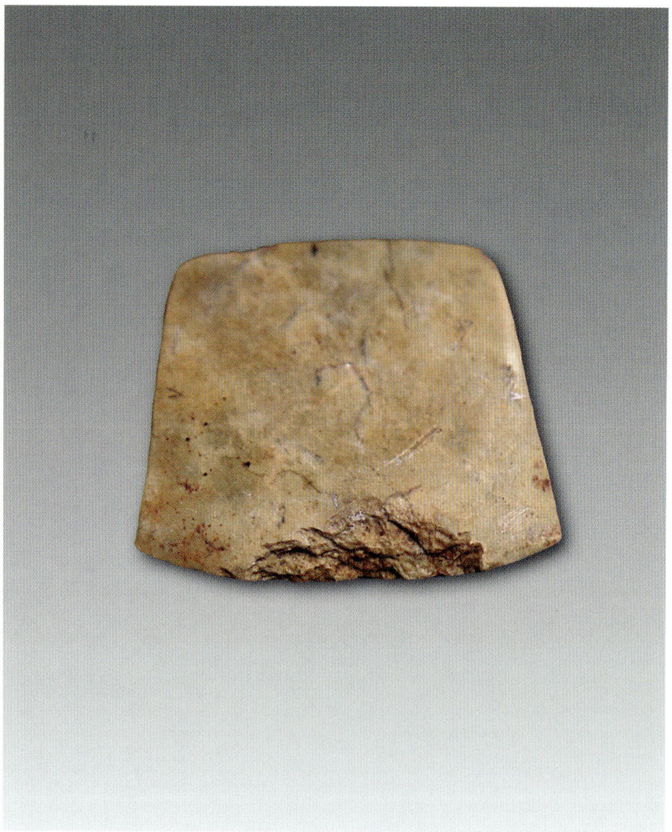

1. 石锛（T2 ⑤ a:5）
1. Stone Adze (T2 ⑤ a: 5)

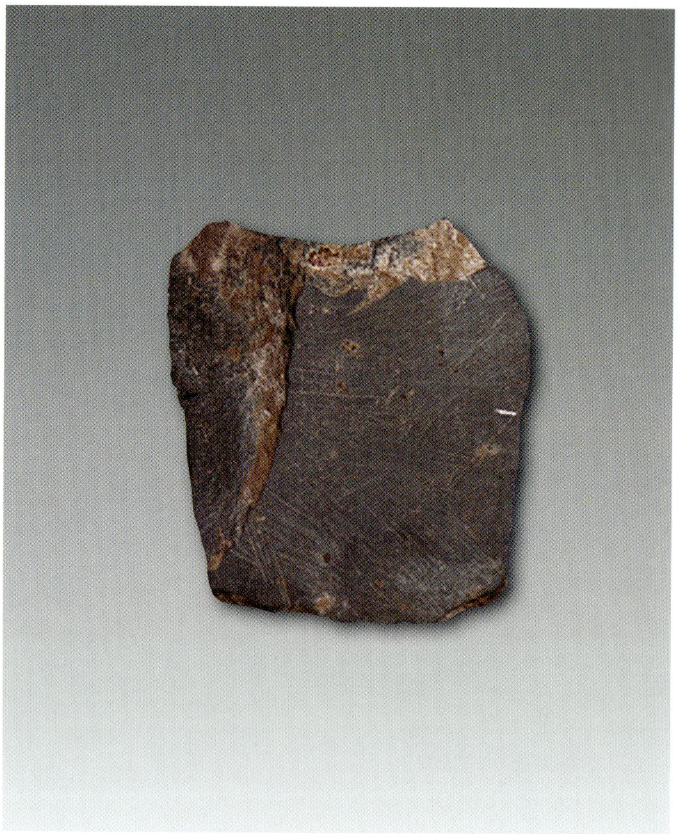

2. 石璧形器（T2 ⑤ a:2）
2. Stone Piece (T2 ⑤ a: 2)

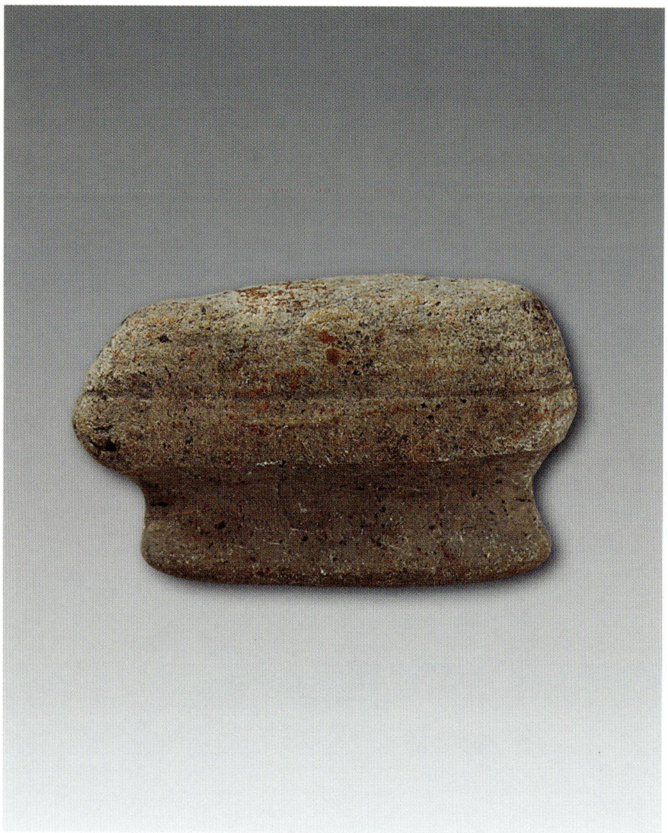

3. 石网坠（T2 ⑤ a:14）
3. Net Sinker (T2 ⑤ a: 14)

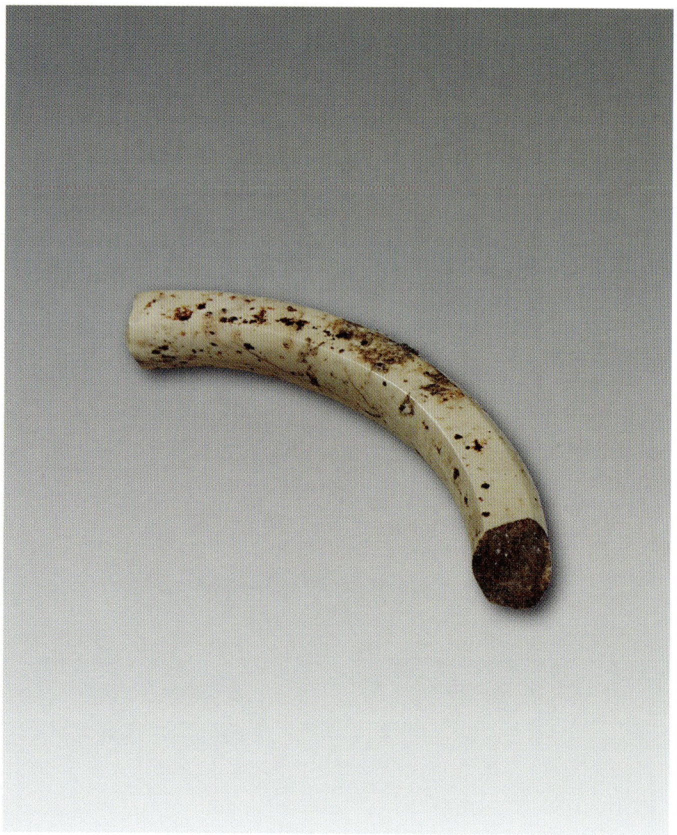

4. 玉环（T2 ⑤ a:9）
4. Jade Ring (T2 ⑤ a: 9)

彩版六二　T2 出土器物
Plate 62　Stone and Jade Tools Unearthed from T2

彩版六三　T2 ⑤ a 层出土陶器纹饰组合

Plate 63　Portfolio of Pottery Patterns of Pieces Unearthed from T2 ⑤ a

彩版六四　T2 ⑤ a 层出土陶器纹饰组合

Plate 64　Portfolio of Pottery Patterns of Pieces Unearthed from T2 ⑤ a

彩版六五　T2 ⑤ a 层出土陶器纹饰组合

Plate 65　Portfolio of Pottery Patterns of Pieces Unearthed from T2 ⑤ a

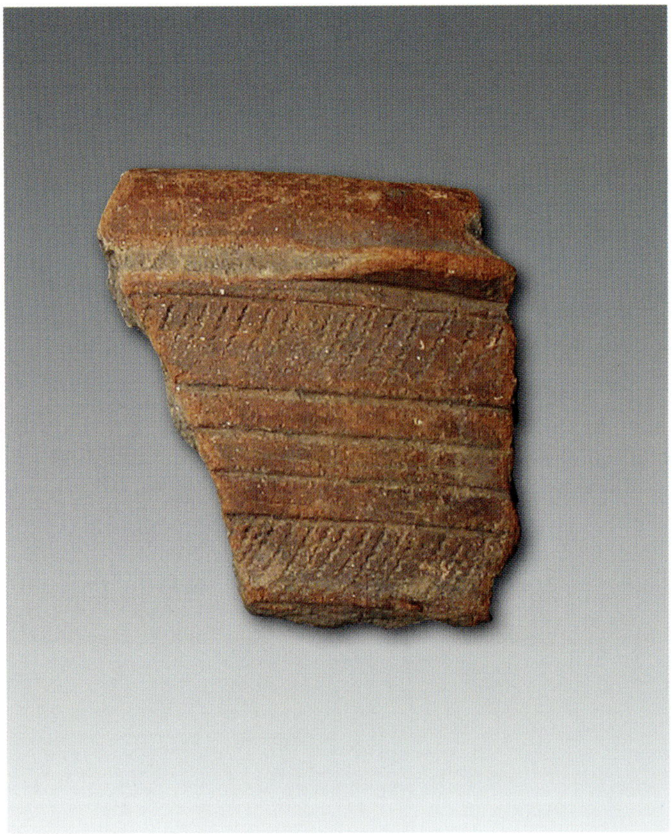

1. T2 ⑤ a:61

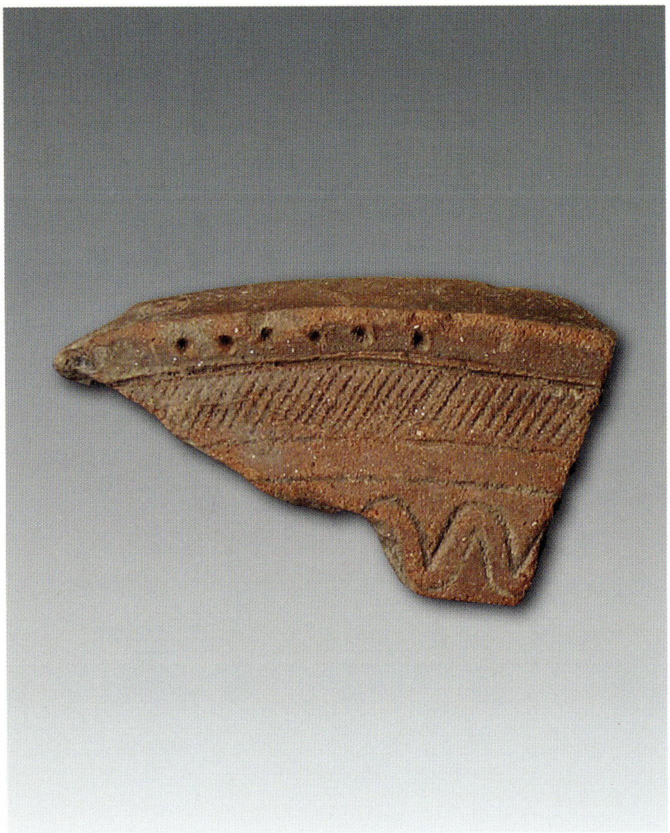

2. T2 ⑤ a:67

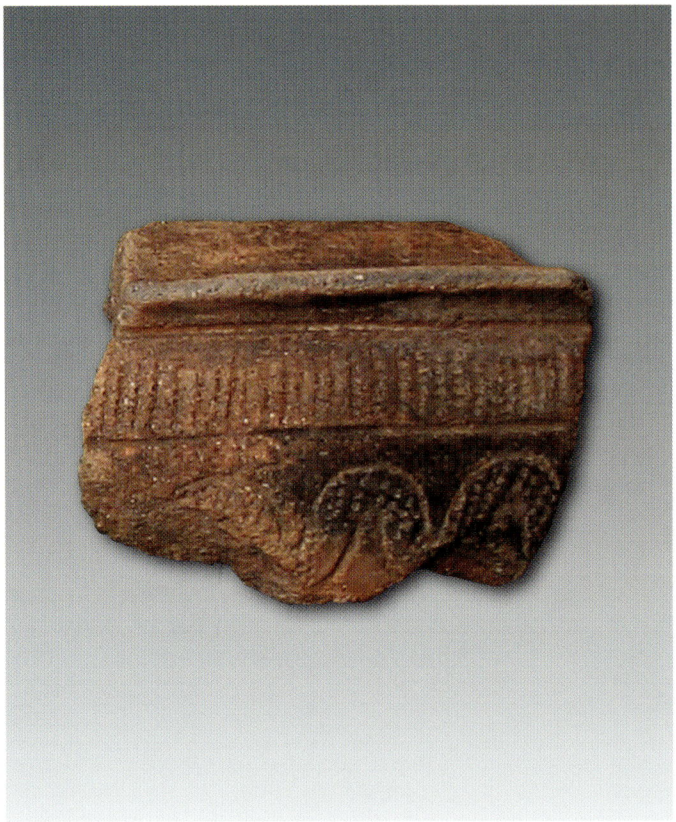

3. T2 ⑤ a:62

彩版六六　T2 出土陶敛口罐

Plate 66　Pottery Contracted Mouth Jars Unearthed from T2⑤a

彩版六七　T2⑤a层出土陶圈足

Plate 67　Pottery Ring Feet Unearthed from T2⑤a

彩版六八　T2 ⑤ b 层出土陶器纹饰组合

Plate 68　Portfolio of Pottery Patterns of Pieces Unearthed from T2 ⑤ b

彩版六九　T2⑤b层出土陶器组合

Plate 69　Portfolio of Pottery Pieces Unearthed from T2⑤b

彩版七〇　T2 ⑤ b 层出土陶器组合
Plate 70　Portfolio of Pottery Pieces Unearthed from T2 ⑤ b

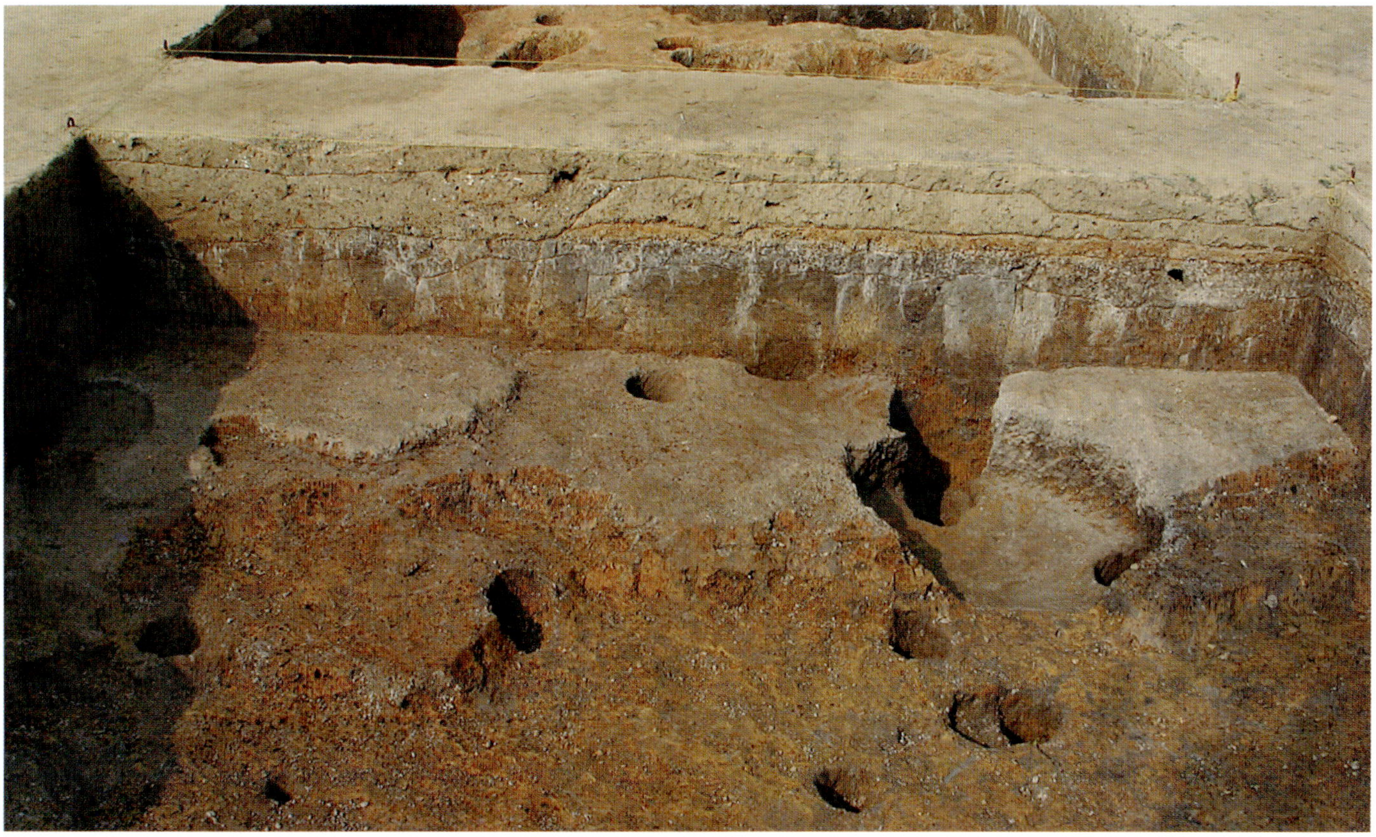

1. T3 北壁剖面
1. Section of North Wall of T3

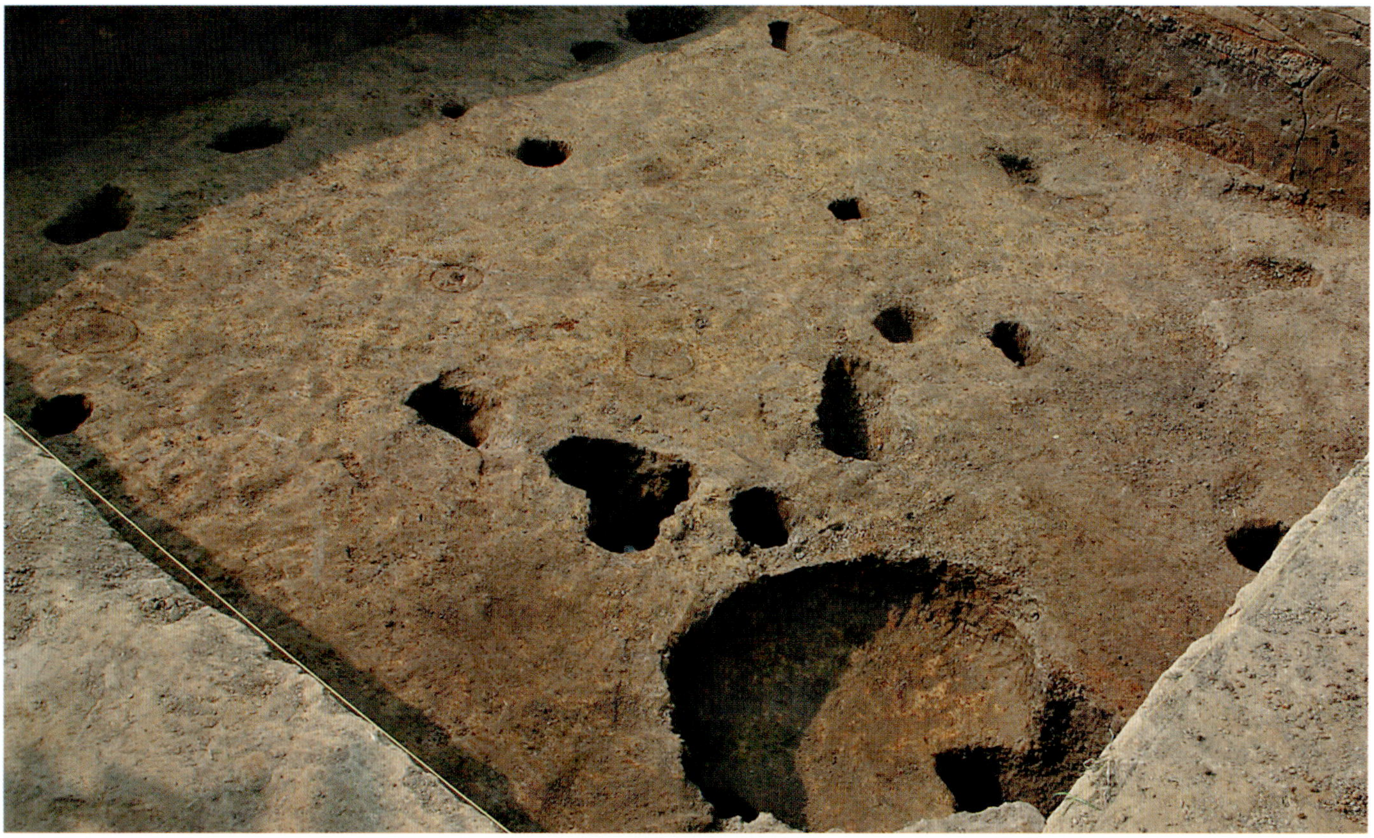

2.T3 ⑤ a 层下遗迹
2. Remains under T3 ⑤ a

彩版七一　T3 北壁剖面及 T3 ⑤ a 层下遗迹
Plate 71　Section of North Wall of T3 and Remains under T3 ⑤ a

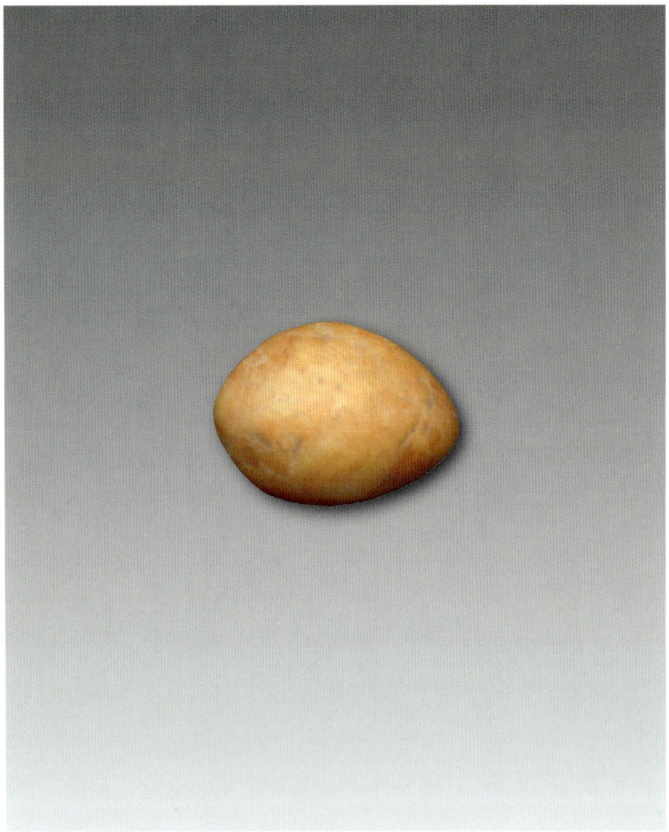

1. 石球（T3 ②:2）
1. Stone Ball (T3 ② : 2)

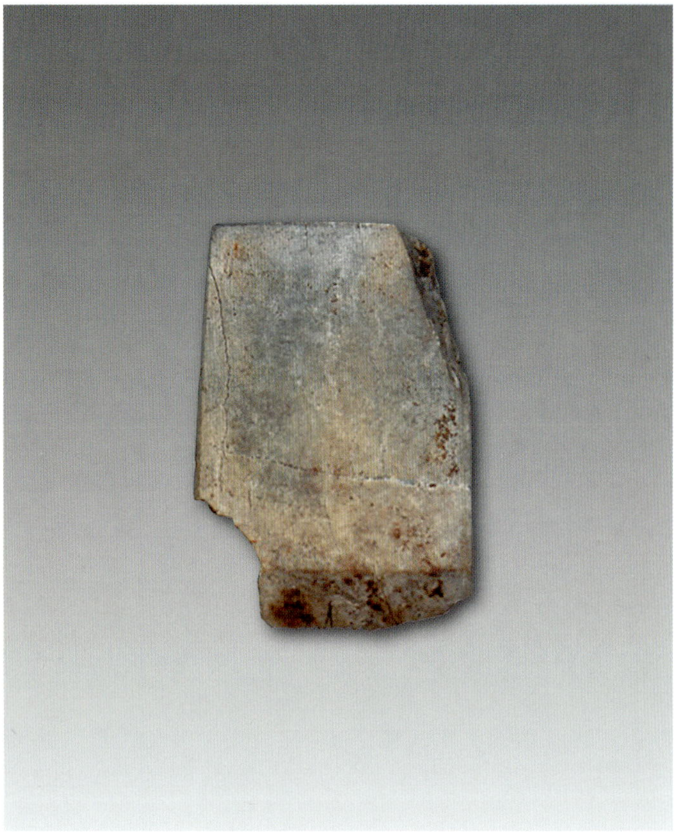

2. 石锛（T3 ⑤ a:5）
2. Stone Adze (T3 ⑤ a:5)

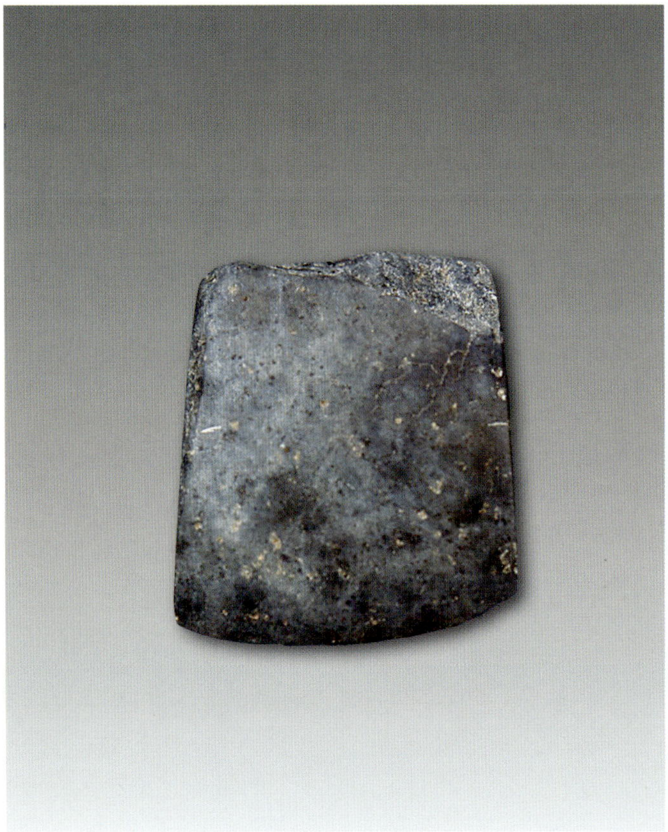

3. 石锛（T3 ⑤ a:3）
3. Stone Adze (T3 ⑤ a:3)

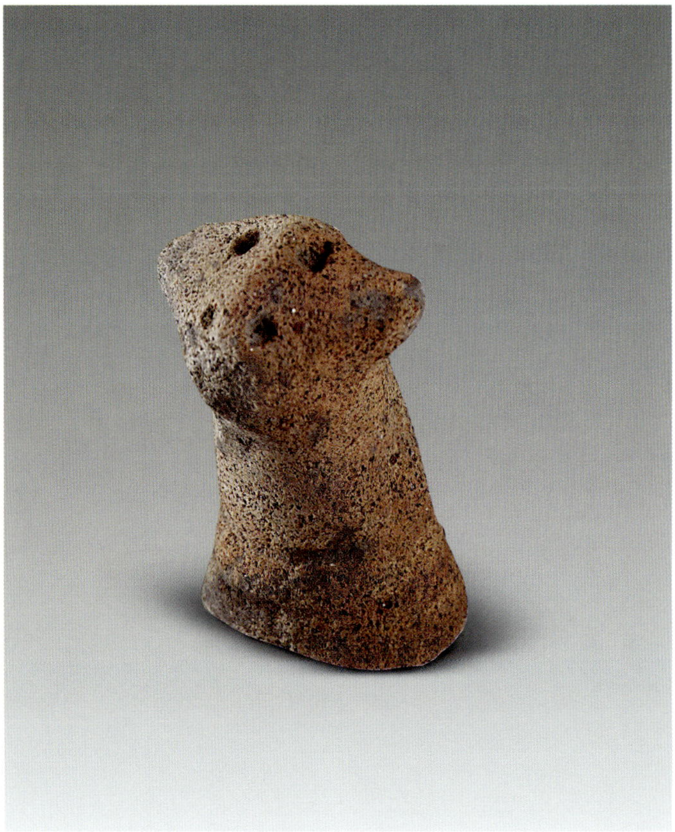

4. 陶器柄（T3 ⑤ a:4）
4. Pottery Utensil Handle (T3 ⑤ a: 4)

彩版七二　T3 出土器物
Plate 72　Stone and Pottery Pieces Unearthed from T3

彩版七三　T3 ⑤ a 层出土陶器纹饰组合
Plate 73　Portfolio of Pottery Patterns of Pieces Unearthed from T3 ⑤ a

彩版七四　T3 ⑤ a 层出土陶器纹饰组合
Plate 74　Portfolio of Pottery Patterns of Pieces Unearthed from T3 ⑤ a

彩版七五　T3 ⑤ a 层出土陶器纹饰组合
Plate 75　Portfolio of Pottery Patterns of Pieces Unearthed from T3 ⑤ a

彩版七六　T3 ⑤ a 层出土陶器组合
Plate 76　Portfolio of Pottery Pieces Unearthed from T3 ⑤ a

彩版七七　T3 ⑤ a 层出土陶器组合
Plate 77　Portfolio of Pottery Pieces Unearthed from T3 ⑤ a

彩版七八　T3 ⑤ b 层出土陶器组合

Plate 78　Portfolio of Pottery Pieces Unearthed from T3 ⑤ b

彩版七九　T3 ⑤ b 层出土陶器组合
Plate 79　Portfolio of Pottery Pieces Unearthed from T3 ⑤ b

彩版八〇　T4 ⑤ a 层下遗迹

Plate 80　Remains under T4 ⑤ a

彩版八一　M1

Plate 81　M1

1.M1墓主人及随葬品
1. M1 Tomb Owner and Burial Objects

2. 加固人骨
2. Reinforced Skeleton

1. 发掘出人骨时的祭祀
1. Ritual on Excavating the Skeleton

2. 搬运人骨前的祭祀
2. Ritual before Moving the Skeleton

彩版八三　M1 清理后祭祀
Plate 83　Ritual at M1

1. 正视
1. Pottery Stem Dish (M1:1)

2. 局部纹饰
2. Part of Pottery Stem Dish (M1:1)

彩版八四　M1 出土陶豆（M1:1）
Plate 84　Pottery Stem Dish (M1:1) Unearthed from M1

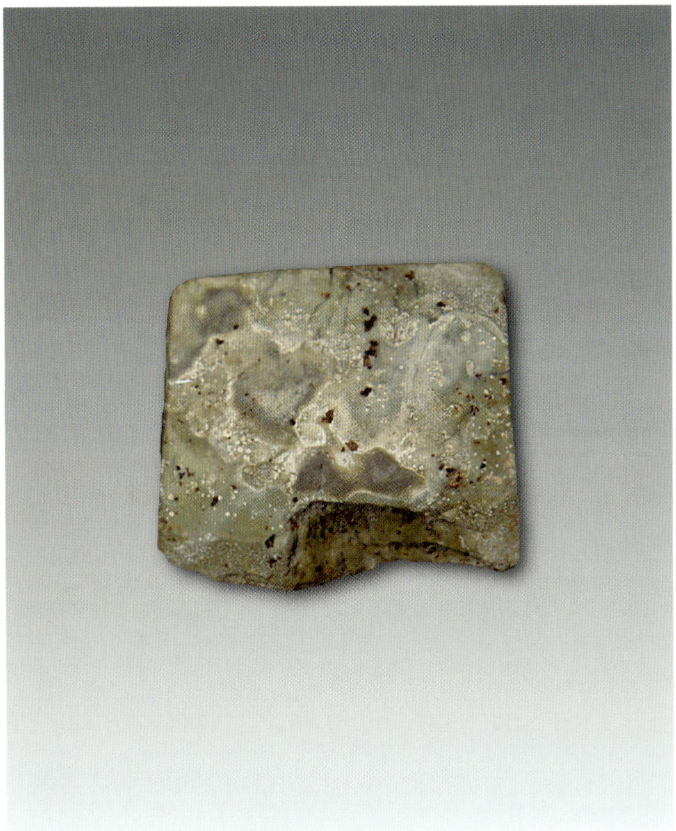

1. 石锛（T4⑤a:2）
1. Stone Adze (T4⑤a: 2)

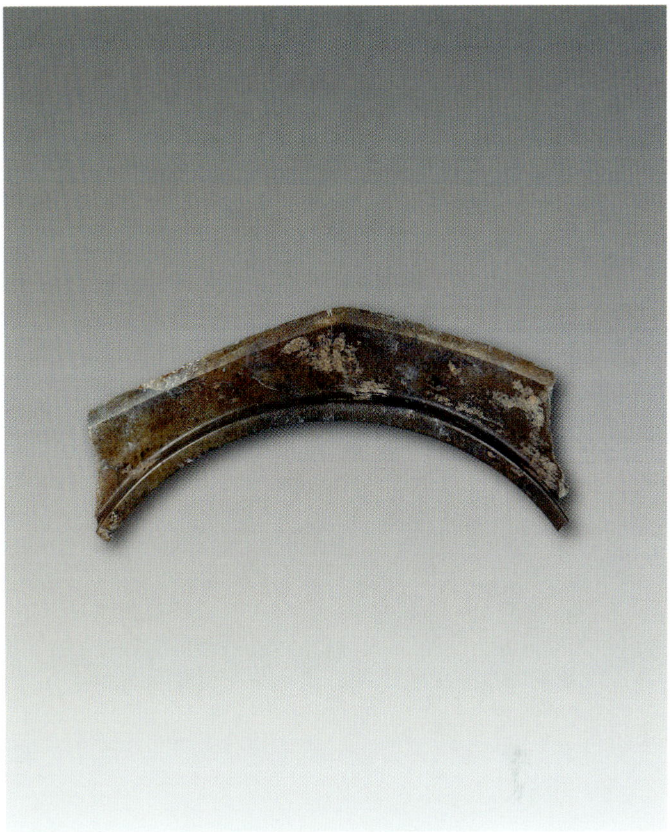

2. T字形玉环（T4⑤a:5）
2. T-shaped Ring (T4⑤a: 5)

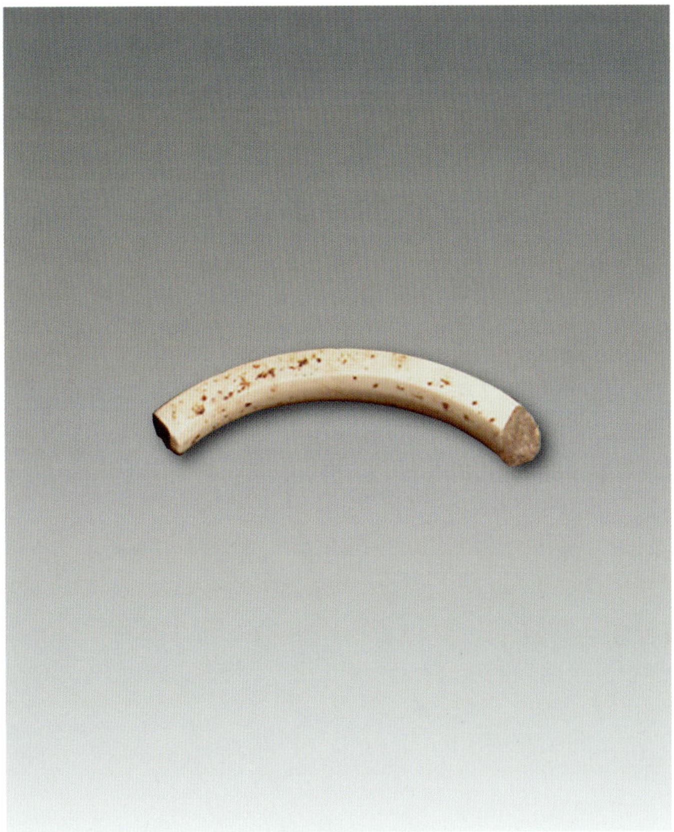

3. 玉环（T4⑤a:1）
3. Jade Ring (T4⑤a: 1)

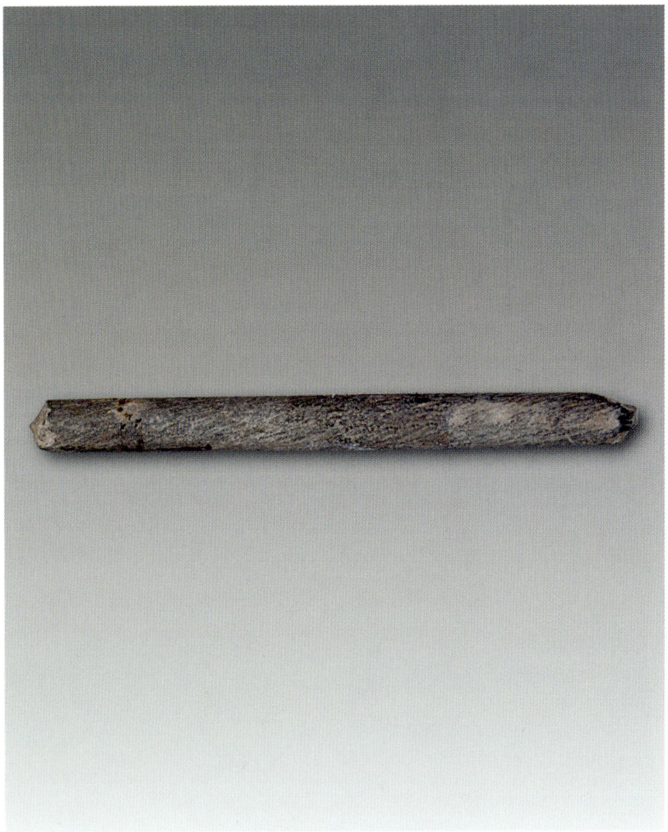

4. 石凿（T4⑤a:4）
4. Stone Chisel (T4⑤a: 4)

彩版八五　T4出土器物
Plate 85　Stone and Jade Tools Unearthed from T4

1. T4 ⑤ a:6

2. T4 ⑤ a:31

彩版八六　T4 出土石锛
Plate 86　Stone Adzes Unearthed from T4

1. T5 西壁剖面
1. Section of West Wall of T5

2. H16

彩版八七　T5 西壁剖面及 H16
Plate 87　Section of West Wall of T5 and H16

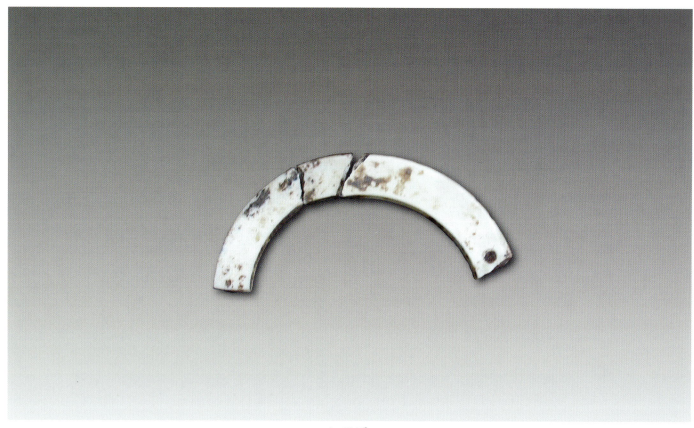

1. 正面
1. Front

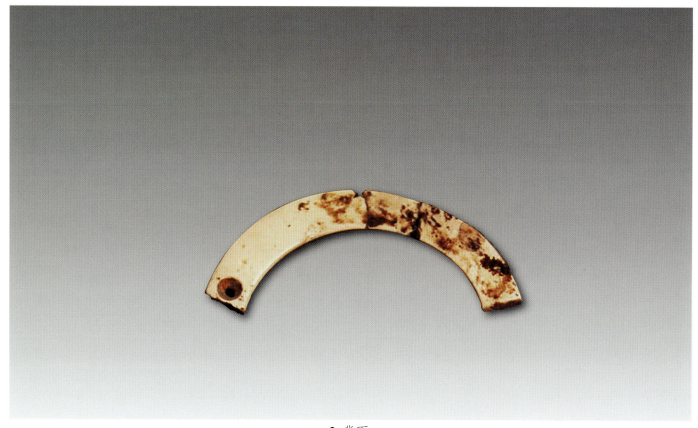

2. 背面
2. Back

彩版八八　H16 出土玉玦（H16:1）
Plate 88　Jade Pendant (H16:1) Unearthed from H16

1. T5 ⑤ a:2

2. T5 ⑤ a:1

彩版八九　T5 出土石锛
Plate 89　Stone Adzes Unearthed from T5

彩版九〇　T5 ⑤ a 层出土陶器纹饰组合
Plate 90　Portfolio of Pottery Patterns of Pieces Unearthed from T5 ⑤ a

彩版九一　T5 ⑤ a 层出土陶器纹饰组合
Plate 91　Portfolio of Pottery Patterns of Pieces Unearthed from T5⑤a

彩版九二　T5 ⑤ a 层出土陶器组合

Plate 92　Portfolio of Pottery Pieces Unearthed from T5 ⑤ a

彩版九三　T5 ⑤ a 层出土陶器组合
Plate 93　Portfolio of Pottery Pieces Unearthed from T5 ⑤ a

1. 钵（T5 ⑤ a:20）
1. Bowl（T5 ⑤ a: 20）

2. 圈足
2. Ring Feet Unearthed from T5 ⑤ a

3. 圈足
3. Ring Feet Unearthed from T5 ⑤ a

彩版九四　T5 出土陶器
Plate 94　Pottery Artifacts Unearthed from T5

彩版九五　T7 内遗迹

Plate 95　Remains of T7

1. 拍（T7 ④ aD1:1）
1. Flapper (T7 ④ aD1:1)

2. 锛（T7 ② :1）
2. Adze (T7 ② : 1)

彩版九八　T7 出土石器
Plate 96　Stone Tools Unearthed from T7